APOLOGETICS

and

CATHOLIC DOCTRINE

APOLOGETICS
SIXTH EDITION

and

CATHOLIC DOCTRINE
FOURTH EDITION

BY

Archbishop Michael Sheehan
(1870 — 1945)
Archbishop of Germia

Revised and Edited
by
Fr. P. M. Joseph

2001

The Saint Austin Press
296, Brockley Road
London, SE4 2RA
Telephone: +44 (0) 20 8692 6009
Facsimile: +44 (0) 20 8469 3609
Electronic mail: books@saintaustin.org
Internet site: www.saintaustin.org

Apologetics	1st Edition 1918	Catholic Doctrine	1st Edition 1923
	2nd Edition 1919		2nd Edition 1941
	3rd Edition 1932		3rd Edition 1962
	4th Edition 1939		
	5th Edition 1962		

ISBN 1 901157 14 8

A catalogue record for this book is available from the British Library.

Nihil Obstat: Rev. J. Rheinberger, D.D., Censor Deputatus

Imprimatur: Most Rev. William Brennan, Bishop of Wagga Wagga, Feast of St Luke, 18th October 2000

The *Nihil Obstat* and *Imprimatur* do not imply agreement with the opinions of the author, but are simply a declaration that the work contains nothing contrary to Catholic faith or morals.

Typeset and printed by NEWTON Design & Print, London, UK. www.newtondp.co.uk

CONTENTS

PART I   APOLOGETICS

NATURAL APOLOGETICS

CHRISTIAN APOLOGETICS

CATHOLIC APOLOGETICS

PART II CATHOLIC DOCTRINE

Tables and Diagrams

The Author

Michael Sheehan was born 17th December 1870 at Newtown, Waterford City, County Waterford, Ireland. His father, Cornelius, born and bred in Newmarket, County Cork, owned an export business. His mother, Ann Lawler, was an Anglican, the daughter of a Church of Ireland minister. Mr and Mrs Sheehan had ten children. In 1880, the family went to reside in Dungarvan, County Waterford.

In Dungarvan, Michael was educated privately and then at the Christian Brothers for eighteen months. He then went to the Augustinian School, Dungarvan, for nearly four years, before going to the seminary of St John's College, Waterford, in 1888. In 1890 he was transferred to the seminary of St Patrick's College, Maynooth, where, in addition to the usual studies of philosophy and theology, he applied his linguistic abilities to Greek, Latin, Irish, French and Italian. Having brilliantly completed the full course there before he was 23, he returned to St John's College and continued to study theology privately, pending canonical age for ordination. He was ordained a priest in 1895 and for a biennium taught liberal arts at St John's. In 1897 he was appointed to the Chair of Ancient Classics in Maynooth. Later he studied Latin, Greek and Sanskrit at the German universities of Greifswald and Bonn, gaining his Ph.D. in Classics at the latter in 1901 with his thesis on the Athenian orator Isocrates. Dr Sheehan was Commissioner of Intermediate Education for Ireland 1906-1922. He was Professor of Greek at Maynooth College 1905-1922, and its Vice-President 1919-1922.

On 22nd February 1922 he was named titular archbishop of Germia when appointed Co-adjutor Archbishop of Sydney, Australia. He was consecrated at Maynooth on 28th May. In August, on his way to Australia, he stopped off at Rome, staying at the Irish College. He had an audience with Pope Pius XI, in which they spoke German.

In Sydney, Dr Sheehan was distinguished for his culture, unfailing piety, gentle kindness, and passionate dedication to the cause of Christian education. In 1924, he re-launched the quarterly journal, the *Australasian Catholic Record*, and became a regular contributor to it, while virtually acting as its editor. He retained episcopal office in Sydney until his resignation on 1st July 1937 after it had been made clear to him by the Apostolic Delegate, Archbishop Panico, that because he was Irish he would not succeed Dr Kelly as Archbishop of Sydney. At the announcement of Dr Sheehan's resignation, it was most likely Archbishop Mannix of Melbourne who authored the public letter to him "from the Bishops and Archbishops of Australia," saying, "The news of your resignation … filled us all with sorrow and consternation, for we realise that your going is an irreparable loss to the Church in Australia—a real tragedy."

Retiring to Ireland, Archbishop Sheehan lived in Dublin, at the Holy Ghost Fathers, but he often visited Ring, County Waterford, where he once used to spend his holidays among its fishing folk. It was in Ring that he had first learnt Irish from an aged woman, and in 1906 had co-founded an Irish College, which is still thriving today. Although he had not spoken Irish in his childhood, he became proficient in it and wrote several works in Irish, including studies of the language.

Dr Sheehan wrote two other books of religious instruction, *A Child's Book of Religion* (1934), and *A Simple Course of Religion* (1937). He had a great interest also in botany and co-authored a book on that subject. His scholarship, clear mind and wonderful expression are exemplified in *Apologetics and Catholic Doctrine*.

Archbishop Sheehan died 1st March 1945 at St Mary's, Talbot Lodge, Blackrock, Dublin, and was buried outside the entrance to St Nicholas' church in Ring.

PREFACE

Apologetics and Catholic Doctrine, printed originally as two volumes by M.H. Gill & Son, Dublin, was a classic high school text in several countries over forty years, and sold well over 450,000 copies. Because of its outstanding clarity, persuasiveness and comprehensiveness, I have long desired to see the book reprinted—but of course this could not be done without some revision of the text. My principle has been to retain the original text as far as possible and to add, change or delete only where necessary.

Additions come from documents of the Magisterium and works of some modern authors. Other additions expand the treatment of some subjects, deal briefly with modern questions, and broaden material from the Bible, the Fathers, the liturgy, canon law, archaeology and Eastern Churches. Parts of the chapter on Marriage have been re-written substantially. Two chapters are entirely new, one on the Bible, one on the Church. Some tables and diagrams have been inserted in the text.

The Scripture quotations and references are changed from the Douay-Rheims translation to the Revised Standard Version. The Denzinger references are updated to the 36th edition, edited by A. Schönmetzer S.J., 1965. These numbers are unchanged in the 37th edition, Denzinger-Hünermann, 1991. All of the lengthy footnotes have been transferred to the main text, to help ease in reading. Dr Sheehan's classical English style has been modified in some places. The many disciplinary, canonical and liturgical changes since the second Vatican Council have been incorporated. The natural sciences have also been updated. This edition draws upon some of the revisions of Fr Bernard Kelly C.S.Sp., who issued a revised edition of the two volumes in 1962.

Deleted from the text are a few passages judged too technical or too subtle, some things no longer applicable, and a great deal of the former scientific references and arguments. Deleted from the footnotes are most but not all of the references to Latin manuals, French and German works, and lesser known books long out of print. Nine-tenths of Archbishop Sheehan's two-part work remain here exactly as he wrote it. As in the original, the text in large type gives a complete but basic treatment of the subject matter—whilst the text in this smaller print is for the more advanced reader.

Translations of the Roman Liturgy have been done afresh from the Latin; no use has been made of the ICEL versions. Excerpts from the *Catechism of the Catholic Church* have been translated from the definitive Latin text promulgated in 1997.

The two Parts of this book stand together, but either Part can be read first. Part II, *Catholic Doctrine*, covers the same material as Parts 1 and 2 of the *Catechism*, namely the Creed and Sacraments. It does not cover in any detail the Commandments and Prayer.

In preparing this new edition, I have received assistance from many people. Before all, I thank the Irish Provincial of the Holy Ghost Fathers for his permission to revise and reprint the text. I also wish to thank Mrs Leanne Nugent and Mr Simon Paton for their generous help in the preparation of this revised edition. I am grateful also to many friends and colleagues who have helped me correct or refine the drafts with the aid of their expertise in the various fields of history, theology and science. The motivation for our work was the propagation of the faith and, in accordance with this, any personal profits from this book will go to Catholic Missions and aid to refugees.

Mr Gregory Byrnes of New South Wales generously supplied, from his personal research, some of the details and dates of Dr Sheehan's life, thereby preventing a repetition of mistakes which have appeared in other biographical notices.

From today's viewpoint it seems remarkable that this book was once a school text for 15 and 16 year olds. For many, it gave the support and knowledge to sustain them in the Faith for a lifetime. They knew the Catholic Religion, and they knew the reasons for it. Both teachers and students who used it have testified to its lasting impression upon them. I hope that its re-issuing will help to restore to today's disinherited young generation their rightful heritage. The structure and sequence of the argument of Sheehan's *Apologetics* have a unique clarity and logical force. The exposition of the deposit of faith in *Catholic Doctrine* is clear and thorough. Objections are faced openly and honestly. Dr Sheehan's whole text breathes a loving confidence in the truth of the Faith founded on Him to Whom all honour and glory is due: Jesus Christ, the same, yesterday, today and forever.

Fr. Peter Mary JOSEPH
Diocese of Wagga Wagga
Australia

ABBREVIATIONS

L = **L**ateran Council IV (held in 1215)
F = Council of **F**lorence (held 1438-1445)
T = Council of **T**rent (held 1545-1563)
V = **V**atican Council I (held 1869-1870)

DS = **D**enzinger-**S**chönmetzer, *Enchiridion Symbolorum* (36ᵗʰ ed.).
The numbers placed after these letters (e.g., T 1820, V 3041, DS 2651) are
the paragraph numbers of Denzinger-Schönmetzer in the *Enchiridion
Symbolorum*, a manual of the official pronouncements of the Church on faith
and morals.

C = **C**atechism of the Catholic Church (promulgated 1992; definitive Latin
text *Catechismus Catholicae Ecclesiae* 1997). The number after C is the
paragraph number within the Catechism.

Can. = The Code of **Can**on Law (the legislation of the Latin Church,
promulgated 1983). The number after Can. refers to the number of the
canon.

S.T. = **S**umma **T**heologica (the major work of St Thomas Aquinas 1224-
74). The numbers and letters after S.T. refer, respectively, to the part,
question, article, and corpus or replies in the work.

Other abbreviations:

d. 430 "died in the year 430"
c. 670 "circa 670" = in the year 670 approximately
f. / ff. after a number, means "and following page/s or verse/s"
Cf. = confer
Ibid. (= Ibidem) the same book or work (as the preceding footnote)
Id. (= Idem) the same author (cited in the preceding work or footnote)
op. cit. (= opus citatum) the author's work already cited
O.T. = Old Testament
N.T. = New Testament
viz. (= videlicet) namely

Biblical quotations are from the Revised Standard Version (Catholic
Edition) Nelson, G.B. 1966.
On a few occasions the Douay translation is used and noted where so.

PART I

APOLOGETICS

APOLOGETICS

INTRODUCTORY CHAPTER

Summary

I.   Apologetics defined; its aim is to prove the divine Authority of the Catholic Church; its study, a duty and a discipline. The nature of its proof; its proof, conclusive but not coercive.
II.   The two methods of proof: (1) the more elaborate method, arguing from the New Testament as history; (2) the simpler method, arguing from our knowledge of the Church herself. - The more elaborate method, adopted in the body of the text; reasons. The simpler method, presented in Chapter 12.
III. The relation of Apologetics to Faith.

I

Apologetics. DEFINITION. Apologetics is the science concerned with the defence of the Catholic religion. Its aim is to prove from reason the divine authority of the Catholic Church. Advancing through a series of connected truths, it concludes that the one and only guide of faith on earth is the Catholic Church, Holy and Infallible. It leads unbelievers to the portals of the House of God, and bids them enter. Within, they hear the Catholic Doctrine, Christ's message to them interpreted by His living representative.

Beginners will note that the words *Apologetics* and *Apology*, though derived from the same Greek root, have come to have very different meanings. *Apology*, as commonly used, may signify nothing more than an excuse, or an appeal for forgiveness, whereas *Apologetics* always denotes a scientific proof or defence of religious truth. "Catholic Apologetics", therefore, is not a mere appeal for the acceptance of Catholicism or a plea for its toleration but a solid demonstration that it is the one and only true religion.

ITS STUDY FOR CATHOLICS: A DUTY AND A DISCIPLINE. We may already possess in simple form an appreciation that our faith in the Church and her teaching is a reasonable faith. Perhaps we have heard it defended by convincing arguments put before us in some brief form, such as the following: (1) "Christ the Son of God founded a Church to teach all mankind. He promised to be with her all days even to the end of the world. Because of this perpetual help, His Church must claim to teach people as He taught them: she must claim to be infallible in her teaching. The Catholic Church is the only religious body in the world that makes that claim. She alone therefore is the Church founded by Christ." (2)"The great

17

antiquity of the Catholic Church, her marvellous growth, her unconquerable endurance, her wondrous holiness, her inexhaustible fruitfulness in all charitable works, her power of holding her vast following together—despite every assault upon her unity—so that, in spite of all manner of differences in race and culture and ambitions, they remain ever one in faith, in worship, in obedience—it is the combination of all these characteristics that sets the Church quite apart from merely human institutions and marks her plainly as the work of God."

But, as we advance in secular knowledge, so also we should advance in our knowledge of our holy religion. We should seize the full content and plumb the depth of these simple proofs; we should familiarise ourselves with the whole network of argument by which our faith is defended. The age in which we live is hostile to God, to Christ, and to His Church. It is our duty, therefore, to master the proofs set forth in Apologetics, so that we may have a fuller vision of the reasonableness of our faith, of the enormous strength of its defences, and of the weakness of the objections alleged against it. It is our duty to remove temptation from our path, and to fortify ourselves against the spirit of infidelity that infects the very air we breathe. It is our duty to acquire sufficient enlightenment to enable us to answer the questions that may be addressed to us by the honest inquirer. The exhortation of St Peter to the early Christians to "be prepared to make a defence to any one who calls you to account for the hope that is in you",[1] is as applicable to us as it was to them. Besides bringing the reward of a duty fulfilled, the study of Apologetics is in itself a valuable mental discipline: it stimulates and develops our reasoning powers by setting them to work at problems of profound importance and of unfailing interest.

Our proof. ITS NATURE. The modern reader, too much impressed perhaps by the methods employed in mathematics and physical science, must be warned against the assumption that, outside the sphere of exact calculation and experiment, complete certainty is unattainable. On reflection he will realise that in the most important affairs of life, truth is established by quite different methods. For instance, a man claims an estate by virtue of a will naming him as the heir; witnesses whose word is reliable testify to the genuineness of the will; and the judge decides, saying, "It is clear that the witnesses have spoken the truth. This man is the heir." The judge is completely certain that his decision is correct, because it is based on the word of persons whose truthfulness and whose knowledge of the facts to which they testify cannot be doubted. And if far greater issues were at stake,—if, for example, there were question of the lawful election or

---

[1] 1 Pet 3:15

authority of a President, or a Parliament, a question affecting the welfare of millions,—a bench of judges with similar human evidence before them, i.e., the evidence of living witnesses and authentic documents, would be equally certain of their decision. The certainty at which one arrives in such cases resembles the certainty which is given to us in Apologetics. In Apologetics we prove the divine authority of the Catholic Church by proving that we have God's word for it. He makes His mind known to us through the language of miracles, and His miracles are attested by people whose truthfulness and impartiality, and knowledge of the facts they report, exclude all reasonable doubt and give us the certainty we require. The reader will therefore understand that human testimony, properly checked, is a most certain means of arriving at the truth.

CONCLUSIVE BUT NOT COERCIVE. Our proof is conclusive. To question it would be unreasonable. But it is not coercive. It cannot force conviction on the prejudiced or the foolish, for prejudice and folly wrap the mind round with an impenetrable casing. Thus, it is a waste of time to argue with one who refuses to listen, or with one who seriously defends an absurdity, who maintains, for example, that a great work of literature is a mere chance arrangement of words, or that thieving and bribery are not vices. Folly is mere imbecility, mere incapacity of understanding, while prejudice acts like a brake on the reason, impeding its natural movement. Manifestly, then, a perfectly valid proof may not carry conviction to all. It deserves, but does not receive, universal assent.

No truth is safe from human perversity. There are men of ability who hold that the truths on which the science of mathematics is built are not eternally true and may some day be shown to be false. There are other men, equally clever, who tell us that the external world (including our own bodies) has no real existence but is a mere fancy or dream of ours. People of such views, however, are rarely met with. They suffer from some twist of mind and are abnormal. Such people can be most enlightening when they speak on their own field of study, but can speak arrant nonsense as soon as they step outside that field. The reader, however, will not feel justified in applying so strong a term as "abnormal" to those who reject our argument at its various stages, but he will realise how easily people deceive themselves and snatch at any excuse to evade the truth. Pascal observes, "Truth is so obscure in these times, and falsehood so established, that, unless we love the truth, we cannot know it."[2]

---

[2] *Pensées*, 860

II

The two methods of proof. Having established the preliminary truths that God exists and that by miracles He can witness to the doctrines which He desires us to believe, we can prove by two methods the divine authority of the Catholic Church:

The more elaborate method in which we argue from the New Testament.
First we show that the writings of the New Testament, considered simply as ordinary human compositions, are truthful and trustworthy. Hence we accept as a faithful report the account which they give of Jesus of Nazareth, His words, and works.

A. We find in these historical documents:
    (1) that Jesus claimed to be God;
    (2) that He made good His claim by miracles and prophecies.
B. Continuing our examination of the New Testament, we find also:
    (1) that Jesus, true God, founded a Church to carry on His work and teaching, and declared that she would last for all time;
    (2) that He gave His Church certain well defined marks or characteristics, so that she could be clearly known to people of all times.

Equipped with the means of identification, we proceed to examine the religious bodies of the present day which claim Christ as their author, and we discover that all the marks imprinted by Him are found in the Catholic Church alone.

The simpler method in which we argue from our knowledge of the Church herself. In this method, we show from the unique and miraculous characteristics of the Church herself that she is sustained and guided by God. The argument is presented in Chapter 12.

The more elaborate method, which we follow in the body of the text, deserves careful study and should be mastered by every educated Catholic: because it meets on their own ground the large number of opponents who hold that in religious matters one should not move hand or foot without the authority of the Bible; because it provides a convenient occasion for dealing with a great variety of objections and difficulties; and, more important still, because it gives us such a knowledge of our Saviour and His work, that we should indeed be hard of heart were we to deny Him the full homage of our mind and love.

III

Apologetics and faith. Suppose an unbeliever is convinced by our argument, and says, "I believe that the Catholic Church is the true Church, because God has said so." Does he thereby make an act of faith—i.e., an act of faith pleasing to God, an act of divine faith, one that is done with the help of God's grace? That will depend on his attitude to God and to the truth which God has revealed. He cannot make an act of faith unless (1) he freely, humbly, and reverently subjects himself to the Supreme Authority of God who knows all things and cannot deceive him, and (2) accepts with good will the truth which God has made known to him. Those conditions, however, he cannot fulfil of himself; he needs the help of God's grace.

Many non-Catholics believe that the Catholic Church is God's representative on earth, and yet they make no act of faith. Their belief may be termed "an act of merely natural faith"; it is not pleasing to God. (An extreme instance of "natural faith" is that of the demons who, while believing in the divine origin of the Catholic Church, are filled with hatred of God and of the truth He has revealed). These people do not welcome the truth God has sent them. Some look on it with indifference, repugnance, or hostility; others shrink from the change of life it would demand of them. Though recognising God as the source of all truth, they seem to forget that He can give the strength to overcome every obstacle. They seem to forget that He is dishonoured by disobedience and by a false trust in His mercy. (These are inferences from the statements of non-Catholics who may not fully mean what they appear to say: we should beware of the sin of harsh judgement. The grace of faith is a free gift of God. He will not deny it to the sincere and conscientious, but He may delay it till the last moment of life when its coming will be known only to the one who receives it.)

Briefly, acceptance of the truth established in Apologetics is not in itself an act of faith. Of itself, it is but an act of the natural reason. It becomes an act of faith only when the two conditions mentioned above are fulfilled. A true act of faith always gives honour to God: it is an act of divine worship.

SEQUENCE OF THE ARGUMENT

Chapters 1 - 10

I. Natural Apologetics

1.   God exists. He is the Supreme Being, intelligent and free, infinite in all perfections. He created the world and all things in it. (Chapter 1)
2.   Man, one of God's creatures, possesses reason and free-will. His soul is spiritual and immortal. (Ch. 2)
3.   Man has duties to God, to himself and to his neighbour; but without a revelation, it would be practically impossible for the generality of mankind to arrive at a sufficient knowledge of these duties and of the truths that underlie them. We have, therefore, an assurance that God in His Mercy must, as a fact, have given the necessary revelation. (Ch. 3)

II. Christian Apologetics

4.   Miracles and prophecies are signs by which a divine revelation may be known with certainty. (Ch. 4)
5.   The New Testament, as history, is trustworthy. (Ch. 5)
6.   The New Testament shows that Jesus Christ claimed to be God. (Ch. 6)
7.   It shows likewise that His claims were proved by miracles and prophecies, and above all by His Resurrection from the dead. (Ch. 7)

III. Catholic Apologetics

8.   The New Testament proves that Christ established a Church, and that He invested her, and her alone, with authority to teach mankind His doctrine. (Ch. 8)
9.   It proves also that Christ gave His Church certain characteristics, one of which was imperishability. His Church, therefore, still exists in the world. (Ch. 9)
10. Of the existing Christian Churches, the Catholic Church is the *only one* that possesses all the characteristics of the institution founded by Christ. Therefore, the Catholic Church is the one and only true Church. (Ch. 10). Further, the Church's marvellous unity, sanctity, miracles, and miraculous endurance are proofs of her credibility as a work of God. (Ch. 12). We can proceed with confidence, therefore, to study the doctrine of the Catholic Church and live by it. (Chs 11, 13, and all of Part II).

The first three chapters may be postponed at the reader's discretion until the remaining portion of Part I and all Part II have been read, but they should by no means be omitted entirely. In addition to the matter which they explicitly cover, they expose the false systems of Atheism and Materialism, which when encountered for the first time by an impressionable mind, unprepared and unassisted, constitute a most grave danger to the Faith. The only remedy is to face such errors squarely, all the better during school years, to rob them of their novelty, and to unmask their absurdity. Young people who go out into the world without this enlightenment are ill equipped for battle and are easily overcome. At a young age, they may or may not succeed in grasping every philosophical point in the arguments: it will suffice, however, to see their main lines and be satisfied of their validity.

SECTION I

NATURAL APOLOGETICS

CHAPTER 1

THE EXISTENCE AND THE NATURE OF GOD
AS SHOWN BY PURE REASON

Summary

A.   The Existence of God:
      Brief treatment of the proofs of the existence of God:
  I.   Proof from order and law in nature
  II.   Proof from motion and change
  III. Proof from causality
  IV. Proof from dependence

     Fuller treatment of the proofs of God's existence:
      First principles.
  I.   Proof from order and law in nature
  II.   Proof from motion
  III. Proof from causality
  IV. Proof from dependence

B.   The nature of God as known from reason: The perfections of God:
Simplicity.   Spirituality.   Infinity.   Unity.   Omnipotence.   Omnipresence.
Omniscience.   Goodness and happiness.   God's perfections in general.

C.   Replies to objections: objections of Kant.   Objection against the argument
from causality.   Objection against the nature of God.

D.   Atheism and its various forms

A. THE EXISTENCE OF GOD

From truths naturally known, we prove the existence of a Living, Personal God, i.e., of a Being endowed with intelligence and free-will, the First or Originating Cause of all things distinct from Himself.[1]

---

[1] Attention is directed to page 119, where it is shown that the Resurrection of Christ enables us to dispense with the philosophical proof for the existence of God given in this chapter.

BRIEF TREATMENT OF THE PROOFS

I

Proof from order and law in nature

PROOF FROM ORDER IN NATURE (usually called the proof from design). In the works of nature, as well as in the works of man, order or orderly arrangement cannot be explained except as being due to the activity of an intelligent designer.

1. Suppose you pay a visit to a bicycle factory. In one of the workshops you see a number of parts, sorted into different collections—a pile of steel tubing, a sheaf of spokes, wheel-rims, hubs, handlebars, pedals, boxes of nuts and screws and so forth. You return some hours later, let us say, and find that the entire assemblage of units has been transformed into a dozen new bicycles, each perfect in every detail: part has been fitted into part with deft adjustment, yielding a result which is a model of ordered arrangement. Could you possibly imagine such an achievement to have been the product of mere chance? No, you would recognise at once that it was the work of an intelligent mechanic.

Order is unity or uniformity amid variety. Order is the result of design. Design may therefore be defined as the planning of order. Order is present when several different things combine to produce a single effect or result. Examples: (1) A watch consists of the case, the dial, the hands, a multiplicity of wheels and other arrangements: each part contributes towards the production of a single result, viz., the convenient indication of the hour. (2) The human body consists of a great number of members and organs, yet all help, each in its own way, towards the well-being of the whole.

Now turn from the bicycles to the human hand that helped to make them, and you will find a far more wonderful instance of order and ingenuity. Every movement of the human hand causes an interplay of finely wrought bones, a contraction or relaxation of pliant muscles, a straining or slackening of fibrous sinews. Its framework is composed of no less than nineteen bones, while eight more of various shapes ensure strength and flexibility in the wrist. Surely *blind chance* can have had no part in the formation of such a highly-complicated and intricate system of bones and muscles, of sinews and arteries, wherein the several units are working harmoniously for the production of each and every movement of the whole. And if we exclude chance, the question immediately arises, where has it come from? Obviously not from man, for it has grown and developed with himself. Who then is the author of that wonderful piece of mechanism?

Who has caused it to grow to its present shape, to develop so many different tissues, to attain such efficiency? The answer springs to your lips. The Maker of the human hand and of the countless other marvels with which the universe is filled can be none other than the great Master-worker, Almighty God.

2. A camera consists of a case in which there is a circular opening for the admission of light. The light passes through the lens, and forms a picture on the sensitive plate. Parallel with this is the instance of the human eye, the eye-ball corresponding to the case of the camera, the pupil corresponding to the circular opening, the crystalline lens to the camera-lens, and the retina to the sensitive plate. In both examples, it will be observed, several distinct things are found united or fitted together to produce a single result, viz., a clear picture on the sensitive plate and on the retina. Could those distinct things have come together by chance? No. It is perfectly plain that such a combination could have been effected only by the intelligent operator. The camera was made by man. The human eye was made by a worker no less real, though invisible.

How did the maker of the camera do his work? He collected the materials he required; he shaped, filed, and polished them with great care, and finally fitted them together. Though you may admire his skill, you are convinced that you yourself with proper training could imitate it. But what of the maker of the human eye? How did *he* do his work? In some most mysterious way which we are quite unable to understand, and which we recognise as far beyond the possibility of imitation, he caused a minute portion of flesh to multiply itself a million times over, and, in so doing, gradually to build up, shape, and perfect every part of the wonderful organ. He who could get a particle of matter to behave in that way is a worker whose intelligence and power it is impossible for our minds to measure. He is the Author and Master of Nature: we call Him God.

PROOF FROM THE LAWS OF NATURE. All nature acts according to law. Astronomy, physics, and chemistry show that inanimate matter, from the stars of heaven to the smallest speck of dust, is, in all its movements and changes, subject to fixed laws. The same holds for living things—plants, animals, and men: each species grows, develops, and acts in the same way. The entire universe is bound together into one vastly complicated whole, and is like a great machine, the parts of which are admirably fitted together. The orderly movement of the heavens, the marvellous structure of living things and their organs, such as the organs of sight and hearing, the wonderful instinct of the lower animals, as instanced in the work of insects and the nest-building of birds, the free activity of man, his great achievements in science, literature, and art—all these marvels are the gifts of nature and in conformity with its laws.

It is unthinkable that laws, producing effects so vast, and yet so orderly in their entirety and in their smallest detail, could have sprung from chance, or from any unintelligent cause we choose to name. They must have been imposed by a wise Lawgiver who so framed them, and so directed them in their working as to achieve the ends desired. That Lawgiver must be a being of vast intelligence. He must possess free-will for he has given that faculty to man. He must possess power beyond our capacity to measure, a power to which our minds can affix no limit.

The great Isaac Newton who discovered the laws of the motions of the heavenly bodies wrote as follows: "This most beautiful system of sun, planets and comets could nowise come into existence without the design and ownership of a Being at once intelligent and powerful. ... This Being governs all things, not as if He were the soul of the world, but as the Lord of everything. ... We admire Him for His perfections, we venerate Him and we worship Him for His Lordship."[2]

II

Proof from motion

Everyday experience shows us that things move. Nothing in the visible world can move entirely of itself, i.e., without help. No moving thing contains in itself the complete explanation of its movement. Consider the particular case of inanimate bodies. They move only as they are moved. They do not move themselves in any way. They get all their motion from without.

Let us apply these observations to the earth and to the heavenly bodies. That some of these bodies are in motion is manifest. The movement of the earth on its axis is a proven fact. Its motion round the sun is likewise certain.

Ask yourself now: how did the earth get its motion? Many physicists say that it got its motion from the sun, which, spinning round, flung it off as a fragment. But from where did the sun get its motion? Some say that the sun got its motion from a larger body of which it once formed a part, while others assert that the sun with its motion is the result of a collision between two stars. But how did the motion of the larger body or the stars originate? Science can provide conjectures, but in doing so, it merely tells us of another moving body or bodies whose motion would equally need

---

[2] *Philosophiae Naturalis Principia Mathematica* (1687), III, Sch. Gen.

explanation. That answer would leave us exactly where we were: we should still be as far as ever from a final and satisfactory explanation of the motion of the earth. The only real reply, which excludes all further inquiry, is that the motion is due immediately or ultimately to some unmoved source of motion, to the first mover.

There must exist, therefore, a being distinct from the world who gave it motion. That being is either the first mover or a being moved by some other. If that mover is moved by another, from where did that other derive his motion? The question as to the source of motion can be answered satisfactorily only when, at last, we reach a first mover who is not moved by any other.

That first mover we call God.

Motion is a form of change. We may present the same demonstration by considering change in general.

Proof from change. Experience shows us that many things in the world change. But change is a reality or event which cannot be explained by reference only to the thing that changes. Hence every example of change which we encounter must be explained by the action of some being outside the thing that changes, and ultimately by the action of an unchanging being.

This proof becomes clearer if we take it part by part.

Experience shows us that many things in the world change: Things that were at rest begin to move, and things that were in motion slow down or accelerate. Cold things become hot and hot things become cold. Pieces of metal become magnetised or lose their magnetism. Livings things die and non-living matter is transformed by assimilation or otherwise into living matter.

Change cannot be explained by reference only to the thing that changes: In a changing object we notice: (a) its condition before the change; (b) the process of change; (c) its condition after the change. How are all these to be explained? Not as consequences of the nature of the thing itself, for whatever belongs to a thing of its nature is always found in it. Hence, by the simple fact that a thing is observed to pass through the stages of first condition, change, and second condition, we know that none of them belongs to it of its nature. The reason why it is in any one stage at a particular moment must, therefore, be sought outside the thing itself. In other words, every thing which changes is indebted for the change to the action of an outside agent.

Change is explained ultimately by the action of an unchanging being: Since the thing that changes does not explain the change that takes place in it, an explanation must be sought elsewhere. Every change depends, therefore, on something other than the thing that changes. This thing on which the change depends is itself subject to change or it is not. If it is, it depends, in its turn, on something for the changes it undergoes, and so on till at length we reach a being that is not subject to change.

A being not subject to any kind of change is a perfect being. Only a being having all perfection, and having it with such necessity as to be incapable of losing any of it or having anything added to it—only such a being is entirely removed from the possibility of change. On this unchanging Being—whom we call God—depends the fact of change in the mutable beings we encounter in the world.

III

Proof from causality

A thing must exist before it can act. Nothing, therefore, can make itself. If we see anything new come into existence, we are sure it must have been brought into existence by something else. That which is brought into existence is often called an *effect*; and what brings it into existence is called a *cause*.

If we find that the cause of any particular effect is itself an effect, our mind is not content: we feel that we have not yet arrived at a satisfactory explanation of the first effect. Take, for example, the electric light that suddenly springs up at the flick of a switch and floods your room at night-time. It is an effect. But what is its cause? The current. But the current is an effect of the moving generator. Now, if the moving generator is the last cause that we can name, we are still without a full and satisfactory explanation of the electric light. Why? Because the generator itself is an effect. Therefore, at the end of our series of questions, we find ourselves in the presence of an effect that needs explanation quite as much as the effect from which we started.

Let us repeat in general or abstract form what we have been saying in the last paragraph: In the world around us, the existence of any particular thing, which we will call A, is accounted for by something else, which we will call B. A is the effect; B is its cause. But suppose B itself to be the effect of C; C the effect of D; D the effect of E, and so on through a long series. If the last cause which we can set down—let us call it Z—has itself been produced by something else, then we are still without a true and satisfactory explanation of A. The complete and final explanation will be found only when we reach a cause which is not an effect, a cause which has not derived its existence from something else. This cause, which we designate the First Cause, accounts at once for the entire series of causes which we have been considering and of any other series which we choose to investigate.

Thus, the First Cause of all things in nature must necessarily be uncaused (if it were caused it would not be the first cause). It was not brought into existence; thus, it must have existence of itself, it must be self-existent. The first cause, the self-existent source of all things, we call God.

IV

Proof from dependence

Everything in the visible world is subject to change and death. Plants, animals, and men come into being, and after a short time perish, while inanimate matter suffers endless changes. No particular thing in the universe has any unbreakable grip on existence. Its existence is an unfastened cloak that may slip from it at any instant: existence is no part of its nature. Everything in the world, therefore, is dependent, i.e., it does not exist of itself, but depends on something else for its existence.

Since dependent beings do, as a fact, exist, and go on existing, and since they do not exist of themselves, they must be held in existence by an independent or necessary being, i.e., by a being who is self-existent, a being to whose nature existence belongs.

Can the self-existent being be like matter, or electricity, or any other lifeless thing we care to name? No; to support in existence all things in the world, including living plants, sentient animals, and rational men, the self-existent being must be a Living Power. He must be the Supreme Being who holds within Himself the source of His own existence.

We call Him God.

Note. Grasp the significance of the truth that we are absolutely dependent on God for our existence. It is the foundation of all religion; it brings sharply before our mind the nothingness of man and the greatness and goodness of God. From it springs the chief of all our duties, the duty of loving Him with our whole heart and soul as the Giver and ever-active Sustainer of our very life and being, and of acknowledging His supreme dominion over us and our total dependence on Him.

FULLER TREATMENT OF THE PROOFS OF GOD'S EXISTENCE

The reader may prefer to skip the rest of this difficult chapter and pass straight to chapter 2.

First Principles. Before giving our fuller treatment of the above proofs, we shall state the first principles on which they are based. First principles are the self-evident truths that serve as the basis of a science. Thus, in Euclid, the axioms are the first principles from which all the propositions may ultimately be deduced. In our proofs, the first principles are chiefly two, viz.:

(1) That our reason and the evidence of our senses are trustworthy.
(2) That anything which begins to exist must have been brought into existence by something distinct from itself (Principle of Causality).

We need not, and in fact we cannot, prove first principles. They shine by their own light. Those who deny their validity put themselves beyond the pale of discussion.

I

PROOF FROM ORDER AND LAW IN NATURE

PROOF FROM ORDER IN NATURE. *Text of St Thomas Aquinas:* "We observe that some things which are without understanding, such as physical bodies, operate for an end, as appears from the fact that always, or more frequently, they operate in the same way to arrive at what is best. From this it is clear that they attain this end not by chance but by intention. Now these things, which do not possess understanding, do not aim towards a purpose unless they are directed by a being endowed with knowledge and intelligence, just as an arrow is directed by the archer. Therefore, there is an intelligent Being, by whom all the things of nature are directed to their end. And this Being we call God."[3]

Order explained by examples. *The camera*. The camera is a familiar object. It consists of a small case into which are fitted a sensitive plate and at least one lens. The plate is a little sheet of glass on which is spread a chemical preparation: it is called "sensitive" or "sensitised" because it retains any picture made on it by light-rays. The lens is of glass or other transparent substance, and has the power of casting on a screen the image of any object placed in front of it. The camera is completely closed but for a small opening in one of the sides. Through this opening, the light-rays enter; they pass through the lens, and fall on the sensitive plate where they make the picture.

Without going into all the details, we may note the following as the essentials of a satisfactory camera:

(1) A case, blackened within.
(2) A circular opening which can be altered in size so as to admit only the exact amount of light required.
(3) A lens of a special curved shape.
(4) A sensitive plate.
(5) An arrangement by which the lens can be adjusted to a particular distance from the sensitive plate, so as to secure the proper focus, and save the picture from being blurred.

---

[3] S.T., i, q. 2, a. 3

All these things were shaped and brought together for the purpose of producing a good picture. We have here an example of order or design, i.e., a combination or arrangement of different things in order to produce a single effect.

The human eye. The human eye is similar in structure to the camera. Note the following points of resemblance:

(1) The eye-ball corresponds to the case.
(2) The pupil corresponds to the circular opening; it is of adjustable size, and can be altered according to the amount of light required.
(3) The crystalline lens, corresponding to the lens of the camera.
(4) The retina, corresponding to the sensitive plate.
(5) An arrangement for focussing. In the camera, this is done by altering the distance between lens and plate; in the eye by altering the curvature of the crystalline lens.

> Here again we have an example of order, because different things are combined to produce a single effect. Each contributes in its own measure towards the same end, viz., the formation of a clear picture on the retina.

Order demands intelligence. How did the camera come to be made? You have your choice of just two answers, viz., that it was made by chance or by intelligence. Now, you know that it could not have been made by chance. Such an explanation is so foolish that you would regard it as a jest. No one has to convince you that the camera was put together by an intelligent workman.

How did the human eye come to be made? By chance? No: that is an absurd reply. The human eye was made by some intelligent being.

The Maker of the human eye possesses power and intelligence without limit. Suppose that all the parts of a camera lay scattered about a table, and suppose you saw them rise up and move towards one another and fit themselves together: would you say that this happened by chance? No; you would say that this happened by some intelligent, though invisible, worker, and you would add that he must indeed possess very wonderful powers.

Now take a step further. Suppose that the case, the lens and the sensitive plate were all ground to the finest powder and mixed thoroughly together. Suppose that the minute fragments of each part sought one another out, and fastened themselves together again; and suppose that each part thus completed took up its proper place so as to give us a perfect camera: would you say that this was due to chance? No, but you would protest that here there was need of a worker, still more intelligent, still more powerful.

But we are not done with our suppositions. There is one more which we must make. Suppose you saw just a single tiny speck of dust on the table before you. Suppose that, having grown to twice its size, it broke up into two particles, and that each of these two particles, having doubled in size, broke up into two others. Suppose that this process of growth and division went on, and that, during its progress, the particles managed to build up the case, lens and plate. Suppose, in other words, that you saw one and the same minute fragment of matter produce such widely different things as the case with its blackened sides, the transparent lens

33

with its mathematically accurate curvature, the sensitive plate with its chemical dressing, the aperture with its light-control, and last of all, the mechanism for focussing. What would you say to such a supposition? You would be tempted at once to stamp it as utterly improbable. You would protest, and with good reason, that only an all-powerful being could get a single speck of dust to behave as we have described, to make it multiply itself, and, while so doing, form unerringly, and piece together, an ingenious mechanism.

But is there really any improbability in the occurrence of which we have just spoken? No: the very eyes with which you have been reading this page are witnesses against you. Each of them began as a single particle of matter: the hidden worker acted upon it, made it multiply itself millions of times and made it develop such utterly distinct things as the eye-ball, the retina, the crystalline lens with its controlling muscles, the contractile pupil, along with other parts equally marvellous which it is unnecessary to mention. The hidden worker is a being whose power and intelligence our minds cannot measure.

The Maker of the human eye is God. He who has made the human eye is a spirit. He is a spirit because He is an active, intelligent and invisible being. He is one to whom nothing is hard or impossible. We call Him God.

FURTHER EVIDENCE FOR THIS CONCLUSION

God's wisdom and power. 1. The human eye, as we have explained, grows from a single particle of matter. But the entire body with its flesh, blood, bone, muscle, its various limbs and organs, grows in precisely the same way. It begins as a single living cell which multiplies itself, and gradually forms every part. That living cell, small as it is, is far more wonderful than any machine that man has ever made. You can show how a watch does its work; you can show how the movement of the spring passes from one part to another, until finally it is communicated to the hands; but you cannot produce a living cell, whose work is wrapt round with mystery—why? Because the mind that made it is too deep for us to fathom. But the mystery lies not only in the *manner* in which the cell works but in the *results* which it produces. As fruit, flowers, foliage, bark, stem and roots come from a single seed, so the wonderful powers of man, his sight, his hearing, his other senses, come from the living cell. The more intricate and ingenious a machine is, the greater testimony it is to the cleverness of its maker. But there is no machine in the world that can be compared with the living cell which builds up a man capable himself of making machines and of attaining to eminence in art and science.

The power displayed in the development of a living cell is on par with the wisdom displayed in its development. It is power exerted, not through hands and muscles, but by a mere act of the will. God commands the development to take place, and nature obeys Him.

Another example. A remarkable instance of design appears in the set of organs for the reception, mastication, and digestion of our food. The mouth, with its flexible muscles by which it opens and closes, receives the food; the tongue and palate register its agreeable or disagreeable taste; the teeth cut and crush it; the salivary glands pour out their juices to prepare it for digestion; the muscles of the throat draw down the masticated food through the alimentary canal to the stomach, where the digestive juices convert it into such a form that it can bring nutrition to every part of the body. This admirable system of organs, all conducing to the achievement of a single purpose, viz., the preservation and strengthening of life, bears the unmistakable impress of design.

2. We have proved God's existence from a few special instances of order, but we could have argued with equal success from *anything whatever* in the visible world: the very stones you tread under foot are made up of molecules each one of which, when studied scientifically, is found to possess a structure that could have been given to it only by a wise architect: it is as clearly the work of intelligence as is the house in which you live.

We read that in olden times a certain man was accused of denying the existence of God. Stooping down, he picked up a straw from the ground: "If I had no other evidence before me but this straw", he said, "I should be compelled to believe that there is a God." He meant that Divine Wisdom alone could have devised the special tubular shape in virtue of which a very small quantity of matter supports an ear of corn, and allows it to toss and sway freely with the breeze.

PROOF FROM LAW IN NATURE. In the proof from *order*, we examined separate things, such as the human eye and human hand. We showed that each is the outcome of design; that each, therefore points to a Designer. In the proof from *Law*, we assume with modern adversaries that all instances of orderly arrangement in the world are due to the operation of Nature's Laws. We prove against them that these Laws themselves give us no final explanation, but demand the existence of an Intelligent Lawgiver. A law of nature, or physical law, may be merely a formal statement of what regularly occurs in nature, or it may denote the cause of such regularity. We use the expression in the latter sense: let us then define a law of nature as "the cause of a certain regularity observed in nature." It must not be inferred, however, that we claim any exact knowledge of the cause of each set of regularly occurring phenomena. That the cause exists we are certain, but as to its precise nature and mode of operation we need not profess to know anything.

All nature acts according to law. That the universe is obedient to law is a truth which forms the very basis of all physical science:
(1) *Inanimate matter is subject to law.* In *astronomy*, the laws of Kepler and Newton have exhibited the heavens as forming so exact a mechanical system that seemingly irregular occurrences, such as eclipses and the return of comets, can be predicted with certainty. In *physics*, the laws of sound, heat, light, and electricity, work so perfectly that results can be calculated in advance with mathematical accuracy. In *chemistry*, substances are found to have definite attractions and affinities and to combine according to fixed laws. In all other branches and sub-divisions of physical science, the same regularity is observed. Everywhere, like agents in like circumstances produce the same effects.

(2) *Animate matter is subject to law.* (a) All living things are subject to fixed laws of nutrition, growth, and reproduction. Plants, animals, and men develop from a single living cell. In the higher forms of life, in man, for instance, that cell multiplies itself many times, gradually building up a great complexity of organs, such as the eye, the ear, the heart and lungs. (b) Every living thing possesses some capacity to repair itself. (c) Among the lower animals, every individual of the same species is endowed with the same set of useful appetites and tendencies in connection with the quest for food, the defence of life, the propagation of its kind, and the care of its offspring. (d) The same holds for man, who, in addition, possesses inclinations in keeping with his rational nature. Impelled by the desire for truth and the love of beauty, his mind builds up many wonderful sciences, and produces all the marvels of literature and art. In its movements it is subject to certain laws, the laws of thought, just as the seed, developing into stem, leaf, and flower, is subject to the laws of growth.

(3) *Animate matter is subject to, and served by, the laws of inanimate matter.* All living things are subject to the laws of inanimate matter. Nutrition, growth, and many other processes take place in accordance with the laws of chemistry. The laws of gravitation and energy are as valid for the living as for the non-living. The tree, for instance, which stores up the energy of the sun's rays, returns it later on when its withered branches burn on the hearth.

Animate matter is served by the laws of inanimate matter. Examples: gravitation has so placed the earth in relation to the sun that it receives the moderate quantity of light and heat necessary for the support of organic life. The air contains in every 100 parts nearly 79 of nitrogen and 21 of oxygen gas, together with .04 of carbonic acid, a minute proportion of ammonia and other constituents, and a variable quantity of watery vapour. In pure nitrogen, man would suffocate; in pure oxygen, his body would burn out rapidly like a piece of tinder; without carbonic acid plant life would be impossible. The plant exhales oxygen and inhales carbonic acid; the animal exhales carbonic acid, and inhales oxygen; thus, each ministers to the life of the other. The water, drawn by evaporation from the sea, drifts in clouds, and descends in rain on the mountains, thus feeding the wells, the streams and rivers, so necessary for living things. Bodies contract with a fall of temperature, and yet water expands when its temperature falls below 4° Centigrade. Hence, ice is lighter than water, and forms a surface-covering which, being of low conductivity, prevents the rapid congealing of the entire body of water and the destruction of living things beneath.

(4) *In conclusion, the whole universe is guided by law.* Everywhere, there is order. Everywhere there is admirable arrangement. Everywhere there are fixed modes of action.

The laws of nature could not have been produced by chance or by a cause acting blindly, which is but another name for chance. Is it necessary to refute the absurdity that chance could have generated a law? Law is the exact opposite of chance. (We leave aside for the moment the rare interferences with the laws of nature that occur when there is a miracle). Fixity is the characteristic of law;

variability, the characteristic of chance: (1) Four rods of equal length, flung aimlessly from the hand, may fall into the exact form of a square. It is barely conceivable that this may happen a hundred times in unbroken succession; but what should be the conceivability of its *only* happening thus? Yet this last must be realised in order to give us the basis of a law. (2) If the generation by chance of such a simple law be impossible, how can we measure the absurdity of supposing that chance could have produced the vast complexity of laws that rule the universe, the laws whose operation guides the course of planets, and accounts for the growth and reproduction of living things, the instinct and tendencies of animals, the work of bees, the nest-building of birds, the activity of the mind of man?

The laws of nature have been imposed by a Lawgiver. The arguments by which we have shown that the laws of nature are not due to chance avail, also, to prove that those laws cannot be due to any unintelligent cause we choose to name. Therefore, they must be due to some great intelligence distinct from matter. They must have been ordained and imposed by a Lawgiver. And, as the statesman frames his legislation for a definite purpose, so also the Lawgiver of the universe imposed His laws to achieve the ends He desired. The orderly arrangement produced by His laws was intentional. It was in accordance with His preconceived plan or design.

Observe how the necessity for an intelligent author of the laws of nature is enforced by considerations such as the following:

(a) Great intelligence and skilful workmanship are required to construct a steam-engine that can feed itself with fuel and water. But immeasurably greater would be the intelligence and power which could make the iron-ore come, of itself, out of the depths of the earth, smelt and temper itself, form and fit together all the parts of the engine, make the engine haul in its store of water and coal, kindle its furnace, and repair its own worn parts. Yet this is an everyday process of nature in the case of living organisms. And as intelligence is needed to guide the hands of the mechanic who builds the engine, much more is needed to combine and direct the lifeless forces of nature in producing more marvellous results.

(b) The lower animals often exhibit instances of wonderful order. They perform with great skill a series of actions for the achievement of a definite purpose. Take the following example: the ammophila hirsuta, a kind of sand-wasp, prepares a worm as food for its larvae by cutting as with a surgical lance and paralysing all the motor-nerve centres, so as to deprive the worm of movement but not of life. The sand-wasp then lays its eggs beside the worm and covers all with clay. It has surgical skill without instruction or practice. It lives for but one season. It has not been taught by its parents, for it has never seen them. It does not teach its offspring, for it dies before they emerge from the earth. It has not received skill by heredity. For what does heredity mean in such a case? It means that some ancestor of the insect, having accidentally struck the worm in nine or ten nerve centres, managed somehow or other to transmit to all its descendants a facility for achieving the same success. But it is mere folly to say that this chance act of the ancestor rather than any other chance act should become a fixed habit in all its progeny. And could the original success have been due to chance? Where the number of points that might have been struck was infinitely great, the chance of striking the nerve centres alone was zero. The behaviour of the larvae is still more astounding. While eating into the live worm, they take care to avoid the vital parts. Were they to injure even one of these, the worm would die, and they would perish for want of fresh food. But perhaps the insect gets its skill by reasoning? No: (1) because reasoning does not give dexterity; (2) because it is impossible that each insect of the same tribe—and all are equally expert—should discover by independent reasoning exactly the same process; (3) because, when the insect is confronted with the slightest novel difficulty, it acts like a creature without reason and is powerless to solve it. Therefore, the intelligence which the sand-wasp exhibits did not originate from the insect itself but in the mind of God: it was He who planned the work: it is He who planted within the insect the instinct to perform these operations.

(c) Man is as much a product of nature as the bee or the flower. The elaborate works of civilisation, the arts and sciences, and all the accumulated knowledge of centuries, are as certainly due to the working of nature's laws or forces, as the honey-cell of the bee or perfume of the flower. Is it for a moment conceivable that those laws were not directed by intelligence, that man and all his achievements could have sprung from a source, blind and lifeless, and, therefore totally inadequate to account for them?

The Lawgiver is God. (1) As the carpenter is distinct from the table he makes, the architect from the house he designs, as every cause is distinct from its effect, so the Lawgiver of the universe must be distinct from the universe and its laws. (2) A scientist of exceptional talent, aided by a perfect apparatus for research, succeeds, after many years of study, in understanding the working of one or two of those laws. Must not, then, the Author of them all be a Being of vast intelligence? (3) That Being must possess free-will. Or else, how does man by a law of his nature come to possess a faculty? And why should the laws of nature be precisely as they are—we see no reason why they might not be otherwise—except from the act of a Being free to choose as He pleases? The Being who possesses these perfections we call God.

II

PROOF FROM MOTION

The existence of motion and change in things around us is proved by innumerable instances.

In the visible world nothing moves entirely of itself, i.e., without help. The nature of the help may be a true cause or a stimulus, or it may consist simply in the removal of an obstacle.

You can divide all things in the world into two classes, viz., things animate and things inanimate, or, things with life and things without life.

(1) No lifeless thing moves without help. This obvious truth can be illustrated by a thousand examples. The marbles with which a child plays are propelled by his fingers; the stone falling through the air is being pulled down by gravity; the ocean liner gliding through the water gets its motion from the engine—and so on for

instances without number. If then you see any quantity of inanimate matter in motion—any quantity great or small—you are certain that it must have got help from without.

(2) No animate or living thing moves without help. This, at first sight, is not so clear, yet a little reflection will show that it is true. Living things move themselves but can do so only by receiving help from outside. Both animals and plants require food; it is the source of their energy; without it they would cease to be living things. Life, or the principle of life, is not like the movement of a particle of matter; life is not energy, but a director of energy. The total energy of a plant or animal during the whole course of its existence (including the store of energy which it may possess at death) is exactly equivalent to the energy which it has absorbed from without; and this equality remains, no matter how the energy may have been expended. The principle of life never begins its work until it is stimulated from outside. One illustration will suffice: take, for instance, the grain of corn in the earth. The living principle in that grain will remain inactive unless the proper conditions of warmth, moisture, etc., are present.

"But", you will say, "what of our free-will? Using the word 'motion' in a broader sense to mean more than the movement of something material, can we not say, and must we not say, that our will moves itself?" Yes, but it never moves itself without help. The will cannot choose between two courses, unless those courses have been laid before it by the intellect. "But what of the intellect? Does it not conceive ideas unaided?" No; it cannot take its first step until it gets information from one or other of the five senses; and the senses themselves would remain forever passive, unless stimulated or affected by things distinct from them. You may urge your objection still further and say: "An angel is not in any way dependent on bodily senses. The intellect of an angel, therefore, can move itself, that is, it can obtain ideas without external help." No; the intellect of an angel could not perform its first act unless it were affected in some way by an object distinct from it. Someone has to make the link between the mind of the angel and the first truth it knows.

There would be no motion in the world but for help given by someone who is outside the world. Since nothing in the world moves of itself, since everything requires help of some kind for its motion, it follows that there must be some Being outside the world who gave it its first motion.

Suppose that there are five children who are willing to obey you strictly: suppose you get each to promise not to speak until spoken to; and suppose you lock all five in a room by themselves: then, no word would ever be spoken in that room, unless someone from outside were to speak to the occupants. It is so with the motion we see in the world. As the silence in the room would never have been broken but for the voice from without, so the motion in the world could never have existed but for the motion given by some Being outside the world.

In the distant past, the universe was formed from a quantity of moving matter. Who gave that matter its motion? Someone who is outside the universe, and is no part of the universe. Someone who is truly called the First Mover.

The First Mover is God. If you suppose that he who gave the world its motion was himself moved by a second being, the second by a third, and so on indefinitely, you make a supposition which leads nowhere, because it would still remain true that there must be some being who is the fountain-head of all that motion; there would still have to be a First Mover. The hands of a watch are moved by one of the wheels, that wheel is moved by another, and so on. But it is quite absurd to think that we can do without the mainspring by merely increasing the number of wheels indefinitely. "But the series of wheels could be infinite", someone may say. Very well; let us suppose so. But let us suppose also that the wheels have the gift of speech and can answer a question. Ask any one of them, "Are you the cause of the motion I see in you?" It will answer, "No", and all the members of the infinite series will give the same reply. We must therefore look outside the infinite series for the source of that motion which we see flowing from member to member.

The First Mover cannot be a lump of inert matter; if he were, his motion would have been derived from without; he could not have been the First Mover.

He is not like us: he is not united to a body; if he were, his knowledge would depend on external stimulus, and he would not be the First Mover. He must be a Being whose knowledge had no beginning, whose mind was never in darkness.

He Himself is the source of all His activity. He is a Spirit, the Lord and Master of the universe: His name is God.

Note. In God, the mind knowing is not distinct from the object known; the mind knowing is God Himself, and the object known is likewise God himself; and through His self-knowledge He has a perfect knowledge of His creatures. This identity in God of the mind knowing and the object known enables us to understand how His knowledge never had a beginning.

III

PROOF FROM CAUSALITY

The only full and satisfactory explanation of the universe is found, as we shall see, in the existence of a First Cause, to whom all things and all changes, all facts and events, are directly or indirectly due.

Take anything you please in the world about you—let us call it A—and try to account for its existence. You discover that it has been produced by B; that B has been produced by C; and C by D. Now, if the last cause named by you in this or any other such series be itself an effect, you are still without a true and full explanation of A, and you will not find that explanation until you arrive at a first cause, a cause which is not an effect, a cause which has not derived its existence from anything else, a cause which is uncaused and self-existent.

If it be objected that A may be caused by B, B by C, and C by A, thus moving in a circle, as it were, we answer: (1) If A had been caused by B, and B by C, it follows that A has been caused by C. But if A is caused by B, then B must have existed before A. If B had been caused by C, then C must have existed before B. Therefore C existed before A, and could not have been caused by it.

The series of effects and causes, A, B, C, etc., leads us therefore to a First Cause which is uncaused. Being uncaused, it was never brought into existence by anything else; it always existed; it has existence of itself; it is self-existent. Just as it is idle to inquire why a circle is round, for it is round of its very nature, so it is idle to inquire why the First Cause exists, for it exists of its very nature. The First Cause is thus self-explanatory, accounting not only for itself but for A and B and C, and for each and every member in any other such series which we choose to set forth.

Now, since there is nothing in the visible world about which we cannot ask the question why it exists, it follows that the independent being, who is the explanation and cause of all things in nature, must himself be distinct from all and superior to all.

Each individual thing in the visible world, as we have seen, needs an explanation, and finds it, directly or ultimately, in the existence of a first cause. But the universe in its entirety likewise needs an explanation: it is not self-explanatory; it is not the full explanation of all that takes place within it. The universe is made up of a certain number of constituents; the action of any one of them (X) may be explained by its properties, and by the influence exerted on it by all the others; the action of the second (Y) may be explained in a similar way, and so on, yet this leaves still unexplained why the constituent X existed at all, and why it had Y, Z, K, etc., acting upon it, and not a totally different set of influencing companions. Hence, the universe, considered as a whole, is not self-explanatory: it needs an explanation just as much as the smallest thing in it. It points beyond itself; it points to an uncaused being outside nature, a being that contains its own explanation, and is the final explanation of everything else, the first and sufficient cause of all things.

Since this being is the author of the order of the universe, the author of the intelligence and free-will of man, he himself, in some supereminent way, must possess intelligence and free-will, for the cause must be sufficient to account for the effect.

This First Cause, this Self-existent and Intelligent Being, we call God.

Note. The reader should observe that a physical cause, that is, a cause whose operation comes under the observation of the senses, can *never* fully account for its effect. Let us take an example: suppose we are asked to account for the letters we see in this printed page. The physical causes of those letters are the printing machine, the ink, the absorbent nature of paper, the computer operator's hands and eyes. But, clearly, these causes do not fully explain how the page became printed. The real cause is not physical. It is the free-will of the printer operator. Note how the example applies to the motion we observe in the world around us: the physicist explains the motion of the train by the motion in the piston of the engine; the motion in the piston by the combustion of diesel fuel; the energy in the fuel (which is nothing more than compressed vegetable matter) by the sun's heat and light; the sun's heat and light, by the motion of the galactic matter out of which it was formed. Therefore, as far as a complete explanation is concerned, we find ourselves at the end of a long series of physical causes, just where we were at the beginning. The motion of the galactic matter requires explanation just as much as the motion of the train. Thus we are driven once more to find the ultimate explanation of all physical phenomena in the will of some all-powerful Being distinct from the world.

We may bring out the point of this argument by means of an illustration used for a somewhat different purpose by W.G. Ward.[4] He supposes a "philosophical" mouse to be enclosed in a pianoforte. The mouse discovers that every sound of the instrument is produced by a vibration of the strings, and the vibration of the strings by taps of the hammers. "Thus far I have already prosecuted my researches", says the mouse. And he goes on with all the blithe optimism of the Atheist: "So much is evident now, viz., that the sounds proceed not from any external agency, but from the uniform operation of fixed laws. These laws may be explored by intelligent mice; and to their exploration I shall devote my life." And so, the mouse, arguing himself out of the old belief of his kind, becomes convinced that the piano-player has no existence.

IV

PROOF FROM DEPENDENCE
(Usually called the proof from contingence)

The meaning of "dependence" and "necessity".
Contrast these two statements: "The sky is clear." "The whole is greater than the part."
The former is a dependent truth; the latter is an independent or necessary truth.

The former *may* be true at this moment, but *need* not be true. Its truth depends on the fulfilment of a condition, viz., that there be no clouds or mist: it is therefore a dependent truth. The latter is true at this moment and *must* always be true; its truth does not depend on the fulfilment of any condition: it is an independent or necessary truth.

(1) If a statement which is now true *was not always true*, we know at once that it is a dependent truth; the very fact that it is a temporary truth shows us that it is not a necessary truth. May we infer from this that every statement that is true for all time must be a necessary truth? No. We can suppose that the statement, "The sky is clear", was always true and always will be true. We can suppose it to be eternally true. But even so, our supposition will not make it an independent truth. It will remain a dependent truth, forever dependent on other truths.

A dependent statement such as, "The sky is clear", no matter how long it may continue to be true, can lose its truth at any instant: our mind admits the possibility without hesitation. But an independent statement, such as "The whole is greater than its part", can never cease to be true; our mind rejects the possibility as absurd and inconceivable. A dependent statement is always reversible; it is subject to death, as it were; it is a perishable truth. In contrast, an independent statement is a truth which is irreversible, imperishable and necessary.

(2) A statement which tells us something that follows from the very nature or definition of a thing expresses an independent or necessary truth. The nature of anything is shown to us in its definition; the definition tells us what precisely the

---

[4] *The Philosophy of Theism*, vol. II, p.173

thing is, or how it is constituted. We define "the whole" as "the sum of two or more parts." *The very nature of "the whole"*, therefore, compels us to assert that "the whole is greater than its part." The assertion is really contained in the meaning or definition of "the whole."

Now look at the other statement, "the sky is clear." We may define the sky as "the visible region above the earth." It is obvious that the nature of what we call "the sky" does not compel us to assert that "the sky is clear." Such an assertion would not follow from our definition of "the sky."

It is the nature of "the whole" to be greater than its part. It is not the nature of the "the sky" to be clear. The truth that "the whole is greater than its part" is true of itself; it does not lean for help on any other truth. The truth that "the sky is clear" is not true of itself; it needs outside help to make it true.

(3) An independent statement *explains itself*: it shines by its own light. It does not force us to look elsewhere for the reason of why it is true. A dependent statement is the opposite of all this: it does not account for itself. It shines by a borrowed light, leaves us dissatisfied, and sends us farther afield until we find a self-explanatory truth.

Now, as a truth may be either dependent or independent, *so too an existing thing may be either dependent or independent*. An existing thing is dependent:

(1) if it exists only for a time; or

(2) if existence does not belong to its nature; or

(3) if it compels us to look outside it for the reason of its existence.

If, therefore, any one of these three conditions has been verified, the thing derives its existence from without.

Everything in the world is dependent. (1) Everything in this world about us is subject to change and death. Plants, animals and men come into existence and pass away. Inanimate matter suffers endless variations; new substances are being constantly built up and broken down. Consider our planet alone: (a) The distribution of land and water is insensibly but constantly changing; (b) the earth's rotatory motion is getting slower and slower, because the tide, the great bank of water piled up by the attraction of the moon, acts like a brake on it; (c) the motion of the earth round the sun is being retarded, because of friction with clouds of meteoric dust: the earth is, therefore, ever being drawn nearer to the sun. Enormous changes will result, after the lapse of ages, as a consequence of (b) and (c). All earthly things are obviously dependent, because their existence is merely temporary; but even if their existence were everlasting, it would still be, as we shall see, a dependent existence.

(2) If we were asked to give the list of things that make up the nature of man or, in other words, if we were asked to set down all those things which constitute a man, we should not mention "existence" as one of them. The description of a man remains precisely the same whether he exists or not, or whether he exists everlastingly or not, and this is true of any particular thing in the world we choose to name. Existence, therefore, does not belong to the nature of man, nor to the nature

of anything else in the world. Hence we say that everything in the visible world is dependent or contingent, i.e., that it *need not exist*. Not merely is there no necessity for its coming into existence, but there is no necessity for its continuing in existence. Nothing in the world exists necessarily. Nothing in the world has any unbreakable grip on existence.

The point of the argument can be illustrated as follows: Suppose that last year a sculptor gave you a full description of a statue he intended making, and that today you are looking at the successfully completed work. Your description of the statue, as it is now, would correspond exactly to the sculptor's description a year ago when the statue had no existence. The description of the statue tells us the nature of the statue, and does not include the statement that "the statue must exist."

To borrow a term from chemistry, the description of a thing's nature may be called its *formula*. The *formula* shows us a *possible* being and nothing more. It shows us a being that can exist; it does not say that the being must exist. We can construct a great number of formulae corresponding to things actually existing, but we know that there must be an indefinite number corresponding to things which, as a fact, have never existed, and never will exist, and yet each one of these unknown formulae would fully describe the characteristics of a particular and possible being.

You may object that the soul of man is immortal, and therefore must go on existing forever without any help. No; that is a false conclusion. The soul of man does not exist of itself; it does not exist without help. If it did, it would never have begun to exist; it would have always existed. But as long as it is kept in existence, it cannot fall to pieces like the body, because it is not made up of parts. Hence, when we say that it is immortal, we mean that it will last forever, unless He who holds it in existence withdraws His help.

(3) If we examine the world at any stage of its history, we shall arrive at the same conclusion. Go back, if you will, to the remote age when, according to scientists, nothing existed but the fiery nebula out of which all things around us today are supposed to have evolved. Here again you find a merely dependent thing: (a) it existed for a time; (b) it was composed of a definite number of particles linked together in definite ways, and the fact that it possessed such a particular arrangement and no other shows its dependence on something outside itself; it needs explanation quite as much as the blast-furnace in a factory. Existence does not belong to its nature.

Suppose we conceive the possibility that, amid all the transformations through which the world has passed, fundamental particles of some simple kind may have persisted fixed and unchanged, serving as the material out of which all else has been made. But these particles, as scientists themselves admit, would be dependent things: (a) they would possess only a definite, *limited* power, a fact which would send our mind in quest of further explanation; (b) the power exerted by them would be described by scientists—to put their view in the simplest form—as a certain amount of activity; but this activity would need explaining quite as much as the activity of our muscles. We might have ruled out the discussion of the nebula and fundamental atoms by simply asserting that the word "existence" will not be found in the description of either of them.

44

Dependent things are held in existence by an Independent Being. Since the visible world with all that it contains is dependent, it must be held in existence by some being distinct from it. If this being were dependent on a second and higher being, the second on a third, the third on a fourth, and so on endlessly, we should thus have an infinite series. But the entire series would be dependent quite as much as any member of it, and would not account for its continued existence. Therefore, no explanation of the continued existence of ourselves and all else in the world can be found, unless we admit the existence of an independent or necessary being, existing of itself, existing of its very nature.

The physical scientist's sphere of inquiry is restricted to the visible world, where he will never find anything but dependent things or activities like those with which we are familiar. His last word will take us no farther than the theory of the Indian sages who said that the earth is supported by an elephant, the elephant by a tortoise, and the tortoise by —?: he will never reach the end of his inquiry, because he will never see the Absolute, i.e., God, in the microscope.

The Independent or Necessary Being is God. The Independent or Necessary Being, the giver of dependent existence and the upholder of every dependently existing thing, from intelligent man down to the least material thing, must be a great living Power: we call Him God. Existence must belong to Him as truth belongs to the statement that "the whole is greater than its part." He must be self-existent. He must be one who cannot, without an absurdity, be divested of His existence. He must, therefore, be identified with existence itself, a concept which excludes every demand for further explanation and sets our mind at rest.

Notes. (1) For the purpose of this argument, it would have been sufficient to show that there is at least one contingent being in the world. From that one contingent being we could have proved the existence of a Self-existent Being.

(2) To the beginner in these studies, the proofs from Motion, Causality and Dependence may seem to be much alike. It is therefore well to point out that each leads to a distinct notion of the Supreme Being:

The proof from Motion shows that *He is not moved or changed by any other being.*

The proof from Causality shows that *He is not produced by any other being.*

The proof from Dependence shows that He exists necessarily—that *He exists without the help of any other being.*

In addition to the proofs for the existence of God set forth above, there are many others. Among them may be mentioned, in particular: the Aesthetic Argument, based on the perception of beauty in the universe; the Ethical Argument, based on the voice of conscience (a favourite of Newman); the Gradations of Being Argument (St Thomas' 4th way); and the Moral Argument or the Argument from the universal belief of mankind. All these arguments, save the last, have in common that they spring from a search for an *ultimate* explanation of reality.

45

B. THE NATURE OF GOD AS KNOWN FROM REASON

By the light of pure reason, we may arrive at some knowledge of the Nature of God from the fact that He is the First Cause, eternal and self-existent.

We can show that, since by the mere act of His will, He can call things out of nothingness into actual existence, and annihilate them at will, He must be the Master of existence, subject to no deficiency and containing within Himself in some higher way every created perfection that can possibly exist. In other words, we can show that He must be infinitely perfect—infinitely perfect in Power and Knowledge and Goodness and in the splendour of Beauty. But, to those who have been taught by Bethlehem and Calvary to know Him and love Him with a warm, personal love, our philosophic arguments must appear to be as chill and formal as the propositions of Geometry. The Incarnation of the Son of God has given sight to us men who were groping in darkness. He who dwelt among us has thrown a light on the Divine Nature which does not shine from the ablest treatise on philosophy.

THE PERFECTIONS OF GOD

Simplicity. God must be simple, i.e., He cannot consist of separate parts united into one whole. In a being so compounded, it is the union of parts that forms the whole. This union would require a cause. But the First Cause is uncaused.

Spirituality. God cannot be matter, because all matter is made up of parts. He is, therefore, a Being with no extension. But He is also an Active, Intelligent Being, because He is the Creator of all things, including the human soul. An Active, Intelligent Being without extension is a Spirit. Therefore, God is a Spirit.

Living in a material world we tend to look on material things—that is, extended things which can be seen and touched—as the most real. In truth, however, spiritual things are more real, more powerful, than material ones. A spiritual being lives more fully and at a higher level than does one bound up with matter.

Infinity. God is infinite, i.e., He possesses every perfection in its highest form—Power, Wisdom, Goodness, Kindness, and Mercy, and the Splendour of Beauty.
(1) We get the measure of a sculptor's ability by comparing the finished statue with the rude block of marble. His ability is in proportion to the distance he places between the perfect work of art and the unshapen stone. The greater the distance, the greater the ability. Now, the Divine Artificer had no material on which to begin His work. The things He made were nothing until He made them. But the distance between "nothing" and actual existence is infinite. God, therefore, produced

something which is at an infinite distance from its previous state. Such an act is infinite and can come only from an Infinite Being.[5]

Note. The arguments set forth below in (2), (3) and (4) rest on the truth, already established, that God is the only being whose nature is such that He must exist, as shown in the proof from dependence. God's nature is what makes Him God and sets Him apart from all else. How then can we best describe His nature? Is it enough to say that He is the most wise or the most beautiful of all beings? No; because we can think of a being as wise or beautiful without having to think of Him as actually existing. Search as we may, there is only one name for God which shows clearly what His nature is, and that name is Existence itself. As wisdom cannot be unwise or beauty unbeautiful, neither can existence itself be non-existing.

(2) We speak of a living plant, a living animal, a living man. Each of these possesses but a share of life, a limited life. But suppose that there were such a thing as life itself actually existing. It would not be a mere share of life; it would not be a limited life; it would be a perfect life. Now, apply this to what we know of God. He is Existence itself. He cannot even be conceived as non-existing. All other things get their existence from Him; their existence is limited. His existence is unlimited. He cannot be short of any perfection, for, if He were, He would have but a share of existence, and would not be Existence itself. Therefore God is infinite, i.e., He possesses, in its highest form, every perfection that can exist.

(3) A being is something that exists or that can be given existence. If it cannot be given existence, it is a mere nothing; it is something inconceivable (like a square circle). God is the Supreme Being. He is Existence itself. He is the Master of Existence. He can give existence to anything that can conceivably exist. If then we suppose Him to be wanting in any conceivable perfection, we are at once confronted with an absurdity, for He would possess the power to call that perfection into existence and should, therefore, already possess it. Not only should He already possess it but He should possess it in a higher form, as may be seen from the following illustration: The beauty of a picture comes from the aesthetic beauty of the painter's mind. His mind is capable of conceiving, in line and colour, countless beautiful designs; and, as the source must be higher than the stream that flows from it, so must his mind be in a higher order of beauty than any or all of the works he is capable of producing. So it is with God. He, the source of all conceivable beings, is above them all, and must possess in a higher way all their greatness and goodness and beauty.

(4) We can put the preceding argument in a slightly different form: if God, the Master of Existence, were imperfect, He could make Himself perfect; He could raise Himself from a lower to a higher state. But the less cannot produce the greater without outside help, and God could have no helper. Outside Him nothing can exist but His own creatures, things to which He has given a small share of being

---

[5] St Thomas, S.T., i, q. 45, a. 5, ad 3

and which He held in existence at every instant by His power. Therefore, the supposition that He could be imperfect is absurd.

Unity. (1) Since God is infinite, He must be One. Two infinite beings, each containing all perfections that can possibly exist, would be a contradiction. If there were two infinite beings, each should possess some perfection which the other did not have, otherwise they would not be distinct. But since each would be infinite, each should possess all perfections. Moreover, each would be independent, and outside the power of the other. Hence, neither could be infinite.

(2) Since God is Being Itself, He must be One, for Being Itself is one. If there were two Gods, each would possess but a share of Being, and neither would be identical with Being Itself.

Omnipotence. God is omnipotent, i.e., all-powerful, because He is infinite. All things that are possible He can do. They are possible only because He can do them. They can come into existence only because He can bring them into existence. He cannot contradict His own Will or Truth. He cannot commit sin, for instance, for the essence of sin is opposition to His Will. Nor can He attempt what is absurd, the making, for instance, of a four-sided triangle. Such a figure is a mere nothing, a contradiction in terms. This is no limitation upon His power, but an affirmation of His consistency and integrity. Human beings, because of the imperfection of their will or understanding, commit sin, or undertake what is intrinsically and ultimately absurd.

Omnipresence. God is omnipresent, i.e., He is everywhere, for He supports in existence everything outside Himself.

Omniscience. God is Omniscient, that is, He knows all things. He is Omniscient because His knowledge is infinite. He does not have a number of distinct ideas as we have, but by one act of His intellect He knows and knew from all eternity all things past, present, and to come.

Goodness and happiness. Goodness is what makes a thing or being truly desirable or pleasing. Since God is infinite, He is goodness without limit. He is infinitely pleasing to Himself and, therefore, He is infinitely happy in the possession of Himself.

Note. The Nature of God is incomprehensible. But so is our own nature. So is the nature of all things around us, from the star to the daisy by the wayside. Sir Isaac Newton, one of the greatest scientists that ever lived, compared himself to a little child picking up a few shells on the shore, while all the depths of the ocean remained hidden from him. He felt that his momentous discoveries had revealed, but without explaining, just one or two facets of the infinitely complicated structure of the universe, while all the rest lay beyond in impenetrable darkness. His knowledge seemed to him as nothing compared with his ignorance. If it is so difficult, then, to know anything worth knowing of the visible world, how incomparably more difficult must it be to understand the Nature of its Author?

The perfections of God in general. (1) We speak of men as possessing various perfections, e.g., wisdom, justice, courage, reasoning power, but not as possessing them in a perfect degree. No man is perfectly wise, just, courageous, logical. May we predicate all these things of God? No, not all, since some of them involve an imperfection. We may say that God is perfectly wise, i.e., that He knows the causes of all things, or that He is perfectly just, i.e., that He rewards and punishes according to merit. But we cannot say that He is perfectly courageous, for courage implies a willingness to face danger, and danger implies a weakness, a condition in which one's life is threatened. Neither can we say that He is perfectly logical, for the epithet implies the power of passing from the known to the unknown, and to God nothing can be unknown.

The perfections, traces of which we observe in men, are therefore of two kinds, absolute and relative. Absolute perfections of their own nature involve no imperfection, while relative perfections do involve an imperfection. The former class God possesses *formally*—that is, He possesses them as they are in themselves. The latter class He possesses *eminently*—that is, He is the source, perfect in itself, whence they are derived.

(2) Some say that the perfections we ascribe to God are merely "anthropomorphic", i.e., imitations of human perfections; that if, for instance, a watch could think, it would have just as much right to argue that the watchmaker was made up of springs and cog-wheels, as we have to say that God possesses intelligence, goodness, justice, etc. We reply (a) that we do not ascribe to God mere imitations of our human perfections; that the perfections we ascribe to God are found in Him in an infinitely higher manner than in creatures; that in creatures intelligence, goodness, justice are distinct qualities, while in God, in some incomprehensible way, they and all perfections are one and the same, identical with His nature or essence; (b) that, if the analogy of the watch were justified, we should be found ascribing to God hands and eyes and bodily organs, but such is not the fact; that, if the watch could reason aright, it would justly ascribe to the watchmaker the beginning of its movement and the orderly arrangements of its parts.

Conclusion. Thus, with no aid beyond the natural light of reason, we have laid bare the foundation on which all religion is built. We have discovered the great fundamental truths that God of His own free will has created the universe; that He has given us every good thing we possess, our life and our very being; that He holds us in existence from instant to instant; that, without His supporting hand, we and the whole world with us would lapse into the nothingness from which He has called us; that He is supreme in goodness, wisdom and power.

Our reason casts us at His feet. It impels us to a great act of loving adoration. It bids us tell Him that we love Him with our whole heart and mind and soul, and that we humbly and gladly acknowledge His absolute dominion over us and our absolute dependence on Him.

Our use of Philosophy. Philosophy is the science which, by the use of reason alone, endeavours to find an ultimate explanation of the world and our knowledge of it. The philosophy which we follow is substantially that of Aristotle; and our proofs for the existence of God rest on the principles which he formulated. Numerous other systems of philosophy have been proposed, but they have been mere fashions of thought, each having its vogue, and each in due course falling into disrepute because of its inherent absurdity. However, Aristotle failed to make full use of his own principles and was thus led to a denial of God's providence. The Catholic Scholastic philosophers who have worked out the foregoing proofs say that their philosophical principles and categories are inherent in nature itself. As we shall now see, Kantian philosophy and its derivatives say that their categories are imposed or created by man's mind. As such, they can make no claim to be accepted universally at all.

C. REPLIES TO OBJECTIONS AGAINST THE PROOFS OF GOD'S EXISTENCE AND NATURE

KANT: HIS PHILOSOPHY; HIS CRITICISM OF OUR PROOFS. **The philosophy of Kant.** Immanuel Kant, a German philosopher (1724-1804), held that space and time are mental forms and nothing more; that they are moulds within our minds, which give our thoughts their special shape or quality. Thus, the world about us, the earth, the sun, the stars, our own bodies, the people with whom we converse, the very book we are reading, are all so many images which our mind has constructed. Similarly, our conviction that time is passing, that we have lived so many years, that such-and-such events belong to this or that point in the past, is merely a notion fashioned by ourselves. Then, does nothing really exist? Yes, he says, there is something really existing outside our mind, acting on it, and giving rise to all the different kinds of ideas we have. This real thing, however, cannot be known as it is in itself.

The successors of Kant, as one would expect, went a step further and denied the existence of the external reality which he postulates. One of his disciples, Fichte (d. 1814), held that we ourselves do not exist, nor anything outside us; that nothing exists but thought. In other words, he maintained that thought exists but not the mind that thinks it. He and those that share his views are called Idealists. Kant was a modified or incomplete Idealist: an Idealist because he said that our ideas are not the images or likenesses of anything real—an incomplete Idealist, because he held that they are derived from some really existing thing even though its nature is unknown to us.

His teaching, logically developed, takes us even beyond the absurdity at which Fichte arrived. It leads to the conclusion, now held by many in the modern world, that truth itself is only the result of a "mould" of the mind, so that a doctrine can be, at one and the same time, both true and false—true for some, and false for others.

No form of Idealism, however plausibly constructed, can ever command wide acceptance. The principles that an external world really exists, and that a true knowledge of it can be obtained through the senses and the intellect, will always be regarded as self-evident and unassailable truths not only by the generality of mankind, but by all sane and profound thinkers. The undoubted hold which Kant still has on a small circle of intellectuals is due to the ability which he displayed in his wide survey of all branches of knowledge, and the ingenuity with which he worked out the details of an elaborate system, based though it was on the shifting sands of falsehood.

Kant's criticism of our proofs of God's existence. Kant did not deny the existence of God, though if he had been logical he would have done so. He put it forward as a practical necessity: if there were no God, he says, there would be no morality, and morality is a necessity of social life.

Kant objects as follows against the proof from order in nature:

A. "The order which we observe in nature is a limited or infinite thing. It might have been produced by a finite being. We are not justified, therefore, in concluding that it must be the work of an infinite being."

Reply: 1. Neither the argument from order nor any of the arguments for God's existence professes to prove that He is infinite. This is quite clear from the italics at the head of this Chapter where we state what we purpose proving. Each argument examines some phase or aspect of the world—its order, its mechanism of cause and effect, its motion, its (instances of) dependence—and shows that each phase finds its ultimate explanation in a being distinct from the world, supreme and intelligent. No doubt, at the close of each argument, we push on to the further conclusion that God is infinite, but that conclusion, though correctly drawn, is not required for our proof of His existence. It belongs strictly to the Section B, "The Nature of God as Known from Reason", where we address ourselves directly to the questions of whether He is one or several, whether He is spirit, whether He is infinite, etc.

2. Let us suppose for the moment that the objection is sound. Let us suppose that the great Designer of the world is a finite being. What follows? A most important conclusion, fatal to materialists, who hold that nothing exists except what we perceive by our senses—the conclusion that, outside the world and distinct from it, there exists some Being of vast intelligence and power, on whom we are utterly dependent.

3. A thing may be finite, and yet the work done in connection with it may be possible only to an infinite being. A grain of sand is only a finite thing, yet to make it from nothing demands infinite power. He who at His word can create a grain of sand is the Master of existence, and with equal ease could give existence to worlds immeasurably greater than ours. Our mind can conceive no limit to His power. So, too, with the ordered universe: the universe is limited, yet the order which it reveals as we have shown above (pp.26-8; 33-5), is due to a power and intelligence to which the human mind can affix no limit. It is due to a Being whose infinity we are unable to question or deny. But we may bring this argument to a sharper point: Life, the source of the marvellous order we observe in plants, animals and men, was introduced into the world at some point of time in the remote past. It was created, and its creation is a direct proof of the infinite power of the Designer.

We have given Kant's objection against the argument from order, because it is one that anyone might reasonably propose. The only other arguments that he notices are those from Causality and Dependence, but his attacks on them are undeserving of an extensive reply.

B.   Kant held that the Law of Causality is merely a conception of the mind. Innumerable examples will show the absurdity of this. Let one suffice. Look at a watch. You see the second-hand moving quickly round its little dial. You attribute its busy movement to the works within; that is, you hold that the works are the cause of the motion of the hand. But Kant would say: "No. Neither you nor any man can ever tell whether the works drive the second-hand or not. All that you can justly assert is that your mind *represents* the works as the cause, and the motion of the hand as the effect." We need not be astonished that Kant should hold such an absurd opinion. In his view, the watch, with its mainspring, wheels, dial, hands, and case, is simply a construction which our own mind has fashioned from some unknown and unknowable reality outside us.

Kant would say also that what we call "causes" must always be things that can be perceived by the senses, and hence that we can never prove the existence of an invisible First Cause. This error too can be swiftly extinguished: our will is imperceptible to the senses, and yet it can work on the muscles of our body, causing movement in our limbs. Neither causes nor effects need be visible: for example, our will can move our intellect to build up a new science. The science would be the product or effect of the working of the intellect; and the working of the intellect would be caused by the will; and yet neither will nor intellect nor science is perceptible to the senses.

C. Apart from the special errors of his philosophy, Kant completely misunderstood the argument from Dependence. He fancied that, when fully analysed, it was identical with a proof put forward by Descartes (1596-1650),[6] who derived his inspiration from St Anselm (c. 1033-1109). The proof may be put as follows: "All, even atheists, understand by the word 'God' a being who contains all perfections. But existence is a perfection; therefore, God must exist." This proof is obviously defective.

In the first place, it is not true that all, even atheists, understand by the word "God" a being who contains all perfections. "Many of the ancients", as St Thomas says, "asserted that this world is God",[7] and therefore supposed Him to be limited.

In the second place, the conclusion, "God must exist", does not follow. All that follows is that those who conceive God as a being possessing all perfections must conceive Him as existing. But to conceive Him *within* our mind as existing is no proof that He actually exists *outside* our mind.

Thirdly, as St Thomas says, the truth of the statement, "the whole is greater than its part", is immediately evident to us, because it is contained in the very

---

[6] What is called "modern philosophy", i.e., philosophy tainted with idealism, owes its origin to the celebrated French mathematician Descartes. He held that extension and motion are the only properties (of bodies) which have any real existence outside our mind.

[7] *Summa Contra Gentiles*, Book I, ch. 11

meaning of "the whole". But the truth of the statement, "God exists", is not immediately evident to us. If, however, we knew the meaning of "God" as fully and clearly as we know the meaning of "the whole", we should see at once that God must possess all the highest perfections including that of perfect existence. We should see that our very idea of Him had flashed into our mind from a being existing outside our mind. His existence would be known to us as immediately as the existence of the book we see before us on the table. But our knowledge of God did not come to us immediately from Himself. In our childhood it came to us through the word of our parents, and later on, when we were able to reason for ourselves, we saw that what they told us was true: a truth based on authority or reasoning is only indirectly known to us. It is not self-evident: St Anselm's basic assumption is therefore false.[8]

The great St Anselm, who first proposed this proof, did not deny the value of the others. It was his laudable purpose to construct a simple argument which would carry conviction to all men, but he did not succeed. He was refuted by St Thomas Aquinas (d. 1274), Bl. Duns Scotus (d. 1308) and many other Catholic philosophers.

AN OBJECTION AGAINST THE NATURE OF GOD

The sufferings of life and the prodigality of nature seem to argue against the wisdom of God. The notion that there are defects in the work of God is due, not to the imperfect character of His design, but to our imperfect understanding of it. We cannot hope to understand God's purpose in everything. His design is not always clear to us. Sometimes we not only fail to discover wisdom in the happenings of life, but seem to find a colossal cruelty in them. "Why", we ask, "is there so much pain and grief in the world?" But, if there were no pain nor grief, there would be no pity nor self-sacrifice, no noble discipline for the soul of man. To complete our answer we must look to Revelation. It will tell us of the fall of man and its consequences.[9]

Sometimes we marvel at the prodigality of nature, and ask ourselves why there are so many useless things in the world. On this point one scientist has remarked that if the animals called labyrinthodonts, which belong to the early geological ages, had been endowed with intelligence, they might have made a strong case against the wisdom of Providence from the lavish waste of fern spores. Yet, all that vegetable waste has given us coal. The animals would have judged wrongly from their not being able to foresee events of what was to them an incalculably remote future. When a brood of young birds die before fledging, their bodies feed a multitude of smaller creatures. These serve for others, and ultimately swarms of bacteria reduce lifeless organic matter to elements which serve to nourish vegetation, which serves to feed worms and other creatures, which again actively minister to the welfare of all the higher animals and of man. Nature is so arranged that the purpose of its First Cause can never be defeated, happen what may.

---

[8] Ibid., start of ch. 11
[9] See Part II, Ch 7, "Original Sin".

Our argument does not require us to prove design in *all* things. It is sufficient to prove it in *some* things. Neither are we called on to prove that the design is perfect. Whether perfect or imperfect, it establishes the existence of a Designer. A manual loom proves the existence of a designer just as well as an electric loom, although the design may be less perfect in the one case than in the other. A dormitory with nineteen beds made and one unmade, makes us just as certain of the activity of a bedmaker, as we would be if the twenty beds were made.

D. ATHEISM

We apply the term *atheist*, not to those who deny the existence of an Ultimate Reality, a First Cause of all things, for there are none such, but to those who deny the existence of a Personal God, Intelligent and Free, to whom men are responsible for their actions.

(1) The fact that the greatest minds in all ages were firm believers in a Personal God refutes the contention that such a belief is the mark of ignorance and low civilisation. Our belief, and the belief of the vast majority of mankind, was the belief: (a) of the ancient philosophers, Plato, and Aristotle, men to whom the modern world owes a debt that cannot be easily estimated; (b) of the world-acclaimed geniuses Leonardo da Vinci and Michelangelo; (c) of the astronomers, Copernicus, Galileo, Kepler, Newton, Leverrier, and Herschel; of the chemists, Berzelius, Dumas, Liebig, Chevreul, Davy, and Dalton; of the zoologist and geologist, Cuvier; of Schwann, the founder of the modern school of physiology; of the physicists, Ohm, Ampère, Galvani, Volta, Faraday, Joule, Clerk Maxwell, and Lord Kelvin; and of Pasteur, to whom humanity is so much indebted for having founded the study of bacteriology.

It is the belief of all the members of the Catholic Association of Scientists and Engineers, founded in the 1990's by physicist Dr Francis J. Kelly in the U.S.A., an association whose members and conference speakers include Celso S. Barrientos, Joseph Batuello, Wilfred G. Chen, Scott R. Chubb, Pierre Conway O.P, William R. Coulson, Peter Hodgson, Dianne Irving, Rex S. Kochanski, Rocco Martino, Edmund J. Mazza, Dunstan Robidoux O.S.B. Also worthy of mention is Hungarian-born physicist and theologian Fr Stanley Jaki O.S.B., who has written much on the relationship between science and religion.

These are but a few of the names that might be mentioned. An exhaustive list would include the greatest statesmen, artists, poets, generals, inventors and scholars of every age.

(2) Atheism is found chiefly among (a) men who find the belief in a Personal God an irksome check on the indulgence of their passions, and (b) students of physical science who, from a too intense concentration on

their own particular line of work, which is concerned exclusively with material things, come to doubt all that is spiritual and moral, everything in fact, except those things to which the tests of the laboratory can be applied.

Atheism is the enemy of human nature. Atheism has already been refuted by our arguments for God's existence, but it can be refuted also by the fact that it is contrary to the well-being and nature of man.

Society is necessary for man, because it is only as a member of society that man can attain to the normal development of his faculties; and society can have no stable and happy existence unless its members observe the moral law. The moral law requires justice and kindness in those who govern, and willing obedience and loyalty in their citizens. It forbids murder, lying, fraud, and every kind of wicked desire. It unites husband and wife in lifelong marriage; it binds the family together, and ensures the proper rearing of children. That society is necessary for man, and that its success depends on the observance of the moral law—these are truths which no sane man denies. They flash out from our very reason, and they cannot be rejected unless we surrender all trust in human intelligence, and confess that the discovery of truth is impossible. But, for the mass of mankind, the observance of moral law, over any great stretch of time, is quite impossible, unless they believe in a Personal God, All-powerful, All-knowing, who will reward the good and punish the wicked. Belief in a Personal God, therefore, is a demand of our very reason and nature, and must be true. "If God does not exist, everything is permitted."[10]

"It may be objected that in many countries today large sections of the population either deny or ignore the existence of God, and yet are well-behaved. We reply that these are people whose good habits have been derived from believing parents or from other Christian influences; that the momentum of Christianity by which they are now being carried along will inevitably spend itself in this or a future generation; and that their Atheism, which removes the only effective check on sin, will inevitably lead to moral degradation and the destruction of human society. Atheism is man's greatest enemy." - So wrote Dr Sheehan for the 1939 edition of this book. We may remark: amid the violence, crime, lawlessness, vandalism, dishonesty, obscenity, scandals and family breakdown of the late 20th century, no-one can deny the prophetic nature of these words and the truth of the teaching that inspired them.

Atheism has taken several forms, which we deal with in the following pages.

MATERIALIST EVOLUTION

Materialists hold that nothing exists but matter and its modifications. In ancient times, the chief materialists were Democritus of Abdera (d. 360 B.C.) and Epicurus (d. 270 B.C.); in modern times, the French Encyclopaedists, Diderot and d'Alembert (c. 1750), Feuerbach (d. 1872), and E. Haeckel (d. 1919). They were succeeded by Marxists and Communists, and other philosophers adhering to secular humanism.

---

[10] Dostoievsky, *The Brothers Karamazov*, Bk 5

In its existing form, Materialism takes its colour from the theory of evolution. It is explained and refuted in the following paragraphs. (The theory of Materialist Evolution is shown in Apologetics to be contrary to reason. The Catholic reader is of course aware that it is contrary to Divine Faith also).

Materialist evolution says that the laws of nature may be due to blind forces inherent in matter itself. We may express the doctrine in the following form: "Nothing exists, nothing ever existed but matter, i.e., nothing but what has extension (length, breadth, and width), and can be perceived by the senses. The universe was once a fiery rotating nebula, a cloud of glowing gas; it matters not how we describe it. Its molecules possessed those chemical and physical forces which, by action and interaction, have gradually evolved the great variety of things, with and without life, which we see in the world at the present day. Living creatures are, therefore, nothing more than cunning mechanisms. Thought and will are mere motions of matter."

Under criticism this theory falls to pieces. Though it has been implicitly refuted by our proofs of God's existence, its defects and absurdities become still more manifest when we reflect on all that it involves.

The theory does not account for the characteristics of the original nebula. We here develop more fully a point on which we touched in the proof from dependence. Granted for the moment that Materialist Evolution accounts satisfactorily for the universe as it now stands, what of the original matter itself? Its motion, its physical and chemical laws, the precise number of its particles and their relative position—all these and other characteristics—call for an explanation, because they of themselves offer none.

(1) The motion of the original nebula must have been in one definite direction: why in that particular direction rather than another? Our reason insists that the direction must have been determined by a cause. Its velocity also was a definite velocity. Why that exact and particular velocity rather than another? Our reason again demands a cause. Why did the original nebula move at all, unless under the influence of an outside cause?

(2) The physical and chemical laws governing the supposed development of the nebula formed one particular set or system. But why that particular system rather than another? Furthermore, the very fact that matter obeyed that particular combination of laws demands an explanation, a cause: it points conclusively to the determining mind of the Lawgiver.

(3) The original nebula was made up of a number of particles in a definite arrangement. There was no absolute necessity for that particular number of particles, or for that particular arrangement of these particles. Fix your mind on any one atom or ultimate particle of the nebula: it gives no explanation of itself, or of its position with regard to the other particles. How did it come to hold the position it occupied? Why did it have the particular particles that were around it, and not a completely different set of neighbours? The same questions may be asked of any

other particle we choose to examine. And why was there the particular number of particles that actually formed the nebula and not a different number?

The original mass of matter, therefore, does not explain itself. It is not by its nature a necessary thing. It calls for an explanation; it requires a cause. And we are back again to the Uncaused Cause, to the Universal Designer, to the Necessary Being.

The theory does not account for the origin of life and reason. The theory assumes quite gratuitously that life had its origin from non-living matter. As the science of biology advances, that unsupported theory is being more and more discounted. There is not a shred of evidence in its favour. On the contrary, it has been demonstrated that the living cell possesses a structure complicated beyond description, and that in its action it differs essentially from any material machine that we know of. Even the most recent advances in biology by the most learned scientists with the best equipped laboratories have brought us no closer to the artificial production of life. Yet we are to imagine that mindless nebula had the power to organise themselves into complex systems that the greatest minds today cannot fully understand or explain. A remarkable illustration of the truth that life can come only from life is found in the aseptic treatment of wounds. This treatment depends on two facts, viz., (i) that if germs are permitted to get into a wound, they may propagate their kind, and so cause putrefaction, often with fatal results to the patient; (ii) that if germs are entirely excluded from the wound, no corruption takes place, and the healing process is unimpeded.

Even if the great chasm between living and lifeless matter were successfully bridged, there would still remain the greater chasms between sentient and non-sentient life, thinking and non-thinking. Spirit differs absolutely from matter (as we shall see in Chapter 2). The human soul, by its ideas of truth and beauty, by its judgements of good and evil, exhibits itself as something completely different from a material thing. A mass of mere matter has in no way the power of a thinking being, and can never give itself these powers. The chasm between them is impassable. It is a maxim in Philosophy, approved by common sense, that, without extrinsic aid, the less can never produce the greater: life, therefore, cannot come from dead matter, nor sentient life from non-sentient, or rational life from irrational, except by the act of some Power capable of breathing into matter these higher activities. - On the other hand, if human intelligence is merely the final product of mindless matter, why should we give assent to its conclusions? The theory of Materialist Evolution formulated by such an intelligence must also itself be a mindless product of evolution and may be a total illusion. The theory is self-destructive.

The theory offers us no more than a series of absurdities. Taking a general survey, see what the theory proposes: the original mass of matter derived its temperature and motion from nowhere. After some time, some fragment of it, by a process inconceivable to the modern chemist, made itself into the first living thing. Somehow or other, that living thing acquired the power of propagating itself, and of developing under a law of unexplained origin, into the higher forms of life, and finally into man himself. Poets, philosophers, scientists, and all their works, are, therefore, the offspring of a mere clod of earth, developing under the influence of a law which sprang out of nowhere, which was imposed by no lawgiver, which wrought and shaped with consummate skill, although there was not a glimmer of intelligence to guide it. The more this Naturalist or Materialist Evolution is examined, the more preposterous it seems. As a final and complete explanation of the world, it is a far greater absurdity than the statement that the paintings of the Sistine Chapel were the work of an unaided paintbrush and buckets of paint. It was much in vogue among the rationalists during the latter years of the 19th century. It was advocated as the full explanation of things, but nowadays the difficulties against its acceptance are admitted to be overwhelming. In those days, scientists felt they were on the verge of a complete explanation of all things, and that it was only a matter of time for this to occur. Since then, they have discovered that the most basic elements of matter—to say nothing of basic life forms—are extraordinarily complex, and defy simple material depictions and explanations.

Even if the fact of an unbroken line of evolution from matter to man were established beyond doubt, the arguments for an Intelligent First Cause would remain unaffected. In fact, if it could be proved that the world passed through this orderly and progressive development, like the seed that becomes the giant of the forest, then the argument for the necessity of a designer, lawgiver and perfecter, so far from losing force, would only receive an intensified cogency. The more vast and complicated the design, and the more intricate the interdependence of order, the clearer becomes the evidence for the mind of the Designer. *However* this world came to be, it cannot be but the work of a vast Intelligence.

PANTHEISM

The chief Pantheists were, in ancient times, Heraclitus (c. 500 B.C.), and the Stoics (a school of philosophy founded c. 350 B.C.); in modern times, Spinoza (d. 1677), Fichte (d. 1814), Hegel (d. 1831), Schelling (d. 1854), Einstein (d. 1955) and others. Pantheism, in the form in which it is commonly professed, is the direct opposite of Materialism. Materialism holds that nothing exists but matter; Pantheism, that nothing exists but spirit, God, the Absolute. "God is everything, and everything is God" sums it up. Therefore, according to the Pantheists, all the phenomena of the universe, all contingent beings, are but manifestations of the Divine Nature; everything is one and the same. The logical issue of these principles is to remove all distinction between right and wrong, and to identify God with all sorts of different things—good and evil, living and lifeless, intelligent and unintelligent, present, past, and future. Pantheists do not shrink from such conclusions, and so set themselves in opposition to the common sense of mankind. It is patently ridiculous to say that a cat is the same real being with the mouse which she devours, and with the dog that worries her, and that cat and dog alike are the same being with the owner who looks after them. It is absurd to maintain that the criminal to be sentenced is really the same being with the judge who pronounces the sentence against him, and with the jailer who carries out this sentence. And who can accept the statement that the atheist is substantially the same being with God, whose existence he denies?

Albert Einstein, had he been a consistent Pantheist, must have held that he and the German Government which banished him for being a Jew—that he and the German scientists with whom he exchanged angry letters on the subject of his expulsion—that he and those unable to understand his theory of relativity—are all the one identical being. Emerson, the American writer, was a believer in Pantheism. In a stanza of one of his favourite poems, he represents the pantheistic God as solemnly identifying itself with several things. Andrew Lang parodied the stanza as follows: "I am the batsman and the bat, / I am the bowler and the ball, / The umpire, the pavilion cat, / The roller, pitch, and stumps and all."

Briefly, Pantheism must be rejected: (1) because it is opposed to the infinite perfection of God: God cannot change; He cannot become greater or less; He cannot be identical with what is limited, whether it be matter or human intelligence; (2) because it destroys God's freedom by representing Him as a kind of intelligent machine with no power of choosing, and as compelled by His nature to produce all the happenings of the world, including the decisions of human beings; (3) because it is opposed to human consciousness, i.e., to the knowledge which a person has of his own mind: every person is conscious of his individuality and of his free will. Every person knows as clearly as he can know anything that he is distinct from the world around him, and that his will is free. If he is deceived in either of these, there is an end of certainty, and all reasoning becomes futile. Further, if his will is not free, he is no longer responsible for his acts, and cannot be punished or rewarded for them, a conclusion opposed to the normal reason of mankind, and therefore unsound.

AGNOSTICISM

The term 'Agnostic' was invented by Thomas Huxley (d. 1895). Herbert Spencer (d. 1903), the chief exponent of Agnosticism, said the final explanation of the world is to be found in an infinite, eternal energy from which all things proceed—the ultimate Reality, unknown and unknowable, transcending human thought. Because of the inconsistency of his exposition, it is difficult to say whether his difference with us is partly a mere matter of words, or whether he is upholding a form of materialism, already refuted. Today, however, the word 'agnostic' means nothing more than to be uncertain as to ultimate truth. An 'agnostic' (from the Greek, meaning: not to know) is someone who says, "I do not know if God exists; I do not know if any religion is true." In itself, therefore, it is not a position of mind, but a refusal to take up a position. It is a declaration of incapacity to make an intellectual decision in the most crucial matter in life. The truth is, however, that many agnostics are, in practical terms, atheists, since they act as if there were no God: they never offer a prayer to God, do not fulfil any religious commandments at all, and do not seek religious instruction. An agnostic, if sincere, has the duty to search for the truth until he finds it—not abandon the search. Often, the profession of agnosticism is only a pretence by which one avoids having to defend the absurdity of atheism, while living no differently from an atheist.

ATHEISTIC EXISTENTIALISM

Atheistic existentialism attempts to reduce a consistent atheistic attitude to its logical consequences. As a philosophy of life, it has been popularised in novels by writers such as Jean-Paul Sartre and Albert Camus. The 'Theatre of the Absurd', of playwrights Samuel Beckett, Harold Pinter and others, is another literary expression of it, using discordant and disconnected dramatic actions to express the absurdity of the human condition. Denying that God exists, the existentialist believes that he is logical in finding the world to be absurd and meaningless. He finds himself committed to the rejection of the ideas of law and value, and is forced to regard life as totally purposeless and meaningless—not even death has a meaning. He cannot even find a reason for taking life seriously. In the end, there is nothing worth living for, and nothing worth dying for. But he is, himself, located in the world and is subject to its various forms of impact. From this situation there is no escape, and human life resolves itself into hopelessness, anguish, dread and disgust.

The absurdity and harm of such conclusions—for even common sense tells us that life has a meaning and value—reveals the utter unthinkableness of atheism. The Catholic will appreciate, however, the significance of the existentialist admission that a universe in which there is no God is meaningless, and that attempts of rationalists to make sense of the universe without reference to God are doomed to failure.

NIHILISM

Nihilism is an attitude or viewpoint denying all traditional values and moral truths. The term was coined by Ivan Turgenev in his novel *Fathers and Sons* (1862) and has been applied since to various radical movements. In rallying against Czarist oppression, the Russian nihilists of the 19th century renounced God, the soul, the State, the Church, morality, nationality and high culture.

In its modern expression, "nihilism is the cult of nothingness; the belief that behind the appearance of reality there is nothing: no God, no truth, no right, no wrong, only sensation and satisfaction."[11] It is the prevailing philosophy of the modern age, and is the source of the modern boredom, aimlessness, confusion, hopelessness, restlessness, and endless seeking for sensuous entertainment. Within nihilism, whether a proposition is true or false is of no interest; all that matters is what a thing does for "Me, now". In nihilist morality, all things are permitted, provided the individual finds them useful. As a philosophy of belief, it falls under all the condemnations of atheism above. As a philosophy of life, it stands condemned by all its modern fruits.

THE NEW AGE

The 'New Age' is a term embracing a variety of modern beliefs and practices which have all the markings of ancient gnosticism, in that they promise a species of enlightenment and salvation outside the sober and traditional Christian religion.

---

[11] B.A. Santamaria, *Australia at the Crossroads*, Melbourne University Press 1987, pp.88-9

The New Age is a mixture of ancient gnosticism, pantheism, modern pseudo-science, occultism, eastern religions, and pop psychology.[12]

Judgement on the New Age. (a) *On the level of reason and religion in general:* the New Age is devoid of logic or intellectual rigour. Its different systems are contradictory of one another. It is but a substitute for religion, it entails no genuine moral commitment, and does not require repentance and penance. It does not face the question of God directly; it does not acknowledge the eternal, free, intelligent Creator worthy of our love, adoration and obedience. It is not focused on any person except one's own ego. The New Age takes no responsibility for the effects it has upon people's lives, it condones the use of mind-bending and mind-numbing drugs and often makes wild claims which it can never fulfil. It exploits people's credulity and demands exorbitant fees for its 'services'. It exemplifies perfectly the dictum: "When people stop believing in God, they don't believe in nothing, they will believe in anything."

(b) *Incompatibility with the Catholic religion:* the New Age seeks sometimes to use the name of Jesus and incorporate Him into its ideas on peace and healing, etc., whilst totally misrepresenting or ignoring Christ's other doctrines and demands, e.g., on the necessity of baptism, the permanence of marriage, the requirement of forgiveness, doing penance, carrying one's cross, worshipping and believing in the one true God, confessing one's sins, avoiding adultery and idolatry, hating sin, refusing to entertain the devil. It depersonalises the Triune God of Christian revelation, who is reduced to some nameless cosmic force. It has no place for the redeeming sacrifice of Christ. It rejects the teaching authority and the institution of the Church. It deforms language by using Biblical and Christian terms but with a new meaning.[13]

The despair ushered in by the various forms of atheism may lead people, in the long run, to recoil in horror from it and seek the meaning of life in God who is its Author and its End.

---

[12] See M. Pacwa S.J. *Catholics and the New Age*, Servant Publications, Michigan 1992.
[13] Cf. *Pastoral Instruction on the New Age*, Archbishop Norberto Rivera Carrera, Mexico City, 1996.

CHAPTER 2

THE HUMAN SOUL AS KNOWN BY PURE REASON

Summary

Brief presentation of the argument.

Detailed presentation:
A. Man's soul is spiritual.
> Meaning of life and soul.
> The soul of man gets its knowledge of material things through the senses, of immaterial things through the mind.
> Man's will is free. How the will is exercised. Definition of free-will.
> How man differs from lower animals; man is progressive, because he is rational; the lower animals are stationary, because irrational.
> Man's work is marked by diversity, because his will is free; the work of animals is marked by uniformity, because they are not free.
> Conclusion: the soul of man is spiritual, because it acts independently of matter and is self-directing. Therefore it can exist apart from the body.
> Objections answered.
B. Man's soul is immortal.

The human soul. We can divide all living things into plants, animals, and men. Plants have the power of growth; animals have the power of growth and sensation; men have the power of growth, sensation and reasoning. Every living thing has within itself the source of its own special power, the source of its own activity. That source, in plants and animals, is called the principle of life; in man, it is called the soul.

We can learn something of man's soul by observing what it enables him to do. We notice that, in contrast to the lower animals, he is not occupied entirely with what his senses tell him. He is not concerned solely with the quest for food and animal pleasures. In his perceptions and desires, he is not pinned down to merely material objects. He can rise above everything in the visible world, and pass into a higher region. He can form ideas of "truth", "justice", "wisdom", "eternity" and countless other such things which he could never have perceived with his eyes or ears or other sense organs. He can think of God and His angels, and he can love them; yet God and His angels are utterly beyond anything his senses can show him. They are not material things with length, breadth and depth. They are living, intelligent beings with no extension; that is, they are spirits. Man's soul, therefore, being fitted by its nature for the contemplation of immaterial things and for intercourse with spiritual beings, must itself be akin to them; it must be immaterial and spiritual; or, more plainly, it must be a spirit.

Not only is the soul a spirit, but it is also an immortal spirit. It is not an extended thing like the eye or the ear; it is not made up of parts that can be taken asunder. It does not perish with the body: "Dust thou art, to dust returnest"[1] was not spoken of the soul. After death it can continue to exercise its higher spiritual activity. It cannot be destroyed by any power except that of God Himself, the Master of existence; and, as the voice of nature confirmed by Revelation tells us, God will never annihilate the soul of man.[2]

A. THE SOUL OF MAN IS SPIRITUAL

The soul or principle of life. We are familiar with the common distinction between things with life and things without life. By life we understand a special kind of activity which manifests itself in various ways, in growth, sensation, free movement, intelligence and reasoning. Plants grow and put forth leaf and flower; animals feel pain or pleasure, and possess freedom of movement; man grows like the plant, he has feeling and movement like the animal, and, in addition, he thinks and reasons. Every living thing—plant, animal, or man—has within itself the principle of its own activity. That principle we call "soul" or "principle of life." Strictly speaking, we may apply the word "soul" to the vital principle of plants and animals, but, in ordinary speech, we confine it to the vital principle of man. Now, we may learn much about the character of a man by reading about his behaviour, without ever seeing him. Similarly, without directly perceiving the human soul, we may discover much about its nature by studying the acts that proceed from it.

The human soul in relation to knowledge. Let us examine the activity of the human soul in relation to knowledge.
THE KNOWLEDGE GIVEN BY THE SENSES. Man is like a city with five gates. Through each gate, messengers come with tidings of what is passing in the outer world. These gates are the five senses, and each sense allows some special kind of knowledge to pass in. Man has no other means than these of knowing anything about the external world. Through the eye he gets a knowledge of colour, through the ear of sound, through the nose of smell, through the palate of taste, and through the whole surface of the body, but particularly through the hands, he comes to know of the resistance, of hardness, and softness of bodies and such like.

The eye is the organ, or instrument, of sight, the ear of hearing, and so on with the rest. Each organ is a part of the body, or, for the sense of touch, the entire body, and is acted on only by things that are themselves bodies—that is, by things that are material, things that have length, breadth and depth. The eye cannot see an object, unless its retina be set in motion by the vibrating ether. The ear cannot hear

---

[1] Gen 3:19

[2] The reader may prefer at this point to pass straight to Chapter 3. (Chapters 1 and 2 are the most difficult of this book).

a sound, unless its tympanum be struck by the air-waves. The nostrils cannot perceive the perfume of a flower, unless the minute fragrant particles actually penetrate to them. The palate cannot taste, and the hand cannot feel without coming into direct contact with their objects.

THE KNOWLEDGE GIVEN BY THE INTELLECT AND REASON. Man knows many more things than the senses tell him. Let us take some simple examples. When we say that "Honesty is the best policy" we understand what we mean by "honesty", and yet we cannot have learned its import by the senses alone. We may be acquainted with an honest man, we may see him do an honest act, but "honesty" itself we have never seen nor heard, nor grasped in any way by the senses. So, too, with such words as "truth", "goodness", "justice" and all the other abstract terms. We may have heard a true statement, witnessed a good deed, or listened to a just judgement. But we have never reached "truth", "goodness" and "justice" themselves with any organs of sense. Or again, we say that "man is a rational animal." No man that we ever saw was without a particular height, complexion, manner, and yet we think of none of these things when we use the word "man." We are thinking of something common to all men, but which, by itself, we have never seen or perceived by any of the senses.

The senses allow knowledge of the outer world to pass into us. Some power within us raises the data supplied by the senses to a higher plane—a plane which the senses themselves could have never reached. That power we variously call intellect, reason or mind. These are simply other names for the thinking or rational soul.

The human soul in relation to the exercise of the will. Let us now examine the activity of the soul in regard to free choice.

MAN'S WILL IS FREE. Man is conscious that his will is free, i.e., that he performs actions over which he has mastery. He is conscious of the power to choose whether he will or will not do a certain act. Every day, in matters trivial or important, he is aware of the exercise of his freedom. When he chooses one course rather than another, he knows that he has acted freely and might have chosen differently. I am writing just now. I am sure that I can refrain from writing if I choose to do so. If our wills were not free, "then counsels, exhortations, precepts, prohibitions, rewards and punishments would be meaningless."[3] When a man violates a law, the State will punish him, not exactly because he has violated it—for it will not punish him, if he is insane—but because he has violated it wilfully and was free to refrain from doing so. We chastise a dog for disobedience, not because we regard him as a free agent and as responsible for his act, but because we wish him to associate disobedience with suffering, and thus, for sensate reasons, to refrain from those acts.

HOW FREE WILL IS EXERCISED: ITS DEFINITION. A young man about to decide, let us suppose, whether he should study music or marketing, tries to take the measure of his aptitude for each of the two careers: he reckons up the years of preparation in each case, the means at his disposal, the chances of a successful career, and then, when he has fully deliberated, he decides—that is, he exercises his free will. So

---

[3] St Thomas, S.T., i, q. 83, a. 1

many points may not have to be considered in other cases, but the process is the same: there is first a deliberation, a weighing of advantages, and then a choice. But the choice is free. A man may select the lower instead of the higher advantage.

As the senses serve the intellect, so the intellect serves the will. It brings before the will the opposing advantages, and the will chooses between them. The advantages may be, and often are, of such a kind as to be manifestly imperceptible to the senses, e.g., the advantages to the mind of studying astronomy rather than pure mathematics. Free-will may, therefore, be defined as *the power of choosing either of two courses represented as good by the intellect*, i.e., as having at least some good aspect. No man ever chooses evil as such. If he chooses what is as a fact evil, he does so because he represents it to himself as good in some way. The evil object is viewed "sub specie boni", as philosophers say, i.e., under a good aspect, or as having the appearance of goodness. That evil things can be so regarded is clear from experience, and, in fact, they must necessarily be represented as good in some way, in order to be capable of being an object of desire for the will. Note that the intellect, in declaring a thing to be "good", sets it down as belonging to a large class of things. That class, to which the general name "good" is given, includes everything man can desire from mere bodily pleasure to the happiness of heaven and the vision of God himself. "Good", therefore, cannot attract the senses, for it cannot be perceived by them. It *can* attract the will. The will has for its object the "good" presented to it by the intellect.

The will of its nature is attracted by what is "good", and is repelled by what is "evil." As we have already conveyed, we take "good" to mean, in this connection, "anything which we believe will bring us happiness", and "evil", "anything which we believe will bring us unhappiness."

If we were offered immediate, perfect, and eternal happiness, our will would not be free to refuse it; nor indeed could our intellect in such a case commit the absurdity of proposing an alternative. This immediate, perfect, and eternal happiness, which is attainable only after death, is what we call "the perfect good". The "good" things of our present life are imperfect; they are all mixed with evil, and, because of this very fact, they leave the will free to accept or reject them. Let us take two examples: (1) A young woman is thinking of becoming a nurse. Her intellect represents the profession as "good" (because it is an honourable and beneficent way of living, etc.), and at the same time as "evil" (because of the intensive study required, the long and late hours on duty, the distasteful nature of some of the work, etc.). Her will is attracted to the "good", and is repelled by the "evil". It is not forced to accept the "good"—because the "good" is mixed with the "evil"; it is not forced to reject the "evil"—because the evil is mixed with "good"; therefore it is free. (2) A man is deliberating whether he will obey God's commandments or not. His intellect puts before his will the "good" of obedience to God, viz., great peace of mind in this life, and perfect happiness after death; but his intellect also puts before his will the "evil" of obedience, viz., the hardships which he must face, the checking of his passions, etc. As in the other case, his will is not forced to accept the "good" or reject the "evil"; therefore, it is free.[4]

How man differs from the lower animals. MAN IS A RATIONAL ANIMAL. THE LOWER ANIMALS ARE IRRATIONAL. Man has the faculty of reason, or the power of deducing new truths from those which he already knows, of passing from the known to the unknown. He is constantly pushing out the frontiers of knowledge. He adds new sciences to those already existing. He invents and perfects implements and machinery, rejecting the old for the new. The lower animals, on the other hand, are confined within the same circle of actions; the variations due to change of habitat, etc., are of little importance. They cannot transcend their instincts and environment, and try another way of life. Bees are today just as they were in the time of Moses and Virgil; spiders, as they were in the days of the Pharaohs; birds build their nests now as they have always built them, in the same shape and with similar materials. The most sagacious of the lower animals, the horse and the dog, which have been in contact with man for countless centuries, exhibit not the slightest progress. The lower animals are not inventive. (This is universally admitted. The rudest implement, discovered deep down in the earth, is accepted by all as conclusive evidence of the work of man). Animals are held in a groove from which they cannot escape. They are stationary, they are enclosed within fixed narrow limits, because they are irrational. Man is progressive, because he is rational, because he sees that a general idea, e.g., "house", may take an infinite number of forms.

MAN IS FREE. THE LOWER ANIMALS ARE NOT. Men apply their minds to an infinity of subjects, and pass from one occupation to another. A man may begin life as a labourer and end as an artist or philosopher. The lower animals, on the other hand, are pinned down to one set of actions. They do not possess free-will. Therefore, the characteristic of their work is uniformity. We admit, of course, that, in the same species of lower animals some individuals behave more sagaciously than others, but such diversity is as nothing compared with the diversity we observe in the work of man. Man possesses free-will. Therefore, the characteristic of his work is diversity. In the lower animals, the absence of free-will is a consequence of the fact that they are irrational.

It may be objected that a hunting dog, e.g., sometimes appears to be deliberate and come to a decision as to which of the two trails to follow. But the appearance of deliberation is due simply to the uncertainty of the animal as to which is the stronger trail. When the stronger trail is discovered, the dog follows it of necessity. The dog's action is determined from without. Man, on the other hand, in exercising free-will, determines himself. He may follow at pleasure the less instead of the greater advantage. Again, the dog's choice is a sensuous choice and must be distinguished from the intellectual choice of free-will. The free-will, even when exercised in choosing between different kinds of food, is acting on the information given it by the intellect. The intellect represents each of the two kinds of food as

---

[4] St Thomas, S.T., i-ii, q. 10, a. 2

"good." "Good", however, is a universal term like the word "man". It denotes a something which the senses cannot perceive. It belongs to the intellect alone.

Conclusion: the human soul is spiritual. The soul is spiritual, i.e., it possesses activity, but it has no extension and is independent of matter in its existence and, to some extent, in its operations.

(1) The soul is spiritual, because some of its actions are independent of matter. It acts independently of matter, because it forms abstract and universal ideas, e.g., "honesty", "truth", "goodness", "man." Such ideas cannot be formed by the senses. They can be formed only by a faculty that resembles themselves in being immaterial. If the soul were a material thing and had extension like the senses, it could never pass beyond the pictures of concrete things with their definite shape, colour, hardness, etc. It could never get a notion of God, or desire Him above all things in the visible world.

(2) The soul is spiritual, because it moves and directs itself, as it does in the exercise of free-will, while matter moves only as it is moved: matter gets its motion and the direction of its motion from without. While the soul is united to the body, the senses supply it with the materials from which it derives its knowledge, but, in its life and action, it is as independent of the senses as the painter is of the people who supply him with his brushes and colours. Man can transcend his bonds with matter and seek an immaterial, spiritual good freely, such as knowledge or virtue. He can move freely toward or away from any material thing. All this shows that the life-principle or soul of man, of which the will is a power or faculty, is superior to and independent of matter. Since it acts independently of the body, it can exist even when the body perishes, and can continue to seek the truth and to love the good.

OBJECTIONS ANSWERED

Objection 1. "The mind cannot act, if the brain be injured. Therefore, brain and mind are one and the same, and what we describe as acts of the mind are merely movements of the brain." REPLY: (1) By way of retort or turning the argument: "The violinist cannot play, if the violin is broken. Therefore the violinist and the violin are one and the same, and what we describe as acts of the violinist are merely movements of the violin."

(2) The conclusion cannot be sound. The brain is matter. Abstract ideas, reasoning, and free-will, are immaterial things. They have no extension. They are utterly distinct from matter, and cannot be identified with it or with any of its states, whether rest or motion.

(3) The conclusion does not follow. In the living man, soul and body are most intimately united together. Every act of the mind, even every act which is beyond the power of matter, is accompanied, or preceded, by some act of movement of the brain, which is an organ or instrument of the whole man. Hence, in the ordinary course of nature, thought becomes impossible, if the brain is seriously injured, or if, as in sleep and unconsciousness, its proper activity is impeded. But does this make

thought identical with a movement of the brain? By no means, as the following illustration will show: Suppose a lighted candle is set in a lantern with a rather dim pane of glass. The candle, though burning with uniform brightness, will show only as much of its light as the glass allows to pass through. If the glass is thoroughly blackened, no light will be seen. As long, therefore, as the candle remains in the lantern, its lighting-power will depend on, but obviously will not be identical with, the transparency of the glass. Now, the soul may be compared to the lighted candle, the body to the lantern, and the brain to the glass. While the soul is in the body, it cannot think unless the brain is in a suitable condition.

Objection 2. "It is assumed that animals have merely material souls or principles of life. Is it not possible that, unknown to us, their souls may have spiritual powers also?" REPLY: To correct a possible misapprehension, the principle of life in a plant or an animal is not material in the sense that it can be seen or felt like a stone. It is a certain kind of activity and has no extension. However, it is correctly called material in the sense that its work has to do exclusively with material things, that it has no powers higher than those of the senses, and that it perishes with the body to which it is united. The possibility that the soul of an animal may be spiritual like ours is like the possibility that stones may be alive without our knowing it, or the possibility that there may be a sewing-machine and a vase of wild roses at the centre of the moon. Such imaginings do not deserve consideration, because there is not an iota of evidence to support them. If the lower animals had spiritual souls like ours, they would be persons, with the same right to life that we have, and to kill them for food would be to commit the sin of murder. However, nothing an animal does gives evidence of any independence of matter. But a thing reveals itself by what it does: "agere sequitur esse" - action follows being. Hence there is absolutely no reason to attribute any spiritual power to animals. To hold that a thing can be other than what its activity indicates, is to make coherent thought an impossibility. In any case, the proof of the spirituality of the human soul rests on our knowledge of *ourselves* and *our* acts, and would not be weakened even by the most extravagant concessions as to the powers of lower animals.

Objection 3. "It would seem reasonable to suppose that man has more souls than one; that he has three distinct souls, each doing its own work—a vegetable soul for growth, an animal soul for seeing, hearing, feeling, and a spiritual soul for thinking and reasoning." REPLY: (1) No biologist would give the suggestion a moment's thought. In every living thing, whether it be plant, animal or man, the different parts or powers co-operate closely with one another for the welfare of the whole, which shows that they must be under the government of a single vital principle. To the biologist, there is no more perfect example of unity than the unit which he finds in each individual living thing. In the living man all the organs assist one another and contribute to his well-being, as we may perceive from a simple example: the eye sees an apple, the hand plucks it and conveys it to the mouth, the teeth chew upon it, the stomach digests it and sends nutriment to all parts of the human system. Thus several distinct members or organs co-operate for the common good. There must, therefore, be some single power that binds them together and makes them do this. That power is the soul.

(2) A man's consciousness—that is, his knowledge of his inward states and acts, tells him that he is one and the same person who thinks and feels. Therefore, he has but one soul for thinking and feeling; but if his soul can combine spiritual with animal powers, there is no difficulty in ascribing vegetative powers to it also.

(3) If a man had three separate souls, he would need a fourth soul to watch over them and act on them so that all three would work together harmoniously for his common welfare. But this fourth soul could not act on the others and direct each in the performance of its proper task, unless it possessed the three powers which we ascribe to the one human soul. Thus, the suggestion is shown to be useless.

Objection 4. "You have said that the soul is not a material thing and has no extension. But it is hard to understand how the soul which has no extension can be present in all the different parts of the body. Would it not be easier to suppose that the soul is in some part of the brain that governs the body from there?" REPLY: No. Such a supposition would be useless. Take any portion of the brain you please. It has length, breadth and depth, and can be divided up into an indefinite number of parts. If the soul can be present in all these, it can equally well be present in every part of the entire body.

B. THE SOUL OF MAN IS IMMORTAL

The soul is immortal. We have proved that the destruction of the body does not involve the destruction of the soul. The soul, unlike the body, is immaterial. It is not made up of parts distinct and separable. Therefore, after death, it cannot perish of itself or through the agency of any creature. God alone can destroy it.

Since the desire of perfect happiness is common to all men, it must spring from human nature itself, and must have been implanted therein by God, whose wisdom and justice exclude the possibility of its universal frustration. Perfect happiness, therefore, is the divinely appointed destiny of man, and must be attainable by all who act conformably to the Divine will. But perfect happiness, i.e., complete and unending happiness, is beyond the reach of man in this world. There must, therefore, be a future life in which it can be found.

Conscience implies the existence of a Supreme Lawgiver who will reward the good and punish the wicked. It cannot be said that, in this life, the good and the wicked are uniformly treated according to their deserts. It happens only too often that the cunning malefactor succeeds in winning wealth and position, and that he ends his life untroubled by remorse and with a minimum of suffering, while the just man lives in toil and penury, and dies after a protracted agony, or freely sacrifices his life in the heroic discharge of duty. The justice of God, therefore, demands that there should be a future state in which this inequality is redressed.

We are certain, then, that there is a life beyond the grave. But is it the Divine will that life should endure for all eternity? Shall the good be granted only a limited period of happiness, undisturbed by the thought of approaching annihilation? No;

their happiness must be of unlimited duration, and must be known to them as such, otherwise it would not be perfect happiness. And as for the wicked, when we consider the infinite majesty of God and His infinite claims to the obedience and gratitude of His creatures, and when we recall their deliberate malice and rejection of grace in this life, we cannot but recognise that their eternal punishment involves no incongruity. It must, however, be admitted that the proof from reason of the immortality of the soul, particularly in its reference to the wicked, presents difficulties which cannot be satisfactorily solved without the aid of revelation. The doctrine that the damned suffer forever will appear less difficult when we understand that their will is immovably fixed in hatred of God, and that their annihilation would necessitate the annihilation of the Saints in Heaven as well. If we could know the truth fully, we should perceive that God's act in annihilating a soul would in some way be an offence against His justice, and therefore a contradiction of His nature.[5]

---

[5] See pp.629-30.

CHAPTER 3

NATURAL RELIGION. ITS INSUFFICIENCY. PROBABILITY OF REVELATION

Summary

I. Natural religion, defined. Its duties discoverable by the unaided reason.
    Man has duties:
    A. Individually and socially, to God.
    B. To himself.
    C. To his neighbour.
II. A full and accurate knowledge of natural religion, practically unattainable
    without revelation:
    A. Man, unaided by revelation, has, as a fact, failed to acquire it.
    B. Its discovery would be fruitless through defective teaching-authority
       and human weakness.
III. The goodness and mercy of God lead us to the assurance that the necessary
    revelation has been made.

I

Natural Religion. Individual and social duties. Natural Religion is the sum of man's duties in so far as they can be ascertained by the light of reason alone. It is the worship of God prescribed by reason alone. Supernatural Religion is the sum of man's duties as defined by Divine Revelation. It is the worship of God prescribed by Revelation.

From the truths already established, we infer that man has duties to God, to himself, and to his neighbour.

A. INDIVIDUALLY, MAN HAS DUTIES TO GOD. (a) In God he recognises a Being of supreme excellence, deserving to be loved above all for His own sake. (b) To God he owes his entire being and its preservation at every instant. (c) To God he owes all his faculties, or powers of acting: every throb of his heart, every glance of his eye, every thought of his mind, even the most trivial movements of soul or body are possible only with divine aid or co-operation. (d) To God he owes his sense of right and wrong, and his sure hope that a good life will bring him everlasting happiness after death. Man, therefore, perceiving his own inferiority and his total dependence on God, is bound to acknowledge His supreme excellence, to recognise Him as his Creator, Preserver, and Sovereign Ruler. He is bound to love Him more than all else, to love Him with his whole heart and soul and mind. He is bound to thank Him and pray to Him as his Benefactor; to honour Him as the source of every perfection, to obey Him as his Master, and to conceive and express sorrow for the offences he commits against Him; in a word to offer Him the supreme homage of adoration.

SOCIALLY, MAN HAS DUTIES TO GOD. (a) A society, in simple terms, is a group of individuals united for a common purpose under a common authority. The Family is a society for the rearing of children under the authority of their parents. The State is a number of families united under one government for the temporal well-being of all. (b) The Family is necessary for the very life of man, the State for his normal development. It is only in a well-ordered state that any degree of civilisation is possible: its members are enabled to provide more conveniently, by division of labour, for the necessities and comforts of life, and to promote by intercourse and mutual training the development of mind and heart. Since society, whether it consist of the Family or the State, is necessary for man, it follows that society is a divine institution. It is a creature of God, indebted to Him for its existence and preservation, and for the benefits it receives. It can think and act through its governing authority; it, therefore, resembles a living person. It is conscious of its debt to God, and is under a like obligation to discharge it. Even from the point of view of worldly advantage, the State should show individual citizens the good example of respect for religion. For, without the aid of religion, the State cannot secure permanently the two conditions on which its existence depends. Those conditions are (1) that the citizens deal justly with one another; (2) that they be loyal to the common authority.

Divine worship, naturally, in the case of individuals, necessarily, in the case of societies, must take some external, sensible form. Man, obeying the instincts God has given him, assumes a reverential posture at prayer, sets apart times and places for public worship, orders special ceremonies and rites, and appoints ministers to take charge of them.

B. MAN HAS DUTIES TO HIMSELF. God has given him his life and his faculties for use, not for abuse. He is, therefore, bound to take reasonable care of his life, to promote the health of mind and body, to be industrious, sober, and chaste.

C. MAN HAS DUTIES TO HIS NEIGHBOUR. Since social life is necessary to man, and since social life is impossible without truthfulness, justice, and obedience to lawful authority, it follows that these virtues, and all others akin to them, are prescribed by our nature, and, therefore, by God.

But even if man were not made for social life, his reason would tell him that his neighbour, being a rational creature and under God's protection, had the same rights as himself to his life, to his property, and to his good name.

The duties of Natural Religion may be summed up in three great commands which God conveys to man through his reason.

(1)   *Honour God.*
(2)   *Subdue your passions.*
(3)   *Do as you would be done by.*

In Natural Religion man would avoid evil and do good for a twofold motive, viz., the love of God and the fear of His judgement after death.

II

Without Revelation, a full knowledge of Natural Religion is practically unattainable.

REVELATION.   A revelation, literally "a drawing back of the veil", is a communication of truth made directly by God to man. It is obvious that God can communicate directly with us, since it was He who gave us power to communicate directly with one another. In reasoning out the chief truths of Natural Religion, we had the advantage of knowing them beforehand through God's revelation to us: we set about the solution of a series of questions, the answers to which we knew in advance. But how should we have fared without this special help? No better than those of whom we shall presently speak.

The chief duties of man according to the law of nature are expressed in the Ten Commandments, the third excepted, but only because of its special designation of the Sabbath. Under Natural Religion, men would be bound to set apart a day from time to time for the public worship of God, but the selection of particular days would be at the choice of each State or Community.

MEN UNAIDED BY REVELATION HAVE, AS A FACT, FAILED TO ACQUIRE A FULL KNOWLEDGE OF NATURAL RELIGION. It is evident from the failure of pagan nations and pagan sages that, without special light from God, man cannot arrive at a full knowledge of Natural Religion. Among all the peoples of antiquity, the Jews alone excepted, the grossest errors prevailed. The Divine Power, in whose existence they believed, was divided, they fancied, among two or more divinities. Their gods were at feud with one another. They were the patrons of theft, lying, and every disgraceful crime, and were offered a form of worship which in certain instances consisted of nothing less than public immorality. Men with such notions of the Deity had no fixed and unalterable standard of right and wrong. There was a universal belief in a future state, but the notion prevailed among cultured peoples, particularly the Greeks, that even for good men life after death was much less happy than life on earth, while less civilised races contemplated an endless career of low, sensual enjoyment. A study of the general character of religion and morality among the pagans of the present day leads us to similar conclusions.

Plato (428-347 B.C.), one of the master-minds of the world, favours in his ideal state a community of wives and the destruction of weakly and deformed children.[1] His great disciple, Aristotle (384-322 B.C.), who systematised so many branches of learning, held the same lax views as to the care of infant life. He allowed the exhibition in the temples of lewd figures of the gods. He had no proper conception of human dignity, and regarded slaves as mere beasts who could be tortured or put to death by their masters without injustice.[2] It is true, however, that the moral code

---

[1] *The Republic*, Book 5
[2] *The Politics*, iv (vii) 16; 17, i. 5

of the Roman Stoic philosophers, influenced possibly by the inspired books of the Jews, was remarkable for its elevation and purity. Still, Seneca (c. 4 B.C.-A.D. 65), one of the leaders of the school, was emphatic in his approval of suicide, while Marcus Aurelius (A.D. 121-180), its last and most perfect representative, hesitates, now approving, now condemning.

BECAUSE OF DEFECTIVE AUTHORITY AND HUMAN WEAKNESS, A FULL KNOWLEDGE OF THE NATURAL LAW WOULD BE FRUITLESS FOR THE MASS OF MANKIND. Through the promptings of nature itself, all men may know the existence of God, or some Supreme Power, and their responsibility to Him. But the other truths and precepts of Natural Religion, the unity of God and the worship He should receive, the duties of man to himself and to his neighbour, all depend on reasoning so manifestly abstruse as to be within the reach of only the exceptional few, of rare talent and ample leisure. Let us make the supposition, which, as a fact, has never been realised, that in some community a gifted man of this description appears, that he masters all the truths of Natural Religion, that he devotes his life to the instruction of his fellows, and that he has no rival in ability to challenge his conclusions and impair his influence. Still his mission would fail for want of authority.

A man tempted to grievous wrong against God, against himself or his neighbour, would say: "This is forbidden by one liable to err like myself. All his reasoning may be false. I will not listen to mere man. I would listen to God, but God has not spoken." But would he listen to God? Taking him as representing the mass of mankind, we are certain that the external help of a revelation would not of itself suffice to keep him in the straight path of duty. So dark is his understanding, so weak is his will, so strong are his passions, that he would need a further help from God, an internal help which would open his mind to the truth and enable him to beat down the evil influences within him.

III

The probability of Revelation and other divine help. Man suffers from a moral sickness. His mind is dark, his will is weak; he is practically incapable of learning the Natural Law, and practically incapable of fulfilling it. An unbeliever might object that a good God would never have created such a poor thing as man, so fickle and prone to evil. The answer is that God did not do so. The first man He created is responsible for the blight that fell on the human race. But the goodness and mercy of God lead us to the assurance that He would come to the rescue of the plague-stricken members of the human race; that He would address to them a word that none could dispute; that He would leave them in no doubt regarding the immortality of the soul and the judgement after death; that He would enlighten them as to all their natural duties; that He would establish among them a perpetual living authority to speak and teach in His name throughout all ages; and that in addition to this outward help He would give a constant inward help, so that men might perceive the truth and have the strength to live up to it.

Socrates (469-399 B.C.), a few hours before his death, while trying to overcome the difficulties of his friends against the doctrine of the immortality of the soul, urged them in gentle and pathetic language to forget their Greek exclusiveness, and to seek for enlightenment not only among their own race but outside the bounds of their vaunted civilisation. One of his disciples, Simmias, suggested that perhaps they might succeed in discovering "some divine word", some divine revelation on which they could place implicit reliance.[3] It seemed as though God, the kind Father of all, had evoked the expression of these thoughts, so that the admirers of Socrates in a later generation might be prepared to see in the Infallible Church which came to birth in despised Judaea the perfect fulfilment of their master's hope.

---

[3] See Plato, *Phaedo*, 78 A, 85 D.

SECTION II

CHRISTIAN APOLOGETICS

INTRODUCTION

God has given a Revelation to the whole human race

We recorded in the preceding pages the failure of the keenest minds among the pagans to arrive at a clear and accurate knowledge of our duties to God, to ourselves, and to our neighbours. We saw that even if they had succeeded in their search, they would have been unable, through want of authority in themselves and a moral weakness in their hearers, to get the mass of mankind to live up to their teaching. Arguing from the mercy of God, we drew the conclusion that He would help human insufficiency, that He would speak to all men and be their teacher, and that He would work on their minds and hearts so that they would see the truth and obey His precepts. Our inference, as we shall see, was correct.

The nature of the Revelation

God might have revealed to man nothing more than the truths and precepts of natural religion. By believing those truths and by obeying those precepts, man would be entitled to very great happiness after death. Freed from all temptation and misery, he would derive an intense pleasure from the contemplation of God, as imagined in His creatures. But God Himself would be hidden from his eyes. God would seem to dwell in some separate world from which he was excluded. God would not be his friend and intimate.

In the revelation which God, as a fact, has given us, He has not only made certain for us the whole content of natural religion, but He has told us many truths which no human mind could have ever discovered, and He has appointed for us a destiny which no creature without His special aid could win. He has promised that we shall see Him as He is with all His perfections, that we shall live with Him for ever and taste of His very own happiness. No human tongue can tell the value of His gift to us, for the gift is God Himself. In His revelation to us, the Bounty of God shines forth no less clearly than His Mercy. His Mercy has healed our wounds and restored us to health, while His Bounty has clothed us and enriched us. It has raised us, poor creatures of the earth, from beggary to royalty; it has made us sons of the Most High, destined for unending happiness in the home of our Father.

Christ, the bearer of the Revelation

Who was the bearer of this revelation? Who was the messenger of God to all mankind? None other than His own Divine Son, Jesus Christ, Our Lord, true God, true Man. Born of the Virgin Mary, He lived and laboured and taught among us, and He died nailed to a cross.

By partial revelations delivered to the Patriarchs of old and to the Jewish people, God had prepared the way for the full and universal revelation which He was to give us through His Son. God had foretold many things about Him so that when He came He might be known. He came to banish the dark ignorance that filled the souls of men. He was the Light of the world, and He still is its Light and will ever be so.

[When we pass on to the next Section, "Catholic Apologetics", we shall find that Christ founded a Church to continue His teaching. He promised it His unfailing support and guidance. He promised that it would last till the end of the world; and since He is God Omnipotent, no power of earth or hell can defeat His promise. Placed in the world by Him to be the one and only Light that shows us the way to eternal happiness, it can have no rival: no other church or religion can be true.]

OUTLINE OF THE PROOF IN CHRISTIAN APOLOGETICS

The course of the argument is set forth in the following summaries of Chapters 4-7. Chapters 4 and 5 contain introductory matter.

Chapter 4. *Miracles and prophecies are sure signs that a Revelation is genuine.* A teacher makes good his claim to speak to us as the messenger of God, if he has the support of miracles and prophecies. Miracles and prophecies, in the sense in which we use these words, are above the capacity of creatures. It is only God who has the power to work a miracle. It is only God who has the knowledge required for the deliverance of a prophecy.

Chapter 5. *The following Books of the New Testament, viz., the Gospels, the Acts of the Apostles, and the Epistles of Saint Paul, tell us the truth about Christ.* For the purpose of our argument, we make no appeal to the inspired character of the books we have named: we regard them as merely secular records of past events. By applying the tests which we would employ in deciding the value of any work on history, we arrive at the conclusion that their account of Christ is true and must be accepted by anyone with an impartial mind.

Chapter 6. *We learn from genuine history that the man Jesus Christ claimed to be God.* In the historical works we have mentioned, the man Christ appears before us as a teacher of religion. He does not present Himself as merely a messenger of God. He claims to be a Divine Person; He claims to be God. He expresses His claim in word and act. He speaks as only God could have spoken; He acts as only God could have acted.

Chapter 7. *By miracles and prophecies, and above all by His Resurrection, Christ proved His claim to be God.* In proof of His claim to be God, Christ worked miracles, prophesied events which came to pass, and rose from the dead. He could not have done so if His claim were false: God would not have lent His divine power and knowledge to an impostor. Therefore, He must be what He claimed to be. He must be a Divine Person. He must be God.

In our study of Christian and Catholic Apologetics, we shall find that the revelation which God gave us through Christ is supported, not only by a single miracle or prophecy, but by many miracles and prophecies whose cumulative effect should compel conviction. It is supported by the great web of Messianic prophecies. It is supported by all the miracles of Christ during His life-time on earth, and by the crowning miracle of His Resurrection from the dead. It is supported by the miraculous spread of Christianity and by the constancy of its martyrs. It is supported by the miraculous nature and vitality of the Church which has survived innumerable dangers, and lives in irrepressible vigour. (See Ch. 12.)

As to the nature of our proof, the reader is referred to the paragraph on this subject in the Introduction to this work. The proof that God has declared Christ to be a Divine Person is conclusive. It is based on evidence so complete, so telling as to leave not the smallest shadow of doubt in any unbiased mind. On evidence of far less compelling force, men have risked the wealth and lives of millions.

CHAPTER 4

THE SIGNS OF REVELATION:
MIRACLES AND PROPHECY

Summary

How Revelation may be known: miracles and prophecies.
Replies to the following objections against miracles:
A. That the evidence for miracles is necessarily unsatisfactory.
B. That miracles are opposed to physical science.
C. That alleged miracles need not be referred to divine authorship.

How a Revelation may be known. We find certain men claiming that God has given them a revelation, and that He has commissioned them to speak in His name to the whole human race. We can know whether a teacher has been sent by God (1) if his doctrine is worthy of its alleged Author; e.g., it should not be ambiguous or trivial; and (2) if it is confirmed by miracles or prophecies.

Miracles. DEFINITION. A miracle is an occurrence outside the course of nature, perceptible to the senses, and explicable only as the direct act of God Himself.

A miracle is obviously a clear proof of the divine origin of the doctrine *in support of which it is wrought*; it is God's *positive testimony* that the doctrine is true, and God cannot testify to a lie.

The *possibility* of miracles cannot be denied by anyone who admits the existence of a personal God: He who fixed the course of nature can alter, suspend or supersede it at His pleasure. The question then to be decided in connection with miracles is not whether God *could* work a miracle, but whether, in a given case, a miracle has occurred or not. In other words, the question of miracles is a question of evidence.

We restrict our inquiry to "evident" miracles. Being perceptible to the senses, they can be adduced as proofs and recognised by everyone without exception. An instance of a "non-evident" miracle would be the change of bread and wine into Christ's Body and Blood. Such a change is not perceptible to the senses. It is known only through faith, and therefore cannot be used as evidence of God's intervention.

In examining a particular miracle for its apologetic value, we have to consider three points:

(1) Did the alleged occurrence actually take place? This reduces itself to an inquiry into the competence and veracity of the witnesses: Did they actually observe what they report? Can their words be trusted?

(2) Was the occurrence positively outside the course of nature or above its power? Without knowing all about nature we can still be absolutely certain that there are occurrences which are outside its course and above its power. We know, for instance, that nature cannot fill up and heal a great wound in a moment of time, or raise a dead person to life. Hence when we find that any such thing has actually taken place, we can assert with the most firm conviction that it must have been due to the direct action of God Himself, who, when He wills, can override the methods of nature and quite exceed its power.

(3) Was the miracle worked in proof of a certain doctrine? Was it clear that the worker explicitly or implicitly wrought the miracle in proof of the truth of his words? Or did the circumstances clearly point to a connection between the miracle and the doctrine? This again is a question of the competence and veracity of the witnesses.

Under these three headings, the evidence in favour of miracles can be so thoroughly tested and controlled that we can arrive at certainty both regarding the miraculous character of the occurrence and its confirmation of a doctrine.

Prophecies. Prophecy also gives us a conclusive proof of divine authority. DEFINITION. Prophecy is the definite prediction of events which depend for their occurrence on the exercise of free will, whether it be the free will of God or of rational creatures, and which are of such a nature as to be beyond the possibility of guess or human foresight.

God alone can know beforehand what a free agent will do and all the particular circumstances of his act. A prophecy, therefore, if fulfilled, is as conclusive of divine authority as a miracle. A prophecy can originate only in God's Omniscience, a miracle only in His Omnipotence.

Objections.

A. *The evidence for miracles is unsatisfactory.*

1. "It is contrary to experience for miracles to be true, but it is not contrary to experience for testimony to be false. That the evidence is false will always be more probable than that the miracle occurred." (David Hume's objection: it made some stir in its day, but has now been abandoned except by the unthinking). REPLY: (a) This objection is merely a statement of antecedent probabilities. But antecedent probabilities must yield to facts. The unlikely and the improbable sometimes happen! Our experience is our knowledge of what we ourselves have seen and observed. When the first aeroplane appeared, those who had not seen it for themselves would rightly have been regarded as unreasonable if they had said:

"This machine is entirely outside our experience. It is therefore more probable that the evidence for its existence is false." Why would they be regarded as unreasonable? Firstly, because they reject the word of thoroughly reliable witnesses. Secondly, because they do not allow for the fact that an inventor may, at any time, construct a machine which will do a work outside all previous experience. Apply the illustration to the case of miracles. A person who refuses to believe in a properly attested miracle is unreasonable. Firstly, because he rejects the word of reliable witnesses; secondly, because he makes no allowance for the possibility that God, the Author of Nature, may, at His own good pleasure, perform a work of which people have never had previous experience. (b) As to probabilities: it is *never* probable that the evidence which the Church requires for a miracle is false. The Church is always slow to pronounce on miracles. But the evidence, once accepted, is of such a kind that, if we refuse to accept it, we can never believe anything that anyone tells us, and must reject all historical truth. As G.K. Chesterton observed, "Somehow or other an extraordinary idea has arisen that the disbelievers in miracles consider them coldly and fairly, while believers in miracles accept them only in connection with some dogma. The fact is quite the other way. The believers in miracles accept them (rightly or wrongly) because they have evidence for them. The disbelievers in miracles deny them (rightly or wrongly) because they have a doctrine against them."[1]

2. "The advance of physical science, and the deeper insight it has given us into the secrets of nature, has been fatal to credulity in every form, to belief in charms, magic, witchcraft, miracles, and astrology. The Christian miracles belong to the childhood of the world, when people were prepared to believe almost anything." (The ordinary rationalist view).

REPLY: (a) The early Christians were by no means credulous in respect of the greatest and all-important miracle of Christianity, viz., the Resurrection of Christ. They were most unwilling to believe it. They accepted it, as we shall see further on, only when overwhelmed by the evidence. The Apostle Thomas and Saul of Tarsus are two notable examples of disbelievers who were convinced by the evidence before their very eyes. But is it true to say that the age in which they lived was the childhood of the world? Not at all. Christianity appeared at a time of advanced civilisation. It was embraced by men adorned with all the intense intellectual culture of Greece and Rome, by legal minds specially fitted for the task of sifting evidence and appraising its value. It was embraced by them because they were convinced that the Resurrection of Christ, its basic miracle, was a fact. (b) As for the contention that the advance of physical science is fatal to credulity: astrology, fortune-telling, spiritism, charms, mascots, and the like have a strong hold over many people living in the age of jet-transport, computers and nuclear physics. In all ages of history, there are credulous people as well as people of critical judgement who know how to sift evidence.

---

[1] *Orthodoxy*, 1908, Ch. IX

B. *Miracles are opposed to physical science.*

1. "Physical science claims that nature acts uniformly. The doctrine of miracles says it does not. Therefore, if we believe in miracles, we must reject physical science."

REPLY: (a) We do not differ with scientists as to the uniformity of nature. We hold with them the general law of nature that the same physical cause in the same circumstances will produce the same effect, but we maintain that, when God intervenes, the circumstances are no longer the same: a new power has been introduced. His intervention is of rare occurrence and does not invalidate the work of a scientist whose conclusions are concerned only with normal cases. (b) Man himself can interfere with the forces of nature. If he holds a stone in his hand, he is preventing the law of gravity from producing one of its effects.

2. "But an interference by God with the course of nature may involve a violation of the Law of the Conservation of Energy. If, e.g., the stones leave the quarry at the mere word of the miracle-worker and make themselves into a house, this must happen through the expenditure of some energy that did not previously exist."

REPLY: (a) The Law of the Conservation of Energy remains intact. If the total energy of an isolated system is observed to increase, the Law of Conservation requires nothing more than that the increase be ascribed to the entrance of some new energy. (b) The miracle referred to may have been due merely to a re-distribution of energy. According to physicists themselves, there are vast stores of energy in the universe on which the Creator could draw, if He did not wish to introduce a new energy. (c) If, on the other hand, God created energy to wreak the miracle, we need have no hesitation in admitting that the miracle is an effect produced independently of the laws of nature. With those laws alone the physicist is concerned, not with an agency extrinsic to them.

C. *Miracles need not be referred to divine authorship.*

1. "Miracles may be the work of evil spirits."

REPLY: Evil spirits can undoubtedly work *apparent* miracles, but evil spirits, like all other creatures, are dependent on God at every instant for their existence and power of acting. God will not permit them to involve us in inevitable deception. Their activity may be detected by the relative triviality or unimportance of the wonder performed, the personal depravity of their human medium, or by the absurdity or wickedness of his doctrine.

2. "Miracles may be due to hypnotism."

REPLY: Hypnotism, as a curative agency, is successful only in certain forms of nervous disease. As a general explanation of miracles it is obviously inadequate.

3. "We do not yet know all the forces of nature. So-called miracles may have been due to occult forces whose operation will some day be fully understood."

REPLY: (a) *We do not know everything that natural forces can do, but we certainly do know some things which they can never do.* We do not know the lifting power of a man, but we do know that no man can lift a ton. We know that natural forces alone will never raise a dead man to life, or build up a piece of living tissue instantaneously. The building up of tissue is a slow and detailed process, every stage of which is perfectly well known. A period of time, more or less protracted, is essential. The instantaneous cure of a wound or a fracture is beyond the category of natural possibilities, unless the whole foundation of our medical knowledge is inaccurate. (b) The objection assumes that miracle-workers had far more knowledge of natural forces than any modern scientist. To ascribe such knowledge to Christ and the Apostles, who, from the human standpoint, were uneducated men and lived at a time when physical science was practically unknown, is to suppose a miracle as great as any. (c) The modern world has witnessed the utilisation of natural forces previously unknown. Still, no natural forces can ever be utilised unless specially constructed instruments or apparatus are employed. But workers of miracles used, in many instances, no means whatever, nothing but a word or a gesture.

4. "The present order of nature, which seems to us to be so fixed, may be subject to occasional, though indeed vastly rare, interruptions. These interruptions, resulting from natural causes, might coincide with what we call miracles, and miracles would thus be susceptible of a natural explanation."
REPLY: (a) The vastly rare interruptions would be far too rare to coincide with the numerous and fully authenticated miracles that have taken place within the last two thousand years. (b) The combined intelligence of all the scientists in the world at the present day would be unable to tell us the precise instant and the precise spot at which any one of the vastly rare interruptions might occur. But apparently this knowledge was possessed most exactly by a band of poor Galileans nearly two thousand years ago and by many others since their time, nearly all of whom were presumably strangers to modern scientific ideas. When they commanded sickness to disappear or life to return, they picked out the precise individuals who were to be restored by an incalculably rare action of natural forces, and they timed their words of command to the very second in which the effects would be produced. Such knowledge would itself have been miraculous.

CHAPTER 5

PROOF OF THE HISTORICAL VALUE OF THE GOSPELS, THE ACTS OF THE APOSTLES, AND THE EPISTLES OF ST PAUL

Summary

The four Gospels, the Acts of the Apostles, and the Epistles of St Paul must be accepted as historical if they satisfy the three tests of (a) genuineness; (b) veracity; and (c) integrity.

A. The Gospels:
- (a) Their genuineness proved by external and confirmed by internal evidence.
- (b) Their veracity established by the character and history of the writers, and by the impossibility of fraud.
- (c) Their integrity assured, chiefly, by the reverence of the early Christians for the sacred text.
B. The Acts of the Apostles and Epistles of St Paul: genuineness, veracity and integrity, similarly established.
C. Confirmation in recent research.

The New Testament may be looked at from two points of view:
1. As consisting of ordinary historical documents;
2. As a series or collection of divinely inspired books, having God as their principal Author.

Inspiration is an influence breathed forth by God on the soul of a writer, so that he expresses what God wishes him to express and nothing else. It is not perceptible to the senses, nor deducible from the text. The fact of its bestowal can be ascertained only from the testimony of God Himself. That testimony He gives through the Catholic Church, as we shall see. From her infallible authority we shall learn of the existence of inspired Scripture and the books of which it consists.

In this chapter we make *no reference to inspiration*. We treat certain books of the New Testament from a human point of view, and we establish by reason that they are trustworthy historical documents.

The tests by which we shall establish the historical value of the New Testament writings.

The four Gospels, the Acts of the Apostles, and the Epistles of St Paul, are the portions of the New Testament writings on which we chiefly rely to prove the divinity of Christ and the authority of the Church which He founded. As the Gospels are of special importance in our proof, we give at some length the arguments which show that, even if we leave aside all question of their inspiration and regard them as merely secular compilations, we must accept them as historical.

The Gospels were authored by SS. Matthew, Mark, Luke, and John.[1] They were placed in that order from the first centuries, because that was taken to be the order of their writing. The Gospels of SS. Matthew, Mark, and Luke are called the Synoptic Gospels, because of their close resemblance in matter and arrangement: they give us, as it were, but one picture, not three distinct pictures, of Christ. St Matthew probably wrote first. St Mark probably wrote between 50 and 60 A.D.; St Luke, some time before the year 60. As Our Lord died about the year 33 A.D., these three Gospels were written within the lifetime of those who had seen and known Him. St John's Gospel, written last, supplements the account of the other three. Its distinctive features are its report of the discourses of Christ, miracles not mentioned by the others (such as the raising of Lazarus), and the prominence which it gives to Christ's Divinity.

     The word "gospel" means "good tidings"; the Gospels convey the good news of the coming of the Redeemer. The writers of the Gospels are called, from the Greek title, Evangelists.

The Acts of the Apostles was written by St Luke not long after he had completed his Gospel.

The Epistles of St Paul were written within the period 50-67 A.D.

A work must be accepted as historical, or, in other words, as a faithful narrative of past events, (a) if it is genuine, i.e., if it is the work of the author to whom it is ascribed; (b) if its author himself is trustworthy, i.e., if it be shown that he was well informed and truthful; (c) if it is intact, i.e., if the text is substantially as it left the author's hand. All these conditions, as we shall show, are fulfilled in the case of the New Testament writings.

A. PROOF OF THE HISTORICAL VALUE OF THE GOSPELS

The genuineness of the Gospels. "Genuineness" has the same meaning as "authenticity". The genuineness, truthfulness, and integrity of the Gospels are most readily demonstrated by showing the impossibility of the opposites, i.e., forgery, untruthfulness and change of text. The Gospels are the genuine work of the writers to whom they are ascribed:

---

[1] The relics of *St Matthew* are in the Cathedral of Salerno, Italy; of *St Mark* a portion are in the Basilica of St Mark, Venice, Italy, but the major portion was returned in 1968 to the Coptic Orthodox Church in Alexandria, Egypt. Relics of *St Luke* are in the Basilica of St Giustina in Padua, Italy. The empty tomb of *St John* is in the ruins of St John's Basilica, Ephesus, Turkey.

I. *External evidence.* The testimony of Christian and non-Christian writers of the first two centuries shows that the Gospels were widely known, carefully studied, and revered everywhere in the Christian world. (For details see small print below).

The fact that the Gospels were held in veneration and were in *practical use* all over the Church within one hundred years of the death of the Apostles, and while their memory was still vivid, is a conclusive proof of their genuineness. Would the Apostles themselves or their immediate successors, who gave their lives to testify to the truth of all that is contained in the Gospels, have allowed a series of forgeries to be published, and palmed off as the inspired Word of God? Would Jewish converts have accepted them, without jealous scrutiny, as equal in authority to their own profoundly revered books of the Old Testament? Would the Gentiles, so many of them men of the highest education, have embraced a religion which made such severe demands on human nature, which exacted even the sacrifice of life itself in witness of the faith, without previously assuring themselves of the genuineness of its written sources? Would learned pagans and heretics have fastened on all kinds of arguments against the Church, and have neglected the strongest of all, viz., that its sacred books were forgeries? Would the faithful throughout the world, at a time when to be a Christian was to be a potential martyr, have all conspired without a single protest to fabricate and accept these books, falsely ascribe them to the Evangelists, and hand down the impious fraud as an everlasting inheritance for the veneration and guidance of their children's children? We must, therefore, either accept the Gospels as genuine, or commit ourselves to a series of puerile absurdities.

The period in which the Gospels were written cannot be described as an age when the human mind was in its infancy. Dr Arendzen writes of it: "The world into which Christ was born was the most refined and cultured history knows. ... The Græco-Roman world was one of astounding peace and well-being, of amazing splendour and political achievement, an age of choice literature, of wonderful works of art, of profound but restless speculation. The three centuries that lie between 40 B.C. and 260 A.D. are in many respects those of the highest prosperity men have ever known."[2] The entire age is still today the object of study by scholars and universities.

Testimony of Early Writers.
(a) Numerous texts from the Evangelists are quoted in the letters of Pope Clement (96 A.D.), St Ignatius of Antioch (once in Syria; now Antakya, Turkey: 107 A.D.), St Polycarp of Smyrna (now Izmir, Turkey: d. c. 155 A.D.), and other disciples of the Apostles; also in the *Shepherd of Hermas* (c. 145 A.D.), the *Letter to Diognetus* (2nd

---

[2] *The Gospels—Fact, Myth, or Legend?*, Sands & Co., London 1929, pp.95-6

cent.), and in the important work entitled *The Didache* or *The Teaching of the Twelve*, written some time between 95-130 A.D.

(b) St Justin of Samaria and Rome, who became a Christian in 130 A.D., says that the Gospels were written by Apostles and disciples, and were read at the meetings of Christians on Sundays.[3]

(c) Papias of Phrygia, Asia Minor, disciple or associate of St John, writing about 120 A.D., explains the circumstances in which the Gospel of St Mark was composed, and refers to a collection of the Lord's sayings in a Hebrew tongue by St Matthew, probably his Gospel, or an early version of it.[4]

(d) Tatian wrote his *Diatesseron*, or harmony of the four Gospels, about the year 170 A.D. The genuineness of the work is not disputed.

(e) St Irenaeus of Lyons (in Gaul, modern France), writing about 180 A.D., says, "Matthew wrote a Gospel for the Jews in their own language, while Peter and Paul were preaching and establishing the Church at Rome. After their departure [or "death": the Gk is uncertain], Mark, also, the disciple and interpreter of Peter, handed down to us in writing the information which Peter had given. And Luke, the follower of Paul, wrote out the Gospel which Paul used to preach. Later, John, the disciple of the Lord, who had reclined on his breast, published his Gospel during his sojourn at Ephesus in Asia Minor."[5] The personal history of St Irenaeus invests his testimony with special importance: a native of Asia Minor, in his early youth he drank in with avid ears, he tells us, the discourses of St Polycarp who was himself a disciple of St John, Apostle and Evangelist;[6] he became bishop of Lyons, and lived for some time at Rome. His testimony, therefore, representing the tradition of East and West and of what was then undoubtedly the heart of Christendom, must be accepted as decisive.

(f) Tertullian of Africa, writing against the heretic Marcion, about 200 A.D., appeals to the authority of the churches, "all of which have had our Gospels since Apostolic times." He speaks of the Gospels as the work of the Apostles Matthew and John, and of the disciples Mark and Luke.

(g) Heretics, e.g., Basilides (d. 130 A.D.), and pagans, e.g., Celsus (d. c. 200 A.D.), did not question the genuineness of the Gospels.

Later testimony is abundant. Probably there is not one of the pagan classics whose genuineness can be supported by such convincing evidence. No one disputes that Julius Caesar was the author of the *Commentaries on the Gallic Wars*, and yet the only ancient references to the work are found in the writings of Plutarch and Suetonius, about one hundred years after its composition.

II. *Internal Evidence.* An examination of the texts themselves proves that the writers were Jews, and were contemporaries, or in close touch with contemporaries, of the events they record:

---

[3] *Apol.* I, 66-67; *Dial. cum Tryph.* n. 103
[4] Quoted by Eusebius, *Hist. Eccles.* III, 39.
[5] *Adv. Haer.* III, 1
[6] Quoted by Eusebius, *Hist. Eccles.* V, 20.

1. The writers were Jews: (a) The Gospels are written in the colloquial Greek of the period, known as Hellenistic or Koine Greek, but show marked traces of Hebrew idiom. The Gospel of St Matthew was first written in Hebrew or Aramaic (now lost), and was shortly afterwards translated into Hellenistic Greek. This popular form of the Greek language was employed during the first century of the Christian era as a literary medium by Jews, such as Philo (d. 50 A.D.) and the historian Flavius Josephus (c. 37-c. 100), but not subsequently. By use of Hebrew idiom in the Gospels, the body is spoken of as "the flesh"; "soul" means life, temporal or eternal; "my soul" is sometimes used as the equivalent of the pronoun "I"; abstract terms are avoided, - thus, "the meek", "the clean of heart", and other such expressions are employed instead of "meekness", "purity" and so on. God is referred to by the use of the word "Heaven", as, e.g., in the phrase, "Kingdom of Heaven", or by use of the passive, e.g., "Ask, and it will be given you" - namely, by God. The Hebrew expression, "Son of ...", is frequently used, e.g., "Son of man" (e.g., Mk 8:31), "son of perdition" (Jn 17:12; 2 Thess 2:3), "sons of the resurrection" (Lk 20:36), "son of peace" (Lk 10:6), "sons of light" (Jn 12:36). These are typical Hebrew idioms, which are found nowhere else in Greek texts. Many other examples could be given.
(b) The writers show no acquaintance with Greek literature or philosophy, but are familiar with the religion, customs, and usages of the Jewish people.

2. The authors were contemporaries, or in close touch with contemporaries, of the events they narrate: (a) Modern scholarship has failed to detect any error on the part of the Evangelists in the countless references to topography and to the political, social, and religious conditions of Palestine at the time of Christ. Those conditions, peculiarly complicated and transient, could not have been accurately portrayed by a stranger to Palestine or by a late writer. The Gospels depict them faithfully: government was administered in part by the Romans and in part by the natives; the Sanhedrin, or great religious council of Jewish judges, still exercised its functions, and was in frequent conflict with the civil officials; taxes were paid in Greek money, Roman money was used in commerce, dues to the Temple were paid in Jewish money; the languages Hebrew and Greek, and, to some extent, Latin, were spoken. In general, public and private life was affected in many ways by the diversity of language and the division of authority. The unsuccessful rebellion against the Romans (66-70 A.D.), which flung a devastating flood of war over the land, sweeping the Holy City and the Temple off the face of the earth, was followed by enormous changes in population and government. A writer, therefore, who was not a contemporary of Christ, or in intimate relations with His contemporaries, would certainly have committed many errors when dealing with the period which preceded that great catastrophe. Recent discoveries have all confirmed the truth of the Biblical accounts. Among numerous discoveries and excavations in the 20th century can be named: the house of Peter, the pool of five porticoes mentioned in St John 5:2, the synagogue of Capernaum, the judgement seat at Gabbatha (Jn 19:13) in the Fortress of Antonia, the inscription of Pontius Pilate at the Roman theatre in Caesarea, and the tomb of the high priest Caiaphas.
(b) The vividness and detail of the narrative can only spring from personal contact with the events recorded.

Trustworthiness of the Evangelists. The Evangelists are trustworthy, because they knew the facts and truthfully recorded them:

1. They knew the facts: SS. Matthew and John had been companions of Christ. SS. Mark and Luke had lived in constant contact with His contemporaries.

2. They were truthful: (a) Their holy lives, and their sufferings in witnessing to the very truths set forth in their Gospels guarantee their sincerity. (b) From the world's standpoint, they had nothing to gain but everything to lose by testifying to the sanctity and the Divinity of Christ. (c) They could not have been untruthful, even if they wanted to: they wrote for contemporaries of the events they narrate, or for men who had known those contemporaries, and could not, without detection, have published a false account. (d) Their narratives appear at some points to be irreconcilable, but can be harmonised by careful investigation. Had the Evangelists been impostors, they would have avoided even the appearance of contradiction. As to variations between the four Gospels in the sayings of Christ, their meaning is not changed by the differing words. Many other variations can be explained by the fact that Christ would have uttered many sayings in various ways as He substantially repeated the same discourses and teachings as He moved from town to town. Every itinerant speaker makes small changes when presenting the same material over and over. (e) They could not have invented their portrait of Christ. His character so noble, so lovable, so tragic, so original, emerging unconsciously, as it were, with ever greater distinctness of outline, as the Gospel narrative proceeds, is, viewed merely as an artistic creation, quite beyond the inventive capacity of men such as the Evangelists were. Besides, every Jew of their day—and the Evangelists were Jews—believed that the Messiah would come to restore the kingdom of David. Not one of them ever dreamt, before the teaching of Christ, that He would come to found, not a temporal, but a spiritual kingdom, to preach meekness, humility, and brotherly love, and to live a life of poverty and persecution, culminating in the agony of the Cross.

The integrity of the Gospels. The Gospels have come down to us intact, i.e., free from corruptions or interpolations. The purity of the text is assured by:
1. The great reverence of the Church for the four Gospels and her rejection of all others. Gospels ascribed to SS. Peter, Thomas and James, and other imitations of Biblical books, were in circulation in the sub-apostolic age, but were discarded by the Church as spurious or false.
2. The practice which prevailed from the earliest times of reading the Gospels at public worship.

3. The wide diffusion of the Gospels among Christian communities all over the world.

4. The substantial uniformity of the text in all manuscripts, some of which date from the fourth century.

Public reading and oral tradition. The memories of the ancients were far better trained and much more employed than those of moderns. In an age when the great majority of people could not read or write, the use of memory was crucial, and it was standard for ordinary people to remember or learn great lists and speeches by heart. Homer's *Iliad* and *Odyssey*, the great ancient Greek epics, were transmitted orally for centuries before being committed to writing. The reliability of oral tradition has only been questioned by an age that has no place for it and demands to see everything in print, with its date and author at the start, before giving credence. The public and weekly reading from the New Testament books ensured both their secure place in the memories of the Christian faithful and the impossibility of substantial change to the text. The value of the guarantee of publicity may be measured from the incident recorded by St Augustine[7] as having befallen one of his colleagues, an African bishop. He says that St Jerome's use of the word "ivy" for "gourd", in his version of the Book of Jonah, caused such dissatisfaction when read out in church, that the bishop, fearing lest he might lose his people, felt compelled to restore the traditional rendering.

Existing manuscripts and codices. Codex Sinaiticus of the mid 4th century contains the entire New Testament. Codex Vaticanus of the same period contains all the Gospels and most of the rest of the New Testament. Codex Alexandrinus of the early 5th century contains almost all the New Testament. Codex Bezae of the 5th century contains, *inter alia*, the four Gospels. Another codex of the 5th century contains three-fifths of the N.T., and another of the 4-5th century contains the four Gospels.[8] The reliability of these earliest *complete* copies of books is indicated by the fact that they closely correspond to earlier *portions* of books.

Discoveries of fragments and portions. We do not have the original manuscripts, but the earlier manuscripts from which our complete texts are descended have not perished without a trace. Since 1890, some 60 fragments and portions of N.T. books, dating from the 2nd-4th century, have been discovered in Egypt. They correspond closely to our texts listed above, and it is a fair inference that the missing portions would show the same correspondence. We now have 76 manuscripts of portions of the New Testament going back to the 4th century or earlier.[9] In 1935, a small fragment—four verses of St John's Gospel, chapter 18—came to light; it is true to our text, and it is dated c. 125 A.D.[10] Another 2nd century fragment contains Jn 18:36-19:7. We also possess, dated c. 200 A.D.: portions of 19 verses of St Matthew; papyri of St John's Gospel containing twelve complete chapters and

---

[7] *Ep.* 71, 5; 82, 35
[8] Cf. *Jerome Biblical Commentary*, 1970, vol. 2, p.581.
[9] Cf. K. & B. Aland, *The Text of the New Testament*, W.B. Eerdmans, Grand Rapids 1989, p.81.
[10] Aland, *op. cit.*, p.57

portions of the other nine; 86 leaves of a codex containing portions of St Paul's letters. From the early 3rd century we have: portions of 30 leaves with parts of the Gospels and Acts; a papyrus codex containing eight complete chapters of St Luke and five complete chapters of St John. From the 3rd century: two leaves of a codex with some of the text of chapters 1, 16 and 20 of John.[11] It is now regarded as practically established that the four Gospels as we know them were circulating in Egypt as separate books within the first half of the second century.

Comparison with Classical Texts. Looking at the table below, we can see that the oldest manuscripts of certain major works of Plato, Caesar, Cicero and Horace date from the 9th century; of Thucydides, Herodotus, Sophocles and Aristotle from the 10th; of Tacitus from the 11th—yet no one doubts that these manuscripts, though ever so many centuries later than their authors' day, are, substantially, the uncorrupted descendants of the originals. No one would ever have thought of questioning the integrity of the Gospel texts, but for the fact that they contain a Divine Law of belief and conduct, irksome to the irreligious. Whoever would dismiss the New Testament must logically reject all written sources of ancient history and literature.

Author	Work	Date of writing	Earliest complete copy	Time span	No. of early mss., complete or partial[12]
Horace	Satires	35 B.C.	9th cent.	850 years	17
Cicero	De Senectute	44 B.C.	9th	900	16
Caesar	Gallic Wars	52 B.C.	9th	950	11
Plato	Republic	375 B.C.	9th	1300	7
Thucydides	Pelopon. War	411 B.C.	10th	1300	13
Aristotle	Poetics	334 B.C.	10th	1300	2
Herodotus	History	440-425 B.C.	10th	1350	11
Sophocles	Antigone	441 B.C.	10th	1550	4
Tacitus	Annals	110 A.D.	11th	1000	34
Evangelists, St Paul, etc.	**New Testament**	**50-100 A.D.**	**4th cent.**	**350 years**	**263 in Greek up to 9th cent.[13]**

---

[11] Listed in Aland, *op. cit.*, pp.96-102.

[12] mss. = manuscripts. This does not include fragments. All manuscript statistics of the ancient classics are taken from the introductions to the critical editions of these texts published by Société d'Édition *Les Belles Lettres*, Paris.

[13] Aland, *op. cit.*, p.106. This figure does not include the even more numerous early manuscripts of translations into Latin, Syriac, Coptic, Armenian, Georgian, Ethiopian, Gothic, Old Church Slavonic and other languages.

In the entire range of ancient literature, the *Iliad* of Homer, committed to writing possibly in the 7th century B.C., is second to the New Testament in terms of the number of ancient manuscripts: we have 372 portions of papyri from the 3rd century B.C. to the 7th cent. A.D., which together give us about 90% of the text. We also have five major manuscripts from the 10th cent. A.D. onward, and about 200 later manuscripts of complete or partial copies of the *Iliad*—but the earliest near complete manuscript is of the 10th cent. A.D.[14]

B. PROOF OF THE HISTORICAL VALUE OF THE ACTS OF THE APOSTLES AND THE EPISTLES OF ST PAUL

The Acts of the Apostles. The opening words of the Acts and the Gospel of St Luke prove identity of authorship. St Irenaeus, who quotes several passages from the Acts, says that St Luke was the companion of St Paul, and the historian of his labours. The Fragment of Muratori, c. 180, which contains a list of New Testament books, says: "But the Acts of all the Apostles are in one book which, for the excellent Theophilus, Luke wrote, because he was an eye-witness of all." Similar statements are found in Tertullian, Clement of Alexandria, Origen and many others. The arguments to prove the integrity of the text and the veracity of the author are similar to those advanced in the case of the Gospels, and need not be repeated. Further, the Apostles guaranteed the authenticity of any written or oral messages by sending them with known and trustworthy members of their own people.[15]

The Epistles of St Paul. Our adversaries admit the genuineness of the epistles to the Romans, Corinthians, Galatians, Philippians, Thessalonians and Philemon. Leaving aside the other epistles, whose authenticity they question or deny, we have more than enough for the purposes of our argument to maintain that the majority of writings which go under the name of St Paul are truly his and bear his imprint, and were held to be so by all Christian readers in the centuries that immediately followed him. The arguments to prove the integrity of the text and the veracity of the author are similar to those advanced in the case of the Gospels, and need no repetition. Further, St Paul warned against false messages or letters, and gave specimens of his handwriting to his addressees as a protection against deception.[16] As for the reliability of St Paul's doctrine: if Christ were not the divine Son of God, Paul of Tarsus could not have deified Him, and the Christians would never have admitted His Divinity, for the first Christians were Jews, highly sensitive to blasphemy. St Paul wrote at a time when very many who had listened to the teaching of Christ Himself were still alive. Had he tried, he could not, undetected, have falsified the doctrine of his Master. Like most of the other Apostles, St Paul suffered and died for the faith which he taught: he was beheaded c. 67 A.D. at Tre Fontane, Rome, where the Basilica of St Paul's-Outside-the-Walls now stands over his relics.

---

[14] P. Mazon, *Introduction à l'Iliade*, Société d'Édition *Les Belles Lettres*, Paris 1959, pp.7-65.
[15] See Acts 15:22-23; 2 Cor 12:17-18; Eph 6:21-22.
[16] See Rom 16:1; 1 Cor 16:21; Gal 6:11; Col 4:18; 2 Thess 2:2; 3:17; Philem 19.

C. CONFIRMATION IN RECENT RESEARCH

In the 19th century it became standard for haughty Rationalists to scoff at Christianity and say that the Gospels were mere mythical stories, only loosely based on history, and not written until one hundred years or more after the original events. But the discovery of earlier and earlier fragments of manuscripts, the confirmation of the New Testament furnished by archaeological research, as well as the citation of the New Testament writings by Fathers of the early 1st century A.D., pushed their successors closer and closer to those dates which traditionally were ascribed to the four Gospels and the Epistles of St Paul.

German church historian Adolf von Harnack (1851-1930), a rationalist scholar of high repute among Protestants and Rationalists, said that the Synoptic Gospels were written before 70 A.D. (i.e., before the fall of Jerusalem). After many years of doubt or denial on the question, he concluded that the Gospel of St John is by him and can be dated 80 onwards. He placed the Gospels of Mark and Luke before the year 60, and Acts in the year 62.[17] Shortly before his death, he signified his acceptance of the tradition that St Luke derived his information on the infancy of Jesus from Mary His Mother.[18]

Early dating of the books of the New Testament is held by numerous modern scholars.[19] Modern research adduces several complementary arguments for the credibility and early dating of the Gospels, Acts, and letters of St Paul:

(1) *Argument from internal indications of dating.* Italian Biblical scholar and Orientalist, Giuseppe Ricciotti, takes as his starting point the conclusion of the Acts of the Apostles. Acts concludes with St Paul in prison, before his trial had taken place and before the general persecution of Christians under Nero, which began in 64. It was written about 62 or 63, therefore. St Luke wrote Acts after his Gospel, as he states at the start of Acts. His Gospel, therefore, cannot be dated after 60, and tradition places it third in the list of Gospels, something confirmed by the Gospel's prologue, which refers to "many others" who have also written narratives of Christ, among whom would certainly be Matthew and Mark. This dating puts Matthew and Mark no later than 60. Ricciotti argues for the following dates: Matthew 50-55; Mark 55-60; Luke c. 60; John c. 100.[20]

(2) *Argument from history.* Anglican bishop J.A.T. Robinson, well-known for the theological liberalism of his book *Honest to God* (1963), in an epoch-making work *Redating the New Testament*, came to the conclusion that the late dating of the Gospels by the school of 'form criticism' is totally dependent upon "the manifold tyranny of

---

[17] *Neue Untersuchungen zur Apostelgesch. und zur Abfassung. der Syn. Evang.*, 1911; *The Date of Acts and the Synoptic Gospels*, Williams & Norgate, London, and Putnam, N.Y., 1911.
[18] *Theologische Quartalsch.*, Tübingen 1929, IV, pp.443-4
[19] See a list of fifteen scholars in J. Wenham, *Redating Matthew, Mark and Luke*, Hodder and Stoughton, London 1991, p.299.
[20] *The Life of Christ*, Bruce, Milwaukee 1947, pp.98-141

unexamined assumptions."[21] Robinson begins his study by noting that in the entire New Testament, "the single most datable and climactic event of the period—the fall of Jerusalem in AD 70, and with it the collapse of institutional Judaism based on the temple—is never once mentioned as a past fact."[22] He proposes the following dates: Matthew 40-60; Mark 45-60; Luke 57-60; John 40-65; and indeed he dates the entire New Testament before the year 70.[23]

(3) *Argument from early patristic tradition combined with internal comparison of the Gospels.* Anglican canon, and Professor of New Testament Greek, John Wenham, arguing from the likenesses and differences between the Synoptic Gospels, and early tradition regarding their order and place of writing, concludes that the Gospel of St Matthew was written around 40, St Mark about 45, St Luke by the mid-50s, and Acts of the Apostles in 62. Early Fathers and writers are unanimous in asserting that St Matthew wrote first, and in a Hebrew tongue. Those who say so include Papias, Irenaeus, Pantaenus, Origen, Eusebius, Epiphanius, and Cyril of Jerusalem. Later writers say the same: St Gregory Nazianzus, St John Chrysostom, St Augustine, St Jerome.[24]

(4) *Argument from Jewish oral and written tradition.* Swedish Biblicist, Birger Gerhardsson, demonstrates the reliability of the sayings of Jesus as recorded in the Gospels from the teaching and memorisation methods of the Jewish rabbis and disciples at the time of Christ.[25] "Turning to Jesus' oral teaching, we must reckon with the fact that he used a method similar to that of Jewish—and Hellenistic— teachers: the scheme of text and interpretation. He must have made his disciples learn sayings off by heart; if he taught, he must have required his disciples to memorize."[26] The same evidence has been presented by Harald Riesenfeld,[27] also of Sweden, and Thorleif Boman of Norway. French scholar Marcel Jousse in his own studies demonstrated the Semitic characteristics and rhythm of the sayings of Jesus as recorded in the Gospels. Other scholars point also to the wide use of shorthand and the carrying of notebooks in the Graeco-Roman world, the practice in schools of circulating lecture notes, and the common practice among the disciples of rabbis to make notes of their sayings.[28]

(5) *Argument from Hebrew basis of the texts.* French scholar Jean Carmignac was struck by the Semitisms (Hebrew or Semitic way of writing and speaking) of the Greek text

---

[21] *Redating the New Testament*, SCM Press, London 1976, p.345

[22] Idem, p.13

[23] Idem, p.352

[24] *Redating Matthew, Mark and Luke*, op. cit., London 1991

[25] *Memory and Manuscript. Oral Tradition and Written Transmission in Rabbinic Judaism and Early Christianity*, Gleerup, Uppsala, Sweden 1961; *Préhistoire des Évangiles*, Cerf, Paris 1981; *The Gospel Tradition*, Gleerup, Lund 1986

[26] *Memory and Manuscript*, op. cit., p.328

[27] *The Gospel Tradition*, Blackwell, Oxford 1970

[28] R.H. Gundry, *The Use of the Old Testament in St Matthew's Gospel*, Brill, Leiden 1967; E.J. Goodspeed, *Matthew, Apostle and Evangelist*, Winston, Philadelphia 1959; R. Riesner, *Jesus als Lehrer*, Mohr, Tübingen 1988

of St Mark's Gospel when in 1963 he began to translate it into Hebrew. His work *The Birth of the Synoptic Gospels* summarises twenty years of research on the Hebrew language background to the Gospels. Carmignac names forty-nine scholars who uphold the Semitic origin of one or other of the Gospels. He adduces multiple examples of Semitisms, and divides them into nine categories: Semitisms of borrowing, imitation, thought, vocabulary, syntax, style, composition, transmission, and translation. In essence, he demonstrates that the Synoptic Gospels can only have taken shape in the Jewish culture of the first half of the 1st century A.D., and thus they evince the authenticity of their content and origin. "In short, the latest dates that can be admitted are around 50 for Mark, ... around 55 for Completed Mark; around 55-60 for Matthew; between 58 and 60 for Luke. But the earliest dates are clearly more probable: Mark around 42; Completed Mark around 45; (Hebrew) Matthew around 50; (Greek) Luke a little after 50."[29] Based upon the same arguments, French philosopher and specialist in Hebrew thought Claude Tresmontant proposes the following dates: Matthew before 36, Mark 50-60, and Luke 40-60.[30]

The Hebrew origins of our Greek manuscripts have been studied by scholars in Jerusalem such as Robert Lindsey, David Flusser, Pinchas Lapide and David Bivin. Lindsey comments, "My own encounter with the strong Hebraism of the Gospels of Matthew, Mark, and Luke came several years ago when I had occasion to attempt the translation of the Gospel of Mark to Hebrew.[31] What first caught my attention was the very Hebraic word order of the Greek text of Mark. Usually I only needed to find the correct Hebrew equivalents to the Greek words in order to give good sense and understanding to the text. In other words, the syntax or word relationships were just such as one would expect in Hebrew."[32] The Greek text reads like a word-for-word translation of a Hebrew text. At times, obscure phrases in Greek can be understood by translating back into Hebrew, thus arriving at a Hebrew idiom or term or saying whose meaning was lost in translation. St Jerome[33] says that he himself made a copy of the Hebrew original of a 'Gospel according to the Hebrews'—a work, now lost, which scholars judge to be akin to St Matthew's Gospel. Other ancient writers, Clement, Origen, Eusebius and Epiphanius, attest to the same or a similar work.[34]

(6) *Argument from internal comparison of language.* French Biblical scholar Philippe Rolland argues, as Ricciotti, for the early dating of Acts and contends that falsification of the facts by Luke was completely impossible, given that many readers and listeners to Acts were eyewitnesses to the events described therein. He accepts

---

[29] *The Birth of the Synoptic Gospels*, Franciscan Herald Press, Chicago 1987, p.61

[30] *The Hebrew Christ. Language in the Age of the Gospels*, Franciscan Herald Press, Chicago 1989, p.324

[31] *A Hebrew Translation of the Gospel of Mark*, 2nd. ed., Jerusalem 1973

[32] Foreword to D. Bivin & R. Blizzard, *Understanding the Difficult Words of Jesus: New Insights from a Hebraic Perspective*, Rev. ed., Center for Judaic-Christian Studies, Dayton, Ohio 1994

[33] *De Vir. Illustr.* c. 3

[34] References given in W. Schneemelcher (ed.), *New Testament Apocrypha*, vol. I, Westminster, Kentucky 1991, pp.134-78. Cf. J.N.D. Kelly, *Jerome*, Duckworth, London 1975, pp.65, 223; J. Quasten, *Patrology*, Vol. I, p.111-2.

the basic argument of J. Robinson regarding the fall of Jerusalem. He then demonstrates the similarity of language between the discourses of St Peter in the Acts of the Apostles and the two epistles by him. He demonstrates likewise the similarity of language between the discourses of St Paul in the Acts of the Apostles and the several epistles by him. He proposes the following dates: Gospel of Matthew in Hebrew, A.D. 40; Greek translation of Matthew, and Gospel of Luke, 63 or 64; Mark, 66 or 67; John, towards 100.[35] These dates are accepted and proposed by Italian Biblical, Oriental and Patristic scholar, Tommaso Federici.[36]

(7) *Argument from dating of papyri.* German papyrologist Carsten Peter Thiede examined three papyrus fragments of the Gospel of St Matthew—acquired in the 1890's in Luxor, Egypt, and now kept at Magdalen College, Oxford—and concluded that they can be dated to about the year 60 A.D.[37]

The reliability of the chief New Testament books established, we can now proceed to examine their contents with security.

[35] *L'origine et la date des évangiles*, Éditions Saint-Paul, Paris 1994, pp.163-4
[36] *Resuscitò Cristo*, Eparchia di Piana d. albanesi, Palermo 1996, pp.166-7
[37] C.P. Thiede & M. d'Ancona, *Eyewitness to Jesus*, Doubleday, N.Y. 1996; *The Jesus Papyrus*, Phoenix, London 1997

CHAPTER 6

JESUS CHRIST CLAIMED TO BE GOD

Summary

That Christ claimed to be God is proved:
I.   (A) From His words as reported in the first three Gospels.
       (B) From His words as reported in the Gospel of St John.
II.   From His acts.
III.   From the belief of His Apostles and disciples.

I

A. THE FIRST THREE GOSPELS TESTIFY
THAT JESUS CHRIST CLAIMED TO BE GOD

Christ claimed to be God, because He made claims that God alone can make.

He claimed to be God, the Judge of all mankind. "When the Son of Man comes in His glory, and all the angels with Him ... before Him will be gathered all the nations, and He will separate them one from another".[1] It is only God who can speak of Himself thus. It is only God who can read the hearts of the countless of millions of mankind, and apportion to each individual his deserts. In the continuation of the same passage, He says that He, "the King", will tell the good on the day of judgement that in befriending the needy they were befriending Him, and He will tell the wicked that in neglecting the needy they were neglecting Him. He identifies Himself, therefore, with God, whom good men please and wicked men displease. He calls Himself, "the Son of Man", a Messianic title.[2]

He claimed to be God the Lawgiver. The Pharisees accused the disciples of Jesus of having violated the Sabbath. Jesus replied that "the Son of Man is Lord of the Sabbath."[3] That is to say, the Sabbath observance may be set aside by Him, viz., God, who instituted it. He said, in the Sermon on the Mount: "You have heard that it was said to the men of old, 'You shall not kill' ... *But I say to you* that everyone who is angry with his brother shall be liable to judgement".[4] And, throughout the discourse, He returns repeatedly to the same emphatic declaration: "You have heard ... *But I say to you*". Had He claimed to be no more than a merely human envoy of God,

---

[1] Matt 25:31-46. The whole passage should be read.
[2] Daniel 7:13-14
[3] Matt 12:8
[4] Matt 5:21-22; cf. vv. 28, 32, 34, 39, 44.

He would never have spoken thus: to do so would have been the vilest blasphemy and arrogance. He would instead have adhered with the strictest reverence and humility to the formula: "But God now bids me to say to you." The words He actually spoke show Him as claiming to enlarge and re-interpret the Ten Commandments on His own personal authority. But such authority can be possessed by God alone, the giver of the Law on Sinai.

He claimed to be Omnipotent. He claimed to be a Divine Person, God the Son, equal in power to the Father. "All authority in heaven and on earth has been given to Me."[5] "All things have been delivered to Me by My Father; and no one knows who the Son is except the Father, or who the Father is except the Son and any one to whom the Son chooses to reveal Him."[6] He claimed to possess a power which only God could possess, power over the angels and all creatures, whether in heaven or on earth. But while making this claim, He stated clearly that He was not the only Person in God. He spoke of Himself as the Son who had received all things from the Father to whom He was mysteriously united in mutual knowledge, and whom He alone at His pleasure could make known to men.

He claimed to be God the Son, one in nature with the Father. (a) One day, near Caesarea Philippi, Jesus "asked His disciples, 'Who do men say that the Son of Man is?' And they said, 'Some say John the Baptist, others say Elijah, and others Jeremiah or one of the prophets.' He said to them, 'But who do you say that I am?' Simon Peter replied, 'You are the Christ, the Son of the living God.' And Jesus answered him, 'Blessed are you, Simon Bar-Jona! For flesh and blood has not revealed this to you, but My Father who is in heaven.'"[7] St Peter had learned the truth about Christ, not from his merely natural powers ("flesh and blood"), but from the revelation given to him by the Father through the Son. Christ had already shown in many ways that He was a Divine Person, God the Son. The expression "Son of God" is used sometimes in the Scriptures in the figurative meaning of "Friend" or "Servant of God." Here, however, there can be no question of such figurative sonship. In this sense, John the Baptist, Elijah and the prophets were "sons of God." Besides, had St Peter used the words in this weaker meaning, he would not have required a revelation from God the Father.

(b) In the hearing of the priests and scribes, Christ spoke a parable to the people. He told how a man planted a vineyard and let it out to tenants, how

---

[5] Matt 28:18
[6] Lk 10:22
[7] Matt 16:13-17; cf. Lk 10:22; Matt 11:27.

he sent servant after servant to them to collect his share of the fruit, how the tenants beat them and drove them away empty-handed, and how at last "the owner of the vineyard said, 'What shall I do? I will send my beloved son;[8] it may be they will respect him.' But when the tenants saw him, they said to themselves, 'This is the heir; let us kill him, that the inheritance may be ours.' And they cast him out of the vineyard and killed him. What then will the owner of the vineyard do to them? He will come and destroy those tenants, and give the vineyard to others."[9] The people caught His meaning. They saw that His parable foretold that the Jews who had slain prophet after prophet, would at last slay the beloved Son of God himself, and so accomplish their own destruction. They cried out: "God forbid!" And the priests and scribes, were it not for the many friends about Him, would have seized Him that instant. They saw themselves in the parable as the slayers of the true Son of God.

(c) When Jesus stood before the Sanhedrin on Good Friday morning, "the High Priest asked Him, 'Are you the Christ, the Son of the Blessed?' And Jesus said, 'I am; and you will see the Son of Man sitting at the right hand of Power, and coming with the clouds of heaven.' And the High Priest tore his mantle, and said, 'Why do we still need witnesses? You have heard his blasphemy. What is your decision?' And they all condemned Him as deserving death."[10] What was the blasphemy? It was the claim of Jesus to be the true Son of God, one in nature with the Father. It was for that blasphemy they condemned Him to death.

B. THE GOSPEL OF ST JOHN TESTIFIES THAT JESUS CLAIMED TO BE GOD

He claimed divine prerogatives. The Jews said to Him: "'You are not yet fifty years old, and You have seen Abraham?' Jesus said to them, 'Truly, truly, I say to you, before Abraham was, I am.'"[11] "The Father ... has given all judgement to the Son, that all may honour the Son, even as they honour the Father."[12] To Nicodemus He said: "He who does not believe [in the Son] is condemned already, because he has not believed in the name of the only Son of God."[13] He speaks of Himself as "the door"[14] through which

---

[8] "Beloved Son" in the Scriptures means "true and only son". Cf. Matt 3:17.
[9] Lk 20:13-16
[10] Mk 14:61-64; cf. Matt 26:63-66
[11] Jn 8:57-58
[12] Jn 5:22-23
[13] Jn 3:18
[14] Jn 10:9

men enter into life. He is "the true vine",[15] we are the branches. He is "the Way, and the Truth, and the Life".[16] Before He suffered, He prayed to His heavenly Father: "Father, Glorify Thou Me in Thy own presence, with the glory which I had with Thee before the world was made. ... All Mine are Thine, and Thine are Mine".[17] Many more texts of like purport from St John and the other Evangelists might be quoted.[18]

The Jews knew He claimed to be God. Jesus said to the Jews: "I and the Father are one." They were about to stone Him for these words, "because", they said, "You, being a man, make Yourself God."[19] Jesus, replying to the Jews who were offended because He had cured a sick man on the Sabbath day, said, "My Father is working still, and I am working." Whereupon they "sought all the more to kill Him, because He ... called God His Father, making Himself equal with God." Jesus, far from saying that they had misunderstood Him, answered: "... for whatever [the Father] does, that the Son does likewise ... For as the Father raises the dead and gives them life, so also the Son gives life to whom He will."[20] When Pilate tried to acquit Jesus, the Jews cried out: "We have a law, and by that law He ought to die, because He has made Himself the Son of God."[21]

II

THE ACTS OF JESUS TESTIFY THAT HE CLAIMED TO BE GOD

Jesus performed His many miracles, not merely as the ambassador of God, but as God Himself: "even though you do not believe Me, believe the works", i.e., the miracles, "that you may know and understand that the Father is in Me and I am in the Father."[22] He allowed men to adore Him as God. When He had given sight to the man born blind, "He said, 'Do you believe in the Son of Man?' He answered, 'And who is He, sir, that I may believe in Him?' Jesus said to him, '... it is He who speaks to you.' He said, 'Lord, I believe'; and he worshipped Him."[23] He forgave sin as of His own independent power. "My son, your sins are forgiven", He said to the

---

[15] Jn 15:1
[16] Jn 14:6
[17] Jn 17:5,10,19
[18] When Christ says (Jn 14:28), "the Father is greater than I", He means, "the Father is greater than I am *as man*." Or it is a mode of saying, "The Father is my origin". See p.385 for a fuller explanation.
[19] Jn 10:30-33
[20] Jn 5:17-21
[21] Jn 19:7
[22] Jn 10:38
[23] Jn 9:35-38; cf. Matt 14:33; 15:25; 17:14.

man sick of the palsy. When the Scribes ask themselves indignantly, "Who can forgive sins but God alone?", He does not deny the assertion implied in their question, viz., "it is only God who can forgive sin", but goes on to reaffirm the claim He has already made. "'But that you may know that the Son of Man has authority on earth to forgive sins'—He said to the paralytic—'I say to you, rise, take up your pallet and go home.' And he rose, and immediately took up the pallet and went out before them all".[24] To Magdalen, who had kissed His feet and bathed them with her tears, He said, "Your sins are forgiven." And to those who sat at table with Him on the same occasion, He said, "her sins, which are many, are forgiven, for she loved much".[25] It is only through love of God that sins are forgiven. Christ, therefore, asserts that love of Him is love of God. In other words, He claims to be God.

III

THE APOSTLES AND DISCIPLES KNEW THAT CHRIST CLAIMED TO BE GOD

No one denies that, after the death of Christ, His followers, both Jews and Gentiles, preached His Divinity, and that they suffered and died in testimony thereof,[26] facts which can be explained only by their knowledge that He Himself had claimed to be the Son of God.

---

[24] Mk 2:5-12
[25] Lk 7:47-8
[26] Acts 3:14-15; 5:41; 7:55-58; 15:26.

CHAPTER 7

JESUS CHRIST, TRUE GOD

Summary

We prove the Divinity of Christ by various arguments:
I.   A. By His miracles.
     B. By His prophecies.
     C. By the fact that He was Himself the fulfilment of prophecy. Note on Jewish groups at the time of Christ.
II. By His Resurrection. Christ claimed to be God. In proof of His claim, He said He would rise from the dead, and did rise from the dead. Therefore, Christ is God. The witnesses to the Resurrection were trustworthy. Refutation of adversaries' Theories: the Deception Hypothesis, the Hallucination Hypothesis, the Trance Hypothesis.
III. By His perfection as a man and as a teacher of natural religion, considered in the light of His claim to be God. Christ, viewed even from a merely human standpoint, was the most perfect man, the most perfect teacher of Natural Religion that ever lived. He said repeatedly and emphatically that He was God. We must, therefore, conclude that His claim was just, that He was God. Otherwise, we are driven to the absurdity of saying that the most perfect of mankind was a maniac or a blasphemer.
IV. By His living force and influence in the world. Note on the various methods of proving Christ's divinity.

I

FIRST PROOF:
MIRACLES AND PROPHECIES PROVE THAT JESUS CHRIST
WAS WHAT HE CLAIMED TO BE—GOD

A. **His miracles prove His Divinity**. During His life on earth, Christ performed many miracles. He healed the sick, the blind, the lame, the dumb, the epileptic, by a mere word, and sometimes from a distance. Specially remarkable was the cure of the man born blind.[1] He raised at least three dead persons to life: the daughter of Jairus, the widow's son in Naim, and Lazarus. He delivered people from evil spirits, thereby showing His dominion over the world of spirits. Many of His miracles were wrought on inanimate nature: He changed water into wine; He fed five thousand with five loaves and two fishes; He stilled a storm with a word; He walked upon the waters. His miracles cannot be explained away:[2]

---

[1] Jn 9
[2] Cf. Ch. 4 on Miracles.

GOSPEL MIRACLES
related in detail

		Matthew	Mark	Luke	John
1.	Water into wine at wedding of Cana				2:1-11
2.	Cure of the nobleman's son				4:46-54
3.	The first miraculous draught of fish			5:1-11	
4.	Cure of the demoniac in Capernaum		1:23-28	4:31-37	
5.	Cure of Simon's mother-in-law	8:14-15	1:29-31	4:38-39	
6.	Cure of a leper at Capernaum	8:1-4	1:40-45	5:12-16	
7.	Cure of a paralytic carried by four	9:1-8	2:1-12	5:17-26	
8.	Cure of the centurion's servant	8:5-13		7:1-10	
9.	Resurrection of widow's son at Nain			7:11-17	
10.	Cure of a man with a withered hand	12:9-14	3:1-6	6:6-11	
11.	Cure of sick man at the Pool of Bethzatha				5:1-15
12.	The calming of the storm	8:23-27	4:35-41	8:22-25	
13.	The Gerasene demoniac delivered	8:28-34	5:1-20	8:26-39	
14.	Cure of the woman with a haemorrhage	9:18-26	5:21-43	8:40-56	
15.	Jairus' daughter raised to life				
16.	Cure of two blind men at Capernaum	9:27-31			
17.	First miracle of the loaves	14:13-21	6:30-44	9:10-17	6:1-13
18.	Jesus walks on the water	14:22-33	6:45-52		6:16-21
19.	Syrophoenician's daughter healed	15:21-28	7:24-30		
20.	Second miracle of the loaves	15:32-39	8:1-10		
21.	Healing of the deaf man		7:32-37		
22.	Cure of a blind man at Bethsaida		8:22-26		
23.	The epileptic demoniac at Tabor	17:14-21	9:14-29	9:37-43	
24.	The Temple tax paid by Jesus and Peter	17:24-27			
25.	Cure of the man born blind				9:1-38
26.	Cure of the dumb demoniac	9:32-34			
27.	Healing of crippled woman on Sabbath			13:10-17	
28.	Healing of a dropsical man on the Sabbath			14:1-6	
29.	The resurrection of Lazarus				11:1-44
30.	The ten lepers			17:11-19	
31.	The blind men of Jericho	20:29-34	10:46-52	18:35-43	
32.	The fig tree made barren	21:18-22	11:12-14		
33.	Healing of Malchus' ear			22:51	

This list does not include: (a) the miracles which concern the Saviour's person, such as His virginal conception and the Transfiguration; (b) the miracles of His glorious life; (c) the probably miraculous happenings which are not presented as such by the Evangelists, for example, Jesus withdrawing Himself from the rage of His enemies; the falling backward of the men at Gethsemane; (d) the countless miracles mentioned *en bloc* in the Gospels, e.g. Matt 4:24; Mark 6:56; Luke 7:21; John 12:37. (Adapted from F. Prat S.J.)

(1) by *the delusion theory* according to which merely natural occurrences were regarded as supernatural by His credulous disciples. The miracles were performed in public and their genuineness was not disputed by Christ's adversaries.[3] Nor (2) by *the theory of diabolical agency*. Christ was holy in His person and in His doctrine,[4] and could not, therefore, have been an emissary of Satan. Christ, by casting out evil spirits, showed that He was not the agent of Satan, but his enemy. Nor (3) by *the theory of hypnotism, or faith healing*. Certain nervous disorders may be cured by hypnotism or suggestion, but the cure cannot be effected instantaneously, nor from a distance. Christ cured all manner of diseases. In many cases the patients were not present and did not even know that He was about to cure them. The theory takes no account of cases of resurrection from the dead.

The miracles of Christ were so frequent, the witnesses so numerous, and the evidence so stark, that not even Christ's enemies disputed the fact of their occurrence. Instead, they ascribed them to the power of the devil, or defied Him to perform another one in His own favour.[5] Many of both the beneficiaries and the eye-witnesses of Christ's miracles were alive for decades after the miracles themselves, and stood as living proofs and witnesses to their occurrence. If, for example, the twelve year old girl raised from the dead[6] lived to the age of eighty-five, this would have meant that she was still alive in the year 100. Quadratus, c. 124 A.D., in a defence of the Christian religion addressed to the Emperor, says, "The miracles of the Saviour always appeared, for they were genuine. Those who were cured and those who were raised from the dead were seen not only while being cured and being raised. They were present, not only while our Saviour dwelt among us, but also for a considerable time after He had departed. In fact, some of them lived to our own day."[7]

Christ appealed to His miracles as a proof that He was sent by God: "these very works which I am doing, bear me witness that the Father has sent Me."[8] Christ's teaching, therefore, was the teaching of God. But Christ taught that He Himself was God. Therefore, Christ is God.

B. **His prophecies prove His Divinity**. Christ foretold many things which came to pass and which no mere man could have foreseen: (1) With reference to Himself, He foretold His Passion, Resurrection, and Ascension

---

[3] Jn 11:47
[4] For the evidence of this, see pp.119-26.
[5] Matt 12:24; 27:39-42; Jn 11:47
[6] Mk 5:35-42
[7] *Apology to Hadrian*, in Eusebius, *Hist. Eccl.* IV, 3, 2
[8] Jn 5:36. Cf. 10:37; Matt 11:4-5.

into Heaven;[9] (2) with reference to His disciples, He foretold that Judas would betray Him, that Peter would deny Him, that all His disciples would forsake Him;[10] (3) with reference to His Church, He foretold that it would grow like a mustard-seed, that it would leaven all mankind, that, like Himself, it would be hated and persecuted by the world, and that the gates of hell would not prevail against it.[11] *The fulfilment of these prophecies proves that Christ's teaching was the teaching of God.* But Christ taught that He was God. Therefore, Christ is God.

His prophecy about Jerusalem and the Jews is particularly noteworthy. He said: "The days shall come upon you, when your enemies will cast up a bank about you and surround you, and hem you in on every side, and dash you to the ground, you and your children within you, and they will not leave one stone upon another in you".[12] And again: "great distress shall be upon the earth and wrath upon this people; they will fall by the edge of the sword, and be led captive among all nations; and Jerusalem will be trodden down by the Gentiles".[13] How accurately these prophecies were fulfilled will be understood by the readers of the *History of the Jewish War*, written at the request of the Roman Emperor Titus, by Flavius Josephus (A.D. c.37-c.100), a Jew who first served against the Romans, was taken prisoner and pardoned. He was with Titus at the siege of Jerusalem. The complete destruction of the city was quite unexpected, as it was the Roman practice to preserve conquered cities and particularly the temples. The Emperor, Julian the Apostate (361-363 A.D.), tried to rebuild the Temple, so that by re-establishing the Jewish state and the Jewish religion, he might falsify the Christian prophecy. Jews flocked in from every side, and assisted with great enthusiasm in the work. Ammianus Marcellinus, a pagan writer, one of the imperial lifeguards, tells us of the issue, one of the most remarkable, as it is one of the best attested events in history: "[Julian] committed the accomplishment of this task to Alypius of Antioch, who had before that been Lieutenant of Britain. Alypius, therefore, set himself vigorously to the work, and was seconded by the governor of the province. Fearful balls of fire, breaking out near the foundations, continued their attacks, till the workmen, after repeated scorchings, could approach no more; and thus, the fierce elements obstinately repelling them, he gave up his attempt."[14]

---

[9] Jn 3:14; Matt 20:18; Jn 6:62
[10] Jn 13:21, 26; Matt 26:34; 26:31
[11] Matt 13:31-33; 16:18
[12] Lk 19:43-44
[13] Lk 21:23-24
[14] *Hist.* 23, 1-3. Newman, *Essays on Miracles*, sect. vii, p.334, quotes several other authorities, Christian and pagan, some of them contemporaries.

C. **Christ Himself the fulfilment of prophecy**. Many Jews were
converted by perceiving that in Christ were fulfilled the prophecies about
the Messiah contained in their sacred books, the books of the Old
Testament. We are not concerned here to prove that these books were
divinely inspired, nor even that they were authentic. It suffices to accept as
true, what no one denies, that the books were in existence long before the
birth of Christ.

The religion of the Jews was a religion of expectation, with the belief in a
Messiah, or a Redeemer to come, as its central doctrine. All that had been
foretold of the Redeemer was accurately fulfilled in Christ. The table below
gives a brief summary of the prophetic description of the Redeemer, and a
selection of the texts recording their fulfilment.

Prophecy of the Messiah	Fulfilment
He shall be a descendant of Abraham. Gen 12:2-3	Matt 1:1
He shall belong to the tribe of Judah. Gen 49:10	Matt 1:2. Lk 3:33
He shall be sprung from the line of David and be heir to his throne. Is 11:1-2	Lk 1:32-33
He shall be born at Bethlehem.[15] Micah 5:2	Lk 2:4-7
He shall be born of a Virgin Mother. Is 7:14	Lk 1:26-27, 34-35
He shall be called the Son of God. Ps 2:7	Mk 1:11
He shall have a precursor to announce Him. Is 40:3-5. Mal 3:1	Mk 1:1-9
He will enlighten the people of Galilee. Is 9:1-2	Matt 4:12-17
He shall heal the broken-hearted and work miracles in their favour. Is 61:1-3; 35:4-6	Matt 11:2-5
He shall be sold for thirty pieces of silver, and the silver shall be used to purchase the potter's field. Zach 11:12-13	Matt 26:15; 27:3-10
He shall be a man of sorrows, despised and the lowest of men. He shall be offered of His own will, and shall not open His mouth; He shall be led as a sheep to slaughter, and shall be dumb as a lamb before His shearer. Is 53	Mk 15:4-5 Lk 23:32-43
His hands and feet shall be pierced, His garments shall be divided, and lots cast upon His vesture. Ps 22 (21):17-19	Jn 19:17-24
His empire shall be multiplied. Is 9:7. He shall be a light to the Gentiles and bring salvation to the ends of the earth. Is 49:6. "The God of Heaven will set up a Kingdom which shall never be destroyed" Dan 2:44. His Kingdom shall be assailed but shall last for ever. Ps 2:1-4. He shall judge all men and crown the just with glory. Is 24, 28	Ongoing and future.

It is manifest that the fulfilment of all these prophecies in an individual
could not have been due to chance or human contrivance, but must have
been the work of God. Christ was therefore the promised Redeemer. He

---

[15] The chief priests and scribes, in answer to Herod, quoted this text to prove that Christ
should be born at Bethlehem: Matt 2:3-6.

had been sent by God. He taught with divine authority. But He taught that He was God, therefore He was God.

The divine origin of Judaism. The Divinity of Christ establishes the divine origin not only of Christianity, but also of the preparatory religion of Judaism. Christ, in His human generation, was a man of the Jewish race. For nearly thirty years He professed and practised the Jewish religion. Therefore, the Jewish religion was what it claimed to be, a religion given to the Jewish race by God, and the accounts of all pre-Christian revelation which its sacred books contain must be accepted as of divine authority. The Divinity of Christ therefore assures us of His own revelation, and of the revelations given before His time to the Jewish race.

In addition to the direct references to the person of the Messiah, listed in the table above, it can be shown that the Jewish religion contains in its general organisation and in its details a foreshadowing of His work, of the Church which He founded and of the Sacraments which He instituted. Furthermore, it will be found that the chief incidents in His life are reflected or typified in the lives of the Patriarchs, Prophets, and Saints of the Old Law.

The prophecies which say that Christ would found an everlasting kingdom and would be the Judge of mankind have, obviously, not yet been fulfilled in the strict sense. It is only at the end of the world that their perfect fulfilment will be attained. They have, however, been fulfilled already insofar as they signify that Christ would *proclaim* Himself to be the founder of an everlasting kingdom and to be the future Judge of mankind. The endurance of His Kingdom on earth, the Church, for 2,000 years is an ongoing fulfilment of the prophecy that His Kingdom shall endure for all time.

But why did not the entire Jewish people perceive that in Christ all prophecy was fulfilled? The question appears even more difficult to answer when we remember that, as the time of Christ's birth approached, hope in the speedy coming of the Messiah had become intense. Response: (1) The Jewish people at the time of Christ were, as a mass, morally corrupt. Flavius Josephus says that, had not the Romans come to punish them, an earthquake, a deluge, or the lightnings of Sodom would have overwhelmed them. Christ denounced them as an "evil and adulterous generation".[16] Their wickedness closed their ears to the message of Christ. (2) They heard with savage bitterness the revolutionary doctrine of Christ that they would no longer stand apart from the rest of the world as God's chosen people, but that the despised Gentiles were to be admitted to the same privilege. This doctrine of Christ was repeated on many occasions.[17] Early in His mission, in the Synagogue of Nazareth, when He spoke of God's mercies to Gentiles in ages past, the people rushed at Him in a body, swept Him to the brow of a precipice, and would have

---

[16] Matt 16:4; cf. Mk 8:38.
[17] E.g., Matt 21:43; 24:14; 26:13

107

flung Him to His death but for an exercise of His divine power.[18] (3) Their leaders, the Scribes and Pharisees, conceived a terrible hatred against Christ, because they were envious of His influence, and because He had unsparingly denounced their arrogance and hypocrisy. They were therefore not disposed to examine His claims impartially. (4) Owing partly to the Pharisees' interpretation of the sacred writings, and partly to the foreign oppression and national pride, the Jewish people had come to think of the Messiah not as one who would deliver them from sin, but as a temporal king who would break the Roman yoke and lead them to world-empire. The triumphs of a Spiritual King were all interpreted as the triumphs of an earthly monarch.[19] Even the Apostles could hardly rid themselves of the popular belief, for they asked Christ before His Ascension, with a pathetic yearning for the fulfilment of a patriotic hope, "Lord, will You at this time restore the Kingdom to Israel?"[20]

The rejection by the Jews of their long-promised Messiah is both a mystery of iniquity and of Redemption. "He came unto His own and His own received Him not."[21] Their sinful disbelief brought down God's judgement upon them, the destruction of Jerusalem, and their dispersion over the face of the earth. Yet God brought good out of evil; He used this very rejection as the instrument of the Redemption, to bring the Kingdom of God to the Gentiles: "through their trespass salvation has come to the Gentiles".[22] Pascal says that God has preserved the Jews as a permanent witness to the truth of the Old Testament.[23] Christ wept tears over Jerusalem.[24] It cut St Paul to the heart to see his own race cut off from Christ and hardened in blindness,[25] and yet he prophesied that before the end of time the Jews will be converted.[26] At the present time, the Jews worldwide are extremely diverse in belief and observance. Some adhere rigidly to the Law of Moses and the Old Testament (Orthodox Jews), others hold to basically the same doctrines but are less rigid in their practices (Conservatives), whilst others are very free in belief (Liberals or Freethinkers). Many Jews have altogether given up looking for a Messiah, and a large number are now atheists.

The second Vatican Council says, "Even though the Jewish authorities along with their followers pressed for the death of Christ, those things perpetrated during His Passion cannot be indiscriminately blamed upon all Jews of that time, nor Jews today. Although, indeed, the Church is the new people of God, the Jews should not be presented as rejected or accursed as if this followed from Holy Scripture. ... Moreover, the Church, which reproves all persecution against any people, mindful of her common heritage with the Jews, and moved not by political considerations,

---

[18] Lk 4:18-30.
[19] See p.89.
[20] Acts 1:6
[21] Jn 1:11 (Douay)
[22] Rom 11:11
[23] *Pensées*, 618, 620, 641, 750, 766
[24] Matt 23:37ff.
[25] Rom 9:1-5
[26] Rom 11:12,15,25-26,31. The prophecy of the Jews' conversion is mentioned in *Nostra Aetate*, Declaration on the Relation of the Church to non-Christian Religions, second Vatican council, 1965, art. 4; also C674.

but by religious and evangelical charity, deplores all hatred, persecutions, and displays of anti-Semitism directed at the Jews at any time or from any one."[27] Addressing a Jewish crowd, St Peter says, "And now, brethren, I know that you acted in ignorance, as did also your rulers. But what God foretold by the mouth of all the prophets, that His Christ should suffer, He thus fulfilled."[28] It is not the Jews who are collectively responsible for Christ's death, but all of us sinners, "for, as our sins consigned Christ the Lord to undergo the death of the Cross, most certainly those who wallow in sin and iniquity crucify in themselves the Son of God anew, for He is in them, and hold Him up to contempt. This guilt, then, can be seen to be graver in us than in the Jews, since as the Apostle witnesses, 'If they had known it, they would never have crucified the Lord of glory';[29] while we, on the contrary, professing to know Him, yet denying Him by our actions, seem in some way to lay violent hands on Him."[30]

Note. **Jewish groups at the time of Christ**. The Jews were divided into various politico-religious groups at the time of Christ.

The Pharisees. The Pharisees ("separated ones") followed the Law of Moses as well as the oral tradition of its interpretation developed by the rabbis (teachers of the Law). The oral tradition they regarded as on the same level as the Law itself—something which Christ attacked when any of these man-made traditions undermined the very purpose of the God-given Law (cf. e.g., Matt 15:1-9). They held to the orthodox doctrines and practices of the Jewish religion, as Christ Himself did. They exerted their influence through the development of education, and fostered synagogue worship, which took place in local Jewish towns. They were distinguished also for their separation from anyone whom they regarded as ritually unclean. Christ denounced their leaders for hypocrisy, for self-righteousness, for mere outward observance of the Law, for their impossible multitude of observances, and for their oppression of the poor.

The Sadducees. The Sadducees were opposed to the Pharisees, and stood for the interests of the priestly aristocracy and the rich. They were powerful as a group in Jerusalem and in the Temple. They performed the Temple service and gave the priestly interpretation of the Law. They accepted only the first five books of the Old Testament and did not accept the oral tradition of the Pharisees and the later Hebrew writings, nor did they believe in angels, the next life, the immortality of the soul, and the resurrection. It was their disbelief in the resurrection which prompted their question to Christ about who would be the husband in the next life of a woman widowed seven times over (Matt 22:23ff.). Their question was posed in order to mock the whole idea of the resurrection by arguing it would usher in absurdities.

---

27 *Nostra Aetate*, art. 4
28 Acts 3:17-18
29 1 Cor 2:8
30 C 598, quoting the *Roman Catechism* of 1566, on which see p.643, n.133

The *Scribes* were teachers and practitioners of law, some of whom adhered to the Pharisees, others to the Sadducees.

The Zealots. This Jewish party of revolt opposed foreign domination of the Promised Land and used violence to attack political enemies. It is possible but uncertain that the apostle Simon the Zealot had once been a member. They were responsible for the revolt against the Romans which led to the destruction of Jerusalem in 70 A.D.

The Essenes. These were a strict Jewish sect, not named in the Bible, who lived in highly organised and disciplined communities, like monasteries. The Dead Sea Scrolls discovered from 1947 onwards, and the excavations of their headquarters there, have provided information on their doctrines and way of life.

The common people generally followed the teaching of the Pharisees but feared their severity at the same time. Jesus had pity on these crowds for they were like sheep without a shepherd.
Of all the Jewish groups, only the Pharisaic tradition survived the fall of Jerusalem.

II

SECOND PROOF: THE RESURRECTION OF JESUS CHRIST PROVES THAT HE WAS GOD

Christ said He would rise from the dead. When the Jews demanded a miracle in proof of His authority, He answered: "Destroy this temple, and in three days I will raise it up." "He spoke", the Evangelist says, "of the temple of His body."[31] Later He speaks more clearly: "An evil and adulterous generation seeks for a sign; but no sign shall be given to it except the sign of the prophet Jonah. For as Jonah was three days and three nights in the belly of the whale, so will the Son of Man be three days and three nights in the heart of the earth."[32] After the Transfiguration, He says to Peter, James, and John: "Tell no one the vision, until the Son of Man is raised from the dead."[33] Before going up to Jerusalem to suffer, He says with perfect distinctness: "Behold, we are going up to Jerusalem; and the Son of Man will be delivered to the chief priests and scribes, and they will condemn Him to death, and deliver Him to the Gentiles to be mocked and scourged and crucified, and He will be raised on the third day."[34] That He had foretold His Resurrection was well known to all, for the Jews, after

---

[31] Jn 2:19,21
[32] Matt 12:39-40
[33] Matt 17:9
[34] Matt 20:18-19

His death, said to Pilate: "We remember how that impostor said, while He was still alive, 'After three days I will rise again.'"[35]

Christ died and was buried. The four Evangelists say that He died on the cross. The soldiers, finding Him already dead, did not break His limbs. One of them opened His side with a spear. When Joseph of Arimathea asked Pilate for permission to bury Him, Pilate, before consenting, despatched a centurion to make sure that He was dead.[36] It was not likely that His enemies would leave their work half finished. In the words quoted above (end of last paragraph) they say "while He was still alive", i.e., they assert that He is now dead. The Roman historian Tacitus (55-120 A.D. approx.) says that "Christ was put to death by Pontius Pilate, the procurator of Judaea, in the reign of Tiberius".[37]

Christ rose from the dead. The Evangelists tell us that the *tomb was found empty* on the morning of the third day; that Christ appeared to Mary Magdalen and the other women; that He appeared to the Apostles and showed them His wounds, "See My hands and My feet, that it is I Myself; handle Me, and see; for a spirit has not flesh and bones as you see that I have";[38] that He conversed with them and ate with them;[39] that He walked with the two disciples to Emmaus, and was recognised by them "in the breaking of the bread."[40] St Paul writes to the Corinthians, "He appeared to *more than five hundred brethren at one time* ... last of all, He appeared also to me."[41] The other Epistles make frequent reference to the Resurrection.

The witnesses to the Resurrection were trustworthy.
(1) *They were not deceivers*: they had no inducement to give false testimony. Their labours and their sufferings are proofs of their sincerity. *They were not themselves deceived*: the supposition is excluded by their numbers, their reluctance to believe, and the length of time Christ was with them after His death.

(2) *God confirmed their honesty*. God Himself showed by miracles that they were neither deceivers nor dreamers but speakers of the truth. Through their hands and in the name of the risen Christ, He wrought many signs and wonders, so that "fear came upon every soul."[42] Note in particular the

---

[35] Matt 27:63
[36] Mk 15:43-45
[37] *Annals* xv, 44
[38] Lk 24:39
[39] Lk 24:43
[40] Lk 24:35
[41] 1 Cor 15:6,8
[42] Acts 2:43

miracle of tongues, the miraculous cure of the man publicly known as having been lame from birth, and the deliverance of all the Apostles from prison—a miracle which has some features in common with Christ's deliverance from the prison of the grave. During the night an angel led them forth, and next morning the servants of the High Priest reported: "we found the prison securely locked and the sentries standing at the doors, but when we opened it we found no one inside." [43]

Christ Risen appeared over 40 days to:	
Probably the Blessed Virgin Mary first and, amongst others:	
1. St Mary Magdalene and the holy women	John 20:11-18 Mark 16:9-11 Matthew 28:1-10
2. Simon Peter (Cephas)	Luke 24:34 1 Cor. 15:5
3. Cleopas and companion on way to Emmaus	Luke 24:13-35 Mark 16:12-13
4. The Apostles and disciples in the Cenacle on Sunday evening (without Thomas)	John 20:19-23 Luke 24:36-43
5. The Apostles next Sunday (with Thomas)	John 20:24-29
6. Seven disciples (Peter, Thomas, Nathanael, James, John, and two others) at Lake Tiberias	John 21:1-23
7. The Apostles in Galilee	Matthew 28:16-17 Mark 16:14-15
8. More than 500 of the brethren together	1 Cor. 15:6
9. St James the Less	1 Cor. 15:7
10. The Apostles on the day of the Ascension	Acts 1:4-11 Luke 24:50-51

(3) *Many former scoffers and enemies became believers*: observe the striking fact that among the thousands of early converts that flocked to St Peter, there were "a great many of the priests."[44] They belonged to the very class that had rejected the miracles of Jesus and had sent Him to His death; but now they broke away from the High Priest and the other leaders who were still fiercely brushing aside every new evidence sent them by God. These new believers were "cut to the heart", while their opponents were enraged, at the

---

[43] Acts 2:7-8; 3:1-10; 5:18-23
[44] Acts 6:7

suspicion of being stained with the blood of God's Son.[45] These converts knew that they were sacrificing all the privileges of their priesthood for a life of persecution. They knew that they would be branded as traitors to their order and their race. How could they have faced such a future? Only because of the sharp command of their conscience. The truth of the Resurrection must have shone out, clear as crystal in their minds. This would have come to pass in either of two ways: either they were convinced that the miracles wrought by the Apostles were genuine, and that, therefore, God Himself had vouched for the truth of their statement that Christ was risen—or else they were convinced, after personally interviewing and cross-questioning the numerous witnesses to the Resurrection (to all of whom they would have had easy access), that there was no flaw in their testimony. However, with the severe choice before them, we may take it as beyond all doubt that many of them would have examined both sets of evidence, and would, moreover, have studied anew the Messianic prophecies and have found their fulfilment in the suffering, yet triumphant, Christ, the Son of God made Man, who died on the Cross and rose from the grave.

The Roman soldiers as witnesses to the Resurrection. St Matthew records that the chief priests and Pharisees, knowing of Christ's announcement that after three days He would rise again, went to Pilate to request a guard for the tomb of Jesus to prevent any theft of His body. Pilate said to them, "You have a guard of soldiers; go, make it as secure as you can."[46] These Jewish leaders had seen the eclipse of the sun, followed by the earthquake, and the veil of the Temple torn into two from top to bottom.[47] They had seen the raising of Lazarus, apart from other prodigies. So, in fear of the Resurrection, a guard was set. We often imagine two soldiers only, but there must have been several, for after the Resurrection, "*some of the guard* went into the city and told the chief priests all that had taken place."[48] What had those Roman soldiers seen? They had seen a glorious angel of the Lord descend from Heaven and roll back the stone of the tomb.[49] But what exactly made them—a cohort of trained Roman soldiers—run in fear from their post? Was it merely the sight of an angel? The story of an angel's appearance would not have worried the Jewish leaders. That story by itself would not prove a resurrection. The soldiers were paid a bribe, not to keep silent about an angel, but to say that the disciples had stolen the body.[50] What, then, did that group of soldiers see? They must have seen, at the very

---

[45] Acts 2:37; 5:33; 7:54
[46] Matt 27:65
[47] Matt 27:45,51
[48] Matt 28:11
[49] Matt 28:1-4
[50] Matt 28:12-13

least, the angel open the tomb to reveal to their own eyes *that it was empty*. They, who had seen how the Jews had "made the sepulchre secure by sealing the stone",[51] now saw with their own eyes that the dead Man inside had vanished! They were frightened by the angel—but even more by what the angel revealed. Or did they also see Christ Risen in glory, and run into the city with the dreadful news that the One whose body they were guarding, they had seen alive in glory? Was it *this* that they were told to say nothing about? No one minded admitting the angel, no one minded even admitting the empty tomb—they had a story to explain *that* away—but what had to be kept silent was the news that He had been seen alive on the third day after His crucifixion.

St Paul as witness to the Resurrection. St Paul's testimony, so valuable in itself, confirms that of the other witnesses. No critic doubts his account of the miraculous vision on the road to Damascus. No critic challenges the authenticity of the great epistles in which, within thirty years after the death of Christ, he preached the Resurrection to the Christians of Rome, Greece, and Asia Minor as the very basis of their faith. No one can question the holiness and complete sincerity of this former persecutor of the Church. It is inconceivable that a man of his strict honesty, high intelligence and learning, would have joined a band of cheats or dupes. It is inconceivable that he who was in touch with the witnesses to the Resurrection could have discovered some discrepancy or suspicion in their testimony, and have suppressed all mention of it. His testimony is quite independent of the Gospels. He wrote some of his epistles before the Gospels were written.

The Resurrection is proved by the miracle of the worldwide belief in it. On the day of Pentecost, in Jerusalem itself, the scene of Christ's shameful death, the Apostles came boldly before the people and put the Resurrection in the forefront of their preaching. On that day three thousand Jews were converted by St Peter to belief in Christ whom, he said, "God raised up, and of that we all are witnesses." And five thousand more were added some days later, when he spoke of Him as "the author of life, whom God raised from the dead."[52] In Palestine and beyond its borders, converts of every rank and race multiplied rapidly. Within a few years they were counted by millions. Within a few centuries, they formed the vast, and still growing majority of the population of the Roman Empire. St Augustine says that had not the Resurrection been a fact, the conversion of the world to belief in it by a few Galilean fishermen would have been as great a miracle as the Resurrection itself. And that miracle of belief, a

---

[51] Matt 27:66
[52] Acts 2:32; 3:15; cf. 4:10.

continuous miracle, gains in impressiveness as the centuries pass. Within the Catholic Church today, there are found 1,000 million believers, and six hundred million more believers outside her fold. Among them are men of every class, some of them of the highest intellect. Thus does God show that His Apostles spoke the truth; thus does He show that Christ our Lord rose from the dead.

These positive arguments are reinforced by the very weakness of the theories proposed by our adversaries to account for the undoubted fact of the empty tomb on Easter morn.

Adversaries' theories.

The Apostles were deceivers (the Deception Hypothesis). This was the earliest attempt to explain away the Resurrection and is an attack on the sincerity of the disciples. The Evangelist says the guards were bribed to make this statement. The guards at the sepulchre said that they fell asleep and, while they slept, the disciples came and removed the body. The story spread widely among the Jews and many believed it. If the soldiers fell asleep, they could not have known what happened during their sleep. All they could have said was that, when they woke, the tomb was empty. They might have added that *probably* the disciples came and stole away the body. Let us assume that they put their statement in some such reasonable form. Can we imagine that the disciples who had shown utter timidity during the Passion would risk liberty, perhaps life, in an attempt to steal the body, and all with a view to fraud? If they really knew that Christ was not risen, then they knew He had deceived them and was not God. What had they to gain by preaching a fraudulent resurrection? Nothing but persecution, incessant labour, and death, not to speak of remorse of conscience. And could the five hundred witnesses have succeeded in their conspiracy of fraud? Impossible: their cruel, skilful, and powerful enemies would have unmasked them. The fact that the Pharisees did not even try to break the testimony of the witnesses by cross-examination is a proof of their conviction that the task was hopeless: the sincerity of the Apostles and disciples was only too manifest. And there is a further point: the silver in their treasury had bribed an Apostle to betray his Master. The silver was still there, and its pull on the avaricious would have been strengthened by the fear of persecution and death. There was no Judas among all the witnesses to the Resurrection. Had there been even one false man among them, he would have broken under the weight of the double temptation. He would have sold his honour and saved his life by concocting a story to discredit his companions.

The Apostles were deceived (the Hallucination Hypothesis). This is the favourite hypothesis of modern adversaries. The followers of Christ, they say, were in a state of tense nervous excitement after the Crucifixion. They believed that their beloved Master would triumph over the grave and come back to them again. It was in answer to their passionate longing for His coming that their imagination produced the vision of the risen Saviour. That an individual might suffer from such an hallucination is possible. That all the Apostles and hundreds of the disciples should suffer from it simultaneously and over a long period is impossible. Besides, the evidence against the existence of any "passionate longing" is overwhelming. The followers of Christ were not expecting His Resurrection. When He was seized by the Jews, they fled in terror, believing that all was over. He had undoubtedly foretold His Death and Resurrection, but they appear never to have reconciled themselves to the thought of His Death, and so did not think of His Resurrection.[53] Mary Magdalen and the other women brought spices to embalm His corpse on the morning of the third day. They, therefore, did not expect to find Him risen from the dead. Magdalen's first thought, when she saw the empty tomb, was that someone had stolen the Body.[54] When Christ spoke to her, she did not recognise Him at first, believing that He was the gardener. Cleopas and the other disciple, as they talked sadly of Christ on the road to Emmaus, told the stranger, as they took Him to be, how they had been amazed by the women's story of the Resurrection. When He revealed Himself to them as Christ, they returned and told the Apostles. The Apostles refused to believe them, just as they had already refused to believe the women.[55] Thomas was not present when Christ first appeared to the Apostles, and protested that he would not believe until he had put his finger "in the mark of the nails" and his hand "in His side".[56] The witnesses, therefore, to the risen Christ were not credulous, but incredulous, and the hypothesis of hallucination is excluded.

Further, the very idea that mass hallucinations can occur has never even been proved: how many times have gigantic crowds assembled for some concert or rally for a beloved hero or performer who has been announced at the last minute as unable to turn up. The crowds are dejected and disappointed, maybe even enraged or in desperate hope for a later opportunity, but has it ever been reported that crowds saw their hero appear just because they were expecting him?

Christ was a deceiver (the Trance Hypothesis). This suggests that Christ did not really die on the cross. He merely swooned—and recovered consciousness in the sepulchre. While the soldiers slept, He pushed aside the stone and rejoined His companions; and so He made on them the impression that He had triumphed over death. The mental anguish which Christ suffered, the scourging, the crowning with thorns, the crucifixion and the piercing of His side with a spear make the trance hypothesis impossible. Suppose for a moment it were true. Could one so severely wounded, so exhausted from the loss of blood, have moved aside the great stone, and have done so without waking the soldiers? The women wondered whether they could find anyone to roll back the stone from the mouth of the sepulchre, "for it was very large."[57] Could He have played the role of victor over death, and walked like one in perfect health with those cruel wounds in His feet? Could He have entered the supper-room through closed doors? Could He have appeared and disappeared at will? Could He make an assembly of disciples imagine that He ascended into heaven in their sight? Are we to suppose that this Man of perfect holiness, who had suffered the agony of the Cross in upholding His claim that He was the Son of God,

---

[53] Matt 16:21-22; Lk 24:13-27,44-46; Jn 20:9
[54] Jn 20:13
[55] Mk 16:11,13
[56] Jn 20:25
[57] Mk 16:4

was a vile impostor; that He could set His followers on fire with zeal to go forth and preach a lie to the world? The hypothesis is unworthy of consideration.

Celsus' objection. Why did not Christ show himself publicly after His Resurrection to His enemies and the entire people? That question was first asked by the pagan, Celsus (d. c. 200 A.D.), and has been repeated by others. (1) God wishes us to turn to Him freely and, as a rule, does not employ a superabundance of means to bend the will of the evil-minded. He is content with giving clear and amply sufficient proofs that faith is reasonable.[58] The rich man in the parable,[59] calling out from hell to Abraham, besought him to send a messenger from the dead to warn his five brothers of the tortures of the damned. Abraham refused, saying, "They have Moses and the prophets; let them hear *them* ... If they do not hear Moses and the prophets, neither will they be convinced if some one should rise from the dead." The Pharisees asked Christ for a sign from heaven and were refused.[60] While He hung on the Cross, they that passed by bade Him come down if He were the Son of God,[61] but He paid no heed to them. But to one adversary He gave an exceptional grace: He appeared to the persecutor, Saul of Tarsus, who became the Apostle Paul.[62] (2) Had Christ appeared to all, the depraved subtlety of men would still have found a means to escape belief. "This is not Christ", they would have said, "but some evil spirit, an emissary of Satan." And unbelievers of later generations would probably ask: "If Christ appeared to all the people after His Resurrection, why does He not appear to everyone now? Why does He not remain on earth always?" Even if He did remain on earth always, these same unbelievers would still persevere in their incredulity, protesting that He was being impersonated by a series of impostors. There are many modern miracles worked in proof of the Catholic religion,[63] and still people manage to withhold belief.

Objection to the consistency of the accounts of the Resurrection. "The Resurrection accounts are contradictory and irreconcilable: for example, the first three Gospels all mention Mary Magdalen and another Mary on Easter morn, but St Mark adds Salome, and St Luke adds Joanna, while St John's Gospel mentions only Mary Magdalen. Again, St Matthew mentions an angel announcing the Resurrection at the tomb, Mark a young man, whilst Luke speaks of two men. Further, St Luke only mentions appearances of Christ Risen in Jerusalem, St Mark records no appearance there, while St Matthew says the disciples met Jesus in Galilee—about eighty miles away. These and other discrepancies and divergences make the whole story untrustworthy."

Reply: The accounts certainly differ, but are not mutually exclusive. As with the rest of the Gospels, the differing accounts can be harmonised, and treated as supplementary to each other, as long as we remember that each one is not claiming to present the whole picture. Policemen and lawyers are familiar with witnesses

---

[58] See p.19 "Our proof is conclusive but not coercive".
[59] The parable of Lazarus and the rich man: Lk 16:19-31
[60] Mk 8:11-13
[61] Matt 27:40
[62] Acts 9
[63] See p.223 ff.

presenting the same event from different angles, their honesty not in question if each one only recounts the portion that he remembers. A series of totally identical accounts of the same event is a sign that witnesses have conferred, or have been trained so as to agree in all respects—while divergences are natural where different people recount memories spontaneously. The seeming differences, therefore, strengthen the case for honesty rather than weaken it.

"Here is an outline of a possible harmony of the Evangelists' accounts concerning the principal events of Easter Sunday: (1) The holy women carrying the spices previously prepared start out for the sepulchre before dawn, and reach it after sunrise; they are anxious about the heavy stone, but know nothing of the official guard of the sepulchre: Matt 28:1-3; Mk 16:1-3; Lk 24:1; Jn 20:1. (2) The angel frightened the guards by his brightness, put them to flight, rolled away the stone, and seated himself above the stone: Matt 28:2-4. (3) Mary Magdalen, Mary the Mother of James, and Salome approach the sepulchre, and see the stone rolled back, whereupon Mary Magdalen immediately returns to inform the Apostles: Mk 16:4; Lk 24:2; Jn 20:1-2. (4) The other two holy women enter the sepulchre, find an angel seated in the vestibule, who shows them the empty sepulchre, announces the Resurrection, and commissions them to tell the disciples and Peter that they shall see Jesus in Galilee: Matt 28:5-7; Mk 16:5-7. (5) A second group of holy women, consisting of Joanna and her companions, arrive at the sepulchre, where they have probably agreed to meet the first group, enter the empty interior, and are admonished by two angels that Jesus has risen according to His prediction: Lk 24:3-8. (6) Not long after, Peter and John, who were notified by Mary Magdalen, arrive at the sepulchre and find the linen cloths in such a position as to exclude the supposition that the body was stolen; for they lay simply flat on the ground, showing that the sacred body had vanished out of them without touching them. When John notices this he believes: Jn 20:3-10. (7) Mary Magdalen returns to the sepulchre, sees first two angels within, and then Jesus Himself: Jn 20:11-17; Mk 16:9. (8) The two groups of pious women, who probably met on their return to the city, are favoured with the sight of Christ arisen, who commissions them to tell His brethren that they will see Him in Galilee: Matt 28:8-10; Mk 16:8. (9) The holy women relate their experiences to the Apostles, but find no belief: Mk 16:10-11; Lk 24:9-11. (10) Jesus appears to the disciples at Emmaus,[64] and they return to Jerusalem; the Apostles appear to waver between doubt and belief: Mk 16:12-13; Lk 24:13-35. (11) Christ appears to Peter, and therefore Peter and John firmly believe in the Resurrection: Lk 24:34; Jn 20:8. (12) After the return of the disciples from Emmaus, Jesus appears to all the Apostles excepting Thomas: Mk 16:14; Lk 24:36-43; Jn 20:19-25. The harmony of the other apparitions of Christ after His Resurrection presents no special difficulties."[65]

Conclusion. We have proved, through the testimony of friends and enemies, that Christ died and was buried. We have proved through the testimony of witnesses who were honest and, at the same time, incredulous,

---

[64] most probably modern Motza-Illit, 3-4 miles from Jerusalem: cf. R. Mackowski S.J., *Cities of Jesus*, Pont. Oriental Institute, Rome 1995, pp.77-97.
[65] A.J. Maas S.J., in "Resurrection", *The Catholic Encyclopedia*, Vol. XII, p.790

and through the success which attended the preaching of the Apostles, that Christ rose from the dead. Christ claimed to be God. In proof of His claim, Christ said He would rise from the dead. He rose from the dead. Therefore, His claim is true.

No one who admits the Resurrection of Christ can deny the existence of God. If Christ rose from the dead, there must be a God who raised Him to life. The existence of God, therefore, is established by the Resurrection quite independently of the philosophical proofs at the beginning of the treatise.

III

THIRD PROOF: THE PERFECTION OF CHRIST AS A MAN AND AS A TEACHER OF NATURAL RELIGION, CONSIDERED IN THE LIGHT OF HIS CLAIM TO BE GOD, PROVES THAT HE WAS GOD

Note. In this section, we disregard for the moment all direct evidence of Christ's divinity. We look at Christ through the eyes of our adversaries. They hold that He was a mere man, a teacher of mere Natural Religion, i.e., a teacher of religious or moral truths that can be discovered by the unaided human intellect. In the interest of our argument, we accept this false view of Him for the time being. In our sketch of His character, therefore, we ignore every word and act of His that show Him to be God. In our account of His doctrine, we allow ourselves to speak inaccurately of Him as a teacher of mere Natural Religion, suppressing everything that would set Him in His true light as a Teacher of Supernatural Religion, as one who taught that no act of ours, however good it may seem to men, is of any supernatural value in the sight of God unless it be inspired by belief in mysteries inaccessible to human reason.

CHRIST VIEWED AS IF HE WERE MERE MAN

His origin, His power over men, His eloquence, His silence. He came from Nazareth, a village in Galilee, the most backward district in Palestine. People asked in wonder: "Can anything good come from Nazareth? ... Is not this the carpenter, the Son of Mary? ... How is it that this man has learning, when He has never studied?"[66] Yet this poor tradesman had a power over the human heart which men could not resist. He called them and they came. They left their homes and their fathers, their boats, their nets and their money and followed Him.[67] He was gifted with a wondrous power of speech. He pressed a world of meaning into a short sentence. He employed the plainest and homeliest illustrations, e.g., the woman searching

---

[66] Jn 1:46; 7:41; Mk 6:2-3; Jn 7:15
[67] Matt 4:18-22; 9:9; Mk 2:14

for the lost piece of money, the patching of an old garment, the shepherd in quest of his sheep.[68] He clothed His thoughts in simple and beautiful language, as where He says of the lilies of the field that "even Solomon in all his glory was not arrayed like one of these."[69] By parables such as that of the Good Samaritan,[70] or the Prodigal Son,[71] He fixed His great doctrine of Love in the minds of the least instructed of His hearers. He touched at times a depth of pathos in such words as: "Come to Me, all who labour and are heavy laden, and I will give you rest.";[72] and, in His last discourse to His disciples, He speaks in the language of grave and tender sadness, full of the sorrow of parting and death, and yet breathing a sublime assurance that His work had not failed.[73] No wonder that people followed Him for days without food. Even His enemies said: "No man ever spoke like this man!"[74] He outmatched them in the gift of eloquence, and confounded them with His quick retort and subtle reply. Often they tried to ensnare Him into some awkward admission, but He baffled them by His wisdom.[75] And He could be silent as well as eloquent. At His trial, He answered when adjured to answer, but He was silent while the witnesses were giving their perjured evidence. There was no need for speech, for they contradicted and confounded one another. Pilate, who knew that their testimony was worthless, still sought to provoke Him to reply, but "He made no answer ... so that the governor wondered greatly."[76] And when Peter had denied Him, He spoke, not with His lips, but with His eyes. It was enough. Peter "went out and wept bitterly."[77]

He was a man of superb courage and stainless character. He was firm but not obstinate. The poor tradesman from Galilee had no fear of the proud and powerful Pharisees. He scourged them in a terrible invective for their hypocrisy, their avarice, and their hardness of heart. He knew that their fury could be sated only by His blood, and yet He never ceased to whip them with the lash of righteous indignation.[78] Several times He was on the brink of destruction. Once a raging mob had swept Him to the verge of a cliff, but, at the last moment, He eluded their grasp.[79] In the

---

[68] Matt 5, 6, 7, 10
[69] Matt 6:26-34
[70] Lk 10:30-35
[71] Matt 15:11-32
[72] Matt 11:28-30
[73] Jn 14, 17
[74] Jn 7:46
[75] e.g., Matt 12:26-28; Lk 13:14-16
[76] Lk 23:9 & Matt 27:13-14
[77] Lk 22:61-62
[78] Matt 23; 16:21; Jn 11:48
[79] Lk 4:30; cf. Matt 12:15; Jn 8:59; 10:39; 11:53.

hour of His Passion, caught in the snares of His enemies, He made no appeal, no apology, no retraction of His doctrine.   No cry for mercy escaped Him when the pitiless scourges lacerated His flesh, nor when His sacred hands and feet were nailed to the Cross. Bitter though His enemies were, they were silent when He challenged them to charge Him with sin.[80] He was the only man that ever lived who could stand up before His enemies and defy them to convict Him of a single fault.   The traitor, Judas, confessed, "I have sinned in betraying innocent blood."[81] At His trial, when His foes strained every nerve against Him, neither Pilate nor Herod could find any guilt in Him:[82]   His character scrutinised in the fierce light of savage hatred showed not a stain. He was no self-seeker, no respecter of wealth. He fled when the multitude sought to make Him king.[83] He had not enough money to live without alms.[84] He could not pay the temple dues without a miracle.[85] He whose ability might have borne Him to the highest position had "nowhere to lay His head."[86] He preferred to be a teacher of truth, to wander about poor and homeless. He was firm, but not obstinate. He refused to abate His teaching to win the companionship of the wealthy young ruler.[87] Yet He knew how to bend when no principle was at stake. He sought to escape, even by hiding, the importunities of the Syro-Phoenician woman who implored Him with piteous cries to heal her daughter, but at last, touched by her profound humility, He yielded.[88]

He was affable, gentle, courteous, and humble. He was a man of loving heart. He did not shun the companionship of any class: He could dine with the respectable rich, and yet His enemies murmured because He also ate "with tax collectors and sinners."[89] Though Jews were not wont to converse with Samaritans, He spoke to the Samaritan woman at the well.[90] He was entertained at the house of His friends, Martha, Mary, and Lazarus.[91] He gently remonstrated with His two Apostles, James and John, for their ambition.[92]   He was courteous to the Pharisee, Nicodemus,

---

[80] Jn 8:46
[81] Matt 27:4
[82] Lk 23:13-15
[83] Jn 6:15
[84] Lk 8:3
[85] Matt 17:24-27
[86] Matt 8:19-20
[87] Lk 10:18-24
[88] Matt 15:24-28; Mk 7:24-30
[89] Matt 9:11; Lk 15:2; 19:7
[90] Jn 4
[91] Jn 11:5
[92] Matt 20:20ff.

because he came to Him with a right intention.[93] He impressed more than
once on His Apostles the need for humility. They were not to lord it over
their dependants like earthly princes, but were to be the servants of their
subjects. He Himself set them the example by washing their feet at the Last
Supper.[94] He was a Man of loving heart. His three years' ministry was an
incessant outpouring of love. The sick and the sinful came in vast numbers
to Him. He healed them of their infirmities. His life was a daily triumph
over sin, sorrow, and disease. He saved from death the unhappy woman,
convicted of a shameful crime: "Let him who is without sin among you",
He said to her accusers, "be the first to throw a stone at her",[95] and looking
into their consciences they slunk away ashamed. He restored to the
widowed mother her only son as he was being carried forth for burial. He
feared not to lay His hands on the foul leper.[96] He wept with passionate
grief over the Holy City, dear to Him and to all Jews as the very hearthstone
of their race: "How often would I have gathered your children together as a
hen gathers her brood under her wings, and you would not!"[97] Some great
light of love must have shone in His face, else, why were little children
brought to Him that He might notice them? He chided the Apostles for
trying to keep them back. He took them in His arms and blessed them.[98]
On the Cross, His heart was still the same loving heart, true to its old
affections, ready to receive the sinner and pardon the persecutor and
calumniator. Amid all His agony, He thought of His Blessed Mother, and
asked St John to be a son to her. With words of sublime hope, He blessed
the contrition of the penitent thief who, only a moment before, had been
reviling Him. He besought His heavenly Father to pardon the very men
who had nailed Him to the Cross, and who, even as He prayed for them,
still pursued Him with mockery, insult, and blasphemy.

Summary: He was the model of all virtues. To a perfect love for God
and submission to His holy will ("Not My will, but Thine, be done"),[99] He
united in a form, never before witnessed, the virtues of humility, courage,
patience, meekness, and charity. He was a brave, strong man, who spoke
His mind fearlessly, and died for the doctrine He advocated. He was gentle,
courteous, affable, and unselfish.   No contradiction, calumny, or
persecution could wring from Him a word or gesture inconsistent with His
dignity as a heaven-sent instructor of mankind. His goodness was without

---

[93] Jn 3:1-21
[94] Jn 13
[95] Jn 8:1-11
[96] Mk 1:41
[97] Matt 23:37. Cf. Lk 19:41-44.
[98] Mk 10:14-16
[99] Lk 22:42

weakness; His zeal and earnestness, without impatience; His firmness, without obstinacy. He was not only a thinker, but a man of action. His eyes seemed ever fixed on heaven, but yet He was full of sympathy for the weakness of His disciples, full of tenderness for the sorrowful and afflicted, and He combined an intense hatred of sin with an intense love for the sinner. He is the model for people of all conditions in all ages, the ideal which, while remaining unattained and unattainable, has been the inspiration of the noblest lives.

THE TESTIMONY OF RATIONALISTS. All who have studied the Gospels, unbelievers as well as believers, are agreed as to the nobility of the human character of Christ. The French rationalist, Ernest Renan, who wrote a life of Christ denying everything supernatural in the Gospels, concluded it by saying, "All the centuries proclaim that among the children of men there is none greater than Jesus."[100]   William Lecky, a rationalist, says: "It was reserved for Christianity to present to the world an ideal character, which, through all the changes of eighteen centuries, has inspired the hearts of men with an impassioned love; has shown itself capable of acting on all ages, nations, temperaments, and conditions; has been not only the highest pattern of virtue but the strongest incentive to its practice; and has exercised so deep an influence that it may be truly said that the simple record of three short years of active life has done more to regenerate and to soften mankind than all the disquisitions of philosophers, and all the exhortations of moralists."[101]

CHRIST VIEWED AS IF HE WERE A TEACHER
OF MERE NATURAL RELIGION

Setting aside for argument's sake all the higher doctrines of Christ, we shall find that He who was perfect as a man was perfect also as a teacher of truths which, in the view of our opponents, may be assigned to the sphere of Natural Religion. He stands alone and unrivalled because of His doctrine of the Law of Charity, His doctrine of the Law of Sincerity, His doctrine of the supreme importance of the human soul, and His ideals of moral excellence. He taught as "one who had authority",[102] not like Socrates and others, as though He were groping for the light. He taught with clearness and decisiveness, and was Himself the model of all His teaching.

His doctrine of the Law of Charity. The Jews of His day held high dispute as to which was the greatest commandment of their Law. Some

---

[100] *Vie de Jésus* (last sentence)
[101] *History of European Morals*, George Braziller, New York 1955, Vol. II, pp.8-9
[102] Mk 1:22

said it was the commandment to offer sacrifice; others, the commandment of Sabbath observance; others again the commandment of Circumcision. Christ swept aside all current opinion as so much rubbish, and laid bare the true foundation of sanctity. "The whole Law", He said, in effect, "is summed up in the one Law of Charity, i.e., the love of God and one's neighbour."[103] But, in His Sermon on the Mount, the first great exposition of His teaching, He gave the Law of Charity a wider interpretation. "Neighbour", with the Jews, had meant a fellow Israelite or a friendly alien. Christ broadened its meaning so as to include every man without exception, good or wicked, friend or foe. Men must love one another, because they are brothers. They are brothers, because they are children of the same heavenly Father[104] who loves them all, who gives the blessings of His Providence, the sunshine and the fruitful rain, to all, unjust as well as just, who goes in quest of the sinner, as the shepherd seeks for His lost sheep, who is no longer robed in the lightnings of Sinai, but shines with the radiance of kindness and love. Men must forgive one another as they hope to be forgiven. For how can they ask of their Father what they themselves refuse to a brother? Christ's Law of Charity, therefore, may be briefly expressed thus: "Love God, for He is your loving Father. Love and be indulgent to one another, for you are all His children. Love and forgive, as you hope to be loved and to be forgiven." Christ, unlike all other teachers, drew people close to God. He taught them to turn to God with a warm, personal love, and to see His image in their fellow-man.[105]

His doctrine of the law of sincerity. Christ would have no mere outward sanctity, the sanctity of the Scribes and Pharisees who made light of internal sin. "You fools!" He said to them, "Did not He who made the outside make the inside also?"[106] God is as much the author of the inner as the outer man, and will have service of them both. We must pluck anger and all uncleanness from our hearts. Our sanctity must be sound to the core.[107]

His doctrine of the supreme importance of the human soul. The human soul is infinitely more precious than anything else in the world. The loss of friends, the loss of all our possessions, the loss of life itself are all as nothing compared with the loss of the soul: "What shall it profit a man, if

---

[103] Cf. Matt 22:37-40.
[104] In Natural Religion, God would be addressed as "Father", because He is the Creator of the human soul, a spirit made to His own image. In Revealed Religion, the word "Father" takes on a higher sense because, by grace, God has made us sharers in His own divine nature. Cf. St Thomas, S.T., i, q. 33, a. 3.
[105] Matt 5-7
[106] Lk 11:40
[107] Matt 5:23-30

he gain the whole world and suffer the loss of his soul? Or what shall a man give in exchange for his soul? Whosoever will save his life shall lose it; and whosoever shall lose his life for My sake and the gospel shall save it."[108] Others before Christ had perceived this truth, but dimly and as through a veil. He was the first to give it clear and fearless expression.

His ideals of moral excellence. Profound reverence for God, perfect submission to His will, and readiness to rise to heroic heights of self-denial in His service were Christ's ideals of moral excellence.

1. (a) Had Christ not been God, or one sent by God, His teaching on natural religion would have failed for want of authority. (b) Clear though His teaching was in its main purport, it is obscure in some points. For instance, we are not always sure whether the heroic virtues which He commends are for all, or only for the few, or how in individual cases His doctrine should be applied. Hence the necessity of having always with us a living, infallible voice authorised to speak in His name, and to give the true interpretation.
2. Socrates (469-399 B.C.) is regarded as the noblest man of pagan antiquity, but he cannot be compared with Our Saviour. Socrates was the foe of pretended knowledge. He urged men to strive after precise ideas of goodness, virtue, justice, beauty, etc. He was put to death by the Athenian democracy in a moment of frenzy, not because of his supposed doctrines or method, but because of the profligacy and disloyalty of some of his admirers. Though superior to his contemporaries in intellectual power, he shared the loose notions of his day in regard to chastity. He concerned himself only with the better educated among the Athenians. Even these he did not so much instruct as stimulate to inquiry. He undoubtedly helped to purify the gross popular notion of the Deity, but his ideas about the future state were vague in the extreme, and he had no conception of the brotherhood of man. Since he was born into a highly cultured state, and had as his contemporaries men of the first rank in philosophy, history, drama and art (e.g., Anaxagoras, Thucydides, Euripides, Myron), the development of his talent was, in great measure, due to environment. Our Saviour, from the human standpoint, enjoyed no such advantage. He spent His youth and manhood among peasants or artisans of little or no education.

THE TESTIMONY OF PHILOSOPHERS AND HISTORIANS. The German philosopher, Immanuel Kant, says: "We may readily admit that, had not the Gospels first taught the general moral principles (i.e., the precepts of natural religion) in their full purity, our intellect would not even now understand them so perfectly." The historian Adolf von Harnack, who does not admit that there was anything supernatural in Christ, cannot find words sufficiently emphatic to express admiration for His moral teaching. His sayings and parables, he says, are simplicity itself in their main purport, and

---

[108] Mk 8:35-37 (Douay)

yet they contain a depth of meaning which we can never fathom. In His personality, He is not like a heroic penitent or an enthusiastic prophet who is dead to the world, but He is a man who has rest and peace in His own soul and who can give life to the souls of others; He speaks to men as a mother speaks to her child. He quotes Goethe, another rationalist, as saying: "Let intellectual and spiritual culture progress, and the human mind expand, as much as it will; beyond the grandeur and the moral elevation of Christianity, as it sparkles and shines in the Gospels, the human mind will not advance."[109] It is unnecessary to quote the opinions of other rationalists. All are agreed that Christ in His character and His doctrine was immeasurably beyond the noblest teachers that ever lived.

Conclusion. (1) It is admitted that Christ was perfect as a man, was unsurpassed, unequalled as a teacher. But Christ claimed emphatically and persistently that He was God. We must admit that His claim was just, that He *was* God, or else face the terrible conclusion that He was a deceiver or a victim to some hallucination. In other words, we must say that the most perfect of mankind was a shameless liar and blasphemer, or a pitiable maniac. Such is the colossal absurdity to which Rationalists are reduced, an absurdity which, when they realise it, must convince them that their entire position is untenable.

(2) The character of Christ—His wisdom, His goodness, His innocence, so absolutely above the limitations and frailties of human nature—a miracle of perfection—is wholly inexplicable without special reference to a unique divine intervention. His very character is a divine testimony to the truth of His doctrine, and to the truth of His claim to be God.

IV

CHRIST, A LIVING FORCE: A PROOF OF HIS DIVINITY

Newman represents Napoleon in the solitude of his imprisonment as communing with himself, thus:

"I have been accustomed to put before me the examples of Alexander and Caesar, with a hope of rivalling their exploits, and living in the minds of men forever. Yet, after all, in what sense does Caesar, in what sense does Alexander live? Who knows or cares anything about them? At best, nothing but their names is known ... Nay, even their names do flit up and down the world like ghosts, mentioned only on particular occasions, or from accidental associations. Their chief home is the schoolroom; they have a foremost place in boys' grammars and exercise books;

---

[109] *What is Christianity?* II (end); Eng. trans., p.4

they are splendid examples for themes … So low is heroic Alexander fallen, so low is imperial Caesar, 'ut pueris placeat et declamatio fiat.'[110]

"But, on the contrary, there is just One Name in the whole world that lives; it is the Name of One who passed His years in obscurity, and who died a malefactor's death. Eighteen hundred years have gone since that time, but still it has its hold upon the human mind. It has possessed the world, and it maintains possession. Amid the most varied nations, under the most diversified circumstances, in the most cultivated, in the rudest races and intellects, in all classes of society, the Owner of that great Name reigns. High and low, rich and poor, acknowledge Him. Millions of souls are conversing with Him, are venturing on His word, are looking for His presence. Palaces, sumptuous, innumerable, are raised to His honour; His image, as in the hour of His deepest humiliation, is triumphantly displayed in the proud city, in the open country, in the corners of streets, on the tops of mountains. It sanctifies the ancestral hall, the closet, and the bedchamber; it is the subject for the exercise of the highest genius in the imitative arts. It is worn next the heart in life; it is held before the failing eyes in death. Here, then, is One who is not a mere name, who is not a mere fiction, who is a reality. He is dead and gone, but still He lives,—lives as a living, energetic thought of successive generations, as the awful motive-power of a thousand great events. He has done without effort what others with life-long struggles have not done. Can He be less than divine? Who is He but the Creator Himself, who is sovereign over His own works, towards whom our eyes and hearts turn instinctively, because He is our Father and our God?"

The argument may be put briefly as follows: The power of Christ over the hearts of men is no natural phenomenon. It is miraculous. It is God's testimony to the Divinity of Christ. The mighty name of Christ shows its power in the savage hatred as well as in the tender love it evokes. Once known, He cannot be forgotten. Those on earth who have revolted from Him cannot tear His image from their minds. They are obsessed by it and rage against it like the demons of hell. He is "a sign of contradiction" (Lk 2:34) that cannot be ignored, a "sign of unbounded envy—and profound compassion—of unquenchable hatred—and unconquered love."[111]

Note. **The various methods of proving the Divinity of Christ.**

God has made known to us by many miracles that Christ is His Son, one in nature with Him. These miracles are not all alike, but may be divided into different classes. Each class gives us a distinct method of proving Christ's Divinity:

---

[110] 'that he is agreeable to boys and becomes a theme.' *A Grammar of Assent*, end of Ch. 10, pp.490-1. The argument was Napoleon's; the words Newman's.
[111] Alessandro Manzoni, *Il Cinque Maggio*, vv. 57-60. Manzoni (1785-1873) is the author of the classic Italian novel *I Promessi Sposi* (1840) (Penguin Books ed. *The Betrothed*).

Miracles relating directly to Christ.

1.   The prophecies made and the miracles wrought by Christ Himself during His life-time on earth, and the miracle of His Resurrection. These are the miracles on which we depend for our main proof above (Sections I, II).

2.   The miracle of the unique personality and perfection of Christ (III).

3.   The miracle of Christ's undying influence in the world (IV).

Miracles relating indirectly to Christ through His Church.

4.   The manifold miracle of the Church, as seen in her several characteristics and age-long vitality, proves that she is from God, and that her belief in Christ's Divinity must be true (Part I, Ch. 12).

5.   The miracles worked in the name of Christ over the centuries of the Church's history (Ch. 12: Miracles in the Lives of the Saints).

SECTION III

CATHOLIC APOLOGETICS

INTRODUCTION

The Catholic Church alone is the authoritative teacher
of the Christian Revelation

THE POSITION OF THE CHURCH IN THE DIVINE PLAN. The Christian Revelation—i.e., the doctrine and the way of life taught by Christ—was not merely for a single nation, nor for the children of a certain epoch: it was for all people, and for all time. To secure that it might be accessible to all in every age, Christ by His divine authority instituted a society, His Church, world-wide and imperishable, which was to be its sole, authentic and infallible teacher.

Its mission was to bring all men the light of divine truth, to show them their heavenly destiny and help them to attain it. Through the Church, God would bestow His gifts on men, making them His sons and co-heirs with Christ, blessing them with the spirit of gentleness and with that peace of heart which the world does not know. And, after death, He would reward them for their faithful and humble service in the Church of His Son by unveiling Himself to them, so that they might be united to Him in eternal love and happiness.

OUTLINE OF THE PROOF IN CATHOLIC APOLOGETICS

Chapters 8 & 9. We have proved that Jesus Christ is God Himself. We shall now prove that for the benefit of all mankind, of every race and generation, He founded an infallible Church to speak and act in His name until the end of the world; and that He gave her certain marks or notes by which she could be easily known. These Marks are four in number, viz., Unity (in faith, government and worship), Universality, Sanctity and Apostolicity.

Chapter 10. The Catholic Church alone possesses these marks. Therefore the Catholic Church alone is the True Church founded by Christ, and is the One and Only Infallible Teacher for all time of His Revelation.

The four notes of the Church are properties or qualities easily perceived. In virtue of Christ's institution, all four together are always present in the true Church but not in any other body. Besides these four notes the Church has other characteristic properties, e.g., Visibility, Imperishability, Infallibility. She has always claimed these characteristics. The absence of any of these notes in a religious society, or the absence of the claim to them, shows that the society is not the Church of Christ.

CHAPTER 8

JESUS CHRIST FOUNDED A CHURCH

Summary

I.   The mission of Christ. He was sent into the world by His heavenly Father to cleanse all men from sin, to make them children of God and heirs to His Kingdom. These blessings He won, and made accessible to every individual, on condition of faith in His doctrine, participation in the sacred rites He instituted, and obedience to His precepts.

II. The mission of the Apostles. Christ preached to only a few. He sent the Apostles to preach to all. He sent them (A) to teach (B) to minister and (C) to govern. They obeyed His word.

III. The foundation of the Church. Christ, by giving the Apostles this commission, thereby founded a society, His Church. Christ saves us through His Church.

I

The mission of Jesus Christ. (1) Jesus Christ, the Son of God, was sent into the world by His heavenly Father: "He who does not honour the Son does not honour the Father Who sent Him".[1] "Do you say of Him whom the Father consecrated and sent into the world, 'You are blaspheming,' because I said, 'I am the Son of God'?"[2]

(2) He came to cleanse us from sin: the angel, addressing St Joseph, said: "She"—the Blessed Virgin—"will bear a Son, and you shall call His name Jesus, for He will save His people from their sins";[3] "the Son of Man came", He said Himself, "to save the lost."[4] He was to save us by His Passion and Death: "the Son of Man came...to give His life as a ransom for many";[5] and at the Last Supper He said, taking the chalice, "this is My Blood of the New Covenant, which is poured out for many for the forgiveness of sins."[6]

(3) He came not only to save us from sin, not only to give us life, but to give us a higher and fuller life: "I came that they may have life, and have it

---

[1] Jn 5:23
[2] Jn 10:36
[3] Matt 1:21
[4] Matt 18:11
[5] Matt 20:28
[6] Matt 26:28

abundantly."[7] He came to make us children of God: "God sent forth His Son", says St Paul, "that we might receive adoption as sons."[8] He came, therefore, to deliver us from sin and to make us children of God and heirs to His Kingdom.

(4) He fulfilled His mission: in His prayer to His heavenly Father at the Last Supper, He said He had "accomplished the work which Thou gavest Me to do."[9]

(5) He has made the blessings which He purchased for mankind, viz., remission of sin and divine sonship, accessible to all on the following conditions:

(a) that they *believe* in Him and His teaching. "this is the will of My Father, that every one who sees the Son and believes in Him should have eternal life";[10] "He who does not believe [My Gospel] will be condemned".[11]

(b) that they *avail themselves of the sacred rites* He instituted: for instance, He says of Baptism, "He who believes and is baptised will be saved";[12] "unless one is born of water and the Spirit, he cannot enter the Kingdom of God";[13] and of the Blessed Eucharist He says, "unless you eat the Flesh of the Son of Man and drink His Blood you have no life in you."[14] (It is sufficient to show, at this point of our argument, that Christ instituted certain sacred rites. We need not inquire into the precise number).

(c) that they *obey* His commandments: "You are My friends if you do what I command you";[15] "He who does not love Me does not keep My words".[16]

As we shall presently see, these three conditions can only be fulfilled by membership in the Church which Christ established. He appointed the Church to convey us His doctrine, sacraments and commandments.

II

The mission of the Apostles. THEIR PREPARATION. Christ did not Himself teach all men. He taught but a few. These He sent forth to teach all the world what He had taught them. He chose twelve men from among the larger following of His disciples: "He appointed twelve, to be with

---

[7] Jn 10:10
[8] Gal 4:4-5
[9] Jn 17:4
[10] Jn 6:40
[11] Mk 16:16
[12] Mk 16:16
[13] Jn 3:5
[14] Jn 6:53
[15] Jn 15:14
[16] Jn 14:24

Him, and to be sent out to preach".[17]   For about three years they lived in closest intimacy with Him, and were trained by Him for their future work: "all that I have heard from My Father", He said to them, "I have made known to you."[18]   Their defects of knowledge or memory were all to be made good: "the Holy Spirit whom the Father will send in My name, He will teach you all things, and bring to your remembrance all that I have said to you."[19]

A. CHRIST SENT THEM TO TEACH ALL MEN. He sent them first to the Jews: "Go nowhere among the Gentiles ... but go rather to the lost sheep of the house of Israel."[20]   Later, He sent them to all mankind. He "died for all".[21] Therefore, He said: "Make disciples of all nations";[22] "go into all the world and preach the Gospel to the whole creation";[23] "you shall be My witnesses in Jerusalem and in all Judea and Samaria and to the end of the earth."[24]

The Apostles obeyed His word, spreading the new message far and wide, so that twenty-five years later St Paul could say to the Romans that their faith was "proclaimed in all the world."[25]   Likewise, he says to the Colossians: "the Gospel which has come to you, as indeed in the whole world ... is bearing fruit and growing."[26]

B. HE SENT THEM TO SANCTIFY MEN BY MEANS OF SACRED RITES. He bade them administer Baptism: "make disciples of all nations, baptising them in the name of the Father and of the Son and of the Holy Spirit".[27] He gave them the power to forgive sins, and, therefore, we must infer that He bade them administer the Sacrament of Penance: "if you forgive the sins of any, they are forgiven; if you retain the sins of any, they are retained";[28] and, after His Resurrection, addressing the Apostles, "He said to them ... that repentance and forgiveness of sins should be preached in His Name to all nations".[29] He bade them imitate Him in the consecration of bread and wine: "and He took bread, and when He had given thanks He broke it and gave it to them, saying, 'This is My Body which is given for

---

17 Mk 3:14
18 Jn 15:15
19 Jn 14:26
20 Matt 10:5-6
21 2 Cor 5:15
22 Matt 28:19
23 Mk 16:15
24 Acts 1:8
25 Rom 1:8
26 Col 1:5-6
27 Matt 28:19
28 Jn 20:23
29 Lk 24:46-7

you. Do this in remembrance of Me'. And likewise the cup after supper, saying, 'This cup which is poured out for you is the new covenant in My Blood.'"[30]

These sacred rites the Apostles administered. We are told, for instance, that they baptised: "those who received his (St Peter's) word were baptised";[31] that they fed the faithful with the Body and Blood of the Redeemer: "the cup of blessing which we bless, is it not a communion in the Blood of Christ? The bread which we break, is it not a communion in the Body of Christ?"[32]

C. HE SENT THEM TO GOVERN. He sent them not only to teach and sanctify but to govern, i.e., to make laws, to judge, to enforce and to punish. For He said to them: "As the Father has sent Me, even so I send you";[33] "all authority in heaven and on earth has been given to Me. Go therefore and make disciples of all nations ... and lo, I am with you always, to the close of the age."[34] Therefore, Christ clothed His Apostles with His own authority, and promised them unceasing support. He had not only been their teacher, but their ruler and master. So, they were to be the spiritual rulers and masters of the world. Again, He said to them: "if he (a sinner) refuses to listen even to the Church, let him be to you as a Gentile and a tax collector."—i.e., let him be excommunicated—"Truly, I say to you, whatever you bind on earth shall be bound in heaven, and whatever you loose on earth shall be loosed in heaven",[35]—giving them thereby supreme power in all spiritual matters: their laws, judgements, sentences or remissions would all be ratified and sanctioned in Heaven.

The Apostles exercised the triple power (legislative, executive, judicial) which He gave them: at the Council of Jerusalem they imposed laws of abstinence on Gentile converts, requiring them to abstain "from what has been sacrificed to idols and from blood and from what is strangled".[36] St Paul determines the qualifications of those who should be admitted to Holy Orders.[37] He delivers to the Corinthians a series of precepts and admonitions—doctrinal, ritual, and moral—concluding with the promise, "About the other things I will give directions when I come."[38]

---

[30] Lk 22:19-20
[31] Acts 2:41; cf. 8:16, 38; 9:18; 10:48.
[32] 1 Cor 10:16; cf. 11:27.
[33] Jn 20:21
[34] Matt 28:18-20
[35] Matt 18:17-18
[36] Acts 15:29
[37] 1 Tim 3:2; Titus 1:6-9
[38] 1 Cor 11:34; cf. ibid. 7, 10, 16.

The Twelve Apostles

B	Bartholomew
A	Andrew
P	Philip
T	Thomas
I=J	John, James, James, Jude, Judas
S	Simon Peter, Simon the Zealot
M	Matthew

- They are listed in Matthew 10:2; Mark 3:16; Luke 6:14; Acts 1:13.

- Peter and Andrew were brothers.

- James and John were brothers, sons of Zebedee. This James is often called James the Greater. He was martyred about the year 44 (see Acts 12:2).

- The other James is sometimes called James the Lesser (Mark 15:40). He was a son of Alphaeus and a cousin of the Lord (Matt 10:3; 13:55).

- Jude was called Judas, but he is often called Jude to distinguish him from Judas Iscariot. His surname is Thaddeus (Matt 10:3).

- Bartholomew is also called Nathanael (John 1:45).

- Matthew is also called Levi (Luke 5:27).

- There are Letters (Epistles) in the New Testament by James the Lesser, Peter, John and Jude.

- The four Evangelists (Gospel writers) are Matthew, Mark, Luke and John. Of these, only Matthew and John were Apostles.

- St Paul (Galatians 1:1), Matthias (Acts 1:26) and Barnabas (Acts 14:14) are also called Apostles, but were not members of the original Twelve.

He cuts off from the faithful and delivers over to Satan (i.e., excommunicates) the blasphemers, Hymenaeus and Alexander,[39] and the incestuous Corinthian.[40] He instructs Timothy as to the trial of priests, forbidding him to receive an accusation "except on the evidence of two or three witnesses."[41] He speaks of coming to the Corinthians "with a rod"[42] and of "being ready to punish every disobedience".[43]

III

The foundation of the Church. Christ, as we have just shown, sent His Apostles into the world, clothed with His own divine authority. In words most solemn, He said to them: "As the Father has sent Me, even so I send you." He sent them out into the "whole world" to "all nations" and promised to be with them "all days" until the end of time. He sent them (1) to teach all men His doctrine, (2) to make all men holy by means of the sacraments which He instituted, (3) to rule in spiritual matters with His authority. In thus sending and equipping them, He founded a religious society, His Church. It was not the Apostles who decided for convenience to organise themselves into a society. Jesus Christ Himself made them into a society, the Church. "Church" comes from a Greek word[44] meaning "belonging to the Lord", i.e., the Lord's House.

In order to understand this we may consider what a society is. A society is a number of people united for a common object to be attained by common means and under a common authority. In a society, therefore, we distinguish four essentials: (1) a number of people; (2) a common object; (3) common means for its attainment; (4) a common authority binding them together. These four essentials were found in the Church from her very beginning. It was Christ who gave them to her. Hence Christ is the Founder of the Church.

The Church is a Society. From the day of the first Pentecost onwards the Church stood out before the eyes of the world as a fully equipped society. It had all the four essentials: (1) *It was made up of a number of people.* Christ chose twelve Apostles, whom He sent, invested with His own authority, to preach to all men. On the first occasion of their exercise of the ministry, thousands joined them. (2) *The members of this body sought a common object,* viz., sanctification and salvation. Christ and His Apostles were one in purpose: "As the Father has sent Me, even so I send you."[45]

---

[39] 1 Tim 1:20
[40] 1 Cor 5:1-5
[41] 1 Tim 5:19
[42] 1 Cor 4:21
[43] 2 Cor 10:6
[44] κυριακον, Kyriakon
[45] Jn 20:21

The object of the society He had called into being was manifestly the object for which He had come into the world, viz., to cleanse men from sin, to make them holy, to make them children of God and heirs to His kingdom. (3) *The common object was to be attained by the employment of common means*, viz., belief in the doctrine of Christ as taught by the Apostles, obedience to His commandments, and the use of the sacred rites instituted by Him and delivered by Him to His Apostles for the sanctification of all the members of the society. (4) *The members were bound together under a common authority*. The Apostles were not sent to act independently of one another, but to govern by their collective authority. Had Christ intended that each of the Apostles should have his own distinct and independent following, He would have founded not one society, but many societies. But He never spoke of more than one. He always spoke of His *Church*, never of His *Churches*; "on this rock I will build My Church."[46] He likened it to "a sheepfold", "a kingdom", "a city", words which imply unity of government or administration.

The Apostles themselves regarded the Church as a single society under their collective authority. At the Council of Jerusalem they issued a decree binding people who had been converted by one or other of the Apostles. The Galatians, although the converts of St Paul, recognised the authority of St Peter and his colleagues, but St Paul explains to them that he and his fellow Apostles are of one mind.[47] St Peter, St Paul, St John and St James wrote authoritative letters to communities which had not been converted by them but by other Apostles. These facts of history establish the existence of a common authority in the society from its very foundation.

Christ is the Founder of the Church. Whoever gives a society its four essentials is the founder of that society. It was Christ who gave these four essentials to His Church. Therefore Christ is the Founder of the Church.

Christ gave the Church the four essentials by which it is constituted a society: (1) because it was Christ Himself who called the first members, the twelve Apostles, the seventy-two disciples, and several others; it was Christ who, though unseen, was regarded as the principal Minister of Baptism, the rite by which every one was admitted as a member to the society; (2) because it was Christ Himself who set up the common object to be attained, viz., the sanctification and salvation of souls; (3) because it was Christ Himself who gave them the common means which they were to employ for its attainment; it was He who gave them the doctrine to be believed, the rites to be employed, the commandments to be obeyed; (4) because it was Christ Himself who gave the government of the Church its authority, its right to demand and exact obedience. The Apostles were not self-appointed, nor appointed by the people, but appointed by Christ. And after their appointment they were not left to their own discretion; they were always attended by the assistance of Christ: "Behold I am with you all days". Their commands were His commands; their government was His government; they ruled as His representatives. Many men have founded societies, but no man has ever founded a

---

[46] Matt 16:18
[47] 1 & 2 Gal

society in the intimate, complete and thorough manner in which Christ founded the Church.

Christ saves us through His Church. Since Christ conveys to us through the Church, and through no other channel, all the blessings He has earned for us on the Cross, we may speak of Him not only as having died to redeem and save us, but also, and more precisely, as having died to give us the Church. St Paul the Apostle says: "Christ loved the Church and gave Himself up *for her* ... that He might present the Church to Himself in splendour". He "gave Himself up *for her*", i.e., He delivered Himself unto death for her, to found her and endow her with all the gifts she possesses.

The Church alone, the ever living representative and agent of Christ on earth, shows us the way to Heaven and gives us every help to get there. She holds in her hands all the blessings of Calvary. We can obtain them from her, but only if, dismissing all arrogance and in the spirit of little children (for only such, Our Saviour says, can enter the Kingdom of God), we fulfil the following conditions: (1) humbly believe her teaching; (2) gratefully receive the Sacraments she offers us; (3) faithfully obey her laws. - Putting these conditions in the simplest form, we should say that to be saved, we must *believe* what the Church teaches, and *do* what she tells us.

CHAPTER 9

THE CHARACTERISTICS OF THE CHURCH FOUNDED BY CHRIST

In these Chapters (8 & 9) we speak of the nature and characteristics of the Church which Christ founded. In Chapter 10 we show which one of the existing churches can lawfully claim to be identical with it.

The characteristics of the Church founded by Christ are set forth in the New Testament which we have proved to be a trustworthy historical document.

Summary

The Church of Christ is:
I.   Imperishable and visible.
II.   (a) One: one Body, one in Government, Faith, Worship.
      (b) Universal or Catholic (membership, therefore, obligatory on all).
      (c) Apostolic.
      (d) Holy: in her Founder, Doctrine, Members.
III. Infallible.

I

THE CHURCH FOUNDED BY CHRIST IS IMPERISHABLE AND VISIBLE

Christ's Church is Imperishable. The existence of the Church, the society possessing the right to speak to the world in the name of God, *was not to be limited to a particular period of time.* This is manifest from the promise of the abiding presence and assistance of Christ Himself and of the Holy Spirit, a presence and assistance which was not to be temporary but perpetual: "Going, therefore, teach ye all nations … and, behold, I am with you all days, even to the consummation of the world."[1] "I will pray the Father, and He will give you another Counsellor, to be with you for ever".[2] "I say to thee", He said to Simon, "thou art Peter"—i.e., a rock—"and upon this rock I will build My Church; and the gates of hell shall not prevail against it";[3] "the gates of hell", that is, death, destruction, the power of its enemies. These unequivocal promises of Christ made to the society which He founded, seal it with the seal of imperishability: it was to last to the end of the world, teaching, sanctifying, and governing men. Had Christ

---

[1] Matt 28:19-20 (Douay)
[2] Jn 14:16
[3] Matt 16:18 (Douay)

intended that His Church should last for only a time, He would have set forth in clear prophecy the signs of its dissolution. The termination of a divine institution should be as marvellous and manifest as its beginning.

His Church is Visible. Christ established the Church as a visible society, that is, as a society which stood out plainly before the eyes of all as an organised body, consisting of teachers and taught, rulers and subjects, who joined in public worship and made open profession of their belief. The Apostles admitted people to membership of the Church by the public rite of Baptism. They made laws affecting the external behaviour of the faithful, and they exacted obedience. They gave the faithful the command of Christ to confess their faith openly: "so every one who acknowledges Me before men, I also will acknowledge before My Father who is in heaven; but whoever denies Me before men, I also will deny before My Father who is in heaven."[4]

II

THE CHURCH FOUNDED BY CHRIST IS ONE, UNIVERSAL, APOSTOLIC, AND HOLY

Christ's Church is One. *General proof of the unity of His Church.* Christ, in His prayer after the Last Supper, said: "I do not pray for these only"—i.e., the Apostles—"but also for those who believe in Me through their word, that they may all be one; even as Thou, Father, art in Me, and I in Thee, that they also may be in Us, so that the world may believe that Thou hast sent Me."[5] Christ, therefore, desired for His Church an absolute unity, a unity which should exclude all division, whether in government, doctrine, or worship, for He likens it to the perfect unity of the Father and His Divine Son, and this unity was to be so evidently miraculous as to afford a proof of the divine authority of Christ Himself.

St Paul is of one mind with his Lord and Master. He holds that unity is the fundamental characteristic of the Church. Over and over again, he compares the Church to a living body: "for just as the body is one and has many members, and all the members of the body, though many, are one body, so it is with Christ. For by one Spirit we were all baptised into one body—Jews or Greeks".[6] He conceives the members of the Church as parts of the same living organism. Vivified by the same spiritual life, they believe the same doctrine, they participate in the same worship, and yield obedience to one and the same authority.

[4] Matt 10:32-3
[5] Jn 17:20-21
[6] 1 Cor 12:12 f. Cf. Eph 4; Rom 12.

Particular proof of the unity of His Church. HIS CHURCH IS ONE IN GOVERNMENT. This particular proposition has already been proved (p.137). To recapitulate: (1) Christ spoke of His *Church*, not of His *Churches*. Therefore, He meant that His Church should be one society under one government, not several societies, each under its own government, distinct and separate from the rest. (2) He compared His Church to a "sheepfold", "a city", "a kingdom", thereby implying unity of government. (3) The Apostles themselves regarded the Church as one in government (see p.137). Further proofs: (4) Christ said that no kingdom divided against itself can endure.[7] Therefore no division in government could be found in the imperishable society established by Him. (5) The Church, St Paul says, must be "one body and one Spirit".[8] It must be like the living body; and as in the living body there is but one governing will, so in the Church there must be but one governing authority.

HIS CHURCH IS ONE IN FAITH. Christ said to the Apostles: "Teach ye all nations … teaching them to observe all things whatsoever I have commanded you."[9] The Apostles, therefore, were to teach everybody the whole doctrine of Christ. They were to insist that everybody should believe one and the same body of truths. The Church of Christ, therefore, must be one in faith.

In the Church, according to St Paul, there must be "one Lord, one faith, one baptism".[10] The Church, he says, in the simile he so often repeats, is a living body; and as, in the living body, there is but one mind, so in the Church there must be but one faith. The faithful, he says to the Romans, "with one voice" are to "glorify the God and Father of Our Lord, Jesus Christ."[11] "I appeal to you, brethren", he says to the Corinthians, "by the name of Our Lord Jesus Christ, that all of you agree and that there be no dissensions among you, but that you be united in the same mind and the same judgement."[12] "Take note of those who create dissensions and difficulties, in opposition to the doctrine which you have been taught; avoid them. For such persons do not serve our Lord Christ".[13]

HIS CHURCH IS ONE IN WORSHIP. This proposition follows directly from the preceding. Worship is nothing more than a practical manifestation of faith. The members of His Church are one in faith. They must, therefore,

---

[7] Matt 12:25; Mk 3:24
[8] Eph 4:4
[9] Matt 28:19-20 (Douay)
[10] Eph 4:5
[11] Rom 15:6
[12] 1 Cor 1:10
[13] Rom 16:17-18

be one also in worship. Their unity of faith excludes the possibility of any disagreement among them as to the rites by which God is to be adored and man sanctified.

Note that, of the three species of unity, unity of faith is the chief. It is, as it were, the root of the other two. Converts to Christianity believed first of all in Christ and His doctrine. Believing His doctrine, they believed, as part of it, that they were bound to worship God in the manner prescribed by Him and to yield obedience to the superiors whom He had appointed for their guidance.

His Church is Universal or Catholic. The obligation of membership.

HIS CHURCH IS UNIVERSAL OR CATHOLIC. Christ gave His Apostles a most emphatic command not to confine their teaching to people of any particular race or social status. He bade them preach the Gospel to "all nations"[14] and to "the whole creation".[15] The Apostles obeyed Him: St Paul applies to himself and his fellow-preachers the words of the Psalmist, "Their voice has gone out to all the earth, and their words to the ends of the world", and he tells the Colossians that the Gospel is believed "in the whole world".[16] The Apostle, we must understand, is speaking, not of an absolute, but of a moral catholicity, i.e., of a membership which, in kind and extent, could be described as catholic or universal, in ordinary speech. The moral catholicity of the Church was to be both social and numerical: it was to be social, in the sense that the membership of the Church should include people of every condition and grade of culture; it was to be numerical, in the sense that the Church would be widely diffused throughout the world. The Church could not have failed to achieve, within a reasonable time after her foundation, a moral catholicity, because her teachers were supported by Christ Himself in their mission to the world, and because her doctrines, being doctrines of God, must have made a powerful appeal to the reason and the heart of all well-disposed men. Since the Church of Christ, being imperishable, still exists in the world, it must, for the same reasons, viz., divine aid and suitability of doctrine to human needs, possess a moral catholicity. It must, moreover, in accordance with the will of Christ that all men be saved, strive by practical and organised effort for the ideal of absolute universality.

THE OBLIGATION OF MEMBERSHIP. The command of Christ to the Apostles to preach the Gospel to "the whole creation" implies a corresponding obligation on the part of all people to hear and obey them,

---

[14] Matt 28:19
[15] Mk 16:15
[16] Ps 19 (18):4; Rom 10:18; Col 1:6

and, therefore, to become members of His Church; "preach the Gospel to the whole creation", said Christ, "...he who does not believe will be condemned."[17] No one, therefore, who comes to know and recognise the true Church, but refuses to join it, can be saved. Neither can any person be saved if, having once entered the Church, he forsake it through heresy or schism or apostasy:[18] "as for a man who is factious, after admonishing him once or twice, have nothing more to do with him, knowing that such a person is perverted and sinful; he is self-condemned."[19] The Church, as St Paul says, is the living body whereof Christ is the Head. Whoever severs himself from the Church, severs himself from Christ, and cannot be saved, for in Christ alone is salvation. "I am the vine", said Christ, "you are the branches. He who abides in Me, and I in him, he it is that bears much fruit, for apart from Me you can do nothing. If a man does not abide in Me, he is cast forth ... The branches are gathered, thrown into the fire and burned."[20]

His Church is Apostolic. In every age the rulers of His Church are clothed in the authority given by Christ to the Apostles.[21] Christ personally taught and formed the Apostles. He made them eyewitnesses to His works. He showed Himself to them after His Resurrection. He gave the Apostles authority to speak in His name. He said to them: "As the Father has sent Me, even so I send you."[22] "He who hears you hears Me, and he who rejects you rejects Me, and he who rejects Me rejects Him who sent Me."[23] As we have seen in the first paragraph of this chapter, Christ placed them in charge of a work that will not be completed until the world ends. The Apostles themselves are dead, yet, according to the terms of His assurance, they must in some sense remain in the world until the end of time. They can remain in the world only through representatives chosen in the manner which, under divine direction, they themselves prescribed. They must, therefore, have made provision that their authority should be passed on to others and transmitted down the whole line of their successors, so that, in every generation, the rulers of the Church could say: "Our authority is the ever living authority of Christ Himself. Our authority is the authority of the Apostles, for we are one with them by lawful succession." The words of Christ make it clear that the Apostles are the last envoys whom God will send to the human race. The authority which He gave them and their successors He will never give to any others. The mission of the Apostles is

---

[17] Mk 16:15-16
[18] See pp.169-170.
[19] Titus 3:10
[20] Jn 15:5-6
[21] The word "apostolic" has other senses also with which we are not concerned at present.
[22] Jn 20:21
[23] Lk 10:16

final and perpetual. That the Apostles elected others to assist them in their work is plain from the Scriptures themselves. That they went further and made definite provision for their succession during all time, can be proved by many authorities, e.g., St Clement, who died about 100 A.D., says, "Christ was sent by God, the Apostles by Christ. They appointed bishops and deacons ... and they made order that when they (the bishops and deacons) died, other men of tried virtue should succeed in their ministry".[24] St Irenaeus, writing towards the end of the second century, speaks of "the bishops and their successors down to our time who have been appointed by the Apostles."[25]

To sum up: the Church is Apostolic (1) in her origin, by being built "on the foundation of the Apostles";[26] (2) in her teaching, which she has received and passes on from the Apostles, the original and irreplaceable eyewitnesses to the life, death and Resurrection of the Son of God; (3) in her Holy Orders and pastoral office handed on by the Apostles to the Bishops.[27]

But in giving the Apostles authority over His Church, Christ did not make them independent of one another: He made them a united body with St Peter at their head. (1) He built His Church on St Peter as its supporting rock.[28] From St Peter, therefore, the other Apostles derived their strength; they belonged to the Church by belonging to St Peter. (2) To St Peter He gave the keys of the Kingdom of heaven, which means that St Peter is master of the gate to that Kingdom, and that only through him could the other Apostles obtain admittance. (3) He gave St Peter His own office of Good Shepherd: "Feed My lambs", He said to him, "tend My sheep",[29] which shows that as He, Christ, had been the one and only Shepherd, so now St Peter was to be the one and only Shepherd in His place, with authority over all, including his brother Apostles, the one supreme Pastor to whom all should listen and whom all should obey. Loyalty to St Peter and his lawful successors was therefore an outstanding characteristic of the Church founded by Christ.

His Church is Holy.[30] THE CHURCH IS HOLY IN HER FOUNDER. Jesus Christ Himself is the Founder of the Church, the Author of her organisation and all her work. He is her permanent Head, communicating

---

[24] *1 Clem.* 42, 44

[25] *Adv. Haer.*, III, 3

[26] Eph 2:20

[27] C 857

[28] For fuller treatment of Scriptural evidence, see pp.188-90.

[29] Jn 21:15-7

[30] Men or things are holy according to the intimacy of their relation to God.

life personally to the members. The Church is holy, therefore, in her system of government, in her doctrine, in her worship, and in her object.

THE CHURCH FOUNDED BY CHRIST IS HOLY IN HER DOCTRINE. Non-believers admit the excellence of Christ's moral precepts, but Christ rose far above the low level of mere natural ethics and taught a far higher doctrine inspired by the Mystery of the Incarnation. Not content with the common virtues, such as truthfulness and honesty which are practised by many pagans, He urged His followers to higher things. He bade them to strive to attain the ideals of heroic virtue. He recommended to them profound reverence for God, leading to a childlike submission which would manifest itself in fraternal charity, meekness, humility, and self-denial in its various forms, e.g., voluntary poverty, forgiveness, submission to persecution, self-sacrifice even unto death to testify to their faith or to relieve the sufferings and save the souls of others.[31] He summed up all these ideals in one: "You, therefore, must be perfect, as your heavenly Father is perfect."[32]

He placed this doctrine of holiness with His other teachings in the custody of His Church: "Make disciples of all nations", He said to the Apostles, "teaching them to observe *all* I have commanded you".[33]

THE CHURCH FOUNDED BY CHRIST IS HOLY IN HER MEMBERS. Christ did not say that all the members of His Church, high and low, would be holy, even in the humblest sense of the word: man may abuse the liberty God has given him, and choose evil instead of good. So, we find that among the Apostles, who had lived in intimate friendship with God Himself, there was a traitor. So, we find that Christ likens His Kingdom (Church) to a net that enmeshes worthless fish as well as good,[34] or to a field wherein the cockle grows among the wheat.[35] Still, *because of His divine assistance*, the Church of Christ, as a whole, must at all times, be remarkable for sanctity. She cannot fail in this object of her existence, and she must exhibit many instances of the realisation of the highest ideals. Heroic sanctity must be manifested among her children in all ages. His Church is "the good tree" that "brings forth good fruit."[36] She will bring forth the good fruit of virtue, for Christ, her Founder who is God Himself, will always be with her.

HER SANCTITY PROVED BY MIRACLES. He will never cease to prove her sanctity by miracles, for He said: "These signs will accompany those who

---

[31] Read the Sermon on the Mount, Matt 5-7.
[32] Matt 5:48
[33] Matt 28:19-20
[34] Matt 13:24-30
[35] Matt 13:47-48
[36] Cf. Lk 6:43f.

believe: in My name they will cast out demons; they will speak in new tongues; they will pick up serpents, and if they drink any deadly thing, it will not hurt them; they will lay their hands on the sick, and they will recover";[37] "he who believes in Me will also do the works that I do; and greater works than these will he do".[38]

III

THE CHURCH FOUNDED BY CHRIST IS INFALLIBLE

The Church founded by Christ is infallible, that is, His Church cannot err in teaching and interpreting, as of faith, the truths which Christ delivered to her keeping.

Indirect proofs. *Proofs from absurdity of the contrary.* (1) If it be admitted that His Church can err in exacting the assent of faith for her doctrine, it follows that God has bound men on pain of damnation to believe what is false, for He said, "He who does not believe will be condemned."[39]
(2) It would follow that there can be no certainty whether any particular doctrine is the doctrine of God.
(3) If there is no organ of infallibility on earth, it follows that Christ's office as teacher ceased when He left the world; but see what this involves. All through the long stretch of centuries, God had been preparing the hearts of men for the coming of His Son, by vouchsafing to them revelation after revelation, and by setting up a whole system of elaborate ceremonial. Yet we are asked to suppose that, in spite of all this, when the Redeemer came at last, He taught infallibly for only a few years a mere handful of people of one generation in a small corner of the world. Common sense rejects such an absence of wise proportion. It justly expects that what God granted to the people of Judea in the days of Christ, He has granted also to people of every generation down to the end of time. It justly claims that God has established an organ of infallibility among us through which we can still hear the infallible voice of His Divine Son.
(4) *Proof from necessity.* In the words of Newman, "A revelation is not given, if there be no authority to decide what it is that is given. ... The absolute need of a spiritual supremacy is at present the strongest of arguments in favour of the fact of its supply. Surely, either an objective revelation has not been given, or it has been provided with means for impressing its objectiveness on the world. If Christianity be a social religion, as it certainly is, and if it be based on certain ideas acknowledged as divine, or a creed ...

---

[37] Mk 16:17-18
[38] Jn 14:12. On miracles in the Church, see pp.223-9.
[39] Mk 16:16

and if these ideas have various aspects and make distinct impressions on different minds, and issue in consequence in a multiplicity of developments, true, or false, or mixed,... what power will suffice to meet and to do justice to these conflicting conditions but a supreme authority ruling and reconciling individual judgements by a divine right and a recognised wisdom? ... Philosophy, taste, prejudice, passion, party, caprice will find no common measure, unless there be some supreme power to control the mind and to compel agreement. There can be no combination on the basis of truth without an organ of truth."[40]

Direct proofs. (1) *Proof from imperishability*. His Church will never perish. She will always teach with divine authority, because Christ has promised to be always with her. Hence, she can never err in her teaching.

(2) *Proof from unity of Faith*. His Church must at all times teach and believe the same body of divine truths. Possessing unity of faith, she must also possess the means by which that unity may be preserved or defended. Owing to the waywardness or wickedness of men, the plainest doctrines of Christianity, as we know from history, and even the writings of St Paul, are liable to constant misinterpretation. Christ's Church therefore is always threatened with error, and error would be fatal to unity. Christ therefore must have empowered His Church to declare with an infallible voice whether a doctrine has been revealed or not, and to expel from her fold and threaten with damnation all who reject her decision.

> Since the Church founded by Christ is Imperishable, it exists in the world at the present day, clothed in all its attributes. It is Visible, One, Holy, Catholic, Apostolic, and Infallible.

---

[40] *An Essay on the Development of Christian Doctrine*, 1845, Rev. ed. 1878, Part I, Ch. II, Sect. II, 12-13.

CHAPTER 10

THE IDENTIFICATION OF THE CHURCH OF CHRIST.
THE CATHOLIC CHURCH IS THE TRUE CHURCH

Summary

I.   The true Church must have all the following marks:
    1. it must be universal.
    2. it must be one: in government, faith, and worship. Also, infallible.
    3. it must be holy.
    4. it must be apostolic.
II.   The non-Catholic Christian Churches:
    A. Protestantism: its origin; its doctrines. It has none of the marks of the true Church.
    B. The Orthodox Church: its divisions, origin, liturgy, doctrines. It has not all the marks of the true Church.
    C. The Branch Theory, viz., that the true Church consists of the Church of England, the Orthodox Church, and the Catholic Church: - rejected, because destructive of unity.
III. The Catholic Church alone has all the marks of the true Church: it is universal, one, holy, apostolic, and founded by Christ.
IV.   'No salvation outside the Church.' An objection and difficulty answered. Relationship of Protestants and Orthodox to the Catholic Church. Conversion. Converts. Enmity against the Church. The Church and civilisation. The ultimate choice.
V.   Objections answered.
VI.   Excursus: the Eastern Churches, Catholic and non-Catholic.

I

Method of identification. The Church of Christ, being imperishable, exists in the world today; and being visible, it stands out plainly before the eyes of all, and can be identified. In the preceding chapter, we set forth all the characteristics of the Church of Christ. In this chapter we make use of *four* of them to prove that His Church is the Catholic Church and none other. His Church must possess four *marks*, i.e., four great, public characteristics: it must be Universal; it must be One—in government, faith and worship; it must be Holy; it must be Apostolic. A church which does not possess *all* these marks or characteristics cannot be the Church of Christ.

    To the four identifying marks we shall add what at first sight might seem to be a fifth, viz., the claim to Infallibility, but it is really a sub-section of Unity. The Church of Christ must be one in faith to the end of time, because He has promised to be with her always. His perpetual help ensures that, in a fickle and ever-changing world, she will always teach His doctrine without the taint of error. His Church, therefore, must claim to possess that perpetual help; she must claim Infallibility, the indispensable shield of her Unity in doctrine. Hence a church that *disclaims* Infallibility is at once incapable of being the true Church.

The divisions of Christianity. Our line of proof. In the world of today, those who believe in the Divinity of Christ and profess to be members of His Church fall into three divisions, viz., Protestants, Orthodox, and Catholics. Which of these groups is the Church of Christ? Or, does it consist of some combination of the three? These are the questions which we will now answer.

We will show (in II) that neither the Protestant nor the Orthodox Church, nor a combination of Protestants, Orthodox and Catholics, can claim to be the Church of Christ. When we have established so much, we have proved by a negative argument, i.e., by the method of rejection, that the Catholic Church must be the true Church. We then proceed to show (in III) that she does actually bear all four marks detailed above.

Note. In Chapter 9 we examined the characteristics of the Church founded by Christ as they are recorded in the New Testament. In this chapter we appeal to our own observations to show that the Catholic Church and she alone has these same characteristics.

II

THE NON-CATHOLIC CHRISTIAN CHURCHES

The true Church is not the Protestant Church nor the Orthodox Church, nor is it a combination of these Churches with the Catholic Church.

THE PROTESTANT CHURCH is not the true Church, and has not even one mark of the true Church: (1) IT IS NOT UNIVERSAL: It is not a universal religion, either racially or numerically. (2) IT IS NOT ONE: It is notoriously not one in *faith* or *worship*, and makes no claim to be. Every shade of opinion and doctrine is found among its leaders and members, some of whom, without any peril to their status as members, reject miracles, deny the Resurrection and deny the Divinity of Christ. From the doctrinal standpoint, Protestantism can be described as a chaos rather than a religion. Nor is it one in *government*, for it is divided into a countless number of totally independent bodies. In fact, there is no one body which can or does call itself, "The Protestant Church". (3) IT IS NOT APOSTOLIC: Its founders and leaders never claimed apostolic succession. It has renounced apostolic teaching. (4) IT IS NOT INFALLIBLE: Not one Protestant body claims infallibility. (5) AS TO HOLINESS: Its founders were notoriously not holy, and it has not produced a succession of Saints or heroically holy people as has the Catholic Church. (6) It rejects even the notion of a "true Church"!

THE ORTHODOX CHURCH is not the true Church: (1) IT IS NOT UNIVERSAL: It is not Catholic or Universal. It is confined chiefly to portions of the Greek and Slavonic races. Its total following does not exceed 160 million. (2) IT IS NOT ONE: It is not one in *government*; it is broken up into a number of divisions, each under an independent authority. It is not really a church but an assemblage of churches. (3) IT IS NOT INFALLIBLE: It does not claim infallibility.

THE TRUE CHURCH DOES NOT CONSIST OF THREE PARTS OR BRANCHES, viz., THE CATHOLIC CHURCH, THE CHURCH OF ENGLAND, AND THE ORTHODOX CHURCH. Such a combination of churches would not be the true Church: (1) It would not be one either in government, faith or worship. (2) It would not have a common organ of infallibility which the three parts would acknowledge as divinely established.

A

Protestantism. ITS DIVISIONS. The Protestant denominations (and their founders) include: *Lutherans* (founded by Martin Luther 1483-1546), *Zwinglians* (Ulric Zwingli 1484-1531), *Calvinists* (= 'Reformed Church', John Calvin 1509-1564), *Presbyterians* (John Knox 1505-1572), *Anabaptists* (Nicholas Stork d.1525, Thomas Munzer c.1490-1525), *Huguenots* (= French Protestants, William Farel 1489-1565), *Dutch Reformed* (1561, Guido de Bres), *Mennonites* (Menno Simons 1492-1559), *Church of England* (= *Anglican*, called *Episcopalian Church* in N. America, *Church of Ireland* in Ireland, *Episcopal Church* in Scotland: Henry VIII, 1534), *Baptists* (John Smyth c. 1544-1612), *Quakers* (George Fox 1624-1691), *Moravians* (Nikolaus Ludwig 1700-1760), *Swedenborgians* (Emmanuel Swedenborg 1688-1772), *Methodists* (John Wesley 1703-1791), *Christadelphians* (John Thomas 1805-1871), *Salvation Army* (William Booth 1829-1912). Derived from Protestant principles are more modern sects, such as: *Christian Scientists* (Mary Baker Eddy 1821-1910), *Jehovah's Witnesses* (Charles Russell 1852-1916), *Seventh-Day Adventists* (W. Ing 1844). The sects and Protestant bodies include a countless and ever-increasing number of smaller associations, impossible to list.

ITS ORIGIN. The Reformation, as the Protestant movement is inaccurately termed, began in Germany in the sixteenth century, and spread thence to Switzerland, France, the Netherlands, Denmark, Norway, Sweden and England. The following were the chief causes of the success of the Reformation:

(a) *The unhappy state of religion at this period.* The numerous richly endowed offices in the Church had attracted unworthy men to her ministry. In many countries, she had become the slave of royal power. Even the Papacy itself was, for a time, in bondage to the crown of France. The loyalty of members had been much weakened by a disastrous schism (the Great Western Schism, 1378-1417) during which there were two, and, for a short period, three rival Popes. Many grave abuses, not, however, at all so grave as the enemies of the Church represented, had arisen in connection with the levying of Papal monies. In general there was much laxity of discipline, and so, in the hour of stress, the Church in many places found herself with bitter enemies in her household and with too few zealous defenders.

(b) *Political considerations.* In Germany, the princes thought that by joining in a religious insurrection they might succeed in casting off the yoke of the Emperor, Charles V (1519-1556)—King of Spain and Emperor of Germany, whose dominions included the Netherlands and parts of Italy—for they knew he would unquestionably defend the old faith. Their designs naturally met with much encouragement in France, where the Emperor's power was a cause of uneasiness. Further, the German princes and with them the king of the united countries, Denmark and Norway, and the king of Sweden, were attracted by the Lutheran doctrine that the king is head of the Church in his own dominions, since it enabled them to consolidate their power and seize the vast wealth of ecclesiastical corporations. While Lutheranism favoured the pretensions of kings, Calvinism, on the other hand, with its denial of royal supremacy and its republican spirit, was of service in what may be described as the anti-monarchical, or anti-imperial, struggle of the Swiss and the people of the Netherlands. In England, Henry VIII regarded the Papal supremacy as an obstacle to his lust and rapacity, and used the great power of the crown to effect a schism. During the reigns of Edward VI and Elizabeth, the doctrines of Luther and Calvin were introduced so that, by a complete separation from Rome in obedience and faith, all foreign interference in the affairs of the kingdom might be permanently excluded.

(c) *The popular character of its doctrines.* The doctrines of the Reformers offered an easy remedy for sin, abolished all irksome duties such as fasting and confession, and flattered national and personal vanity by denying the authority of the Pope, and by investing the individual with the power of choosing and interpreting his own faith.

(d) *Humanism or the revival of learning.* Humanism, though favoured by many learned Catholics, and patronised by Popes, caused a ferment of intellectual unrest throughout Europe. It prepared the minds of men to admit novelties in faith as willingly as they had admitted them in the department of secular knowledge.

(e) *The personality of Luther.*[1] Martin Luther (1483-1546), the leader of the revolt, was a man of great natural ability. He had all the qualities of a successful demagogue—vast energy, effrontery, coarseness of manner, power of invective, quick wit, cutting

---

[1] See *Luther* by Hartmann Grisar S.J., 6 vols. (trans. by E. M. Lamond) Kegan Paul, London 1913-1917.

sarcasm, an unrivalled grasp of popular and forceful diction, fanaticism, fractiousness, and utter want of self-restraint. His imperfect theological training, his ignorance of the early history of the Church, his incapacity for exact reasoning—all these defects, while they helped to blind him to his iniquity, have left their clear imprint on the illogical system of doctrine which he constructed.

Luther opened hostilities in 1517 by denouncing a Papal proclamation which granted an indulgence, on the usual conditions of confession and communion, to all who should assist by their contributions, or by their prayers if they were too poor to contribute, in the charitable work of rebuilding St Peter's, Rome. Although the object was worthy of the support of Christendom, the Pope found himself heir to the dissatisfaction created by his predecessors' exactions and misapplications of Church monies. Luther, at first, had the sympathy of some well-meaning men, but lost it as soon as he showed that his design was not reformation but destruction. His movement threatened at one time to overrun all Europe with the exception of Italy, Spain and Portugal. But a reaction set in, which wrested from it half its triumphs, and pressed it back to those Teutonic areas from which it has not since notably advanced. At the Council of Trent, where the true reformation took place, the Church cast the slough of abuses, and in a brief time, through the zeal of her missionaries, repaired her losses in the Old World by successes in the New. It cannot be said that Luther and his associates were actuated by piety or by zeal for religion. Most of them, in fact, were men of loose morals, remarkable even in that corrupt age for profligacy, and not one of them could make any claim whatsoever to sanctity.

ITS DOCTRINES. The following are the chief tenets of Luther:
(1) The Bible privately interpreted is the sole rule of faith.
(2) Man is made holy by faith alone without good works. His soul is always in the state of sin: faith does not remove sin, but merely hides it from the eyes of God. Man's will is not free.
(3) The Church is invisible (consisting of the just alone), although individual congregations are visible. All believers are equally priests, and need no special spiritual power to act as pastors or presbyters. The State has supreme power in all church appointments.
(4) There are three sacraments, viz., Baptism, Eucharist, and Penance, but they do not confer grace in the Catholic sense.

Calvin (1509-1564) agreed with Luther as to (1), but added to (2) that man is predestined by God, independently of his own acts, to salvation or perdition. He also held that (3) the Church is visible (but there is also an invisible church consisting of the elect alone), and independent of the State. Presbyters elected by the people thereby receive the spiritual authority of bishops. (4) the Lutheran list of sacraments must be reduced to two, viz., Baptism and the Eucharist.

It would be impossible to give a brief and clear account of all the extraordinary transformations through which Protestant doctrine has passed from its origin down to the present time. A great number of German Lutherans now hold that Christ founded no Church, that religious belief is a matter of private opinion, or sentiment, and may be quite false. The Church of England is, in the main, liberal or rationalist (Broad Church). It downplays or rejects the supernatural (the mysteries of the Trinity and the Incarnation, the inspiration of the Bible, etc.). A small section of its members (the High Church or Ritualist party) copies the ceremonies of the Catholic Church. While some High Church Anglicans hold almost all the doctrines of Catholicism, except the Primacy and the Infallibility of the Pope, others are frankly rationalist. The Evangelical or Low Church party professes a mild form of Calvinism.

The Protestant Church is not the true Church. Protestantism, as a doctrinal system, is perhaps the weakest heresy ever proposed. *It has not even one of the essential marks of the true Church.*

(1) *It is not Infallible*: It repudiates all claim to infallibility. Confessedly, therefore, it may teach false doctrine, and can be no guide to truth. It leaves the ultimate decision on every point to the individual judgement.

(2) *It is not Apostolic*: It does not claim to be apostolic. Neither Luther nor Calvin received lawful appointment to teach. Luther, indeed, appears to have claimed a direct commission from God Himself, saying he was the instrument of God, chosen to reform the Church which had been corrupted since Apostolic times.[2] Needless to say, his pretension was not supported by miracles.

A section indeed of the Anglican Church (the High Church party) claims apostolicity. But England was converted by emissaries from the Holy See. Her Church retained apostolicity, therefore, only so long as she remained in communion with Rome. Rome gave her apostolic authority and Rome could and did deprive her of it. She was thrust off the Rock of Peter; she was put out of the Church of Christ.

Some members of the Church of England argue that their Bishops, since they occupy the ancient Cathedrals of Catholic days, must continue to possess the apostolic authority of their predecessors. This is what Newman calls "bricks-and-mortar" apostolicity. By the same argument a usurper could claim lawful succession because he resides in the ancient royal palace. Similarly it could be argued that milk put into a jug a month ago, and left exposed to the air, must be still good milk because the jug has not changed. If the Church of England says, "I am apostolic, because my doctrine is apostolic", how can she prove her doctrine apostolic without the gift of infallibility? And how, without the same gift, can she guarantee in a world of crumbling faith that her doctrine will continue to be apostolic to the end of time? In any case, the Catholic Church has declared her orders to be null and void.[3]

---

[2] *Kirchenlexikon*, 2nd ed., VIII, 325. Cf. H. Grisar S.J., *Luther*, vol. 2, 2nd ed., Kegan Paul, London 1918, pp.91-94.

[3] "orders" = the sacrament of Holy orders. See below, p.164.

(3) *It is not Catholic.* It is not catholic, either racially or numerically. Not racially, because the religion is practically confined to portions of certain races, although many other groups quickly pass both in and out of membership. Nor numerically, because the total of its adherents is about 420 million, divided up into over tens of thousands of independent bodies, each of which must be regarded as a separate Church.

(4) *It is not One.* If, as may be asserted, those 420 million really form but one Church, then that Church has not the unity of the Church of Christ. It is notoriously not one either in government, faith, or worship. Its tenet that private judgement is the final arbiter of faith is a principle of destruction, ever creating new bodies, and ever making the entire Protestant following more and more unlike the one, living body of Christ, the true Church.

(5) *As to Holy.* It is not holy in the sense explained in the preceding chapter. There are, of course, many Protestants who lead most upright lives, but their probity is not due to the principles of Protestantism as such, but to good traditions inherited from Catholicism. Some praiseworthy efforts have been made by some Anglicans and Protestants, in spite of much official discouragement, to imitate the Catholic religious communities in their practice of poverty, chastity and obedience. If Protestantism as such had any power to make men holy, we should expect to find a pre-eminent degree of sanctity in its founders and chief promoters. But enthusiasm itself has failed to detect such a quality in Luther, Calvin, Henry VIII, or Elizabeth I.

The root error of Protestantism is its false rule of faith. The Protestant doctrine regarding the source of Christian truth is known as *Sola Scriptura*, "Scripture alone". (Its doctrine regarding the means of salvation is known as *Sola fides*, "Faith alone", which we treat elsewhere.[4])

The doctrine of the Protestant Reformers that the Bible, *privately interpreted* by each reader, is the sole rule of faith, i.e., that it is the one and only sure and easy means of determining what we should believe, implies: (a) that all truths necessary for salvation are found in the Bible (principle of *Sola Scriptura*), and (b) that everyone can and ought to ascertain those truths for himself by reading the Bible (principle of *Private Interpretation*). For myriad reasons, both implications are false:

Bible alone. As to (a), the Bible cannot be the only store-house of divine truth for the following reasons:

---

[4] See p.446.

(1) The Bible itself says nothing of the kind. In fact, it says the contrary. St Paul writes to the Thessalonians, "So then, brethren, stand firm and hold to the traditions which you were taught by us, either *by word of mouth* or by letter."[5] St Paul tells Timothy, "what you have *heard from me* before many witnesses entrust to faithful men who will be able to teach others also."[6] He tells the Thessalonians, "you know what *instructions* we gave you through the Lord Jesus."[7] Later he tells the Thessalonians that the man of sin will appear and, "you know what is restraining him now"[8]—but what that is must have been told them orally, for it nowhere appears in his letters. He also tells the Corinthians, "About the *other things* I will give directions when I come."[9] And St John ends his Gospel: "But there are also *many other things* which Jesus did; were every one of them to be written, I suppose that the world itself could not contain the books that would be written."[10] He later closes a letter, "Though I have much to write to you, I would rather *not use paper and ink*, but I hope to come to see you and talk with you face to face".[11] At the end of his third epistle, he says the same again.[12]

(2) The Bible itself gives us no satisfactory proof of its inspiration, or even a list of its contents. We require some living authority to say to us: "This collection of books, consisting of these parts, has God for its author." The collection of books itself cannot say this. It was the living authority of the Church herself in the early centuries which gathered together the writings now called the New Testament and declared them to be inspired. But for her acceptance and recognition of them, their inspiration would have remained unacknowledged, and there would have been no such book as that which is now known as the New Testament. As St Augustine said, "I would not believe in the Gospel had not the authority of the Catholic Church moved me to do so."[13] Catholics and Orthodox have several books in the Old Testament which Protestants exclude from theirs.[14] Only a living authority can say whose list of books is correct.

(3) Christ did not send the Apostles to write but to preach. Most of the Apostles wrote no inspired Scripture. They never came together to write a systematic book of all that they believed and taught.

---

[5] 2 Thess 2:15
[6] 2 Tim 2:2
[7] 1 Thess 4:2
[8] 2 Thess 2:6
[9] 1 Cor 11:34
[10] Jn 21:25; cf. 20:30.
[11] 2 Jn 12
[12] 3 Jn 13
[13] *Contra ep. Manich.* 5, 6 quoted in C 119.
[14] Cf. p.268.

(4) Most of the New Testament did not begin to come into existence for two or three decades after the Ascension; was there no access to Christian truth before then? Yes: in the preaching of the Church—which preceded the writing of Sacred Scripture.

(5) For three centuries after Christ there was no universal agreement over the authentic books of the New Testament.

(6) The doctrine is of no practical help when, as in every generation, new questions arise and need an authoritative response which is not explicitly contained in the Bible. To choose but a few examples: what is Christian teaching on gambling, Sunday rest, repeating Baptism, organ transplants, praying to the Holy Spirit, telling a lie to protect the innocent?—none of which is mentioned in the Bible.

(7) The doctrine was completely unknown to the early Fathers of the Church. In fact, they regularly appeal to ecclesiastical Tradition as a rule of faith in the interpretation of difficult and disputed texts.

(8) The "Bible alone" doctrine was almost unheard of until Martin Luther in the 16th century after Christ.

(9) If "Bible alone" be true, all Christians for up to fifteen centuries were in gross error as to the source of their faith, until God sent Luther to put Christians right. This means that, for all those centuries, Christ failed to keep His promise that the Holy Spirit would lead the Apostles to the whole truth and be with them forever, and that He Himself would be with them to the end of the world.[15] As a result, the "Bible alone" doctrine destroys belief in Christ *and* the Bible.

Private Interpretation. As to (b), there can be no obligation upon everyone to search for divine truth in the Bible, for the following reasons:

(10) Christ never said that the ability to read was necessary for salvation. He never commanded us to discover by reading the Bible what we should believe. Such a command would have been a grievous hardship at a time when there were no printed books, when manuscripts were so expensive, and most people were illiterate. Mass literacy is a phenomenon only of the post-Renaissance age.

(11) Since most people do not read Hebrew, Aramaic and Greek, it is not the Bible itself, but a *translation* of the Bible that they will be reading. And

---

[15] Matt 16:18-19; 18:18; 28:20; Jn 14:16,26; 16:13

God has not guaranteed the infallibility or flawlessness of any translation. Hence, again, the Bible separated from the Church is no guide at all.

(12) As every Biblical scholar knows perfectly well, there is no book in the world more difficult than the Bible. It is a sheer absurdity to say that ordinary people, with no knowledge of Hebrew or Greek, archaeology, ancient history or the writings of the Fathers of the Church, are competent to interpret it.

(13) The Bible refers to its own obscurity: St Peter himself says that in the epistles of St Paul there are "some things in them hard to understand, which the ignorant and unstable twist to their own destruction, as they do the other Scriptures."[16]

(14) St Peter also rules out private interpretation: "no prophecy of Scripture is a matter of one's own interpretation, because no prophecy ever came by the impulse of man, but … from God."[17]

(15) St Philip likewise did not counsel private interpretation. When the Ethiopian man in Acts 8:31 said, "How can I understand (the prophet Isaiah), unless someone guides me?", St Philip did not say, as a good Protestant would have, "The Holy Spirit will enlighten you; keep on reading"—but in accordance with the need for an official and correct interpretation, St Philip began to instruct him in the true meaning of the prophecy and told him the Good News, after which the man was immediately baptised.

(16) The practical proof of the insufficiency of the Bible as a rule of faith is the diversity of belief among Protestants, every extravagance of doctrine being professedly based on someone's interpretation of the sacred text— and no agreed authority to settle disputes even over fundamental doctrines.

(17) If every sincere interpretation is to be ascribed to the Holy Spirit, this can only mean that God the Holy Spirit inspires totally irreconcilable and contradictory understandings—an unthinkable absurdity.

The Protestant doctrine is shown to be wrong on other grounds also, which we deal with in other chapters of this book: we have shown from chapter 8 up to this chapter 10 that Christ founded a living, visible, hierarchical, teaching Church—which means that any attempt to reduce the Christian

---

[16] 2 Pet 3:16
[17] 2 Pet 1:20

religion to a single book is flawed at its roots and is contrary to the clear teaching of Christ found in the Bible itself.

The Catholic Rule of Faith is the teaching authority of the Church.

The substitution of private judgement for a living infallible teaching authority is the root-error of Protestantism. Its destructive force is seen, not only in the multiplication of bodies and sects, but in the denial of the Divinity of Christ, the inspiration of the Scriptures, and other doctrines, regarded by the early Reformers as fundamental.

OBJECTION: "St Paul says, 'All scripture is inspired by God and profitable for teaching, for reproof, for correction, and for training in righteousness, that the man of God may be complete, equipped for every good work.' (2 Tim 3:16-7) Therefore the Bible alone is sufficient." (This is the favourite objection of most Evangelicals). REPLY: (1) This text says the Scriptures are "profitable" for certain purposes; it does *not* say that they *alone* will suffice or that they are the *sole* rule of faith. It says all Scripture is inspired by God. It does not say "*only* Scripture"; it does not say that God never commissions anyone else to speak in His name. (2) St Paul elsewhere insists on his oral teaching: 2 Thess 2:15; 2 Tim 2:2, quoted in the section above. (3) The preceding verse, 3:15, shows St Paul is speaking here of the *Old Testament*: "from childhood you have been acquainted with the sacred writings which are able to instruct you for salvation". Hence, if St Paul's words are to be taken in this overstated meaning of the objection, he would be saying that the New Testament is not a necessary part of the rule of faith! (4) Even if he meant the body of writings called the "New Testament", some of it, including later epistles by St Paul himself, did not yet exist. (5) Further, some of those already written, and the later ones, would not be recognised definitively for two or three centuries. Hence, to quote this text does not answer the question: "what books constitute 'all Scripture'?"

B

The Orthodox Church. ITS DIVISIONS. The (Eastern) Orthodox Church consists of several independent churches, viz., the Patriarchates of Constantinople, Alexandria, Antioch, and Jerusalem; and the Churches of Russia, Serbia, Romania, Bulgaria, Georgia, Cyprus, Greece, Poland, Albania, Czech Republic and Slovakia, the Orthodox Church in America, and various others.[18] The Orthodox Church is a collective term for a variety of national or regional Churches which share the same faith and sacraments, as well as the Byzantine (= Constantinopolitan) liturgical, canonical and spiritual tradition. It is often called the *Greek* Orthodox Church—but this is only one branch of it, as we can see. (The reader must not confound the separated Greek Orthodox Church with the Greek *Catholic* Church. All over the East, side by side, we find both the Orthodox Churches separated from the Pope,

---

[18] See pp.177-8 for a full list.

and the Eastern Catholic Churches united to the Pope and differing from the Western Church merely in matters of ceremony, discipline and spiritual traditions).

ITS ORIGIN. In the year 867, Photius, the Patriarch of Constantinople (reigned 858-67, 877-86), aided by his partisans, held a council presided over by the Emperor at which sentence of deposition and excommunication was pronounced against the Pope, Nicholas I.[19] That rupture was healed, but began again in 1054 under the Patriarchate of Michael Cerularius (reigned 1043-59), who attacked Latin usages and closed the Latin churches in Constantinople.[20] He was excommunicated. The division resulting was never overcome, and continues to the present day. The split became definitive in the popular mind of the east after the sacking of Constantinople by the Latin Crusaders in 1204. "The actual schism between Old Rome and the Greek East took shape between the 9th and the 13th centuries. It is quite impossible to fix upon any one particular incident as the precise cause of the schism, rather the whole period from 863 to 1204 saw the fomenting of a spirit of schism; a poisoning and estranging process with which the churchmen colluded."[21] The schism between the Orthodox and Catholic Churches "was the result of a centuries-long process of estrangement between the two communions. Such events as the excommunications of 1054 between the Patriarch of Constantinople and the papal legate were only high points in this process. Moreover, each Orthodox Church has its own history concerning the rift with Rome. There was, for example, never a formal separation between Rome and the Patriarchate of Antioch, although Antioch came to share the common Byzantine perception of the schism. Today it is widely agreed that there were significant non-theological factors at play in this gradual alienation between east and west. These included the cutting of ordinary contact imposed by political developments, and the loss of the ability to understand the Greek or Latin of the other church. But doctrinal issues were also involved".[22] Issues of doctrine included Roman Primacy, and the use of the word *filioque* to describe the eternal procession of the Holy Spirit, and its addition to the Creed (see p.317). Two major attempts at reconciliation took place, at the Second Council of Lyons (1274) and the Council of Ferrara-Florence (1438-9), but were short-lived on account of their rejection by the general Orthodox people. Since the break with Rome, the separated Greeks speak of themselves as members of the "Orthodox Church" or "The True and Apostolic Church." Strictly speaking, the term "*Greek* Orthodox" is inaccurate, since the majority of them are not Greeks, but Slavs.

Many of the separated Eastern Christians over the centuries have returned to allegiance to Rome, while retaining their traditions, rite and proper liturgical language. They number about 15 million in all and are known under the general name of Eastern Catholics. Scattered all over the East, therefore, there are many communities of Catholics who celebrate Mass in their own language and with

---

[19] Cf. F. Dvornik, *The Photian Schism*, Cambridge 1948, 1970.

[20] J.D. Faris, *Eastern Catholic Churches: Constitution and Governance*, St Maron Publications, N.Y. 1992, p.22

[21] Lawrence Cross, *Eastern Christianity: the Byzantine Tradition*, E. J. Dwyer, Sydney; Philadelphia, 1988, p.18

[22] R.G. Roberson, *The Eastern Christian Churches: A Brief Survey*, Pont. Oriental Institute, Rome 1993 (4th ed.), pp.27-8

ceremonies which differ in unessential details from the Latin Rite. See the Excursus in Section VI of this chapter.

LITURGICAL RITES. Between the fourth and the tenth century, Constantinople developed its own rite, known as Byzantine, and adopted Greek as the liturgical language. In the ninth century, Sts Cyril and Methodius converted the Bulgarians and Moravians, used the same rite, but translated the liturgy into Slavonic. From Bulgaria, the Byzantine-Slavonic rite spread into Serbia and Russia.

THE ORTHODOX DOCTRINES. The Orthodox Churches are one in faith and tradition with Catholics on most points. They possess the same Scriptures in both the Old and New Testament.[23] They profess the Nicene Creed and the doctrines proclaimed at the first seven Ecumenical Councils, up to and including Nicea II, held in 787. They revere and study the Fathers of the Church. They have a genuine hierarchy of Bishops. They celebrate seven sacraments, have male and female religious orders, cultivate religious art, practise devotion to the Blessed Virgin and the Saints, visit holy places, practise fasts and conduct pilgrimages, etc. The chief difference is the doctrine of the Primacy and Infallibility of the Pope. Another very important difference is their permission of divorce and remarriage. They hold that the only infallible authority in the Church is a General Council consisting of the bishops of the entire Church, Greek and Latin. Hence, since they regard the Latin, or Catholic, Church as in error, and hold no communion with it, they maintain that, at the present time, no organ of infallibility exists, and they reject the decrees of all councils in which their bishops took no part. They hold that the Primacy of the Roman Pontiff is not of divine, but of ecclesiastical, institution, and was transferred, at least, as regards the Greek, or Eastern, Church, to the Patriarchate of Constantinople. The Primacy of that Patriarch, however, they interpreted merely as a primacy of honour, without jurisdiction: the Churches of Russia, Greece, and the Balkans, i.e., the majority of the Orthodox, are completely separated from her and from one another.

Differences between the Catholic and Orthodox Churches. Some of the differences over the centuries—of greater or lesser moment—have concerned the following: (1) the Primacy and Infallibility of the Bishop of Rome—a specifically Catholic doctrine. The division between East and West means that the Orthodox accept only the first seven Ecumenical Councils, while Catholics recognise twenty-one; (2) the addition of "filioque" in the Nicene Creed: this is reproved by the Orthodox, since they believe that the Holy Spirit proceeds from the Father but *not* "from the Son" also, and that a Creed promulgated by a General Council should not be modified; (3) the use in the Roman Church of *unleavened* bread at Mass; (4) the Orthodox belief in the necessity of the *epiclesis* (the invocation of the Holy Spirit

---

[23] Unlike Protestants, whose O.T. is smaller. See p.268.

during the Eucharistic Prayer) for the consecration to take place; (5) the method of Baptism; the Orthodox often insist on immersion as of divine institution; (6) the Roman practice of delaying Confirmation, which the Orthodox (likewise Eastern Catholics) administer straight after Baptism; (7) Communion under one kind only, often reprobated by the Orthodox who always administer the Body and Blood of Christ together (generally with a spoon); (8) the Orthodox under certain circumstances will recognise dissolution of a sacramental marriage and permit a second marriage; (9) the Immaculate Conception; its definition is not accepted by the Orthodox, even if they are inclined to accept the content of the doctrine; (10) the exact concept and purpose of Purgatory; (11) other fine points over the state of the soul between death and the general resurrection; (12) the Orthodox do not recognise the doctrine and granting of indulgences; (13) the Orthodox sometimes will not accept the validity of a sacrament, even of Baptism, administered outside their community; on the other hand, in practice, they recognise Anglican orders, which the Catholic Church does not; (14) the practice of seeking to make the Orthodox become Catholic; the existence of Eastern rite communities of people who have returned to union with Rome—some Orthodox object to the existence of these Churches with their parallel structures in predominantly Orthodox territory; (15) differing ecclesiology: the Orthodox have no notion of the universal church, but only local churches.

The Orthodox Church is not the true Church.

(1) IT IS NOT ONE: It has no claim to unity of government. It is divided into several churches, each claiming independence. It is not really a Church but an assemblage of Churches.[24] There is no one agreed authority among them. Nor are they absolutely one in doctrine: Constantinople and Russia disagree as to the validity of Baptism conferred by a Protestant or Catholic. There are several other points of difference which we need not detail.

(2) IT IS NOT INFALLIBLE: The Orthodox Church does not claim infallibility. Since its separation from Rome, it recognises no living teaching authority competent to decide matters of faith or morals infallibly. It has no structure for judging the orthodoxy or otherwise of its bishops or theologians. As a result, it has issued no authoritative and binding statements on newly disputed points of doctrine or vital issues of modern morality. It is devoid of clear and authoritative doctrine on birth control, the indissolubility of marriage, IVF, artificial prolongation of life, fine points of medical and health ethics, and a host of issues that have arisen in the modern technological world. Patriarch Bartholomew, the Greek Orthodox archbishop of Constantinople, was asked where the Orthodox Church stands on birth control. He replied, "According to a long-held tradition, the Orthodox Church avoids dictating or making categorical decisions of a social or ethical

---

[24] Cf. Donald Attwater, *The Christian Churches of the East. Vol. 2: Churches not in Communion with Rome*, Bruce, Milwaukee 1948.

nature."[25] Such neutrality was totally unknown to the Fathers of the Church, and represents a renunciation of teaching authority.

(3) IT IS NOT CATHOLIC: It is not catholic either racially or numerically. Not racially, because it is confined chiefly to portions of the Greek and Slavonic races, and their descendants in the lands where they have migrated. Nor numerically, because its total following is no more than 160 million. The missionary efforts of the Orthodox are negligible.

(4) IT IS NOT FULLY APOSTOLIC: It claims apostolicity, but does not possess it fully. It is apostolic in: (a) the transmission and succession of Holy Orders; and (b) most, but not all, of its doctrine. However, it is not apostolic in: (c) unity with the successor of Peter, the chief of the Apostles. The Orthodox, broken up as they are into independent Churches, admit that, unlike us Catholics, they have no central See communicating apostolic authority to the rest. While they maintain that their doctrine is apostolic, no Church has any certainty that its doctrine is apostolic and will remain so to the end of time, unless it can show that its authority to teach is derived from the Apostles and is guarded by the gift of infallibility.

(5) AS TO HOLINESS: The average level of sanctity among the practising laity of the Orthodox Churches is unquestionably high. This we may explain by the fact that it has preserved almost all the doctrines and devotions of the Catholic Church, that it has valid episcopal and priestly orders, and so still disposes of many of the means of grace. Yet it must seem singular even to the Orthodox themselves that, since they snapped the link with Rome, their Church appears to have remained in spiritual stagnation: it has had relatively few miracles strictly authenticated and only a few saints whose sanctity has been tested so severely as in the Catholic Church. It has developed no new and beautiful devotions, or new religious orders for the needs of the times, such as we expect to find in a truly living Church that enjoys God's blessing. It seems unable to accept genuine doctrinal development, but only those branches of the seed of the Gospel that appeared in the first millennium.

The root-defect of the Orthodox Church is its rejection of a supreme spiritual authority, the Papacy—the great unifying bond of the Church of Christ. At the time of their separation, the Orthodox formed one body, united around the Patriarchate of Constantinople. Their unity, however, was not a unity of obedience, but of reverence, and has been riven to fragments by secular princes who required that each kingdom should have its own separate and subservient church.

C

The Branch Theory. Since the Oxford Movement (1833-1845), it has been a favourite theory with Anglican theologians of the Ritualist or High Church party that the Church of Christ resembles a tree with three great branches, viz., the Church of England, the Eastern Orthodox Church, and the Catholic Church. The

---

[25] TIME, 5 May 1997, p.50

branches are distinct, yet they are of one tree, because each has apostolic succession,[26] and all share in the same sacramental life. Each is *the* Church of Christ in its own domain, so that men are bound on pain of schism to be members of it, not of another branch. The Church of England is for Englishmen and the Commonwealth, the Orthodox Church is for Greeks and Slavs, and the Catholic Church is chiefly for the Latin races. This theory, they believe, reconciles the present divided state of the Church with the doctrine that she is one and continuous. But the difficulties against it are insuperable. In fact, it is mentioned here rather as a matter of historical interest than as having any serious place in religious controversy. It is ignored or rejected by the majority of Anglicans; it has not been accepted by the Orthodox, and it is utterly repudiated by the Catholic Church. We are asked, then, to conceive a "branch" Church whose branches refuse to acknowledge its existence. Such a church would possess no unity of government: it would consist of mutually hostile bodies, each seeking the correction of the other two, and would be utterly unlike the Church of St Paul, the one living body of Christ, one in heart and mind. It would not be one in faith, for its creed would be a mass of ludicrous contradictions: its Catholic members would hold, while the Orthodox and Anglicans would reject, the Primacy and Infallibility of the Pope; and the official Anglican Church would regard as obligatory hardly any doctrine professed in common by Orthodox and Catholics. A member of the Anglican Church may hold, without imperilling his status, almost anything he pleases on the necessity and efficacy of Baptism, the Real Presence and the Eucharist, the sacramental nature of Matrimony, the divine institution of the Episcopacy, the Resurrection of Our Lord and even His Divinity. Moreover, he is bound to tolerate every doctrine which a court, appointed by the civil authority, may decide is tenable. It was this last consideration which finally moved Henry Manning (later Cardinal of Westminster) to become a Catholic.[27]

The analysis of the theory yields so many absurdities that it need not be considered further. We merely note in conclusion the following points: (1) The assumption that the Anglican Church has a sacramental life, that its Bishops and Priests are validly ordained, with powers to consecrate and absolve, is rejected by the majority of Anglicans themselves—and the Catholic Church has expressly pronounced against the validity of Anglican orders: see below. (2) The theory makes the extravagant supposition that faith varies with nationality, that Christ wished men to believe one thing because they were born in England, and quite the opposite because they were born in Italy. (3) The three "branches" would possess no common organ of infallibility. - It is unnecessary to consider whether the true Church may consist of a combination of some two of the three Churches. The arguments against any such theory may be easily deduced from what has been already said.

Notes. *The term 'Roman Catholic'* was not used by the Fathers, but first appeared in the 16th century and was used by Anglican divines (theologians) to make room for their claim that they were "*English* Catholics", while those in union with Rome were

---

[26] As to the Anglican claim to apostolicity, see p.153.
[27] Cf. J. Pereiro, *Cardinal Manning. An Intellectual Biography*, Oxford 1998, pp.108, 166.

"*Roman* Catholics". Well aware that the title "Catholic" goes back to the second century, they did not want it used by Catholics in their country. It was an attempt to claim that there could be varying, even contradictory, forms of "Catholic". Later, other disparaging terms would be invented, such as "Romanist" and "Papist". For the most part, "Roman Catholic" is confined to the English language, although some Orthodox in their polemics with the Catholic Church have adopted the term as well. The Catholic Church herself in her official Council and Papal documents does not use the term. Catholics themselves should do likewise. The first writer to use the term, "Catholic Church" was St Ignatius of Antioch (d. 107): "Where the bishop appears, there let the people be, just as where Jesus Christ is, there is the Catholic Church."[28]

Anglican orders. In 1896, in his Apostolic Letter *Apostolicae Curae*, Pope Leo XIII ruled definitively, and infallibly therefore, on the invalidity of Anglican orders.[29] For this reason, in official dialogue with Anglicans, the Catholic Church by no means regards them as being on an equal footing with the Orthodox. In official Church documents, Protestant and Anglican bodies are called *communions* or *communities*, but not *Churches*. The Catholic Church reserves the word *Church* for those bodies that have a genuine episcopacy and Holy Orders. The non-Catholic Eastern bodies are called *Churches* since they possess these.

III

THE CATHOLIC CHURCH IS THE TRUE CHURCH

Since the true Church is not the Protestant nor the Orthodox Church, nor any combination of Protestants, Orthodox and Catholics, it must be the Catholic Church. Besides, the Catholic Church has all the marks of the true Church.

THE CATHOLIC CHURCH IS UNIVERSAL, ONE, HOLY, APOSTOLIC, AND FOUNDED BY CHRIST

(1) SHE IS CATHOLIC OR UNIVERSAL. The notion Catholic is found in the Scriptures, not expressly but equivalently. "The *Catholic* Church" is the short way of saying "The *Teach-ye-all-nations* Church." (a) She is catholic in desire, for she has at all times endeavoured to fulfil the command of Christ to teach all nations. She has always felt that she had a duty to the heathen which she dared not neglect. She has never been content simply to retain her members, but is ever seeking new converts from all angles and in all nations. (b) She is socially or racially catholic because, unlike other

---

[28] *Ep. ad Smyrn.*, 8
[29] DS 3319. Cf. Cong. for the Doctrine of the Faith, *Commentary* on *Ad Tuendam Fidem*, 1998, art. 11.

Christian bodies, she is not confined wholly or chiefly to a single people, but is found in every continent. She belongs not to any nation, but to the world. She counts her members in every station of life, the poor and the illiterate as well as men and women eminent in every calling. So powerful over the hearts and minds of men is the attraction of her doctrine and institutions that even her adversaries are forced to recognise that power, but her only spell is the spell of Christ to whose office of charity she has succeeded. She is to her followers what Christ was to the poor of Palestine: a light, a refuge, and a hope. (c) She is numerically catholic. Her following numbers about 1000 million, and far exceeds that of any other Christian denomination.

(2) SHE IS ONE IN GOVERNMENT, FAITH, AND WORSHIP. (a) *She is one in government.* The people are joined to their priests, the priests and people to their Bishops, and all are subject to the Pope, the centre of authority, the bond of apostolic unity, the successor of St Peter, and the Vicar of Christ. (b) *She is one in faith.* All her members, whether they be cultured Europeans or children of the forest, are bound by the same doctrines and profess the same faith on penalty of exclusion from her fold. The Catholic Church bears the message of Christ and, courageous and plain-spoken as Himself, insists that it be received in its integrity. She shuts her ears to the sensual who look to her in vain for an accommodation in her moral teaching. She ignores the claims of false science and the demands of corrupt politicians. She maintains, in season and out of season, as the divinely appointed teacher, the revealed truths of the Holy Trinity, the Incarnation, and all the profound mysteries of her creed. Therein lies the miracle of her unity: that she holds her vast following together while teaching what is hard to believe, while prescribing what is hard to practise, while rejecting all compromise in faith or morals. (c) *She is one in worship.* Her sacraments and sacrifice are everywhere the same, and everywhere the faithful have access to the same ministrations. There are differences of language and ceremonial, but nothing that affects essentials. She makes the highest as well as the lowest, the Cardinal as well as the peasant, the president as well as the janitor, kneel as humble penitents before her priests, and she brings them all to the altar to be fed with the Bread of Life. The Church is absolute in regard to worship, as she is in regard to faith. Since her sacraments are the means given her by Christ for the sanctification of men, she sees that none of them be made void but that each be applied as He intended. Her faithful followers bear her yoke of worship as willingly as they bear her yoke of faith, thus exhibiting to the world the miraculous spectacle of a vast number of people, representing so many phases of human weakness, united, not for any material gain or sensual pleasure, but to participate in mysterious rites

that may seem unreal, perhaps even repellent, to those who cannot see with the eyes of faith.

The Catholic Church therefore has the mark of Unity with world-wide Catholicity and this alone is enough to identify her with the Church which Christ founded.

(3) SHE IS HOLY. She is holy, because she teaches, in addition to the other doctrines of Christ, His counsels of perfection, and succeeds in getting many of her children to practise them. It is part of her *very system* to bless and encourage all who strive to attain to the higher Christian ideals, the ideals of intimate union with God, of fraternal charity, and self-denial in its many forms: she is in truth the mother of saints and martyrs. Hence, we see in her fold those great religious societies of men and women who, seeking fuller freedom to surrender themselves to the sanctifying action of the Holy Spirit, bind themselves by vows of poverty, chastity, and obedience. They devote their lives to such practical works of charity as the education of youth, the relief of the poor, the support of families in crisis, the care of the sick and the aged, provision for refugees and victims of war, and the rescue of the victims of sin. Others, following the vocation to the contemplative life, spend their days in mortification and prayer. The Church is "the good tree" of the Gospel. She is the tree that, standing by the living waters, brings forth fruit in abundance. Christ Himself is with her and within her, and is multiplied in her children.

The holiness of the Church is manifested especially in the heroic sanctity and great number of the canonised saints whom she has guided to a perfection of sanctity beyond the powers of our frail fallen nature. (This point is developed in Ch. 12, pp.219-23).

Finally, the Catholic Church declares that Christ, in accordance with His promise, never ceases to attest her sanctity by miracles. We need not enter into a discussion of particular cases. It is sufficient to say that many of the miracles wrought in her communion cannot be believed, unless we are prepared to reject everything founded on human testimony. Further, the very fact of her making such a claim is in itself an evidence of her truth. (See Ch. 12, pp.223-9).

(4) SHE IS APOSTOLIC. Compare the government of the Catholic Church today with the government of the Church of Christ at its foundation. Christ placed His Church under the supreme government of St Peter assisted by the Apostles:[30]   the Catholic Church today is under the government of the lawful successors of St Peter and the Apostles. In other words, she is apostolic.

---

[30] See pp.188-90 for Scripture evidence.

That the Pope and the Bishops are the lawful successors of St Peter and the Apostles is proved as follows:

The Catholic Church alone claims the apostolicity given by Christ to His Church, i.e., to be governed by the successor of St Peter. (a) As we saw in the preceding chapter, Christ placed His Church under the government of the Apostles with St Peter as the chief Pastor and Ruler. He promised to be with them "all days, even to the consummation of the world",[31] thus implying that St Peter and his brother Apostles would continue to rule the Church until the end of time. But since the Apostles are dead, how do they still rule the Church? There is only one answer: they rule the Church, and will ever continue to rule it, through their lawful successors. "Their lawful successors" are those whom Christ accepts as lawful successors. (b) The Catholic Church alone claims that she is ruled by the successor of St Peter. She claims that the Pope has succeeded to the office of St Peter: that the Pope is the supporting rock of the Church; that he holds the keys of the Kingdom of Heaven; that he is the Shepherd of the whole flock of Christ, and that his brother Bishops are subordinate to him as the other Apostles were to St Peter. The Catholic Church claims that Christ accepts the Pope as the successor of St Peter, and the Bishops as successors of the other Apostles.

The claim of the Catholic Church must be true. The Catholic Church's unique claim to possess the precise form of apostolicity given by Christ to His Church must be true, because, if it were false, the Church which He built on the rock of Peter would no longer exist in the world, and—a gross absurdity—Christ would have failed to keep His promise that she would last forever.

Christ with His omnipotence will see to it that St Peter and the Apostles will always be represented in lawful succession by the Pope and the Bishops. This is beautifully summed up in the celebrated phrase of St Ambrose (d. 397), "Ubi Petrus, ibi Ecclesia", "Where Peter is, there is the Church."[32]

Christ will see to it that no vital interest of His Church will ever be endangered through the personal defects or failings of any of St Peter's successors.

The Catholic Church's apostolicity has never suffered, and will never suffer, interruption. The apostolicity of the Catholic Church was not broken for any period in the past, and will not be broken during any time in the future. This is obvious from the words of Christ: He did not promise His help

---

[31] Cf. Matt 28:20.
[32] *Enarr. in Ps.* 40, n.30 (PL 14, 1082)

merely for this century or that, or for this year or that, but for *"all days"* till the end of time (Matt 28:20).

It is an historical fact no longer disputed that, at the present day, no See in the world but the See of Rome is linked in unbroken succession to an Apostle. Constantinople, called by courtesy apostolic, was obviously not founded by an Apostle, since the city itself was founded by Constantine in the 4th century. Antioch, St Peter's first bishopric, fell away from the Church in the Monophysite heresy of the fifth century.[33] A similar fate befell Alexandria, founded by St Mark under the direction of St Peter. Jerusalem, the See of St James, had only a brief existence, perishing utterly at the destruction of the city by Titus in 70 A.D. There are no others.

But suppose that some non-Catholic Church could point to a central see tracing its succession step by step back to one of the Apostles other than St Peter: would such a Church be apostolic? No; it would have lost its apostolicity and catholicity at the precise moment when it severed the vital link of allegiance to the See of Peter, Christ's Vicar on earth.

(5) THE CATHOLIC CHURCH WAS FOUNDED BY CHRIST. Everyone knows that the Protestant form of the Christian religion began with Martin Luther in the 1500's. As Cardinal Newman pointed out, all heretical bodies are named after their founder, locality or doctrine.[34] The Lutheran and Calvinist churches, e.g., are named after their *founders* Luther and Calvin. The Church of England (Anglican Church)[35] and Russian Orthodox Church, e.g., are named after the *place* of their origin. The Presbyterian, Congregational, Baptist and Methodist churches, e.g., are named after their particular *doctrines* regarding, respectively, presbyters, the congregation, baptism, and method. The Catholic Church is named after no particular place or doctrine, since it is universal and has not isolated any one doctrine from the rest; it takes its name from no mere man, but was founded by Christ. Since the time of Newman, countless new Protestant groups, as well as semi-Christian sects, have arisen. Some of them, e.g., Assembly of God, Jehovah's Witnesses, Worldwide Church of God, are not named after any particular person, place or doctrine—but one thing they, and all Protestant bodies, have in common is that *the date of their foundation can be given.* And it is not the year 33 A.D., and the founder is not Jesus Christ. Only the Catholic

---

[33] The heresy of Eutyches, condemned at the General Council of Chalcedon in 451. Eutyches denied the two distinct natures in Christ, saying that His Humanity was absorbed in His Divinity. See p.386.

[34] *The Development of Christian Doctrine*, 1845, Rev ed. 1878, Part II, Ch. VI, Sect. II, 6. Longmans ed., p.255

[35] = *Episcopalian Church* in N. America since they believe in the episcopacy (hierarchy of bishops); called *Church of Ireland* in Ireland, *Episcopal Church* in Scotland.

Church goes back in every respect of her foundation to Jesus Christ Himself. No other person can be adduced as her founder.

> **Conclusion**. Christ who is God founded a Church. He promised it would last to the end of time. Therefore, His Church exists in the world at the present day.
>
> Christ imprinted certain marks on His Church so that people could always identify it. No church, therefore, can be His Church, unless it possesses *all* those marks.
>
> The Catholic Church alone possesses them. Therefore, the Catholic Church is the one and only true Church of Christ.

IV

"Outside the Church there is no salvation."[36] Before the death of Christ, those who died in a state of grace could not enter Heaven. By faith and contrition, they were justified (i.e., made just and righteous), but after death they had to wait in the Limbo of the Fathers, also called the bosom of Abraham (Lk 19:22). They received grace on earth in consideration of the merits of the Redeemer to come, but until the Redeemer's death, they could not receive its chief benefit, the vision of God in Heaven.

Since the coming of the Saviour, God commands all men to be members of His Church. Those who deliberately disobey Him will be lost eternally. But, since He condemns no man except for a grave fault, He will not condemn those who through inculpable ignorance are unaware of His precept, who serve Him faithfully according to their conscience, who have a sincere desire to do His will and, therefore, implicitly, the desire to become members of His Church. The ancient phrase, "Outside the Church there is no salvation", was addressed to those already in the Church, lest they be tempted to join heretical bodies or abandon the faith. It was not a statement that all non-Catholics were condemned.

Pope Pius XII appealed thus to non-Catholics: "We invite them all, each and every one, to yield their free consent to the inner stirrings of God's grace and strive to extricate themselves from a state in which they cannot be secure of their own eternal salvation; for, though they may be related to the Mystical Body of the Redeemer by some unconscious yearning and desire, yet they are deprived of those many great heavenly gifts and helps which can be enjoyed only in the Catholic Church. Let them enter Catholic unity, therefore, and joined with us in the one organism of the Body of Jesus Christ, hasten together to the one Head in the fellowship of most glorious love. We cease not to pray for them to the Spirit of love and truth, and with open arms we await them, not as strangers, but as those who are coming to their own father's house."[37]

---

[36] St Cyprian, *Ep*. 73, c. 21; Origen, *Hom. in Josue*, 3,4.
[37] *Mystici Corporis*, 1943, Part III

The second Vatican Council twice declared the necessity of the Church for salvation: "Hence those people could not be saved, who, not ignorant that the Catholic Church has been founded as necessary by God through Jesus Christ, would still refuse either to enter it or to remain in it."[38]

Let us consider the following cases: (1) A man, born of Protestant parents, is baptised; lives his life as a Protestant, without ever having a grave doubt that he is in the wrong; makes, before death, an act of perfect contrition for grave sins committed or an act of perfect charity. Such a man will be saved, for he dies in the state of grace. (2) A heathen has never heard the name of Christ. He obeys the natural law according to his lights. He dies a heathen, to all appearances. The Divine Mercy will not suffer such a man to be lost. It is a recognised principle that God, because He wills that all be saved, does not deny grace to him who does his best. He will infallibly give him who is faithful to the natural law sufficient illumination and aid to enable him to make the acts of faith and charity necessary for salvation. The act of charity includes the desire of full compliance with the Divine Will; it includes, therefore, the desire of baptism.[39] In the view of the fact that the Church stands plainly before the eyes of men like a city on a mountain-top, that the words of her ministers have gone forth to the ends of the earth, we speak only of those who have truly remained ignorant of Jesus Christ and His Church. For those deprived of the abundant graces at the disposal of those who belong to the visible membership of the Church, salvation is not easy. (3) Children who die unbaptised are, according to the common teaching, admitted to a state of natural, but not supernatural, happiness. The Church has never said that they are sent to a place of suffering. (See pp.481-2).

OBJECTION: "All religions are equally good. Believers in other religions, or in no religion, should be left alone, in good faith. It is enough if they are sincere. No one has the right to disturb them or criticise their beliefs or try to change them." REPLY: Sincerity alone is never enough: Hitler and Stalin were sincere. Sincerity is no obstacle to causing harm. Sincere people can be dangerously mistaken, can do great harm, and can lead others to do the same. Sins and false ideas always harm human beings and human happiness, even if the perpetrators are unaware of it and are not culpable. No one *really* believes that sincerity is enough: anyone who needs an electrician or builder or doctor or chef, wants not just a sincere person of good intentions, but a knowledgeable and reliable person, competent for the job. Now if sincerity by itself is insufficient in all these areas of life, it cannot be sufficient in the most important matters in life: the truth about God and man and Christ, the truth about right and wrong, holiness and sinfulness, salvation and damnation. As for the claim that all religions are equally good: no one who is logical can state this sincerely—since it is equivalent to saying that truth and error are equally good, that to worship God or the devil are equally good, that to offer prayers or practise

---

[38] *Lumen Gentium* (on The Church) 1964, art. 14; *Ad Gentes* (on Missions), 1965, art. 7; cf. C 846.

[39] This paragraph, "Let us ...", up to this point, stands as Dr Sheehan wrote it for the 1939 edition.

human sacrifice are equally good, and that a religion which condemns such indifferentism to truth is just as good as a religion which approves it.

DIFFICULTY: "If non-Catholics and even non-Christians can be saved, why bother to seek converts at home and send missionaries abroad?" REPLY: Simply: because our religion is true, and this is the command of Christ. More fully: *In terms of salvation:* (1) the Catholic religion, because it has *all* of Christ's teachings and *all* the means of salvation, gives greater *helps* to salvation and *assurance* of it; and (2) it enables people to reach *a higher degree of glory* which they shall enjoy for all eternity. *In terms of this life:* (3) it gives the *peace* and *blessings* of the true faith on earth; and (4) *God* desires to be *known, loved and served* in this life—as well as in the next.

We must never let any theory about the salvation of non-Catholics undermine our apostolic and missionary endeavours. Since Christ gave us the command to go and teach all nations, and since all people have a right to know God their Father, Jesus Christ their Saviour, and Mary their Mother—we must fulfil the command of Christ and seek to bring as many as possible to the one true religion, for "God our Saviour ... desires all men to be saved and to come to the knowledge of the truth."[40]

THE RELATIONSHIP OF PROTESTANTS AND ORTHODOX TO THE CATHOLIC CHURCH. While not being members of the Catholic Church, these Christians are our brothers, for they are in *partial* but imperfect communion with the Catholic Church by virtue of their baptism.[41] They possess "many elements of truth and sanctification"[42] within their own communities, but whatever truth they have, they have received from the Catholic Church, since those things truly belong to and come from the Catholic Church. "All of these, which come from Christ and lead back to Him, belong by right to the one Church of Christ."[43] The Catholic Church ardently prays that all Christians may be one and enter into *full* communion with her. "For it is only through Christ's Catholic Church, which is the universal help towards salvation, that the fulness of the means of salvation can be obtained."[44]

CONVERSION. Outstanding have been the many converts to the Catholic Church over the centuries, especially those who have entered the Church at great personal sacrifice. Of course, a change from Catholicism to another non-Catholic body involves heresy or schism, and can never be justified: such changes are always accompanied by *moral* difficulties; the *intellectual* conversion has barely any credibility. The declaration of a staunch Anglican here is significant: "A man who is converted from Protestantism to Popery [Catholicism], may be sincere: he parts with nothing: he is only superadding to what he already had. But a convert from Popery to Protestantism, gives up so much of what he has held as sacred as any

---

[40] 1 Tim 2:3-4
[41] *Unitatis Redintegratio*, Decree on Ecumenism, Second Vatican Council 1964, art. 3
[42] *Lumen Gentium*, Dogmatic Constitution on the Church, Second Vatican Council 1964, art. 8
[43] *Unitatis Redintegratio*, art. 3; cf. C 819.
[44] Ibid., art. 3; C 816

thing that he retains: there is so much laceration of mind in such a conversion, that it can hardly be sincere and lasting."[45]

THE WITNESS OF CONVERTS. The array of converts in the last century alone is a witness to the perennial attraction of the Church to those in relentless search of ultimate and certain Truth. Among these countless converts from all sorts of backgrounds, religions and countries can be named: from *England*: Mother Janet Erskine Stuart, Mgr Robert Hugh Benson, Fr C.C. Martindale, Christopher Dawson, Katharine Asquith (née Horner), Alfred Noyes, J.B. Morton, G.K. Chesterton & Frances Chesterton, Dorothy Collins, Mgr Ronald Knox, Vernon Johnson, Maurice Baring, Arnold Lunn, Sheila Kaye-Smith, Eric Gill, David Jones, Douglas Hyde & Carol Hyde, Elizabeth Anscombe, Peter Geach, Edith Sitwell, Fr Frederick Copleston, Graham Greene, Donald Attwater, Lord (Frank) Longford, Anne Fremantle, Christopher Hollis, Evelyn Waugh, Penelope Betjeman (née Chetwode), Edward Sackville-West, Leonard Cheshire V.C., Sir John Biggs-Davison, Philip Trower, Alec Guinness, Diana Dors, Michael Dummett, John Saward, Fr Aidan Nichols, Phyllis Bowman, Denis & Valerie Riches, Lord (Kenneth) Clark, Malcolm & Kitty Muggeridge, Stratford & Leonie Caldecott, William Oddie, Ann Widdecombe, John Gummer, Charles Moore, Paul Goodman, General Sir Charles Guthrie, Shirley Williams, Katharine Worsley the Duchess of Kent, Josephine Walpole, Fr Graham Leonard, two other former Anglican bishops and hundreds of Anglican clergymen. *Scotland*: Bruce Marshall, A.J. Cronin, Bishop Henry Grey Graham, Compton Mackenzie, Hamish Fraser, James Adam, Muriel Spark, Fr Ronald Walls, Fr William Anthony, Fr Gordon Brown, Hayden Ramsay, Alasdair MacIntyre. *New Zealand*: James K. Baxter, (Fr) Wilfrid Fitzgerald, Fr David Jillett, Mother Xavier OSB, Fr Rory Price, Fr David Hercus, Kenneth & Mary Prebble, John Jensen, Tom & Gillian Drummond, Don Cowan, Matthew Mawkes. *Australia*: Sir Gilbert Murray, Fr Leslie Rumble, Arthur Streeton, James McAuley, Les Murray, Bruce Dawe, Fr James Tierney, Mons. Peter Elliott, Bishop Geoffrey Jarrett, Fr John Parsons, James Bogle, Fr Brian Harrison, John Finnis, Stuart & Tracey Rowland, Thomas Forgan, Peter Birrell, A.D. Hope, Beatrice ("Bee") Miles, John Niland, Sir Ronald Grieve, Marion Selwyn, Ralph Marsh, John Ducker, Barrie Unsworth, John MacBean, John Menadue, Wayne Hudson, Keith Wilson, Michael Birt, Christopher Pearson, Susan Moore, Fr John Fleming, Michael Daniel, Archie Cameron, John Dayle, Tim Fischer, Malcolm Turnbull. *Nigeria*: Cardinal Francis Arinze. *S. Africa*: Roy Campbell, Fr Elias Friedman, Archbishop George Daniel. *Italy*: David Guido Nacamuli, Giovanni Papini, Mons. Salvatore Garofalo, Israel Eugenio Zolli the Chief Rabbi of Rome, Arrigo Minerbi, Vittorio Messori. *France*: Jacques & Raïssa Maritain, Fr Louis Bouyer, Julien Green, André Frossard, Jean Daujat, Cardinal Jean-Marie Aaron Lustiger. *Germany*: Gertrud von Le Fort, Dietrich von Hildebrand, Karl Stern, St Edith Stein, Rosa Stein, Maria Alice Reis, Sr Amelie Adelgundis Jaegerschmid, Erna Hermann Haven, Erik Peterson, Hilda Graef, Colonel Herbert Kappler, Erich von Petersdorff, Siegfried Spiegel; four Protestant ministers: Rudolf Goethe, Martin Giebner, Georg Klünder, Heinrich

---

[45] Dr Samuel Johnson in James Boswell, *The Life of Samuel Johnson*, Everyman 1946, Vol. I, p.377, A.D. 1769, Aetat. 60

Schlier. *Holland:* Hilda van Stockum, Vonne van der Meer. *Sweden:* Mother Elisabeth Hesselblad, Fr Lars Rooth. *Finland:* Birgit Klockars, Fr Finn Arvé. *Norway:* Sigrid Undset. *Denmark:* Johannes Jørgensen. *Iceland:* Halldór Laxness. *Russia:* Achmed Abdullah, Helen Iswolsky, Waldemar Gurian. *Japan:* Dr Takashi Nagai, Shusaku Endo. *China:* John Chin Hsung Wu. *Canada:* Herbert C.F. Bell, Anton Pegis, Fr Alan McCormack. *U.S.A.:* Clare Booth Luce, Louis Budenz, Bella Dodd, Emily Holmes Coleman, Francis Parkinson Keyes, Fulton Oursler, Dorothy Day, William C. Kernan, Fr Arthur Klyber, William Congdon, Walker Percy, Fr Avery Dulles, Gary Cooper, John Wayne, Fr Raphael Simon, Martin & Ronda Chervin, Paul Waldmann, Valerie Wiener, Debra Herbeck, H. Lyman Stebbins, James Likoudis, Sheldon Vanauken, Freda Mary Oben, Jeffrey Rubin, Warren Carroll, Peter Kreeft, Paul Vitz, Fr George Rutler, Fr Jay Scott Newman, Ruth Pakaluk, Celia Wolf-Deviner, Thomas Howard, Dale & Elena Vree, Gerry Matatics, Scott & Kimberly Hahn, Elizabeth Fox-Genovese, Stephen Mosher, Wilton Wynn, Steve Wood, Helen Hitchcock, Fr Richard Neuhaus, Nora Hamerman, Bernard Nathanson, Rebecca Jackson.[46]

THE ENMITY AGAINST THE CHURCH: A WITNESS TO HER TRUTH. The Catholic Church also bears the mark of opposition. Like her Divine Founder she is a "sign of contradiction" (Lk 2:34). Even the most religiously illiterate person knows that it is only the Pope and the Catholic Church that have any coherent and authoritative teaching on the burning issues of the day. The very dissent whipped up against the Pope when he speaks is proof that he speaks with a voice that disturbs consciences with the authority of Christ Himself. No other Christian leader arouses the fury of the modern enemies of Jesus Christ as does the Vicar of Christ, the Pope. "One thing in this world is different from all other. It has a personality and a force. It is recognised, and (when recognised) most violently loved or hated. It is the Catholic Church. Within that household the human spirit has roof and hearth. Outside it, is the Night."[47]

THE CATHOLIC CHURCH AND CIVILISATION. The Catholic Church is the great civiliser and has been the inspiration of the greatest elements of Western civilisation. The appreciation of this led Lord (Kenneth) Clark to become a Catholic on his deathbed. It is to the Catholic Church ultimately that Europe owes all that made it great and distinctive. It was this insight that inspired Hilaire Belloc to write that, "The Faith is Europe and Europe is the Faith." Of course he did not mean that the two could really be so literally identified, and that the Faith could only be European in expression. As he explained, "I have never said that the Church was necessarily European. The Church will last for ever, and on this earth, until the end of the world; and our remote descendants may find its chief membership to have passed to Africans or Asiatics in some civilisation yet unborn. What I have said is that the

---

[46] For some conversion stories, see *Surprised by Truth* ed. by Patrick Madrid, Basilica Press, San Diego 1994. 23 Jewish conversions are related in *Bread from Heaven* ed. by Ronda Chervin, Remnant of Israel, 3050 Gap Knob Rd, New Hope, Kentucky 1994.
[47] Hilaire Belloc (1870-1953) *Essays of a Catholic*, Ch. xv, p.305

European thing is essentially a Catholic thing, and that European values would disappear with the disappearance of Catholicism."[48]

The Catholic Church does not exist primarily for the sake of civilisation, but for the salvation of souls. However, even on the basis of civilisation, we can recognise the necessity of the Church's power and influence for good, and the inability of any other philosophy, religion or institution to hold out against all that is anti-human. Without the supernatural, the natural order itself cannot survive. Evelyn Waugh, upon his conversion in 1930, could already see the same truth: "in the present phase of European history the essential issue is no longer between Catholicism, on one side, and Protestantism, on the other, but between Christianity and Chaos. ... In the eighteenth and nineteenth centuries the choice before any educated European was between Christianity, in whatever form it was presented to him ... and ... a polite and highly attractive scepticism. So great, indeed, was the inherited, subconscious power of Christianity that it was nearly two centuries before the real nature of this loss of faith became apparent. Today we can see it on all sides as the active negation of all that Western culture has stood for. Civilisation ...the whole moral and artistic organization of Europe—has not in itself the power of survival. It came into being through Christianity, and without it has no significance or power to command allegiance. ... It is no longer possible, as it was in the time of Gibbon, to accept the benefits of civilisation and at the same time deny the supernatural basis on which it rests. ... Christianity... is in greater need of combative strength than it has been for centuries."[49]

THE ULTIMATE CHOICE: BETWEEN LIGHT AND DARKNESS. Those who examine seriously the claims of the Catholic Church come to realise that the choice is between Her—and Nothing. Cardinal Newman recorded that, while an Anglican, he "came to the conclusion that there was no medium, in true philosophy, between Atheism and Catholicity, and that a perfectly consistent mind, under those circumstances in which it finds itself here below, must embrace either the one or the other."; - "there are but two alternatives, the way to Rome, and the way to Atheism: Anglicanism is the halfway house on the one side, and Liberalism is the halfway house on the other."[50]

V

OBJECTIONS ANSWERED

Objection against the infallibility of the Church. "The Church claims that, in virtue of her gift of infallibility, her teaching never varies, that the faith of her children is always the same. This cannot be true, because from time to time she enlarges her creed by new definitions. Since the definition of the doctrine of the

---

[48] Letter to the *Catholic Herald*, 1936
[49] *The Essays, Articles and Reviews of Evelyn Waugh*, ed. by D. Gallagher, Methuen 1983, pp.103-5
[50] *Apologia Pro Vita Sua*, Ch. IV (1841-45)

Immaculate Conception in 1854, all Catholics are bound to believe it. Before the definition they were free to reject it."[51]

REPLY: The Church's teaching never varies. She never contradicts herself, as the other bodies do. She never adds anything to the revealed truth given her by Christ. Her definitions are nothing more than fuller and more precise explanations of doctrines contained in the Deposit of Faith. The doctrine of the Immaculate Conception, for instance, is but a part of the doctrine always held by the Church that Mary is the Mother of the Redeemer promised in Genesis 3, that she is the new Eve, full of grace and sanctity, and that she loosed the knot of sin which Eve had fastened on the human race. The Church has not set forth the explicit and exhaustive meaning of all the profound truths entrusted to her. It is only as controversy, or some new devotion arises, that she declares whether a particular doctrine is, or is not, implicitly contained in those truths. Thus, as time advances, her teaching grows in explicitness or clearness, and this is what we understand by the *development of doctrine*. It is a development that goes on without any increase or contradiction of revealed truth.

Once the Church issues a definition, it is clear to any doubters there may have been among her children that the doctrine must henceforward be held as of Catholic faith on pain of heresy. It is true therefore that a new definition creates a new obligation. But the new obligation cannot weigh as a burden on the mass of the faithful who, in virtue of collective infallibility in belief, have always believed all the doctrines explicitly or implicitly contained in the Deposit of Faith. It can affect but the very few who, as a fact, have not been one in faith with the Church. And even these, loyal Catholics as we assume them to be (for of others there is no question), will gladly relinquish an unwitting error, and will acquiesce at once in the infallible decision. - John Henry Newman's classic work, *An Essay on the Development of Christian Doctrine* (1845), was written as an answer to the objection in his own mind. Upon its completion, he entered the Catholic Church.

Objection against the unity of the Church. "The Church has not always been one in government. During the Great Western Schism (1378-1417), the allegiance of the faithful was divided between two, and even three Popes."

REPLY: Catholics were divided on a question of *identification*, not of *principle*. All acknowledged that there could be only one lawful Pope in the Church, but, owing to political disturbances and difficulties of communication, they were unable to identify him among the rival claimants. One of these was the lawful Pope, possessing apostolic succession and authority. The Schism, although it was the source of many evils, proves God's solicitude for the preservation of the Papacy, for no human dynasty could have survived such a trial.

Objection against the catholicity of the Church. "If the Church is from God, and has been sent by Him to preach to all nations, how is it that all nations do not accept her teaching? Why has she failed to convince the majority of mankind?"

REPLY: As Christ, the Son of God, was sent by His heavenly Father to preach to the Jews, so were the Apostles and their successors sent by Christ to preach to all

---

[51] See also "Objections against Papal infallibility", p.206.

nations. And as Christ, though He was God himself, failed to convert the majority of the Jews, so has the Church failed to gather into her fold the majority of the human race. The command received by Christ from His Father did not imply that all, or even the greater number, of those who heard Him would receive His words. Neither does the command given by Christ imply that His Church will be more successful in her mission than He was in His. In fact, Christ Himself foretold that the Apostles would be treated as He had been treated. He sent them to preach to the world, but He warned them that the world would hate them (Jn 15:18 ff.; Matt 24:9).

How is this hostility or aversion to be explained? Its causes are chiefly the following: (a) *Ignorance* of Catholic Doctrine and of the arguments by which its truth is defended. (b) *Prejudices* against the Church—often the result of early training— which clog reason and prevent it from accepting the proofs set forth in Apologetics.[52] (c) *Intellectual Pride* or an excessive confidence in one's own judgement: a person afflicted with this vice regards any effort to convince him of error in his religious convictions as an insult to his intelligence and an offence against his dignity. His state of mind is the very opposite to that childlike humility which Christ requires of those who seek His Kingdom. (d) *Want of courage*: people are appalled by the strictness of the Catholic Moral Law (e.g., the law of Confession, the laws regarding Marriage), and by the hardships which are often involved in conversion (e.g., the opposition of family and friends, loss of means of livelihood). It is God's grace alone that enables the non-Catholic to break through these obstacles.

It is only on the day of General Judgement that God's dealings with the whole human race will be fully known. Only then shall we see how He used the Church as His agent of mercy to mankind, how through her prayers, her Sacraments and the Sacrifice of Mass, He gave the blessing of a happy death to heretics and pagans, to those who retained but a vestige of her teaching, to those who in their invincible ignorance bitterly opposed her, to those who seemed hopelessly involved in grossest error. Only then will the Church, the Spouse of Christ, shine forth triumphant as the beneficent mother of grace to all men of good will.

Objection against the holiness of the Church. "Many immoral people are members of the Church. If she is called the Mother of Saints, she would with greater justice be called the mother of sinners."
REPLY: The glory of the saints is the glory of the Church: it was she who showed them the way to the great heights of holiness; it was she who, through Christ her Head, upheld them with grace and saved them from fainting on their toilsome journey. The fact that they represent every order of society and every degree of intellectual ability, and that in them are found instances of triumph over all manner of weakness and sin, proves that there is no one on earth who cannot become a saint, if he will only listen to the Church's instructions and accept her aid. And what of the sinners of her fold? Has she to bear their shame? No; no more than Christ has to bear the shame of Judas; no more than the Apostles had to bear the shame of those Christians whose crimes they denounced. If there are bad people in the

---

[52] See pp.283-6.

Church, they themselves are to blame. Saints are saints because they listen to the voice of the Church: sinners are sinners because they refuse to hear or heed her. Though sinners are numerous in the Catholic Church, it cannot be maintained that this is the result of her teaching or her discipline. On the contrary, everything in her tends to produce saints. Saints are the fruits of the Church; sinners are not her fruits: they are sinners precisely because they choose to put themselves outside the pale of her influence, by refusing to follow her teaching and submit to her laws. In any case, since the human will is free, and since the temptations of "the world, the flesh, and the devil" are very strong, we need not be surprised that sinners should be found in the Church. Our Saviour Himself compared her to a harvest field, in which weeds are intermingled with the wheat (Matt 13:24-42).

VI

EXCURSUS: THE EASTERN CHURCHES

Although not part of Apologetics, it may be fitting here to outline the various Oriental (= Eastern) Churches, both Catholic and non-Catholic. Above, we treated of the Orthodox Church, which is only one portion, albeit the major one, of non-Catholic Eastern Christianity. Here, we propose a fuller scheme of things:[53]

The non-Catholic Eastern Churches.
I.   The Assyrian Church of the East: is not in communion with any other Church. It separated over the Council of Ephesus (held in 431), and used to be called the Nestorian Church. However, it does not hold the heresy known as Nestorianism.
II. The five ancient oriental Churches are each independent but in communion with each other, and have in common that they did not accept the Christological definitions of the Council of Chalcedon (held in 451). They used to be called the Monophysite Churches. However, their doctrine is not monophysite. They are:
     1. The Armenian Apostolic Church
     2. The Coptic Orthodox Church
     3. The Ethiopian Orthodox Church
     4. The Syrian Orthodox Church ("Jacobite")
     5. The Malankara Orthodox Syrian Church
III. The Orthodox Church is a collective term for a variety of national or regional Churches which share the same faith and sacraments, as well as the Byzantine (= Constantinopolitan) liturgical, canonical, and spiritual tradition. They accept the first seven General Councils, up to and including Nicea II (held in 787).
     A.   The Autocephalous Churches (generally accepted as fifteen): The Patriarchates of (1) Constantinople (2) Alexandria (3) Antioch (4) Jerusalem;

---

[53] Cf. R.G. Roberson, *The Eastern Christian Churches: A Brief Survey*, Pont. Oriental Institute, Rome 1993 (4th ed.); Donald Attwater, *The Christian Churches of the East. Vol. 1: Churches in Communion with Rome*, Bruce, Milwaukee 1947.

and the Orthodox Church of (5) Russia (6) Serbia (7) Romania (8) Bulgaria (9) Georgia (10) Cyprus (11) Greece (12) Poland (13) Albania (14) Czech and Slovak Republics; and (15) the Orthodox Church in America.

B.   The Autonomous Churches (each dependent on an autocephalous Church): The Orthodox Church of (1) Mount Sinai (2) Finland (3) Japan (4) China.

C.   Canonical Churches under Constantinople:

(1) American Carpatho-Russian Orthodox Greek Catholic Church   (2) Ukrainian Orthodox Church of America (3) Ukrainian Orthodox Church of Canada   (4) Russian Orthodox Archdiocese in W. Europe   (5) Albanian Orthodox Diocese of America   (6) Byelorussian Council of Orthodox Churches in N. America.

D.   Churches of Irregular Status:

(1) Old Believers (2) Russian Orthodox Church outside Russia (3) Ukrainian Autocephalous Orthodox Church (4) Byelorussian Autocephalous Orthodox Church (5) Macedonian Orthodox Church (6) Old Calendar Orthodox Church (Greece and Romania).

Together the non-Catholic Oriental Christians number about 190 million, of whom about 30 million belong to the five ancient oriental Churches.

The Catholic Eastern Churches.

There are twenty-one Eastern Catholic Churches, all of which are in communion with the Holy See and recognise the Primacy of the Pope. They often used to be called 'Uniate' Churches, a term which they themselves do not use. In 1992, Eastern Catholics numbered about 15 million faithful. Each of these 'sui iuris' ('in its own right; distinct; self-governing') Churches has a liturgical, theological, spiritual and disciplinary patrimony, known as its 'rite'. A 'sui iuris' Church is a community of faithful united by a hierarchy according to the norms of law, and recognised by the supreme authority of the Church (the Pope or a General Council). The second Vatican council decree on Eastern Churches says, "these Churches are of equal rank, so that none of them is superior to the others because of its rite."[54]   All of them fall under the Pope's jurisdiction via the Sacred Congregation for the Oriental Churches, Rome. However, the Pope does not appoint Eastern bishops. Their ecclesial life is governed by the *Code of Canons of the Eastern Churches* promulgated by Pope John Paul II in 1990, and by their own particular laws. They are governed in diverse fashion; six of the twenty-one are headed by a "Patriarch".

The various Churches of the East originate from five ancient traditions:

I.   *Alexandrian:* 1. Coptic 2. Ethiopian
II.   *Antiochian:* 3. Syrian 4. Maronite 5. Syro-Malankara
III.   *Armenian:* 6. Armenian
IV.   *Chaldean:* 7. (Assyro-)Chaldean 8. Syro-Malabar

---

[54] *Orientalium Ecclesiarum*, 1964, art. 3

V. *Byzantine*: 9. Byelorussian 10. Bulgarian 11. Greek 12. Hungarian 13. Italo-Albanian 14. Melkite 15. Romanian 16. Ruthenian 17. Slovak 18. Ukrainian 19. Yugoslavian 20. Albanian 21. Russian.

Of the twenty-one, only the Italo-Albanians and the Maronites have no corresponding Orthodox counterpart. The Maronites have always been in communion with Rome.[55]

Comparison with the West. In the West, there is only one 'sui iuris' Church, known as the Roman, or Latin, or Western, Church. Catholics of the Latin Church number about 990 million. Its Patriarch is the Bishop of Rome, who at the same time enjoys jurisdiction over the whole universal Church. Certain actions the Pope does as Patriarch of the West (issue liturgical directives for the Roman Rite, appoint Western bishops, e.g.); other actions the Pope does in exercise of his office as Supreme Pontiff (issue universal encyclicals, define doctrines, e.g.). On another level, the Pope sometimes acts in his capacity simply as the Bishop of the diocese of Rome, as, for example, when he visits a Roman parish or meets with his auxiliary bishops.

Note on the word "rite". The word "rite" can refer to the *church grouping* as such, or to its particular form of the *liturgy* which might be shared by a number of Churches. For example, the different *Byzantine* Churches follow the same liturgical rite. Within the Latin Church, the *Roman* "rite" of Mass predominates, but there are other "rites" of Mass used by members of the Latin Church: the Mozarabic (used in a part of Spain), the Ambrosian (used in Milan), the Lyonnais (used in Lyons, France), the rite of Braga (in N. Portugal)—and others (such as the Gallican), which have passed into history. There are also variations of the Roman Rite of Mass within medieval religious orders: the Carthusian, Cistercian, Norbertine, Carmelite and Dominican. Official documents now use the word *Church* for the particular body of faithful, and reserve the word *rite* for a particular liturgical and spiritual tradition.

Worldwide statistics on religion.[56] Non-Christian: 1,000 million atheists, or no religion; 1,000 million Moslems; 766 million Hindus; 337m Buddhists; 20m Sikhs; 18.2m Jews of all groups.
    Christian: 1,800 million Christians altogether, of which there are: 1,004 million Catholics, 357m Protestants, 187m Eastern Orthodox, 56m Anglicans, 22m marginal Protestants, 170m Christians with syncretist beliefs (i.e., mixed up with other religions).

---

[55] Bishop P. Dib, *History of the Maronite Church*, (French orig., Beirut 1962, Eng. trans. by Rev. S. Beggiani) Detroit 1971, pp.9-41
[56] Based on *International Bulletin of Missionary Research*, Virginia 1996, ed. by David Barrett.

APOLOGETICS ENDS. CATHOLIC DOCTRINE BEGINS

Our treatise on Apologetics ends with Chapter 10. We have proved that the Catholic Church is the Church of God, i.e., that she speaks to us in His name and with His authority. The argument may be briefly summarised as follows: Jesus Christ put forward the claim that He taught with divine authority, that He was sent by God, that He was God Himself. God showed by miracles, and by the Resurrection especially, that this claim was just. It follows, therefore, that the Church founded by Christ is the Church founded by God. We have established that the Catholic Church alone is identical with the Church of Christ. Hence God, by testifying to the truth of Christ's claim, has testified likewise to the truth of the Catholic Church.

The Catholic Church claims that she has a divine mission and that she teaches with divine authority. As a different form of argument, in Chapter 12 we will show how God has confirmed her claim by the marvels of her worldwide unity, her sanctity, her endurance, her martyrs and abundant miracles.

Both arguments yield the same conclusion—God has revealed that the Catholic Church is His Church. And the certainty of this conclusion is based on the positive action of God, for He has given His positive miraculous support both to the Founder of the Church and to the Church herself. He, the source of all the truth, has shown us the reasonableness of our faith in the Catholic Church. With Richard of St Victor, a great theologian of the twelfth century, we can say: "O Lord! if we are mistaken in our belief, it is Thou who hast led us astray, because this our Faith is proved by signs which Thou alone couldst have worked."[57]

What fruit have we gathered from this study of Catholic Apologetics? It has enabled us to see in a clear vision the extraordinary strength and solidity of the defences of the Church, and the weakness of the arguments alleged against her. It has enabled us to intensify the certainty which we already possessed that our faith in her is reasonable, and it has given us some idea of the divine beauty of the Bride of Christ. As the English martyr-priest St Edmund Campion exclaimed in his famous *Brag* of 1580: "when you shall have heard these questions of religion opened faithfully, which many times by our adversaries are huddled up and confounded, (you) will see upon what substantial grounds our Catholike faith is builded, how feeble that side is which by sway of the time prevaileth against us, and so at last for your

---

[57] *De Trin.*, lib. i., cap. 2

own souls ... will discountenance error when it is bewrayed, and hearken to those who would spend the best blood in their bodies for your salvation."[58]

Once we have made an act of divine faith in the revealed truth that the Catholic Church is the living representative of Christ, we can learn from her the other truths that God has revealed and we can make acts of faith in them. Being infallible, her word or her belief that they have been revealed suffices for a Catholic. He accepts her teaching as the teaching of God and believes it on God's authority. And if he studies his religion in approved textbooks, he will be shown how to meet the objection that the Church's doctrine changes from age to age, or that it is an offence against human reason. He will be shown that through the writings of the Fathers and the books of the New Testament her doctrine can be traced back historically to the days of the Apostles, and that it is either in accordance with reason or never in conflict with it.

In Chapter 11, we deal with the nature and extent of the Church's infallibility. Obviously she is qualified to tell us how she interprets that gift; in which of her members it resides; and from what sources she derives her doctrines. We also give her teaching on the Primacy and the Infallibility of the Pope. In Chapter 12, we review the living marvel of the Church through the ages. In Chapter 13, we present the Church's doctrine regarding her sacred book, the Bible, a chief source of her doctrine and life. In Chapter 14, we set forth her doctrine on the subject of Faith. Though, strictly speaking, Chapters 11, 13 & 14, being a part of Catholic Doctrine, belong to Part II of this work, their close relationship to what has preceded justifies their insertion here. Chapter 11 deals with matters of special interest to the defenders of the Church's claims. Chapter 13 gives the ground rules for understanding and interpreting the Bible, the sacred Book which Catholics and Protestants hold in common, while disagreeing much about its doctrines. Chapter 14 emphasises the truth that only God's grace can build the bridge that leads from the territory of Apologetics to that of Faith.

---

[58] From the *Brag*. full text in *Edmund Campion* by Evelyn Waugh, London 1935.

CHAPTER 11

THE CHURCH'S TEACHING AND GOVERNING AUTHORITY

Summary

I.   The Church's infallibility. Its nature and extent:
- A. The teaching of the Church.
- B. The source of the Church's infallibility.
- C. The subject of the Church's infallibility: the Church Believing, the Church Teaching.
- D. The object of the Church's infallibility: the Deposit of Faith together with all teachings necessary for its custody.

II.   The Primacy of the Pope:
- A. The doctrine of the Primacy defined by the Church.
- B. This doctrine found in Sacred Scripture:
    - (1) The Primacy promised to St Peter: "Thou art Peter", etc.
    - (2) The Primacy conferred on St Peter: "Feed My lambs."
    - (3) Acceptance of the doctrine of the Primacy by the Apostles.
    - (4) This Primacy to be exercised to the end of time.
- C. The Doctrine of the Primacy found in Tradition.

III.   The infallibility of the Pope:
- A. The doctrine of Papal infallibility defined by the Church.
- B. This doctrine found in Scripture.
- C. This doctrine found in Tradition.
- D. Twofold teaching authority of the Pope.

IV.   The authority of Bishops.

V.   The levels of the Magisterium: ordinary and extraordinary; authoritative and infallible.

VI.   Difficulties answered: Claims of erroneous or changed teaching. Some misconceptions removed. Objections answered: cases of Galileo, Liberius, Honorius; pseudo-philosophical objections. The Inquisitions: intolerance and cruelty.

I

THE CHURCH'S INFALLIBILITY: ITS NATURE AND EXTENT

A. **The teaching of the Church.** The Church teaches as of Faith:

(1)   that the Church is infallible (unable to err) in her solemn and her ordinary teaching;[1]

(2)   that her infallibility extends to all that is in Scripture and Tradition;[2]

---

[1] V 3011

[2] T 1507; V 3020

(3)   that her infallibility extends to all that is necessary to guard and explain the Deposit of Faith.[3]

B. **The source of the Church's infallibility**. When Christ commanded His Apostles to teach the whole world and every nation in it, promising to be with them in their work of teaching, "all days, even to the consummation of the world",[4] His command and His promise were addressed not only to them, but also to their lawful successors. He is with them through the Holy Spirit: on the night of His Passion He said, "I will pray the Father, and He will give you another Counsellor"—or Paraclete, i.e., another Comforter, or Helper—"to be with you for ever ... the Spirit of truth ... He dwells with you, and will be in you ... The Holy Spirit, whom the Father will send in My name, He will teach you all things, and bring to your remembrance all that I have said to you."[5]—i.e., 'My entire revelation—all that you shall have heard from Me up to the moment of My Ascension into Heaven.' "When the Spirit of truth comes, He will guide you into all the truth".[6] Hence, by appropriation,[7] the perpetual assistance of the Holy Spirit is named as the Source or Principle of the Church's infallibility.

C. **The subject of the Church's infallibility**. Since the Church founded by Christ is a society consisting both of believers and teachers, the infallibility which He gave her will protect her from error both in belief and in teaching. The members of the Church in whom infallibility resides are called the subject of infallibility. Infallibility resides in what is called the "Church teaching" (*Ecclesia docens*) and the "Church believing." By the "Church teaching" we mean the official teachers of the Church, the successors of the Apostles, viz., the Pope and the Bishops who are united under his leadership. By the "Church believing" we mean the entire body of the faithful who believe their teaching and cannot err as a united body.

THE INFALLIBILITY OF THE CHURCH BELIEVING. The infallibility of the Church believing resides in the entire body of the faithful, yet no individual member of the Church is infallible in belief, not even the Pope himself. He with the Bishops united to him are infallible as *teachers* but not as *believers*. The Pope as a private doctor (*doctor privatus*) can err; he will never, however, bind the faithful to a false belief. "The whole body of the faithful, who have an anointing from the Holy One,[8] cannot err in belief,—and it

---

[3] V 3020, 3042, 3070; DS 3116; C 2035
[4] Matt 28:20 (Douay)
[5] Jn 14:16-17, 26
[6] Jn 16:13
[7] See p.315.
[8] Cf. 1 Jn 2:20.

manifests this characteristic of its own by means of the supernatural sense of the faith (*sensus fidei*) of the whole people, when, 'from the bishops to the last of the faithful'[9] they exhibit their universal consent in matters of faith and morals."[10]

THE INFALLIBILITY OF THE CHURCH TEACHING. The Church may convey her infallible teaching to us either on her *solemn* or her *ordinary* authority. With her *solemn* authority she commands us to believe all doctrines contained in the four Creeds, or expressed in definitions of Popes or General Councils.

Creeds. The Apostles', the Nicene, the Athanasian, and the Creed or Profession of Pius IV. The last-named, issued in 1564, repeats the Nicene Creed and gives a summary of the doctrines defined by the Council of Trent. Pius IX inserted in it an acceptance of the decrees of the Vatican Council, "in particular of those affirming the Primacy and Infallibility of the Roman Pontiff", and Pius X appended to it a solemn repudiation of the errors of Modernism.

General or Ecumenical Council: a meeting of a large number of bishops, representative of the entire Church, assembled at the summons or with the approval of the Pope, and passing doctrinal or disciplinary decrees which he confirms. That the concurrence and approval of the Pope are necessary for the work of a General Council follows from the doctrine of Apostolicity. A local or provincial or particular Council or Synod may have its definitions solemnly approved by the Pope, in which case they acquire a solemn authority. E.g., the decrees of the Second Council of Orange, France, were approved by Pope Boniface II in 531 and given ecumenical authority.

With her *ordinary* authority the Church commands us to believe the doctrine which the Pope and Bishops throughout the world, in the everyday exercise of their pastoral office, unanimously teach as revealed truth.

Not absolute, but practical unanimity, is required. A Bishop teaches his subjects not only personally and by pastoral letters, but through his priests and school teachers and through the catechisms or text-books which he prescribes. The Bishops of the Church are not infallible individually but collectively and as forming a united body with the Pope. It is their living union with him that gives them their infallibility.

DIFFERENCE BETWEEN SOLEMN AND ORDINARY TEACHING. The Church is as infallible in her ordinary teaching as she is in her solemn teaching. The only points of distinction between the two which we need note are: (1) Her solemn teaching is made known at once to all the faithful by a most public

---

[9] St Augustine, *De praed. sanct.* 14, 27
[10] *Lumen Gentium*, Vatican II, Dogmatic Constitution on the Church, 1964, art.12

and solemn declaration, definitively excluding the possibility of holding any contrary doctrine. It is thus a most effective organ of infallibility, a most effective means of combating widespread error. (2) Her ordinary teaching, though less effective as an organ of her infallibility, is of greater importance, because it is her ordinary, everyday means of propagating and preserving the faith, and has gone on without interruption since Apostolic times. (3) Her solemn teaching is of rare occurrence and is never more than a clear and emphatic explanation of doctrines that have always formed part of her ordinary teaching.

ORDINARY TEACHING. Almost all the great doctrines of the Church are taught with her solemn authority. Among those which are proposed to us on her ordinary authority are: (1) the spirituality of the soul; (2) the particular judgement after death; (3) the entrustment of human beings to guardian angels; (4) the evil of murder of an innocent; (5) that it is never permitted to do evil (commit sin) that good might come of it; (6) that Christ is the Founder of the Church; (7) that there will be no new Revelation or Covenant to supersede that of Christ; (8) that the Blessed Virgin Mary is spiritual mother of all Christians.

Most of the above can be found clearly in Sacred Scripture. There are likewise many other affirmations in Sacred Scripture which have not become the object of a solemn definition, since they have been peacefully possessed by the Church and have not required it. For example, the Bible and the Church teach that Jesus Christ is the one and only Saviour of the human race.[11] This doctrine is part of the ordinary, infallible teaching of the Church, and so far has not needed explicit definition.

It may be asked how we are to ascertain what the Church teaches on her ordinary authority. The simplest answer is that the body of it can be found in the *Catechism of the Catholic Church* promulgated by Pope John Paul II. The *Catechism* gives all the chief doctrines of the Church, along with much explanation and illustration. Further explanation of the many points contained in this *Catechism* can be found by consulting the original documents from which much of it is compiled. They are listed at the back of the *Catechism* and are cited in its footnotes.

A Pope or a General Council may propose a doctrine for our acceptance without binding us to an assent of faith. This is usually called "provisional teaching"; see below, "The twofold teaching authority of the Pope" p.196.

D. **The object of the Church's infallibility**. The truths which the Church teaches infallibly are called the object of infallibility. They may be

---

[11] E.g., Jn 14:6; 1 Tim 2:5; Acts 4:12

divided into two classes: (a) all doctrines in the *Deposit of Faith*, i.e., all doctrines delivered by Christ to the Apostles. They are the sum of His public revelation to mankind. Any subsequent revelations which God may grant are private, and form no part of the Deposit of Faith; (b) "secondary objects": all doctrines, or statements, which, though not found in the Deposit of Faith, are necessary for its safe custody because they are presupposed by Revelation or intimately connected to it.

Note that the Church's infallibility extends only to matters of *faith and morals*. It does not include the *discipline* of the Church, i.e., Church-made laws and regulations, particular ceremonial directives and options, and so forth. Needless to say, it does not extend to other *prudential decisions and judgements* of Popes and Bishops, the Holy See's concordats with States, Vatican foreign policy, and so on. That is, the Church is infallible in her *teaching*, but not in the exercise of her *government*.[12]

The Deposit of Faith[13] comprises all doctrines found in the Bible and in Tradition. (1) The Bible consists of the inspired books of the Old and the New Testament; God Himself is its author. (2) Tradition includes the Sacred Scriptures, but also embraces all those truths which, though never committed to writing under divine inspiration, have been handed down within the Church from age to age in various ways. Many of them are found in: (a) the works of the Fathers of the Church, those learned and saintly ecclesiastical writers who lived before A.D. 750 and whose orthodoxy is specially recognised by the Church: Pope St Gregory the Great, the last of the Latin Fathers, died in 604; St John Damascene, the last of the Greek Fathers, died in 749; (b) the Acts of the Martyrs, which record in several instances the express doctrines for which the martyrs suffered; (c) Professions of Faith, and the teaching of Popes and Councils. (d) Many of them also are attested by early paintings and inscriptions, found in the Catacombs and elsewhere; (e) the practices and customs of the Universal Church, as well as the sacred liturgy.

Catholics call the Bible and Tradition "the sources of Faith". They are the two channels by which the doctrine of Christ comes down to us, and the Church is the divinely appointed guardian and interpreter of both: "revelation is transmitted integrally either *in written form or in oral tradition* through the legitimate succession of bishops and above all through the watchful solicitude of the Roman Pontiff himself".[14]

The "primary object of infallibility" is the Deposit of Faith, i.e., all that is in Scripture and Tradition. The Church's "infallibility extends as far as the deposit of

---

[12] Further explained, pp.205-6. Cf. DS 3116.
[13] Cf. 1 Tim 6:20.
[14] *Lumen Gentium*, art. 25, second Vatican Council 1964

divine Revelation; it also extends to all those elements of doctrine, moral doctrine included, without which the saving truths of the faith cannot be preserved, explained, or observed."[15] Examples of such are:

(1) *theological conclusions*, i.e., a conclusion drawn by applying a truth of reason to a doctrine, e.g.- Man's will is free.—Christ is true man.—Therefore Christ's human will was free.

(2) *dogmatic facts*, e.g., the truth of certain historical facts, such as the validity of a Papal election or of a particular General Council; a declaration that a certain proposition is false, or that a certain work contains error. It has been the common teaching of theologians that a canonisation is an infallible proclamation of a dogmatic fact. A canonisation is a solemn declaration that a member of the Church is now in Heaven and is enrolled in the "canon" (official list) of saints, for public veneration and invocation by all the faithful.[16]

(3) *truths of reason* or philosophy, e.g., concerning the knowability of God, the power of the human mind to know truth, the validity and meaning of concepts such as "nature", "person", "substance", which are enshrined and used within defined dogmas.

These elements—or "secondary objects of infallibility"—call for our "definitive assent", our "full and irrevocable acceptance". They are not directly *revealed* truths, but are truths infallibly taught nevertheless. Without them, the Faith cannot stand. (Imagine the havoc wrought to the Faith if someone were to say, for example, "I *would* believe the teaching of the Council of Trent on Original Sin, but I do not believe that Council to be valid.")

II

THE PRIMACY OF THE POPE

A. **The teaching of the Church**. The first Vatican Council (1870) defined:[17]

(1) that Christ appointed St Peter visible Head of the Church;

(2) that St Peter received from Christ a Primacy, not only of honour, but of jurisdiction, i.e., he received from Christ supreme authority to teach and govern the whole Church;

(3) that he has, in virtue of the same divine institution, a perpetual line of successors in the Primacy;

(4) that his successors are the Roman Pontiffs.

---

[15] C 2035; cf. DS 2896, V 3045; L. Ott, *Fundamentals of Catholic Dogma*, Mercier Press, Cork 1957, pp.8-9. Cf. *Doctrinal Commentary* on the *Professio Fidei*, art. 11, Congregation for the Doctrine of the Faith, 1998.

[16] Cf. C 828.

[17] V 3055, 3058, 3064

Christ Himself is the invisible Head of the Church. All power in the Church is derived from Him. He will remain with it forever, guiding, governing, and supporting it.

As stated above, when the Church solemnly defines a doctrine, she simply declares that it is revealed by God, i.e., that it is part of the teaching delivered by Christ to the Apostles, that it has always been believed by the faithful, and that it is found in Scripture or Tradition, or in both together. This *infallible* statement is sufficient for a Catholic. Now certain that God has revealed the doctrine, he believes it on God's authority. The following demonstrations are offered simply for fuller instruction.

B. The doctrine of the Primacy is found in Scripture.

(1) THE PRIMACY PROMISED TO ST PETER. Peter's original name was Simon. It was Our Lord who gave him a new name to express his new mission: "Jesus looked at him, and said, 'So you are Simon the son of John? You shall be called Cephas' (which means Peter)."[18] "Cephas" meant *rock* in Aramaic, and "Peter" was the same in Greek. When Christ said to His disciples, "Who do you say that I am?" Simon Peter answered, "You are the Christ, the Son of the living God." And Jesus said to him, "Blessed are you, Simon Bar-Jona! ... And I tell you, You are Peter [i.e., the Rock], and on this rock I will build My Church, and the powers of death shall not prevail against it. I will give you the keys of the Kingdom of Heaven, and whatever you bind on earth shall be bound in heaven, and whatever you loose on earth shall be loosed in heaven."[19] The text must be interpreted as follows:

(a) Christ compares His Church to a house which shall be built on a rock. As the rock gives stability to the house,[20] so shall St Peter give stability to the Church, the divine edifice, and be its foundation and support. He shall make the Church proof against all assaults, and so firm, that the gates of hell—i.e., death, the power of its enemies—shall never destroy it. The sustaining strength of St Peter, therefore, shall be felt in every part of the Church and by every member of it without exception. In a society, it is the Supreme Authority which gives stability, hence St Peter's office in the Church shall be that of Supreme Authority. He shall shield the Church from the great evil of heresy: he shall, therefore, be the teacher of the entire Church, and shall never teach any doctrine but the true doctrine of Christ. He shall shield the Church from the great evil of schism: he shall be the ruler of the entire Church, never tolerating a rival authority, never allowing the Church to break up into independent sections. He shall cast out the

---

[18] Jn 1:42
[19] Matt 16:15-19
[20] Matt 7:25 "the house did not fall, because it had been founded on the rock."

188

heretical and the rebellious, and hold the faithful firmly together, one in faith and obedience.

(b) The promise of the Primacy is directly stated in the words: "I will give you the keys of the Kingdom of Heaven", i.e., the keys of the Church. The keys were regarded by the Jews, as they are regarded by us, as a symbol of ownership or supreme authority. He who holds the keys is the master of the house. St Peter, therefore, shall be master or ruler of the Church.

(c) He shall receive the powers of "binding" and "loosing", i.e., he shall have power to issue decrees; to make laws or annul them; to judge, condemn, or acquit; to grant or withhold absolution from sin. The same powers of binding and loosing are, indeed, promised to all the Apostles in Matthew 18:18, but because they were first promised to St Peter, the rock and the holder of the keys, it is clear that his fellow-Apostles are to exercise them subordinately to his authority. We make a like comment on the words of St Paul that the Church is built "upon the foundation of the Apostles."[21] It is built on them as forming a united body under the Primacy of St Peter.

(2) THE PRIMACY CONFERRED ON ST PETER AND HIS SUCCESSORS. Christ promised the Primacy to St Peter on hearing him make a profession of faith in His Divinity. He fulfils the promise on hearing him make a triple protestation of love for Him. "Feed My lambs", He said to Peter, "tend My sheep."[22] St Peter was thus made shepherd of the whole flock of Christ. Christ had spoken of Himself as the Good Shepherd, the "lambs and the sheep" being the Apostles and all others who believed in Him. But now He makes St Peter the Good Shepherd in His stead. All, including the Apostles, are to listen to his teaching and obey his commands. This Primacy, like the Church herself, must last until the end of time, and must, therefore, be passed on to successors of Peter.

(3) THE DOCTRINE OF THE PRIMACY WAS ACCEPTED BY THE APOSTLES. The Primacy of Peter was taken for granted in the Apostolic college. He is always mentioned first in the lists of the Apostles, although he was not the first whom Christ called. He proposes the election of the successor to Judas. He preaches the first Apostolic sermon on the feast of Pentecost, and he works the first Apostolic miracle in the name of Jesus. He receives the first Jewish converts and the first Gentile converts into the Church, declaring that salvation is for all men alike. At the council of Jerusalem,

---

[21] Eph 2:20
[22] Jn 21:15-17

"after there had been much debate", he gives the discussion a decisive turn and draws the others with him. All this points clearly to the conclusion that St Peter was recognised as the head of the Apostles.[23]

(4) THIS PRIMACY IS TO BE EXERCISED TO THE END OF TIME. ST PETER'S OFFICE IN THE CHURCH IS PERPETUAL. (a) The 'lambs' and 'sheep', i.e., the members of the Church, shall always need the shepherd's care to shield them from the wolf and lead them to wholesome pastures. Their shepherd, therefore, St Peter, through his successors, shall always be with them. (b) The Church, *and, with it, its foundation and support*, is to last until the end of time. St Peter, therefore, through his successors, shall always be with the Church, guarding its life, and giving it strength to withstand its enemies. He, through them, shall be the source of its imperishability. And who is his successor? The successor of St Peter is the Bishop of Rome, the city where Simon Peter was martyred about 70 A.D. and buried under the site of what is now St Peter's Basilica.[24]

C. **The doctrine of the Primacy is found in Tradition.** (1) *From the 5th century onward* the Primacy of the Pope as the successor of St Peter was universally admitted. At the Council of Ephesus in 431, Philip, the Legate of Pope Celestine (422-432), said, and no voice was raised in protest: "No one doubts, nay but all ages know, that the holy and most blessed Peter, prince and head of the Apostles, the pillar of faith and the foundation of the Church, received from Our Lord, Jesus Christ, the keys of the Kingdom ... His successor in order, and the holder of his place, our holy and most blessed Pope, Celestine ... has sent me".[25]

St Cyril of Alexandria (d. 444), pre-eminent among the Eastern Patriarchs, said that Pope Celestine was "the chief Bishop of the whole world."[26]

At the Council of Chalcedon in 451, when the letter of Pope Leo I (440-461) had been read, the assembled bishops cried out: "Peter has spoken through Leo."[27]

(2) *In the 4th century*, the evidence, though less in volume, is equally decisive. At the Synod of Aquileia in 381, St Ambrose tells the Emperors, "the Roman Church is the head of the whole Roman world."[28]

"I speak", said St Jerome to Pope Damasus (366-384), "with the successor of the fisherman and the disciple of the cross. Following no one as my chief but

---

[23] Lk 6:14; Acts 1:15; 2:14, 41; 3:6; 10:1-48; 15:6 ff.

[24] Cf. J.E. Walsh *The Bones of St Peter*, Doubleday, N.Y. 1982, for an account of the discovery in the 20th century of the ancient tomb and bones of St Peter under the basilica after the archæological investigations which began there under Pope Pius XII.

[25] Mansi, IV, 1294

[26] PG 77, 1040

[27] Act. II: Harduin, II, 306

[28] *Ep.* xi, 4

Christ, I am joined in communion with Your Beatitude, that is, with the See of Peter. I know that on that rock the Church is built."[29]

St Basil urges the same Pope to deal with troubles that had arisen in the Churches of Asia Minor. He adds that he requests nothing new, and quotes as a precedent for the Pope's intervention the action of his predecessor Pope Dionysius (259-269).[30]

The Emperor Constantine sent the Donatist schismatics to Rome, to be judged by Pope Melchiades (310-14).[31]

Optatus of Milevis (c. 370) says Siricius succeeds on the one throne that St Peter sat on first, and he "is our comrade today, with whom, together with us, the whole world agrees in the society of one communion, by exchange of letters."[32]

At the Council of Nicea in 325, Hosius of Cordova "held the place of the Bishop of Rome, with the priests Vito and Vincent." He signed first, "in the name of the Church and Rome, the Churches of Italy, Spain and the West."[33]

Carvings and ornamentations in the Catacombs dating from this century represent St Peter as the Moses of the New Testament receiving the New Law from Christ; and Moses as the Peter of the Old Testament. Peter was the leader of the Christians, as Moses was the leader of the Jews.[34] It has been calculated that there are more than three hundred representations of St Peter in the early Christian art of the catacombs—a number exceeded only by depictions of Christ Himself.[35]

(3) *In the 3rd century*, St Cyprian (d. 258) says there is "one Church founded by Christ our Lord on Peter, by the source and reason of unity."[36] He says the Roman See is "mother and root of the Catholic Church".[37] He speaks of those who "bring letters to the throne of Peter and the chief Church, whence priestly unity came forth."[38] Tertullian c. 200 writes, "Was anything hidden from Peter who was named as the rock on which the Church was to be built, and who possessed the keys of the Kingdom of Heaven together with the power of binding and loosing in heaven and on earth?"[39]

Other testimonies could be adduced from matters arising with Pope Zephyrinus (199-217), Tertullian (d. c. 220),[40] Pope Callistus (217-22),[41] and Dionysius of Alexandria (d. c. 264).[42]

---

[29] *Ep.* xv, ad Damasum, 2: PL 22, 355-6

[30] *Ep.* lxx: PG 32, 435; cf. *Ep.* lxix, 1: PG 32, 431.

[31] Cf. Eusebius, *Hist. Eccl.*, X, c. 5, §§18-20.

[32] Opt. Mil., II, c. 3

[33] Mansi, II, 805; II, 692, 697

[34] L. Hertling S.J. & E. Kirschbaum S.J., *The Roman Catacombs and their Martyrs*, DLT, London 1960, p.243. Cf. photo in the *Catechism*, preceding #1691.

[35] Hertling & Kirschbaum, *op. cit.*, p.243

[36] *Ep.* lxx, 3 (ed. Hartel)

[37] *Ep.* xlviii, 3

[38] *Ep.* lix, 14

[39] *De Praescriptione*, 22

[40] *Adv. Prax.*, I; *De Pudic.*, I, 21

[41] *Philosophumena*, IX, 12

(4) *In the 2nd century* the evidence is not so clear, because the Church suffered much from persecution, and communication with the Pope was difficult; and because circumstances provided little occasion for the exercise of the Papal prerogative. There was, however, a development in government as well as in matters of faith. Opposition, as it arose from time to time, called forth a more explicit statement of doctrine, and a clearer enunciation of the relations of the Pope to the universal Church. Let us quote St Irenaeus (d. c. 202), who speaks of "the greatest and oldest Church known to all, founded and established by the two most glorious apostles, Peter and Paul, at Rome".[43]

Pope Victor I of Rome (189-99) had considered excommunicating the Quartodecimans in Asia for what he regarded as dissident behaviour, but St Irenaeus, among others, urged him not to, without calling into question his power to do so.[44]

St Ignatius of Antioch (d. 107), in his epistle to the Romans, speaks of the Church which, "presides in the land of the Romans ... presiding over love" - "love" being his name for the Church.[45] He also refers to Peter's authority in Rome, by saying, in the same letter, "I am not commanding you as did Peter and Paul."[46]

(5) *Even in the 1st century*, this primacy was exercised: the remarkable fact is that, while St John the Apostle was probably still living in Ephesus, Pope Clement in Rome, about the year 96, writes, *as one commanding*, to the Church of Corinth in Greece, and tells them, "If any disobey what He (Christ) says through us, let them know that they will be involved in no small offence and danger; but we shall be innocent of this sin".[47]

In conclusion, we note: (a) that the belief in the Primacy of the Pope, universal in the 5th century and distinctly expressed in the 4th and earlier, if it is not as old as the Church, must have been fraudulently invented during the ages of persecution; in other words, either we must admit the Apostolic origin of the doctrine, or else maintain the gross absurdity that it was forged at a time when the chief office among Christians was the surest road to martyrdom; (b) that, since the Church is infallible, a doctrine universally taught and believed at any time as part of the faith of the Church must be true; and (c) that St Peter must always have a living successor to act as the supporting Rock of the Church; that this living successor must be none other than the Bishop of Rome, for he alone of all the bishops in Christendom has ever claimed the title.

On the basis of this overwhelming evidence, we may appreciate the dictum of Cardinal Newman: "To be deep in history is to cease to be a Protestant."[48]

---

[42] Athanasius, *Ep. de sent. Dionysi*, 13: PG 25, 499
[43] *Adv. Haer.* III, 3, 2
[44] Eusebius, *Hist. Eccl.*, V, c. 24, §§9, 12-17
[45] *Ad Rom.*, salut. Cf. *Trall.* xiii, 1.
[46] *Ad Rom.*, 4,3
[47] *I Clem. ad Cor.* 59, 1
[48] *An Essay on the Development of Christian Doctrine*, 1845, Rev. ed. 1878, Intro., 5, p.8

III

THE INFALLIBILITY OF THE POPE

A. The teaching of the Church on Papal infallibility.
The doctrine defined by the first Vatican Council may be briefly stated as follows: The Pope is infallible when he speaks *ex cathedra*, i.e., when, as Pastor and Teacher of all Christians, he defines, in virtue of his supreme Apostolic authority, a doctrine concerning faith or morals to be held by the Universal Church.

The full text says, "it is a divinely revealed dogma that when the Roman Pontiff speaks *ex cathedra*—i.e., when exercising his office as pastor and teacher of all Christians, he defines, by his supreme Apostolic authority, a doctrine concerning faith or morals which must be held (*tenenda*) by the universal Church—he enjoys, through divine assistance, that infallibility promised to him in blessed Peter and with which the divine Redeemer wanted His Church to be endowed in defining doctrine concerning faith or morals; and therefore that the definitions of the same Roman Pontiff are irreformable of themselves and not from the consent of the Church. If anyone should presume however to contradict this Our definition—which may God forbid—let him be anathema."[49]

Hence, there are four conditions for the exercise of Papal infallibility, which we may summarise under the headings of (1) office, or *subject* of infallibility (2) mode, or *act* of speaking infallibly (3) content, or *object* of infallibility, and (4) recipient.[50]

(1) Office: the Pope must be speaking *ex cathedra*, i.e., from his position as *Supreme* or *Universal* Pastor,—not simply as a private theologian, or Bishop of the diocese of Rome, or Sovereign of Vatican City State, or Archbishop and Metropolitan of the Roman Province, or Primate of Italy, or Patriarch of the West.
(2) Mode: he must be *defining* a doctrine, not merely expounding, commenting, observing, exhorting or discussing, etc. In defining, he conclusively pronounces a doctrine with precision and certainty, enunciating it as a final and definitive judgement of truth, to the exclusion of alternatives and the elimination of doubt. No special formula is required for a definition; nor is it necessary to attach an anathema; nor does the Pope have to say—just as no Pope ever has—that he is speaking infallibly.

---

[49] DS 3074-5. For a full explanation of this definition, the theologian can consult Fr. J.T. O'Connor, *The Gift of Infallibility*, St Paul's ed., Boston 1986, which contains an English translation of the discourse given by the *Relator*, Bishop V. Gasser, who presented and explained the proposed text to the Fathers of Vatican I.
[50] The three words in italics are used by Bishop Gasser. See Fr. O'Connor, *op. cit.*, pp.45-6.

(3) Content: the doctrine must concern *faith* or *morals*. It need not be a *revealed* doctrine; it may be something already known by human reason, e.g., the immortality of the soul; a point of the natural law such as the evil of murder, theft, etc.[51]
(4) Recipient: it must be addressed to *all* the Church, not merely one segment of her.

In a way, (4) can be subsumed within (1), for the Pope necessarily addresses *all* the faithful when he speaks by virtue of his *supreme* office. Reducing these conditions to the first three only, Vatican II summarises the doctrine thus: "The Roman Pontiff, head of the college of bishops, enjoys this infallibility in virtue of his office, when, as supreme pastor and teacher of all the faithful (=1)—who confirms his brethren in the faith—he proclaims by a definitive act (=2) a doctrine concerning faith or morals (=3)."[52]

In order to express the doctrine in a way that helps prevent misunderstanding, rather than say that the Pope *is* infallible (which can sound like he always is), we should say that the Pope *can speak* infallibly.

Strictly speaking, a doctrine is not itself "infallible"; a doctrine is either *true* or *false*. Infallibility belongs to *persons*; by extension we apply the word "infallible" to the *doctrines* they enunciate.

B. The doctrine of Papal infallibility is found in Scripture.
(1) St Peter, always living in his successors, is the rock on which the Church is built. He shall, through the assistance of Christ, always with him, save the Church from heresy.[53] He, the one and only source of stability, cannot be a false or doubtful guide. He must, therefore, be able to speak infallibly.
(2) Christ gave to St Peter and his successors "the keys of the Kingdom of Heaven." He thereby gave them the power of binding the consciences of men. He promised that whatever obligations they might impose would be confirmed in heaven. In other words, He promised to support and guide them in teaching the truth so that they would only impose a just obligation. But the Head of the Church is the chief teacher of the Church and, from time to time, binds all the faithful to believe his teaching with an assent of faith. Since, from the promise of Christ, he cannot bind them to error, he must himself be secured against error in his teaching: he must, when binding all the faithful, be infallible.

---

[51] The definition of Vatican I uses the word *tenenda* (requiring to be held), used for *any* truth to be held; not *credenda* (requiring to be believed), a word reserved for *revealed* truths. *Id.* pp.68-9, 76, 82-3
[52] *Lumen Gentium*, Vatican II, Dogmatic Constitution on the Church, 1964, art. 25. Canon 749 §1 adopts this very text.
[53] See above, pp. 188-90.

194

(3) The Pope is the Pastor of the Universal Church. "Feed My lambs", said Christ to St Peter, "feed My sheep." He has the command of Christ to feed all the faithful with spiritual nurture, to teach them all the doctrines of Christ, to administer to them the sacred rites which Christ instituted, to govern them in the form, and under the laws, prescribed by Christ. But, if the Pope were to err in his *ex cathedra* teaching, he would not be the pastor, but the poisoner, of his flock. Therefore, he must possess infallibility on those solemn occasions.

(4) Christ said to St Peter, "Simon, Simon, behold, Satan demanded to have *you* [plural], that he might sift *you* [pl.] like wheat, but I have prayed for *thee* [singular] that *thy* faith may not fail; and when *thou* hast turned again, confirm *thy* brethren."[54] Christ says that the Apostles would be assaulted by Satan, but He had prayed that St Peter's faith in particular should not fail, and His prayer was effective. He as Man had uttered a request which He as God had already decided to grant. This is clear from the command He gave to St Peter to confirm the others in the faith. Equivalently, His words would run: *"with the faith I have gained for thee, confirm thy brethren."* St Peter, therefore, was made infallible. He was to use his gift of infallibility to shield the faith of his brethren from the assaults of Satan. His office passed to his successors. As long as the Church exists, it will be assailed by the enemy of truth. It will, therefore, always need an unerring guide, a Peter living in his successors who shall confirm his brethren.

(5) Independently of the text, "Thou art Peter", etc., we proved that the Church is infallible.[55] But, in an infallible Church, the supreme judge of doctrine must be infallible when giving final judgement. The Pope is the supreme judge of doctrine because, as the supreme ruler, his decision on all questions affecting the teaching, the governing, or the sanctifying office of the Church, must be final. As Vatican I says, it is the infallibility *of the Church* that the Roman Pontiff possesses, when he speaks *ex cathedra*.

Although Christ made all the original Apostles infallible, St Peter alone was to transmit his infallibility to his successors. The idea, taught by some Protestants, that St Peter's infallibility, like that of the other Apostles, was a personal prerogative, and therefore intransmissible, is irreconcilable with any reasonable interpretation of the text.

C. **The doctrine of Papal infallibility is found in Tradition.**
The voice of tradition, as in the case of the Primacy, grows clearer with the progress of the centuries.

(1) *Towards the end of the 2nd century*, St Irenaeus (d. c. 202) praises the See of Rome as "the greatest and oldest Church known to all", and says, "For to this Church,

---

54 Lk 22:31-32 (RSV, adapted)
55 See pp. 146-7.

because of her mightier rule, every Church must resort [or, must agree], that is, those who are faithful from all sides".[56] He also lists the succession in the Church of Rome: he lists Peter, Linus, Anencletus, Clement, Evaristus, Alexander, Sixtus, Telesphorus, Hyginus, Pius, Anicetus, Soter, "and now, in the twelfth place after the Apostles ... Eleutherus." Irenaeus concludes, "In this order, and by the teaching of the Apostles handed down in the Church, the preaching of the truth has come down to us."[57]

(2) *About the beginning of the 3rd century*, Pope Zephyrinus condemns the Montanists, who thenceforward are regarded as outcasts from the Church. (They led an apocalyptic movement, with severe moral teaching, claiming a new coming of the Holy Spirit was imminent). St Cyprian (d. 258) says the African schismatics, "had not considered that the Romans are those whose faith is praised by the Apostle [Paul], to whom perfidy cannot have access."[58]

(3) *In the 4th century*, the Synod of Milan, about the year 389, was equally aware of the impossibility of Rome's erring in the faith: "let them believe the Apostles' creed, which the Roman Church always keeps and preserves incorrupt."[59] Pope St Julius remonstrated in 342 with the Eusebians: "Why were we not written to concerning the Church of Alexandria? Or are you ignorant that this has been the custom first to write to us, and then what is just shall be decreed from this place ... For what we have received from the blessed Apostle Peter, that I make known to you."[60]

(4) *In the 5th century*, the bishops at the Council of Chalcedon (451) in the words already quoted said, "This is the faith of the Fathers; this is the faith of the Apostles. We all believe thus; the orthodox believe thus. Anathema to whoever does not so believe. Peter has spoken through Leo."[61]

From this century onward the doctrine was universally acknowledged in the practical life of the Church. It was accepted at the third Council of Constantinople (680-681), and all but defined in express terms by the Council of Florence (1438-1445), which declared that "the Roman Pontiff is the successor of blessed Peter, Prince of the Apostles and the true Vicar of Christ, the head of the whole Church, the father and teacher of all Christians, and that to him, in blessed Peter, there was given by Our Lord Jesus Christ full power to feed, rule and govern the universal Church."[62]

D. **Twofold teaching authority of the Pope**. The Pope does not always speak with his charism of infallibility. He possesses a twofold teaching

---

56 *Adv. Haer.*, III, 3, 2. In either interpretation the words refer to a higher doctrinal authority.
57 *Adv. Haer.*, III, 3, 3
58 *Ep.* lix, 14: CSEL, III, p.683
59 Ambrose, *Ep.* xlii, 5
60 Athanasius, *Apologia contra Arianos*, 21, 33
61 Act. II: Harduin, II, 306
62 DS 1307. For a full series of ancient texts regarding Papal primacy and jurisdiction see J. Shotwell and L. R. Loomis, *The See of Peter*, Columba University Press, N.Y., 1927, 1991.

authority, viz., supreme or infallible, and ordinary. When he employs his ordinary authority, he is authoritative but not infallible and does not, of course, bind us to an assent of faith or an irrevocable assent. He does not bind the Church solemnly in an address intended for a particular audience or in teaching contained in an Encyclical Letter which is only incidental to the main theme. Still, we must give his ordinary teaching an interior, religious assent.[63] The obligation arises (1) from the obedience which we owe, as dutiful children, to lawful ecclesiastical authority, and (2) from prudence, which forbids us to set our opinion against the great authority of the Pope, familiar, as he must be, with the traditions of the Church, and aided, as he is, by the counsel of eminent theologians. Should it happen— in the nature of things, it must happen rarely—that learned Catholics see, or think they see, grave reasons for doubting some point in the ordinary teaching of His Holiness, they may represent their views to him, but must do so privately, respectfully, and with a profession of complete willingness to accept his final ruling in the proper spirit of obedience.[64] Vatican II gives three indications of the degree of authority enjoyed by statements of the ordinary Papal magisterium: one ought "sincerely adhere to decisions made by [the Pope], conformably with his manifest mind and intention, which is made known principally either by the *character of the documents* in question, or by the *frequency* with which a certain doctrine is proposed, or by the *manner* in which the doctrine is formulated."[65] Pope Pius XII reminded Catholics that Our Lord's declaration to the Apostles, "He who hears you hears Me",[66] is valid also for the ordinary teaching of the Popes. So, he said, "When the Supreme Pontiffs in their acts intentionally pronounce a judgement on a hitherto disputed point, then it is clear to all that, according to the intention and will of these Popes, the matter can no longer be held to be a question for free discussion among theologians."[67] The authority of the Pope's teaching is not based on his argumentation. He may or may not use the best arguments, and we may or may not have the education to appreciate his reasons. But even if his exposition is faultless, arguments are always convincing to some and obscure to others. We are not bound to accept the arguments as such, but the conclusions and doctrines proposed for belief.

The Pope teaches the Church with his ordinary authority either directly, or through one of the Roman Congregations, i.e., through one of the committees of qualified ecclesiastics who assist him in his work. The Congregation for the Doctrine of the Faith (formerly known as the Holy

---

[63] Cf. *Lumen Gentium*, art. 25.
[64] This sentence stands as Dr Sheehan wrote it for the 1939 edition.
[65] *Lumen Gentium*, art. 25
[66] Lk 10:16
[67] *Humani Generis*, 1950: DS 3885

Office) is concerned with doctrine. It issues documents and statements on doctrinal and moral issues, with the authority and approval of the Pope. The Pontifical Biblical Commission, founded in 1902, ceased being an organ of the magisterium in 1971 and was made purely advisory.[68]

Note that the ordinary teaching of the *Pope* is to be carefully distinguished from the ordinary teaching of the *Church*. As explained above, the *Church* is infallible in all her teaching whether Solemn or Ordinary.

Extent of Papal infallibility. Papal infallibility, like that of the Church, extends only to faith and morals, but not to government. "These examples of human weakness are rare on the chair of St Peter; but history records them, and the Church's children have no reason to cover them up, since they know that He who has assured the Roman Pontiffs of infallibility in teaching of the faith, has not at all protected them from every defect in the exercise of the supreme government".[69]

Bad Popes. The Pope himself may give bad example and even scandal to the Church. He may compromise with her enemies and mislead the faithful. Sacred Scripture records how the first Pope, St Peter, compromised with Christians who were insisting upon Jewish practices, and was rightly and publicly rebuked by St Paul.[70] However, the number of bad Popes is surprisingly low. Of the 264 popes up to John Paul II, more than eighty are canonised saints and only about six were bad Popes who led immoral lives, so that Dr Rumble observes, "the proportion of Popes who have been really unworthy of their office works out at about one in forty, whereas the proportion of failures among the apostles chosen by Christ Himself was one in twelve."[71]

Provisional teaching. Apart from teaching timeless doctrine as such, "the Magisterium can intervene in disputed questions that involve, in addition to fixed principles, certain conjectural and contingent elements".[72] On those occasions, "The willingness to give sincere submission to this teaching of the Magisterium in matters not *per se* irreformable must be the rule."[73] This is the submission required, e.g., when the Holy Office (Congregation for the Doctrine of the Faith) gives an answer to a 'loaded question' (i.e., loaded

---

[68] Paul VI, *Sedula Cura*, 1971
[69] *Institutions Liturgiques*, Dom Prosper Guéranger OSB (1805-75), Vol. III, ch. iii
[70] Gal 2:11-16; cf. Acts 10:9-11:18.
[71] Leslie Rumble MSC, *Questions People Ask*, Chevalier Books, Sydney 1972, p.148
[72] *Donum Veritatis*, "The Ecclesial Vocation of the Theologian", Congregation for the Doctrine of the Faith, 1990, art. 24
[73] Ibid. 24

with stated presuppositions) or says that X "may not be held safely" or "taught safely."

Discipline. "… decisions of the Magisterium in matters of discipline, even though they do not enjoy the charism of infallibility, are not therefore devoid of divine assistance, but call for the adherence of Christ's faithful."[74] Such adherence requires obedience, but not necessarily agreement with the point of discipline.

IV

THE AUTHORITY OF THE BISHOPS

The Bishops, Successors of the Apostles. The Pope, the Bishop of Rome, is the successor of St Peter; the bishops, not taken singly, but collectively and in union with the Pope, are the successors of the other Apostles. The Pope receives his authority directly from Christ; the bishops receive their authority from the same divine source, upon their consecration as bishop. The Pope is the supreme pastor; they retain their divine authority as long as they remain loyal to the Holy See (Rome). The bishops of the Western Church are generally appointed by the Pope. In the East, bishops are appointed under the procedures proper to each Eastern Church.

The nature of their authority. A Bishop, on taking possession of the diocese assigned to him, becomes the spiritual ruler and teacher of its Catholic inhabitants. He can make laws and regulations for his subjects, and he is their authentic teacher on faith and morals. As an individual, he is not indeed infallible, yet this will cause no anxiety to his people who know that, in the case of error, a higher authority or the supreme head of the Church can intervene to protect them. But pending an appeal to a senior Bishop, such as a Patriarch or Pope, the clergy and the laity are bound to obey their Bishop, because he has authority (1) to teach Catholic Doctrine, and (2) to decide whether any particular question belongs to the sphere of faith or morals. To deny him this latter power would be tantamount to asserting the Protestant claim to the right of private judgement. "Bishops who teach in communion with the Roman Pontiff are to be revered by all as witnesses of divine and Catholic truth; the faithful, for their part, are obliged to submit to their bishops' decision, made in the name of Christ, in matters of faith and morals, and to adhere to it with a religious submission

---

[74] *Donum Veritatis*, 17

of mind.”[75]   In ecclesiastical matters, St Thomas says, “one who is not an equal can reprove privately and respectfully. … It must be known, however, that where there is an imminent danger to the faith, prelates [bishops] must be rebuked even publicly by subjects. Hence, even Paul, who was subject to Peter, rebuked him in public, on account of the imminent danger of scandal concerning the faith”.[76] St Thomas also says, “it is better for a prelate to be deposed or a deacon cut off from the Church, than the Church be scandalised.”[77]

The authority to teach and govern is called Jurisdiction. A Bishop’s jurisdiction extends only to his own subjects and diocese; that of the Pope extends to the universal Church.

V

THE LEVELS OF THE MAGISTERIUM

The levels of the Church’s Magisterium (Teaching Authority).[78] The Pope and Bishops are the divinely ordained teachers of Christ’s faithful, and hold the office of the Magisterium or Teaching Authority in the Church. However, they do not always act at the same level of authority or call upon the fulness of their office whenever they proclaim Christian doctrine. They may act and teach at different levels according to the needs of the Church, their own intentions, and the solemnity desired. When they exercise their magisterium in an ordinary fashion, they must receive a religious assent from the people. When the Pope and Bishops exercise their magisterium in unison at an ordinary level, or at an extraordinary level, they must receive an unconditional assent, for at those times they *infallibly* speak the truths of the Christian religion.

The following table sets forth these various levels and required responses. It is based on the second Vatican Council’s dogmatic constitution on the Church, *Lumen Gentium*, art. 25 (quoted below), and should be read in conjunction with it.

Vatican I says, “by divine and Catholic faith, all those things must be believed which are contained in the written word of God or in Tradition, and are proposed by the Church—either in a solemn decree, or in her ordinary and universal magisterium—to be believed as divinely revealed.”[79] This corresponds to levels 3, 4 & 5 in the table. A teaching declared to be revealed requires “divine and Catholic faith”—*divine*, because it is based on faith in God who reveals, and *Catholic*,

---

[75] *Lumen Gentium,* art. 25

[76] S.T., ii-ii, q. 33, a. 4, ad 2

[77] *Lectura super Matt.* 18:9, n. 1500

[78] In this section we re-present and make a resumé of many points already made in this chapter.

[79] DS 3011

because it is based on faith in the Catholic Church which declares that God has so revealed. A "heretic", strictly speaking, is someone who obstinately denies, or places in doubt, such a teaching (nos. 3, 4 & 5).[80] Such an obstinate denial or doubt is a mortal sin and puts one outside the Church.

Teacher:	Level of Magisterium:	Degree of certitude:	Assent required:
1. Bishops	Ordinary	Authoritative	Religious submission of intellect and will
2. Pope	Ordinary	Authoritative	Religious submission of intellect and will
3. Bishops proposing definitively, dispersed, but in unison, in union with Pope	Ordinary and universal teaching of the Church	Infallible	Faith
4. Bishops, in union with Pope, defining doctrine at General Council	Extraordinary (and universal teaching of the Church)	Infallible	Faith
5. Pope *ex cathedra*	Extraordinary (and universal)	Infallible	Faith

"Extraordinary" teaching (nos. 4 & 5) is also known as "solemn" teaching, or doctrine defined *de fide* (as of faith, belonging to faith). Ordinary and universal teaching (no. 3) is not said to be defined, but is equally *de fide*.

A denial of any doctrine contained in Scripture or Tradition, whether or not the Church has explicitly declared it to be revealed, is an "error in faith" and is mortally sinful.

At nos. 3, 4, & 5, faith is demanded if the doctrine is part of the Deposit of Faith. But if the doctrine is not revealed, but only connected to Revelation, "definitive assent" is demanded. This is the assent given to the "secondary objects of infallibility".[81] A denial of any "secondary object of infallibility" taught at levels 3, 4 & 5 is an "error", a "denial of Catholic doctrine", entails loss of full communion with the Church, and is similarly a mortal sin.[82] Definitive assent is given to such teachings because it *is a consequence of our faith* in the Holy Spirit's assistance to the "Church of the living God, the pillar and bulwark of the truth."[83]

Nos. 3, 4, & 5 are called "universal" because they are directed to the Church universally, not just a particular segment of her. At times, no. 2 may be directed to the universal Church, e.g., encyclicals addressed to the whole Church.

Synonymous with "infallible" are such terms as: irreformable, irreversible, definitive, irrevocable.

---

[80] Can. 751
[81] See above, pp.186-7
[82] Cf. Can. 750 §2, 752, 1371 §1; *Ad Tuendam Fidem*, art. 4, Pope John Paul II, 1998, & accompanying *Doctrinal Commentary* on the *Professio Fidei*, Congregation for the Doctrine of the Faith, 1998.
[83] 1 Tim 3:15

The following quotations from *Lumen Gentium*, art. 25, given in their original order, illustrate each of the five rows in turn:[84]

(1) "Bishops who teach in communion with the Roman Pontiff are to be revered by all as witnesses of divine and Catholic truth; the faithful, for their part, are obliged to submit to their bishops' decision, made in the name of Christ, in matters of faith and morals, and to adhere to it with a religious submission of mind."

(2) "This religious submission of the will and intellect must be given, in a special way, to the authoritative magisterium[85] of the Roman Pontiff, even when he does not speak *ex cathedra* in such wise, indeed, that his supreme magisterium be acknowledged with respect, and that one sincerely adhere to decisions made by him, according to his manifest mind and intention…".

(3) "Although the bishops, taken individually, do not enjoy the privilege of infallibility, they do, however, proclaim infallibly the doctrine of Christ on the following conditions: namely, when—though dispersed throughout the world but preserving the bond of communion amongst themselves and with Peter's successor—they are in agreement, in their authoritative teaching concerning matters of faith and morals, that a particular teaching is to be held definitively."

(4) "This is still more clearly the case when, assembled in an Ecumenical Council, they are, for the universal Church, teachers and judges in matters of faith and morals, whose decisions must be adhered to with the submission of faith."

(5) "The Roman Pontiff, head of the college of bishops, enjoys this infallibility in virtue of his office, when, as supreme pastor and teacher of all the faithful—who confirms his brethren in the faith (cf. Lk 22:32)—he proclaims by a definitive act a doctrine concerning faith or morals."

The rows of the table (across-ways) express co-terminous terms. Thus, e.g., a Papal or an episcopal statement on the ordinary level cannot *per se* demand the assent of faith; there cannot be ordinary but infallible Papal teaching; there cannot be a solemn Papal teaching which was not declared infallibly; there cannot be a solemn declaration of a General Council that was not infallibly uttered, and so on.

VI

DIFFICULTIES ANSWERED

Claims that the Church has erred, or changed her teaching. We sometimes hear that "the Church has admitted her teaching was wrong" or "the Church has changed her teaching". From what is written above, it is clear that no *infallibly taught teaching* could be wrong or overturned.

---

[84] Sources for levels 1-5 can also be found in Canon Law: (1) Can. 752, 753 (2) Can. 752 (3 & 4) Can. 749 §2, 750 (5) 749 §1, 750. Likewise in *Profession of Faith*, Congregation for the Doctrine of the Faith, 1989; *Donum Veritatis*, Congregation for the Doctrine of the Faith, 1990: (1 & 2) 17, 23.3 (3, 4 & 5) 15, 23.1, 16, 23.2; *Ad Tuendam Fidem*, John Paul II, 1998, & accompanying *Doctrinal Commentary* on the *Professio Fidei*, Congregation for the Doctrine of the Faith, 1998.

[85] *authenticum magisterium*. *Authenticus* is mediaeval Latin for *authoritative*.

Provisional teaching can be revised, but this is not usually what people have in mind. To avoid confusion, we must distinguish and keep separate four areas:[86]

(1) the *teachings* of the Church (as taught by the teachers at nos. 3, 4 & 5 in the table above). The infallibly taught doctrines cannot change. Any claim that they have changed is simply mistaken, and no official and solemn Church declaration could ever be adduced to maintain such a claim.

(2) the *rules* or legislation of the Church (often called *discipline*). These *do* change, and have regularly changed over the centuries, some of them differing from one country to another even at the same time. Among countless examples are: the Holy Days of obligation outside of Sunday; the penance required on Fridays; the length of the fast prescribed before Holy Communion; the rules and ceremonies connected with a mixed marriage (i.e., of a Catholic and non-Catholic); the liturgical laws governing Mass and other rituals; Communion for the laity under one or both kinds; the celibacy of the clergy in the Latin Church; the age fixed for Confirmation and first Communion, etc. We *believe* the teachings of the Church; we *obey* the legislation of the Church. We are not bound to agree with the legislation, but we must always observe it and speak of it respectfully, even if we hope for a change in some point or other. Many disciplinary norms are not simply arbitrary determinations, but have a foundation in doctrine and tradition. Some of the more important legislation (e.g., clerical celibacy) might never change, and if the Supreme Pontiff declares that the Church has no intention of changing something, a good Catholic will not foment division and discontent by prolonging the debate.

(3) the wisdom or *prudence* of the Church's leaders. Christ never promised that the pastors of the Church would always act with prudence and effectiveness. The wisdom of certain decisions (not doctrinal or moral) is open to discussion. Thus a new bishop or Pope is free to change his predecessor's directives. Church historians are always discussing the wisdom or otherwise of the Church's policies in her dealings with different governments, movements and cultures over the centuries.

(4) the teachings of *individuals, writers* and *schools of thought*. None of these is guaranteed any infallibility. Even Doctors of the Church—including St Thomas and St Augustine—have been mistaken on some points, and were corrected later on when the Church gave a definitive teaching. Sometimes opinions or theories arise in the Church and become so widespread that

---

[86] Cf. *Catholic Apologetics Today*, Fr. W. Most, TAN 1986, p.163 ff.

people mistake them for an actual teaching of the Church. (This is what happened in the Galileo controversy: high-ranking ecclesiastics presumed a *particular* interpretation of Biblical passages to be the *Church's* interpretation—see below). At other times, people presume that what *they* were taught is Church teaching, and that any differing idea *must* be false. Sometimes a phrase such as "No salvation outside the Church" receives a gross misexplanation (e.g., that only Catholics can get to Heaven), and many people then think that is 'Church teaching'.[87] One can guard against such mistakes by reading the official documents of the Church. In Part II of this work, each chapter opens with what the Church teaches infallibly in her solemn or her ordinary teaching. After that comes the theological explanation of that teaching—which can never be as definitive as the teaching itself.

Misconceptions as to Papal infallibility. To remove, first, some gross misconceptions: Papal infallibility does not imply impeccability, or sinlessness. The Pope is infallible in doctrine, but not impeccable in conduct. He must work out his salvation "in fear and trembling" like other men, sharing with St Paul the apprehension "lest, perhaps, when I have preached to others, I myself should become a castaway."[88] Neither does Papal infallibility imply a power to make new revelations, i.e., to disclose divine truths previously unknown. The whole Christian revelation was delivered to the Apostles. The Pope, in the exercise of infallibility, merely explains a point of it definitively, without adding anything to it. The Pope has no power to add, change or eliminate any doctrine, but only to guard, expound, explain, defend or define doctrine. The whole deposit of Catholic faith is not at the mercy of whoever happens to be in the Chair of Peter, so to speak. Campaigns to convince the Pope to change a solemn Church doctrine of faith or morals betray a fundamental error, viz., that the truth can be changed by say-so; ironically, it attributes to the Pope more power than he has ever claimed. A doctrine of faith or morals is not true because the Pope solemnly teaches it; *he teaches it because it is true*. His teaching of it may be *how* we come to know of it; but it would be true even if he never said it. Asking the Pope to change definitive Church teaching is as futile as asking him to change the law of gravity.

Nor are the Pope's infallible utterances inspired. For inspiration it is required that the writer or speaker be moved by God Himself to write or speak and be so guided by God that he expresses what God Himself wishes to express and nothing more. God is the author of inspired utterances. He is not the author of Papal definitions, but He guarantees them against error. Further, a Papal definition has but the one meaning intended by the Pope. A passage of inspired Scripture, on the other hand, may have, not only its literal meaning, but also a meaning of a higher order. For instance, the account of the sufferings and rejection of the Prophet Jeremiah is historical narrative, but also a type or image of the future sufferings of the Saviour. Or, when Christ addressed His Mother and said, "Behold

---

[87] For the example given, see C 846-7.
[88] 1 Cor 9:27

your son", His words applied literally to St John by her side, but expressed a spiritual meaning also, viz., that Mary publicly became the spiritual Mother of mankind at that moment.

Infallibility does not mean that the Pope knows more about the Catholic religion and the Bible than anyone else. "A Pope might be quite ignorant and a very poor theologian. He may make a mistake as private theologian;[89] only God will take care that he does not commit the whole Church to it. Papal infallibility is a negative protection. We are confident that God will not allow a certain thing to happen; that is all. It does not mean that the Pope will always give the wisest or best decision ... He may not speak at all; he may preserve a regrettable silence, just when it would be greatly to the good of the Church if he did speak. But if he does speak, and if he speaks in such a way as to commit the Church, then what he says will not be false."[90] "From all these we should not however conclude that this divine assistance is merely of a negative character, as if it merely prevents an arrival at an erroneous definition; it *positively* guides the Pope also to a correct knowledge and presentation of the truth Christ entrusted to the Church."[91]

Limits to Papal authority. "The Pope's authority, in the first place, is limited to matters of *religion*, that is of faith and morals, and such things as Canon law, liturgy, marriage cases, ecclesiastical censures and so on, which are part of faith and morals. The Pope has no authority from Christ in temporal matters, in questions of politics... He has no authority from Christ to teach mathematics, geography, history. His authority is ecclesiastical authority; it goes no further than that of the Church herself. But even in religious matters the Pope is bound, very considerably, by the divine constitution of the Church. There are any number of things that the Pope cannot do in religion. He cannot modify, nor touch in any way, one single point of the revelation Christ gave to the Church; his business is only to guard this against attack and false interpretation. We believe that God will so guide him that his decisions of this nature will be nothing more than a defence or unfolding of what Christ revealed. The Pope can neither make nor unmake a sacrament, he cannot affect the essence of any sacrament in any way. He cannot touch the Bible; he can neither take away a text from the inspired Scriptures nor add one to them. He has no fresh inspiration nor revelation. His business is to believe the revelation of Christ, as all Catholics believe it, and to defend it against heresy. He cannot take away the divine authority of any of his fellow-bishops as long as they are Catholic bishops in normal possession of their sees; though he can, as chief authority of the Church on earth, under certain circumstances try, suspend or depose an unworthy bishop.[92] The Pope can, in extraordinary circumstances, rearrange dioceses; he cannot abolish the universal episcopate. The Church of Christ, by her founder's constitution, is ruled by bishops who are the successors of the apostles, among

---

[89] as Pope John XXII did in three sermons in 1331-2, but later retracted. Cf. DS 990-1 & its introduction.
[90] Adrian Fortescue, *The Early Papacy*, London 1920, 3rd ed. Saint Austin Press, U.K. 1997, p.39
[91] Bishop L.Z. Legaspi, O.P., *The Church We Love*, University of Santo Tomas, Manila 1982, p.250; 1997 ed., p.273
[92] Pope John Paul II deposed a French bishop in 1995.

whom, as among the apostles, one of their number is chief. Each Catholic bishop receives his jurisdiction from God; though he must use it in the union of his fellow-bishops, and in canonical obedience to the Bishop of Rome, who is his chief. The Pope is not, in the absolute sense, head of the Church; the head of the Church is Jesus Christ our Lord, as our English catechism says. The Pope is the vicar of that head, and therefore visible head of the Church on earth, having authority delegate from Christ over the Church on earth only; just as every diocesan bishop has authority delegate from Christ over his diocese only. If the Pope is a monarch he is a very constitutional monarch indeed, bound on all sides by the constitution of the Church, as this has been given her by Christ."[93]

Objections against Papal infallibility. Protestants mention four Popes as having erred, viz., Paul V and Urban VIII, who condemned Galileo; Liberius and Honorius, who are said to have fallen into heresy, the former into Arianism, the latter into Monothelitism. Our general reply is that the conditions required for an infallible decision were not present in any of these cases:

Paul V, Urban VIII: and Galileo. Paul V in 1616 and Urban VIII in 1633, acting through the Congregations of the Holy Office and the Index, condemned as heretical the teaching of Galileo (1564-1642) that the sun is immovable, and that the earth rotates daily on its axis. The astronomer would most certainly have escaped all censure but for his imprudence in applying his doctrine to the interpretation of the passage of the Book of Joshua (10:12ff.) where it is said that the sun stood still. He undoubtedly suffered for his opinions in the sense that, for many years, he had to endure much mental distress. As for physical punishment, he was not "tortured" nor "cast into a dungeon", as our enemies used to say, but was kept for a short time in honourable confinement. Nicolas Copernicus (1473-1543) and Cardinal Nicholas of Cusa (1401-64), his predecessors in astronomical research, had advocated the same opinions without molestation. His condemnation does not affect the doctrine of the infallibility of the Pope, for the Popes in question did not teach *ex cathedra*. A Pope cannot delegate his infallibility to a Congregation. He must, himself, personally address the Universal Church, and require that his teaching be accepted by all its members with absolute assent. This condition was not verified in the case of Popes Paul and Urban. That there was no question of an irreversible decision is perfectly clear from the words of Cardinal Robert Bellarmine (1542-1621), a member of the Congregation of the Holy Office which condemned Galileo, and now a canonised Saint. Writing to Galileo's friend, Foscarini, he says that there would be no objection to putting forward the new system as the best explanation of celestial phenomena, provided no reference were made to the apparent conflict with the Bible. And he continues: "I say that if a real proof be found that the sun is fixed, and does not revolve around the earth, but the earth around the sun, then it will be necessary very carefully to proceed to the explanation of the passages of Scripture which appear to be contrary, as we should prefer to say that we have misunderstood these rather than pronounce that to be false which is demonstrated."

---

[93] A. Fortescue, *op. cit.*, pp.27-8

But, though the condemnation of Galileo proves nothing against the infallibility of the Pope, may it not be said that it proves the hostility of the Church to scientific progress and freedom of research? In reply, we put forward the following considerations: (1) Since the great majority of contemporary physicists and astronomers treated Galileo's opinions with derision, the most that can reasonably be urged against the Church in not immediately adopting them is that she was not in advance of her age. In fact, some of Galileo's arguments were undoubtedly worthless, and have been since abandoned. Of Galileo's contemporaries, Bacon, the so-called coryphæus of modern methods, was hostile to him as any. It is surely an ironic comment on the whole incident that, according to Einstein, it would not have mattered a pin's point whether it was said that the earth goes around the sun, or the sun around the earth.[94]

(2) No Protestant can complain of the Church's treatment of Galileo in view of the attitude of the Reformers to Copernicus who, some generations earlier, had advocated the same opinions. Luther denounced him as an arrogant fool who sought to overthrow all scientific astronomy, and who contradicted Holy Writ. Melanchthon wished his pestilent doctrines to be suppressed by the civil power.

(3) When physical science appears to demand a new interpretation of some statement in the Scriptures bearing on natural phenomena or such like, the attitude of the Church, as any impartial non-Catholic would admit, must be cautious and conservative. Her procedure will be exactly as Cardinal Bellarmine describes it (see quotation above). She will disregard the unsupported word of one or two scientists; she will move only when she is assured that unanimity of scientific teaching demands a revision of the received interpretation.

(4) The Church may, by her slowness to accept what is new, cause a temporary retardation of progress, but she rightly regards the custody of faith as something immeasurably more precious than the interests of physical science. And, for her, the custody of faith is bound up with veneration for antiquity. Hence, even though no point of faith be at issue, she will not abandon the ancient interpretation except under the pressure of irresistible evidence.

(5) For every one case put forward against the Church, there could be adduced ten thousand against scientists who have erred on all sorts of matters. How many theories put forward by scientists in one generation have had to be abandoned by the next! How many lives in the past were lost through medical science's false diagnoses and mistaken remedies! If science dare tell the Church to cease work for her few mistakes, then science itself should have ceased long ago.

It may be asked why the Pope does not pronounce at once infallibly on all questions submitted to him. The answer is that, although it is within his power to deliver, when he pleases, an infallible decision, he holds himself bound to refrain from exercising his infallibility until he has first done all that human industry can do, by studying and careful inquiry, to ascertain the mind of the Church. God does not wish His human instruments to be merely passive. He wishes them to be active, to think and reason. Hence, even the inspiration of the Biblical writers did not exclude industry and research. It follows, therefore, that the Pope's infallible decisions,

---

[94] Einstein and Infeld, *The Evolution of Physics,* Cambridge University Press 1938, p.224

except in cases of manifestly corrupt doctrine, must be of rare occurrence, and that, in dealing with the numerous questions submitted to him, he must, as a rule, employ his ordinary or non-infallible teaching authority.

Pope Liberius (351-366). Liberius, on refusing to confirm an Arian formulary of faith, was exiled in 355 by the Emperor Constantius. (The Arians denied the divinity of Christ). Two years later the Pope was permitted to return to Rome. Some say, while others, and very weighty authorities, deny, that he purchased his liberty by acceding to the Emperor's wishes. Let us suppose that he did sign the formulary: (1) It cannot be shown that it contained anything erroneous: many of the Arian formularies were unobjectionable; (2) He did not sign as a teacher of the Universal Church; he signed as a prisoner and under compulsion. Manifestly it cannot be held that, in such circumstances, he intended to bind the consciences of all the faithful.

Pope Honorius (625-638). Honorius wrote two letters, one to Sergius, an advocate of the Monothelite heresy, another to Sophronius, the champion of orthodoxy, in which he forbade further discussion and declared that "there is but one Will in Christ." (The Monothelites taught that there was no distinct Human Will in Christ; that it was absorbed in the Divine. In other words, they taught that Christ was not true man). Honorius was anathematised as a heretic by the General Council of Constantinople, 680-81. His case, however, yields no argument against Papal infallibility: (1) Honorius did not pronounce a definition *ex cathedra*, for, he said expressly, "It does not behove us to settle the question whether the number of operations in Christ is one or two." He had been misinformed by Sergius as to the point at issue, and thought that the controversy was, as he observed, "a war of words" to be settled by "grammarians". (2) His words bear an orthodox sense; they were written to contradict the false doctrine, ascribed by Sergius to his opponent, "that there are two *conflicting* Wills in Christ." (3) The decree of the Council of Constantinople must be regarded as condemnatory of the conduct of Honorius, not of his teaching as head of the Church. So much is clear from the words of Pope Leo II who explained that he had confirmed the decree, because Honorius had been negligent "in extinguishing the rising flame of heresy." The decree of a General Council is infallible only in the sense in which it is ratified by the Pope. It is, however, much disputed whether the Fathers of Constantinople intended to stigmatise Honorius as a heretic in the modern acceptation of the term. The word seems to have been applied in those days to anyone whose action, apart from any positive teaching, was thought to favour heresy or schism.

It is most striking that, with all the long history of the Church before them, vigilant opponents have been unable to discover any serious objections against Papal infallibility. Below we give two objections, pseudo-philosophical in character.

(1) "No one can interpret infallible teaching satisfactorily unless he is himself infallible."
REPLY: Christ did not give the individual members of His Church any special gift of infallible interpretation, because the gift would have been superfluous. He made

His Church a living, efficient teacher and gave her the power to express herself in language so clear as absolutely to exclude all danger of misinterpretation. Some of her followers have tried occasionally to misconstrue her teaching by a false subtlety, but they have always been exposed in the end. No person of normal intelligence—let him be an atheist if you will—who is given an ordinary course in Catholic Doctrine from an official textbook, can ever have the slightest doubt as to what precisely the Church asks us to believe. Of course he will not understand *how* her teaching e.g., about the Trinity, the Incarnation, the Real Presence, etc., can be true. That is not the point. What he will understand, and understand without the slightest trace of uncertainty, is the statement of her doctrine. When she says, for instance, that Christ, true God, true Man, is present in the Blessed Eucharist under the appearance of bread and wine, her statement, as a statement, will be perfectly plain to him. He will know exactly what Catholics have to believe. His certainty as to what the Church teaches is an absolute certainty; it is an indestructible certainty, because he will deny the possibility of his having misunderstood the words in which the doctrine is expressed. - The objection does not tell against Catholics but against those Protestants who profess to receive infallible teaching from the Bible, and who differ so widely in their interpretation of it. The Bible cannot speak to them; it cannot correct their errors.

(2) "The proof of infallibility can be constructed only by our own fallible reason, and therefore can give us nothing higher than a very probable conclusion."
REPLY: Our reason is fallible—undoubtedly. Still, our fallible reason can lead us to absolutely certain conclusions, as can be shown by an abundance of examples from daily life: the courts of law, for instance, will supply us with many decisions which cannot be challenged by anyone who has studied the evidence impartially; the symptoms of a patient enable the physician to identify the exact illness. Neither courts nor physicians claim infallibility, but at times they do claim certainty beyond reasonable doubt. Yet it would be impossible to find in ordinary human affairs any evidence so compelling as that by which we prove the divine origin of the Catholic Church with all her characteristics, including her claim to infallibility. The evidence leaves us no alternative—unless we regard as an alternative the supreme absurdity that the God of truth has deceived us. To the impartial mind, the evidence is irresistible, and gives a certainty impossible to overthrow.

The mendicant, the Roman, and the Spanish Inquisition.
The mendicant or medieval Inquisition. During the 12th and 13th centuries, violent sects, the Cathari and Albigensians, made their appearance in several parts of southern Europe. They attacked the clergy, destroyed churches and monasteries, opposed child-bearing as a curse, advocated various immoral practices (including concubinage, euthanasia, and 'religious' suicide by starvation), and encouraged revolt against civil authority. They set themselves up as a State within a State, for they regarded themselves as exempt from taxes, and not bound by oaths or allegiance to anyone except their own members.[95] The whole fabric of society, political and religious, was threatened with disruption. To meet so grave a peril, the

---

[95] E. Vacandard, *The Inquisition* (trans. by B.L. Conway), Longmans, N.Y. 1907, pp.50-74

Church, in concert with the secular governments, established c. 1232 the Inquisition (run chiefly by members of the mendicant orders, the Franciscans and Dominicans) to try charges of heresy. Its tribunals were set up in several countries, as need arose. Its object was primarily corrective. If the heretic were prepared to recant his errors, it imposed a penance, sometimes very light, such as fasting or a pilgrimage, and reconciled him with the Church. If he were obdurate, it pronounced him guilty of heresy, and handed him over to the State for punishment. The State passed sentence, and its judgements were severe—flagellation, confiscation of property, temporary or perpetual imprisonment, or death itself. Officially, the Church never condemned anyone to death, but she undoubtedly approved of the stern repression of heresy by the State, and believed that, in the circumstances of the age, she was justified in her approval. The activity of this Inquisition continued intermittently until the sixteenth century.

The Roman Inquisition.[96] In 1542, Pope Paul III established the Congregation of the Inquisition to control and co-ordinate the activities of the Inquisitions operating in the Italian States, and to be a final court of appeal in heresy cases. This institution came to be known as the Roman Inquisition. Part of the function of its modern successor, the Congregation for the Doctrine of the Faith (the Holy Office) in Rome, is to inquire into the orthodoxy of writings, and to condemn them and discipline their authors if anything is found contrary to Catholic faith or morals.

Our adversaries point to these Inquisitions as a proof of the intolerance and cruelty of the Church.
(1)   As to the charge of intolerance:
(a) A man is said to tolerate what he believes to be an error when he is able, but unwilling, to suppress it. The Church, commissioned by Christ to preach the Gospel, and clothed with infallibility, can never be unwilling to suppress erroneous doctrine. The Church and every lover of truth must necessarily be intolerant of error. The so-called tolerance of the present age is not tolerance in the strict sense. It is due either to the incapacity to enforce, or to utter indifferentism in religious matters.

(b) The objection of intolerance ignores the conditions of that age. Apart from a small Jewish minority, whom the Inquisition did not affect, Europe was Catholic, with no century-old non-Catholic bodies with an accepted right to legal recognition. Hence, by establishing the Inquisition, the Church did not deny religious freedom to groups, such as Jews, having an accepted status. A crisis had arisen: the appearance, within the Catholic body itself, of sects hostile to the natural law and civil order no less than to the Church. The Church sought the help of the State in suppressing them.

---

[96] Cf. J. Tedeschi, *The Prosecution of Heresy. Collected Studies on the Inquisition in Early Modern Italy*, Medieval & Renaissance Texts & Studies, Binghamton, N.Y. 1991; E. Peters, *Inquisition*, Uni. of California Press, Berkeley 1989.

(c) Every society's tolerance necessarily has limits—otherwise it ceases to be a society. In the second Vatican Council's document on religious liberty, which many mistakenly take as a charter for religious indifferentism, the Catholic Church *still* declares, and reasonably so, that religious freedom may be impeded coercively by the State when a religious body, under the pretext of religion or not, is guilty of harming the common good: (i) by abusing its own rights or violating the rights of other groups, e.g., by dishonest coercion, unworthy persuasion, or false propaganda; (ii) by threatening the public peace, or (iii) by undermining public morality.[97] While that decree "leaves intact the traditional Catholic teaching on the moral duty of individuals and societies towards the true religion and the one Church of Christ",[98] the Church has always taught that the faith must be received freely, or not at all. Hence, Canon Law old and new declares that no one may be obliged to embrace the faith against his will, and no one after the age of reason may be baptised except after instruction and with his consent.[99]

(2)   As to the charge of cruelty:
(a) *The Church has the right to legislate and punish*: The Church, established by Christ as a complete society, is empowered to make laws and inflict penalties for their violation. Heresy not only violates her law but strikes at her very life, unity of belief.

(b) *The activity of the heretics was criminal*: When Christianity became the religion of the empire, and still more when the peoples of Northern Europe became Christian nations, the close alliance of Church and State made unity of faith essential not only to the ecclesiastical organisation, but also to civil society. Heresy, in consequence, was a crime which secular rulers were bound in duty to punish. It was regarded as worse than any other crime, even that of high treason. For society in those times, it was the equivalent of anarchy. "In 1224, even a semi-atheist like the Emperor Frederick II had heretics burnt alive. Any attack on the Catholic Church was an attack against state security, and anyone attacking the Church was, *ipso facto*, subject to the terrible penalties exacted by the civil authorities. Not only society, but the whole of cultural, civil and religious life was strictly dependent on the Church. An enemy of the Church was thus by definition an enemy of civilisation, guilty of undermining the very foundations of social living. In relation to this, it should be remembered that the Albigenses [12-13th cent. heretics] were not pacifist free-thinkers; on the contrary, their intolerance knew no bounds. The spread of their organisation constituted a major threat to society, undermining its very bases. Furthermore, we should also recall the law of physics: 'every action gives rise to an equal and opposite reaction': the same law applies to the interplay of historical forces. If the Albigenses called retribution upon themselves, they had only themselves to blame with their continual violence and systematic disloyalty. ... It is right to pity them, but absurd to cast them as the innocent victims of papal intolerance and the ambitions of the French kings."[100] Still, it is an undoubted fact

---

[97] *Dignitatis Humanae*, Decree on Religious Liberty, 1965, art. 4, 7. Cf. C 2104-9.
[98] *Dignitatis Humanae*, art. 1
[99] Cf. Can. 748 §2, 851, 852, 865 (CIC 1917, can. 752, 1351).
[100] V. Gamboso, *Life of St Anthony*, Padua 1991, pp.74-5

that for centuries the principal teachers of the Church shrank from such stern measures against heresy as torture and capital punishment, and yielded only under pressure from civil powers. Hence, it cannot be said that the Inquisition was due solely to the initiative of the Church.

(c) *The methods of the Inquisition were just, legal, and mild for the times.* The Inquisition was milder in its methods than the secular courts. The rights of the accused were better guaranteed in the Inquisitions than in the ordinary civil trials of the major European countries. Suspects were not arrested until careful investigation. The Inquisition gave the heretic ample time to defend himself or to recant. Its officers were bound under most severe penalties to move by slow delays, so as to give the accused every opportunity of retraction, whereas the civil authority, when it acted, as it often did, without any reference to the Church, gave no time for repentance. The accused was guaranteed a defence lawyer, paid for by the Inquisition if unable to afford it himself. "This provision was anything but negligible when it is recalled that in a country like England the right of the accused to be defended was recognized only in 1836. Torture, which was a juridical practice applied in all tribunals, was inflicted only in precisely determined cases, namely when there were good grounds to suspect that the accused was lying or at least hiding part of the truth. Even in these cases, however, he could be tortured only after certain procedures had been followed. These involved, *inter alia*, the favorable vote of the diocesan ordinary or his representative."[101] Thus, the Inquisition marked an improvement on the treatment meted out to heretics. Before its institution, summary executions by the State or by the enraged populace were the order of the day. Further, the Inquisition punished false accusers. Whatever its defects, the Inquisition provided that cases of heresy would be judged by competent and impartial judges.

Its penalties. While we admit that condemned heretics were treated with what, by modern standards, was great severity, the penalties were by no means harsh, when judged by the standards of the time. Besides, the accounts given of the numbers who suffered under the various Inquisitions are often exaggerated. Let us look at some statistics, in contrast to wild propaganda and popular claims: in Toulouse, of 930 heretics convicted by the inquisitor Bernard Gui from 1308-1323, 42 were put to death.[102] In Pamiers, from 1318-1324, of 64 persons convicted, five were executed.[103] Although the Inquisition never operated in England, in comparable heresy trials conducted in Kent, 1511-12, before Archbishop Warham of Canterbury, 53 suspects were examined, of whom 5 refused to abjure and were handed over to the State for execution as heretics; the other guilty parties were given penances.[104] In 1538, the Inquisition of Valencia, Spain, convicted 112 persons, of whom 14 were sent to the stake.[105] Over the years 1536-1794, the Portuguese Inquisition tried roughly 31,000 persons, of whom 6% were handed over to the secular arm for the death sentence: 4% were executed, and 2% burnt in

---

[101] J.W. O'Malley S.J. (ed.), *Catholicism in Early Modern History 1500-1700*, Center for Reformation Research, St Louis 1987, p.260

[102] E. Vacandard, *op. cit.*, p.143

[103] J.M. Vidal, *Le tribunal de l'Inquisition de Pamiers*, Toulouse 1906, p.235

[104] N. Tanner S.J. (ed.), *Kent Heresy Proceedings 1511-12*, Kent Archaeological Society 1997

[105] E. Vacandard, *op. cit.*, p.145

effigy because they were dead already or missing.[106] Of the first 1,000 accused who appeared before the Aquileia-Concordia Inquisition in the Venetian Republic in the years 1551-1647, four were sent to the stake.[107] Of the more than two hundred sentences of the tribunals throughout Italy issued from 1580-1582, four imposed the death penalty.[108]

It was only those unrepentant to the end who were burnt alive. Generally, execution took place by hanging or beheading *before* the burning at the stake.[109] Seldom enough, too, is the Church credited with the care she took regarding conditions in Inquisition prisons.[110] Further, the Inquisitions often admitted appeals against the sentence, whereas most civil courts allowed no appeal against sentences for certain crimes. "Relatively few encounters with the Inquisition ended at the stake. This was a fate reserved for the relapsed, the impenitent, and those convicted of attempting to overturn a few central doctrines of the Church. But even in these cases lesser forms of punishment often prevailed."[111] The lesser punishments were generally medicinal and spiritual: public abjurations of error, penances, work in a charitable institution, a cycle of prayers and devotions.[112]

(d) *Reply to Protestant objectors.* In the days of the Roman Inquisition, Protestants dealt with their opponents exactly as Catholics dealt with theirs, but often far more cruelly, with sessions of prolonged torture on the rack, etc. Protestants regularly put Unitarian heretics to death for their heresy: for example, Calvin had Michael Servetus burnt at the stake in 1553; King James I, an Anglican, had two Unitarian heretics burnt at the stake in 1612; in Scotland, the Presbyterians hanged Unitarians until as late as 1696. But, while the severity of Protestants was indefensible, on their own grounds, since they maintained the liberty of private judgement and, therefore, admitted that their victim might be right and they themselves wrong, the severity of Catholics, on the other hand, was consistent with their doctrine that they alone possess divine truth, and that the heretic working amongst Catholics is necessarily a source of moral or spiritual infection, a slayer of souls, and, therefore, more dangerous than the thief or murderer. The Roman Inquisition ceased executing heretics close to the end of the pontificate of Urban VIII (d. 1644).[113] Protestant England continued to put Catholic priests to death for their priesthood: the last Catholic executed for his religion there being St Oliver Plunkett in 1681. Penal laws against Catholics remained in force in Britain until 1791.

(e) *Reply to non-Christian objectors.* The criminal law of the Middle Ages was much more severe than that of the present day, the death penalty being exacted for

---

[106] J. Tedeschi, *The Prosecution of Heresy*, op. cit., p.126; cf. also J. Lucio de Azevedo, *História dos Cristaōs Novos portugueses*, Lisbon 1975, p.489: cited in *Catholicism in Early Modern History 1500-1700*, op. cit.

[107] J. Tedeschi, *op. cit.*, p.103

[108] Ibid., p.261

[109] Cf. J. Tedeschi, *op. cit.*, pp. 124, 153.

[110] E. Vacandard, *op. cit.*, pp.137-43

[111] J. Tedeschi, *op. cit.*, p. xi; cf. pp. 151-2.

[112] J. Tedeschi, ibid., p.151

[113] Lord Acton, *Essays on Church and State*, Hollis and Carter, London 1952, pp.256-7

burglary, blasphemy, vandalism and even petty theft. From the modern standpoint, they were truly merciless times. But what of the values and boasted clemency of our own 'enlightened' age? A future generation may pass a most severe judgement on *us* for: the legalised murder of millions of helpless infants in their mothers' wombs; the enforced sterilisation of handicapped people; the involuntary euthanasia of people deemed 'useless' (well documented in several countries, but never are the guilty doctors prosecuted); the destruction of children's innocence through exposure to obscenity; the glorification of base immorality and gratuitous violence under the name of 'entertainment'; the idolisation of 'stars' who lead lives of sheer depravity; the widespread sale of mind-destroying drugs; the plague of divorce and the attendant abandonment of children; the degradation of motherhood and family; the relegation of many old people to a life of loneliness and isolation; the bombing of entire cities in wars—and countless other modern evils unimagined by past generations.

More human beings are killed by abortion now *every week* in the world, than in all the Inquisitions ever. Are we in any position to condemn past ages so self-righteously? Is the modern outrage at the Inquisition sincere, or is it a cover-up for today's far more appalling crimes?

(f) *General reply:* Let us suppose all the charges alleged under the heading of cruelty to be fully established. Let us accept as true all the gross exaggerations of unprincipled adversaries as to the number of victims of the Inquisition, and the nature of the punishments to which they were subjected. What follows? Nothing against the Church as a divine institution.[114] Nothing against her claim to doctrinal infallibility. Much, perhaps, against the personal wisdom and clemency of her rulers. But, even though such personal failure be admitted, it serves only to emphasise the fact that the weakness and errors of individuals can never bring the Church to ruin.

The Spanish Inquisition. When our opponents speak of the cruelty of the Catholic Church, they usually have in mind the proceedings of the Spanish Inquisition, a tribunal established by Ferdinand and Isabella in 1478, at the request of their subjects and with the approval of the Holy See. Its purpose was to unmask and punish pretended converts from Judaism or Islam. Many of these possessed great wealth and influence, and held high office in the State and even in the Church. Their plots and secret machinations threatened to reverse the dearly-bought victory which the Spaniards had won over the Moors after a struggle of nearly eight centuries. The Inquisitors were ecclesiastics, but they held office at the pleasure of the Spanish crown. Pope Sixtus IV (1471-84), who declared that his sanction for the erection of the tribunal had been obtained on false pretences, protested more than once against its severity, but without avail. The complete lack of Papal control over the Inquisition is evident from the fact that when the Primate of Spain, Archbishop Caranza of Toledo, was imprisoned by the Inquisition in 1558, the

---

[114] Consider the dread punishments inflicted by God under the Old Law: cf. Ex 21-22; Lev 18:29; 20:27; Deut 3:5; 17:2-6; 1 Sam 6:19; 2 Sam 6:7. Cf. the deaths of Ananias and Sapphira under the New Law (Acts 5).

Pope could not procure his release for eight years, despite repeated requests. Since it was more a political rather than an ecclesiastical institution, the Church cannot be held responsible for its proceedings.[115] In any case, the Spanish Inquisition was not an instrument of religious fanaticism tyrannically imposed on society. Like the Venetian Inquisition, it enjoyed the support of the populace as a whole—civil authorities and citizens alike—because they saw heresy as creating not only religious and social disturbances and disintegration, but also as leading to political upheaval.[116]

After the Reformation, the Protestants counter-attacked Catholic Spain via the printing press, with a continuous stream of crude and venomous anti-Spanish invective. The Inquisition provided a ready focus for the propaganda. The popular image of the Inquisition comes especially from the 1567 document, *A Discovery and Plain Declaration of sundry subtle practices of the Holy Inquisition of Spain*, conveniently authored under a pseudonym, 'Montanus', who posed as a victim. The image presented in that work has persisted ever since, Protestant propagandists thereafter continuing to outdo one another in manufacturing lurid accounts of ghastly Inquisitorial tortures. Juan Antonio Llorente, the chief witness on whom some Protestants rely, was appointed Secretary to the Inquisition at Madrid in 1789, but was dismissed in 1801 through his misconduct. Although Spanish, he sided with the French in their invasion of Spain in 1808. His work, *A Critical History of the Inquisition*, published in 1817 in Paris, his place of retirement, was prompted by a desire of revenge. Apart from his undoubted animus, the fact that Llorente destroyed the records on which he purported to base his statistics makes his testimony very suspicious.

According to Prof. Henry Kamen, an English Jew, of the Barcelona Higher Council for Scientific Research, historians now studying in depth all the files of the Spanish Inquisition have produced findings demolishing the Inquisition's previous image.[117] According to Prof. Stephen Haliczer of the Northern University of Illinois, the Spanish Inquisition rarely used torture at all. An analysis of 7,000 cases from Valencia, for example, revealed that 2% involved torture, and then for no more than fifteen minutes. 1% experienced torture more than once. This was far less than other tribunals of the time. Edward Peters says that the Spanish Inquisition "acted with considerable restraint in inflicting the death penalty, far more restraint than was demonstrated in secular tribunals elsewhere in Europe that dealt with the same kinds of offenses", and its "torture appears to have been extremely conservative and infrequently used." He concludes that its "use of torture was well under that of all contemporary secular courts in continental Europe, and even under that of other ecclesiastical tribunals."[118]

Between 1550 and 1700, 1,483 of 49,092 cases (less than 3%) concluded with the death sentence. However, of these, only 776 were actually put to death. In the

---

[115] Cf. F. Hayward, *The Inquisition*, Alba House, N.Y. 1965; W.T. Walsh, *Isabella of Spain*, Sheed & Ward, London 1935, Chs. xii, xiv-xvi, xix.

[116] N. Davidson, "Il Santo'Uffizio e la tutela del culto a Venezia nel '500", *Studi Veneziani* 6 (1982) pp.87-101: cited in *Catholicism in Early Modern History 1500-1700*, op. cit.

[117] Cf. H. Kamen, *The Spanish Inquisition. A Historical Revision*, Yale University Press 1997.

[118] *Inquisition*, op. cit., pp.87, 92

215

other 707 cases, the guilty party was already dead or missing.[119] On average, about five persons a year were put to death during that century and a half. To put this in context, during the same period in the rest of Europe, cruel punishments were commonplace: in England, execution was the penalty for damaging a shrub in a public garden; in Germany, those returning from banishment had their eyes gouged out; in France, sheep stealers were disembowelled. The Inquisition, however, had a rule-book, *Instructiones*, specifying legal and illegal procedures. Inquisitors who broke the rules were dismissed. As for prisons, a document from Barcelona, says Prof. Haliczer, records that prisoners in secular courts would blaspheme in order to be sent to Inquisition prisons.[120]

---

[119] G. Henningsen, "El «Banco de datos» del Santo Oficio. Las relaciones de causas de la inquisición española (1550-1700)", *Boletín de la Real Academia de la Historia* 174 (1977) pp.547-70 at p.564: cited in *Catholicism in Early Modern History*, op. cit.; cf. also J. Tedeschi, *The Prosecution of Heresy*, op. cit., pp.104, 126.

[120] Cf. BBC documentary, 1996, *The Myth of the Spanish Inquisition*.

CHAPTER 12

THE MARVEL OF THE CHURCH

This Chapter belongs to Apologetics, and is placed here as a completion of our treatment of the Church. In itself it is a complete argument for the credibility of the Catholic Church as a work of God.

Proof by the simpler method that the Catholic Church is the living work of God: arguments from her miraculous unity in government, faith, and worship; from the heroic sanctity of so many of her children; from the numerous miracles accompanying her; from her miraculous stability and the endurance of the Papacy in particular; from the willing witness given to her faith by so many martyrs.

Summary

I. The miracle of the Catholic Church's unity in (a) government (b) faith (c) worship.
II. The miraculous sanctity of so many of her members.
III. The numerous miracles accompanying the Church's mission.
IV. The miracle of the Church's stability; the endurance of the Papacy.
V. The miracle of the rapid propagation of Christianity and the fortitude of so many martyrs dying for the faith of the Church.

I

THE HAND OF GOD IS SEEN IN THE MIRACLE OF THE CHURCH'S UNITY

Miraculous unity in government. To unite a vast multitude of men in working out a particular end without the incentive of earthly advantage, to maintain among them agreement of opinion and unanimity of purpose, to organise them and hold them together beneath a single government in spite of human weakness, racial prejudice and great world changes—this surely needs more than human intellect can devise or human ingenuity achieve.

But we see all this in the Catholic Church—the greatest of all societies. We see her faithful members[1] acknowledging the sway of one ruler, yielding a ready obedience not through fear of armed force, nor through the urge of national sentiment, nor in the hope of earthly gain. We see them as one in professing their submission to the Successor of Peter, although on all other matters they are sharply divided. She numbers amongst her multitudinous members men of every nation and every race,

---

[1] We speak in this section of the millions of faithful Catholics, but not of those who proclaim themselves "dissenters".

men who differ in culture, in language, in customs, and in political ambitions. The Church is daily confronted with difficulties and campaigns which have shattered kingdoms and empires, yet her sovereignty goes on with a permanence and a stability which are the envy of the statesman and the politician, and which manifestly proclaim the guidance and support of God.

Miraculous unity in faith. In the faith professed by the vast multitudes of the children of the Catholic Church, we see displayed the same miraculous unity. Pandering not to man's base passions, teaching doctrines repellent to human frailty, swerving not a hair's breadth from the truths she has defined, she is yet the teacher to whose words millions listen with reverent docility.

The human mind is fickle and wayward. Opinions shift and alter in endless diversity; individual differs from individual: what is asserted in one place is denied in another; what is held today is abandoned tomorrow. Yet, in spite of this natural restlessness and disunion, the faithful children of the Church never change in their belief. Conquering the natural desire to exalt private judgement and follow its dictates, they humbly listen to the voice of their Mother: overcoming the natural reluctance to believe what cannot be entirely understood, they, at her command, profess with alacrity their belief in the most profound mysteries. This unanimity in faith, this cordial submission of the intellect on the part of such great multitudes, can have but one explanation, viz., the direct and constant assistance of God Himself.

Miraculous unity in worship. As her faith is one and unchanging, so too is her worship. In its essentials, it is the same in every land. All over the earth, she gathers her children around the altar to join with her in offering the same Great Sacrifice, the memorial and perpetuation of the Sacrifice of the Cross; and she presents to them the same seven Sacraments, the same seven channels by which the grace of the Redeemer is conveyed to their souls. She binds them all, learned and simple, great and lowly, to kneel at the feet of her priests, and confess their most secret sins. That people in such numbers should suppress their inherent desire for novelty and individualism, their personal likes and dislikes, their ingrained reluctance to reveal their hidden wickedness, and take on themselves the yoke of a uniform worship, with all its severe exactions—that is a phenomenon for which no human or natural explanation can be found.

The Church, therefore, in her triple unity of government, faith and worship, is a living miracle of God.[2]

---

[2] See Ch. 10 for a further presentation of this triple unity.

II

THE HAND OF GOD IS SEEN IN THE MIRACULOUS SANCTITY OF SO MANY OF HER CHILDREN

The holiness of the Catholic Church has always been so marked and unrivalled, that it cannot be explained as the effect of any merely human cause. It is a standing miracle of God's power and goodness.

Holiness implies sincere attachment to God, as our dear Father and Friend. It carries with it necessarily the avoidance of sin, because sin is hateful to Him; yet the mere avoidance of sin does not alone suffice for holiness. In ancient and modern history, we find several instances of men remarkable for kindness, truthfulness and justice; but while we willingly admit that no serious fault can be laid to their charge, we search the record of their lives in vain for the evidence of that burning personal love of God which is found in the Saints of the Church. It is hard indeed to keep the soul free from sin, hard to conquer the desires of the flesh, hard to resist the attractions of the world. Yet such avoidance of sin, though a great and noble achievement, is still but a first feeble step in the direction of heroic sanctity. Morality alone is not holiness: no one would be content to speak of Christ as a moral man. He was something far more: He was holy.

But, granted for the sake of argument that there may have been persons outside the Church equal in holiness to the Saints, the truth still remains that the instances are most rare, and therefore cannot have been due to one perpetually-operating cause. In the Church, on the other hand, the instances are numerous. They appear unfailingly, generation after generation, springing up in every rank of society, and presenting us with every phase of character and ability. The Church is the one and only fertile field of saints on earth; she is the garden of God in the desert of the world.

From where do her flowers of sanctity derive their life and beauty? Not from her doctrine alone; not from any rules of life which she has formulated or sanctioned; for none of these is a secret. Her teaching and her methods are accessible to all, and may be, and have been, copied by others. But she has one thing which no outsider can imitate or reproduce: it is the special help which she gets from God, which is obtainable in her fold alone, and which, passing into the souls of her children, awakes in so many of them the radiance of a peerless sanctity. In outward form, other religious bodies may resemble her, but they differ from her as a lady's picture differs from the living woman, or as the idle machine differs from another that is connected with the power source.

Look over the great list of saints from the period of the Reformation down to our own times. Many of their names are known to unbelievers as geniuses in the spiritual order, and are honoured by them almost as much as by ourselves. Sir Thomas More has been reckoned one of the greatest Englishmen of all time. He was an internationally recognised scholar, humanist and wit. He was a man renowned for his friendship, justice and legal genius. Beheaded rather than renounce the Catholic Faith, he made jokes even as he approached the block on which to lay his head. The seraphic Teresa of Avila and her contemporary and kindred spirit, St John of the Cross, have been declared Doctors of the Church for their outstanding spiritual doctrine, and are revered and read by Catholics and non-Catholics alike. Legendary are the names of that tireless missionary Francis Xavier, and the soldier-saint Ignatius of Loyola, founder of the renowned Jesuit Order. Who has not heard of St Vincent de Paul, the Christ-like friend of the poor and afflicted, whose name has been adopted by the Society of those today who care for the poor in their districts? And who has failed to hear of St Jean Vianney, the Curé d'Ars, who did battle with the devil in his isolated rural parish and converted thousands of sinners? Who does not know the story of Father Maximilian Kolbe, that heroic man of Auschwitz in 1941, who offered his life in place of a fellow prisoner condemned to death by starvation? The fame of Blessed Pio of Pietrelcina is universal, the Franciscan Capuchin popularly known as Padre Pio (1887-1968). He bore in his body for fifty years the painful stigmata—the five wounds of Christ—and was renowned in his lifetime for countless cures and miracles. Yet these saints are but a few from a roll of hundreds, many of whom have founded orders and societies which perpetuate their virtues; and as Christ lived in them, the founders, so He now lives in their spiritual children.

The title of "Saint" is not given lightly. The level of sanctity demanded is nothing less than heroic. The process of inquiry is meticulous and complex, making hasty and superficial judgement an impossibility.[3]

No cause for canonisation can be opened until five years have elapsed since the candidate's death. At the request of the promoters of the cause, the diocesan inquiry may then be opened by the local Bishop, and the candidate may be known as the "Servant of God". For a claimed martyr, the object of the diocesan inquiry is threefold, viz., the candidate's life, martyrdom, and reputation for martyrdom. For martyrdom, it must be ascertained, first, that the killer hated the Faith, and second, that the victim died as a witness to the Faith or a Christian virtue. For all other causes, the objects of inquiry are the candidate's life, heroic virtues and reputation for holiness.

A *Postulator*, or representative of the promoters of the cause, is appointed to study the case and help gather the proofs. The *Postulator* is

---

[3] The process is outlined in the 1983 Apostolic Constitution *Divinus Perfectionis Magister* of John Paul II, and the 1983 Norms for diocesan inquiries as decreed by the Sacred Congregation for the Causes of Saints.

assisted by the promoter of justice, the notary, the judge-instructor, the episcopal delegate, and other experts as needed. All evidence, written and oral, favourable and unfavourable, is collected. All the faithful, indeed all people, are bound to bring forward anything they may know against the sanctity or miracles of the candidate. Witnesses are summoned to give depositions and be examined under oath. The only secrets to be held back from the inquiry are those of the confessional and spiritual direction. At least two theological experts must examine the candidate's published writings and report if they have found anything contrary to Catholic faith or morals. A specially appointed historical commission gathers any and every document relevant to the life of the Servant of God as well as any unpublished writings. Thus, witnesses, documents and experts are all examined. For candidates who are not martyrs, their whole life is subjected to a thorough examination. Objections made against their virtues must be answered to satisfaction.

Private devotion to the Servant of God may be encouraged, but it is forbidden to forestall the judgement of the Church by conducting public ecclesiastical celebrations in honour of the Servant of God. It is likewise forbidden to use the title of Venerable, Blessed or Saint, or to depict the Servant of God in art with a halo or other signs of sanctity, or to decorate the tomb with votive offerings.

Once the local inquiry is complete, the cause is presented to Rome, where the Sacred Congregation for the Causes of Saints will decide if the cause may continue, and if so, will appoint a *Relator* to direct the writing of the *Positio super Martyrio*, an account of martyrdom, or, for non-martyrs, the *Positio super Virtutibus*, a critical account of the life and works of the Servant of God. In the latter case, the theological virtues (faith, hope and charity), the cardinal virtues (prudence, justice, temperance and fortitude), and other pertinent virtues, are all made the subject of investigation, because it is necessary to establish that each and all have been practised in a heroic degree. This account is read by several theological consultors who independently give written judgements. The *Promotor Fidei* (Promoter of the Faith)—once popularly known as the Devil's Advocate—presides over the experts examining the case. Assisted by their judgements, the Cardinal and Bishop members of the Congregation for the Causes of Saints may then approve the cause and recommend a favourable judgement to the Pope. Thus, if the candidate satisfies the proofs of martyrdom, or passes the test of all the virtues, the title of *Venerable* is bestowed by the Pope.

For martyrs: a Venerable martyr may be beatified by the Pope and so receive the title of *Blessed.* Beatification gives permission for local and restricted cult.

For non-martyrs: even when the searching tests above have been completed, the Church is not yet satisfied. All possible human testimony has been called upon and has been found favourable. The Church now seeks divine testimony, and it is only when God has granted an indubitable miracle in response to the invocation of the candidate's name, that the Church is at last satisfied that the case has been established, that the person whose life has been under examination is worthy to be beatified. If the miracle is of a cure, it must not only be inexplicable to medical science, but rapid, complete and lasting.

For all Blessed: To proceed to canonisation and so receive the title of *Saint*, it is necessary to verify a miracle wrought through the intercession of a Blessed. Canonisation mandates universal cult. Thus the Church's highest honour comes to no one, however holy, except through a careful process culminating in the attestation of a divinely wrought sign.

The completeness of the examinations made by the Church appears in the following facts regarding the diocesan investigation for the beatification of Therese of the Child Jesus (d. 1897): 108 sessions were held of 5-6 hours each, and 45 witnesses were examined (exclusive of the doctors). The report of the whole as forwarded to Rome filled 3,000 pages in close writing—and this for a woman who lived but twenty-four years, and spent her entire time from the age of fifteen in a single convent.

In the face of those apparently impossible exactions on frail human nature, there are now 185 with the title of Blessed, and 78 others who are now Saints, who were declared so during the course of the 19th century. In the 20th century, more than 1,600 were declared Blessed, and more than 460 others were enrolled among the ranks of the Saints.[4]

Outside the Church there have been holy people to whose good deeds we pay the tribute of our sincere respect, but who has ever heard of an official inquiry into their lives to ascertain whether publicly and privately they truly lived up to their reputation? And as to miracles wrought in their honour after death, who has ever heard of an inquiry into such evidence of divine approval?

The Church is, and always has been, the one and only Mother of Saints that there is in the world—the one and only Mother of men whose lives have been in themselves miracles of holiness—the one and only Mother of men whose sanctity has been attested after death by the direct intervention of God Himself. She is proved to be in possession of a perpetual and unfailing divine help, and therefore of a perpetual divine approval.

The constant succession of miracles which God has granted to the children of His Church is in itself an all-sufficient proof of her divine

---

[4] *Index ac Status Causarum*, S. Congregation for the Causes of Saints, Vatican City, 1988; *Supplementa*, ann. seq.

authority. The evidence for multitudes of these miracles is such that no unprejudiced mind can refuse to admit its cogency. In causes for canonisation, the miracles alleged are subjected to a complete and critical examination in all their aspects. Scientific experts are called to sift the evidence and a single flaw entails absolute rejection.

III

THE NUMEROUS MIRACLES WHICH ACCOMPANY THE CHURCH'S MISSION

We spoke above of the miracles wrought by the intercession of the Saints after their deaths; they are but a few of a countless number of miracles which have accompanied the Catholic Church throughout her history, and above all in the lives of her holy ones.

Miracles in the lives of the Saints. The lives of the saints are replete with miracles—divine confirmations of their holiness and mission. One only has to read a life of *St Francis of Assisi* (d. 1226) or *St Anthony of Padua* (d. 1231) to see holy lives accompanied by abundant miracles. For the last two years of his life, St Francis bore the five stigmata of Christ, which he received in a vision. His gentleness, poverty, and seraphic love are legendary all over the world.

St Joseph of Cupertino (d. 1663), also Franciscan, became famous for his ecstasies, miracles and supernatural gifts. His gift of levitation in prayer attracted crowds whenever he went to say Mass. It occurred at least seventy times and was reported by numerous eyewitnesses over several years.

St Frances of Rome (d. 1440) regularly experienced visions and ecstasies, and had the gift of prophecy. She had also the gift of healing, and the sick often had recourse to her. Similar prodigies are recorded in the lives of St Margaret of Cortona (d. 1297), St Clare of Montefalco (d. 1308), Blessed Lydwina of Schiedam (d. 1433), St Mary Magdalen dei Pazzi (d. 1607) and St Veronica Giuliani (d. 1727).

St Charbel Makhlouf (d. 1898), a Maronite monk of Lebanon, was often called upon to pray over the sick and dying. He healed some sick people pronounced incurable, cured two madmen by reading a chapter of the Gospel over each one, and conferred the gift of speech upon an eight year old boy mute from birth. He miraculously delivered the monastery fields from a swarm of locusts, and on one occasion when the other monks playfully put water into his kerosene lamp, Father Charbel lit it and it worked as usual.[5] In 1950, fifty-two years after his death, an unknown

---

[5] Fr Mansour Awad, *Three Lights from the East*, USA 1990, p.87

monk appeared in a photograph taken at his monastery. When shown to the older monks, they recognised the man at once as Fr Charbel.[6] His tomb is a place of pilgrimage for Catholics, other Christians and Moslems alike.

Blessed Padre Pio (d. 1968) was surrounded by supernatural manifestations all through his priestly life: he had battles with the devil; he enjoyed visions of Our Lord and Our Lady, and various saints and angels; he knew of hidden things and could read hearts and minds, often prophesying to people in the confessional and answering their doubts and queries even before they had a chance to tell him their problems. At times he read and understood letters in a language he did not know at all. His prayers were often answered miraculously. He sometimes bilocated (appeared in two places at once)—there are many accounts of people who saw or heard the Franciscan friar in different parts of the world, warning them of mortal danger or leading them out of harm's way, while he himself was in his isolated friary in southern Italy. Of many cures attributed to him, the most astounding one is of Gemma di Giorgi, born in Sicily in 1939. She was blind from birth and doctors had declared her case to be hopeless, since she had no pupils in her eyes. In 1947, she was taken to Padre Pio and, though no pupils appeared, was cured of blindness during the visit to him.[7] In 1998, she appeared on television during a program on Padre Pio, still seeing, and still without pupils. We may adapt and apply to her the words of Our Lord concerning the man born blind (Jn 9:3): "She was born blind that the works of God might be made manifest in her."

There are saints who went for years without food, living only on Holy Communion. Accounts of these and other marvels might invite scepticism were there not living eyewitnesses, rigorous tests, and irrefutable evidence. Miracles do not belong to the age of fable and ignorance—whenever that was meant to have been. They belong to all ages, and, whatever may be alleged—rightly or wrongly—against past miracles, modern-day miracles have been scrutinised with all the rigour of modern science and technology.

We appeal to the miracles in the lives of the saints, and yet miracles are not necessary signs of sanctity. Some well-known saints—Sts Edmund Campion and Thomas More—are not credited with any vision or miracle at all in their lifetime. Yet one need only peruse a Dictionary of Saints to see how numerous are the miracles surrounding the Catholic saints. Unless we are going to say that God Himself has lent His power to uphold fraud, we must either discount human testimony altogether or acknowledge that the Church to which the Saints belonged is the living House of God.

---

[6] J. Eid, *The Hermit of Lebanon Father Charbel*, N.Y. 1955, p.34, photo p.140
[7] E. White, *Padre Pio: A Biographical Sketch*, Capuchin Friary, San Giovanni Rotondo, Italy 1986, pp.36-7

Incorrupt bodies of the Saints. The saints are the special friends and servants of God. Often God has signalled His favour by miracles during their lifetime, but also by miracles connected with their bodies after death—those bodies which were temples of the Holy Spirit, bodies in which they glorified God, and which are destined for a glorious resurrection at the end of the world. The bodies of more than one hundred Saints, Blessed and Venerable have remained incorrupt over a long period of time without the application of any preservatives or treatment. The first known case is the virgin martyr *St Cecilia* who died c. 177 A.D.

"Most of the incorruptibles … are neither dry nor rigid but quite moist and flexible, even after the passage of centuries. Moreover, their preservations have been accomplished under conditions which would naturally foster and encourage putrefaction, and they have survived circumstances which would have unquestionably necessitated and resulted in the destruction of others."[8] Some have eventually decomposed after years of exposure, but dozens of them are still on display in churches and chapels, permanently defying the laws of nature.

Two of the more extraordinary cases are those of St Andrew Bobola (d. 1657) and St Charbel Makhlouf. *St Andrew* was tortured at length, hideously mutilated and finally put to death by a sword. "His body was hastily buried by Catholics in a vault beneath the Jesuit church at Pinsk, where it was found forty years later perfectly preserved, in spite of the open wounds, which would normally foster corruption. Although his grave had been damp, causing his vestments to rot, and in spite of the proximity of decaying corpses, his body was perfectly flexible, his flesh and muscles soft to the touch, and the blood which covered the numerous wounds was found to be like that which is freshly congealed."[9]

St Charbel was buried shortly after his death in 1898, but after a mysterious light appeared about his tomb for the next forty-five nights, his body was exhumed four months after death, and was found to be in perfect condition, although it was floating on mud in a flooded grave. Thereafter, his body remained in perfect condition and exuded a slow constant flow of liquid, a mixture of perspiration and blood, until it was interred again in 1927. In 1950 it again started to exude a liquid that found its way into the oratory where pilgrims came to pray. The tomb was re-opened and still the body was as fresh as on the day of death. So it remained until it finally decomposed in 1965, the year of his beatification. Thus did a hermit, who sought only prayer, penance and solitude, become one of the best known figures in all the Middle East. "He who humbles himself will be exalted."[10]

---

[8] J.C. Cruz, *The Incorruptibles*, TAN Books, Illinois 1977, p.33
[9] Idem, p.36
[10] Lk 18:14

The book cited by no means contains an exhaustive list. Several others have been found since its writing, and other incorrupt bodies belong to holy people not yet officially recognised by the Church. Two more of recent note are Sr Rita Dolores Pujalte and Sr Francisca Aldea, martyred by the revolutionaries in Spain in 1936 and beatified in 1998. Their incorrupt bodies are in Villaverde near Madrid.

Miraculous relics. Apart from prodigies associated with entire corpses, God has been pleased to glorify His saints even by means of smaller pieces or articles connected with them.[11] Pre-eminent among them is the regular miracle connected to *the blood of St Januarius* (San Gennaro), the bishop of Benevento, Italy, martyred in 305. His relics, including his blood stored in two glass vials, are kept in the Cathedral of Naples. Three times every year, his blood mysteriously liquefies, remains liquid for some time, and then hardens again. This liquefaction happens: on the Saturday before the first Sunday in May and over the eight days following; on the saint's feast day September 19 and through the octave; and on December 16. The phenomenon has been observed every year since 1389, and only fails to occur before an approaching disaster for the city of Naples. It is an unparalleled miracle occurring publicly three times every year before thousands of people. A non-Catholic visitor from England who came to witness the phenomenon in 1987 remarked that he had no difficulty in accepting the genuineness of the miracle because, he said, a body so large and historic as the Catholic Church would not be so silly as to put her reputation at stake for the sake of a petty fraud. Similar miracles occur, also in Naples, with the blood of two other early martyrs, St Pantaleon and St Patricia.

Since her death at the age of twenty-three in 1870, *the voice of St Clelia Barbieri*, foundress of the Little Sisters of Mother of Sorrows, has been heard by individuals and groups on many occasions. Especially at Le Budrie di San Giovanni in Persiceto (near Bologna, Italy), the town of her birth and the location of her first religious house, her voice has been heard accompanying the Sisters in hymns, religious readings and conversations. She was heard thus for the first time on July 13, 1871, the first anniversary of her death, accompanying the prayers of the Sisters in their chapel. Many who have heard her voice over the years have given sworn testimony before ecclesiastical tribunals. The voice of the young foundress has also been heard by her Sisters, as well as priests and laity, in the religious congregation's houses in Asia and Africa.

The Shroud of Turin bears all the marks of a man crucified according to the ancient Roman practice and is perfectly consistent with the Passion of

---

[11] For the examples following, cf. J.C. Cruz, *Relics*, Our Sunday Visitor, Indiana 1984.

Jesus as recorded in the four Gospels. It bears the evidence of a scourging, a crown of thorns, crucifixion by three nails, a lance through the heart after death, and coins minted under Pontius Pilate placed over the eyes. The Shroud is the burial cloth of this man and bears the negative imprint of his body—an image that modern science is unable to explain or reproduce, since it is made of a substance undefined and formed by a process completely unknown. Learned and scientific studies have been written on the mysterious nature of this Shroud. The anatomical accuracy, the perfect consistency with the effects of crucifixion upon the body, the Jewish features of its majestic face, the three-dimensional properties of the image—all of which have only been discovered from 1898 onwards when it was photographed for the first time—place the Holy Shroud beyond the possibility of fraud, and even beyond the possibility of being man-made. To suppose that a medieval forger could have made an image beyond the understanding or powers of 20th century science is to suppose as great a miracle as any. The more reasonable explanation for this miracle is that Our Lord left us the image of His holy face, not seen upon this earth since His ascension, as a relic for our veneration and a stimulus to faith. To an age of unbelief and secular science, God has proposed the mysteries that lay hidden in the Holy Shroud for nineteen centuries. It corroborates the Gospels, vindicates faith and is authenticated by the science that it surpasses.

Similar in some respects to the Holy Shroud is the miraculous *image of Our Lady of Guadalupe*. At a time when the Reformation in Europe was wreaking havoc upon Christendom, the conversion of the Americas was heralded by the miraculous appearance of the Mother of God in 1531, outside Mexico City, to a poor Aztec peasant named Juan Diego. On 12th December that year, Our Lady told him to gather flowers at the top of Tepeyec hill nearby—a summit which was normally rocky and devoid of flowers. He went there to pick the flowers, and placed them in his *tilma* (a cloak), and went at once to the Bishop, as Our Lady told him to. When received by the Bishop, he opened the *tilma* and there was imprinted upon it a beautiful 4½-foot image of the Lady who had announced herself to Juan Diego as "the perfect and perpetual Virgin Mary, Mother of the true God". In the next seven years, eight million Aztecs were converted to Christ. This miraculous image has been venerated ever since, and is visited by thousands every day. The *tilma* itself on which it is imprinted should have corrupted centuries ago and yet it remains untouched by time. The image has been studied by scientists, and the colourings found to be made of substances unknown to science. In 1791, a goldsmith cleaning the frame accidentally spilt nitric acid on the left side of the *tilma*, but the only harm was a faint stain which has faded very slowly. In 1962, a magnification of the eyes of Our Lady of Guadalupe revealed the images of three people, one of whom is Juan Diego himself, recognised from the likeness to early portraits of him. This hidden testimony to the image's authenticity was unknown for the first four centuries of its existence. Other extraordinary qualities and symbolism have been noted in it over the centuries.

Miraculous apparitions. The sanctuary of Lourdes, France, where the Blessed Virgin Mary appeared to 14 year old St Bernadette Soubirous in 1858, identifying herself as "the Immaculate Conception", has become one of the most popular shrines in Christendom. On February 25 that year, Bernadette scratched into the ground as Mary told her to, and a spring of water began to flow where none had been before. From that time on to today, miracles of healing, and other blessings, have been reported by visitors to the spring and shrine. An international medical commission is based there to study claims of miraculous cures, and when they are verified, the evidence is kept there for public scrutiny. Sixty-six cures have passed the rigorous tests required.

Knock, in County Mayo, Ireland, in 1879, was the site of a silent apparition, lasting two hours. St Joseph, the Virgin Mary, St John, and the Lamb of God accompanied by angels, were witnessed by fifteen people young and old. Since then, Knock has become a place of pilgrimage where numerous cures, graces and conversions are attested.

At Fatima, Portugal, three young children reported seeing a beautiful lady in 1917, who appeared to them six times and identified herself as "the Lady of the Rosary". Our Lady promised a miracle on October 13, 1917, in confirmation of her message, and before 70,000 people, the sun did a dance in the sky, sent forth rays of different colours, and seemed to plunge to earth.

Similar accounts could be given of approved and verified appearances of the Blessed Mother at Guadalupe (1531) in Mexico; Rue de Bac (1830) in Paris; La Salette (1846) and Pontmain (1871) in France; Beauraing (1932-33) and Banneux (1933) in Belgium.

Eucharistic miracles. One of the most stunning declarations of Our Lord was given at the synagogue in Capernaum: "I am the living bread which came down from Heaven; if anyone eats of this bread, he will live for ever; and the bread which I shall give for the life of the world is My flesh."[12] In confirmation of these words, Jesus had worked the miracle of multiplication of the loaves of bread. Through the history of the Church, He has worked other miracles to illustrate and confirm the truth of these words, that the Holy Eucharist is no mere symbol, but is His living flesh. There are more

---

[12] Jn 6:51

than thirty Eucharistic miracles which have been documented, studied and venerated ever since their occurrence.[13]

The first known one occurred in the eighth century A.D. in Lanciano, Italy, during a Mass said by a Basilian monk tormented by doubts about the Real Presence. When he consecrated the bread and wine, they changed visibly into human flesh and blood before his eyes. The Flesh and Blood are still on permanent display in the church, 1,300 years later. Scientific tests ordered by the Holy See in 1970 produced the following conclusions: the flesh is real human flesh, consisting of the muscular tissue of the heart; the blood is real human blood, with the constitution and properties of freshly shed blood; the flesh and blood have the same blood type AB; their preservation over twelve centuries' exposure to nature without the use of preservative is inexplicable to science.

Other miracles are documented of hosts bleeding and leaving permanent stains; stolen hosts changing appearance, thus stunning their thieves and leading them to repent; hosts removing themselves from harm; and stolen hosts preserved for centuries after their robbery. Each episode is a unique demonstration of the Real Presence of Jesus Christ in the Blessed Sacrament, the treasure of treasures of the Catholic Church.

IV

THE HAND OF GOD IS SEEN IN THE MIRACLE OF THE CHURCH'S STABILITY AND THE ENDURANCE OF THE PAPACY

The endurance of the Catholic Church is the marvel of her adversaries. It is only the hand of God that could have brought her safe through perils which have proved fatal to merely human institutions. Often she seemed rent with schism or corrupted by heresy. The pallor of death seemed to have come upon her, but, sustained by her divine vitality, she cast off disease as a garment, and rose from her bed of sickness, renewed in youth and Pentecostal zeal. She is like the house of which Christ speaks in the Gospel: "and the rain fell, and the floods came, and the winds blew and beat upon that house, but it did not fall, because it had been founded on the rock."[14] Often have her children heard the demons' exultant cry that, at last, she was whelmed in the wave of death. But the tempest passed, and day broke anew, and the eyes of men beheld her still firmly fixed as of old on the rock of Peter, triumphant amid the wreckage of her enemies.

One of the most beautiful and eloquent testimonies to this perennial and miraculous endurance of the Church and the Papacy was penned by a

---

[13] cf. J.C. Cruz, *Eucharistic Miracles*, TAN Books, Illinois 1987; R. & P. Lord, *This is My Body, This is My Blood, Miracles of the Eucharist*, Journeys of Faith, USA 1986.
[14] Matt 7:25

Protestant writer, Lord Macaulay:[15] "There is not, and there never was on this earth, a work of human policy so well deserving of examination as the Roman Catholic Church. The history of that Church joins together the two great ages of human civilization. No other institution is left standing which carries the mind back to the times when the smoke of sacrifice rose from the Pantheon, and when camelopards[16] and tigers bounded in the Flavian amphitheatre.[17] The proudest royal houses are but of yesterday, when compared with the line of the Supreme Pontiffs. That line we trace back in an unbroken series, from the Pope who crowned Napoleon in the nineteenth century, to the Pope who crowned Pepin in the eighth; and far beyond the time of Pepin the august dynasty extends, till it is lost in the twilight of fable. The republic of Venice came next in antiquity. But the republic of Venice was modern when compared with the Papacy; and the republic of Venice is gone, and the Papacy remains. The Papacy remains, not in decay, not a mere antique, but full of life and youthful vigour. The Catholic Church is still sending forth to the furthest ends of the world missionaries as zealous as those who landed in Kent with Augustin, and still confronting hostile kings with the same spirit with which she confronted Attila. The number of her children is greater than in any former age. Her acquisitions in the New World have more than compensated her for what she has lost in the Old. Her spiritual ascendency extends over the vast countries which lie between the plains of the Missouri and Cape Horn— countries which, a century hence, may not improbably contain a population as large as that which now inhabits Europe. The members of her communion are certainly not fewer than a hundred and fifty millions;[18] and it will be difficult to show that all the other Christian sects united, amount to a hundred and twenty millions. Nor do we see any sign which indicates that the term of her long dominion is approaching. She saw the commencement of all the governments, and of all the ecclesiastical establishments, that now exist in the world; and we feel no assurance that she is not destined to see the end of them all. She was great and respected before the Saxon had set foot on Britain, before the Frank had passed the Rhine, when Grecian eloquence still flourished at Antioch, when idols were still worshipped in the temple of Mecca. And she may still exist in undiminished vigour when some traveller from New Zealand shall, in the midst of a vast solitude, take his stand on a broken arch of London Bridge to sketch the ruins of St Paul's."

Macaulay continues: "… It is not strange that, in the year 1799, even sagacious observers should have thought that, at length, the hour of the

---

[15] Essay on Leopold Ranke's *History of the Popes* (1840)
[16] giraffes
[17] the Colosseum
[18] now 1,000 million

Church of Rome was come. An infidel power ascendant, the Pope dying in captivity, the most illustrious prelates of France living in a foreign country on Protestant alms, the noblest edifices which the munificence of former ages had consecrated to the worship of God turned into temples of Victory, or into banqueting houses for political societies.... But the end was not yet. ... Anarchy had had its day. A new order of things rose out of the confusion, new dynasties, new laws, new titles; and amidst them emerged the ancient religion. The Arabs have a fable that the Great Pyramid was built by antediluvian kings, and alone, of all the works of men, bore the weight of the flood. Such as this was the fate of the Papacy. It had been buried under the great inundation; but its deep foundations had remained unshaken; and, when the waters abated, it appeared alone amidst the ruins of a world that had passed away. The republic of Holland was gone, and the empire of Germany, and the great Council of Venice, and the old Helvetian League, and the House of Bourbon, and the parliaments and aristocracy of France. Europe was full of young creations, a French empire, a kingdom of Italy, a Confederation of the Rhine. Nor had the late events affected only territorial limits and political institutions. The distribution of property, the composition and spirit of society, had, through a great part of Catholic Europe, undergone a complete change. But the unchangeable Church was still there."

The dangers to the Papacy came from within as well as from without. As an elective monarchy, notoriously the most unstable of all forms of government, it attracted the ambition of worldly ecclesiastics and, for a time during the Middle Ages, became a prize for which rival monarchs intrigued, each trying to secure it for his own minion. It was, therefore, threatened with the twofold evil of an unworthy occupant and a disappointed faction. Hence, we find that there have been a few incompetent and even wicked Popes, and that disastrous schisms have occurred from time to time. Any one of these schisms, any one of these Popes, if he had held a secular throne and were equally unfit for his office, would have brought the most powerful dynasty crashing to the ground. Moreover, the Papacy was threatened with another and, perhaps, greater, because more constant, danger, viz., the danger arising from ordinary human infirmity, for the Pope as a teacher, when not exercising his gift of infallibility, is liable to the errors of common men: St Peter was upbraided to the face by St Paul for his mistaken indulgence to the prejudices of Jewish converts, and some of his successors, though acting like him with the best intentions, seemed to bring the Church to the very brink of peril by their imprudence. In the long history of the Papacy, there have been errors of policy which would have cost a temporal monarch his throne. It seems as though God wished to make of the occasional weakness of the Papacy a motive of credibility, a proof that the Church is divinely supported. "God chose what is foolish in the world", says St Paul, "to shame the wise, God chose what is weak in the world to shame the strong, God chose what is low and despised in the world, even things that are not, to bring to nothing things that are, so that no human being might boast in the presence of God",[19] i.e., so that no one could take credit to himself for what had been the work of God. Again, we read in the Book of Judges how the Lord said to Gideon: "The people with you are too many for me to give the Midianites into their hand, lest Israel vaunt themselves against Me, saying, 'My own hand has delivered me'."[20] So He bade him keep only 300 men of the assembled host of 32,000. Gideon obeyed, and with this insignificant force he put a great army to rout. And as the hand of God was manifest in the triumph of Gideon in spite of inferiority of numbers, so has it been manifest in the survival of the Papacy in spite of the occasional weakness or unworthiness of those who have sat on the throne of Peter.

We may summarise the argument as follows: (1) The Papacy, the foundation on which the Church is built, is the only institution which has survived all the vast social and political changes and revolutions in the life and government of Europe since the days of the Roman Emperors. (2) It has survived in spite of persecution and political intrigue; in spite of heresy and schism among its subjects; in spite of the worldliness and the weakness or incompetence of some of the Popes. (3) It has survived, not as a mere shadow of its former greatness, but in unimpaired vigour. - Such a survival is miraculous. The Papacy and the Church over which it presides must, therefore, be the work of God.

The above proof from the Church herself as a living fact, as a successful achievement, is ever gathering force with the lapse of centuries. The first Vatican Council puts the apologetic argument very concisely in its chapter on faith: "To enable us to fulfil the duty of embracing the true faith and of persevering steadfastly in it, God established the Church through His only-begotten Son, and endowed her with manifest marks of her establishment, so that she can be recognised by all as the guardian and teacher of the revealed word. For to the Catholic Church alone belong all those marks, so many and so marvellous, which have been divinely established for the evident credibility of the Christian faith. Indeed, through her wonderful expansion, her outstanding holiness and inexhaustible fruitfulness in all good works, her worldwide unity and unconquerable endurance, the Church is herself a great and perpetual motive of credibility, and an unassailable witness to her divine mission. ..."

"Now this evidence is efficaciously supported by power from on high. For our most kind Lord not only rouses and helps the erring by His grace, that they may be able to 'come to the knowledge of the truth' (1 Tim 2:4), but by His grace confirms those whom 'He has brought from darkness into His marvellous light' (1

---

[19] 1 Cor 1:27-29
[20] Judges 7:2

Pet 2:9), that they may persevere in this same light, and He abandons no one, unless He is abandoned. Therefore, the situation of those who have adhered to Catholic truth by the heavenly gift of faith, is by no means on a par with those who, led by human opinions, follow a false religion; for the former, who embraced the faith under the teaching authority of the Church, can never have just cause for changing this faith or calling it into question."[21]

When English Prime minister William Gladstone (1809-1898), angered by the decree of the first Vatican Council (1870) and by the publication of a list of propositions condemned by the Holy See, asked contemptuously whether Rome could hope "to refurbish her rusty tools" and harness the avenging power of God to her excommunications in the modern world, he was reminded by Newman that the Pope who, in the Middle Ages, made Henry, the German Emperor, do penance bare-foot in the Snow at Canossa, had had his counterpart in that other Pope who, in the nineteenth century, and by an actual interposition of Providence, inflicted a "snow-penance" on the Emperor Napoleon. We quote the memorable words of the Protestant historian, Alison:[22] "'What does the Pope mean', said Napoleon to Eugene, in July 1807, 'by the threat of excommunicating me? Does he think the world has gone back a thousand years? Does he suppose the arms will fall from the hands of my soldiers?' Within two years after these remarkable words were written, the Pope did excommunicate him, in return for the confiscation of his whole dominions, and in less than four years more, the arms did fall from the hands of his soldiers; and the hosts, apparently invincible, which he had collected, were dispersed and ruined by the blasts of winter. 'The weapons of the soldiers', says Ségur, in describing the Russian retreat, 'appeared of an insupportable weight to their stiffened arms. During their frequent falls they fell from their hands, and, destitute of the power of raising them from the ground, they left them in the snow. They did not throw them away: famine and cold tore them from their grasp.'... There is something in these marvellous coincidences beyond the operations of chance, and which even a Protestant historian feels himself bound to mark for the observation of future ages. The world had not gone back a thousand years, but that Being existed with whom a thousand years are as one day, and one day as a thousand years."

And as He was with Pope Gregory in 1077, and with Pope Pius in 1812, so He was with Pope John Paul, a Slav elected to the papacy in 1978 from the midst of a communist empire that seemed permanent and intransigent, but which came apart in 1989. And so shall He be with some future Pope again, when the need shall come, and show to His enemies that His arm has not forgotten its strength.

---

[21] DS 3012-4
[22] *History of Europe*, Ch. 60

V

THE MIRACLE OF THE RAPID PROPAGATION OF CHRISTIANITY
AND THE FORTITUDE OF SO MANY MARTYRS
DYING FOR THE FAITH OF THE CHURCH

Tacitus says that in the first persecution of the Church (64-68 A.D.) under Nero "a vast multitude of Christians" were put to death.[23] Some, he says, were thrown to dogs, some crucified, and some were burned as torches in Nero's gardens. Fifty years later, Pliny, the Propraetor of Bithynia in Asia Minor (modern Turkey), reports to the Emperor Trajan that he is startled and perplexed by the number, influence, and pertinacity of the Christians he finds in his district and in the neighbouring province of Pontus.[24] St Justin Martyr, writing about 150 A.D., says, "There is not a single race of men, whether barbarians or Greeks, or whatever name they may be called, or of waggon-dwellers or shepherds or nomads in tents, among whom prayers and eucharists are not offered to the Father and Maker of the Universe through the name of the crucified Jesus."[25] Around the year 197, in his classic *Apology* of the Christian religion, Tertullian could boast, "We (Christians) are but of yesterday, and we have filled every place among you—cities, islands, fortresses, towns, market-places, the camp itself, tribes, companies, the palace, the senate, the Forum,—we have left to you nothing but the temples of your gods."[26] At the conversion of the Emperor Constantine in 324 A.D., about one-twelfth of the Roman world was Christian. The proportion had risen to one-half about the year 400 A.D. Three decades later an imperial document declared that paganism had almost completely disappeared. The triumph of the new creed was social as well as numerical. Gradually it had worked its way upwards from despised toilers to proud officials, from uncultured Jews to learned philosophers.

Such a rapid and world-wide revolution cannot be explained by natural causes:

(1) The founder of the religion was, in the eyes of the world, a poor Galilean tradesman. Four of His Apostles were fishermen, and one a petty tax collector. When Sts Peter and John, after the first Christian miracle, were arraigned before the Council, wonder was expressed that such "uneducated, common men"[27] had the presumption to preach a new Gospel. The same charge was repeated many times in the years that followed. "Christians", said their opponents, "are fools … the lowest dregs

---

[23] *Annals* xv, 44. Tacitus lived c. 55-120 A.D.
[24] Lib. 10; *Ep.* 97
[25] *Dial. cum. Tryph.* n. 117
[26] *Apol.* 37
[27] Acts 4:13

of people ... unpolished boors, ignorant even of the sordid arts of life; they do not understand even civil matters, how can they understand divine? ... They have left their tongs, mallets, and anvils to preach about the things of heaven."[28] Such was the character the Christian teachers bore. Against them were pitted the power, wealth, intelligence and organisation of the Roman Empire.

(2) The doctrine preached by the Apostles was new and repellent to the worldly-minded. It demanded faith and humble submission, brotherly love and self-sacrifice unto death, from a people sunk in materialism, lustful, proud, revengeful, and almost incapable of an elevated concept of the Deity. It urged them to smash to pieces the long hallowed images of gods that were nothing more, they were now told, than personifications of the powers of nature and of base, human passions. It bade them forsake their ancient religion, so flattering to the senses, with its noble temples, its stately ritual, its days of public amusement, and attach themselves to a joyless band of despicable men whose eyes were fixed on the things of another world, and who bowed down in worship before the image of a crucified malefactor.

But, it may be objected, perhaps the very corruption of the world at the time made men sick of vice and long for a great moral reform. We reply: (a) that at Rome in those days, the Stoic philosophers taught a very pure system of morals, and yet they made no impression on the masses; (b) that admiration for Christian morals is very far removed from full faith in Christian teaching and from the practice of Christian precepts; (c) that we cannot conceive how, without the grace of the Holy Spirit, men could ever have overcome their repugnance for what must have seemed the unspeakable folly or blasphemy of its central doctrine that a Galilean workman was the Son of God.

But, again, it may be urged that the rapid propagation of Christianity can be explained by the ease and security with which men could travel in those days to all parts of the Roman Empire. We reply: (a) that other religions, e.g., the worship of Mithra and Isis, enjoyed similar facilities, and yet failed to win and retain world-wide acceptance; (b) that while Roman roads and Roman security on land and sea helped to speed the Christian messenger to the furthest limits of the earth, all such advantages were far more than countervailed by the edge of the Roman sword. Ten times, that vast empire concentrated all its might on the destruction of the infant Church, and, ten times, the followers of the poor Galilean emerged triumphant.

---

[28] For references, see Newman, *Grammar of Assent*, Ch. 10.2, p.468. The noble Roman pagans regarded Christ also as just one of the rabble, because He had been a carpenter. They despised all hand-workers and grouped them under the symbol of the ass, the poor farm-drudge; but, as Chesterton says in one of his great poems, that humble creature had his day of honour when there were palms before his feet.

"You put Christians on crosses and stakes", says Tertullian, "You tear the sides of Christians with your hooks. ... We lay our heads upon the block. ... We are thrown to wild beasts. ... We are burned in the flames. ... We are condemned to the mines. ... We are banished to islands." "But carry on, good officers, you will grow in the esteem of the people if you sacrifice Christians at their wish: crucify us, torture us, condemn us, grind us to dust; your injustice is the proof that we are innocent. ... Nor does your cruelty, however exquisite, avail you; it is, rather, an incitement to us. The more often we are mown down by you, the more we grow in number: the blood of Christians is the seed."[29]

The persecution of Christianity, in its severity and duration, in the number, quality, and fortitude of its victims, forms a unique episode in history.   From A.D. 64 to A.D. 313, Christians endured 129 years of persecution and 120 of tranquillity. The hostility of the Empire, over those three centuries, broke out with especial violence on ten separate occasions. "The very young and the very old, the child, the youth in the heyday of his passions, the sober man of middle age, maidens and mothers of families, boors and slaves as well as philosophers and nobles, solitary confessors and companies of men and women—all these were seen equally to defy the powers of darkness to do their worst. ... They faced the implements of torture as the soldier takes his place before the enemy's battery. They cheered and ran forward to meet his attack, and, as it were, dared him, if he would, to destroy the numbers who kept closing up the foremost rank, as their comrades who had filled it fell."[30]   But their courage was not the courage of a hardened soldier. He has been trained to valour; he goes into battle, not as a lamb to slaughter, not as a passive victim merely to suffer and to die, but with weapons in his hands, prepared to give blow for blow. And in fulfilling his duty, he is supported by the conviction that to stand his ground is safer than to retreat, or he is moved by shame of cowardice, or by desire to win the applause of men. The martyrs, however, from the world's standpoint, had everything to lose and nothing to gain from their fortitude. Many of them no more than poor little children—they suffered themselves to be smeared with pitch and set alight, to be flung into boiling cauldrons, to be torn to pieces by the beasts of the amphitheatre, and all this amid the execrations of the crowd who cursed their obstinacy and promised them every reward if they would but yield. All their strength came from the one thought, the one image of their Crucified Saviour whom they loved with an impassioned love. But how, without the inspiration of God, could that same thought have "entered into myriads of men, women, and children of all ranks, especially the lower, and have had the power to wean them from

---

[29] Tertullian, *Apol.* 12 and 50
[30] Newman, *Grammar of Assent*, Ch. 10.2, pp.477-8

their indulgences and sins, and to nerve them against the most cruel tortures, and to last in vigour as a sustaining influence for seven or eight generations, till ... it broke the obstinacy of the strongest and wisest government which the world has ever seen?"[31]

The exact number of martyrs in those first three centuries is impossible to calculate, but it has been estimated that possibly 100,000 executions took place,[32] or between one hundred and two hundred thousand.[33] Yet even that number of martyrdoms by itself fails to provide a sufficient picture of the persecutions, because for each one martyr there were perhaps several others who suffered confiscation of goods or property, expulsion from public offices or employment, false accusations, denial of legal and civic rights, imprisonment, torture, banishment or condemnation to slave labour in mines.[34]

To put the whole argument briefly: the *rapid propagation of Christianity* among all classes throughout the world *was miraculous*: (1) because its preachers were men of no worldly influence; (2) because its chief doctrine was strange and repellent, while its system of morals was severe and offered no bribe to human infirmity; (3) because it was resisted by all the power of the Roman Empire.

The *fortitude of the Martyrs was miraculous*: (1) because the persecutions extended over three centuries; (2) because vast numbers of every rank and age suffered, including children of tender years; (3) because their constancy was proof against the most terrible tortures; (4) because they were unmoved in the face of the attractive rewards promised them, if they yielded; (5) because, in the throes of death, they gave a beautiful and superhuman manifestation of Christian virtue, of the joyful acceptance of death and suffering, of seraphic love, of profound humility, and of the very spirit of Christ on the Cross, praying with full heart for the salvation of their enemies, and blessing the very hands that were red with their blood. - It is the combination of all these features, a combination unique in human history, that sets beyond the possibility of doubt the miraculous character of the endurance of the early Christians. The persecutions to which other religions have been subjected were either not so lasting, or not so severe or not so willingly borne, and were certainly never accompanied by a great, steady, and continuous effulgence of Christian virtue.

In the early history of Christianity, therefore, we are confronted with two great miracles: the miracle of propagation and the miracle of endurance.

[31] Ibid., p.465
[32] L. Hertling S.J., 'Die Zahl der Märtyrer bis 313', *Gregorianum* xxv (1944) 103-29
[33] I. Lesbaupin, *Blessed are the Persecuted*, N.Y. 1987, p.14
[34] Ibid., p.14. Cf. S. Tromp S.J., *De Revelatione Christiana*, Gregoriana, Rome 1950, pp.362-5.

These two irresistible testimonies from God confirm that the Christian religion was true, and that Christ, its Founder, was, as He claimed, the Son of God, equal to His Father.

But the age of the martyrs in the Church was not just in the first three centuries: martyrs have not been wanting in any age.

The conversion of Constantine did not put an end to persecution, but simply transferred it.

In the *4th century*, the Persians used to persecute Christians as suspect of collaboration with the Christian emperors. Sozomen and St Athanasius record the martyrdom of Catholics by Arian heretics in various parts of the Roman Empire. In North Africa, St Optatus and St Augustine attest to Catholics martyred by Donatist heretics. In Alexandria, a group of pagans seized a number of Christians, whom they cajoled to offer sacrifice to Serapis, and upon their refusal put them to death.

5th century. Under the Vandal regime, from the time of Gaiseric in 429, Catholics suffered much persecution in Africa from the Arians. Bishops especially were persecuted for their attachment to Rome. Under the seven years' rule of Huneric, Catholics were excluded from political and administrative positions, and nearly 5,000 clergy and faithful were condemned to exile. Those who resisted received 550 lashes or were burnt alive.

6th century. The Maronite Catholic Church on 31st July every year commemorates the feast of their 350 monks killed for the faith in Syria by monophysite heretics in 517. In Ethiopia in 523, a convert to Judaism, Dunaan, besieged Najran and decreed death for every Christian who would not apostasise: 4,000 men, women and children were slain. The Lombards invaded Italy in 568 and for many years thereafter attempted sporadically to force pagan rites upon local Christians, and killed about four hundred who refused to do so, as related by the contemporary St Gregory the Great. Earlier in the century, the great philosopher Boethius was martyred by Theodoric, an Arian Goth; and St Herculanus, bishop of Perugia, was also a victim of Gothic persecution.

7th century. This century saw the rise of Mohammed and the religion of Islam founded by him. Before his death in 632, Mohammed had become religious and political ruler of Arabia. Under the Caliphs, his successors, Islam set out to conquer the world: the Persian Empire was taken, Syria fell in 634, Palestine in 637, Egypt in 640, North Africa in 695, and Spain in 711. From Spain, the Moslems crossed the Pyrenees and overran all the south of France. The Moslem take-over of North Africa saw the annihilation of what in the time of St Augustine in the 5th century had been a thriving Christian region of more than 350 dioceses. Islam was destined to become the most enduring threat to the Church through all her history. In every generation, for another 900 years, a violent assault would be made upon Christendom from some quarter of the Moslem world. When a *jihad* or Moslem holy war is in progress, prisoners can be given the alternative of instant conversion to Islam or instant death. From the 7th century on, many Christians have been martyred in these circumstances. In other parts of the Church about this time, St Kilian and his companions were martyred in Germany. St Anastasius was martyred in Persia in 628 after a series of relentless tortures which he bore with such patience and tranquillity as to astonish his captors.

8th-11th centuries. Just as the Arian heretics had martyred Catholics in the 4th century, so in the 8th century the Iconoclast heresy was the cause of persecution. In the Byzantine empire, many clerics, monks and devout lay people obtained the martyr's crown under the Iconoclasts. St Paul of Cyprus, one of these many martyrs, was given the choice of trampling upon a crucifix or being tortured upon the rack. During the 9th-11th centuries, the Church continued to give the witness of the martyrs' blood in two main connections. The first was the struggle with Islam, in which martyrs were faithful unto death in Spain and other territories held by the Moslems. The second was the slow spread of the missions in central and northern Europe, during which heroic missionaries were martyred, as for example, St Boniface, the 'Apostle of Germany', killed by the pagans at Dokkum in the Netherlands in 754. In other separate events, bishops upholding Christian teaching were put to death: St Lambert, bishop of Maastricht, was murdered in Liège c. 705 in revenge for having denounced an adulterous marriage; in 1079, St Stanislaus, bishop of Cracow, was killed by King Boleslaus II for opposing the king's lustful abduction of another man's wife.

12th century. St Thomas à Becket, archbishop of Canterbury, shed his blood for the freedom of the Church when assassinated in 1170 in his cathedral by a group of soldiers sent by Henry II. Blessed Charles the Good was martyred in 1127 in Bruges, Flanders, for his Christian virtue and justice. St Botvid, a Swedish layman, was killed in 1100. St Henry, bishop of Uppsala, Finland, was martyred c. 1156.

13th-15th centuries. In the high medieval period, the Cathar or Albigensian heresy infected some parts of Europe. In Toulouse, France, in 1242, a group of twelve Catholics, including St William Arnaud, was martyred by these dualist heretics. Russia gained further martyrs when the Tartars invaded the country. In 1220, six Franciscans sent by St Francis to preach to the Moslems in Spain and then Morocco were decapitated and thus became the first martyrs of the Franciscan order. In 1227, seven Franciscans—St Daniel and his companions—went to Morocco as missionaries to convert the Moslems, and were captured, imprisoned, threatened and decapitated. In the year 1261 alone, more than 200 Franciscans were martyred in north Africa, and a short time later 190 Dominicans. In 1480, Mohammed II's men took the city of Otranto in the Kingdom of Naples: they slew all the priests and 800 men of the city, they sawed in two the aged Archbishop of Otranto, whom they found praying before the altar; they butchered many captives who refused to become Moslems and threw their corpses to dogs.

It would be an endless task to list the martyrs under Islam, but they have given witness in literally every century, and in almost every country where Christian missionaries have gone, or in which Christian communities, like the Catholic Maronites of Mount Lebanon, have lived under Moslem rule.

The other abiding cause of martyrdom has been persecution by heretics, arising from among hitherto Catholic populations. For example, in Prague, in 1420, sixty-four friars were burnt to death when their monastery was set alight by Hussite heretics.

16th century onwards. With the opening up of the New World and the Far East to European contact from the 16th century onwards, new mission fields and new martyrdoms have figured in Catholic history. In Japan, where evangelisation was begun by St Francis Xavier in 1549, the first martyrs suffered towards the end of the century. St Paul Miki and his twenty-five companions were crucified at Nagasaki, Japan, in 1597, and died with prayers, hymns and acclamations on their lips. 1622 was the year of the Japanese "great martyrdom" which saw a host of priests and lay people, including five-year-old children, put to death by a whole variety of means. The martyrs of Japan in the 16th and 17th centuries run into the thousands. 26 have been declared Saint and 205 are Blessed. Every refined and exquisite torture was used against these martyrs to make them apostasise and trample upon a religious image.

In India, the first Franciscan missionaries were martyred by Moslems in 1521. Hindus murdered Jesuit missionaries in India also.

The first martyrs of the New World were three Franciscans killed by Caribs in the Antilles in 1516. Massacres on the mainland of South America soon followed. Friar Juan de Padilla in 1544 was the first martyr of North America.

The Protestant Revolt which began under Luther in 1517 ushered in a new era of persecution for Catholics in Europe. Lutherans and Calvinists persecuted Catholics in Germany, Switzerland, Denmark and Norway, destroying or confiscating churches and Church goods, and driving religious out of their monasteries and convents onto the streets. The followers of Calvin martyred many Catholics in present-day Holland, Belgium and Luxembourg. In all of the provinces of France, there were Catholics massacred by the French Calvinists, known as Huguenots. Cardinal de Lorraine could say at the Council of Trent, "Three thousand French religious have undergone martyrdom for refusing to betray the Apostolic See." In 1571 Jeanne d'Albret decreed the abolition of Catholic worship in her kingdom of Béarn. Countless Catholics of all ages and states were massacred. In Hungary, Catholics were persecuted by both Lutherans and Calvinists.

Under Henry VIII in England, St John Houghton was the first to be martyred, when the Carthusian monks of the London Charterhouse were put to death for refusing to renounce the supremacy of the Pope. They were followed by St John Fisher the Bishop of Rochester, and Henry VIII's own friend and onetime Lord Chancellor, Sir Thomas More. That was in 1535, and the English and Welsh martyrdoms continued until William Howard, the last victim, in 1680. In that century and a half, a vast number of British Catholic priests and lay people were regularly fined, hunted, persecuted, imprisoned, tortured and executed—the executions often imposed by hanging, drawing and quartering. Many met their horrible deaths after torture upon the rack to make them betray other Catholics. More than 600 were put to death, of whom 318 are certified martyrs. Forty of these martyrs of England and Wales were canonised in 1970, and 85 were beatified in 1987. In Scotland, St John Ogilvie was tortured for months before undergoing execution for the faith in 1615. St Oliver Plunkett, Archbishop of Armagh and Primate of Ireland, was the last Catholic executed at Tyburn, London, in 1681. All of these martyrs could have saved their skins and put an end to their tortures at once if they renounced the Catholic religion or agreed to attend Anglican services. In 1992, Pope John Paul II beatified seventeen Irish Catholic martyrs, a selection of 259 who were martyred in the years 1537-1713. One of the Blessed was Archbishop Dermot O'Hurley of Cashel, whose feet were boiled in oil to make him recant his religion. Steadfast to the end, he was finally hanged in 1584.

17th century onwards. There were martyrs amongst Eastern Christians who returned to unity with Rome, among whom is counted St Josaphat, beaten by a mob and shot dead in Vitebsk, Russia in 1623. St Andrew Bobola, who helped bring many Orthodox into the Catholic Church, was murdered by Cossacks in 1657 with merciless and prolonged torture and mutilation, until he was finally beheaded. In Ethiopia in 1638, Franciscan missionary priests were martyred. The first martyr of China was the Dominican priest, Francisco de Capillas, in 1648. He was followed by numerous others, especially in the 18th and 19th centuries. Several Spanish and Portuguese missionaries were martyred in Central America by the natives. In Paraguay, three Jesuits who had conducted the famed "Reductions"—settlements of native Christians—were killed by hostile locals. Legendary too are the Canadian and North American martyrs, St Isaac Jogues, St Jean de Brébeuf and their companions, who lived and worked among the Hurons and Algonquins, but were tortured and killed by members of the Huron and Iroquois tribes in the years 1642-49. In the Philippines, the first martyr of the Visayas, the 18-year old mission volunteer, Pedro Calungsod, was speared to death in 1672.

18th century onwards. The martyrs of the French Revolution are an abundant host, of whom the Church has officially recognised, among others, the sixteen Carmelite nuns of Compiègne, four Daughters of Charity of Cambrai, eleven Ursuline nuns of Valenciennes, the religious of Orange, the martyrs of Laval, 99 martyrs of Angers, and three bishops along with 188 companions at Paris (the September Martyrs of 1792). In India, the fifty years to 1799 under the Rajah of Mysore, saw a severe persecution which brought death to thousands upon thousands of Christians, and reduced others to slavery. Vietnam was the site of a series of persecutions over the years 1745-1862, the martyrs including St Theophanes Vénard who was beheaded at the age of thirty-one. From 1820-1841, the sovereign tried to obliterate the Christian faith from his country. Christians were called upon to renounce their religion and trample upon the crucifix. Death was decreed for all priests. 117 martyrs of Vietnam were canonised by John Paul II—the largest single group canonised together—but these are only a tiny proportion of the tens of thousands over the years there, many of whom endured atrocities of diabolical cruelty.

19th century. In Africa, where missions greatly expanded in the late 19th century, the blood of the martyrs has again proved to be the seed of the Church. The White Fathers' mission to Uganda brought many converts. Under the despot Mwanga, about a hundred Christians were most brutally put to death there in the years 1885-87. Most of the victims were very young or newly baptised by the French missionaries. In 1964, Pope Paul VI canonised twenty-two of them—Charles Lwanga and his companions—and remarked that the accounts of their glorious martyrdom read like the annals of martyrdom in Africa in the first centuries of Christianity. In Korea, the 19th century saw thousands of martyrs. St Andrew Kim Taegon, martyred in 1846, was among 103 Korean martyrs canonised in Korea itself by Pope John Paul II, in the first Papal canonisation to take place outside Rome. By 1858, the Church in Japan, once accredited with 1,800,000 members in the 16th century, seemed almost completely annihilated. She again suffered a spate of persecution from 1869 to 1871: several thousand Catholics were exiled or deported. Many others died on account of privations or tortures. Religious liberty arrived in 1889. In the South Seas, on the island of Futuna in 1841, the French Marist priest St Peter Chanel was clubbed to death and became the first martyr of Oceania. When new missionaries arrived soon after, the whole island was converted.

Yet these are but a selection of the martyrs of the first 19 centuries.
The 20th century alone would require entire volumes: it is estimated that there have been more martyrs for Christ in the 20th century than in all the previous centuries put together. Early in the century, the virgin martyr, eleven year old St Maria Goretti, was stabbed fourteen times with a knife, and when her mother told her in hospital that she had to forgive her assassin, she replied, "I have already." And as St Stephen's martyrdom won the conversion of Saul, so Maria's won the conversion several years later of her murderer Alessandro Serenelli. He was eventually released from prison, thereafter led an exemplary Catholic life and lived to see her canonisation attended by Maria's mother and family. Other virgin martyrs have followed Maria's example, among them Blessed Karoline Kózka in 1914, Bl. Antonia Mesina in 1935 and Bl. Pierina Morosini in 1957.

Persecution on differing scales has brought martyrs in such countries as Thailand, Indonesia, East Timor, the Philippines, Spain, Nigeria, Sudan, Egypt, Algeria, El Salvador, Mexico, Chile, Peru and several other countries of Latin America and Africa.

Severe persecution took place in Thailand in the 1940's. Among the martyrs are Bl. Philip Sipong and six companions. Bl. Miguel Pro S.J. was executed by firing squad in 1927, one of 25 beatified Mexican martyrs from the years 1920-1930. In the religious persecution of the years 1936-39 in Spain, twelve bishops, nearly 7,000 priests and religious men, 283 nuns and 5-6,000 lay people of Catholic Action, were put to death—many of them in the classic circumstances of martyrdom: offered life if they renounced their faith but death if they upheld it. Of these, 218 have been beatified.

Many Catholics too were martyred under the Nazis. The most famous of the Christians of Jewish origin to suffer was the philosopher and Carmelite nun, St Edith Stein, put to death at Auschwitz in 1942. She had been rounded up along with other Jewish Christians in revenge for the Dutch bishops' pastoral letter denouncing the deportation of Jews by the Nazis. Among other martyrs under Nazism officially recognised by the Church are the Franciscan priest St Maximilian Kolbe—starved almost to the point of death, and then killed by injection at Auschwitz in 1941—and the Carmelite priest Titus Brandsma, given a lethal injection in 1942. Among Poles murdered by the Nazis in the years 1939-45 were six bishops, 2,030 priests, 243 nuns, 173 brothers and 127 seminarians. The Nazi concentration camp of Dachau in Bavaria held, amongst others, at least 2,600 Catholic priests from 24 nations—of whom about 1,100 perished or were executed while there.

The victims of the Soviet Union and the whole communist empire from its emergence in 1917 to its collapse in 1989 are beyond imagining. Persecution on a grand scale brought large numbers of martyrs in such diverse countries as Russia, China, Mongolia, Vietnam, Laos, Cambodia, North Korea, Croatia and Cuba. Entire books have been written documenting the tales of communist persecution, show trials, imprisonment, forced labour, torture, and executions. The Church suffered persecution in Albania, Bulgaria, Romania, Czechoslovakia, East Germany, Hungary, Yugoslavia, Poland, and in all the provinces of the U.S.S.R., including Byelorussia, Moldavia, Lithuania, Latvia, Estonia and Ukraine. Members of the college of cardinals proved themselves worthy confessors of Christ under persecution: Cardinal Stepinac in Croatia, Cardinal Beran in Czechoslovakia, Cardinal Mindszenty in Hungary, Cardinal Wyszynski in Poland, and Cardinal Slipyj in Ukraine. In Ukraine, after 1941, ten bishops, more than 1,400 priests, 800 nuns and tens of thousands of Catholics laid down their lives. In 1945, the entire Ukrainian Catholic hierarchy was arrested, tried under false charges and deported to Siberia. In Albania, the persecution of religious believers was perhaps the most relentless in all the world. All religious buildings were closed or taken over for secular use. Almost all priests were killed or imprisoned. In 1973, one of the few surviving priests, Fr Shtjefen Kurti, was put on trial at the age of seventy and later executed by a military firing squad, for baptising a child. In China, the Catholic Church has faced violent persecution throughout the second half of the 20th century. Heroic bishops, priests, religious and laity have been put to death and many have endured decades of imprisonment.

As noted earlier, Islamic persecution over the centuries has been continuous, and the number of martyrs countless. Still today much persecution takes place and many martyrdoms occur in Islamic countries, of which only a fraction are ever publicly recorded. Often converts to Christianity must flee their homes lest even their own family members murder them for renouncing Islam. In Saudi Arabia, Christians have no religious freedom and are frequently subject to mistreatment and legal penalties. In India and Pakistan, murders of Christians or of family converts from the Hindu religion to Christ occur so often as to go unreported, and on many occasions the murders take place with impunity. Officers of the law are not interested in the deaths of Christians. Priests and religious in India defending the rights of the poor and oppressed have been tortured viciously and killed.

And the martyrdoms continue: it is estimated that every two weeks at least one Catholic missionary somewhere is put to death out of hatred for the Christian religion. The Congregation of Propaganda Fide counted thirty-one priests and religious murdered for the faith in the year 1999—fifteen in Africa, ten in Asia, and six in Latin America.

These countless deaths have not been without fruit. Now as earlier, the blood of martyrs is the seed of Christians: apart from that major fruit garnered by the martyrs themselves—undying glory in Paradise—the Church universal has continued to expand: in Africa, Catholics numbered two million at the start of the

20th century, and now number 110 million. "Christus vincit, Christus regnat, Christus imperat!" Christ conquers, Christ reigns, Christ rules!

Can any merely human belief and power have sustained such a vast array of martyrs? Have they not been divinely sustained to witness to a divine message? The survival and endurance of the Church have made clear to the world that she owes nothing to human agency, and that man did not build what man has been powerless to destroy.

There stand before us: Jesus Christ, the Faith, and the Church. There has been no other Person in history, no other Belief, no other Body, for whom so many men, women and children of the most diverse countries and epochs have been willing to sacrifice so much, suffer such torments and lay down their lives, rather than commit betrayal. This is God's testimony to His Son, His Truth and His Church, the love of whom can be planted deeper than any other love in the human heart.

*   *   *

Any one of the special characteristics outlined above would alone suffice to justify the claim of the Catholic Church. Each one is in itself a moral miracle, i.e., a miracle of human behaviour. Each one is in itself a proof of God's special and extraordinary support. But it is the combination of all, their mass effect, which makes the argument absolutely overwhelming.

The Church presents to the unprejudiced inquirer the unmistakable marks of her divine mission. From her brow there flashes forth the light of truth that brings assent. Truly she is "the standard set up unto the nations[35] who calls unto herself all those who do not yet believe, and gives to her own children the full assurance that the Faith they profess rests on solid foundations."[36]

Summary

We who are Catholics believe that the Catholic Church is the one and only Church of God.

We believe, because God has testified that what we believe is true.

He has conveyed His testimony to us in many ways, but chiefly by setting before our eyes the unique characteristics of the Church herself, viz., her miraculous unity with worldwide Catholicity, her sanctity, her gift of miracles, her unconquerable

---

[35] Cf. Isaiah 11:12.
[36] V 3014

endurance, and the number and fortitude of her martyrs.

We bless and thank Him for giving us the light to see so clearly the imprint of His hands. We bless and thank Him for inclining our hearts to submit to His Church, and to love her as our Spiritual Mother.

In short, the unique and marvellous characteristics of the Catholic Church cannot be due to the operation of any natural cause. They can be explained only by the action of some great, living, intelligent being, the master of the human mind and heart, the Lord of destiny and of history. That being we call God.

CHAPTER 13

THE BIBLE

Summary

I.   The teaching of the Church.
II.   What is 'the Bible'. Inspiration and human co-operation. Inerrancy.
III. Sacred Scripture and Sacred Tradition. The relationship and differences between the two.
IV.   The content of the Bible. The Old Testament and history of Israel. The conquest of Canaan. Covenant. God's promises to the Jews. The New Testament. Differences between the Old and New Testaments.
IV.   Difficulties in the Bible. Diverse genres of books in the Bible. The historicity of the Old Testament. The historicity of the Gospels.
VI.   The interpretation of the Bible entrusted to the Magisterium. Reading the Bible in context. The four senses of Sacred Scripture: literal, allegorical, moral, anagogical. Rationalist criticism. False principles of interpretation.
VII. The Canon. Differences between content of Catholic and Protestant Bibles. Differences between Bibles. Chapter and verse. Reading the Bible.
VIII. Objections answered.

I

The teaching of the Church. The Church teaches as of Faith:

(1)   that the books of Sacred Scripture, with all their parts, being inspired by God, have God for their author, and are the Word of God;[1]

(2)   that the Bible is free from error;[2]

(3)   that the canon of Scripture contains the 46 books of the Old Testament and the 27 of the New;[3]

(4)   that the official interpretation of Scripture has been entrusted to the magisterium (teaching office) of the Church;[4]

(5)   that no one may interpret a text of Scripture in a manner contrary to a teaching of the Church;[5]

(6)   that no one may interpret a text of Scripture in a manner contrary to the unanimous consent of the Fathers;[6]

(7)   that the teachings of the Church are consistent with the Bible;[7]

---

[1] T 1501, 1504; V 3006, 3029 (T = Council of Trent; V = first Vatican Council. 1501 = paragraph no. in Denzinger: see list of abbreviations at start of book).
[2] DS 3291-3
[3] T 1501-4; cf. C 120.
[4] T 1507; V 3007
[5] T 1507; V 3007
[6] T 1507; V 3007

(8) that the truths which God has revealed are found in Sacred Scripture and Tradition;[8]

(9) that the fact that God has spoken to us can be most certainly known from miracles and prophecies;[9]

(10) that the Bible contains accounts of genuine miracles and prophecies by Moses, the Prophets, Christ and the Apostles;[10]

(11) that the Old Testament is fulfilled in the New Testament and Jesus Christ.[11]

II

What is meant by "the Bible". The Bible is inspired by God. Human co-operation with Inspiration. Inerrancy of the Bible.

THE BIBLE. The word *Bible* comes from the Greek word meaning *book*. The collection of Jewish and Christian sacred writings came to be known as the "Books" (*Biblia* in Greek) and became *Bible* in English, with its equivalent in other languages. The Latin word for writings, *Scripturae*, came to be reserved for the inspired writings, and became *Scriptures* in English. The Bible is not just *one* book but a collection of many and diverse books, written by different authors over several centuries for different audiences. "The Church accepts and venerates as inspired the 46 books of the Old Testament and the 27 books of the New."[12] (The O.T. has 45 books if *Jeremiah* and *Lamentations* count as one). Although composed of many books, the Bible is, at the same time, *one* Book, because it contains one Revelation and has one divine Author. The Bible is unique, therefore, and in the sacred liturgy, in theology and the life of the Church, no other writing, however beautiful or inspiring, can ever take the place of Sacred Scripture.

THE INSPIRATION OF THE BIBLE. God is the author of the books of Sacred Scripture. God inspired the books, or rather, He inspired the human writers who recorded what He wanted them to write. For this reason, the sacred texts are said to be the "Word of God". By appropriation,[13] inspiration is attributed to God the Holy Spirit. The first Christians knew that the Old Testament writings had been inspired by God the Holy Spirit:

---

[7] Ordinary and universal teaching of the Church. Cf. V 3070, C 85-6.

[8] V 3006, T 1501

[9] V 3009, 3033-4; Pius IX, DS 2778

[10] V 3009, 3034

[11] Ordinary and universal teaching of the Church. Cf. C 128-30.

[12] C 138

[13] On appropriation, see p.315.

St Paul says, "All scripture is inspired by God".[14] Sts Peter and Paul and others, when quoting the Old Testament, say, "as the Holy Spirit said, …".[15] Our Lord Himself had done the same: He quoted a psalm of King David, saying that David spoke, "inspired by the Holy Spirit".[16] Our Lord showed that He recognised the authority of the Jewish books by quoting them as the Word of God. The New Testament frequently quotes the Old Testament. Later books of the New Testament refer to other earlier books of the New Testament as "Scripture".[17]

INSPIRATION DOES NOT EXCLUDE HUMAN CO-OPERATION AND LABOUR. Inspiration does not mean "dictation". God did not dictate the Sacred Writings word for word, as a businessman dictates a letter to a secretary. "Now in composing the sacred books, God chose certain men whom He employed, as they used their faculties and powers, so that, as He acted in them and through them, they, as true authors, consigned to writing all those things and only those things, which He wanted written."[18] God used men as His instruments, but used them as free intelligent beings, respecting their intelligence, free will and other human faculties. They inquired and researched as necessary, like any writer preparing a work. The human authors, though moved by God, wrote in their own manner, using their own thoughts, images and words. Under God's inspiration, they wrote in one or other of the literary forms with which they were familiar.

THE BIBLE IS INERRANT, I.E., IT CONTAINS NO ERROR. From what has been said, it clearly follows that the Bible, being the Word of God, cannot contain any error. Pope Pius XII likens Sacred Scripture to the Incarnation thus: "Just as the substantial Word of God became like men in every respect except sin, so too the words of God, expressed in human languages, became like human language in every respect except error".[19] The inerrancy of Scripture is explicitly upheld in every Papal encyclical treating of the topic.[20] The difficulties in the texts cannot lead us to reject any part. Sacred Scripture is absolutely binding: Our Lord declares, "Scripture cannot be

---

[14] 2 Tim 3:16

[15] Cf. Acts 1:16; 4:25-6; 28:25; 2 Pet 1:21; Heb 3:7-11; 10:15-17.

[16] Mk 12:36

[17] 1 Tim 5:18 cites Deut 25:4 and Lk 10:7 equally as "Scripture". 2 Peter 3:15-6 ranks the letters of St Paul with "the other Scriptures".

[18] *Dei Verbum*, Dogmatic Constitution on Divine Revelation, Second Vatican Council, 1965, art. 11

[19] *Divino Afflante Spiritu*, 1943, Part II

[20] Cf. *Providentissimus Deus*, Leo XIII 1893; *Pascendi*, St Pius X 1907; *Spiritus Paraclitus*, Benedict XV 1920; *Divino Afflante Spiritu*, Pius XII 1943; *Humani Generis*, Pius XII 1950. Cf. Congregation for the Doctrine of the Faith, *Doctrinal Commentary* on the *Professio Fidei*, 1998, art. 11: "the absence of error in the inspired sacred texts".

broken",[21] i.e., rejected. How, then, are we to explain the *apparent* (but not real) inconsistencies and internal contradictions within the Bible? That there are several to which we do not have an answer is nothing new: St Justin Martyr (c. 155 A.D.) says, "since I am completely convinced that no text of Scripture contradicts another, if a text of Scripture is brought forward and there be a pretext for saying it contradicts another text, I shall admit rather that I do not understand what is recorded."[22]

In attempting to overcome difficulties, we must avoid false paths. Pope Leo XIII declares, "It is absolutely wrong either to limit inspiration to certain parts only of Sacred Scripture or to concede that the sacred writer himself has erred. Equally intolerable is the theory of those who, in order to free themselves from these difficulties, do not hesitate to maintain that divine inspiration pertains to matters of faith and morals and nothing more". He continues, "indeed, far from being compatible with any kind of error, divine inspiration by its very nature not only excludes every error, but necessarily prevents and excludes it just as it is necessarily impossible for God, the supreme Truth, to be the author of any error whatsoever."[23] The same Pontiff says, "all the Fathers and Doctors were so utterly convinced that the original texts of the divine Scriptures are absolutely immune from all error that they laboured with no less ingenuity than devotion to harmonise and reconcile those many passages which might seem to involve some contradiction or discrepancy".[24] He then quotes St Augustine writing to St Jerome: "I most firmly believe that none of the [Biblical] authors has erred in writing anything. If I come across anything in those Scriptures which troubles me because it seems contrary to the truth, I will unhesitatingly lay the blame elsewhere: perhaps the manuscript is untrue to the original, or the translator has not rendered the passage faithfully, or perhaps I have not understood it."[25]

Vatican II declares, "Therefore, since everything which the inspired authors or sacred writers affirm, must be held as affirmed by the Holy Spirit, consequently it must be acknowledged that the books of Scripture teach the truth firmly, faithfully, and without error, that God willed to be recorded in the form of Sacred Scriptures, for our salvation's sake."[26] This declaration contains three propositions:

---

[21] Jn 10:35
[22] *Dial. cum Tryph.* c. 65
[23] *Providentissimus Deus*, 1893: DS 3292
[24] Ibid.: DS 3293
[25] *Ep.* 82 ad Hieron.: DS 3293. For fuller treatment, cf. Fr W.G. Most, *Free From All Error*, Franciscan Marytown Press, Illinois 1985.
[26] *Dei Verbum*, art. 11

(1) everything affirmed in the Bible is affirmed by the Holy Spirit (*inspiration*);

(2) hence, the Sacred Books teach the truth firmly, faithfully and without error (*inerrancy*);

(3) God willed these Sacred Scriptures for our salvation (*salvific purpose*).[27]

III

Sacred Scripture and Sacred Tradition. Their relationship and differences.

SACRED SCRIPTURE AND SACRED TRADITION. In contrast to the Protestant position of "Scripture alone", the Catholic Church regards Scripture and Tradition as equally important fonts of the one Revelation given by Christ and entrusted to the Apostles. The Council of Trent declared, "Our Lord Jesus Christ, the Son of God, with His own lips first proclaimed the Gospel, promised beforehand through the prophets in the Sacred Scriptures; then through His Apostles He commanded it to be preached to every creature as the source of the whole of both saving truth and code of morals. Recognising that this truth and code are contained in written *books* and in unwritten *traditions* which have come down to us, received by the Apostles from the mouth of Christ Himself, or handed on as it were by the Apostles themselves at the dictation of the Holy Spirit:—the Council, following the example of the orthodox Fathers, accepts and venerates with like sentiment of devotion and reverence all the *books* of both the Old and New Testament, since the one God is the author of both, as well as those *traditions* concerning both faith and morals, as either orally from Christ, or dictated by the Holy Spirit and preserved in continuous succession in the Catholic Church."[28]

THE RELATIONSHIP AND THE DIFFERENCES BETWEEN SCRIPTURE AND TRADITION.

What each one is. "Sacred Scripture is the speech of God as put down in writing under the inspiration of the divine Spirit; while Sacred Tradition transmits integrally to their successors the word of God entrusted to the Apostles by Christ the Lord and the Holy Spirit".[29] "Tradition" can have two meanings: the *act* of transmitting the Revelation from God, and the *content* of that Revelation.

Scripture is inspired; Tradition is protected from error. Scripture is inspired by God the Holy Spirit; Tradition is not inspired, but by the assistance of the Holy

---

[27] Cf. B.W. Harrison, *The Teaching of Pope Paul VI on Sacred Scripture*, Pont. Athenaeum S. Crucis, Rome 1997, Ch. 5, pp.163-94.

[28] DS 1501. On "Tradition", see p. 186.

[29] *Dei Verbum*, art. 9

250

Spirit, the Church, which is "the pillar and bulwark of the truth",[30] is guaranteed against error in her exposition of Tradition. Hence, Scripture must always be read and interpreted 'in the Church', not outside or against the Church; and Tradition must always be expounded in conformity with Scripture and never contrary to it.

What they form together. "Sacred Tradition and Sacred Scripture make up a single sacred deposit of the Word of God, entrusted to the Church".[31]

Through Tradition, Scripture is known. "By means of the same Tradition, the complete canon of the Sacred Books is made known to the Church".[32] Without Tradition, we could not know of inspiration, nor identify the inspired books, nor know of the characteristics that come from inspiration, such as inerrancy. In this sense, we can say that the Bible is a part of Tradition and a product of it.

Through Tradition, Scripture is understood and applied. "By means of the same Tradition ... the Sacred Scriptures themselves are more deeply understood and constantly made operative in the Church".[33] Many things in the Bible cannot be understood apart from Tradition, which provides norms of interpretation and an equally binding rule of faith.

Tradition can be known through the Fathers and the life of the Church. "The sayings of the holy Fathers attest the life-giving presence of this Tradition, whose riches are infused into the practice and life of the believing and praying Church."[34]

Scripture remains an inviolable and irreplaceable rule of faith. Since "the apostolic preaching, which is expressed in a special way in the inspired books, was to be preserved in continuous succession until the end of time",[35] the Church remains always bound to the Holy Bible as a rule of faith and can never contradict it or discard it.

Not everything can be known with certainty by Scripture alone. "The Church does not draw her certainty about all revealed truths through Holy Scripture alone."[36] St Augustine says, "There are many things which the universal Church holds, and therefore rightly believes to have been taught by the Apostles, even though they are not found written down."[37]

Common origin and purpose; close relations. "Sacred Tradition and Sacred Scripture, then, are tightly connected and mutually related. For both of them, issuing from the same divine well-spring, somehow coalesce into one,

---

[30] 1 Tim 3:15
[31] *Dei Verbum*, art. 10
[32] *Ibid.*, art. 8
[33] *Ibid.*, art. 8
[34] *Ibid.*, art. 8
[35] *Ibid.*, art. 8
[36] *Ibid.*, art. 9
[37] *De Bapt. contra Donat.*, V,23,31

and tend towards the same goal."[38] It is impossible for one to contradict the other, and hence unlawful to attempt to set up one against the other. *Both are necessary.* "Hence, both must be received and venerated with like sentiment of devotion and reverence."[39]

IV

The content of the Bible in the Old and New Testaments. Conquest of Canaan. The Covenant. God's promises. Differences between the Old and New Testament.

THE OLD TESTAMENT AND HISTORY OF ISRAEL.

1. *In the Beginning.* The Old Testament recounts the creation of the world and of man by God. Man sinned and lost God's friendship, but was promised a Saviour by God. Sin spread and so God punished the world by the great Flood—but Noah, by means of the ark, saved mankind from extinction in the waters. God made a covenant with man after the Flood, and man made a new start. But man in his arrogance attempted to build a city and a tower without God, and therefore was dispersed over the face of the earth. (Recounted in *Genesis*).

2. *Abraham, Father in Faith.* Some time after 2,000 B.C., God called Abraham, and summoned him to leave Ur[40] in Mesopotamia to go to the fertile land of Canaan. God made a covenant with him, promising him the land of Canaan, a son and countless descendants, and that the nations of the earth would be blessed in him. Abraham was called to father a new chosen race, through whom mankind would be reunited as children of God. He was the first Israelite, therefore. The descendants of Abraham would be variously known as the Chosen People, Hebrews, Israel, Judah, or Jews. Abraham was succeeded by his son Isaac, followed by Jacob, to whom God gave the name, Israel. Jacob had 12 sons, from whom came the 12 tribes of the House of Israel. During a time of famine in Canaan, Jacob's family had to migrate to Egypt for food. Initially they were welcomed there, through the providential presence of the younger brother, Joseph, in Egypt, but a later Pharaoh subjected the Hebrews to forced labour. (*Genesis*)

3. *Egypt and the Exodus under Moses.* After the Hebrews had endured several hundred years' slavery in Egypt, God called Moses, with the assistance of his brother Aaron, to lead them from Egypt back to their Promised Land, Canaan. Led by Moses, the Hebrews left there on the first Passover night, c. 1300 B.C., crossed the Red Sea and spent forty years in the wilderness of

---

[38] *Dei Verbum*, art. 9
[39] *Ibid.*, art. 9; T 1501
[40] Ur of the Chaldees = present-day Tell Mugheir (= Tell el-Muqayyar) in southern Iraq

Zin. At Mount Sinai (also called Mt Horeb), God established a covenant with the Chosen People and gave the Ten Commandments: God promised them a homeland, His blessing and protection, and they promised Him fidelity to the commandments, ceremonies, sacrifices and observances that He prescribed for them. Through Moses, and later through the Prophets, God revealed Himself to His Chosen People as the one, true and living God, as a provident Father and just Judge. He taught them also to look for the promised Saviour, and thus through the ages He prepared the way for the Gospel.[41] Moses died just before his people's entry into Canaan. (*Exodus-Deuteronomy*)

4. *Conquest and Settlement of Canaan.* Joshua succeeded Moses and led the conquest of the Promised Land. During the period of the Judges, the twelve tribes dispersed throughout the land and established themselves amidst the pagan Canaanite cities. Their presence in Canaan had to be maintained amidst threats from Philistines, a people come into the land from the west around 1200 B.C. (*Joshua, Judges*)

5. *The Kingdom of Israel under David.* Around 1030 B.C., Samuel, the last of the Judges, anointed Saul to be Israel's first king, to unite the Israelites against the Philistine threat. After Saul died in battle against the Philistines, David, of the town of Bethlehem and the tribe of Judah, was proclaimed king of all Israel, around 1000 B.C., choosing Jerusalem as capital, on the mountain called Zion. God made a covenant with him, and promised that the Messiah would be descended from him. David reigned for forty years. His son Solomon built the Temple which God consecrated by His glory. Under Solomon, who reigned until 922 B.C., Israel reached its height of stability, prosperity and might, and stood proud of its land, king and Temple. (*1,2 Samuel, 1 Kings, 1,2 Chronicles*)

6. *The Divided Kingdom.* As punishment for sin, the kingdom of Israel divided: upon the death of Solomon, the ten northern tribes, under Jeroboam, formed a northern kingdom, known as "Israel" (or Ephraim), and separated themselves from the southern kingdom, "Judah". In the north, rivals from diverse families seized power in a series of violent revolutions. Eventually, the northern kingdom fell under the aggression of Assyria in 721 B.C. Its capital, Samaria, was overrun and Israel's leading citizens were led into captivity. (*1,2 Samuel, 1,2 Kings; Amos, Hosea* in north; *Isaiah, Micah*, in south)

---

[41] Cf. *Dei Verbum*, art. 3.

7. *The Kingdom of Judah.* The leadership of Hezekiah (716-687 B.C.), a king devoted to the spiritual reform of his people, brought Judah through a difficult period, in which they survived Assyrian threats. He was succeeded by the apostate King Manasseh. King Josiah (640-609 B.C.) brought great reforms. He was killed by Necho, the Egyptian pharaoh. The southern kingdom, including Jerusalem and its Temple, fell in 587 B.C. to the Babylonians who had wrested rule from Assyria, and so the Chosen People were deported to Babylon (modern Iraq) for half a century. (*2 Kings, 2 Chronicles, Jeremiah, Daniel, Nahum, Habakkuk, Zephaniah*)

8. *The Babylonian Exile.* Cyrus II of Persia defeated Babylon in 539 B.C., and the following year decreed the freedom of the Jews to return to their homeland. (*Lamentations, Ezekiel, Ezra*)

9. *Reconstruction and Persian Rule.* The faithful remnant of the people rebuilt Jerusalem and re-dedicated a modest Temple there in 515 B.C., and the Covenant was renewed. The walls of Jerusalem were not rebuilt for another century. Under the Persians, the Jews were free to govern themselves in religious matters. Zerubbabel the governor and Joshua the priest led the resumption of Jewish life at the start; the governor Nehemiah and the priest-scribe Ezra led the reforms in the years leading to 400 B.C. (*Esther, Ezra, Nehemiah, Joel, Obadiah, Haggai, Zechariah, Malachi*)

10. *Greek Rule.* Alexander the Great took over the Persian empire; he conquered Palestine in 332 B.C. The Jews then learnt Greek, which became the international language for the eastern Mediterranean, and would remain so till the time of Christ and beyond. Then there were more Jews outside Palestine than within. In Alexandria, by 250 B.C., the Hebrew Scriptures had been translated into Greek. The Seleucid dynasty that eventually succeeded Alexander's rule in Palestine tried to impose Greek culture upon the Jews, and persecution reached a climax under Antiochus IV Epiphanes, 175-164 B.C., who desecrated the Temple. Many conformed, but the Maccabees led a heroic revolt, re-dedicated the Temple, and the Jews gained a century of independence until the Romans came. At this time, Jewish traditions were formed that gave rise to the distinct groups of the time of Christ: Pharisees, Sadducees, Zealots and Essenes.[42] (*1,2 Maccabees*)

11. *Roman Rule.* In 63 B.C., the Roman armies under the general Pompey took control of Jerusalem from the descendants of the Maccabees. Palestine was placed under the authority of the Roman governor of Syria. It was under Roman rule that Christ the Lord was born. The Romans

---

[42] See pp.109-10.

destroyed Jerusalem in A.D. 70, carrying the majority of Palestinian Jews into captivity. The Arch of Titus still stands today in the Roman Forum as a commemoration of this Roman conquest.

There are other narrative and wisdom books of the Old Testament not mentioned in this outline of Israel's history, among which are the books of Tobit, Judith, Job, Proverbs, Ecclesiastes, the Song of Solomon, Wisdom, Ecclesiasticus, Jonah, and the book of Psalms, containing 150 psalms, many of which were written by King David.

THE CONQUEST OF CANAAN. The land promised to the Jews has been variously known as the Promised Land, Canaan, Israel, Palestine, Judea, and today, the Holy Land. Egypt controlled Canaan long before the Jews settled there. The land of Canaan was successively invaded by: (1) Israel, 13th cent. B.C. (2) Assyria, 8th cent. B.C. (3) Babylon, 6th cent. B.C. (4) Persia, 6th cent. B.C. (5) Greece, 4th cent. B.C. (6) Rome, 1st cent. B.C.

THE COVENANT. Central to the Bible is the notion of covenant. This is why the two parts of the Bible are called the Old and New Testaments, which is to say, Old and New Covenants. In the Old Testament, God makes a series of covenants, with Adam, Noah, Abraham, Moses and David—the covenant with Israel under Moses being the central one. In the ancient East, "A covenant was an agreement or promise between two parties, solemnly professed before witnesses and made binding by an oath expressed verbally or by some symbolic action."[43] The parties were obliging themselves to some particular behaviour, and recognised that violation of a covenant would entail punishment. "As a result of a covenant, a new relationship was established between the parties."[44] At Mount Sinai, after the Exodus from Egypt, a sacred pact was made between God and Israel, which was, however, essentially different from human agreements. In the Mosaic covenant made at Sinai, the parties were not equal and mutually dependent. It was a pact freely initiated, and conferred, by the graciousness of God. It bound Israel to God, and God to Israel, without limiting the sovereignty of God. Israel's pledge of obedience to the covenant was based on gratitude for God's mighty acts of deliverance of her from Egypt. Thus the Ten Commandments are prefaced with the declaration, "I am the Lord your God, who brought you out of the land of Egypt, out of the house of bondage."[45] To express the relationship established by the covenant between God and Israel, the Old Testament describes God as a father and

---

[43] M. Guinan, *Covenant in the Old Testament*, Franciscan Herald Press, Chicago 1975, p.8. Cf. the covenants in Gen 21:22-23; 31:43-54; 1 Sam 18:3-4; 1 Kgs 20:34; Mal 2:14.
[44] Guinan, p.8
[45] Ex 20:1; Deut 5:6

Israel as His son; or God as the bridegroom and Israel the bride; God as the shepherd and Israel His flock.[46]

GOD'S PROMISES TO THE JEWS. Through their history from the covenant of Sinai onwards, God sent His Chosen People messengers, called "prophets", to recall Israel to fidelity to that covenant. Through the Prophets and through the inspired writings of the Old Testament, God promised Israel:[47]

a *Messiah*—who would be Jesus Christ of the tribe of Judah, God the Son Himself as King and Shepherd of His People;

to restore the *Kingdom* of Israel—which would be realised in the Church, the Kingdom of God on earth;

a new *Covenant*—established by Christ and sealed in His own Blood;

a new *Sacrifice*—offered by Christ the High Priest and renewed in the Holy Eucharist;

a new *Law*—the New Law of the Gospel, perfecting the Law of Moses;

the sending of a new *Spirit* within His People—the Holy Spirit sent by Christ upon the Apostles and the Church.

THE NEW TESTAMENT. The New Testament records the fulfilment of the prophecies and purpose of the Old Testament.

Its chief books are the four *Gospels* by Matthew, Mark, Luke, and John. The word Gospel comes from God-spel in Old English meaning Good Tidings, Good News. God sent His Son, born c. 6 B.C.[48] of the Virgin Mary in Bethlehem (the city of King David, in the *south*), and reared in Nazareth (in Galilee, in the *north*). Born of God the Father, and of no human father, He is true God. Descended from Adam and born of the Virgin Mary, He is true man. Descended from Abraham, He is a true Jew. A son of Mary and Joseph, He is of their tribe, the tribe of Judah. A descendant of King David, He is of the royal line.

Jesus gathered twelve apostles around Him (symbolically, like the twelve sons of Jacob—fathers of the New Israel) and conducted His Public Ministry for about three years, c. A.D. 28-30. He instructed the people by His example, discourses, precepts and parables. He confirmed and illustrated His teaching by numerous miracles, and then, in obedience to God the Father, submitted to His enemies, was tried, maltreated and crucified. He rose again from death on the third day, appeared to the

---

[46] Hos 11:1; Hos 1-3; Jer 2:2; Ezek 16; Ezek 34

[47] Cf. e.g., Gen 3:15; 49:2,8-10; Num 24:15-17; 2 Sam 7:16; Isa 11:1-2; Jer 31:31-33; 32:40; Ezek 34:11-16; 36:24-27; Dan 2:44; Mal 1:10-11; Ps 2:7; 89 (88); 110 (109); 132 (131):11-14; Lk 24:27,44-45; Jn 5:39; Acts 28:23.

[48] Ancient miscalculation causes this unfortunate discrepancy. We do not know the exact dates of Christ's life with certainty.

disciples, and ascended into Heaven forty days later, whence after nine days He sent the Holy Spirit.

The *Acts of the Apostles*, written by St Luke, recounts the coming of the Holy Spirit and the growth of the Church in the generation immediately after Christ. It records in particular the preaching of St Peter and the missionary journeys of St Paul.

The *Letters of St Paul, St James, St Peter, St John, St Jude* confirm the revelation of Christ, shed light on His life, death and resurrection, preach the saving power of His work, and explain and apply His teachings more fully to Christians.[49]

The *Apocalypse*, or *Book of Revelation*, written by St John, depicts in symbolic language the struggle between the Church and her enemies, and the glorious consummation of history and the Church at the end of time.

DIFFERENCES BETWEEN THE OLD AND NEW TESTAMENTS. The Old Testament was the divinely ordained preparation for the coming of the Saviour of man, Christ the Lord. In it, He and His Kingdom are prefigured by 'types' and pre-announced in prophecy. As St Augustine said, the New Testament lies hidden in the Old, and the Old is made manifest in the New.[50] The Old Testament is fulfilled in the New, and can only be properly understood in its light. At the same time, the New Testament can only be understood with the light shed upon it by the Old Testament.

Jesus our Lord perfected the Law given by Moses.[51] Not everything, therefore, in the Old Testament applies today as it did at the time it was given. To explain more fully, we may say that, in the Old Testament:

(1) *Some things are perennial*: they applied then, now and for all time, e.g., the Ten Commandments. Christ confirmed them as well as explained them more fully in the light of the New Law. To the rich young man, who asked what he must do to inherit eternal life, Christ quoted the Decalogue and told him, "If you would enter life, keep the Commandments."[52] In the Sermon on the Mount, Christ quoted well-known texts of the Old Testament and gave them a deeper and fuller interpretation.[53] The truths

---

[49] Cf. *Dei Verbum*, art. 20.
[50] *Quaest. in Hept.* II, 73: "… et in Vetere Novum lateat, et in Novo Vetus pateat." Cf. *Dei Verbum*, art. 16.
[51] Cf., e.g., Gal 3:13; 3:23-5.
[52] Matt 19:17-19
[53] Matt 5-7

revealed by God about Himself and about the creation of the world and of man remain forever true.

(2) *Other things have been superseded and abolished*: the abolition of the Ritual Law of the Jews was signalled by the miraculous rending of the veil of the Temple at the death of Christ.[54] By the Ritual or Ceremonial Law is meant all the rituals and ceremonies of the Old Testament, e.g., animal sacrifices, the Jewish Passover, rules of purity regarding food and leprosy and corpses, etc. The abolition of these precepts regarding food was announced by Jesus when He declared, "whatever goes into a man from outside [i.e., food] cannot defile him"; rather it is "evil thoughts" and deeds coming "from within". St Mark explains, "Thus He declared all foods clean."[55] The Epistle to the Hebrews declares, "In speaking of a new covenant, (God) treats the first as obsolete." Referring to the old sacrifices preceding the sacrifice of Christ, the same Epistle says that Our Lord, "abolishes the first in order to establish the second."[56] Along with the Ceremonial Law, the judicial precepts of the Old Law were also abrogated—all the legal prescriptions regulating Jewish life, after the manner of civil law, i.e., all the laws and penalties regarding civil and domestic life.[57] St Paul insists that Christians are no longer under the Old Law: "now we are discharged from the law ... so that we serve not under the old written code but in the new life of the Spirit."[58] In contrast to the Ritual and Judicial Law now abolished, the Natural Law, or moral law, as expressed in the Commandments, remains unchanged and unchangeable.

The Old Testament was provisional and incomplete; God taught the Jews in stages. So, for example, God gave the *lex talionis* (the law of revenge, 'an eye for an eye, a tooth for a tooth'[59])—not to teach the Jews revenge, but to *limit* retaliation and regulate it, lest they take *two* eyes for an eye, and so on. When Christ appeared, He taught the higher and perfect law of not returning evil for evil.[60] The love of neighbour in the Old Testament did not always extend to non-Jews. God, the author and Lord of life, even commanded the Jews to exterminate certain races in warfare, since contact with these idolatrous and immoral peoples would have been fatal to the Israelites.

Under the terms of the Old Covenant, God promised temporal rewards, such as long life and health, to those who observed His

[54] Matt 27:51
[55] Mk 7:18-23
[56] Heb 8:13; 10:9
[57] St Thomas, S.T., i-ii, q. 104, a. 4
[58] Rom 7:6; cf. Gal 3:23-5.
[59] Ex 21:23-5; Lev 24:19-20
[60] Matt 6:38-9; Rom 12:17; 1 Pet 2:23; 3:9

258

commands.   Now, under the rule of grace, we are promised spiritual rewards.

(3) *Some things were tolerated:* God tolerated divorce among the Jews: "For your hardness of heart Moses allowed you to divorce your wives, but from the beginning it was not so"[61]—said Our Lord at the moment when He withdrew this toleration and restored marriage to its pristine state.   At certain times in the Old Testament, God "overlooks" immorality, dishonesty and mistaken notions.

(4) *Some things have been transformed:* now that the New Law is in force, certain provisions of the Old Law no longer apply in the same way.   E.g., the Sabbath day of rest and worship has been transferred from Saturday to Sunday.

In all these matters we need the living Tradition of the Church as a guide to the interpretation and use of the Old Testament for today.   Some sects have arisen, trying to revive and enforce provisions of the Old Testament that were only meant to be "provisional" until the coming of Christ took away the need for them.

V

Difficulties in the Bible.   Diverse genres of books in the Bible.   The Gospels' historicity.

DIFFICULTIES IN THE BIBLE.   Neither the Church nor any of the Popes has claimed a complete knowledge and understanding of the Bible.   The great and learned St Augustine said that in the Bible, his ignorance was greater than his knowledge.[62]   In many passages, the Church has not given a definitive teaching or interpretation.   Many things are obscure and difficult, and probably will remain so until the Second Coming, when all shall be made clear.   The difficulties are basically of five kinds:

Textual difficulties. While no manuscript can claim to be the very first copy, our ancient manuscripts are reliable, but do contain slight errors by copyists, and so differ from each other at certain points.   By comparing all the ancient copies, scholars try to ascertain which reading is closest to the original text.

Literary difficulties. The human limitations and character traits of the authors, the different times and cultures in which they wrote, and the language and

---

[61] Matt 19:8
[62] *Ep.* 55 ad Ianuar. (end)

modes of expression, all contribute to obscurity and difficulty in understanding the subject matter of the Bible. These difficulties can be resolved, insofar as possible, by the study of ancient languages, history, archaeology, and literary forms or genres. Sometimes we must ask: are these words to be taken literally or metaphorically? Is this book or passage meant to be history in the strict sense, or is it an allegory or parable, or is it a combination of history and parable? The answers help us to know what the human author intended to say and how. This is called the "literal sense".

Difficulty in reconciling the Bible with other sources of knowledge. Seeming conflicts between science and the Bible can arise from time to time. St Augustine advises, "Whatever they (scientists) have been able to demonstrate of natural science with solid proofs, let us show that it is not contrary to our Scriptures; but whatever they maintain in any of their treatises which is contrary to our Scriptures, that is, to the Catholic faith, let us believe without hesitation that it is completely false, and show this by some means."[63] At other times, archaeological and historical sources produce evidence difficult to reconcile with the Biblical evidence. The resolution of difficulties is the work of scholarship and of time.

Difficulty in reconciling certain texts with each other. Some texts of Sacred Scripture seem to conflict with other texts. Sometimes, in both the Old and New Testaments, the same events are recounted more than once but in different ways. The Fathers of the Church always attempted to harmonise such texts, knowing that there could be no real contradiction. See the example given of the various accounts of the first Easter Sunday on p.117.

Theological difficulties. Textual and literary study of the Bible simply prepares the ground for what the Church has always regarded as the most important branch of Bible study: the religious or theological meaning of the texts. Obscurities in this field are due to the mysterious and elevated nature of the subject matter. As well, St Augustine says, difficulties have been put there purposely by the Divine Author Himself, both to stimulate us to study and examine them with close attention, and also to give us a salutary experience of the limitations of our minds and thus exercise us in proper humility.[64]

DIVERSE TYPES OF BOOKS. Some of the difficulties in the Bible will be diminished if we remember that not everything in the Bible is meant as strict and literal historical fact—especially portions of the Old Testament.

---

[63] *De Genesi ad litt.*, I, 21: DS 3287
[64] *Ep.* 149 n.34 ad Paulinum; *De Diver. Quaest.* q.53 n.2; *Enarr. in Ps.* 146 n.12

We said above that, under God's inspiration, the sacred writers wrote in some one or other of the literary forms with which they were familiar. Every literary form has its own style, its own type of message to convey, and its own manner of expressing this message. We find this illustrated in the teaching of Our Blessed Lord. At one time He spoke plainly and directly (e.g., "love your enemies"); at another He used simple illustrations (e.g., "the Kingdom of Heaven is like leaven which a woman took..."), simple stories (the parables), or symbolic actions (e.g., cursing the fig tree). The sacred writers do the same, making use of the various types of literature common in their time. Thus, the New Testament contains historical books (the Gospels & Acts), letters (of St Paul & other apostles) and a prophetic book (the Apocalypse). Each kind of inspired literature has its own appropriate mode of expression. As we shall see in Part II, Ch. 4, the Book of Genesis does not describe creation in the manner of a scientist or modern historian, but in a popular style and language. Sometimes, the expressions are obviously figurative. No one who reads in the Bible of God's 'right arm', 'finger', 'hand' or 'face'[65] would think that God really has two arms and hands and so on. It is plain, too, that the book of the Apocalypse is not meant to be a literal account of historical events, but a symbolic portrayal of their inner significance. We must remember, finally, that the human authors of the Bible wrote in times different from ours, in a different culture and circumstances, and in a different language. Hence, at times they made use of literary forms to which we are not accustomed. We cannot, therefore, expect to see at once the exact meaning they intended to convey in everything they wrote.

The historicity of the Old Testament. Modern research, says Pope Pius XII, "has clearly shown that the Israelite people singularly excelled the other ancient nations of the East in their mode of writing history, both by reason of its antiquity and by reason of the faithful record of the events: qualities which no doubt issue from the gift of divine inspiration and the peculiar religious purpose of Biblical history. Nevertheless, no one who has a correct idea of Biblical inspiration will be truly surprised to find, even in the Sacred Writers, as in other ancient authors, certain fixed methods of expounding and narrating, certain definite idioms, especially those proper to the Semitic tongues, approximations, and certain hyperbolic modes of expression, indeed at times even paradoxical, by which things are impressed more deeply on the mind. For of the modes of expression which, among ancient peoples, and especially those of the East, human language was accustomed to use to express its thought, none is excluded from the Sacred Books, provided the way of speaking adopted in no wise contradicts the holiness and truth of God." For, the Pope says, "the ancient peoples of the East, in order to express their ideas, did not always employ the same forms and modes of speech which we use today, but rather those used by the men of their times and countries." Knowing these literary manners

---

[65] e.g., Ex 33:23; Ps 98:1 (97:1); Isaiah 14:27; Lk 11:20

leads to correct interpretation and helps to resolve difficulties: "Not infrequently—to mention but one instance—when some persons reproachfully charge the Sacred Writers with having strayed from historical truth or reported things inaccurately, upon investigation it turns out to be nothing else than those customary modes of expression and narration proper to the ancients, which used to be employed in the mutual dealings of social life and which in fact were sanctioned by common usage."[66]

Not every Old Testament narrative is meant to be strictly historical: the literary genre of the book of Job, for example, is subject to discussion. Pope Leo XIII commends the rule laid down by St Augustine: not to depart from the literal and obvious sense, unless reason makes it untenable or necessity dictates.[67] In 1905, the Biblical Commission decreed that the books of the Bible regarded as wholly or partly historical, are to be accepted as history properly so called, containing objective truth, unless "it can be proved by solid arguments that the Sacred Writer did not intend to give a true and strict history, but rather, under the guise and form of history, to set forth a parable or an allegory or something distinct from the strictly literal or historical meaning of the words."[68]

THE HISTORICITY OF THE GOSPELS. Unlike much other ancient history, the New Testament was written within the lifetime of contemporaries. There were no accounts handed on for generations before being written down—living eyewitnesses abounded. There were no speeches composed for literary effect or to fill in gaps—actual speeches were recorded because they expressed divine and inspired teaching. In describing attendant details, the Evangelists use hyperbole[69] and approximations,[70] sometimes stylised ones[71]—they frequently say 'all' when they mean many, or even some[72]—but faithfully record the sayings and deeds themselves of Our Lord. The Church insists on the historicity, i.e., the historical accuracy, of the Gospels of Sts Matthew, Mark, Luke and John: "Holy Mother Church has firmly and with absolute constancy held, and holds, that the four Gospels just named, whose *historicity* she unhesitatingly affirms, *faithfully* hand on what Jesus the Son of God, while living among men, *really* did and taught for their eternal salvation, until the day He was taken up. ... The sacred authors wrote the four Gospels, selecting some things from the many handed on by word of mouth or already in writing, reducing some to a synthesis, expounding them with a view to the situation of the churches, and keeping the form of proclamation accordingly, but always such that they told us *true*

---

[66] All quotes from *Divino Afflante Spiritu*, 1943, Part II.

[67] *Providentissimus Deus*, 1893; *De Genesi ad litt.*, VIII, 7: DS 3284

[68] DS 3373

[69] e.g., Matt 3:5; 8:34; 21:10; Lk 4:22; Jn 21:25; Acts 2:5; 21:30

[70] e.g., Matt 15:38; Mk 6:44; Acts 19:7

[71] e.g., Matt 1:17

[72] e.g., Matt 4:23; 13:34; Mk 1:5; Lk 1:65; 2:38; 3:15; 3:21; 4:28; 4:37; 5:17; 8:37; Acts 19:10; 21:30

and *real* things about Jesus."[73] The sacred writers themselves insist that they are recording exactly what they have seen and heard.[74] Two of the Evangelists—St Matthew and St John—accompanied Christ during His public life. St Luke says at the start that his own account is in accord with those "who from the beginning were eyewitnesses and ministers of the word". The Gospel of Mark is that preached by St Peter. [75]

VI

The interpretation of the Bible entrusted to the Magisterium. Reading in context. The four "senses" of Sacred Scripture. Rationalist criticism. False principles of interpretation. Catholic response.

THE INTERPRETATION OF THE BIBLE HAS BEEN ENTRUSTED TO THE MAGISTERIUM. From the difficulties enunciated above, it is clear that the Bible needs interpretation and explanation. The official interpretation has been entrusted to the magisterium (teaching office) of the Church, held by the Pope and bishops.[76] "It is clear, therefore, that in the most wise disposition of God, sacred Tradition, sacred Scripture and the Magisterium of the Church are so connected and associated with each other, that no one stands without the others".[77]

During the years 1902-1971, the Pontifical Biblical Commission was entrusted with giving authoritative replies to queries regarding the Bible. In 1971, Pope Paul VI made it a purely advisory body to the Sacred Congregation for the Doctrine of the Faith, so that it no longer exercises any magisterial function.[78]

READING THE BIBLE IN CONTEXT. When reading and studying the Bible, it is important to avoid isolating individual texts from their context. Each part of the Bible must be understood within the content and unity of the whole Bible, within the living Tradition of the Church, and in coherence with the truths of the faith among themselves and within the whole plan of Revelation.[79] In commenting on a text of St Paul, St Athanasius says that here, as in all Scripture passages, we must note *on what occasion* the author

---

[73] *Dei Verbum*, art. 19 (italics added). Cf. C 126.
[74] Cf. Jn 1:14; 19:35; 21:24; 1 Jn 1:1-3; 2 Pet 1:16 ff.; Lk 1:1-3. Cf. also Part I, Ch. 5.
[75] Cf. Eusebius, *Eccl. Hist.* II, 15, 1; III, 39, 14; VI, 14, 1; VI, 25, 3; St Irenaeus, *Adv. Haer.* III, 1, 1; III, 13, 3; Tertullian, *Adv. Marcion.*, IV, 2; IV, 5.
[76] cf. C 85.
[77] *Dei Verbum*, art. 10; cf. C 95.
[78] Motu Proprio, *Sedula Cura*, 1971
[79] Cf. C 112-4.

spoke, *to whom* he was writing, and *why* he wrote, lest we miss his real meaning.[80]

THE FOUR SENSES OF SACRED SCRIPTURE. The *Catechism* explains that, according to an ancient tradition, one can distinguish between two senses of Scripture: the literal and the spiritual.[81] The spiritual can be subdivided into the allegorical, moral and anagogical senses.

1. The *literal* sense is the meaning of the words themselves. The literal or *historical* sense is the basis for the other senses. St Gregory the Great says, "from the history, one rises to the mystery".[82]

The *spiritual* sense: not only the words of Scripture, but the things and events of which it speaks can themselves be signs:

2. The *allegorical* or *typological* sense: the words and events of the Old Testament bear a deeper meaning in the light of their fulfilment in Christ. The manna from heaven prefigured the true Bread from heaven, Christ Himself in the Blessed Eucharist. Jerusalem and Israel were a 'type' (prefiguring image) of the Church, the new Israel. Adam prefigured Christ: St Paul says, "Adam was a type of the One who was to come."[83] The paschal lamb of Exodus was a type of Christ, the Lamb of God.

3. The *moral* or *tropological* sense: all of Scripture is written for our edification and instruction in faith and virtue. We must live by the Word and Bread of God. Jerusalem, in the psalms, for example, can be interpreted as an image of the righteous soul wherein God dwells.

4. The *anagogical* sense (from the Greek *anagoge* meaning a *leading upwards*): the words and realities of the Old and New Testaments have an eternal significance, lead us to our heavenly destiny and prefigure our heavenly homeland. The bread from heaven and the true Bread in the Holy Eucharist prepare us for the heavenly banquet. Jerusalem and the Church on earth are a sign of the heavenly Jerusalem.

Thus, "Jerusalem" can be interpreted as 1. a city in Israel; 2. an image of the Church; 3. an image of the soul; 4. heavenly glory.

The four senses are found in Sacred Scripture, but this does not mean that the four senses are present in all passages of the Bible. Some have four, others fewer, others have only the literal one.[84]

RATIONALIST AND FORM CRITICISM.[85] Over the past 200 years, a constant assault has been made upon the Bible by scholars and literary men. Many of the leading figures have been or became Deists, pantheists, agnostics or atheists. Only a few can be mentioned here. We may start with the Deist rationalist scholar H.S. Reimarus (1694-1768), a typical man of the so-called Enlightenment, who held the chair of oriental languages at Hamburg. A selection of his writings was published a few years after his death. According to him, Jesus was a fiery political agitator, but

---

[80] *Orat. contra Arian.* I, 54
[81] Cf. C 115-8.
[82] *In Ezech.* Lib. I, hom. VI, 3: "ab historia in mysterium surgit."
[83] Rom 5:14
[84] St Thomas Aquinas, *QQ. de quolibet* VII, q. 6, ad 5
[85] Cf. Giuseppe Ricciotti, *The Life of Christ*, Bruce, Milwaukee 1947, pp.179-216.

His rebellion against the Romans collapsed with His crucifixion, and so the disciples stole His body, invented the story of the Resurrection and turned Him into a spiritual and religious leader. The Apostles, then, were mere frauds who simply invented the stories of miracles and other supernatural interventions. This manifestly crude attack upon Christianity was not followed by most subsequent critics, for whom the Apostles were well-intentioned self-deceivers rather than frauds. But the conclusions of these later scholars about the origins of Christianity were no less radical or subversive. Ferdinand Baur (1792-1860), for instance, of Tübingen university, Germany, founder of the Tübingen school of Biblical thought, said that the Gospels were written between the years 130-170 A.D., and that St Paul is the real author of Christianity. It is to St Paul, he said, that we owe the doctrines of the Divinity of Christ, a visible Church, and the Sacraments. His pupil David Strauss (1808-74), also of Tübingen, went even further. He said that the Gospels were Christian myths, on a par with pagan myths, committed to writing some time in the years 150-200. They portray an ideal Christ, while of the real Christ we know nothing. (This view, now totally discredited by modern archaeology and the discovery of early manuscripts, still survives as the basis of some romances and so-called Biblical 'studies').

Albrecht Ritschl (1822-89), founder of a 'liberal school', was willing to admit that there was a solid historical core to the New Testament, but held that the New Testament contained mythical elements also. So the search began for the 'historical Jesus', culminating in the work of Adolf von Harnack (1851-1930). The 'historical Jesus' which emerged from the liberal studies of the Gospels was a purely human prophet, the teacher of a simple doctrine of brotherhood and the Heavenly Father's love. He was not divine and certainly did not make true prophecies, work genuine miracles or teach dogmas. He had been an attractive religious person, around whom all sorts of legends grew up. 'Liberal' studies emphasised the parables and spiritual teachings of Jesus, while anything of a supernatural or credal character was treated as non-historical.

Johannes Weiss (1863-1914) argued against the liberal version of Jesus, and said that Christ had been a rabbi of the Jewish apocalyptic tradition, who believed in the imminent end of the world and a new age heralded by His death. Albert Schweitzer (1875-1965) gave these views their classic expression in his *Quest for the Historical Jesus* (1906). Its basic message was that the quest was over. As historical documents the Gospels were all but worthless.

It was into these currents of thought that Alfred Loisy and other Catholic modernists were swept at the end of the 19th century. Pope St Pius X condemned Modernism in his encyclical *Pascendi* (1907). In *Lamentabili*, the same year, he condemned a list of modernist errors, many of which touched upon Biblical studies, the inspiration and inerrancy of Scripture, and the Biblical evidence for the life, teachings and mission of Christ.

The theories of Weiss and Schweitzer prepared the ground for the method of Biblical study known as 'form criticism' (*Formgeschichte* in German), as well as the 'demythologised' Christianity of the Protestant Biblical writer Rudolf Bultmann (1884-1976), whose very definition of history excluded miracles and supernatural events. For form critics, the Gospels belong to the genus of popular literature. They are collections of short self-contained passages drawn from oral tradition, all of which have undergone so much re-working by the early Christians that we can no longer be sure what their original content was. In this view, the origins of Christianity are not in Christ but in the early Christian communities.

The modern-day descendants of these schools of thought are the Biblical critics who deny the historical reliability of the New Testament, the miracles and exorcisms of Christ, the authenticity of the Gospel accounts and sayings, and the existence of any genuine prophecies made before the event. In short, they deny or explain away the supernatural element of Sacred Scripture, and even many natural elements.

False principles of interpretation. Catholic scholars have not been immune to these false principles and conclusions. The Pontifical Biblical Commission in 1964 identified six false principles of interpretation, often allied to the 'form history' or 'form critical method'. "Certain exponents of this method", it said, "led astray by rationalist prejudices, refuse to admit (1) that a supernatural order exists, (2) or that a personal God intervenes in the world by Revelation properly so called, (3) or that miracles and prophecies are possible and have actually occurred. (4) Others proceed from a false notion of faith, as if faith did not care for historical truth, and is even irreconcilable with it. (5) Others deny almost *a priori* the historical value and character of the documents of Revelation. (6) Finally, others, downplaying the authority of the Apostles as witnesses of Christ, and their office and influence in the primitive community, extol the creative capacity of the community itself. - All these aberrations are not only opposed to Catholic doctrine, but are also devoid of any scientific foundation".[86]

Catholic response. To the Catholic, it will be obvious that these ideas are subversive of the very foundations of Christianity. They are also incompatible with the doctrine of inspiration and inerrancy, implying as they do that God has been party to a misrepresentation of the life of His Son. It would mean, further, that despite Christ's promises to be with His Church and send it the Spirit of truth, all Christians—Popes, bishops and faithful—totally misunderstood the Gospels for 18 centuries until the form critics arrived on the scene. In answer to the form critics we can point out:

(a) *The teaching of the Church.* The Church has always maintained that the Gospels bear witness in the first place to the teaching of the Apostles as received from Christ. "In keeping with the Lord's command, the transmission of the Gospel took place in two ways: — *orally* 'by the Apostles who handed on by the spoken word of their preaching ... what they themselves had received from Christ's lips, way of life and works...'; — *in writing* 'by those Apostles and men associated with the Apostles who, under the inspiration of the Holy Spirit, committed the message of salvation to writing'."[87] St Justin c. 155 calls the Gospels read on Sundays, "the memoirs of the Apostles".[88]

---

[86] *Instruction on the Historical Truth of the Gospels*, Pontifical Biblical Commission, 1964: DS 3999a (numbers added).
[87] C 76, quoting *Dei Verbum*, art. 7
[88] *Dial. cum Tryph.*, 100; 103; *Apol.* I, 66, the latter quoted in C 1345.

266

(b) *The historical impossibility of an unhistorical account.* The early date of composition of the Gospels does not allow sufficient time for the working of the processes by which popular traditions change their content. While the Evangelists may have used some matter from oral tradition in compiling the Gospels, there are no grounds for asserting that this material was substantially modified before being incorporated into their work. The Evangelists were eyewitnesses or received their accounts from eyewitnesses: if they drew upon second or third-hand sources, they were not dependent on them, but were able to test and judge their accuracy. St Luke, whose Gospel is, in substance, that of the other Evangelists, makes it quite clear at the start of his Gospel that he reviewed and checked everything from the beginning. The Gospels were written within the lifetime of hostile witnesses who would have pointed out significant changes, had any been made. The Evangelists themselves and the Christian community, believing that Jesus was their Lord and God, would not have dared to change the story of His life. Friendly witnesses as much as hostile—not to mention the other Apostles—would have indignantly rejected any false accounts or fabricated sayings.

(c) *The ancient belief of Christians.* Not a single one of the early Fathers ever interpreted the Gospels in the manner of the form critics and their predecessors. Had the Gospels belonged to some special form of literature that was unhistorical and mythical, the Fathers—much closer in time and culture—would have certainly known it and interpreted the Gospels accordingly.[89]

VII

The canon. Differences between Protestant and Catholic Bibles. Variations between Bibles. Chapter and verse. Reading the Bible.

THE CANON. A canon is a fixed measure or rule. Applied to the Bible, it means the fixed collection of books recognised as divinely inspired. The Protestant rejection of certain books of the Bible moved the Church to define the contents of the entire canon for the first time in 1546, in the first year of the Council of Trent.[90] The list of books given was the same as that recognised by the Council of Florence in 1442.

The Old Testament canon. The majority of the first Christian Jewish converts were Greek-speaking and used the Septuagint version of the Jewish scriptures, the Greek translation made more than two centuries before Christ. This is the version generally cited in the New Testament itself. After the fall of Jerusalem, Jews generally fell back upon the Hebrew scriptures, and eventually excluded those written in Greek, as well as a few others. With the exception of a few books (1 Esdras [= 3 Esdras in Latin], 3 & 4 Maccabees, Odes of Solomon, Prayer of Manasseh), the contents of the Septuagint were eventually used and accepted by Christians as canonical. All of the Old Testament as listed by Trent was recognised by the councils of Rome in 382, of Hippo in 393, Carthage III in 397, Carthage IV

---

[89] See also Part I, Ch. 5.
[90] DS 1501-4

in 419, and in a letter of Pope Innocent I in 405.[91] However, these early lists were not issued as binding upon the universal Church. Some later lists omit certain books. St Jerome (d. 420) had doubts about a few Old Testament books but included them in his Latin translation of the Bible nevertheless. As late as 743, St John Damascene omitted some books from a list of the Old Testament.[92]

The New Testament canon. Although the apostolic writings were very quickly diffused as they were written over the years of the 1st century A.D., it would be three hundred years before the inspired writings now known as the New Testament were gathered into one volume. The four Gospels, Acts, and the major epistles of St Paul, were quickly recognised and copied, but for a long time there were doubts about some of St Paul's other epistles and some of the Catholic epistles (i.e., of Sts James, Peter, John, Jude), Hebrews and the Apocalypse. To complicate things further, some clever forgeries were accepted for a time by some communities; some genuine writings were doubted in some regions for centuries, whilst in some places other early Christian writings by bishops and holy men were read along with the inspired texts. In short, there was no 'canon' for three centuries. Gradually, the forgeries were excluded, the genuine texts came to be accepted, and the non-inspired texts were no longer read in church. A number of lists of recognised books survive from the first centuries, but the earliest one which lists all the New Testament books as we have them today is in a letter of St Athanasius written in 367. An identical list was promulgated by a council of Rome under Pope Damasus in 382. The same list was recognised by the councils of Hippo in 393, Carthage III in 397, Carthage IV in 419, and in a letter of Pope Innocent I in 405.[93] Gradually, this was the list which became universally recognised, and finally canonised by Trent.

The history of the canons of the Old and New Testament is further proof that the 'Bible alone' is an untenable and unworkable doctrine: for several centuries there was no certainty as to what constitutes the Bible. It was the Church which fixed the canon of her books. It is self-contradictory, therefore, to accept the books of the Catholic Church and yet reject her authority.

DIFFERENCES BETWEEN CATHOLIC AND PROTESTANT BIBLES. The Books of the New Testament are the same for Catholics, Protestants and Orthodox. In the Old Testament, however, on account of the tradition inherited from Luther, Protestant Bibles do *not* contain the following seven Books, and portions of two Books, which the Catholic Church accepts: Tobit, Judith, Wisdom, Ecclesiasticus (Sirach), Baruch (Chs 1-5) with the Letter of Jeremiah (= Baruch, Ch. 6), 1 & 2 Maccabees; additions to Daniel (parts of Ch. 3; Chs 13, 14), additions to Esther (10:4-16:24).

Some Protestant Bibles include the above books as an appendix, under the heading, "Apocrypha" (i.e., spurious, not genuine, Books). Under

---

[91] DS 179, 186, 213
[92] *De Fide Orthodoxa*, IV, 17
[93] DS 180, 186, 213

this heading, they will generally include the following, which are *not* considered canonical by the Catholic Church: 1 & 2 Esdras (also known as 3 & 4 Esdras), The Prayer of Manasseh.

Protestants exclude certain O.T. books on the grounds that they only accept the books which have Hebrew texts, but in this they are inconsistent: parts of *Daniel* and *Ezra* were written in Aramaic, not Hebrew, and are accepted by Jews and Protestants.[94] Moreover, in the years 1896-1900, about two-thirds of a Hebrew text of *Ecclesiasticus* were discovered, and yet this book remains excluded from Protestant Bibles. More Hebrew fragments of it were discovered in 1931, 1958, 1960 and 1963.[95] Further, fragments of Hebrew and Aramaic texts of *Tobit* (probably written originally in Aramaic) were found at Qumran, among the famous discoveries that began there in 1947. Our Greek texts of *1 Maccabees, Judith* and *Baruch* were also made from Hebrew originals, now lost, and there is nothing to prevent a future discovery of them also. The acceptance by the early Christians of *Tobit*, for example, is attested by quotations from it by the Fathers from the time of St Polycarp (d. c. 155),[96] and representations of its principal scenes in the Catacombs.[97] There is also a sarcophagus of the early 4th century in Le Mas d'Aire, France, where Tobit is depicted along with other Old Testament figures.[98] The Septuagint version of Scripture, the Greek translation made more than two centuries before Christ, which contains *all* the books in the Catholic O.T. canon, was accepted by the early Christians, and used in their quotations from the Old Testament. 85% of the O.T. quotations in the N.T. are taken from the Septuagint version.

VARIATIONS BETWEEN BIBLES. Some books have alternative names: the book of Ecclesiastes is also known as Qoheleth; Ecclesiasticus is also known as Sirach; Canticle of Canticles can be called Song of Songs, or Song of Solomon; the Apocalypse is also known as Revelation.

Other names of books vary somewhat in their English form: e.g., Tobit/Tobias; Isaiah/Isaias; Hosea/Osee; Obadiah/Abdias; Jonah/Jonas; Zephaniah/Sophonias; Haggai/Aggeus; Zechariah/Zacharias. Some Biblical names vary in spelling: e.g., Noah/Noe, Joshua/Josue.

Translations that follow the names and division of the ancient Vulgate Bible (e.g., the Douay, Knox, Confraternity editions) name and number some books differently from modern Bibles, which generally follow the Hebrew names and divisions. So: 1 & 2 Paralipomenon = 1 & 2 Chronicles; 1 Esdras & 2 Esdras (or Nehemiah) = Ezra & Nehemiah; 1 Kings = 1 Samuel 2 Kings = 2 Samuel

---

[94] *Jerome Biblical Commentary*, 1970, vol. 1, pp.430, 448
[95] Ibid. pp.541-2
[96] *ad Phil.* 10. Cf. Origen (d. 254) *Contra Celsum*, V, 19.
[97] e.g., Cubicle III of the Catacombs of Domitilla, Rome, mid 3rd cent.
[98] *Encyclopedia of the Early Church*, James Clarke & Co., Cambridge 1992, vol. 2, fig. 311

3 Kings = 1 Kings

4 Kings = 2 Kings.

The abbreviations for certain books vary somewhat; e.g., in some older books, "Thren." is an abbreviation for the Book of Lamentations, following its Greek title.

Certain books vary somewhat in their Hebrew, Latin or Greek versions. Thus, certain passages appear in one but not in another, and verse numbers differ accordingly. This is true especially of the books of Tobit, Judith, Esther, and Daniel. The Vulgate version of Tobit seems to follow an earlier Aramaic text in parts. The Vulgate version of Judith was made from an Aramaic text which omits passages present in the Greek that follows an original Hebrew, now lost.

Further, the Hebrew and Greek Bibles divide the 150 Psalms differently, so that the numbers do not always match up. Thus:

Hebrew	Greek & Latin (Vulgate)
1-8	1-8
9-10	9
11-113	10-112
114-5	113
116	114-5
117-146	116-145
147	146-7
148-150	148-150

Most modern books follow the Hebrew numbering.

CHAPTER AND VERSE. The division of books of the Bible into chapters was made in the 13th century; the subdivision of chapters into verses was first done in the 16th century. It should be noted that the divisions are often arbitrary. Sometimes between different versions of the Bible, especially in the Old Testament, the verse numbers do not agree exactly.

READING THE BIBLE. St Paul says, "All scripture is inspired by God and profitable for teaching, for reproof, for correction, and for training in righteousness, that the man of God may be complete, equipped for every good work."[99] It is the wish of the Church that the faithful read the Scriptures frequently. However, since the Scriptures contain "some things in them hard to understand, which the ignorant and unstable twist to their own destruction",[100] it would be a mistake to expect to understand readily all that one reads in the Bible. It is to the Church and not to the individual

---

[99] 2 Tim 3:16-7

[100] 2 Pet 3:16

Catholic that God has entrusted the two sources of Revelation—Scripture and Tradition—and so we should read the Bible in union with the Church's teaching and understanding, and never pitted against it. As God has given us the Bible for our instruction and formation, we should make a point of reading it, in a spirit of faith, humility and docility, in union with the Church, and prayerfully. The Bible is, in the words of Leo XIII, "a Letter written by our Heavenly Father, and transmitted by the sacred writers to the human race on its pilgrimage so far from its heavenly homeland."[101]

The Scriptures have always been read and explained in the sacred Liturgy from the very beginning of the Church. One of the best ways of reading the word of God is to read it as it is presented to us by the Church in the Liturgy, i.e., in our daily Missal. There we find those passages of Scripture which the Church, guided by the Holy Spirit, has specially chosen as best adapted to our needs at each period of the year. It is a very profitable exercise to read the readings of the Mass privately, some time before going to Mass itself.

VIII

OBJECTIONS ANSWERED

(1) "Could physical science, astronomy, geology, etc., some day disprove the chief doctrines of religion?" REPLY: No. Natural science deals solely with matter under some aspect or other. But religion and its fundamental truths—the existence of God, miracles, the spirituality of the human soul, the Divinity of Christ—all these lie completely outside its sphere. The physicist can no more apply his tests to them than he can examine an abstract idea under a microscope.

(2) "But could these sciences disprove some statement as to natural phenomena made by the Sacred Scriptures which the Church holds to be the inspired word of God?" REPLY: We can face all such questions with a tranquil mind. God is as truly the Author of nature as He is of inspiration, and God cannot contradict Himself. Scientists may *seem* to prove a contradiction between the Sacred Scriptures and the results of their investigations, but the contradiction is merely apparent, and can be readily solved by the following considerations:

(a) The Scriptures were written to instruct mankind in faith and morals. They are not a handbook of science, and are not to be judged as such. Further, since they were written for ordinary men, they make use of ordinary language, and, in scientific matters, follow the style of popular narration. Like scientists themselves when not writing scientifically, they speak, e.g., of the rising and setting of the sun, and employ all the so-called inaccuracies of common speech.

---

[101] *Providentissimus Deus*, 1893

(b) They contain many figurative expressions and passages, allegories and other forms of transfigured speech which, of course, must not be taken literally.

(c) They contain explicit quotations from non-inspired sources. These, although inserted in the text under the guidance of the Holy Spirit, must not be regarded as conveying an inspired meaning, unless it is plain that the sacred writer adopts them as his own. The Biblical Commission was asked whether, with a view to solving difficulties (arising chiefly in connection with some parts of the Old Testament), implicit or unacknowledged quotations from an uninspired source could be admitted. The answer, given in 1905, was that they could be admitted, provided that "it be proved by solid arguments and to the satisfaction of the Church: 1. that the sacred writer really does quote the words or documents of another [i.e., of one not inspired]; and 2. that in doing so he does not approve of them or adopt them as his own".[102]

In our reading of the Old Testament it is well to bear these points in mind. We are not at liberty to decide definitively for ourselves whether a passage is figurative or not, or how it is to be interpreted. In all such matters we must accept the guidance of the Church. We shall find (Part II, Ch. 4) that under her direction we shall have no difficulty in meeting the objections of scientists, which are almost exclusively concerned with the opening chapters in the Book of Genesis. The Church, in interpreting a passage of Scripture *dealing solely with natural phenomena*, will be guided by physical science; but she will not accept mere theories or hypotheses.[103] She will accept only a demonstrated truth, and only when she is fully satisfied that it has been demonstrated. She does not need human science for infallibility. Still she holds that God expects her to use all diligence, and to seek knowledge from every available source, before giving her final decision. She will listen to the scientist on a point in physics, just as she will listen to the grammarian, the linguist, or the philologist, on a question connected with the meaning of words.

(3) "Could modern methods of criticism, with their elaborate examination of documents, language, style, historical and geographical allusions, etc., prove that some of the sacred books are forgeries?" REPLY: The hopes entertained by unbelievers that modern methods, when applied to the writings of the New Testament, would finally dispose of the traditions as to their date, authorship, and historical value, seemed to them at first to promise realisation, but, as already noted, have ended in nothing, a result which the humblest Catholic could have foretold. In the early decades of the 19th century, rationalist critics placed the Synoptic Gospels as late as 150 A.D., but their successors, generation after generation, have been forced by the imperative demands of scholarship to push back the date further and further,[104] so that it now coincides with what has always been held within the Church, viz., that the Synoptic Gospels were written within one generation (i.e., forty years) after the Ascension of Christ.

---

[102] DS 3372
[103] pp.206-7
[104] See p.93.

In secular history, old traditions have, in recent centuries, vindicated their claim to respect. Troy, Mycenae, and the Labyrinth of Crete belonged almost to fairy-tale until the excavations of Schliemann and Evans.

CHAPTER 14

FAITH

Summary

I. The solemn teaching of the Church.
II. The Act of Faith.
    A. The Act of Faith: its nature. The Catholic Rule of Faith. Extent of Infallibility. Private revelations.
    B. The Act of Faith is reasonable. It is reasonable in itself; it is not unreasonable in its object, i.e., in the truths proposed for belief. Faith and reason.
    C. How the Act of Faith is made: A convert's first act of faith; the dispositions necessary; how he makes his act of faith; the certainty it brings him. A Catholic's act of faith; how he makes it; the certainty it brings him.
    D. The Acts of Faith which are necessary for salvation, either necessary absolutely or because commanded by the Church.
III. The Virtue of Faith. Definition. The Virtue of Faith, a precious gift, but may be lost; consequent duties; how the Virtue of Faith may be lost; how the Virtue of Faith may be guarded; temptations against faith; how we live by faith and thus increase the Virtue of Faith.
IV. Errors as to the nature and effect of faith.

I

The solemn teaching of the Church. The Church teaches solemnly:

(1) that faith is a divine virtue by which we believe revealed truth, not because it is known to us by the natural light of reason, but because it is known to us by the authority of God who can neither deceive nor be deceived;[1]

(2) that the virtue of faith is infused into the soul with sanctifying grace,[2] and is lost only by a grave sin of unbelief,[3] which a person commits by deliberately doubting or rejecting a truth which he knows God has revealed;[4]

---

[1] V 3008

[2] T 1530

[3] T 1544

[4] Heresy is the sin committed by a Catholic who obstinately doubts or denies any article of Catholic Faith. Apostasy is the total rejection of the Christian Faith by one who has been baptised. Cf. Can. 751.

(3) that, without a gift from God consisting in His enlightening and helping grace, no one can make an act of faith profitable for salvation;[5]

(4) that the grace thus given to a person does not deprive him of liberty, but is a help which he freely accepts, and with which he freely co-operates;[6]

(5) that his act of faith is not a blind movement of the mind,[7] but is in conformity with reason;[8]

(6) that the virtue of faith can remain even when grace is lost by mortal sin;[9]

(7) that the fact of God's existence can be most certainly known from created things;[10]

(8) that the fact that God has spoken to us can be most certainly known from miracles and prophecies;[11]

(9) that the truths which God has revealed are found in Sacred Scripture and Tradition;[12]

(10) that among these truths there are Mysteries which, in this life, the mind of man, no matter how far it may advance in knowledge, can never comprehend;[13]

(11) that opinions proposed by human sciences, when contrary to revealed doctrine, may not be held as true, and the Church can proscribe (condemn) such opinions;[14]

(12) that the dogmas proposed by the Church for belief can develop but cannot change in their meaning.[15]

The two truths that God exists and that God has spoken are the foundations of faith. It is to them that the first Vatican Council refers when it says that it is the office of right reason to prove the "foundations of faith".[16]

---

[5] T 1553
[6] V 3035
[7] V 3010
[8] V 3009
[9] T 1544, 1578
[10] V 3004, 3026
[11] V 3009, 3033-4; Pius IX, DS 2778
[12] V 3006, T 1501
[13] V 3015, 3041; Pius IX, DS 2851, 2856
[14] V 3017, 3042
[15] V 3020, 3043. The meaning of the expressions in the Church's Solemn Teaching given above will become clearer in the course of this chapter.
[16] DS 3019

II

THE ACT OF FAITH

A. THE ACT OF FAITH: ITS NATURE

The Act of Faith: its main features. (1) FAITH IS BASED ON THE WORD OF GOD. When we make an act of faith, we accept a doctrine as true, because God, who knows all things and cannot lie, affirms it. In the world of today, God does not speak directly to us with His own voice. He speaks to us through other men, the Pope and the Bishops of His Church; but when we accept *their* word, we accept it as the word of God. God's spokesmen may be very learned men, yet it is not because of their learning that we believe, but because God speaks to us through them. The doctrine which they convey to us derives no authority from them, for they are mere channels of divine truth. Its authority, i.e., its claim on our belief, comes from God alone. We believe, not because man has told us, but because God has told us. We believe because we revere God's supreme authority, and welcome the revelation He in His goodness has deigned to give us.[17]

(2) FAITH GIVES CERTAINTY. He who makes an act of faith, he who believes, has no doubt whatever in his mind. To quote the words of Cardinal Newman: "He is as certain that the doctrine taught is true, as that God is true; and he is certain, *because* God is true, *because* God has spoken, not because he sees its truth or can prove its truth."[18] Thus, the outstanding characteristics of the act of faith are: (a) that it is based entirely on the word of God, and (b) that it absolutely excludes all doubt or hesitancy. The Angelic Doctor, St Thomas, says, "the certainty which comes through the divine light is greater than that which comes through the light of natural reason."[19]

(3) FAITH AND DIFFICULTIES. With regard to temptations against faith, we should keep in mind that in matters of faith, "Ten thousand difficulties do not make one doubt."[20]—so wrote Cardinal Newman. Doubts come from the will; difficulties from the intellect. Doubts arise from a reluctance to bow to divine authority, as, e.g., when one is unwilling to accept the evidence God gives that He is speaking to us. Difficulties arise from embarrassment of the mind, as, e.g., when one feels unable to reconcile the mercy of God and the eternity of Hell, or to reconcile divine doctrine with

---

[17] Second Council of Orange, DS 375-7. Cf. St Thomas, S.T., ii-ii, q. 5, a. 2, ad 2.
[18] *Discourses to Mixed Congregations*, X, p.195
[19] S.T., ii-ii, q. 171, a. 5, ad 3
[20] *Apologia pro Vita Sua*, 1864, p.239

the teaching of physical science. A doubt cannot be cured except by a change of heart; a difficulty, on the other hand, can be removed by fuller instruction. Of course, not all of our questions will be answered in this life. Many things may remain puzzling and mystifying to the end, but by faith we have the certainty that there always is an answer or explanation—even if we ourselves do not have it—and that answer is in God. "Have you been able to examine all these objections [against Revelation]? Objections of fact, chronology, history, natural history, morality, etc. Have you discovered all the arguments of opponents, and have you discovered they are false, inconsequential? ... Even if you have, that will not be enough to have faith in the Scriptures. It is possible, it is unfortunately possible that in generations to come ... there will be men who will devise new arguments against the truth of the Scriptures; they will fossick through history, ... they will claim to have discovered facts which mean the things asserted in the Scriptures appear false. Now you must swear that these books, which have not yet been written, will be full of errors: do you swear it? If you refuse to, then you must admit that you do not have faith."[21]

(4) FAITH AND FEELING. Faith is not feeling; indeed, it may at times go contrary to feeling, or we should say, feeling may incline us against faith. Faith is a habitual virtue, feelings come and go. In themselves, feelings can be no sure guide to ultimate truth. Feelings may or may not help faith. "The Catholic Church is the exponent of *Reality*. It is true. Its doctrines in matters large and small are statements of what is. This it is which the ultimate act of the intelligence accepts. This it is which the will deliberately confirms. And that is why Faith through an act of the Will is Moral. If the Ordnance Survey Map tells us that it is 11 miles to a place, then, my mood of lassitude as I walk through the rain at night making it *feel* like 30, I use the Will and say, 'No. My intelligence has been convinced and I compel myself to use it against my mood. It is 11 and though I feel in the depths of my being to have gone 20 miles and more, I *know* it is not yet 11 I have gone'."[22]

The Act of Faith: its definition. An act of faith is an act by which we, with the help of God's grace, firmly and piously believe, on His word, truths revealed by Him. (1) It is an act for which divine grace is absolutely essential. Every act of faith is a step towards heaven, but we cannot take even one step in that direction by our natural strength: we need the special help from God called divine grace. Since, therefore, the act of faith is above our *natural* powers and needs the assistance of

---

[21] Alessandro Manzoni, *Osservazioni sulla morale cattolica* ("Observations on Catholic Morality") 1819

[22] Letter of Hilaire Belloc to G.K. Chesterton (1874-1936) upon the latter's conversion in 1922.

God's grace, it is termed a *supernatural* act. (2) It is made by our intellect at the command of our will, and God's grace works both on our intellect and on our will. It is by an act of our intellect or understanding that we accept or acknowledge the truth He has revealed to us; it is by an act of our will that we decide to accept it. His grace gives us a gentle submissiveness[23] so that we freely, piously and reverently resolve that our intellect shall not be guided by its own natural light, but that it shall take His word as the sole reason for assenting to the truth revealed. (A person could make an act of faith without grace, but it would be an act of merely human faith and not count for salvation, because it would not have that kind of submissiveness and assent which God's grace alone can give). (3) Its motive, i.e., the reason why we believe, is the perfect knowledge and truthfulness and supreme authority of God who cannot deceive us and cannot Himself be deceived. (Thus, it is evident that the act of faith is an act of divine worship, giving God a praise that can be given to Him alone). (4) Its object, i.e., the sum of the truths which we must believe, comprises all truths contained in the Deposit of Faith. By the Deposit of Faith we mean that collection of revealed truths which, whether found in Scripture or Tradition, the Church commands us to believe with an assent of faith. (When we believe in general all that the Church proposes for our belief, we believe *implicitly* each truth. But for some of these truths an *explicit* act of faith is necessary[24]).

God has appointed the Church to teach all mankind the truths which He wishes them to believe. He has appointed her to teach them with an infallible voice, and to be their one and only guide to Heaven. The Faith, therefore, of which we speak throughout this treatise, may be more fully described as Faith, Divine and Catholic.

The Catholic Rule of Faith. The Rule of Faith is the test by which we can determine exactly the truths which we are bound to believe. The Catholic Rule of Faith is the teaching of the Church, the living representative of Christ on earth. When she declares that God has revealed a particular doctrine, we are certain that He has revealed it, and that we are bound to believe it. Catholics need not, and, in fact, usually do not, study the evidence from Scripture and Tradition for the revelation of every article of Catholic belief. They inquire whether the infallible Church teaches that a particular truth has been revealed by God, and, if they find that she does, they believe it on God's authority. This Catholic Rule of Faith manifests the wisdom and goodness of God, for it meets the needs of both the learned and the uneducated.[25]

Extent of infallibility. As explained on pp.185-7, the Infallibility of the Church extends to truths outside the Deposit of Faith. The Church can declare infallibly

---

[23] This is what is meant by the Second Council of Orange and the first Vatican Council when they speak of *suavitas in consentiendo et credendo* ("ease in assenting and believing") as the gift of the Holy Spirit: see DS 377, V 3010.

[24] See p.288.

[25] See pp.157-8.

that, e.g., a certain book contains heretical or immoral doctrine. We are bound under grave obligation to accept such a declaration as true, but we do not, and cannot, give it an assent of faith, i.e., of Faith Divine and Catholic—since it is not a truth revealed by God. We give it, however, a definitive assent. We believe it on the authority of the infallible Church.

PRIVATE REVELATIONS. God may, and sometimes does, grant revelations to private individuals. Those who receive them, and are perfectly certain that they come from God, are bound to believe them. The Church never imposes on Catholics the obligation of believing anyone's Private Revelations, even those of the great Saints. She gives her approval to them only when she is satisfied after rigorous examination of their spiritual utility and of the evidence on which they depend, as, e.g., in the case of revelations connected with the devotion to the Sacred Heart. It is forbidden, as well as sinful, to propagate Private Revelations which have received a negative judgement from the local Bishop, the conference of Bishops or the Vatican's Congregation for the Doctrine of the Faith. The authority to rule on the genuineness of a private revelation rests first with the *local Bishop*; very rarely does the Pope himself make a pronouncement. Even should the local authority mistakenly disapprove of a genuine revelation, obedience to the Church remains paramount. There can be no sin in *not* propagating a Private Revelation. After error itself, the first sign of a false mystic is wilfulness and disobedience. "Satan can even clothe himself in a cloak of humility, but he does not know how to wear the cloak of obedience".[26]

The Popes may choose to show their approval of certain revelations, *after* the decision of a local Bishop or conference of Bishops, by speaking of them, or by placing a new feast in the liturgical calendar, or by visiting the places intrinsically connected with them (e.g., Guadalupe, Paray-le-Monial, Rue de Bac, Lourdes, Knock, Fatima, Beauraing, Banneux). Private Revelations "do not belong to the deposit of faith. It is not their role to 'improve' or 'complete' Christ's definitive Revelation, but to furnish help so that it may be more fully applied to life in a certain period of history."[27] Catholics ought be extremely cautious in giving credence to visions and messages before they have received approbation from the Church. The devil rejoices when Catholics reject the tried and true means of spiritual growth to chase after the extraordinary and the unapproved. The Church is extremely careful before approving a Private Revelation, for she knows how "even Satan disguises himself as an angel of light".[28] She must avoid both credulity and unfounded scepticism. "Do not quench the Spirit, do not

26 *Diary of Bl. Sr Faustina Kowalska*, Marian Press, Massachusetts 1996, par. 939
27 C 67. Cf. St Thomas, S. T., ii-ii, q. 174, art. 6, ad 3.
28 2 Cor 11:14

despise prophesying, but test everything", directs St Paul.[29]   And St John warns, "Beloved, do not believe every spirit, but test the spirits to see whether they are of God".[30]   Christian faith cannot accept revelations which claim to correct the teaching of the Church or enjoin disobedience to the lawful directives of her pastors.

B. THE ACT OF FAITH IS REASONABLE

The Act of Faith is reasonable in itself. It is reasonable for us to accept truth on the word of God, because every day of our lives we accept truth on the word of man. The greater and, by far, the more important part of the knowledge we possess is the gift of others. However acute our senses may be, however brilliant our powers of understanding, the store of information which we can brand as peculiarly our own is as nothing compared with that which we have derived from our fellow men. It is to their testimony that we are indebted for all our knowledge of the distant past, for much of our knowledge of the immediate present, for almost everything we know of the conclusions of science, and for all that mass of practical and moral certainty on which we regulate our daily lives. We are certain, e.g., that we are the children of those whom we call our parents, or that the books we read are the exact reproductions of their authors' manuscripts. If, then, we accept truth so freely from men, how could it be unreasonable to accept it from God? Dependence on others is, in fact, a law of our very nature. Nothing, therefore, could be more reasonable, more human, so to speak, than the Act of Faith.

The higher the authority, the more reasonable is the act of submission to it. No authority can be higher than God's. Men are fallible. God is infallible. Therefore, if it is certain that God has spoken, not only would it be reasonable to believe on His word, but it would be the height of unreason and folly to refuse to believe. We insult a man by saying: "You are deceiving me. I refuse to believe you." The insult is all the greater in proportion to the man's uprightness, dignity, and superiority over us in knowledge. What, then, must be the insult to God of deliberately rejecting His word?

The Act of Faith is not unreasonable in its object. There are only two grounds on which it is contended that the Object of Faith is unreasonable, viz., that it includes (1) mysteries, and (2) doctrines which may some day be disproved by secular science. We will show (1) that belief in mysteries is

---

[29] 1 Thess 5:19-21
[30] 1 Jn 4:1. See pp.323-4 on the devil's power to deceive.

280

not unreasonable, and (2) that faith and secular science can never be in conflict.

FAITH IN MYSTERIES IS NOT UNREASONABLE. A mystery is a doctrine beyond mortal comprehension. Our reason cannot prove it to be true; our reason cannot prove it to be false. Yet, convinced of the veracity of God, and of the infinite superiority of His knowledge to ours, we can believe it to be true, as a blind man believes what we tell him of the twinkling star or the colours of a sunset. He cannot prove or disprove our statements; he believes, because he is certain that we have knowledge which he has not, and that we are telling the truth.

It is as reasonable to admit the mysteries of religion as the mysteries of physical science. In almost every science that we study, we are confronted with the mysteries of space and time and their limits. Nature is full of mysteries: a tiny seed falls to earth and puts forth a tender sprout. In the course of years it becomes a great tree with its tangle of roots, its trunk and spreading boughs, its flowers and fruit, and reproduces itself a thousandfold. The very nature of the force of gravity which drew the seed to the earth in the first instance, and the processes of growth and reproduction which it exhibits, are mysteries for which scientists have no explanation, and are but a few amid a countless number. But, if the admission of mysteries is no argument against the validity of physical science, how could it tell against the reasonableness of religion? If the works of God are incomprehensible, how much more incomprehensible must not God Himself be?

It is reasonable for man to expect mysteries in the true religion. God is so far above us that it is only reasonable to expect that there would be certain truths concerning Him which would surpass the powers of human reason. If a religion had no mysteries, its divine origin would be open to suspicion. If all its doctrines could be clearly and fully proved from reason, then they might have all been discovered by reason; they might have come from man, and not from God. Mysteries, therefore, so far from intimidating belief, are an incentive to it.

It is not unreasonable that God should require us to believe mysteries, for such belief leads us to a higher worship of Him. (a) God, in bidding us believe what we cannot comprehend, exacts from us a homage most natural and fitting for us to render. Our belief in mysteries is a bowing down of our reason, the highest faculty we have, in the presence of God's infinite knowledge. It is an admission of the imperfection and limits of our understanding, and a grateful acceptance, on His word, of truths which we need to know; it is the expression of our complete trust in our heavenly

Father; in a word, it is the most perfect acknowledgment we can make that we are God's creatures, that we absolutely depend on Him as the source of all truth and all being. It is a submission most strictly demanded by God, and blessed by Him when given. Note the strong words of Scripture: "Without faith it is impossible to please God"; "He who does not believe will be condemned"; "Blessed are those who have not seen and yet believe."[31]

(b) Belief in mysteries *tends vastly to increase our reverence for God:* the wonder we feel at what reason tells us of His Nature deepens into profound awe when we learn through faith that He is One and Three.

(c) Belief in the mysteries involved in our Redemption *urges us to abandon all selfishness and to give God all the love of our hearts.* The plan of the Redemption was that the Second Person of the Blessed Trinity should become man to atone for our sins and to make us Children of God; that God the Son should be born into the world like any helpless little infant; that He should die on the Cross, and rise from the grave—but how many mysteries are there here? And yet the great lesson of love they convey goes straight to every heart.

A father says to his child who fears to go out in the dark, "Give me your hand, and come with me." The child asks no more. It does not want a scientific explanation of the black shadows. So we, too, with a child's humility, do not seek to understand the impenetrable mysteries of God. Our reason has no protest to make: its murmurs are stilled. Satisfied of His love and wisdom, we place our hand in His. We know He will guide us aright.

FAITH AND SECULAR SCIENCE CAN NEVER BE IN CONFLICT. The God of revelation is the God of creation. The truths of faith and the truths of secular science come to us from God, the former through revelation, the latter through human reason. Truth cannot contradict truth. It has been well said, "God is not afraid of your reason: He made it." Faith is to Revelation as reason is to science. Through faith we know and believe the supernatural truths revealed by God; through reason we know and hold the natural truths of the world about us. Faith and reason have as their object *two different orders of knowledge:* faith's object is the supernatural order; reason's object is the natural order. There may be an apparent, but there can never be a real, conflict between the doctrines of faith and the findings of secular science. "This specious contradiction chiefly arises either because the dogmas of the faith are not understood and explained in accordance with the mind of the Church, or false opinions are mistaken for the

---

[31] Heb 11:6; Mk 16:16; Jn 20:29; cf. 3:18.

conclusions of reason."[32]   Seeming conflicts can arise when exponents of one order step outside their field into the other order.   Apparent conflicts also arise because we do not see all truths perfectly clearly in this life, and so cannot see how to reconcile all points of our knowledge.   In some matters, revelation and human sciences overlap, and so there may be two sources of truth on the same subject: e.g., the sacred history of the Old Testament, and the evidence from archaeology;   our knowledge of God from philosophy, and our knowledge of Him from revelation.   Both are valid and both are necessary.   "Faith and reason are like two wings by which the human spirit is raised up to the contemplation of truth."[33]

Vatican I's doctrine on the relationship between faith and reason can be summarised in the following points: (a) There is no true disagreement between faith and reason.   (b) Reason establishes the foundations of faith.   (c) Reason, using faith, develops the science of divine things.   (d) Faith goes beyond reason, elevates it, furnishes it with much knowledge and never contradicts it, but illuminates the conclusions of reason in the light of a picture more vast.   (e) Faith delivers reason from errors, protects it, confirms its conclusions and makes them more secure.[34]

C. HOW THE ACT OF FAITH IS MADE

Prefatory note.   *The veracity of God.*   We have shown how we can establish from reason the existence of God and the possibility of revelation.   The veracity of God is usually taken as self-evident.   If a proof be required, it might be put in the following form: (I.) If God is not truthful, we cannot trust Him.   If we cannot trust Him, we cannot trust the senses and the reason He has given us, and must believe that they may be constantly deceiving us.   We must, therefore, become uncertain of everything, even of our own existence.   But this conclusion is absurd.   Therefore, the supposition that gave rise to it, viz., that God is not truthful, is also absurd.   (II.) God is infinite understanding.   He knows all truth.   He is the infinitely complete representation of all truth.   He loves Himself necessarily, and with an infinite love, as the God of truth.   It follows from His very nature that He must abhor all falsehood, and that His every utterance must be true.

A. **A convert's first Act of faith**.   We contemplate the case of an unbeliever, one devoid of all faith, who is convinced from reason of the existence and veracity of God and the possibility of revelation.   We suppose him to be about to make *an act of faith in the Church as a divinely appointed teacher.*

THE DISPOSITIONS WHICH HE REQUIRES.   The seeker after faith should be a man of good will.   "Good will" includes: (a) *Prayerfulness and humility*: the man of good will

---

[32] V 3017

[33] *Fides et Ratio*, Pope John Paul II, 1998, art. 1

[34] DS 3015-20, 3041-3. Cf. C 159.

prays to God for light and guidance. He approaches the things of God with the humility and trustfulness of a child. He is ready to admit the fact of revelation, if it is borne to him on testimony which he would acknowledge as decisive in all the important affairs of life. His humility will consist chiefly in the consciousness of his own infirmity, of his incapacity to discover all religious truth by the unaided reason, and of the weakness of his will and its tendency to evil. The humble man seeks God. The proud man, on the other hand, expects that God will seek him, that God will submit His revelation to him to be judged by any standard he chooses, to be accepted or rejected according as his arrogance directs, as though he were the master and God the pupil, as though his decision were of importance to God, but of little interest to himself. (b) *Earnestness and conscientiousness*: he uses all diligence to ascertain the truth and is willing to accept it in spite of old associations and prejudices, and in spite of any irksome duties which its discovery might entail. (c) *Cleanness of heart*: he leads a good life. He puts a check on the indulgence of his passions, because he knows that one of the greatest obstacles to Christian belief is unchristian conduct. In arriving at these dispositions he has the help of God's grace.

HOW HE MAKES HIS ACT OF FAITH. Let us suppose that, while continuing steadfastly in these good dispositions, he carefully examines the arguments for believing in the Church as a divinely appointed teacher, and puts the result of his investigation in some such form as the following: "Relying on the testimony given to me as to the origin of the Church, the sufferings and virtues of her children, and her triumphant survival down to the present day, I am convinced she is from God. In the miracles I see in her, I recognise God's way of telling me that she is right when she claims to be the teacher whom He himself has appointed as His representative on earth. I ought therefore to believe in her." But this conviction which he has reached under God's grace, is not in itself an act of faith. Many men get so far and no further, for it is one thing to recognise a duty and quite another to fulfil it. The act of faith, as the Church teaches, cannot be made without a further and higher grace, i.e., without a very special help from God, which He will not deny to one of good dispositions. The man of whom we speak will, therefore, receive the grace of a gentle submissiveness, moving him to honour God by freely, piously, and reverently submitting his mind to God's word. This grace enables him to give effect to his conviction, and to say: "I do believe that God has given me the Church to be my teacher. I believe it on the word of the good God Himself who can neither deceive nor be deceived." This is the act of faith.

Converts are led to the Church in a great variety of ways: some are attracted by her claim to infallibility, some by the consistency of her doctrine, others by her reverence for antiquity, or by her love for the poor and afflicted, or by her moral teaching. In the case given above, we supposed the future convert to begin his inquiry, convinced of the possibility of revelation. It must be admitted, however, that it is the absence of that very conviction which keeps many learned unbelievers outside the Church.

THE CERTAINTY WHICH THE ACT OF FAITH BRINGS HIM. Reason has led him to faith, but his faith does not rest on reason. It rests on the authority of God who is worthy of all reverence and love, and who can neither deceive nor be deceived. (It is not implied that perfect love for God is required, but there must be at least some low form of love, akin to that which is found in attrition, some affection for spiritual good, a desire to enter on the true worship of God). Reason has made him quite certain that God has spoken, and that it would be wrong and foolish to deny it. Once he is convinced of this, he has opened a door that admits him to a far higher and different kind of certainty, the certainty that God's word gives him.[35] Resting solely on that infinitely secure authority, he gives a most firm assent to the truth that God has revealed. He believes it, not because of any argument or reasoning, *but precisely because God says it is true.* Divine grace has so strengthened his will that it can command the assent of his intellect; divine grace has so enlightened his intellect that it obeys, and accepts as true even that which it cannot understand. In giving such graces, God does not force the soul to yield to them. The soul may, to its own great unhappiness, reject them. St Augustine spoke a profound truth when he said: "Thou hast made us for Thyself, O God, and our heart is restless till it rest in Thee".[36] When a man attains to faith, his mind slips into the socket that God has made for it. It rests securely there, and can never be dislodged except through its own grave fault.

Note. *Grace: how far needed for faith.* Faith helps us to become sons of God, a dignity whose attainment is absolutely beyond our natural powers. To make an act of faith, therefore, we need that special divine aid called grace. This is the defined doctrine of the Church. We shall understand it better when we read the chapter on Grace in Part II. But grace, in the full sense of the term, is not required for the good dispositions that precede the act of faith, because they are not absolutely above the reach of human nature. Yet so weak is fallen man that he cannot, of his own strength, arrive at them and persevere in them. He needs a special help from God which, since it is quite exceptional and gratuitous, is correctly called grace, though it is grace of a lower kind. (This grace is a "healing grace" because God gives it to heal the weakness caused by Original Sin. It is the teaching of the Church that, without God's special help, an unbeliever cannot keep the Ten Commandments for long. It follows that for the more difficult work of persevering in the good dispositions that precede faith, he would need this help still more). Most probably too he receives a further help of a similar character enabling him to discover, without difficulty, the arguments that prove the reasonableness of belief, to hold them all clearly before his mind and perceive their force. These arguments are technically called "the motives of credibility". The case given is that of one devoid of all faith. A baptised Protestant who already believes some revealed truths would undoubtedly receive greater help. He would receive the higher kind of supernatural grace during the entire progress of his conversion.

---

[35] "Higher certainty" does not mean "a greater absence of doubt". That would be a serious mistake. Doubt is absolutely excluded both from the act of reasoning that precedes faith and from the act of faith itself.

[36] *Confessions* 1,1

The act of faith is preceded by an act of reasoning. An act of sound reasoning always precedes the act of faith, otherwise it would not be a prudent or sensible act. (An act of reasoning, explicit or implicit, is necessary for the act of faith, and yet it is no part of it. The following illustration may help: In a lighted lamp, the light is like the act of faith; the oil that produces the light is like God's grace; the vessel that holds the oil is like the act of reasoning. Though the vessel contributes nothing to the light, yet there could be no light without the vessel; and if, at any moment while the light is burning, the vessel is shattered, the light will go out). The act of faith, therefore, is reasonable, i.e., it can be justified by arguments which impartial minds would recognise as cogent. In making an act of faith, we need not have definitely before our minds the reason why we make it: as a sick man may take medicine without recalling why he takes it, so we can make an act of faith without thinking clearly either of the acts of reasoning that precede it, or of the divine authority on which it rests.

Why so many are convinced of the truth and yet are unbelievers. Why is it that so many people see clearly the force of the arguments, e.g., for the Divinity of Christ and the divine authority of the Church, and yet fail to make acts of faith? Because they do not have the precise dispositions that open their soul to the grace of God: their lives may be blameless, except insofar as they have no sincere practical desire of the truth. They are absorbed in the cares of the world, or are immovably fastened to false convictions, their reason frozen by prejudice, their imagination so stained and warped by early training that, even though convinced that they should believe, they cannot bring themselves to do so. For example, some Protestants, especially Fundamentalists, are taught that the Pope is the Antichrist.[37] This belief so grips their imagination that the very thought of examining the claims of the Catholic Church strikes them with panic. These 'willing, but unwilling' offer "no imaginary case; there is many a man who has ground enough to believe, who wishes to believe, but who cannot believe. It is always indeed his own fault, for God gives grace to all who ask for it, and use it … As then men may be convinced, and not act according to their conviction, so may they be convinced, and not believe according to their conviction … The arguments for religion do not compel anyone to believe, just as arguments for good conduct do not compel anyone to obey. Obedience is the consequence of willing to obey, and faith is the consequence of willing to believe; we may see what is right, whether in matters of faith or obedience, of ourselves, but we cannot will what is right without the grace of God."[38]

Some "wish" to believe, but they do not wish fully and sincerely. They do not have a true will to believe but only an inclination. A man may know the way of salvation, and yet refuse to follow it, just as he may see what medical treatment he needs but obstinately refuse it.

Exceptional graces. God may grant, as an exceptional favour, the gift of faith to people of evil dispositions: St Paul, while engaged in persecuting the Church, received the grace of conversion through the dying prayer of the first Christian

---

[37] Cf. J.H. Newman, *Apologia*, p.52 (History of opinions 1833-39).
[38] Newman, *Discourses to Mixed Congregations*, XI, pp.224-5

martyr, St Stephen. St Augustine was snatched from heresy and vice through his mother, the gentle St Monica, who had prayed and wept for him over a dreary stretch of years. And, as we might expect, God does not deny a similar favour to men of "good will". He often bestows on them a sudden illumination of the mind, accompanied by an impulse to the will, enabling them to see and embrace the truth at once without passing through any prolonged process of reasoning.

B. **A Catholic's Act of faith.** Let us take the case of a Catholic child who has received in Baptism the gift of faith.[39] Blessed by Divine Providence which has made him the child of Catholic parents, he is helped by every influence around him—his home, his school, the church he frequents—along the path that leads to God. He is not tied up in the network of error and prejudice from which the convert disengages himself, often after bitter anguish and with the loss of lifelong friends. His Baptism, by giving him the Virtue of Faith, has prepared him for the Act of Faith.

How he makes his Act of Faith. He learns from his parents and teachers the natural truths that lead up to the Act of Faith, viz., that God exists, that God has spoken, that God is truthful. He learns from them all the great truths of religion without at first any clear understanding of the divine authority on which they rest. But, when still very young, aided by the gift of faith which he possesses, he comes to accept them as his instructors themselves accepted them, not on the word of man, but on the word of God himself. As he grows older, he grasps without difficulty some simple and telling arguments from reason in defence of the faith, e.g., "The Catholic Church must be from God, because it has lasted in vigour all the centuries from the time of Our Lord"; "the Catholic Church must be the true Church, because she is the only one that claims to speak, as one from God should speak, with unerring voice." These very arguments themselves, while they help to secure him throughout his life against temptation to unbelief, serve also to stimulate him to make, but always with the aid of divine Grace, new and more vivid acts of faith.

A child behaves reasonably in accepting his parents' word as to what God has revealed. But if, as a fact, God has not revealed what they say, the child gets the credit of submissiveness to God's authority, but his act of belief is an act of faith only in appearance, since it is not ultimately based on the Word of God.

The certainty which the Act of Faith brings him. His mind, as already explained in the case of the convert, has found the place that God has made for it. God will keep it there until death, secure against all the attacks of earth and hell. It can never be cast forth except through its own treachery.

---

[39] See below, "The Virtue of Faith", pp.289-92.

D. THE ACTS OF EXPLICIT FAITH NECESSARY
FOR SALVATION

The Act of Faith which is absolutely necessary for salvation. No one who has come to the use of reason can be saved, unless he makes a definite or explicit act of faith in the existence of one God who will reward the good and punish the wicked. As we are told in the Epistle to the Hebrews, "without faith, it is impossible to please God. For whoever would draw near to God must believe that He exists and that He rewards those who seek Him"[40] and also, therefore, punishes them that avoid Him. This explicit act of faith is as necessary for salvation as eyes are for sight. Without it, salvation is absolutely unattainable.

By "faith", we do not mean "faith alone", i.e., dead faith, faith devoid of hope and love. There must also be *hope*, which is expressed in the belief that "He rewards those who seek Him". There must also be the holiness that comes from *charity*. Hebrews also says, "Strive ... for the holiness without which no one will see the Lord."[41] St Paul speaks of "faith working through love."[42] Without the love of God, salvation is impossible: "if I have all faith", says St Paul, "so as to remove mountains, but have not love, I am nothing."[43] Implicit always in this love or charity is repentance and contrition for sin: Our Lord warns, "unless you repent you will all likewise perish."[44]

Notes. (1) The question may be asked: when did God reveal the truth that He is a rewarder of the good and a punisher of the wicked? The answer is that He revealed it in His dealings with Adam and Adam's children. It passed from them to their descendants, and is widespread among the human race today. It is not a truth which the human reason alone could have discovered, because the rewards and punishments in question are closely associated with the gain and loss of God's grace; and God's grace by which we are truly made His children, one in nature with Him, can be known only through revelation.

(2) The act of faith in God the Judge, accompanied by an act of charity or perfect contrition, suffices for the salvation of those who may never even have heard the name of Christ. Hence it is easy to understand how very many outside the visible membership of the Church may be saved. However, it is not lawful, outside a case of extreme necessity, to administer Baptism to an adult without giving previous instruction in the mysteries of the Trinity and the Incarnation. See p.142, "The obligation of membership", and p.169, "Outside the Church there is no salvation."

---

[40] Heb 11:6
[41] Heb 12:14
[42] Rom 5:6
[43] 1 Cor 13:2
[44] Lk 13:3

Acts of faith, necessary because commanded by the Church. The Church, while urging all her children to obtain as full a knowledge of her teaching as their ability and opportunities allow, requires them to know substantially and to believe: (a) the articles of the Apostles' Creed, (b) the doctrine of the Sacraments (in particular, of Baptism, Penance, the Blessed Eucharist, and of the other sacraments when their reception becomes necessary), (c) the Ten Commandments, (d) the doctrine conveyed in the Lord's Prayer. - To know and believe these truths and precepts is necessary for salvation, but not in the sense explained above. The necessity springs from the commandment of the Church. Those who fail to obey her without grave fault will not be lost.

III

THE VIRTUE OF FAITH

The Virtue of Faith defined. Faith is a supernatural virtue infused into our souls by God which makes us able and willing to give an unhesitating assent to all the revealed truths which He has commanded the Church to propose to us for belief. It is a virtue, i.e., it is not a single *act*, but an abiding *power* in the soul (technically it is called a *habit*). It is supernatural, i.e., no creature can claim it as a natural right. It is a pure gift of God's mercy, which we could never merit, and to which we could never attain, by our natural powers. It is infused into the soul by the Sacrament of Baptism. (Or, for an adult, as a consequence of the act of charity. The convert from unbelief who has made his first act of faith, but has no opportunity of receiving the sacrament of Baptism, will, if his dispositions continue to be good, obtain from God all the grace necessary to enable him to make the act of charity).

The Virtue of Faith is a precious gift, but may be lost. Consequent duties.
The Virtue of Faith is a precious gift. It places us within the sound of God's voice, and it opens our ears to receive it. Every day of our lives we should thank Him for having made us children of His Church and partakers in His sacraments, for having set us on the true path that leads to Him. But this precious gift may become clouded or be lost. It will stay with us, as long as it is our sincere will that it should stay. It will grow weaker or vanish utterly if our will becomes indifferent or hostile to it. It is a lighted lamp which God places in our hands to guide our footsteps through the night of the world. We can make it burn clear or dim. We can extinguish it at our pleasure, but we cannot re-light it; it is only God who can do that. "It is

impossible",[45] as the Holy Spirit tells us, i.e., practically impossible, impossible without a miracle of grace—"It is impossible to restore again to repentance those who have once been enlightened (*by grace of Baptism*), who have tasted the heavenly gift (*Holy Communion*), and have become partakers of the Holy Spirit (*Confirmation*), and have tasted the goodness of the word of God (*instruction*) and the powers of the age to come (*all the graces of religion*), if they then commit apostasy, since they crucify the Son of God on their own account and hold Him up to contempt", i.e., because they are like the Jews who denied Him, who mocked Him, and crucified Him.

Above, we have distinguished *living* faith from *dead* faith. Faith is living when accompanied by charity, i.e., when the soul is in the state of sanctifying grace. Faith is dead when sanctifying grace has been lost. But this *dead* faith is nonetheless a great mercy, for it leaves the way to salvation still open, and can become *living* again by penance, by a return to the love of God. Faith does not disappear utterly from the soul except through a sin of heresy or apostasy.

HOW THE VIRTUE OF FAITH MAY BE LOST. God never suffers any soul to lose the gift of faith, the key to so many other precious gifts, the foundation of the whole spiritual life, except through her own fault. Faith is lost only by a mortal sin of unbelief, but this unbelief is usually preceded by one or a number of things: (1) Indolence in not acquiring a sound knowledge of Catholic doctrine. (2) Reading irreligious books and journals—the Church warns us especially against these: they are poison to the faith. She forbids the reading of irreligious books, not because she is afraid that they might prove her doctrine to be false, but because she knows that lack of expert knowledge exposes Catholics to the danger of being deceived (see under 3). She forbids it also, because it is disloyal in a child of God to associate with His enemies open or hidden: when we read a book, we are in the company of the writer;—no mother would permit her son to consort with those who would try to turn him away from the love he owes his father. (3) Engaging in religious controversy with trained opponents when not qualified by a rigorous scientific training. We should give the honest inquirer any information we possess, but we should be firm in refusing to discuss religion with trained enemies. The average layman is not qualified for religious controversy. Like an honest witness in the hands of a clever lawyer, he may be trapped into all manner of admissions and contradictions by a skilful opponent, and may, ultimately, ascribe his discomfiture to the weakness of his cause, and not to his own ignorance and inexperience.[46]

---

[45] Heb 6:4-6

[46] However, the Church from the earliest times has found some of her ablest defenders among the laity, specially trained for their work. Any layman who feels that he has a marked aptitude for theological study should by all means equip himself under proper direction as a

(4) Forming marriage or social ties with the irreligious, with anti-Catholics or atheists. (5) Adopting an attitude of criticism or unfriendliness to the Church, seeking out and relating with approval, instead of deploring, and praying for the cessation of, those scandals which "must needs come"[47] in an institution whose ministers, though the instruments of God, still retain the ordinary frailty of human nature. Such an attitude of mind is a grave danger, not only to him who entertains it, but to all those with whom he associates. (6) Pride, manifesting itself in a reluctance to accept what cannot be proved from reason. (7) A dissipated or sinful life, neglect of prayer and the sacraments.

HOW THE VIRTUE OF FAITH CAN BE GUARDED. We can guard our precious gift of faith by avoiding the dangers and evils already referred to. In brief, a good life is the best preservative of faith. Good will leads to faith, and good will preserves it. Faith is nourished in particular by suffering and self-sacrifice. This is true of nations as well as of individuals. Genuine faith grows strong under persecution. When persecution ceases, voluntary suffering and self-denial must take its place, if faith is to continue vigorous. The faith of a country which enjoys complete religious liberty is safest when many of its people join those religious orders in which severe mortification is practised, or face the perils of the mission in foreign lands. Their example, the example of living, vivid faith, is a light and an incentive to all others.

TEMPTATIONS AGAINST FAITH. We must be patient and prayerful amid difficulties and temptations. The enemy of our souls naturally desires to attack our faith, for he knows that it is the foundation of our spiritual life, and that, when he has robbed us of faith, he has robbed us of all. Many of the saints have suffered grievous trials from these assaults (e.g., Sts Jeanne Frances de Chantal, Vincent de Paul, Alphonsus Liguori, Therese of Lisieux). The grace which held them firm is within our reach also. In temptation, (1) we should pray for this grace; (2) we should make acts of faith: "I believe. Lord, help my unbelief"; (3) as Saints and theologians warn us, we should never reason with such thoughts, but should treat them as we would impure temptations; (4) we should beware of the presumption of trying to solve our difficulties by our own efforts, but should seek the help of one in whose learning and piety we can fully confide.

controversialist. Next to prayer and the example of his own good life, he can render no greater service to his faith. Witness the example of author Mr Frank Sheed (1896-1981), founder of the Catholic Evidence Guild.
[47] Cf. Lk 17:1.

HOW WE LIVE BY FAITH AND THUS INCREASE THE GIFT OF FAITH. The just man lives by faith—so teaches the Holy Spirit.[48] To live by faith implies that the great truths which God in His goodness has revealed to us are not forgotten, but on the contrary are so frequently present to us in prayer and daily meditation that they influence our life and action. To the man who lives by faith, the divine truths are more real, more impressive, more inspiring and more important than the things he sees and hears and feels, the things that beat on his senses in life's daily round. His mind is filled with the thought of God's presence, and his heart is set on the observance of God's law. Trials and reverses he accepts as from God's hand, knowing they are but crosses given to him to make him more Christ-like. His life of faith is stimulated and intensified by the Sacraments of the Church and especially by the Sacrament of the Blessed Eucharist. And as he grows in holiness, his gift of faith increases. In fact, every time he receives a Sacrament worthily, he thereby makes a great practical act of faith in Christ the Redeemer, the Author of all the Sacraments, and the Cause of all their graces.

IV

Errors as to the nature and effects of faith. Luther and the early Reformers held: (a) that man is made just or holy by faith alone;[49] (b) that this justifying faith consists in nothing more than trust in divine mercy; (c) that a man's sins are forgiven, because he believes for certain that they are forgiven. These and other like doctrines, which were absolutely novel, and which have not the slightest support either in Scripture or Tradition, were solemnly condemned by the Council of Trent (1545-1563).

The Modernists (Loisy and others) hold that each believer receives his own special revelation through his own mind, and that faith is, as it were, the reaction within the soul resulting from such revelation. Hence they maintain that the Object of Faith varies for individuals, that one man may hold as true what all others reject. This teaching, one of a whole series of heresies and rationalist errors, denies that Christ bequeathed to us any fixed and unalterable body of truths to be interpreted by an infallible Church. Pope St Pius X condemned Modernism in his encyclical *Pascendi* of 1907. This condemnation is approved by common sense, which revolts from the notion that God should bind one man to give his body to be burned rather than admit a certain doctrine, and that He should bind another to make the same supreme sacrifice rather than deny it.

Note. Different senses of the word "faith". "Faith" as used in this chapter may denote either the Act of Faith, the Virtue of Faith, or the truths of Faith. In all cases, the precise sense can be easily inferred from the context. Sometimes in the

---

[48] Cf. Heb 10:38.
[49] See p.446.

Scriptures the word means "trust in God", but this trust itself is based on the Virtue of Faith, faith in the merciful promises which God has revealed to us. In one instance (Rom 14:22-23), the word is used as the equivalent of "conscience".

PART II

CATHOLIC DOCTRINE

GOD IN HIMSELF

CHAPTER 1

THE DIVINE ESSENCE AND ATTRIBUTES

Summary

I.   The solemn teaching of the Church.
II.   The Self-existence and Infinity of God.
III.   The Divine Essence: essence defined; the essences of creatures not fully known to us; the Essence of God, incomprehensible. According to the common teaching, self-existence constitutes the Divine Essence. God's names and titles.
IV.   The Divine Attributes: Quiescent Attributes: *Eternity, Immensity* and *Omnipresence*, and *Immutability*. Operative Attributes: *Knowledge* and *Will*. Other attributes: Power, Holiness, Majesty, Wisdom & Goodness, Justice, Providence, Truth, Mercy.
V.   A difficulty against God's foreknowledge answered.
VI.   Love and service of God. Sins against God.

I

The solemn teaching of the Church. The first Vatican Council (1870) says, "The holy, catholic, apostolic, and Roman Church believes and confesses that there is one, true and living God, the Creator and Lord of heaven and earth, omnipotent, eternal, immeasurable, incomprehensible, infinite in understanding and will and every perfection, ... a spiritual substance*, one, absolutely simple and immutable, really and essentially distinct from the world, in Himself and of Himself supremely happy, and unspeakably above all things that are, or can be conceived outside Himself."[1]

The same Council moreover solemnly teaches:

(1)   that God knows all things: past, present and future, including the future free actions of His creatures;[2]

(2)   that the one true God, our Creator and Lord, can be known with certainty by the natural light of human reason from created things.[3]

These truths, expressing the perfections of God, and so fully and emphatically set forth in the infallible decision of the Council, can be established by reason,[4] but, to many minds,

---

[1] V 3001
[2] V 3001, 3003
[3] V 3026

the proof is difficult and obscure. We accept them with all the certainty of faith, because they have been revealed to us by God.

*Substance, here, has a technical meaning. It does not necessarily mean something solid and material, such as wood and iron. It is the opposite of *accident*. An *accident* is something which cannot exist by itself, but only in something else: e.g., our height, weight, and colour are accidents, because they cannot exist apart from our bodies. So, too, motion is an accident, because it cannot exist apart from a moving body. A *substance* is something which exists by itself and not in anything else: thus, wood and iron are substances; our souls are substances; angels are substances; God is a substance. He is not bodily, but "a spiritual substance" in the words of Vatican I, or in the words of our Divine Lord, "God is spirit" (Jn 4:24).

II

God is the self-existent, necessary Being. It is a fundamental doctrine of our faith, revealed to us by God Himself, but discoverable even by unaided human reason,[5] that God owes His existence to no other; that He is the only being who has within Himself the source and fount of His own existence.[6] God's words to Moses declare that self-existence belongs to Him alone. Moses had asked God to tell him His name. God answered: "*I Am who I Am*", and He said: "Say this to the people of Israel: '*I Am* has sent me to you.'"[7] It is because of God's self existence that Scripture so often declares that He is the "the Alpha and the Omega, the first and the last",[8] and that all creatures "are accounted by Him as less than nothing and emptiness."[9]

God alone exists in the fullest, truest sense, deriving His existence from no one else. He is existence itself. All other beings derive their existence from Him. In God "we live and move and have our being."[10]

The infinity of God. Infinity belongs to all the Perfections of God, and is reflected, but ever so imperfectly, in the works of His hands. Think of all the power that lives in the wind and the lightning, in the volcano, the earthquake, the ocean, in the on-rushing planets and stars; think of all the wisdom manifested in the orderly movements of the universe, in the growth and preservation of living things; of all the beauty that has ever shone on land or sea, and of all the fair visions and noble ideals that have ever filled

---

[4] See "The Nature of God as Known from Reason", Part I, pp.46-50.
[5] Proofs from dependence, pp.31,42-5.
[6] The ordinary teaching of the Church.
[7] Exod 3:14
[8] Is 41:4; 44:6; Apoc 1:8; 21:6; 22:13
[9] Is 40:17
[10] Acts 17:28

the mind and thrilled the heart of man; of all the knowledge and ingenuity of the philosophers, statesmen, and inventors of all the ages; think of all the love of martyrs and heroes for faith and country; of all the love of mothers for their children, love, proof against every trial, patient and tender in sickness, pitiful and true even in dishonour; think of all this power, wisdom, beauty, pity, kindness and love, and suppose it magnified and multiplied countless times over, and all concentrated, in some unspeakable way, in one being as the source of all, and you are still no appreciable step nearer an adequate idea of the Infinite Perfection of God. Your mind is still hovering in the shadows, still only straining towards the light, and has caught but the weakest, poorest glimmering of His Glory. When favoured with some obscure vision of His face, His saints have been so overwhelmed with rapture, so pierced by a very agony of joy, that their souls seemed to them to tremble on the verge of annihilation. "Man", He said, "shall not see Me and live."[11] It is as though the soul of mortal man, when in the presence of the infinite beauty of the Divine Essence, becomes forgetful of its task of maintaining and directing the activity of the senses and the various processes of corporeal life, and seeks to draw together all its forces and to exhaust its whole being in one supreme act of love.

III

Essence defined. The essences of creatures, not fully known to us. The essence of God, incomprehensible. The names and titles of God.

DEFINITION. The essence of a thing is that which makes it be what it is, and marks it off from all other things. Thus, the essence of a line is a length without breadth; the essence of a man is a rational soul united to a body. "Nature" is another name for essence, but, in the strict sense, it signifies essence as the source of action or operation: thus, we say that the soul belongs to the essence of man, but that thought and sensation belong to his nature. A true definition of a thing is a statement of its essence.

THE ESSENCES OF CREATURES, NOT FULLY KNOWN TO US. We do not know fully the essence of any creature. In the case of man, e.g., while we know some important truths about "soul" and "body" and their union, we are still ever so far from an exhaustive knowledge of these things. Did we know them fully, we should know all about their origin; we should know how God created soul and body and joined them together. Such knowledge, however, as we shall presently see, is unattainable for creatures. Even mathematical and geometrical essences, although, in a sense, the creation of our own minds, we do not know fully. If we did, we should know at once, and as self-evident, all the properties of a circle, for example, from its definition. We should know at once the equality of chords equidistant from the centre, the equality of angles in the same segment, etc. Though our

---

[11] Exod 33:20

knowledge of essences is imperfect, it is nevertheless true and very important, because it enables us to unify, to bracket under one head, or trace to a common source, all that we know of each thing.

THE ESSENCE OF GOD, INCOMPREHENSIBLE. We know something about the Essence of God, but so little that we justly describe His Essence as incomprehensible. It is easier, says St Thomas, to say what God is not, than to say what He is;[12] and St Augustine says, "If you understand, it is not God."[13] - (a) God possesses formally or eminently[14] all the perfections found in creatures. Yet they do not exist separately in Him; all are identical with the Divine Essence. How this can be we do not understand. (b) "God is spirit", said Jesus to the Samaritan woman, "and those who worship Him must worship in spirit and truth."[15] He is a Spirit, absolutely pure and simple. The human soul is not an absolutely pure spirit, because it is united to matter. It is not an absolutely simple spirit, because, though not made up of separate parts, it is divided, so to speak, within itself in many ways: it possesses distinct faculties or powers of action, intellect distinct from will, and both are distinct from the faculties concerned with growth and nutrition. Furthermore, in both men and angels, the acts of each faculty are distinct from the faculty itself: the act of understanding, e.g., is distinct from the intellect, just as motion is distinct from the body moved. But in God there are no such distinctions; Will and Intellect, the act of willing and the act of understanding, every act which we ascribe to God, is identical with His Essence. If we could comprehend one act of God, we should comprehend God Himself.[16]

Although we can never understand God and can never grasp the infinity of His Perfection, we can learn something about Him, and we can deepen our knowledge by pondering on what He has told us of His perfections. Yet, while so doing, we are, as it were, taking the idea of God to pieces. We are contemplating and loving and worshipping Him under a thousand different aspects. We are employing a piecemeal method which has been imposed on us by the feebleness of our mind, and which tends to obscure that most profound truth, viz., that all His perfections are identical with Himself,—that all are one in adorable simplicity.

Self-existence constitutes the divine essence. Though God is incomprehensible, we can name one of the divine Attributes or Perfections which, according to the common teaching, is the root of all the others, and is, therefore, the Divine Essence. That Attribute is Self-existence. It marks off God clearly from all creatures; and

[12] cf. *Sum. c. Gent.* lib. I, 14; S.T., i, q. 3, prol.
[13] *Sermo* 52,6,16: PL 38,360. St Augustine, A.D. 354-430, born in Thagaste, Numidia, now Souk Ahras in Algeria; later Bishop of Hippo, modern Bone, also called Annaba, in Algeria. His body is in the church of S. Pietro in Ciel d'Oro, in Pavia, Italy.
[14] See pp.46-50.
[15] Jn 4:24
[16] Therefore, to understand fully what a creature is, we should understand fully the act of creation, i.e., God Himself. This truth is expressed in the oft-quoted lines of Alfred Tennyson: Flower in the crannied wall, / I pluck you out of the crannies, / I hold you here, root and all, in my hand, / Little flower—but *if* I could understand / What you are, root and all, and all in all, / I should know what God and man is.

from it we can prove that He must possess every perfection. In Part I, we proved that God, being self-existent, must be identified with Existence itself, and that, since He is existence itself, He must be infinite in all perfections.[17] "We may name Him the Good, the Holy, or the Wise", says St Bernard, "but all is said, when we say that HE IS."[18]

God's name and titles. In the Old Testament, the Creator was known as "God" (in Hebrew, *El*) and by a number of other titles in Hebrew, among which are: the Mighty One, the Powerful One, the Lord, the Almighty, the Most High, the Holy One.

To Moses, God revealed His Name, written with four consonants, YHWH, i.e., "*I Am who I Am*".[19] Hebrew was originally written with consonants only. A system for indicating vowels arose much later. We cannot say with certainty what were the vowels in the name of YHWH. Today, the form of Yahweh or Jahveh is thought to be closest to the original. The name of YHWH was considered so sacred that the Jews avoided using it in speech, and the utterance of it was reserved to the High Priest and, even then, once a year secretly, on the Day of Atonement. When reading the sacred texts, the Jews did not pronounce the name of Yahweh but substituted the Hebrew title, "Adonai" ("the Lord"). The Greek translation of the Old Testament, known as the Septuagint, translated Yahweh as Kyrios ("the Lord"). Christians continued this custom of saying "the Lord", rather than using the Hebrew name of God. In the Middle Ages, the vowels of 'Adonai' were added to the consonants of 'Yhwh', and thus arose the hybrid form of Y-a-h-o-w-a-h, which became Jehovah, found in some older books and hymns.

In the New Testament, Jesus assumed the name of Yahweh ("I Am") for Himself, and the Jews rightly recognised in it a claim to divinity.[20] More often in the Gospels, Jesus refers to God as His Father, and He teaches us similarly to call God, "Father", a name evoking majesty, familiarity and trust.

IV

The divine attributes, how distinguished. Bearing in mind that the divine Attributes or Perfections have no really distinct existence in God, but that all are concentrated in One, and that they are nothing more than the different aspects under which the human mind imperfectly perceives the Divine Essence, we may divide them into two classes, viz., the Quiescent Attributes, i.e., the Perfections which belong to a state of rest, and the Operative Attributes, i.e., the Perfections which belong to action. To them we may add others which again express the very being of God or the characteristics of God in His relations with us.

---

[17] pp.46-50
[18] *De Consid.* I, 6
[19] Exod 3:14
[20] Jn 8:58

The quiescent attributes.[21]

ETERNITY. God is eternal.[22] In God, there is no beginning, no end, no succession. His Eternity is not endless time; it is essentially distinct from time, and cannot be measured by it. As we cannot say that a square is a multiple of a straight line, that it consists of an infinite number of straight lines laid side by side, so we cannot say that eternity is made up of an infinite number of years. In us, living creatures, there is a constant succession; for our present is being always renewed, and our past always being added to. We live only in the immediate present; all our yesterdays are dead; all our tomorrows are unborn. But in God there is no succession, no yesterday, no tomorrow, all is *now*. We hold but the minute fraction of our lives, the fraction that belongs to each passing moment, while God possesses His whole Life, in all its perfection, at one fixed, unchanging instant. "Of old Thou didst lay the foundation of the earth, and the heavens are the work of Thy hands. They will perish, but Thou dost endure; they will all wear out like a garment. Thou changest them like raiment, and they pass away; but Thou art the same, and Thy years have no end."[23]

IMMENSITY AND OMNIPRESENCE. Immensity means that God from all eternity had the *power* of being everywhere. Omnipresence means that in the created world God *actually is* everywhere. God possessed immensity before the world began. He did not possess Omnipresence until the world was created; His Omnipresence flows from His Immensity. God is present in the created world in a threefold sense: (a) *In His knowledge,* since He knows all things: "before Him no creature is hidden, but all are open and laid bare to the eyes of Him."[24] (b) *In His power,* since He maintains all things in existence: He upholds "the universe by His word of power."[25] (c) *In His essence,* since He is in every part of the universe, in every part of every creature, far more perfectly than the soul is in every part of the body: "in Him we live and move and have our being."[26] "Whither shall I go from Thy Spirit? Or whither shall I flee from Thy presence? If I ascend to Heaven, Thou art there! If I make my bed in Sheol, Thou art there! If I take the wings of the morning and dwell in the uttermost parts of the sea, even there Thy hand shall lead me, and Thy right hand shall hold me. If I say, 'Let only darkness cover me, and the light about me be night', even the darkness is not dark to Thee, the night is bright as the day; for darkness is as light with Thee." [27]

IMMUTABILITY. In virtue of His eternity, His being outside time, God is immutable (unchangeable). Every change involves a loss and a gain: something is renounced and something is acquired. But God, Who enjoys every perfection to fulness, cannot lose anything nor gain anything that He does not already have. Therefore, He cannot change. We speak of Him, now as wrathful, now as merciful, now as

---

[21] *Simplicity* is one of the Quiescent Attributes, p.46.
[22] Cf. Rom 16:26.
[23] Ps 102 (101):25-27
[24] Heb 4:13
[25] Heb 1:3
[26] Acts 17:28
[27] Ps 139 (138):7-12

just, but the change is in us, not in Him. The force of gravity holds a statue firm on its pedestal; but, if the statue is pushed forward, the same force of gravity will shatter it to fragments. It is so with the soul. While it obeys the law of God, it is safe. If it violates it, disaster follows, not because of a change in God, but because of a change in the soul.

Operative attributes: knowledge and will.

KNOWLEDGE. (1) *The Objects of divine Knowledge:* (a) God, and God alone, knows Himself fully: "no one comprehends the thoughts of God except the Spirit of God."[28] God's self-knowledge is the source of His infinite Happiness, for it makes Him conscious that He possesses the highest good. The philosopher Aristotle realised that the divine intellect must contemplate what is best and highest. The act of the intelligence is to understand, and God understands what it is to understand. "Therefore the supreme intellect understands itself, if it is that which is best; and its understanding is an understanding of understanding."[29]

(b) God is Omniscient, i.e., all-knowing. He knows all reality, i.e., He knows the past, the present, and the future, "even", says the first Vatican Council, "those things which will take place through the free action of creatures."[30] Hence, the Gospel says, "Jesus knew from the first who those were that did not believe, and who it was that should betray Him."[31] In virtue of God's Eternity, the past and the future are always present to Him. Compare the lives of all men that have ever been or shall ever be, to parts of the circumference of a circle; the all-seeing mind of God is at the centre; it is equally near to all, and has all equally under observation. Or we may compare ourselves to people on the side of a road watching a street procession passing in stages, while God is like the man in an air balloon above who sees the entire procession in one view: from his vantage point, there is no before or after, no succession of one after another. The entire procession is present to his sight. For this reason God knows the future absolutely—because it is not future to Him; it is all present.

(c) God knows all that is possible. He knows not only what man has done, but what man might have done in different circumstances: "if the mighty works done in you had been done in Tyre and Sidon, they would have repented long ago in sackcloth and ashes."[32]

(d) God knows with absolute certainty, for God is Truth itself. St Augustine says, "[divine] truth can neither deceive nor be deceived."[33]

(2) *The One-ness of divine Knowledge.* God knows all things through one glance, one single thought, one act of understanding. That one act of understanding, however, is identical with Himself.

---

[28] 1 Cor 2:11
[29] *Metaphysics*, Bk 12, ch. 9
[30] DS 3003
[31] Jn 6:65
[32] Matt 11:21
[33] *Enarr. in Ps* 123,2; V 3008

WILL. God's will is free, but only in respect of things outside Himself. (1) God was free in creating the world.[34] He had no need of it, and might have created a different world. He had no need of man, but having created him, He could not, by reason of His Goodness and Wisdom, leave him unprovided with the means of attaining the end for which he was created.

(2) *God's love.* (a) *God loves Himself.* To love is to appreciate the goodness in another. God loves Himself, for He is the Infinite Good. He has no choice but to love Himself. He cannot love a finite good in preference to Himself, for the finite good is of necessity less desirable, less lovable than its source, the Infinite Good: compared with the Infinite Good, the finite good is as nothing. There is thus no rivalry between them. God must therefore love Himself. He loves Himself as He deserves to be loved, that is, with an infinite love. Holiness is love of God, the Infinite Good. God loves Himself with a perfect love, and is, therefore, all holy. (b) *God loves His creatures.* To love is to will what is best for another. God loves Himself for His own sake. He loves His creatures, not for themselves, but because they are images, however feeble, of His infinite goodness. In fact, God's love is the cause of goodness in creatures. He is just; patient with sinners; truthful; faithful to His promises; merciful and kind—no one can be so kind as He. God Himself has taught us these sublime truths. He has taught us what we most require to know, viz., how much He loves us. Many times in the Old Testament He speaks of the affection and pity with which He enfolds us, poor children of the earth; but His love found its supreme expression in the Incarnation. God so loved the world as to give His Only begotten Son to suffer and die for us sinful men; and not only to suffer and to die for us, but to teach us with His own sacred lips in a new and far clearer way the lessons of Divine Mercy and Love. St John says simply, "God is love".[35] It is because He loves us that God wills to make us share, as His children, in His own beatitude: "See what love the Father has given us, that we should be called children of God; and so we are."[36] St Leo the Great says, "the gift surpassing all gifts is that God calls man His child, and that man calls God his Father."[37]

Other attributes.

POWER. There is no limit to the power of God. He is Omnipotent, i.e., all-powerful. He can do all things possible, and has manifested the infinity of His power in the act of creation and in the splendours of the cosmos, which is as nothing when compared to its Maker. Omnipotence does not include the power to perform absurdities or contradictions, e.g., construct a square circle. A square circle is no-thing, does not exist, and is a contradiction in terms. God the Supreme Being cannot act against His nature or against the very laws of being.[38]

---

[34] V 3025; cf. St Thomas, S.T., i, q. 19, a. 3.
[35] 1 Jn 4:8,16
[36] 1 Jn 3:1
[37] *Sermo* VI de Nativit.
[38] Cf. p.48.

HOLINESS. In all religions there is a special sensibility, arising from man's God-given religious sense, to the distinction between the sacred and the profane. The notion of 'sacred' or 'holy' expresses that which is segregated, set apart, reserved. Something holy belongs to God by nature, or by consecration to Him, and so cannot be treated with the familiarity of worldly use. In Sacred Scripture, we learn that God is the All-Holy One. Holiness is the very identity, essence and being of God. "I am God and not man, the Holy One in your midst".[39] There is no one greater than God. Thus, when taking an oath, He said: "The Lord God has sworn by His holiness",[40] meaning He has sworn by His very self. No one is like God. God is separated from all that is not God, from all that is created and finite: God is transcendent and "dwells in unapproachable light".[41] Holiness expresses the sublimity of His nature and moral perfection which excludes sin and implies every virtuous quality.

MAJESTY. The majesty of God is His holiness revealed, and, when revealed, makes known to man his own unholiness and littleness, thus arousing fear and trembling. "God is light and in Him is no darkness at all."[42] Before even a small revelation of God's infinite majesty, Moses, Elijah, Isaiah, Ezekiel, and the whole community of Israel, trembled with awe and covered themselves, daring not even to look upon God.[43] At the Transfiguration of the Lord, and the voice of the eternal Father, the Apostles "fell on their faces and were filled with awe."[44] In the city of Heaven, "the glory of God is its light."[45]

WISDOM AND GOODNESS. God is all-wise and all-good. St Paul exclaims, "O the depth of the riches and wisdom and knowledge of God! How unsearchable are His judgements and how inscrutable His ways! For who has known the mind of the Lord, or who has been His counsellor?"[46] God mysteriously disposes all things to our good and our salvation: "We know that in everything God works for good with those who love Him".[47]

JUSTICE AND RIGHTEOUSNESS. Justice is the virtue of giving to each one what is his due. Righteousness is moral perfection. God is just, and utterly pure and upright. He judges each person impartially and acts in favour of those oppressed by injustice. "The decrees of the Lord are truth and all of them just."[48] Yet God goes beyond strict justice; He lavishes His gifts upon us. That we can merit at all is itself a gift. No act of generosity goes forgotten or unrewarded by God. His rewards are out of all proportion to our deeds. For a temporary service, He gives an everlasting prize.

---

[39] Hos 11:9
[40] Amos 4:2; cf. 6:8.
[41] 1 Tim 6:16
[42] 1 Jn 1:5
[43] Ex 3:6; 34:8; 1 Kgs 19:13; Is 6:5; Ez 1:28; Ex 20:18-26
[44] Matt 17:6; cf. Apoc 1:17.
[45] Apoc 21:23
[46] Rom 11:33-4; cf. Is 40:13-4.
[47] Rom 8:28
[48] Ps 19:9 (18:10) (Grail trans.)

The "wrath of God"[49] is reserved for the unjust and the ungodly who resist Him. The wrath of God is the revulsion of the all-holy God towards all that is unholy; it is the manifestation of the divine displeasure at violation of the divine will.

PROVIDENCE, KINDNESS AND BOUNTY. Our Saviour speaks eloquently of our Heavenly Father's providence and generosity: "Therefore I tell you, do not be anxious about your life ... Look at the birds of the air; they neither sow nor reap nor gather into barns, and yet your heavenly Father feeds them. Are you not of more value than they?"[50] "Why, even the hairs of your head are all numbered."[51] He tells us that our Heavenly Father knows what we need even before we ask,[52] and so we can pray to Him in trust and confidence. Divine Providence wants to bestow upon us not just our daily bread, but even heavenly riches.[53]

TRUTH AND FIDELITY. God is Truth itself, and He is true to His word and His promises. He cannot lie or deceive. St Paul says, "if we are faithless, He remains faithful—for He cannot deny Himself."[54]

MERCY. Mercy is compassion for the weak and needy. God is Mercy itself. He is "the Father of mercies and God of all comfort".[55] He is "rich in mercy".[56] Our Lord recounts parables to convey to us the delight that God has in forgiving the sinner. There is no sin too great for God to forgive. The Church declares that God "manifests His omnipotence above all in sparing and having mercy".[57]

V

A DIFFICULTY AGAINST GOD'S FORE-KNOWLEDGE. Fatalists object, "If God foresees that I shall be saved, then I shall certainly be saved, and need not work for my salvation. If God foresees that I shall be lost, then no effort of mine can save me."
REPLY: Things will happen, not because God foresees them; He foresees them, because they will happen. God foresees the yield of every acre; but, if the farmer on that account were to sow no seed, God would foresee that the soil, owing to the farmer's laziness, would bear no crop. It is so with us. God foresees our salvation or damnation as resulting from our own behaviour. St Augustine answers the difficulty thus: "Just as you do not compel past events to happen by your memory

---

[49] Cf. Jn 3:36; Rom 1:18; Col 3:6.
[50] Matt 6:25-6
[51] Lk 12:7
[52] Matt 6:8
[53] Lk 11:13
[54] 1 Tim 2:13; cf. Heb 6:18.
[55] 1 Cor 1:3
[56] Eph 2:4
[57] *Missale Romanum*, 1975, p.365: Collect of 26th Sunday of the year. *Missale Romanum*, 1962: Collect of 10th Sun. after Pentecost.

of them, so God does not compel future events to happen by His foreknowledge of them."[58]

We may illustrate the difficulty and its solution by another example. No one would reason with himself thus: "God foresees whether or not I shall be run over by a bus in the streets today. My destiny is fixed. Therefore, no matter what I do, I cannot escape it. It makes not the slightest difference whether I keep to the footpath or walk in the centre of the traffic neither looking nor listening." God foresees that you will not be run over, because He foresees the precautions you will take to avoid it. Napoleon, who had some shrewd thoughts on religion, said that no one was a fatalist, for if a man were a fatalist and wanted to descend from the upper storey of a house, he should think it just as safe to fling himself out through the window as to come down by the stairs.

Fatalism, like determinism, is a philosophy that some men profess to hold, but do not really adhere to in their own lives. It is a pretentious philosophy that one can profess from an armchair or lectern, but would never dare to act upon or live by.

VI

LOVE AND SERVICE OF GOD. In the first three commandments, God says, "I am the Lord your God: 1. You shall have no other gods before me. You shall not make for yourself graven images, you shall not bow down to them or serve them. 2. You shall not take the name of the Lord your God in vain. 3. Observe the sabbath day, to keep it holy."[59] - What Moses declared to the Jews, Jesus declared to be the first and greatest commandment: "The Lord our God is one Lord; and you shall love the Lord your God with all your heart, and with all your soul, and with all your might."[60] Belief in the infinite greatness of God leads us to supreme adoration of Him, and the full service of our lives. Belief in His holiness urges us to the observance of promises and vows made before Him. Belief in God's love and goodness leads us to love Him in turn. Belief in His bounty and Providence impels us to thanksgiving and trust. Belief in His creation and Fatherhood leads us to respect all things as works of His hands and to love all people as members of our family, children of the same heavenly Father. Belief in His veracity and wisdom invites us to faith in His word, and obedience to His commands. Belief in His Fatherly care and interest moves us to pray to Him and converse with Him.

Sins against God. All sins offend God, even those most secret, but some sins are more particularly directed against God Himself. Contrary to belief in the one true God are polytheism (belief in many gods), atheism (denial of God) and agnosticism (denial that He can be known). Contrary to worship of the one true God are idolatry (adoration of a false god or a mere creature) and superstition (aberrant worship: belief that certain practices magically constrain God in determined ways, or that merely outward performance is adequate before God). Contrary to hope and trust in God are despair, presumption, divination, and putting God to the test.

---

[58] *De libero arbitrio*, Book 3, xi
[59] Cf. Ex 20:2-8; Deut 5:6-12; C 2051-2.
[60] Deut 6:4-5; Matt 22:36-8

Contrary to love of God are irreligion, indifference and ingratitude. Contrary to service of the all-holy God is the violation of just vows. Contrary to God's veracity are perjury (lying under oath), teaching false doctrine, and denying or wilfully doubting God's revelation. Contrary to His holiness and majesty are blasphemy (attacks upon God or His Saints), sacrilege (violation of something sacred) and simony (buying or selling spiritual things). Contrary to the third commandment is a refusal to rest and worship on Sunday in the manner prescribed by the Church.[61]

St Augustine says, "the essence of religion is to imitate the one whom you adore".[62]

---

[61] Cf. p.48.
[62] *The City of God*, Bk 8, Ch. 17: "cum religionis summa sit imitari quem colis".

CHAPTER 2

THE BLESSED TRINITY

Summary

I.   The solemn teaching of the Church.
II.   The Trinity, a mystery, not a contradiction. The doctrine explained. The Trinity in relation to Divine Understanding and Will.
III. The doctrine, a chief article of Faith, and an incentive to piety.
IV. The Trinity in relation to the works of God, the divine attributes, and the divine Missions.
V.   Errors.

I

The solemn teaching of the Church. The Church teaches solemnly:

(1)   that in God there are Three Divine Persons, really distinct and equal in all things, the Father, the Son, and the Holy Spirit;

(2)   that the Father is not the Son, the Son is not the Holy Spirit, the Holy Spirit is not the Father or the Son;

(3)   that each of the Divine Persons is one and the self-same God;

(4)   that the Three Divine Persons are co-eternal;

(5)   that the Father comes from none other; that the Son is begotten eternally of the Father; that the Holy Spirit comes eternally from the Father and the Son as from one source;

(6)   that all the attributes of the Divine Essence are common to the Three Divine Persons.[1]

This solemn teaching of the Church is more fully expressed in the first section of the great *Athanasian Creed*,[2] which is as follows:

Whosoever wishes to be saved, must, before all things, hold the Catholic Faith.
And unless a man shall have kept this Faith, entire and undefiled,
he shall, beyond all doubt, perish everlastingly.
Now the Catholic Faith is this,
that we worship One God in the Trinity and the Trinity in Unity,
neither confounding the Persons nor dividing the Substance.

---

[1] L 804-5, and the Creeds.
[2] DS 75. On the four solemn formularies or Creeds, see p.184. The *Quicumque* or so-called Athanasian Creed was actually written after St Athanasius (d. 373) in Latin, some time from the late fourth to the sixth century. Long usage has given the *Quicumque* Creed great authority as a source of Catholic belief.

The Person of the Father is distinct, the Person of the Son is distinct, the Person of the Holy Ghost is distinct;
but of the Father and of the Son and of the Holy Ghost
the Divinity is One, the Glory equal, the Majesty co-eternal.
As the Father is, such is the Son, such is the Holy Ghost:
Uncreated is the Father, Uncreated is the Son, Uncreated is the Holy Ghost;
Infinite is the Father, Infinite is the Son, Infinite is the Holy Ghost;
Eternal is the Father, Eternal is the Son, Eternal is the Holy Ghost;
And yet not Three Eternals, but One Eternal.
As there are not Three Uncreated, nor Three Infinites, but one Uncreated and One Infinite.
Likewise, Almighty is the Father, Almighty is the Son, Almighty is the Holy Ghost;
And yet not Three Almighties, but One Almighty.
So the Father is God, the Son is God, the Holy Ghost is God;
And yet there are not Three Gods; there is but One God.
So, the Father is Lord, the Son is Lord, the Holy Ghost is Lord;
And yet there are not Three Lords; there is but One Lord.

For, as we are compelled by Christian truth to confess that each Person is God and Lord;
so are we forbidden by the Catholic religion to say that there are Three Gods or Lords.
The Father is made by none; not created, nor begotten.
The Son is from the Father alone; not made, nor created, but begotten.
The Holy Ghost is from the Father and the Son; not made, nor created, nor begotten, but proceeding.
Therefore, there is One Father, not Three Fathers;
there is One Son, not Three Sons;
there is One Holy Ghost, not Three Holy Ghosts.

And in this Trinity there is none before or after, none greater or less;
but all Three Persons are co-eternal and co-equal.
So that, in all respects, as is aforesaid,
we must worship both the Unity in Trinity and the Trinity in Unity.
Let him, then, who wishes to be saved, hold thus of the Trinity.

II

The Trinity is (1) a Mystery, (2) not a contradiction. (1) The doctrine of the Trinity is a mystery, because it contains two truths which our reason cannot reconcile, viz., (a) that there is one God, and (b) that each of the Three Divine Persons is God. These truths, taken separately, we can understand, but not when taken together. We can understand that there is one God, and that each Divine Person is God, but not that each is one and the self-same God. (2) The Trinity is a mystery, but not a contradiction. It would be a contradiction if it said that God is One in exactly the same way in which He is Three. But it does not say this. It says that God is One in nature, Three in person.

The doctrine of the Trinity explained. We can explain the *doctrine*, but not the *mystery*, of the Blessed Trinity. The doctrine is contained in the statement that "in one Divine Nature there are Three distinct Persons." We explain a doctrine by giving the meaning of the terms that express it. Thus, we explain the doctrine of the Trinity by showing what is meant by *nature*, what is meant by *person*,—that is, by showing what precisely is conveyed in the assertion that there are *three* Persons in *one* Nature. But we cannot explain *how* the doctrine can be true, for that is a mystery. Two questions therefore have to be kept carefully apart, viz., "What does the doctrine mean?"; "How can the doctrine be true?" We can answer the first question, but not the second.

NATURE. The essence of man is that which makes him what he is and marks him off from all other things. His essence consists in the union of a body with a spiritual soul. This union of soul and body enables him to move, to feel, hear and see, to think and reason; in brief, it enables him to act as a man. His essence, considered as the source of action, is his nature. The nature of man therefore is that which enables him to act as a man. Likewise, the nature of an angel is that which enables him to act as an angel; the nature of God is that which enables Him to act as God.

PERSON. It is a man's nature that enables him to act, but the acts which he performs do not belong to his nature or to any part of his nature; they belong to him as a *person*. Thus, when you move your arm or when you utter a word or when you solve a problem, you do not say: "My arm has moved" or "My tongue has spoken" or "My mind has solved a problem", nor do you say: "My nature—my soul united to my body—has done these things", but you say: "*I* have moved my arm, *I* have spoken, *I* have solved a problem", that is, "I as a person have done these things." *Person* is therefore distinct from *nature*. It may be regarded as a something added to intelligent nature and as always accompanying it—as something through which we are constituted the owners of our acts, or the owners of our nature. It is because you are a person that you are responsible for your acts, and can be praised or blamed for them.

Every creature, therefore, that possesses an intelligent nature is a person. Every angel is a person; every human being—even the unborn child or one who is insane—is a person. Once the intelligent nature exists, the person exists, although through some defect or obstacle the person may be incapable of acting intelligently.

A fuller explanation of *person* can be found in Catholic treatises of Philosophy, wherein is explained how the notion of *person* includes completeness, distinction, singularity, wholeness, perfection, unity, incommunicability, uniqueness and dignity.

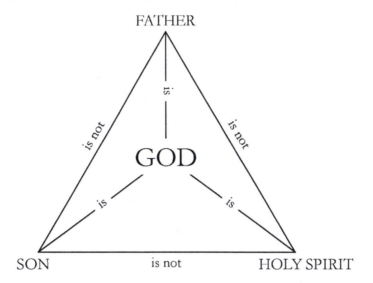

THREE PERSONS IN ONE DIVINE NATURE.   Every work which you do through your human nature is work of a single person;   but every work which God does through His Divine Nature is the work of Three Persons. If you plant a tree, you can say: "I have planted this tree".   On the other hand, God, when He created the world, could have said: "We Three, the Father, the Son, and the Holy Ghost, have created the world."   None of the Divine Persons can use the Divine Nature to act alone.   Thus, for instance, the Father could not alone have decided to create the world.   He could have decided only by an act of the Divine Will, but since the Divine Will is identical with the Divine Nature, its every act belongs at once and equally to all Three Persons.   Similarly with the Divine Understanding and with all the other powers of the Divine Nature: every act proceeding from them belongs at once and equally to all Three Persons.   Briefly we can say that everything which God does as God is done by the Blessed Trinity.

THREE PERSONS ARE EQUAL IN ALL THINGS, AND YET ARE REALLY DISTINCT FROM ONE ANOTHER. The Three Divine Persons are equal in all things, because each is God, each is infinitely perfect.   Yet they are really distinct because the Son has come from the Father, and because the Holy

Ghost comes from the Father and the Son. Therefore, directing our attention exclusively to the relations which they bear to one another, we can say of any one of them what we cannot say of either of the two; of the Father we can say: "He has begotten the Son"; of the Son, "He is begotten of the Father"; of the Holy Ghost, "He proceeds from the Father and the Son."

The doctrine of the Incarnation helps us to see that the Three Divine Persons are really distinct. It teaches that one, and only one, of the Divine Persons—God the Son—was made Man. Christ through His human nature was able to act as Man, and His acts as Man belonged to Him alone. It was He alone who lived and laboured on earth; it was He alone who suffered and died on the Cross for us; it was He alone who redeemed us.

Our word *person* is derived from our knowledge of creatures. We use it when speaking of the Blessed Trinity, not because it is in itself adequate, but because, as St Augustine says, it is the least inaccurate term we can employ.[3]

Let us try to realise how difficult it is for us to know anything about the mysteries of God. Suppose that a triangle described in a limited plane possessed intelligence. Suppose that it could know everything about lines and plane figures, and could even measure the entire surface on which it dwelt. But if it were told that solid figures existed, possessing a new dimension of which it knew nothing, it would at once be confronted with mysteries—mysteries which, indeed, it could accept as true, but without comprehending them. It could not even picture a solid angle, or fully understand that a solid could never be measured by a plane. Why? Because the solid figures belong to a higher order of things. It is so with us. God belongs to a higher order of being and can never be fully known by any creature.

The Trinity in relation to the divine understanding and will. St Thomas, developing a thought suggested by St Augustine, has been followed by all theologians in his exposition of the relation of the Holy Trinity to the Divine Understanding and Will:- God is a Spirit, and the first act of a spirit is to know, to understand. Now, God knowing Himself from all eternity, brought forth the full knowledge of Himself. This knowledge of Himself was not a mere passing idea, such as we have, but His own Image, His own very Substance, a Living Person. God knowing Himself is God the Father; God known to Himself is God the Son. God the Father and God the Son loved one another from all eternity, for each beheld in the other the Supreme Goodness of the Divinity. Their mutual Love is their own very Substance, a Living Person, the Holy Spirit. Thus, with the utmost imperfection, we conceive the Blessed Trinity to be the eternal outcome of the Divine Understanding and the Divine Will. But the mystery remains unsolved: we cannot answer the questions, "How can the Image of God be a Living Person?"; "How can the mutual love of God and His Image be a Living Person?"

---

[3] *De Trinitate*, V, 9; VII, 4,7; VII, 4,9

TRACES OF THE TRINITY IN CREATION. We find in creatures many faint resemblances to the Blessed Trinity: the soul must exist before it can know itself; it must know itself before it can love itself. The soul as existing, and before it possesses self-knowledge and self-love, may be compared to God the Father; its self-knowledge, to God the Son; its self-love, to God the Holy Spirit. Numerous other examples may be found: (a) the three states of matter: solid, liquid and gas; (c) a solid's three dimensions: length, breadth and depth; (c) a line with its two extreme points and their connection; (d) the metaphysical components of composite being: act, matter and form; (e) the three prime colours found within white light: violet, green and red; (f) the triad of: political, economic and social; (g) the three elements of music: melody, rhythm and harmony; (h) the cognitional acts of experience, insight and affirmation.

III

The Mystery of the Trinity, a chief Article of Faith, and an incentive to piety. Some authorities say that God withheld His revelation of the Trinity from the Jews because of their tendency to polytheism, i.e., belief in more Gods than one. The mystery of the Blessed Trinity, obscurely indicated in the Old Testament, and clearly revealed in the New, is a fundamental article of the faith delivered to us by our Saviour. "I and the Father are one", said Christ, the Son of God. The Apostles knew that the Holy Spirit He sent was also divine: in Acts, St Peter says, "Ananias, why has Satan filled your heart to lie to the Holy Spirit? … You have not lied to men but to God."[4]

When we come into the world, we are baptised in the name of the Father, and of the Son, and of the Holy Spirit. During life, we profess our faith in the divine mystery every time we make the Sign of the Cross, and every time we say, "Glory be to the Father, and to the Son, and to the Holy Spirit." On our death-bed the priest will comfort our departing soul with the words: "Even though he has sinned, he has not denied the Father, the Son, and the Holy Spirit." We praise and adore Him who has revealed Himself to us under the loving name of the Father. We praise and adore the Son who became our brother, and humbled Himself even unto the death of the Cross for our salvation. We praise and adore the Holy Spirit who, dwelling in the Church and in our hearts, holds us together, one in divine faith and love: "Thee, God, the unbegotten Father; Thee, the Only-begotten Son; Thee, the Holy Ghost, the Comforter; the holy and undivided Trinity, with full heart and voice we praise and bless: Glory to Thee for evermore."[5]

---

[4] Jn 10:30; Acts 5:3-4; Cf. also Mk 1:11; Matt 28:19; 2 Cor 13:14.
[5] Antiphon to the *Magnificat* at Vespers of Trinity Sunday.

IV

The Trinity in relation to the works of God, to the divine attributes, and to the divine missions.

THE TRINITY IN RELATION TO THE WORKS OF GOD. The Trinity may be described as the internal activity of God, the activity of God within Himself, in which each Divine Person has His own particular share. All works outside God, i.e., all His dealings with creatures, their creation, preservation, sanctification, etc., are common to the whole Trinity. The divine decree to send a Redeemer into the world, the formation of the Human Nature of Christ in the womb of Mary, the joining of that Human Nature to God the Son in Personal union, the decision to accept the Sacrifice of the Cross as satisfaction for the sins of men—all this being the work of God, as God, is common to the Three Divine Persons. On the other hand, as already stated, the acts of Christ as Man, the acts done through His Human Nature, are His alone. But, by appropriation, we speak of the Father, since He is the Head of the whole Trinity, as the Author of Creation, and of the Holy Ghost, since He is Divine Love, as the Author of our sanctification.

"APPROPRIATION" means assigning a work, name, or attribute to a Divine Person as though belonging to Him alone, whereas it belongs really to all Three Divine Persons. In such appropriation, we are guided by our notion of the relations which each Divine Person bears to the others. - It should be remembered that in assigning a work to a Divine Person, as though He alone were the Author of it, we do so under the guidance of the Sacred Scriptures and of Christ Himself. Appropriation helps us to keep before our mind the relations of the Divine Persons to one another, thus leading to a more explicit faith in the Blessed Trinity. It saves us from forgetting or neglecting any one of the Divine Persons, and helps us to discharge the chief duty of our religion, viz., to give each of Them the homage of our adoration and love.

THE TRINITY IN RELATION TO THE DIVINE ATTRIBUTES. By appropriation, we assign to the Father Omnipotence and Eternity; to the Son, Knowledge and Wisdom, since it is through Understanding He is begotten of the Father; and to the Holy Ghost, who is the mutual love of Father and Son, we assign Charity and all the divine attributes associated with it.

THE TRINITY IN RELATION TO THE DIVINE MISSIONS. A divine Mission is the sending of a Divine Person into the world for some special work, or to exist in some new way, among men. The Son can be sent by the Father; the Holy Ghost, by the Father and the Son; the Father comes, but is not sent. The Three Divine Persons enter into the soul with sanctifying grace, the Father as coming of Himself, the Son and the Holy Ghost as sent. This sublime union of the soul with the Blessed Trinity is revealed to us in the words of Christ: "If a man loves Me, he will keep My word, and My Father will love him, and we will come to him and make our home with him."[6] God the Son was sent into the world by the Father. As God, He

---

[6] Jn 14:23

had always existed in the world since it was made; but at the Incarnation, He began to dwell in the world *as Man*, which had not been the case before. As Man, He is still with us in the Most Adorable Sacrament of the Eucharist. The Holy Ghost, sent by the Father and the Son, descended on the Apostles at the first Pentecost. The tongues of fire and the rushing wind were the signs of His coming. The words *coming* or *sending* indicate a new mode of presence of the Divine Persons in a creature or creation. At Baptism of an infant, God takes up His abode in the soul in a *new* fashion, namely as that of Father, via the Christian seal and indwelling by grace.

The Holy Spirit is spoken of as the Paraclete or the Comforter or Advocate. The same title is also given to God the Son. It should be carefully noted that when we speak of the Holy Spirit as coming to the Apostles, we do not mean that He alone of the Blessed Trinity entered the souls of the Apostles. On the principle of Appropriation, explained above, we ascribe to Him a work done by all Three Divine Persons together. It is only by assuming a created nature that a Divine Person can act alone.

It was our Saviour Himself who taught us to speak of "the coming" and "the sending" of the Divine Persons. They are mysterious words whose sense we can but faintly perceive. They are not to be understood literally: since God is everywhere, the Blessed Trinity is everywhere. There can therefore be no question of a *coming* or *sending* in the ordinary sense. What then was our Saviour's meaning? We can answer in part by saying that the words help to express the relations of the Divine Persons to one another: the Father is said to come of Himself, because He is the Head of the Trinity; the Son is said to be sent by Him, as indicating that the Son is begotten of the Father; the Holy Spirit is said to be sent by the Father and the Son, as indicating that He proceeds from them. Thus, the words help us to understand the *doctrine* of the Blessed Trinity, and to make acts of faith in the *mystery*. It would be an error to say that the Father, by some act peculiarly His own, sent the Son into the world, or that the Father and the Son, by some act special to themselves, sent the Holy Spirit. Such acts could be performed only through the Divine Nature, and would therefore belong equally to the Three Divine Persons.

V

Errors. The doctrine of the Holy Trinity was or is denied by various persons and groups:
(1) The Monarchians (c. 200) held that in God there is only one Person.
(2) The Modalists (Sabellius and others) attempted to give the teaching of the Monarchians a more reasonable form by asserting that the Father, Son, and Holy Spirit were mere modes or manifestations of the same Divine Person.
(3) Arius (c. 250-c. 336, a priest of Alexandria, Egypt) maintained that the Son was a mere creature. Macedonius (d. c. 362, Bishop of Constantinople), his follower, enlarged his master's impious doctrine, holding that the Holy Ghost too was a creature and inferior to the Son. Arius was condemned at the First General Council of the Church, held at Nicea (now Iznik, N.W. Turkey) in Bithynia, Asia Minor, in 325. Macedonius was condemned at the Second General Council of the Church,

held at Constantinople (now Istanbul, Turkey) in 381. - The Creed which we recite in the Mass was drawn up at these two Councils. St Athanasius[7] was the great defender of the faith in those days.

(4) Modernists, some Protestants (e.g., Unitarians) and some sects (e.g., Jehovah's Witnesses) hold, against the plainest teaching of Scripture and Tradition, that the doctrine of the Trinity did not attain the form in which it is now professed in the Catholic Church until the fourth century, and that the early Christians regarded Christ, not as God, but as a divine ambassador, and the Holy Ghost as nothing more than the power or activity of God. Modernism, founded on an altogether false notion of the development of the doctrine, (i) denies that the Church is infallible, and (ii) issues in the absurd conclusion that, in the 1st century, a Christian would have given his life rather than assert the Divinity of Christ, and, in the 4th century, rather than deny it. In answer: we admit that there has been a true and thoroughly reasonable *development of doctrine*: see the example of the definition of the Immaculate Conception, pp.174-5, "Objections Answered." But *development* is nothing more than an unfolding, a fuller and more precise explanation, delivered as the need arises, of the doctrines committed by Christ to His Apostles. It *never* implies that there can be any contradiction between the teaching of the Church in different ages. Development is to be distinguished from mutation or aberration or transformation. We can illustrate the development of doctrine from geometry. Pythagoras to his great joy discovered the truth now known to us as *Euclid*, Book 1, 47. Had he been asked where that truth existed before his discovery of it, he would have answered, "It was contained in the axioms, that is, in the self-evident truths on which the science of geometry is based. It is not a new truth but a truth newly ascertained." It is clear that the recognition for the first time of a truth of geometry does not mean renunciation—or even the slightest modification—of what has been held hitherto. The previous truths are retained, but built upon and applied more widely.

The Greek Orthodox, and other Orthodox generally, still hold that the Holy Spirit proceeds from the Father alone, or from the Father through the Son, and not equally from both. This error of theirs was corrected several times by the Church, in particular, at the Councils of Lyons (1274), and Florence (1439), at which they themselves were present. The word *filioque* ("and from the Son"), which they reject, was later added to the Nicene Creed, when the Pope confirmed what had already become popular usage. St Thomas Aquinas (1224-74) defends the Catholic doctrine in part II of his work *Contra errores Graecorum*.

---

[7] Lived 295-373 A.D., Bishop of Alexandria, Egypt. His relics are in the church of St Zachary in Venice, Italy.

GOD THE CREATOR

CHAPTER 3

THE ANGELS

Summary

I.   The teaching of the Church: the nature of angels; their trial; good and wicked angels.
II.   The good angels.
III. The Devil: his names; exorcism and possession. The demons' power and limits.
IV.   The doctrine of the Church as to the existence and number of the angels, and their relations with mankind, is in consonance with reason.
V.   Spiritualism: Does it rest on a basis of fact? What is the value of spiritualistic communications? The teaching of the Bible and of the Church. Ghosts and Poltergeists.

I

The teaching of the Church about the angels. The Church teaches as of Faith:

(1)   that angels are intellectual beings created by God, and, in their nature, of higher dignity than man;[1]
(2)   that the good angels are sent by God to aid man;[2]
(3)   that some of the angels sinned, viz., the devil and other demons, who were created good by God but became evil through their own fault.[3]

The further knowledge of the angels, which we gain from Holy Scripture, the Tradition of the Church, and from the works of learned and saintly writers, may be summarised as follows:

The angels and their trial: they are pure spirits, created at the beginning of time.[4] They were endowed with sanctifying grace[5] to enable them to merit, after a period of probation, the happiness of the vision of God. Those who failed in the test were condemned to eternal punishment, and are known as

---

[1] L 800; V 3002. The Nicene Creed refers to the angels when it says, "Maker ... of all that is, visible *and invisible*".
[2] A doctrine of Faith contained in the ordinary and universal teaching of the Church.
[3] L 800
[4] L 800
[5] St Thomas, S.T., i., q. 62, a. 3

318

demons or devils: "God did not spare the angels when they sinned, but cast them into hell".[6] "Now war arose in heaven, Michael and his angels fighting against the dragon [the Devil]; and the dragon and his angels fought, but they were defeated and there was no longer any place for them in heaven."[7] (This passage must not be taken in a strictly literal sense. It represents symbolically the contest between obedience and disobedience to God in the angelic world. The fallen angels had committed some sin of pride, the sin of striving to be their own masters, and to be happy without God's help).

The good angels: the number of angels who remained faithful was very large: Christ Himself spoke of "legions of angels"[8] and the prophet Daniel says of God that "a thousand thousands served Him, and ten thousand times ten thousand stood before Him".[9] God employs the assistance of the good angels in the government of the world and the protection of mankind.[10]

The Guardian Angels: from birth[11] each person is accompanied throughout life by a Guardian Angel,[12] who shields him from the assaults of demons and even from temporal evils, except insofar as God permits them for his spiritual advancement. The Guardian Angel suggests good thoughts to him, offers his prayers and good works to God,[13] adding them to his own most powerful intercession,[14] gives him special aid in the last hour of life, and leads his soul after death to the throne of the Most High, or to the chastening fires of Purgatory. The Guardian Angels are commemorated in the liturgy on October 2.

The fallen angels: while the good angels seek to draw man to God, the wicked angels or demons are ever plotting his spiritual ruin[15] by endeavouring to fill his mind with evil thoughts, to fix his attention on temporal success, to turn him away from prayer. God, to try those whom He loves, may allow evil spirits to afflict them,[16] and, as a punishment for heinous sin,[17] He may

---

6 2 Pet 2:4

7 Apoc 12:7-8

8 Matt 26:53

9 Dan 7:10

10 Cf. Ps 91 (90):11-12; Heb 1:14.

11 S.T., i., q. 113 a. 5

12 Matt 18:10: Christ says that the little children's "angels always behold the face of my Father who is in heaven." Cf. Job 33:23; Acts 12:15; Heb 1:14.

13 Tobit 12:12-15; Zech 3:1-5; Rev 8:3-4

14 Read the book of Tobit where the help given to us through the ministry of angels is graphically described. The Catholic doctrine on the subject is beautifully put in Newman's poems *The Dream of Gerontius* (1865) and *Guardian Angel* (1853).

15 Cf. Gen 3; Matt 4:1; Jn 13:2; Acts 5:3; 1 Pet 5:8.

16 Read the history of Job. St Paul too was harassed by an angel of Satan: 2 Cor 12:7-9

17 Or for other reasons, in extremely rare cases, in the designs of Divine Providence.

permit an evil spirit to take up its abode in the body of the sinner (*demonic* or *diabolical possession*), to torture him, and subject him to very grievous temptation.

II

The good angels.

STS MICHAEL, GABRIEL, RAPHAEL. Sacred Scripture names three good angels: Michael (Hebrew for, "Who is like God?"), Gabriel ("Strength of God") and Raphael ("Healing of God").[18] Their feast day is September 29. Only these three are publicly venerated by name. The Church does not permit the public use of any other angels' names from apocryphal works or private revelations.

CHOIRS OF ANGELS. Since Scripture uses nine different names in speaking of the angels,[19] theologians conclude that there are nine angelic choirs corresponding to these different names: Seraphim, Cherubim, Thrones, Dominations, Virtues, Powers, Principalities, Archangels, and Angels. Writers are not agreed upon their exact order.

THE GUARDIAN ANGELS AND OTHER GOOD ANGELS. It was an angel who announced to Mary that she was to be the Mother of the Redeemer. It was an angel who brought the word to the shepherds that the Divine Child was born. It was an angel who informed St Joseph of the Divine Incarnation, and advised him when and where to escape with Mother and Child. Scripture says, "For He will give His angels charge of you to guard you in all your ways. On their hands they will bear you up, lest you dash your foot against a stone."[20] The Church, to express her gratitude for the protection afforded by the angels, and to implore their aid, has founded feasts in their honour. The Feast of St Michael and all the Angels was celebrated as early as the sixth century. A special feast in honour of St Michael is of much higher antiquity. The liturgies of the Eastern Catholic Churches are replete with references to the angels. That the Guardian Angel is not alone in discharging the office of conducting the soul to Heaven or Purgatory may be inferred from Lk 16:22, where Christ says that the soul of Lazarus "was carried by the angels to Abraham's bosom", and from the final prayers at a Requiem Mass: "Hasten to meet him, angels of the Lord! Receive his soul and present it to God the Most High ... May choirs of angels welcome you ... May the angels lead you into Paradise." It is generally held that Guardian Angels are given to societies as well as to individuals, and that St Michael is the Guardian Angel of the entire Church; also, that every religious order within her fold, and every nation and kingdom, enjoys the protection of a special Guardian Angel. Portugal has a feast in honour of its Guardian Angel.

---

[18] MICHAEL: Dan 10:13; 12:1; Jude 9; Rev 12:7. RAPHAEL: Tobit 5:4; 12:15. GABRIEL: Dan 8:16; 9:21; Lk 1:19, 26
[19] Gen 3:24; Is 6:2; Eph 1:21; Col 1:16; Jude 9
[20] Ps 91 (90):11-12

REAL ANGELS AND 'NEW AGE' ANGELS. Angels are spiritual beings enjoying the vision of God and fully prepared to execute His will. If, by God's Providence, an angel appears for a time in human form to do some particular work—as St Raphael in the Old Testament book of Tobit—he retains his angelic nature. An angel cannot *become* a human being, nor a human being become an angel. An 'angel', therefore, claiming to be the spirit of a dead person is lying. 'New age' angels, as depicted in television and films, are a mixture of truth and fantasy. True angels are not subject to human passions and rivalry, they cannot fall in love with human beings, nor become totally enmeshed in human affairs. The angels contacted and promoted in 'new age' circles are either purely imaginary, or, worse, demons posing as benevolent powers.

III

The Devil. *The Names for the Devil.* The leader of the rebellious angels is variously named the serpent,[21] Satan[22] (Hebrew, "enemy"), the Devil[23] (Greek, "slanderer, accuser"), the dragon,[24] Beelzebul[25] (a Philistine idol; the word means "lord of flies"), Lucifer (Latin, "the light bringer" from Isaiah 14:12-15, which, however, refers primarily to King Nebuchadnezzar: "How art thou fallen from heaven, O Lucifer … thou saidst in thy heart … I will be like the Most High. But yet thou shalt be brought down to hell." (Douay)). He is also known as the Evil One,[26] the father of lies,[27] the prince of this world,[28] the god of this world,[29] and the tempter.[30] The other angels who followed Satan into rebellion are called devils, demons,[31] fallen angels, impure or unclean spirits[32] and other terms. The Fathers apply to the devil the words of Jeremiah 2:20, *"Non serviam"* ("I will not serve")—words which God speaks to the prophet to indicate Israel's disobedience.[33]

The Scriptures say explicitly that the treachery of Judas and the lie of Ananias were suggested by the devil.[34] St Peter speaks of him as "prowling around like a roaring lion, seeking some one to devour".[35] He tempted even Christ Himself;[36] and,

---

[21] Gen 3:1
[22] Job 1:6; Mk 1:13
[23] Wis 2:24; Matt 4:11
[24] Rev 20:2
[25] Lk 11:15 f.
[26] Matt 13:19
[27] Jn 8:44
[28] Jn 12:31
[29] 2 Cor 4:4
[30] Matt 4:3
[31] Lk 8:33
[32] Mk 6:7
[33] Milton in *Paradise Lost* puts on the lips of the devil, "All good to me is lost; Evil, be thou my good" (IV, 109-10) and, "Better to reign in Hell, than serve in Heaven" (I, 263).
[34] Jn 13:2; Acts 5:3
[35] 1 Pet 5:8
[36] Matt 4:1

under the form of a serpent, by seducing Eve he brought about the fall of our First Parents.[37]

Exorcism. When the Church authoritatively commands the Evil One in the name of Jesus Christ to leave a person or object, it is called *exorcism*. Exorcism banishes the devil, withdraws people and things from his dominion, and protects against his power.[38] An exorcism may be *public* (with an authorised form in a rite), or *private*. When public, it may be *simple* (as within the rite of Baptism), or *solemn* (in case of possession). The reality of diabolical possession and exorcism is clearly set forth in Sacred Scripture: Our Lord questions devils, or at times forbids them to speak; He casts them out and gives His Apostles power over them.[39] The power which Christ gave to His Apostles He has given to His Church: see the instruction in the *Roman Ritual* for the exorcism of evil spirits. A possessed person must co-operate with the help furnished by the Church by making a good Confession, by Mass, prayer, use of the sacramentals, and by observance of the Commandments. In our own day, instances of possession have been proved by abundant evidence. A successful exorcism can take minutes or hours, or longer; each case is different. Only a priest lawfully deputed by his bishop may perform an exorcism.[40] It is presumptuous, dangerous and disobedient for a layman to undertake such a ritual. Lacking authority from the Church to exorcise, he may expose himself to the power of the demon, whom he imitates by disobedience. The well-known lengthy prayer of Pope Leo XIII against Satan and the rebellious angels is not for use by the laity.[41] The short prayer of Leo XIII to St Michael is recommended for general use.

We should note that Satan cannot, even in the case of possession, *compel* any one to commit sin. He may force his victim to do many things that are in themselves sinful, but cannot force him to approve of them. A demon may take possession of the *body*, but never of the *soul*. God has placed man's faculty of free-will absolutely beyond the reach of evil spirits. If we misuse it, the fault is ours alone.

Signs of Possession. Among others may be listed: speaking or understanding languages unknown to the person; showing knowledge of distant and hidden things; exhibiting strength far beyond one's age and condition; a vehement aversion to the sacred; disturbances by what seems to be an alien personality at times inhabiting or taking over the body and its organs; behaviour inexplicable to the science of psychiatry, coupled with the failure of all medical and psychiatric treatment; violent reaction to an exorcism. Possession can usually be traced back to some dabbling in the occult (e.g., a seance, or use of a ouija board). Not without reason, the Church

---

[37] Gen 3. The devil and demons are mentioned in the Vatican II documents, *Sacrosanctum Concilium*, art. 6; *Lumen Gentium*, 5, 16, 17, 35, 48, 55; *Ad Gentes*, 3, 9, 14; *Gaudium et Spes*, 2, 13, 22, 37.
[38] Cf. C 1673.
[39] Matt 11:18; 12:22 f.; Mk 5:2 f.; Lk 8:27 f.; Acts 16:18; 19:13
[40] Can. 1172; *Rituale Romanum: De Exorcismis et Supplicationibus Quibusdam*, 1999, art. 13
[41] Sacred Congregation for the Doctrine of the Faith, 29 Sept. 1985

warns all people, Christians or not, to have *nothing whatsoever* to do with seances, fortune-telling or the occult in any form.

The Power of the Evil Spirit. The modern world, because it ignores or belittles or even denies the dread power and activity of the devil, greatly favours the machinations of that cruel and malignant foe. He and his fellow-angels, though blasted by the anger of God and flung down from their supernatural estate, still retain the mighty faculties which they received at their creation, and which place them vastly above us in knowledge and power, making them most dangerous adversaries. How formidable is their hostility we learn from the Holy Ghost Himself, who warns us that "we are not contending against flesh and blood, but against the principalities, against the powers, against the world rulers of this present darkness, against the spiritual hosts of wickedness",[42] and that "the devil prowls around like a roaring lion, seeking some one to devour."[43] Pope Paul VI described the Devil as "an effective agent, a living, spiritual being, perverted and perverting. A terrible reality. Mysterious and frightening."[44]

But the Holy Ghost shows us how we may defend ourselves. He calls on us to use the means that God has given us: "Put on the whole armour of God, that you may be able to stand against the wiles of the devil."[45] And what is this armour of which He speaks? It is the grace placed within our grasp by the sufferings of Christ on the Cross—the grace of Faith—the grace we obtain through prayer and the Sacraments—in particular through the Blessed Eucharist—and through the sacramentals instituted by the Church.[46] St John Chrysostom says that the devils shrink in terror from the worthy communicant.[47] The faithful and practising Catholic need fear nothing from the witchcraft and sorcery practised by others: indeed, in Africa, witchdoctors lament the impotence of their sorcery against faithful Christians! "Everything which defends us from sin protects us of itself from the invisible Enemy. Grace is the decisive defence."[48]

What the devils can and cannot do.[49]
The devils *cannot* do the following:
(1)   Produce any kind of *truly* supernatural phenomenon.
(2)   Create a substance, since only God can create.
(3)   Bring a dead person back to life, although they could produce the illusion of doing so.
(4)   Make truly prophetic predictions, since only God knows the future absolutely, and those to whom He chooses to reveal a portion of it. However, the Devil's power of intelligent conjecture about the future might *appear* to mere mortals a prophecy.

---

[42] Eph 6:12

[43] 1 Pet 5:8

[44] General Audience, 15 Nov. 1972

[45] Eph 6:11

[46] See Sacramentals, p.471.

[47] *Hom. ad Antioch*, 61; *Catech. Bapt.* III,12

[48] Pope Paul VI, General Audience, 15 Nov. 1972

[49] Taken from Jordan Aumann O.P., *Spiritual Theology*, Sheed & Ward 1980, pp.420-1.

(5)   Know the secrets of a person's mind and heart.   However, their shrewd intelligence and observation may enable them to deduce many things about a person.

The devils *can* do the following:
(1)   Produce corporeal or imaginative visions.
(2)   Falsify ecstasy.
(3)   Instantaneously cure sicknesses that have been caused by diabolical influence.
(4)   Produce the stigmata.
(5)   Simulate miracles and the phenomena of levitation and bilocation.
(6)   Make people or objects seem to disappear by interfering with a person's sight or line of vision.
(7)   Cause a person to hear sounds or voices.
(8)   Cause a person to speak in tongues.
(9)   Declare a fact which is hidden or distant.

Whatever nature or science can cause, the devils too are able to cause, according to what God may permit.   Confer the Book of Exodus where the magicians and sorcerers of Pharaoh were able to accomplish *some* of the prodigies wrought by Moses and Aaron.[50]   Close to 200 A.D., Tertullian writes, "first of all, they [the demons] make you ill; then to get a miracle out of it, they prescribe remedies either completely novel, or contrary to those in use, and thereupon withdrawing hurtful influence, they are supposed to have wrought a cure."[51]   The rituals and formulas prescribed by the devil and his agents have no intrinsic force, but are mere devices employed by the devil: (1) to deceive and degrade the gullible; (2) to increase his hold over his victims and extract their subservience; (3) to ape the rituals of the Church; (4) to gain for himself the worship due to God alone.

Satan and his minions, for all their power, are but finite creatures of God, and can act only as God permits.   God checks their craft and ever-watchful hatred through the armour which, for the sake of His Divine Son, He has given us.   Those who refuse that armour are defenceless against the assaults of the legions of Hell.   "The devil is like a mad dog, but he is chained. ... He can, therefore, only seize and devour his prey if you venture too near him, and that is why his usual tactics are to make himself appear as a lamb."[52]   Wherever they are, or are acting, the demons are always enduring the pains of Hell.[53]

---

[50] Ex 7:11-12; 7:22; 8:7; 8:18-19; 9:11
[51] *Apol.* 22
[52] *The Way of Divine Love*, 1949, Ch. III.6, p.99
[53] The Venerable Bede, *In Epist. Jacob.*, c. iii

IV

The Catholic doctrine about angels is in consonance with reason.
THE EXISTENCE OF ANGELS. (1) *If there were no angels, most of God's works would be known to Himself alone.* Man is the only creature in the visible world capable of knowing and praising God in His works. But man's knowledge of nature is infinitesimal. His little mind works from the meagre data supplied by the senses. He sees, as it were, but the glisten of a dew drop, while the great ocean of truth is hidden from his gaze. It therefore appears natural to suppose the existence of higher beings who survey the whole scheme of creation, who see, with a superhuman intelligence, the wisdom and goodness of God mirrored everywhere, and make of every marvel they behold a theme of divine praise. Thus, the doctrine of the existence of angels gives the material world with all its vastness a new significance, for we conceive it as a book wherein the angels read of their Creator. (2) *If there were no angels, the scale of creation would seem incomplete.* Grouping minerals, plants, and lower animals together under the heading of things "purely material", we set them down as forming the first degree of creation; next above them we place the "material-spiritual" creature, viz., man; but, to complete the scale or gradation, our reason expects to find a third order of creatures, viz., those which are "purely spiritual".[54]

THE GREAT NUMBER OF ANGELS: *suggested by the great number of things in the material world.* When we consider the infinite variety of forms and the orderly arrangement that God has given to matter, we are led on to the thought that He, who was so prodigal in the creation of inert and unintelligent things, must have also created a higher world in which as great a diversity of being is found, and as wonderful an order prevails—a world consisting of a vast number of pure spirits, endowed each, in its own way, and in its own degree, with a capacity to know, serve, and love Him, a world bearing far more clearly than ours the imprint of the Divine Intelligence.

THE RELATIONS OF THE ANGELS WITH MANKIND: *suggested by their present state.* It is reasonable to hold that the good angels sympathise with man in his struggle against sin, for they themselves have felt the stress of temptation; and that they are eager to aid him, because they desire to promote the external glory of God, and to see His Will done on earth as it is in heaven. It is equally reasonable to hold that, while the good angels are all love and pity for man, the demons are all envy and hatred, grudging him the happiness which they have lost, laying every snare for his feet, and seeking to separate him forever from God.

V

Spiritualism. Spiritualism is the name given to the belief and practices of those who profess to hold communication with spirits or with the souls of the dead. (Of the two words "spiritualism" and "spiritism", the latter is the more correct, but the former may be said to have the sanction of a wider usage). The communication, it

---

[54] Cf. St Thomas, S.T., i., q. 50, a. 1; *Sum. Cont. Gent.* Book II, ch. 91.

is said, usually takes place through a person called a medium; but the spirits themselves, it is claimed, sometimes appear under a corporal form, or manifest their presence by sounds, and in various other ways. In its modern form, spiritualism takes its beginning from the early decades of the 1800's. It represents the ancient effort of man to seek for knowledge at forbidden sources.

DOES SPIRITUALISM REST ON A BASIS OF FACT? The great magician Harry Houdini (1874-1926) attended over 300 seances in order to contact his deceased mother, but detected fraud at every one. After this he conducted a crusade against mediums as charlatans.[55] Some of these mediums had fooled scientists who had examined them. Fraud has been proved in so many cases, that one might be tempted to dismiss the entire subject as unworthy of attention. It must, however, be admitted that in some cases the evidence points very strongly to the interference of a hidden intellectual being. Instances of this kind have been vouched for by witnesses whose word we cannot reject, unless we are prepared to deny the value of all human testimony. Among them are men of high standing in physical science, who are accustomed by life-long training to the rigorous examination of phenomena, and who should be qualified to decide whether a given manifestation can be accounted for on purely natural grounds or not.

Spiritualism appears to attract many men of science, because it offers them evidence which they can test personally and by methods akin to those they employ in their laboratory work. Probably, if God consented to work miracles under their direction and in their presence, they would become members of His Church. But God has already fully proved the truth of His Church by miracles of which they can learn, if they have the proper dispositions. God does not suffer Himself to be made the servant of every man and to be placed at his beck and call.

WHAT IS THE VALUE OF SPIRITUALISTIC COMMUNICATIONS? Although accurate information on matters of a purely private nature is sometimes given, e.g., as to the welfare and doings of absent friends, the communications never possess any public interest whatsoever. ("Accurate information is *sometimes* given", we say, but, as a rule, the information is absolutely false, or mixed up with heartless fraud and manipulation). When not trivial, silly or obscene, they are mere repetitions, very poorly expressed, of doctrines already well known, or of pantheistic or gnostic errors. The higher intelligences with which spiritualists profess to deal have contributed nothing whatsoever to human progress. They have given us no new invention or cure; they have added nothing to science or art; they have propounded no teaching which would be of the slightest help in making men lead better lives. One has only to read the records of spiritualist communications to be convinced that, if they emanated from spirits at all, the spirits must have been of a very degraded order. Examples might be quoted, but they are too gross and ludicrous for a text like this. Enough has been said to indicate that the mere word of any of these spirits must be regarded as utterly untrustworthy. This is especially true in regard to the statement made by a spirit that it is the soul of a particular person who is dead: (1) No satisfactory proof of such identity has ever been given.

---

[55] He wrote *A Magician Among the Spirits*, 1924.

If the spirit reveals information supposed to be the exclusive possession of the deceased, this proves nothing, because such information may be accessible to evil spirits. Equally worthless is the 'voice' or 'handwriting' of the deceased: one's voice and handwriting are determined by the characteristics of one's earthly physiology. A disembodied spirit has no voicebox or hands; the realistic imitation of them is not beyond the power of the evil spirits. (2) The Church's doctrine on the destiny of man after death is absolutely inconsistent with the belief that the souls of those who died in the state of grace can be summoned back at the whim of any human medium and for the mere purpose of engaging in the heretical, trivial, and often ludicrous communications of a spiritualistic seance. Hence, if there is no fraud by the medium, the intelligences manifested on such occasions must be identified with the wicked angels (or possibly the souls of the damned)—a conclusion which is confirmed by the false or obscene doctrine they frequently enunciate.

The teaching of the Bible. The Bible condemns necromancy (summoning up the dead), spiritualism, astrology, witchcraft and sorcery on numerous occasions: "do not turn to mediums or wizards; do not seek them out to be defiled by them: I am the Lord your God." (Leviticus 19:31). "A man or a woman who is a medium or a wizard shall be put to death" (Lev 20:27). "There shall not be found among you anyone who … practises divination, a soothsayer, or an augur, or a sorcerer, or a charmer, or a medium, or a wizard, or a necromancer. For whoever does these things is an abomination to the Lord." (Deuteronomy 18:10-12).[56]

The teaching of the Church. The Catechism declares: "All forms of divination are to be rejected: recourse to Satan or demons, conjuring up the dead or other practices falsely supposed to 'unveil' the future. Consulting horoscopes, astrology, palm reading, interpretation of omens and lots, … recourse to mediums … are in contradiction with the honour and respect, joined to loving fear, that we owe to God alone."[57] The use of ouija boards and other occult practices fall under this condemnation. The Catechism also censures magic, sorcery and the wearing of charms.[58]

The Church has officially condemned spiritualistic practices, even if communication with Satan is excluded, and sought with good spirits only. A 1917 decree of the Holy Office, which is binding in conscience on all the faithful, declares it unlawful to assist, with or without the agency of a medium, at spiritualistic seances or manifestations of any kind whatsoever, even if they have the appearance of honesty or piety. The decision further states that by "assisting" is meant: "asking questions of souls or spirits, hearing responses or *merely looking on*, even though one may have made a tacit or express protest that one wishes to have no dealings with evil spirits."[59]

---

[56] Other condemnations can be found in Ex 22:18; Lev 19:26; Deut 12:31; 2 Kgs 17:17; 21:6; 23:24; 1 Chron 10:13; 2 Chron 33:6; Is 8:19; 19:3; Jer 27:9-10; 29:8; Mal 3:5; Gal 5:19-21; Rev 21:8.
[57] C 2116
[58] C 2117
[59] DS 3642

Theologians point out: (1) that the sole object of the spirits evoked at seances is to draw man away from God by getting him to accept their word as a substitute for the divinely appointed authority of the Church; (2) that Satan is skilled in deception, and often assumes a benign appearance—"for even Satan disguises himself as an angel of light"[60]—to win the confidence of his victims, with a view to their degradation and ultimate destruction.[61] Those who indulge in spiritualism usually experience severe psychological disturbances and lose all peace of mind, apart from the danger of being vexed or possessed by the Devil; (3) that Satan and his minions are never allowed to use their superhuman intelligence to interfere with the general course of the world. They cannot act in such a way or give such information as would seriously disturb the lives of men—hence the insignificance of the communications ascribed to them. Consider the results which would ensue if, in the rivalry of politics, commerce or warfare, either side could learn the secrets of the other through the agency of spirits.

Hypnotism (which is sometimes erroneously confounded with spiritualism) is a form of nervous sleep, artificially induced, in which the powers of understanding and will are so much in abeyance that the subject easily submits to the suggestions of the hypnotiser. It can be used profitably for some psychological or psychosomatic disorders. In the hands of the unscrupulous practitioner, it may, as is only too evident, be applied to immoral purposes. But the fundamental reservation about its use is the fact that it involves the surrender of one's will-power to another. Hence, although the Church has not condemned it, she warns us of its dangers.[62] Hypnotism should only be used (1) when all other remedies fail, (2) when the hypnotist is a qualified doctor of good reputation, (3) when the subject gives full consent. The use of hypnotism out of curiosity or for entertainment is not justified and can be harmful and degrading to the subjects.[63]

Ghosts and poltergeists. A ghost is a vague and translucent figure of a dead human being, permitted by God (if real) or imagined by the 'observer'. Ghosts cannot be human souls as such, for the soul is spiritual and therefore invisible. Their appearance often ceases after a house blessing or the offering of Masses for the person it is supposed to be. This would suggest that they are manifestations of evil (but relatively harmless) spirits, or of souls in Purgatory needing prayers.[64]

---

[60] 2 Cor 11:14

[61] The devils' *modus operandi* is well expressed by Banquo in *Macbeth*: "...'tis strange: / And oftentimes, to win us to our harm, / The instruments of darkness tell us truths, / Win us with honest trifles, to betray's / In deepest consequence." Act I, sc. III, 122-6. This is well illustrated in the account by Herodotus (*History*, I, 46-54, 91) of King Croesus of Lydia, who put the oracle of Delphi to the test with a difficult but trivial question, and received precise and correct information—but subsequently, in a matter of great moment, the oracle deceived him with a clever and ambiguous answer that led him into disaster.

[62] Holy Office decree 1899; cf. DS 2823-5; Pius XII, Feb. 24, 1957.

[63] See *Hypnosis: Fact and Fiction*, F.L. Marcuse, Penguin 1977.

[64] The ghost of Hamlet's father is such a soul: he had died "unaneled" (i.e., without the final anointing, Act I, sc. V, 77) and had to be purged for a term (I, V, 9-13). Shakespeare's father and most likely Shakespeare himself were committed to the Catholic religion.

Poltergeist is a German word meaning noisy spirit. Poltergeists are blamed for strange noises and for objects being mysteriously moved or lost. Where such disturbances are not attributable to some extraordinary telekinetic power operating at random, they may be caused by evil spirits of a very degraded sort who seek only to cause mischief and annoyance. A priest's private exorcism and blessing will usually put an end to any disturbances, or at least mitigate them.[65]

An alternative explanation for psychic and mysterious phenomena—where fraud or the devil have been ruled out—is that the human soul, on abnormal occasions, acts in the manner of a pure spirit, learning and effecting things while by-passing its union with the body.[66]

---

[65] *Ghosts and Poltergeists*, Herbert Thurston S.J., Burns & Oates, London 1953 (ed. by J.H. Crehan S.J.). The author is unable to come to any certain conclusion to explain the phenomena.
[66] *Occult Phenomena in the Light of Theology*, Alois Wiesinger O.C.S.O., Burns & Oates, London 1957. Possibly a final answer shall elude mankind always. "There are more things in heaven and earth, Horatio, / Than are dreamt of in your philosophy": *Hamlet* I, V, 167-8

CHAPTER 4

CREATION AND ITS PURPOSE.
THE ORDER OF THE CREATION.

Summary

I.   The solemn teaching of the Church: God created all things.
II. God's Act of Creation. God's primary purpose in creating was His external glory. His secondary purpose was the happiness of rational creatures. His creative act is continuous. He exercises a providence over all that He made.
III. The order of the Creation: The Bible account. It contains a principal and a subordinate element. The account given by scientists: it cannot be in conflict with the principal element in the Bible account; it is not in conflict with the subordinate element. The seven day week.

I

The solemn teaching of the Church. God created the whole world.[1] It had no existence until, by an act of His own free-will, He called it into being. He created the sun, earth, moon, planets, stars and all things in the universe. He created the first living things from which all existing plants and animals are descended. He created man to His own image and likeness. He created the angels.[2] He created all things for His external glory.[3] He exercises a providence over all His creatures.[4]

II

God's act of Creation. God created all beings *ex nihilo*, i.e., from nothing. By His almighty power He summoned them into being from non-being. Whenever man 'creates', he uses some pre-existing material and refashions it. But God created the universe from no pre-existing material.

The universe is not eternal, but was created in time—or rather, with time—since time began when the world began: "In the beginning God created the heavens and the earth."[5]

God's primary purpose in creating. God's primary purpose in creating was His external glory. His external glory is His splendour, as manifested

---

[1] The Creeds
[2] L 800, V 3001-2
[3] V 3002
[4] V 3003
[5] Gen 1:1. Cf. St Augustine, *De Civ. Dei*, XI, 6.

outwardly in His creatures. All the works of His hands reflect in their very being and nature His power, wisdom and goodness: His power has raised them from nothingness to existence; His wisdom has designed the nature of each and appointed its purpose; His goodness is the source of all the gifts bestowed on them through His wisdom and His power. All created things are therefore images of their Maker, each in its own imperfect degree. But the word "image" is applied with special appropriateness to men and angels, because, through their understanding and free-will, they have been raised above all other creatures. They have been made personal agents, and have been given a closer likeness to God. The lowliest of mankind, by his very nature, endowed as it is with a spiritual soul, gives God greater glory than the whole material universe with all its vastness. Further, the lowliest of mankind, by a simple act of the love of God, gives Him greater glory than He receives through all the secular learning of scientists and philosophers. The likeness becomes closer still when those noble faculties are correctly used, i.e., when we employ our mind and will in knowing and loving God, for we are thus, in our little way, made active imitators of Him who has an infinite knowledge and love of His Own Divine Goodness. All men therefore whose mind and will work as He would have them work reflect Him more perfectly, and therefore advance His external glory. They further advance it by teaching others to know and love Him.

All creation, all things are good in themselves, although they may be misused. Seven times the inspired writer says, "And God saw that it was good".[6] Each time, God saw that it was good in itself as proceeding from His hand, and because it was a step in the preparation of the universe for the appearance of mankind, for the Incarnation of God Himself in Jesus Christ, and for the unfolding of the history of salvation to culminate in the Church Triumphant, gathered forever around the throne of the Lamb and the vision of the Blessed Trinity.

God's external glory, as arising from His rational creatures, reaches its highest expression in the Blessed in Heaven who enjoy the direct vision of His unveiled Loveliness. Unlike those on earth, they possess a knowledge of Him that can never grow dim or clouded, and a love of Him that can never prove untrue. They have attained to that perfect exercise of the mind and will for which He made them. *God's internal glory* is His intrinsic splendour, or, more strictly, His appreciation and praise thereof. According to the accepted teaching of theologians, the Son is begotten of the Father by way of understanding, and the Holy Spirit proceeds by way of love. Hence in the very life of the Holy Trinity, we have infinite knowledge and infinite love, and therefore infinite glory. We should notice that self-complacency in God follows necessarily from His knowledge of Himself as an infinitely perfect Being, the source of His own existence and of all His perfections;

---

[6] Gen 1:4, 10, 12, 18, 21, 25, 31

whereas self-complacency in a creature, if it springs from the notion that the creature is the sole author of its excellence, is mere folly, for the creature has nothing of its own.

The word "glory" in its everyday use is similarly applied. It denotes splendour, or the manifestation of splendour, or its appreciation and praise. So we speak of the glory of an artist's talent, or the glory of his works which are its expression, or the glory which he wins from the public.

God's secondary purpose. God's primary purpose in the whole plan of creation was the manifestation of His splendour, but in the creation of men and angels He had a secondary purpose also. He made them, not only that they might by their nature testify to His glory, but that they might win everlasting happiness for themselves.

God's primary purpose cannot be defeated, but His secondary purpose may, because it depends for its attainment on the proper exercise of free-will. But if His rational creatures abuse their freedom, the failure is theirs, not His. Even in their failure, they manifest His Justice by the punishment which sin entails.

Creation was an act of love. "God in His goodness and omnipotence", says the first Vatican council, "drew creatures from nothing, not to increase His happiness, not to gain anything, but to manifest His perfection by the blessings He bestows on creatures."[7] His chief blessing was conferred on His rational creatures, men and angels. To them He gave a nature capable of receiving the further gift of Grace, and therefore of being raised to the sublime dignity of divine sonship.

God's creative act is continuous. Since God alone is self-existent, we and all other creatures, animate and inanimate, spiritual and material, owe our existence to Him. Existence is no part of our nature; therefore, we need the sustaining hand of God from instant to instant. So fully are we dependent on Him that, if it were not for His unceasing help, we should be unable to perform even the most trivial action. God's creative act, in our regard, is therefore continuous. Technically, we say that to God we owe our existence and our conservation: "God who made the world and everything in it ... Himself gives to all men life and breath and everything ... In Him we live and move and have our being."[8] Our existence is as the light from a light bulb: just as there is no light unless the electric current is supplied, so we have no existence unless God continuously supplies it to us. "The fool says in his heart: there is no God",[9] but the greater fool is he

[7] DS 3002
[8] Acts 17:24, 25, 28
[9] Ps 14 (13):1

who, while knowing his utter dependence on God, refuses to be subject to Him and to obey Him.

God exercises a providence over all His creatures. That God exercises a providence or ever-watchful care over all His creatures follows of necessity from His infinite goodness and wisdom. He, the infinitely wise and good, who has made all things and holds all things in being, must necessarily desire that they attain the end for which He made them. His providence extends to all His creatures, but in a particular way to man: Christ said, "Are not two sparrows sold for a penny? And not one of them will fall to the ground without your Father's will. But even the hairs of your head are all numbered. Fear not, therefore; you are of more value than many sparrows."[10] Man is more precious in the eyes of God than the birds of the air, because to man He has given a higher nature and a higher destiny. God in His providence orders the events and circumstances of our lives down to the smallest detail, so as to draw the sinner towards repentance, and the just to higher sanctity. If it pleases Him to send us sorrow or pain, we must accept it with loving resignation, full of faith that He knows what is best for us and that there is no one so kind as He.

III

The Bible account. We read in the first chapter of Genesis that "In the beginning God created the heavens and the earth. The earth was without form and void, and darkness was upon the face of the deep." Then follows a brief account of the six days' work. The common interpretation is that the world, or matter in a state of chaos, was created by God before the six days' work began. The six days' work was, therefore, a work of organisation or development. The account shows us the order in which the chief things in the world were created:

(1) On the first day, He said: "'Let there be light,' and there was light … and God separated the light from the darkness. God called the light Day and the darkness He called Night."

(2) On the second day, He said: "'Let there be a firmament[11] in the midst of the waters, and let it separate the waters from the waters.'"

(3) On the third day, He made dry land appear from out of the waters, and bade it bring forth the green herb and the fruit-tree.

(4) On the fourth day, He said: "'Let there be lights in the firmament of the heavens to separate the day from the night' … and God made the two

---

[10] Matt 10:29-31.

[11] A *firmament*. By this name is here understood the whole space between the earth and the stars. The lower part of this space separates the waters that are upon the earth from those that hang above in the clouds. See also p.335.

great lights, the greater light to rule the day, and the lesser light to rule the night; He made the stars also."
(5) On the fifth day, He said: "'Let the waters bring forth swarms of living creatures, and let birds fly above the earth …' And God created the great sea monsters and every living creature that moves, with which the waters swarm … and every winged bird."
(6) On the sixth day, He made "cattle and creeping things and beasts of the earth" and "God created man in His own image."

Finally, on the seventh day, "He rested … from all His work which He had done."

"He *rested*", that is, He ceased to make or create any new kinds of things. Though, as our Lord tells us,[12] He is working still, viz., by conserving and governing all things, and creating souls.

In the Bible account, there is a principal and a subordinate element. In the Bible account, we must carefully distinguish what is principal from what is subordinate.

The principal element. The Jews to whom the narrative was primarily addressed were surrounded by idolatrous peoples who believed in the existence of many gods, and paid divine worship to all kinds of creatures, to the sun and moon, plants and animals, and images of wood and stone. Hence, the sacred writer, under the guidance of the Holy Spirit, impresses on the Jewish race, with greatest emphasis, that there is but one God, and that He created the whole visible universe with everything in it, living and lifeless. The expression of this great truth is the chief element in his narrative, hence the constant repetition of the words: "God made", "God said and it was so." All else is secondary or subordinate.

The subordinate element. The subordinate element is the popular dress in which the inspired message is clothed. Though, for convenience sake, we designate it "the subordinate element", it is nevertheless as truly a part of inspired Scripture as the principal element; it is the medium through which the Holy Spirit has chosen to speak to us.

The Church, while insisting that the account of the creation in Genesis is in a certain sense historical—i.e., neither fictional nor legendary, but a true narrative of actual events—tells us at the same time that we may regard it as popular in form. Popular form implies popular expression and popular order. (1) *Popular expression*, that things and happenings are described not in strict scientific language but as they would appear outwardly to the senses, and be commonly spoken of and understood by ordinary people. Thus,

---

[12] Jn 5:17

e.g., God is represented as speaking, and as taking counsel with Himself; the moon is represented as one of the two greater lights in the heavens. (2) *Popular order*, that events—and these only the most important—are set down in an order, not necessarily chronological, but suited to the understanding of a primitive people, and so to mankind generally.

Popular vs scientific. In ordinary language we say "the sun is in the middle of the sky." Were we to use accurate scientific language we should speak somewhat as follows: "The earth has so turned on its axis, that our meridian is now directly opposite the sun." The account of creation offers an example of this in its use of the word 'firmament'. To the uninstructed eye the heavens appear at night as if there were in the sky a vast concave structure in which the stars are fixed. This structure— something like the inner part of a hollow sphere—is what is meant by the firmament. Similarly the Old Testament speaks of the 'upper waters' (the source of rain) which are above the firmament.

Popular history vs mythology. Pope Pius XII in *Divino Afflante Spiritu* 1943, stressed the importance, for a correct understanding of the Bible, of a knowledge of the various literary forms used by early writers. There are many literary forms in the Bible, and the sacred writers, primarily interested in theological truth, did not always treat of historical matters in the way a modern historian does. The same Pope also said, "The first 11 chapters of Genesis, although it is not right to judge them by modern standards of historical composition, such as would be applied to the great classical authors, or to the learned of our own day, do nevertheless come under the heading of *history*; in what exact sense it is for the further labours of the exegete to determine. These chapters have a simple, symbolic way of talking, well suited to the understanding of a primitive people. But they do disclose to us certain important truths, upon which the attainment of our eternal salvation depends, and they also give *a popularly written description* of how the human race and the Chosen People came to be. It may be that these ancient writers of sacred history drew some of their material from current popular stories. So much may be granted; but it must be remembered that they did so under the impulse of divine inspiration, which preserved them from all error in selecting and assessing the material they used. These excerpts from current stories, which are found in the sacred books, must not be put on a level with mere myths, or with legend in general. Myths arise from the uncontrolled imagination; whereas in our sacred books, even of the Old Testament, a love of truth and simplicity shine out, so as to put these sacred writers on a demonstrably higher level than their profane contemporaries."[13]

The Church has also declared that the word "day" need not mean a solar day of 24 hours, and that it can be lawfully interpreted as signifying a long period of time.[14] It has long been observed that, since the sun itself was not created until the fourth "day", the word "day" could not mean the solar day

---

[13] Pius XII, *Humani Generis*, 1950: DS 3898-9
[14] DS 3519

before then. (Some writers who think themselves clever make this point as if they were the first to notice it. It was known to Origen, d. 254, and to St Augustine, d. 430).[15]

Beyond these general directions and a general condemnation of all methods of interpretation which would impute real error to the Sacred Writings, the Church has decided nothing as to how the subordinate element in the Scriptural narrative is to be understood.

The account given by scientists of the order of Creation. The account given by scientists of the development of our world is contributed in part by astronomers, in part by geologists. Astronomers seek to explain the processes and stages by which the solar system, planets, satellites and other cosmic bodies and gases came to be as they are today. Geologists seek to explain the formation of the earth and its levels, the sea, land masses, and life forms. Scientific accounts do not dispense with the necessity of a Creator, however. Unless we admit His existence, we leave unexplained: (a) the origin of matter; (b) the origin of its motion and energy; (c) the origin of vegetable and animal life, and the spiritual soul of man; (d) the origin of the wonderful order that pervades the universe.

Science cannot be in conflict with the principal element in the Bible account. Physical science, as we have already learned,[16] deals only with causes whose operation comes under the observation of the senses. It shows how one lever in the machinery of the world is moved by another, the second by the third, and so on, but it cannot tell us how the last lever is moved. Its investigations are entirely confined to an examination of these levers. It deals only with things that happen within the visible world. As long as it keeps to its proper work, it cannot assert or deny anything about the existence or acts of God who is a Being distinct from the visible world, and, therefore, outside its scope. Hence, it cannot touch the doctrine of creation, which is the chief element in the Biblical narrative. It follows therefore that the authority which a man may have gained in the field of physical science forsakes him the moment he passes beyond the limits of his subject. If he ventures to discuss questions outside the realm of physics, the value of his speculations will depend, not on his ability as a scientist, but on his ability as a philosopher; but since in philosophy he will be dealing with a type of evidence quite unfamiliar to him and for which he is not fitted by his previous training, his conclusions will, as a rule, be amateurish.

Science is not in conflict with the subordinate element, as is shown by either of two interpretations. The only difficulties which scientists can raise are connected with the order followed by the sacred writer. We give two interpretations, both in conformity with the decisions of the Pontifical Biblical

---

[15] Origen, *De Principiis*, IV, 16; *Contra Celsum* VI, 50 & 60. St Augustine, *De Genesi ad litteram*, V, 1; IV, 33

[16] p.41

Commission early in the 20th century, and both free from the charge of conflict with physical science.

FIRST INTERPRETATION: *The order followed in Genesis results from the grouping together of similar works.* The inspired writer of Genesis opens his narrative with the words: "In the beginning God created the heavens and the earth. The earth was without form and void, and darkness was upon the face of the deep." This primitive world or Chaos consisted, therefore, of three layers: above was a dark space; beneath the dark space was water; beneath the water was earth. The rest of the account tells in popular form how the present world was produced from the original Chaos. This work of development is described as having taken place in six days, the expressions "first day", "second day", etc., being used, not to signify days of twenty-four hours each, but to indicate the order in which the writer chose to set down the events of creation. St Augustine says that God made all things instantaneously, although, for the purposes of narration, the narrative separates them in time.[17]

I. The sacred writer tells how each layer in turn was divided: on the first day, the dark space was divided into day and night; on the second, the water was divided into the water below (sea) and the water above (clouds, air); on the third, the earth was divided into land under water and land over water (dry land with its concomitant vegetation).

II. Next, he tells us how, on each of the three following days, each region was peopled with its proper occupants: on the fourth day, the sun was created to rule the day, and the moon with the stars, to rule the night; on the fifth, fishes were placed in the sea, and birds in the air (sky); on the sixth, animals and man appeared on the dry earth.

We may tabulate the interpretation thus:

Day	Regions	Day	Occupants
1.	Day & Night	4.	Sun (for Day) Moon with stars (for Night)
2.	Sea & Sky (Air)	5.	Fishes (for Sea) Birds for Sky (Air)
3.	Land under water Land over water, with vegetation	6.	[*No occupants for Land under water, because insignificant or unknown*] Animals and man (for Land over water)

This interpretation, which is given by St Thomas,[18] has much to recommend it: (1) It is suggested by the very words of Sacred Scripture: "So the heavens and the earth were finished and all the furniture of them" (Gen 2:1 Douay)— the "furniture" being the occupants. (2) It represents the sacred writer as impressing most strongly on his people that God made everything in the world and gave each thing the place it occupies. (3) It arranges events in an order which a primitive people could readily

---

[17] Cf. *De Gen. ad litt.* I, 15-16; II, 15; IV, 32, 33, 35; V, 5. Cf. St Thomas, S.T., i., q. 74, a. 2.
[18] S.T., i., qq. 65-74

understand, and easily retain. (4) It will never require re-adjustment to suit the views of scientists.

SECOND INTERPRETATION: *The order followed in Genesis is in its broad lines a chronological order.* Let us note the following most remarkable points of agreement between the Biblical and the scientific accounts: (1) both accounts represent the world as gradually developing from chaos to order; (2) both represent lower forms of life as appearing before higher: vegetation before fishes; fishes (and monsters of the deep) before birds and mammals; (3) both state that man was the last of all to appear. To these we may add the creation of light on the first day. The inspired writer speaks as though he were an observer on the surface of the primitive earth. He sees the sunlight penetrate the dense vapour for the first time; but the sun itself is not yet visible as a distinct object, and will not be seen until the fourth day. In this interpretation, as the first, we may take "first day", "second day", etc., to denote the order, in this case roughly chronological, in which the writer records events.

This interpretation, regarded by many as satisfactory, is perhaps less so than the first.

The week of seven days. God instituted the Jewish week of seven days as a memorial of the successive periods of Creation: "Six days shall work be done", He said, "but the seventh day is a sabbath of solemn rest, holy to the Lord … It is a sign … that in six days the Lord made heaven and earth, and on the seventh day He rested."[19] Through His Church, God has ordered us to continue the observance of the week of seven days. In the hymns of the Divine Office for the Vespers of the days of the week, beginning with the Sunday hymn, *Lucis Creator*, the Church commemorates the works of Creation, deducing from each a spiritual lesson. But God has given us a new Sabbath with a new significance. The new Sabbath (Sunday) commemorates the Redemption, a work of greater love than the Creation itself. Thus the Church speaks of God as having wonderfully created us, but as having still more wonderfully redeemed us.[20] Its commemoration has been fittingly assigned to the first day of the week, for it was on that day that Light came forth from the tomb, the same day that God created physical light, the image of His Son, who is "the Light that shines in the darkness" (Jn 1:5), the spiritual Light that pierced the darkness of a sinful world. The ancient Sabbath paid homage to God as having completed the work of Creation, while the Christian Sabbath pays Him homage as having begun in the Redemption a new and more glorious work.

---

[19] Ex 31:15-17
[20] Roman Missal, 1969, Collect of Christmas Day Mass. *Missale Romanum*, 1962, Offertory.

CHAPTER 5

THE ORIGIN OF LIFE AND THE ORIGIN OF LIVING SPECIES (PLANTS AND LOWER ANIMALS)

Chapters 5 and 6 deal chiefly with the question whether God created life and all living species by His direct creative act or through powers given by Him to creatures.

Summary

I.   The origin of life: The teaching of the Church. What scientists say.
II. The origin of living species (plants and lower animals):
  A. The teaching of the Church on the origin of species. A Catholic may hold either permanentism or theistic evolution.
  B. Difficulties with the general theory of evolution.
  C. Evolution not proved scientifically but useful as a working hypothesis. If evolution has occurred, God is its Author.

I

The Teaching of the Church on the origin of life. The Church teaches that life, as well as every other form of activity, must be traced to God as its ultimate source, as the fount and well-spring of created being with all its modifications. But whether the first animate thing that appeared in the world received its life from Him by a direct creative act, or through the interplay of powers or properties *which He had already communicated to matter*— that is a question which she leaves open. She allows us the freedom to choose between these alternatives as scientific evidence may direct.

What scientists say. It was the ancient view, and the view of most scientists until recent centuries, that spontaneous generation, or the production of life from inanimate matter, did as a fact take place. It was thought that maggots and worms sprang forth spontaneously from putrefying flesh, and that the moist earth could generate mice and frogs. These examples were eventually disproved, but until the 19th century, the belief still persisted that bacteria could arise spontaneously. But in 1864, the devout Catholic scientist Louis Pasteur (1822-1895) published the results of his investigations, showing by a series of masterly experiments that in all the commonly alleged instances of spontaneous generation, life originated, not from dead matter, but from living germs. One of his experiments was the following: he procured a flask with a long neck curving downwards, and poured into it a liquid which, in ordinary circumstances, corrupts rapidly. He boiled the flask and its contents, so as to destroy any vestige of life that might have been present. His purpose in having the neck bent was to prevent germs floating in the air from falling in, and at the same time to allow the liquid in the flask any stimulus to the generation of life which, as some claimed, pure air might afford. He found that matter thus protected remained indefinitely without any manifestation of life. On the other hand, when the neck of the flask was broken off, so that germs could fall in, life quickly developed. The practical outcome of his experiments was aseptic surgery, the preserved food (canning) industries and the process of 'pasteurisation'.

Through Pasteur's work, the dictum, *omne vivens e cellula,* or "all life comes from a living cell", is now accepted as true by scientists. Some of them, however, while admitting that the process no longer occurs, still cling to the belief that it may have taken place in conditions that no longer exist. This, needless to observe, is a mere gratuitous assertion, against which the following considerations may be urged: (1) Scientists regard the laws of nature as invariable, and therefore as always producing the same effect in the same conditions. But the conditions which, according to scientists themselves, prevailed when life had its beginning on earth can be reproduced in our laboratories; yet no chemist has so far succeeded in making a living thing from dead matter. (2) The living cell, so complicated in its structure that it has been compared to a fully equipped battleship, could not have been built up except through the direct act of an intelligent being.

Many of those who cling to the idea of spontaneous generation are agnostics, and hence are unwilling to admit the clear evidence for God's existence that appears in the direct creation of life. Hence, they hold fast to the idea of spontaneous generation; but they fail to observe that spontaneous generation itself affords them no refuge from the truth which they are trying to evade, because, ultimately, it would have to be referred to the action of an Intelligent Creator.

If, in spite of difficulties which at present seem insurmountable, chemists succeed some day in making a living thing from non-living elements, our position as Catholics will not, as indicated in the preceding paragraph, be affected in the slightest degree. Some early Fathers, St Thomas and some of the great doctors of the Church had no difficulty whatsoever in holding spontaneous generation, since they regarded it—as we would also, if it were ever proved—*as a process arising from powers implanted in matter by the Creator.*

II

A

The teaching of the Church on the origin of species. The Church, while teaching as of faith that God created the living things from which all existing plants and lower animals are descended, leaves us free to hold either the theory of permanentism or the theory of theistic evolution. According to the theory of permanentism, God by a direct act, or series of acts, created each species separately. According to the theory of theistic evolution, He caused some or all species to develop in course of time from one or more directly-created primitive stocks, or from inanimate matter.

Permanentism is so called because it says that the species existed *permanently.*

Theistic evolution is so called because it says that *God* is its cause (theistic = pertaining to belief in God).

Note. *The teaching of the Church on the question of evolution is quite simple, but is frequently misrepresented in books and magazines. At the same time, alleged scientific results, and mere theories, are submitted uncritically to the public as 'facts' and 'discoveries'. Hence the enormous confusion on the subject.*

Certain Protestant groups, in the past and today, have condemned the theory of evolution as such. The Catholic Church has never condemned the theory of evolution as such. She has condemned as contrary to faith the theory of materialist or atheistic evolution, which is another thing altogether.

Atheistic evolution denies, or ignores, the existence of a Personal God, and claims that life in all its forms has developed under the operation of blind forces or causes. We have proved (pp.55-8) that this theory is opposed to reason. We now know that it is opposed to faith also.

Permanentism or theistic evolution: the views of theologians. Many of the Fathers of the Church held the doctrine of permanentism, but St Augustine (354-430) favoured a theory which bears a resemblance to some aspects of theistic evolution. He held that each species of animals was created originally in a rudimentary state, and later on was given its perfect form. He does not tell us whether the development was gradual or instantaneous, but once the development was attained, the species remained fixed. He believed, apparently, that the species originated in something like a seed, which he calls the *ratio seminalis* (seminal reason),[1] a latent source of activity inserted by God into matter during the work of Creation.

The theory of theistic evolution is held by some modern Catholic writers. But as stated in the extreme form which derives all plants and lower animals from one and the same common origin, it is, so far, entirely unsupported by scientific evidence. But if, against all present probabilities, the theory should become an established truth, it would only serve to give us a more exalted idea of the power and wisdom of the Creator who so framed His laws as to draw a single particle of inert or primitive organic matter slowly upwards to higher and higher forms of life.

B

Difficulties with the general theory of evolution. There are some major difficulties with the theory of evolution, but they are not given wide publicity. A major cause of obscurity is the attitude of many evolutionists who, since they regard rejection of their theory as disloyalty to science, have created an atmosphere in which unbiased judgement has become difficult. In spite of this, some competent scientists have produced works

---

[1] Cf., e.g., *De Genesi ad litteram*, Bk. V, ch. v, 14; ch. xxii, 45.

demonstrating the inadequacies of any theory of evolution. Among more recent studies may be counted *The Intelligent Universe* by Fred Hoyle;[2] *Evolution: a Theory in Crisis* by Michael Denton;[3] *Darwin on Trial* by Phillip E. Johnson;[4] *In the Beginning* by Walt Brown;[5] *Darwin's Black Box: the Biochemical Challenge to Evolution* by Michael J. Behe.[6] Here we can only draw upon some of their many and developed arguments. To begin to judge Darwinism intelligently, we must first define our terms—something many scientists, untrained in philosophy and logic, do not do.

DEFINITIONS. The word "evolution" can mean a number of things:
1. Evolution of certain characteristics and diversities within species.
2. Evolution of the human body from some ape-like animal.
3. Evolution, by *natural* processes,[7] of living cells from dead matter, of plants from living cells, of animals from plants, and finally of man from animals, as the explanation for the whole variety of living plants, animals and men, and fossils of extinct species of all three. This may be called the *general* theory of evolution.

The *first* is an oft-observed phenomenon, often appealed to by evolutionists as a basis for their claims, but quite irrelevant to a proof of the second or third claims. All traditional Christians, who recognise Adam and Eve as the first parents of the human race, admit therefore that all the varieties of human races come from them. The admission of characteristics and variations developing *within* species is not contested by anyone, and is not the issue in a debate about evolution. This first meaning we can set aside as irrelevant, therefore, although we may have to refer to it when examples of it are adduced in an invalid attempt to prove evolution in the second or third sense.

The *second* is a historical and scientific question, as well as a religious one. The Church so far has not ruled it out as contrary to the teaching in the Book of Genesis. (We deal with this meaning of evolution in the next chapter).

---

[2] Michael Joseph Ltd., London 1983. Sir Fred, a man of no religion, founded the Cambridge Institute of Theoretical Astronomy.

[3] Burnett Books, G.B.; Adler & Adler, U.S.A., 1986. The author is a medical doctor and scientist, of no religion.

[4] Regnery Gateway, Washington D.C., 1991. The author is a law professor at the University of California, Berkeley.

[5] Center for Scientific Creation, Phoenix, U.S.A., 1995. Pp.1-17, 37-58 deal with evolution. The author is a mechanical engineer.

[6] The Free Press, New York 1996. The author is an Associate Professor of Biochemistry at Lehigh University, Pennsylvania.

[7] i.e., without divine intervention

The *third* meaning includes the second, and is a gigantic claim, yet to be proved, not least of all because the first element of it, viz., life emerging from dead matter, has neither been observed within nature nor achieved by science. (We deal with this meaning of evolution in this chapter and in *Apologetics*, Ch. 1). The second and third meanings involve a substantial *transformation* of one thing into another.

The name and theory of *evolution* became famous with the publication of *The Origin of Species* in 1859 by English scientist Charles Darwin (1809-1882). He followed that work up with *The Descent of Man* in 1871.

The alleged causes of evolution. Evolution, in the third sense, was supposed by Darwin to have occurred by two processes:
(1) survival of the fittest, also called natural selection.
(2) transformation of species, i.e., from one species into another. Supposing that life arose from dead matter, this would then explain how basic cells evolved into the whole range of the plant world, animal kingdom and human race. Darwin called this, "descent with modification".

Replies. In answer to (1) survival of the fittest: the famous explanation turns out to be a tautology. (Some scientists who believe in evolution have openly admitted this).[8] Who are the fittest? Answer: those that survive. What does this explain? Nothing: it is merely the observation that, in particular regions, certain species predominate and others are scarce or extinct—something for which reasons need to be found. It asserts that, *within* biological species, fluctuations occur of certain characteristics of certain animals. It does *not* mean that one species became another, that reptiles became birds, for example. It means merely the observation of the occurrence of evolution in the *first* sense given above. "Natural selection merely preserves or destroys something that already exists."[9] It explains nothing about how the species came to exist, and explains nothing about supposed mutations turning one species into another.

In answer to (2) transformations into new species:
(a) *No verification.* Not a single instance has been proved: every claim, when analysed, can be shown to be merely evidence that Y came after X, or is very much like X, and is therefore descended from X. This is begging the question; it is not a proof. Extinction of species is observed frequently; production or appearance of new species, never.
(b) *Limits of mutations.* Every attempt to provoke evolutionary change of species has failed: the mutations effected by breeding experiments either never go beyond the basic design of the creature, disappear in later generations, are quite useless, cause harm, render the new form sterile, or produce monsters that cannot survive. Mutations have only been observed to occur *within* species (evolution is verified only

---

[8] Cf. P.E. Johnson, *Darwin on Trial,* Regnery Gateway, Washington D.C., 1991, p.20.
[9] Idem, p.31

in the first sense). No mutation has ever produced new species, new organs, greater complexity, more viability, or major changes. Fruit flies are the most common object of breeding experiments, yet "Fruit flies refuse to become anything but fruit flies under any circumstances yet devised."[10]

(c) *Distances between species.* The isolation and distinctness of different types of organisms, the existence of clear discontinuities in nature, self-evident even to the non-scientist, is inexplicable if there are meant to be gradual changes and definite steps linking one species to the next.

(d) *Lack of evidence in fossils.* The fossil record to date has such huge gaps, i.e., there are no huge numbers of extinct transitional or intermediate forms which the theory demands must be there. On the contrary, very few even alleged intermediate forms have been found, and all of these are contested.[11] The intense search for fossils and the study of them since Darwin's time has produced three conclusions, all incompatible with evolution: (i) stasis, i.e., stability: fixed forms of life, keeping to stable patterns and not showing directional change or significant change; (ii) sudden appearance, i.e., species appear fully formed and complex when they are discovered; (iii) sudden disappearance, rather than gradual obsolescence when confronted by the development of new forms: there appear to have been a series of mass extinctions in the history of the earth—so extensive in fact, that far more species have perished than survived.[12]

Strictly speaking, the study of fossils never reveals anything more than a succession of types. It does not and can not show one type evolving into another. In other words, it presents facts without an explanation. Evolution, on the other hand, is an attempted explanation of facts, and must be judged as such.

(e) *Microbiology shows that gradual improvement by evolution is impossible.* Biochemical systems are *irreducibly* complex. An *irreducibly* complex system is one that is made up of several inter-dependent parts, linked in such a way that the absence of any one part means that the whole system ceases to function. For example, a mouse-trap—composed of a base, metal hammer, spring, sensitive catch, holding bar—if it is missing one part, cannot catch mice. The eye, similarly, is a useless organ until *all* its parts are in place, and not only must all its parts be there, but the entire corresponding parts of the brain that receive and process the data from the eye must also all be in place. No gradual process of natural selection could have formed and refined an irreducibly complex system in a step-by-step fashion, because it does not work unless all its parts are already present. While some structures within nature and man might be explained by natural selection, the *irreducibly* complex systems (such as the systems which control vision, photosynthesis, blood clotting, immunity, and cellular transport) could not have evolved, but must have been designed by an Intelligent Designer who intervened to create those systems or to cause them to arise at a set time.[13] Darwin himself wrote, "To suppose that the eye with all its inimitable contrivances for adjusting the focus to different distances, for

---

10 F. Hitching, *The Neck of the Giraffe: Where Darwin Went Wrong,* Ticknor and Fields, New Haven, Connecticut 1982, p.61
11 W. Brown, *In the Beginning,* pp.45-50, gives 47 quotes from scientists attesting that transitional forms have not been found.
12 Johnson, pp.50, 56-7, 170-1
13 Cf. M. Behe, *Darwin's Black Box.*

admitting different amounts of light, and for the correction of spherical and chromatic aberration, could have been formed by natural selection, seems, I freely confess, absurd in the highest degree."[14] To this we may add: the development of the eye in pairs, and the necessary corresponding parts of the brain for the reception and analysis of what the eyes see, are further proof that chance or blind forces are incapable of forming such a complex organ as the eye and the even more complex mechanism of the brain, without which the eye would be a useless organ. Despite his comment, Darwin proceeded to uphold natural selection as an explanation of the eye. But as Isaac Newton asked, "Was the eye contrived without skill in optics, and the ear without knowledge of sounds?"[15] Design in fulfilment of a function is the unmistakable and undeniable mark of the Intelligent Designer.

Other alleged causes of evolution. The sheer lack of fossil and biological evidence for evolution as explained by Darwin led some scientists to formulate theories about evolution that ran totally contrary to the former explanations. Instead of supposing gradual changes over millions of years, these scientists postulated "macromutations" (big changes) or "saltations" (big leaps), by which a new type of organism would suddenly appear in a single generation. Darwin himself said that if such evolution occurred, his theory was finished, since a saltation is equivalent to a miracle.[16] Without invoking divine intervention, science cannot explain how a living creature, an intricate assembly of interrelated parts, could generate by chance, or blind forces, a new organism with a new complex assembly of different interrelated parts. Saltation means, for instance, that a snake's egg could hatch and a bird emerge.[17] The evolutionary 'theory' of saltation is, therefore, not even worthy of being called a theory, but is merely a supposition to escape a difficulty. A later theory called "punctuated equilibrium" has been proposed: it is a similar hypothesis which explains nothing, but hides the lack of evidence behind an impressive pseudo-scientific term.[18]

C

Evolution not proved scientifically but useful as a working hypothesis.

NO SCIENTIFIC PROOF OF EVOLUTION. Evolution may be a fact, but there is as yet no scientific proof of it. A scientific proof will be forthcoming only when some incontestable law of nature has been discovered, which can be tested by experiment, and which will account for all the transformations alleged by evolutionists. While there may be evidence for the modification of living things within many of the smaller groups, there is no evidence as

[14] *The Origin of Species*, The Modern Library, N.Y., Ch. VI, p.133
[15] *Opticks* (1704) McGraw-Hill, N.Y. 1931, pp.369-70
[16] P.E. Johnson, *op. cit.*, p.33
[17] Proposed by some scientists: cf. Johnson, p.40.
[18] See also S.L. Jaki OSB, *The Savior of Science*, Scottish Academic Press, Edinburgh 1990, Chs. 4 & 6.

to how any of the greater groups originated. Mutations *within* species have been observed; mutations that transform one plant or animal into a *different* species have not been observed. When astronomers tell us of the changes that have taken place in the stellar universe, they ascribe them to the law of gravitation and other well-known and unquestioned physical laws which, they justifiably assert, must have been working in the past as they are working today. But the evolutionists so far have failed to discover any true and verifiable law of development. Had they succeeded, the animated controversy over the causes of evolution would be at an end. Many biologists believe that evolution has occurred, but they do not agree on its cause. In fact, there are several competing and mutually contradictory theories—enough in itself to show that evolution has not been proved to the satisfaction of scientists themselves. Pope John Paul II referred to this plurality when he said, "And, to tell the truth, rather than *the* theory of evolution, we should speak of theories of evolution."[19] "The versions of 'evolution' promulgated by Richard Dawkins and Stephen Jay Gould, for example, have hardly anything in common except their common adherence to philosophical materialism and their mutual dislike for supernatural creation."[20]

The differences among biologists as to the cause of evolution become intelligible when we consider the extraordinary complexity of the subject of their investigations: they are working on the fringe of a greater mystery than that which confronts the student of inanimate physics, viz., the mystery of life.

EVOLUTION, USEFUL AS A WORKING HYPOTHESIS. A working hypothesis is a tentative or provisional supposition. In physical science, a working hypothesis is indispensable for progress: it stimulates inquiry by raising a number of questions that call for an answer, and it enables the investigator to arrange and classify what would otherwise be a mere assemblage of disjointed observations. Evolution as a working hypothesis has led to the founding of several new sciences—or new lines of investigation—and has helped push out the frontiers of knowledge. On the other hand, when held to against the evidence, it has stifled the presentation of contrary evidence and held back scientific progress. Popular scientific writer Stephen Jay Gould epitomises the irrational dogmatism of evolutionists when he writes, "Our continuing struggle to understand how evolution happens ('the theory of evolution') does not cast our documentation of its occurrence—(the 'fact of evolution') into doubt."[21] The phrase "documentation of its occurrence" is pure bluff: scientists have *theorised* but have not *documented* a single

---

[19] Message to the Pontifical Academy of Sciences, 1996
[20] P.E. Johnson, *Defeating Darwinism by Opening Minds*, InterVarsity Press, Illinois 1997, p.114.
[21] Quoted in S. Jaki, *op. cit.*, pp.250-1.

example of one species becoming another. To rephrase Gould's type of argumentation in legal terms, this is equivalent to saying, "Sir, we *know* you are guilty of committing the crime. We *cannot* explain how you did it, we have no evidence of your movements at the time, but we have no one else to blame, and therefore we *must* find you guilty and sentence you. Our continuing struggle (for lack of documented evidence) to understand how you did it, does not cast doubt upon the 'documented' fact that you did it (for we never relied upon the evidence to come to our conclusion)."

IF EVOLUTION HAS OCCURRED, IT IS THE WORK OF GOD. As was shown in *Apologetics*, Ch. 1, every creature, whether animate or inanimate, is dependent on God at every instant for its existence and its activity. It therefore follows that, if we assume evolution as a theory, we must assert that God is its author. It must have been He who gave the living thing its capacity to vary, and so ordered its surroundings, and all the influences affecting it, as to make it develop precisely as it did. If evolution did occur, divine intervention would have been necessary for: (a) creation itself of the first matter from which the whole universe is composed; (b) the appearance of basic life; (c) the elevation of vital organisms to plant level; (d) the elevation of plants to animal level; (e) the elevation of an animal body to be fit for animation by a human soul; (f) the creation of the soul of the first man, something which could never arise from sub-human life, since it is spiritual.

CHAPTER 6

THE ORIGIN OF MAN. THE UNITY OF ORIGIN
OF THE HUMAN SPECIES.

Summary

I.   The origin of man.
     A. The teaching of the Church on the origin of the soul and body.
     B. The teaching of Scripture. Remarks.
     C. Atheistic evolutionists and the origin of the human soul.
     D. Theistic evolutionists and the origin of the human body.   Scientific
         difficulties with this position.
     E. The Church and the evolution of the human body.
II. The unity of origin and the antiquity of the human species; the teaching of the
     Church. What scientists say.

I

A

The Teaching of the Church. *The Origin of the Human Soul.* The Church
teaches:
(1)   that God directly created the soul of Adam;
(2)   that God directly creates every human soul;
(3)   that the human soul is spiritual.[1]
The Church has condemned the doctrine that our souls, like our bodies, are
derived from our parents,[2] or that they existed before they were united to
our bodies.[3]

The Origin of the Human Body.   The Church requires us to believe in the
"special creation" of Adam, i.e., she requires us to believe that Adam came
into being through no merely natural process but through some special
intervention on the part of God. As we have seen, God created the soul of
Adam, as He creates every human soul, immediately out of nothing (*direct
creation*). But in forming the body of Adam, He made use of material already
existing (*indirect creation*). The Biblical Commission says also it must be held
that God by a special act formed the body of Eve from the body of Adam.

---

[1] The doctrine of the spirituality of the human soul is implied in the definition pronounced by
the Council of Vienne (A.D. 1311-1312) and confirmed by the Fifth Council of Lateran
(A.D. 1512-1517): see DS 900, 1440.
[2] DS 1007
[3] DS 456

Hence, as we shall see below in further detail, if evolution has occurred, it can only mean evolution of the *body*, not of the *soul*.

The Unity of Origin of the Human Species. The Church teaches that the present human species is descended from Adam and Eve.[4]

B

The Teaching of Scripture. The Church is true to Scripture in claiming unique character for the creation of Adam and Eve. The narrative of Genesis represents God as creating all living things, except man, through some virtue which He had communicated to matter: "*Let the earth put forth vegetation … and fruit trees. … Let the waters bring forth* swarms of living creatures, and let birds fly above the earth. … *Let the earth bring forth* living creatures according to their kinds: cattle and creeping things, and beasts of the earth" (Gen 1:11, 20, 24). But when the sacred writer comes to the creation of man, he is moved by the Holy Spirit to choose a different form of words: "Then God said '*Let us make man in our image, after our likeness;* and let them have dominion over the fish of the sea, and over the birds of the air, and over the cattle, and over all the earth'" (Gen 1:26, 27); and in the further account which he gives in the following chapter, he says, "then the Lord God formed man of dust from the ground, and breathed into his nostrils the breath of life" (Gen 2:7). Of the creation of Eve, he says that the Lord God, having cast Adam into a deep sleep, took from him a rib which He built into a woman (Gen 2:21-22).

REMARKS. (1) THE DIGNITY AND UNIQUENESS OF MAN, MADE IN THE IMAGE OF GOD. All creatures, even the very lowest, are a reflection of their Maker. He has made them existing substances, and therefore in some degree like Himself who is the Divine Substance, perfect and self-existing. But to man He has given a further and higher resemblance to Himself. He has made man like to Himself: (a) in his soul, which is a simple and immortal spiritual substance, thus reflecting the Infinite Spirit and His divine simplicity and eternity; (b) in the soul's faculties, intelligence and will, those powers to seek the Truth and to love what is spiritually Good; and (c) as a fitting complement to those great gifts, He has robed man in the mantle of His own Kingship, making him lord of the world. And this royal dignity is not restricted to the soul of man: his body, because of its service in aiding him to acquire and manifest knowledge and goodness, is destined by God for union with the soul in eternal life. The Scripture narrative brings out all this in sharp relief, and reason approves, for no one can

---

[4] See below, p.357.

dispute the pre-eminence and uniqueness of man among created things. - In the light of the Incarnation, we can discern a further way in which man is made in the image of God: St Paul says, "Adam was a type of the One who was to come."[5] God became man, and so every human person is made *in the image of God Incarnate*, for Jesus Christ, a member of our human race, is our elder Brother,[6] like unto us, and we unto Him.

Appreciating the dignity of man made in the image of God, we can appreciate the heinousness of the sin of murder (deliberate killing of an innocent) in any form: homicide, abortion, infanticide, or euthanasia. Human life is a sacred gift from God. No one may take his own life or that of another. From conception until death, innocent human life deserves respect and the protection of law. "The prohibition of murder does not cancel the right to render an unjust aggressor unable to inflict harm. Legitimate defence is a grave duty for whoever is responsible for the lives of others or the common good."[7] However, sacred though life be, it is not the *supreme* good. We are not bound to do *everything* to save our life or that of another: in serious illness, one is not bound to accept expensive and burdensome treatments;[8] in grave need, one may risk one's life to help others, or even make the supreme sacrifice. The Church honours the martyrs because they sacrificed their lives rather than give up greater and higher goods: the Faith, and union with God. The good of human life is ordained unto eternal life.

(2) THE EXACT METHOD OF CREATION OF MAN AND WOMAN. The Church's Magisterium does not bind us to the immediate and obvious literal sense. The description of God as *breathing on* a human image of clay, or as *building up* or *closing up* a woman from a part of Adam's body, need not be taken according to a slavishly literal interpretation. It expresses in vivid and popular form the truth that the Divine Omnipotence acted in some special way on a portion of matter to make it a fitting receptacle for the soul of Adam, and that it multiplied, in a manner utterly mysterious, some part of Adam's body to make the body of Eve. We may illustrate, perhaps obscurely, from the multiplication of a single living cell which ultimately becomes a complete human body. The body of Eve was not built up by the mere addition of extraneous matter. This is clear from the words spoken by Adam when God brought her to him: "This now is bone of my bones and flesh of my flesh."

---

[5] Rom 5:14. "Type" here means pre-figuring image.
[6] Cf. Rom 8:29.
[7] C 2321
[8] cf. C 2278.

(3) THE MYSTICAL MEANING OF THE TEXT. Since Eve was derived from Adam, it follows that he is the fountain-head of the whole human race. He is thus a type, i.e., a prophetic image, of Christ, as Eve is a type of the Church. Our physical life we trace to Adam; our spiritual life we trace to Christ. Eve was the spouse of Adam; the Church is the spouse of Christ. Through Adam and Eve, we were born into the family of man; through Christ and His Church, we were born into the family of God. The Fathers compare the sleeping Adam to the dead Christ on the Cross, and the origin of Eve to the origin of the Church: as Eve came from the side of Adam, so did the Church come from the side of Christ. They regard the flow of blood and water that gushed forth at the thrust of the soldier's spear as representing the final payment made by Christ for the setting up of His Church, and as expressing the cleansing and nourishing power of her Sacraments. Thus the words of Genesis have not only a literal but a typological or spiritual meaning as well. (It is not legitimate to hold that the words of Genesis should be interpreted *only* in a spiritual sense).

C

Atheistic evolutionists and the origin of the human soul. Atheistic or agnostic evolutionists say that man has derived his principle of life, his soul, from lower animals. This would raise beasts to the level of man or lower man to the level of beasts. In the first alternative, beasts would be like children with brains seriously injured; they would possess rationality but be unable to manifest it, and it would be the sin of murder to kill them. In the second alternative, man would not have a spiritual soul. He would not be responsible to God for his actions; he would live and behave like a savage creature of the jungle, acknowledging no other man's right to life or property. His one governing principle would be, 'might is right and woe to the weak.' The absurdity of such repellent views is exposed by their consequences.

In *Apologetics*, we proved from reason that man has a spiritual soul (Chapter 2), and that consequently he is able to understand the great truths and commands of Natural Religion (Ch. 3). His spiritual soul sets him apart from the lower animals. The chasm between him and them is a chasm that cannot be bridged. Human ingenuity has never succeeded, and never will succeed, in getting the cleverest lower animals to grasp general ideas and to hold a rational conversation with us by signs. We hear now and then of "inventive animals" which are said to deliberate and choose means for the attainment of an end. It is stated, e.g., that an untrained chimpanzee fitted one stick into the hollow of another in order to get a banana which was out of reach of either stick by itself. But this proves nothing. Wonderful things are also done by very young children while still unable to reason, which shows that no process of reasoning is required. Adults also while fumbling without plan or purpose have often chanced on a useful discovery. The main argument, however, against the "inventive animals" has already been given, viz., that they cannot be taught to speak to us by signs or symbols; they never reach the level of education to which deaf and dumb children can be brought. Animal communication consists only in signifying a present emotion, feeling or desire, while men are able to transmit ideas and concepts relating to the past, present or future. No one animal could ever communicate to another animal the story of its life. An animal is totally immersed in its environment, while man can transcend his situation.[9]

Darwin, who reduced man to the level of beasts, was depressed by the implications of his theory of evolution. He said, "With me the horrid doubt always arises, whether the convictions of man's mind which has been developed from the mind of lower animals are of any value or at all trustworthy".[10] Therefore, according to him, if we are nothing but improved beasts, we are not sure of any of our convictions, not sure of our responsibility for our actions, not sure even that the theory of evolution is true! He should have gone a little further and said that a hypothesis issuing in such conclusions is self-destructive and should be abandoned. His words betray a vague suspicion that truth and science are unattainable to our senses and can be reached only through the exercise of some higher power in us. Darwinism, in its atheistic form, has had a most pernicious influence on morals.

D

Theistic evolutionists and the origin of the human body. Theistic evolutionists hold that the first man was evolved, or rather, his body developed, from some ape-like creature. As yet, the Church has not ruled this out as contrary to the teaching of the Bible.

Objections and difficulties connected with evolution of the human body. The arguments against the general theory of evolution apply also to man's alleged descent from ape-like creatures. They are given in Ch. 5. Against the evolution of man's body in particular, we may begin by setting out the dishonesty and desperation that have been at work in attempts to prove it.

The 'missing link'. Darwinism gave rise to the search for the 'missing link': not one link, however, but very many would be necessary to link the ape to man—and to date not a single one has been found. The fossil record shows gaps and discontinuities. The attempts to find links between man and other primates have failed. Two of the best-known 'discoveries' promoted as 'evidence' of man's evolution were later exposed as frauds: the famous "Piltdown man" of 1912-15, and "Nebraska man" of 1922. Piltdown man was cited in text-books and articles for forty years as evidence of man's descent from apes.[11] The skull was of a modern man, the jaw that of a recent ape, and the teeth had been filed down to make them look like human teeth. Nebraska 'man' was a tooth, the tooth of a peccary, an extinct wild pig. From one tooth, however, scientists managed to draw

---

[9] Cf. pp.66-7.
[10] *Life and Letters of Charles Darwin*, D. Appleton and Co., N.Y. 1898, Vol. I, p.316, cf. p.313.
[11] Ph. Johnson, *Darwin on Trial*, Regnery Gateway, Washington D.C. 1991, pp.5, 6, 80

an entire man with distinctive features! Since then, other 'missing links', "Neanderthal man", the "Australopithecines", "Java man" and "Peking man", once all presented as wonderful scientific discoveries, have all had to be discarded or re-classified in the light of prolonged scrutiny. "Java man", found in 1891, is now recognised to be a gibbon, and its discoverer Eugene Dubois admitted forty years later that he had withheld parts of other thigh bones of gibbons found in the same area. "Peking man" is now considered by many experts to be the remains of apes. "Ramapithecus" was cited from 1961 to 1977 as an ape-like ancestor of man. The 'ancestor' consisted of a mere handful of teeth and jaw fragments, and not even a portion of the skull. It is now agreed to be from an ape.[12]

Popular presentation and intellectual honesty. The series of neat drawings that so commonly appear in text-books showing an ape slowly move upright and modify his shape and features until *Homo sapiens* (rational man) appears, *is nothing but a series of imaginary drawings*, since the so-called 'missing links' are still missing! Such drawings in books, and similar displays in museums, have had a powerful impact on the public imagination, but are simply dishonest as a depiction of known history. Even the very phrase 'missing link' implies that we *know* of the link, only that we cannot find it. A theory may quite reasonably direct our investigations, so that we search for confirming evidence, but until the evidence is found, scientists must speak of their *theory* of evolution, not of the *fact*. A detective does not speak of a man under investigation as "the criminal", but as "the suspect". When the suspect is arrested, he becomes "the accused"; when he is held and tried, he is "the defendant", uncertain of the outcome, but he is not "the convicted criminal" until the evidence has been presented and affirmative judgement has been given. Likewise, evolution remains a theory of scientific investigators, a hypothesis directing their research, but they cannot call a theory a proven fact until the indisputable evidence, as opposed to imaginary drawings, is produced. "The important claim of Darwinism is not that relationships exist, but that those relationships were produced by a naturalistic process in which parent species were gradually transformed into quite different descendant forms through long branches (or even thick bushes) of transitional intermediates, without intervention by any Creator or other non-naturalistic mechanism. If Darwinism so defined is false then we do not have any important scientific information about how life arrived at its present complexity and diversity, and we cannot turn ignorance into information by calling it evolution."[13]

Scientists are not agreed on evolution. Disbelief in evolution is not unscientific. Some prominent scientists of the past and present who have openly stated their opposition to it on scientific grounds are: Prof. Louis Bounoure, Director of Research at the National Centre of Scientific Research, France; Sir Ernst Chain, Nobel Prize winner along with Fleming and Florey for penicillin; Prof. Albert Fleishman, Zoology and Comparative Anatomy, Earlangen University, Germany; Sir Ambrose

---

[12] Walt Brown, *In the Beginning*, Center for Scientific Creation, Phoenix, U.S.A. 1995, pp.11, 50
[13] Johnson, p.89

Fleming, physicist, inventor of the thermionic valve; Dr Paul Lemoine, President of the Geological Society of France, an editor of the French Encyclopaedia; Prof. Heribert Nilsson, Swedish geneticist, Lund University; Prof. W.R. Thompson of Canada, Director of the Commonwealth Institute of Biological Control; Roberto Fondi, Professor of Paleontology, University of Siena, Italy.

Behind any theory about the origin of species: the origin of life itself. Atheistic evolution requires that all the necessary elements of life were there at the beginning of time. Still, given all the necessary chemical compounds, this does not explain how life began: scientists employing the full power of their intelligence and techniques cannot produce even the simplest forms of life. How then could unguided, mindless matter have done so? To suppose that lifeless matter achieved life by itself is to suppose as great a miracle as any. English scientist and science fiction writer Sir Fred Hoyle says, "A junkyard contains all the bits and pieces of a Boeing 747, dismembered and in disarray. A whirlwind happens to blow through the yard. What is the chance that after its passage a fully assembled 747, ready to fly, will be found standing there? So small as to be negligible, even if a tornado were to blow through enough junkyards to fill the whole Universe."[14]

Dr Michael Denton expresses it thus: "The intuitive feeling that pure chance could never have achieved the degree of complexity and ingenuity so ubiquitous in nature has been a continuing source of scepticism ever since the publication of *The Origin of Species*; and throughout the past century there has always existed a significant minority of first-rate biologists who have never been able to bring themselves to accept the validity of Darwinian claims... Perhaps in no other area of modern biology is the challenge posed by the extreme complexity and ingenuity of biological adaptations more apparent than in the fascinating new molecular world of the cell. ... To grasp the reality of life as it has been revealed by molecular biology, we must magnify a cell a thousand million times until it is twenty kilometres in diameter and resembles a giant airship large enough to cover a great city like London or New York. What we would then see would be an object of unparalleled complexity and adaptive design. On the surface of the cell we would see millions of openings, like the port holes of a vast space ship, opening and closing to allow a continual stream of materials to flow in and out. If we were to enter one of these openings we would find ourselves in a world of supreme technology and bewildering complexity. We would see endless highly organized corridors and conduits branching in every direction away from the perimeter of the cell, some leading to the central memory bank in the nucleus and others to assembly plants and processing units. We would see that nearly every feature of our own advanced machines had its analogue in the cell: artificial languages and their decoding systems, memory banks for information storage and retrieval, elegant control systems regulating the automated assembly of parts and components, error fail-safe and proof-reading devices utilized for quality control, assembly processes involving the principle of prefabrication and modular construction. In fact, so deep would be the feeling of *déjà-vu*, so persuasive the analogy, that much of the terminology we would use to describe this fascinating molecular reality would be borrowed from the

---

[14] *The Intelligent Universe*, Michael Joseph, London 1983, p.19

world of late twentieth-century technology. What we would be witnessing would be an object resembling an immense automated factory, a factory larger than a city and carrying out almost as many unique functions as all the manufacturing activities of man on earth. However, it would be a factory which would have one capacity not equalled in any of our own most advanced machines, for it would be capable of replicating its entire structure within a matter of a few hours. To witness such an act at a magnification of one thousand million times would be an awe-inspiring spectacle... Is it really credible that random processes could have constructed a reality, the smallest element of which—a functional protein or gene—is complex beyond our own creative capacities, a reality which is the very antithesis of chance, which excels in every sense anything produced by the intelligence of man?"[15] Belief in atheistic evolution requires far more faith than belief in God.

The alternative to evolution. Evolutionists say: "Admitting that we have not succeeded as yet in explaining away the differences between man and the ape, we maintain that the similarities cannot be accounted for *physically* except on the hypothesis of evolution—which we must hold, because there is no rival in the field." Their opponents can reply: "The *assumption* of evolutionists that the origin of man can, and must, be traced to *physical* causes may have to be rejected as quite unsound. Scientists may in course of time come to the conclusion that no physical cause can be assigned for the origin of man, and that it is a mystery as inscrutable as the origin of matter or the origin of life. But it is conceivable that, while recognising the mystery of man's origin, they may ultimately succeed in demonstrating that the precise formation of man's body—his brain and nervous system, the organs of sense and all the organs, together with the mechanism of bone and muscle—is not merely in exact harmony with his requirements as a rational animal, but is the *only* possible formation it could have received to make it fit in with the laws of nature. If it is ever given to us to understand the whole scheme of creation, we may find that all the diversified forms of animate and inanimate matter, and all the laws that govern them, fit together, minister to one another, and constitute a unity as perfect and harmonious as the deductions of mathematical science. Thus there would be a scientific reason for stating that God made man as he is, as a necessary consequence of the laws which He Himself had imposed on the world— and the transition to the correct doctrine that 'God made the world for man's use and benefit' would be easy. Some scientists have remarked that it looks as if the world had been prepared for man's coming."

As musical compositions, though independently written, will show a resemblance because of their conformity with the same laws of harmony, so

---

[15] *Evolution: A Theory in Crisis*, Burnett Books, G.B.; Adler & Adler, U.S.A., 1985, pp.327-8-9, 342

too man and the lower animals *must be somewhat alike* because of their adaptation to the same system of physical and chemical laws. But similarities, of themselves, do not mean that one came from the other, or that both came from a common ancestor. They do, however, argue for a common Designer.

The evolutionists whose words are paraphrased above speak of evolution as a *hypothesis*. That is the designation which the scrupulous investigator employs. It is only the presumptuous who represent it as a scientifically established truth.

E

The attitude of the Church on evolution of the human body.
(1) The teaching of the Church on the origin of the human body has been given above, I. A. Following her ordinary practice, she takes the words of Holy Scripture (Gen 1 & 2) in their obvious sense, until the necessity arises of seeking a different interpretation. In the case before us, the necessity would arise only if it were proved on strict historical evidence that Adam was born of lower animals—which is surely a ludicrous supposition, since there could be no historical evidence without contemporary human witnesses. But though the proof is inconceivable, the *theory* of the evolutionary origin of his body does not, in itself, involve an absolute impossibility, and, so far, has not been publicly and explicitly condemned by the Church. Pope John Paul II distinguished between the possibility of the evolution of man's *body*, and the impossibility of evolution of the *soul*.[16] He referred to Pope Pius XII, who in 1950 directed, "the teaching of the Church leaves the doctrine of evolution an open question, as long as it confines its speculations to the development, from other living matter already in existence, of the human *body*. (That *souls* are immediately created by God is a view which the Catholic faith imposes on us). In the present state of the scientific and theological disciplines, this question may be legitimately canvassed by research, and by discussion between experts in both fields. At the same time, the reasons for and against either view must be weighed and adjudged with all seriousness, fairness, and restraint; and all must be ready to accept the judgement of the Church, as being entrusted by Christ with the office of interpreting the Sacred Scriptures authentically and of guarding the dogmas of the faith. There are some, however, who take rash advantage of this liberty of debate, by treating the subject as if the whole matter were closed—as if the discoveries hitherto made, and the arguments based on them, were sufficiently certain to prove, beyond doubt,

---

[16] Message to the Pontifical Academy of Sciences, 1996

the development of the human body from other living matter already in existence. They forget, too, that there are certain references to the subject in the sources of divine revelation, which call for the greatest caution and prudence in discussing it."[17] Pope John Paul II summarised his predecessor thus: "Pius XII added two methodological conditions: that this opinion should not be adopted as though it were a certain and proven doctrine, and as though one could totally prescind from [i.e., ignore] Revelation with regard to the questions it raises."[18]

(2) The Church does not interfere with the investigations of Catholic biologists, who, as loyal members of hers, are always ready to accept her guidance and decisions. She allows them to conjecture, observe and experiment as they please. Since all truth is from God, she welcomes every truth they may incidentally discover, even in pursuit of a theory such as the evolution of the human body. She blesses their work, and imposes no restriction on them except the restriction imposed by physical science itself, viz., that they are not to confound guesses and probabilities with conclusive demonstration.

We need not delay over the fantastic idea that God might at some time or other give a private revelation affirming or denying the evolutionary origin of the body of Adam. He gives private revelations to encourage devotion, but the Church does not draw upon them to settle disputes about the faith. (On Private Revelations, see p.279).

II

The unity of origin of the human species. THE TEACHING OF THE CHURCH. The Church teaches that the present human species is descended from Adam and Eve. Such, indeed, is the obvious sense of Sacred Scripture: before the creation of Adam, "there was no man to till the ground";[19] Eve is "the mother of all the living",[20] and St Paul says, "The God who made the world ... made from one every nation of men to live on all the face of the earth", and, "sin came into the world through one man".[21] Moreover, the doctrines of Original Sin and the Redemption require us to believe that we are all sprung from Adam: we sinned in Adam, because he was our parent; and, because we inherited his sin, we had need of Redemption. Seven times in Romans 5:12-19, St Paul speaks of Adam as

---

[17] *Humani Generis*, 1950: DS 3896
[18] Message to Pont. Acad. of Sciences, 1996
[19] Gen 2:5
[20] Gen 3:20
[21] Acts 17:24, 26; Rom 5:12

"one man". The Council of Trent's solemn decree on Original Sin begins by speaking of the sin of "the first man Adam".[22]

Belief in the descent of all men from one man Adam is called 'monogenism'. It is upheld in the *Catechism of the Catholic Church*.[23] 'Polygenism' (belief in several original ancestors) is contrary to the teaching of the Church. Pius XII declared, "Christ's faithful cannot embrace a theory which involves the existence, after Adam's time, of some earthly race of men, truly so called, who were not descended from him as the ancestor of all men, or else supposes that Adam was the name given to a multiplicity of original ancestors."[24]

WHAT SCIENTISTS SAY. (1) Scientists have not proved the multiple origin of the existing human species. The vague conjectures in which a few of them indulge need not be considered. (2) The fact that all men all over the world, even the least civilised, have the gift of speech and the power to grasp intellectual and moral truths, tends to show that we are all members of the same family, and is, therefore, fully consistent with the doctrine revealed to us that we are descended from a single pair of ancestors. This argument, which is confirmed by world-wide similarities in ancient traditions and folklore, is not affected by differences of race and language. Though there is no certainty yet as to how the different races originated, all races are true to a common type, despite their definite varieties and considerable differences. The human races are all capable of breeding with one another. Difference in language is due chiefly to geographical separation. As the study of philology and linguistics advances, the kinship is gradually being established between all languages, even between those which at one time were thought to be totally unrelated. The more recent researches into human genetic structure would very much favour the common origin of the human race.

Note. A *species* is a group which has something in common with other groups, but is distinguished from them by something which it alone can possess. Mankind is a species. Man is defined as a rational animal. The word "animal" tells us what he has in common with other living creatures; the word "rational" tells us what is exclusively his. From this definition of species, it is clear that no species shades off into another: e.g., there cannot be such things as "three-quarters-brute, one-quarter-man", "half-brute, half-man", "one-quarter-brute, three-quarters-man". If a creature is a brute, it is not a man; if it is a man, it is not a brute.

Difficulty. "If Adam and Eve had only Cain and Abel, where did everyone else come from?" *Reply.* The account in Genesis does not purport to list all their children by name, but makes it clear that there were others: Gen 4:17 mentions that Cain had a wife. Gen 4:25 mentions the birth of Seth, another son of Adam and Eve. 4:26

---

[22] DS 1511
[23] C 374, 375, 376, 379, 390, 391, 404
[24] *Humani Generis*, 1950: DS 3897, cited in footnote to C 390.

mentions Seth's son, Enosh. Finally, 5:4 says, "Adam ... had other sons and daughters."

The antiquity of the human species. The age of the human species is a question on which the Church has never given any decision, and may be left to the investigation of scientists.

CHAPTER 7

OUR FIRST PARENTS: THEIR GIFTS AND THEIR FALL

Summary

I.   The solemn teaching of the Church.
II. The gifts bestowed on our first parents: Sanctifying Grace, Integrity, Immortality, Happiness, Enlightenment. The nature of their gifts. Their happiness.
III. The Fall of our first parents. Original Sin: its meaning; the gravity of the sin committed by Adam; its chief consequence; how it is transmitted to us. The doctrine of Original Sin a mystery. The doctrine of Original Sin so reasonable, and in conformity with human experience. The miseries of life are due to Original Sin; how God enables us to profit by them.
IV. Objections answered: the Scripture narrative of the Fall is not opposed to reason; the doctrine of Original Sin is not opposed to the Justice of God; nor is it opposed to His Mercy; nor is it inconsistent with scientific discoveries.

I

The solemn teaching of the Church about our first parents. The Church teaches solemnly:[1]
(1) that God gave Adam Sanctifying Grace and immunity from death;
(2) that by his sin he lost these precious gifts, became an enemy of God, a slave of the devil, and was changed for the worse in soul and body;
(3) that he transmitted his guilt and its evil consequences to all his posterity;[2]
(4) that man has not lost, however, his free will.

II

The gifts bestowed on our first parents: Sanctifying Grace, integrity, immortality, happiness, enlightenment.
THE GIFT OF SANCTIFYING GRACE. This was the most precious of all the gifts bestowed by God on our first parents. It made them "partakers of the divine nature",[3] so that God Himself was present in their souls as in a temple, and was united to them in the most intimate friendship. It was His design that, after a short period of probation, they should pass painlessly out of this world into Heaven, and dwell with Him as a child with its father,

---

[1] T 1511-2, 1555
[2] Cf. also C 374-390, 396-421.
[3] 2 Pet 1:4

beholding Him, not "in a mirror dimly", or through a veil, but "face to face",[4] and thus be made sharers in His own eternal bliss. Such a happiness is, without Sanctifying Grace, beyond the reach of any creature, even the most exalted of the angels. What would have proved a great danger to their gift of Sanctifying Grace was removed by their gift of integrity.

THE GIFT OF INTEGRITY[5] (*Complete control over the lusts of the flesh*). As in the state of innocence their will was obedient to God, so also their passions were obedient to their will: the appetites of the flesh, which man shares with brutes, were strictly subject to the coercive check of reason. Their gift of integrity, since it suppressed all hostility in their lower or animal nature, gave them a fitness for Sanctifying Grace, and was the firm pedestal on which it rested. In the fallen state, the passions are rebellious. They fret under control, attract men powerfully to sin, and are no friends to Sanctifying Grace.

THE GIFT OF IMMORTALITY AND HAPPINESS (*Immunity from suffering and death*). They were free from all such evils, not because their bodies were themselves insensible to pain or incapable of corruption, but because God either shielded them from harm or provided them with such a knowledge of natural causes and with such preventive remedies against sickness and decay that they were able to live in unimpaired vigour, avoiding all that was hurtful or deadly.

THE GIFT OF ENLIGHTENMENT. "(God) filled them with knowledge and understanding … and they will praise His holy name, to proclaim the grandeur of His works. … He bestowed knowledge upon them … and showed them His judgements. Their eyes saw His glorious majesty, and their ears heard the glory of His voice. And He said to them, 'beware of all unrighteousness'."[6] God gave them the gift of speech. He gave them such a knowledge of religious and moral truths as was necessary for their own enlightenment and for the instruction of their children. He gave them such a knowledge of secular science as was needed for their happiness, or as befitted the circumstances of their life and work.

St Augustine believed that in power of intellect Adam surpassed his fallen descendants even more than "the bird outstrips the tortoise in speed."[7] St Thomas says that Adam, unlike us, had no need to draw out any proof of God's existence,

---

[4] 1 Cor 13:12
[5] Integrity means completeness, the absence of defect. In some authors, "Integrity" is the general name for all the gifts (except Sanctifying Grace).
[6] Ecclesiasticus (Sirach) 17
[7] *Contra Iul. op. imp.*, V, i

but that he perceived that truth the very instant he became aware of the finite things about him and was conscious of his own power of understanding. Thomas says that Adam had a full knowledge of all subjects suitable for human instruction.[8] Our physical scientists propose theories which have only a short life, but Adam had a grasp of the fundamental principles which they are trying in vain to reach. A few Catholic writers, influenced by the opinions of palaeontologists, have attempted to belittle the intelligence of Adam. They seem to think that he may not have been much above a simpleton, but their views are untenable. Since Adam must have had a clear knowledge and appreciation of the gift of Sanctifying Grace, and must have been fully aware of his responsibilities as the head of mankind, he cannot have been a dullard. Nor would God have allowed the act of a dullard to involve the whole human race in disaster.

The nature of their gifts. Of the gifts conferred on our first parents, Sanctifying Grace was *supernatural*, the others were *preternatural*. A supernatural gift is one which *no* creature as such can claim as a natural right. The direct vision of God in His unveiled beauty is a supernatural gift; so too is the Sanctifying Grace which prepares the soul for it. A preternatural gift, on the other hand, is one to which *a particular* creature has no title, but which may be enjoyed as a natural right by some higher creature. Thus, for example, our first parents' preternatural gift of enlightenment belonged, even in a higher form, and as of natural right, to the lowest of Angels. The preternatural gifts left our first parents on the created level; their supernatural gift raised them up to the divine level, the level of God Himself.

Their happiness. St Augustine says, in words no less true than poetical: "Man lived in Paradise as he pleased, as long as his pleasure lay in what God had ordered. He lived in the enjoyment of God, the source of all the good there is in man. He lived free from want, and might have so lived for ever. Food was at hand, lest he should hunger; drink, lest he should thirst; the tree of life, lest old age should undo him. His senses and feelings were undisturbed by bodily decay. He feared no disease from within, no assault from without. In his flesh was perfect heath; in his soul, perfect peace. As Eden was unvisited by excess of heat or cold, so the will of him who dwelt there was untroubled by fear or greed. No sadness was his, no mere empty pleasure: a steady tide of unceasing joy flowed out to him from God whom he loved with the glowing love that comes from a pure heart, a good conscience, and faith undimmed by falsehood or insincerity. Man and wife were there, one in mutual trust, one in honourable love, one in the guard

---

[8] S.T., i, q. 94, aa. 1, 3

they kept over mind and body, one in the easy service of obedience to God's command."[9]

III

The Fall of our first parents. We assume that the reader is acquainted with the Bible text on the temptation and sin of our first parents. The Church, through the Biblical Commission,[10] lays down certain principles to guide us in its interpretation.[11] She tells us that we cannot question the literal and historical meaning of the narrative when it relates to facts touching the foundations of religion. Among these facts she enumerates: (1) the unity of the human race; (2) the original happiness of our first parents in the state of justice (sanctifying grace), their integrity, and immortality; (3) the command issued by God to test their obedience; (4) their temptation by the devil under the form of a serpent;[12] (5) their transgression and its punishment; (6) the promise of a Redeemer. - With regard to the other details the Church has said nothing. Pending explicit direction from her, we are free to follow any interpretation not in conflict with Catholic principles.

Original Sin: its meaning. The gravity of the sin committed by Adam. Its chief consequence. How it is transmitted to us.
THE MEANING OF ORIGINAL SIN. "Original Sin" may denote either (1) the actual sin committed by our first parents, or (2) the unhappy state to which that sin reduced them and their posterity.

THE GRAVITY OF THE SIN COMMITTED BY ADAM. Adam committed a most grievous sin, (1) because God Himself had impressed on him the gravity of the offence by declaring the punishment which it would entail: "of the tree of the knowledge of good and evil you shall not eat, for in the day that you eat of it you shall die";[13] i.e., he was threatened with immediate spiritual death, and with the sentence of physical death; (2) because the command was easy to obey; (3) because Adam was not the victim of passion or caprice, but acted from cool reason and on full deliberation, which showed the calculated malice of his sin; (4) because he sought to be like God in the knowledge of good and evil, so that he might be his own director and attain to perfect happiness by his own enlightenment and

---

[9] *The City of God*, Bk 14, xxvi
[10] Decree of 1909: DS 3514. On the Biblical Commission, see p.263.
[11] Cf. the principles followed by the Church in interpreting the Biblical account of Creation, Ch. 3.
[12] Cf. "Objections answered", p. 368.
[13] Gen 2:17

unaided effort; (5) because he sinned, not as a private individual, but as the representative of the human race.

His sin, as St Thomas points out, was a sin of pride manifesting itself in an act of disobedience.[14] The desire to be like God in the manner appointed by Him is the best of all desires, but Adam desired to be like Him in a manner He had forbidden. (The same desire to have our own way, to be our own master, is present in every grave sin).

ITS CHIEF CONSEQUENCE. All the gifts we have mentioned were lost *to us* by the sin of Adam; of these, Sanctifying Grace was the chief. Everyone born of him in the ordinary course of nature, the Blessed Virgin alone excepted, is from the first moment of existence *in the state of sin*. Not that the child merely by being born is in the position of one who has committed actual sin, but that it begins its life in a condition brought about by the actual sin of Adam, and, therefore, contrary to the will of God. It is in this sense we say that all men are "children of wrath" (Eph 2:3). It was God's will that every member of our race should become His adopted child destined for the happiness of the Beatific Vision. That purpose was frustrated by Adam. But God's mercy and love intervened, and, through the Redemption, restored us to the unspeakably precious gift of sanctifying grace.

HOW IT IS TRANSMITTED TO US. Original Sin is not transmitted to us through our soul, because our soul is directly created by God. It is transmitted to us through the bodily element, the flesh we have inherited from Adam. The moment he sinned, he lost his dominion over his bodily inclinations. His flesh was now in a state of rebellion against his spirit, craving for its own pleasures and gratifications, and it is that rebellious flesh which we have derived from him. Our soul did not exist before our conception. It sprang into existence only in the precise instant of its union with the contaminated bodily element. The entire living man, soul and body, produced by that union was therefore, from the very first, in a condition not intended by God. We may compare His action in creating our soul to the night-atmosphere which causes dewdrops to appear on a poisonous surface. The dewdrops from the first moment of their existence are poisoned; but that is not the fault of the atmosphere; it is the fault of him who strewed the poison. God decreed from all eternity to create human souls. He did not revoke that decree, but foreknowing that the soul of each one of us would be stained by the flesh of Adam, He formed the supplementary decree to repair the evil through the grace of Redemption. It is better for man, as St Thomas says, "to be born with an infected nature

---

[14] S.T., ii-ii, q. 163, a. 2

than to be non-existent, chiefly because, through grace, he can escape damnation."[15]

Notes. Original sin is usually spoken of as the sin of our first parents but it is more correctly described as the sin of Adam. It was Adam who, as the head and representative of our race, brought ruin on us by his sin. Had Eve alone sinned, her guilt would not have been transmitted to her children. If Adam had remained faithful, each one of his descendants would have been subjected like himself to some trial of loyalty to God, before being confirmed in the possession of his gifts.[16]

We normally say 'fallen' or 'weakened' or 'wounded' human nature, and usually avoid saying 'corrupted' or 'depraved'—since human nature in its natural state can attain to natural goods and virtues. The 'corruption' or 'depravity' is not total but relative only, i.e., by comparison with its original condition. - God could have originally created man in that state in which he now enters the world. Baius was condemned by Pope Pius V for asserting that God could not have.[17]

The doctrine of Original Sin is a mystery. If Original Sin meant nothing more than physical sickness or weakness inherited from Adam, the doctrine would not appear to be incomprehensible: we could understand how his sudden fall from peace and happiness to direst misery and remorse would have profoundly altered him for the worse, to the detriment of all who were to be descended from him. But the chief feature in Original Sin is not that we are sharers in Adam's physical infirmity, but that, without any personal fault of ours, we are sharers in his fault—"sharers in his fault", in the sense that we are born in such a condition that without help from God to which we have no claim, we are incapable of reaching the supernatural end to which God calls all men in Adam and without which they cannot attain their fullest happiness. That is the mystery. It is a truth revealed to us by God which we cannot comprehend. It is parallel to the other truth, equally mysterious, that if Adam had not sinned, he would have transmitted to all his posterity the divine gift of Sanctifying Grace. It is parallel also to the Mystery of the Redemption, because Christ is the new Adam who has made good the losses we sustained through Original Sin.

---

[15] S.T., i-ii, q. 83, a. 1, ad 5
[16] St Thomas, S.T., i-ii, q. 81, a. 5; i, q. 100, a. 1
[17] DS 1955

ORIGINAL SIN

Adam and Eve enjoyed:	By their sin they lost these and so we are born:	Now:
Sanctifying Grace	**without Grace**	**Baptism restores Grace**
and ... Integrity Immortality Happiness Knowledge	and subject to ... Concupiscence Death Suffering Ignorance	but ... not the other gifts until the next life

The Biblical basis for the gifts:

GRACE:
Adam and Eve were united to God at the start in most intimate friendship. Only after their sin, "the man and his wife hid themselves from the presence of the Lord God." Gen. 3:8

INTEGRITY:
Gen. 2:25: "the man and his wife were both naked, and were not ashamed."

IMMORTALITY:
Gen. 2:9: "the tree of life also in the midst of the garden". Gen. 2:17: "but of the tree of the knowledge of good and evil you shall not eat, for in the day that you eat of it you shall die." (i.e., they were immortal until this transgression). Cf. also Gen. 3:19,22.

IMMUNITY FROM SUFFERING:
Gen. 2:9: "And out of the ground the Lord God made to grow every tree that is pleasant to the sight and good for food". Gen. 2:16: "You may freely eat of every tree of the garden".

ENLIGHTENMENT:
Gen. 2:15: "The Lord God took the man and put him in the garden of Eden to till it and keep it." Gen. 2:20: "The man gave names to all cattle, and to the birds of the air, and to every beast of the field."

The doctrine of Original Sin is so reasonable. There is no other explanation so satisfying, to explain the permanent imperfections and evils of this world and human life. The very word *religion* contains the idea of Original Sin, for re-ligion means that by which one seeks to be linked again[1] to the divine. All religions represent man's quest for reunion with God, and a desire to see the saving sacred enfleshed. Some of the pagan religions may contain elements of that primitive Revelation given to Adam. Whilst some Mysteries of Faith remain elusive, the stark facts of imperfection, sin and evil, led G.K. Chesterton to say, with a note of hyperbole, "Certain new theologians dispute original sin, which is the only part of Christian theology which can really be proved. Some ... admit divine sinlessness, which they cannot see even in their dreams. But they essentially deny human sin, which they can see in the street."[2]

Cardinal Newman writes, "To consider the world in its length and breadth, its various history, the many races of man, their starts, their fortunes, their mutual alienation, their conflicts; ... the greatness and littleness of man, his far-reaching aims, his short duration, the curtain hung over his futurity, the disappointments of life, the defeat of good, the success of evil, physical pain, mental anguish, the prevalence and intensity of sin, the pervading idolatries, the corruptions, the dreary hopeless irreligion ... - all this is a vision to dizzy and appal; and inflicts upon the mind the sense of a profound mystery, which is absolutely beyond human solution. What shall be said to this heart-piercing, reason-bewildering fact? I can only answer, that either there is no Creator, or this living society of men is in a true sense discarded from His presence. ... - *if* there be a God, *since* there is a God, the human race is implicated in some terrible aboriginal calamity. It is out of joint with the purposes of its Creator. This is a fact, a fact as true as the fact of its existence; and thus the doctrine of what is theologically called original sin becomes to me almost as certain as that the world exists, and as the existence of God."[3]

The doctrine of Original Sin is in conformity with human experience. Man's personal and communal experience is a testimony to the fact of Original Sin, for which the following pointers can be adduced: (a) the traditions of ancient peoples about a primordial tragedy and a Paradise Lost, e.g., Prometheus and the Titans, Pandora's box, Elysium, and the Golden Age; (b) the sense of shame attached to the urges and requirements of man's bodily nature; (c) man's inescapable awareness of a propensity to evil even in the face of clear knowledge of what is right.

The miseries of life, due to Original Sin; how God enables us to profit by them. It is only by accepting the revealed doctrine of Original Sin that we can understand why the world is marred by so much wickedness and unhappiness. Because of the frustration of God's purpose by the sin of Adam, man is burdened with a fallen human nature, and is at feud even with

---

[1] Latin, *re-ligare*: to link, bind, tie again.
[2] *Orthodoxy*, 1908, Ch. II
[3] *Apologia Pro Vita Sua*, Ch. V (Position since 1845), Longmans, pp.242-3

the material surroundings in which he lives. Within himself, he feels the strong pull of evil passions, and, in the course of his life "in this vale of tears",[4] he has to bear much sorrow and suffering. Such is our unhappy lot.[5] But God enables us to turn to profit these very consequences of original guilt. He gives us grace to battle against temptation, and to win a reward all the greater in proportion to the severity of the struggle. He uses pain and sorrow to open our hearts to tenderness and sympathy, to teach us that this world offers us no lasting happiness, and to make us look with the eye of hope to our true home where He "will wipe away every tear ... and death shall be no more, neither shall there be mourning nor crying nor pain."[6] Pain is indeed a cruel discipline which He would have spared us, but, under His loving Providence, it is become like the plant whose root is bitter, but whose fruit is sweet.

IV

Objections answered.
OBJECTION AGAINST THE REASONABLENESS OF THE SCRIPTURE NARRATIVE. "The Bible account of the Fall opens with the words: 'Now the serpent was more subtle than any other wild creature that the Lord God had made. He said to the woman: Did God say, You shall not eat of any tree of the garden?' Eve replies saying that they are free to eat of all trees except for one which God had commanded them not to touch, lest they die. 'You will not die', answers the serpent, 'For God knows that when you eat of it you shall be like God, knowing good and evil.' Eve eats the fruit, and gives to Adam, who also eats. God speaks to them. He condemns the serpent, saying: 'Because you have done this, cursed are you above all cattle, and above all wild animals; upon your belly you shall go, and dust you shall eat all the days of your life.' On all this it may be remarked: (1) animals do not speak except in fables and folklore; (2) the serpent is not the subtlest of animals; (3) the serpent, as the very name (*serpere*, Latin - to creep) indicates, was a creeping animal before the Fall quite as much as after; (4) if the serpent that tempted Eve was not a real serpent but an evil spirit disguised as a serpent, the whole serpent-tribe should not have been punished and pronounced accursed among all cattle and beasts."

[Note. We shall treat this objection at considerable length in order to give an idea of how other seemingly serious objections against the teaching of Scripture are examined and refuted. A Catholic should always approach objections with a mind docile to the Church and filled with the conviction that she possesses the truth, and that he must accept her decision. Even if, after study, he is not clear on the solution of certain difficulties, he knows that there *is* a solution.]

---

[4] From the *Salve Regina* (Hail, Holy Queen)
[5] St Thomas, S.T., i-ii, q. 85
[6] Rev 21:4

REPLY: (1) The talking animals of folklore are merely a literary device that gives pleasure by its quaintness but deceives no one. Even the primitive peoples are aware that animals have not, and cannot have, a gift of rational speech. They know that a parrot can repeat words, but they also know that it does not understand what it says, and cannot carry on a conversation. When therefore the inspired word of God represents an animal as speaking, we at once perceive that the literal interpretation must be excluded.

(2) "Subtlest" means "craftiest." In popular speech, the serpent is justly described as "the subtlest of all animals." His cunning is proverbial. Our Lord spoke about the simplicity of the dove and the craft of the serpent.

(3) "The serpent was a creeping animal before the Fall quite as much as after." The inspired writer of Genesis, says that, on the fifth day, i.e., before the creation of man, "God made ... *everything* that creeps upon the ground" (Gen 1:25). On that day, therefore, God made the reptiles from which all those in the world at the time of Moses (when the account was recorded) were descended. It follows that the serpent which was condemned to crawl cannot have been of the animal kind. The word must refer to a being of a different order, and the "crawling" to a spiritual, not a physical, humiliation.

(4) God's sentence was not directed against a mere animal but against a wicked spirit. He did not curse or punish the serpent-tribe. This is clear from what we read elsewhere in the Scriptures: Psalm 148, e.g., calls on all creatures, living and lifeless, including "beasts and all cattle, *creeping things* [which includes serpents] and flying birds" (v. 10), to chant the praise of their Creator. (The call of the Psalmist to irrational and inanimate creatures to sing the divine praises is but an expressive way of declaring that these things by the very nature God has given them are witnesses in the sight of men and angels to His power and wisdom. It is true that man looks on certain animals as his enemies, and turns with repugnance from certain material things as hateful and disgusting. But all these are God's creatures, good in themselves and beloved of Him. So far as they inspire fear or loathing, they serve as a means in the hands of God to chastise us for our sins. But for the Fall, man would be at peace with the world. Serpents and other animals would still be noxious, but he would have the power of easily avoiding them or of holding them in subjection.)

But the objector will urge that "it is most improbable that the evil spirit would have taken the form of a serpent rather than that of a man."

To this we reply as follows:

(a) Where is the improbability? The form of a serpent is no more alien to a spirit than the form of a man.

(b) In permitting Satan to tempt Eve, God did not allow him to overpower her imagination by an appearance of beauty or magnificence. The humble shape which he was compelled to assume left her mind perfectly open to the wholesome thought that she was in the presence of one who was no worthy rival of God but a mere creature like herself—one therefore who was guilty of great wickedness in disputing the divine command and urging its violation. Besides, God, foreknowing the fall of our first parents, desired that they and their descendants should hold before their mind the picture of the Evil One as a treacherous and dangerous reptile. Contrast

369

this picture with another God has given us: at the Baptism of His Son in the Jordan, the Holy Spirit appeared in the form of a dove, a radiant image symbolising love and innocence and peace.

(c) The doctrine that Satan "under the form of a serpent" tempted Eve has undoubtedly been revealed by God: no reasonable interpretation of the passage in Genesis could lead to any other conclusion. Besides, it is expressly repeated by St Paul: "But I am afraid that as the serpent deceived Eve by his cunning…".[7]

Outside the few points decided by the Church, she allows her scholars to propose any interpretation of the narrative of the Fall which accords with reason and Tradition, and shows reverence for the word of God. One of these interpretations is as follows: "The most important words in the passage are those referring to Our Lady and the future victory over Satan through her Divine Son: 'I will put enmity between you and the woman, and between your seed and her seed; he shall bruise your head, and you shall bruise his heel.'[8] The obviously spiritual meaning of these words points the way to a spiritual interpretation of the complete passage. The Scripture says: 'Now the serpent was more subtle than any other wild creature that the Lord God had made. He said to the woman: Did God say, You shall not eat of any tree of the garden?' The serpent here spoken of, as the subsequent narrative shows, is not a mere brute beast, but a malignant being endowed with reason who knows how to entice Eve to grasp at what seems to be a higher spiritual good. He is none other than Satan himself, correctly described as being 'more subtle than any other wild creature.' The sentence which God pronounces on him draws its terms from animal life but is purely spiritual in meaning. It is not a pronouncement against the serpent-tribe: 'The Lord God said to the serpent: Because you have done this, cursed are you above all cattle, and above all wild animals; upon your belly you shall go, and dust you shall eat all the days of your life. I will put enmity between you and the woman, and between your seed and her seed; he shall bruise your head, and you shall bruise his heel.' That is: 'Because you have done this thing, you are made more vile than the beasts of the earth; you shall go upon your belly in humiliation, and you shall eat the dust of defilement and degradation. I will put hatred and hostility between you and the woman, and between your followers and her sons. You shall be at the heel of her son, seeking to slay him with the venom of your wickedness, but he shall tread upon your head.' Satan therefore shall be punished in the spiritual order after the fashion of the noxious reptile whose shape he had assumed. His power shall be broken by the Redeemer, the Son of God, born of Mary."

Satan's guilt has remained unchanged since his fall. His temptation of Eve was not a new sin, but a new manifestation of his hatred of God. His punishment for it did not increase his suffering, but showed in a new way God's anger towards him.

It may be well to point out to those who make such a difficulty about "the serpentine form" that the description can be justified without supposing a complete

---

[7] 2 Cor 11:3; cf. Apoc 12:9; 20:2.

[8] Gen 3:15 (RSV) "… *he* shall bruise" may also be translated as "*she* shall crush" (Douay).

resemblance. Some indeed argue for a dragon-like form, since elsewhere the devil is called "the dragon".[9]

Those who urge scriptural objections such as the foregoing fail for the following reasons: (1) They depend on the English translation, interpreting it as though it were the original, and making no allowance for the great difference between the ancient and modern turns of speech; (2) they work from isolated passages without regard to what is stated elsewhere in the Bible; (3) they ignore the ancient commentaries of the Fathers of the Church, and the writings of those approved Catholic scholars who have made a profound study of the sacred text.

OBJECTIONS CONTESTING THE JUSTICE OF GOD.

1. "The punishment which God inflicted for eating a bit of fruit was excessive."

REPLY: (a) The objection depends upon a literal interpretation, but even on that score: an act trivial in itself may change its character because of the motive and circumstances. To hoist a bit of colourful cloth over your house is in itself a very small matter, just a sign that you favour that particular kind of decoration, but if the colours happen to be those of a country with which your people are at war, your act will be regarded as the outward expression of grave disloyalty, and you will find yourself facing a charge of treason. Similarly, to eat a bit of fruit is in itself of no great account, but the act of our first parents in eating the fruit, clearly and most emphatically forbidden by God under a dire threat, was the outward expression of grave insubordination. (b) The Church has never said that the expressions, "the tree of knowledge of good and evil" and "its fruit" are to be literally interpreted: see above, "The Fall of our first parents." The prohibition was not an arbitrary rule from God, for that fruit was no mere food hanging on a tree, but the fruit from the "the tree of knowledge of good and evil". Hence to eat it meant to arrogate to oneself the power to determine good and evil—a prerogative belonging to God alone. Adam's sin of eating it, therefore, involved trespassing the limits of his creaturely status, refusing to be subject to the laws of creation and to the moral norms inscribed therein by God. It meant pride, defiance, and contempt for God.[10]

2. "God has dealt *unjustly* with the human race. He has punished innocent children for the sin of their parents."

REPLY: Just as children may inherit their parents' wealth, so too they may inherit their parents' debts and be liable for them. These debts, if not paid, pass on to yet another generation. Thus, it is taken for granted that posterity is liable for its ancestors' debts. To employ another illustration: An aristocrat bestows his favour on two of his servants, man and wife, both of lowly station. On condition of fidelity to him, he promises to adopt them as his heirs, to raise them and their children to noble rank (*Sanctifying Grace*); he gives them house and lands, and provides them with every comfort (*the other gifts*). They prove ungrateful and disloyal. The aristocrat withdraws his promise of adoption, deprives them of their riches, and reduces them to the level at which he had found them. He has deprived them and their descendants of nothing but privileges to which they never had any

---

[9] E.g., Rev 20:2
[10] Cf. C 396-8.

claim except the claim which would have risen from the faithful observance of the condition he had imposed. - But note: The parable must not mislead us into supposing that Adam and Eve, like the servants, lived for some time without any special privileges. From the beginning they enjoyed sanctifying grace and the other gifts, and, therefore, owed all the more gratitude to God.

OBJECTIONS CONTESTING THE MERCY OF GOD.

1. "The doctrine of Original Sin implies that man received immunity from pain as a free gift which God might have withheld. It follows, therefore, that God might have created man subject to pain, a conclusion which cannot be reconciled with the Divine Mercy."

REPLY: The argument against the Divine Mercy might be valid if, in the case supposed, suffering were useless and brought no reward. But suffering would not have been useless: as in the present world, it would have been a great civilising influence, a teacher of kindness and virtue. Nor would it have failed of its reward: God, even though He had destined man for nothing higher than natural happiness after death, would have given him, either in this life or the next, an ample recompense for every sorrow.

2. "Admitting that, as regards man, the existence of pain is satisfactorily explained, we are still confronted with the difficulty of pain in the lower creation. Why does a good God make animals suffer?" (Note. This particular difficulty belongs to Chapter 1 of this text and to *Apologetics*, Chapter 1, p.53 , but some further light is thrown on it by the doctrine of Original Sin).

REPLY: We should note the following points, not as removing the difficulty, but as lessening its force: (a) The lower animals are not at all so sensitive to pain as we: hence, we greatly exaggerate their sufferings by ascribing them to feelings such as ours. For instance, a crab will continue to eat, and apparently relish, a smaller crab, while being itself slowly devoured by a larger one. If a wasp while drinking honey be snipped in two, it will continue to drink as though nothing had happened. A fish just escaped from the hook will often return to the bait as greedily as ever. An insect will allow itself to be burned limb for limb in a candle flame. The writhings of animals are sometimes merely muscular, and are no certain indication of suffering. Both parts of a severed worm will wriggle equally, though surely the hinder part cannot have any sensation. Civilised man is far more sensitive to pain than the savage, and, as the difference between them is only one of degree, whereas that which exists between the savage and the lower animals is one of kind, it may be reasonably argued that the sufferings of the latter are not very considerable. The keenness of human pain is due in great part to rationality. The brute suffers in the passing instant; it does not link up what is gone with what is to come, and is not tortured by the thought that it is a cause of grief to others. Man, on the other hand, suffers intensely from the memory of what is past, from the anticipation of what is before him, from the very longing for the end of his misery, from self-pity, and from the reflection of his sorrow in the faces of those about him, or indeed, it may be, from their indifference or hostility.

(b) While their nervous system has given them a capacity for pain, it has also given them a capacity for pleasure, and it cannot be questioned that, in the animal-world as a whole, the ordinary state is one of happiness, and not of misery. If, then, it be said that they suffer unmerited pain, it can also be said that they enjoy, and in a much fuller degree, unmerited happiness.

(c) Pain is useful to animals, as a warning of disease and danger. In the present order of the world, it is in fact the shield of life. These general considerations, however, do not dispose of the fact that, in the lower creation, there are instances of positive suffering for which we can see no explanation. But, firmly believing in the goodness of God, we are convinced that He never subjects to needless pain the lowliest and least sensitive of living things: if we could read His mind aright, we should see that even the gnat with a broken wing is a necessary and indispensable part of the whole working plan and working of the world. Seemingly trivial things do, in our own experience, produce vast effects: the pressure exerted by the finger of a little child may seem of small account, yet when applied to an electric button it is sufficient to release all the powers of mischief in a missile and lay the great buildings of a city in ruins. Somewhat in this way, we conceive the least things in the world to be inextricably bound up with the greatest.[11] All are knit together, all serve one another, with the perfection beyond our understanding. Pain and all else (except sin) that we designate evils are not really evils, though they seem so to us. We, with our little minds, discern but dimly the design of God in the happenings of the world. We see, as it were, the wrong side of a piece of tapestry. Though we may succeed in making out the main lines of the pattern, we are tempted to regard as ugly and meaningless the knots and threads, the bare patches and misshapen fragments of colour. But what a change when we turn to the other side! The very things that appeared to mar the harmony of the whole are now found to be a necessary part of it. God will show us some day, if we deserve it, the place in His design, and the high and far-reaching purpose, of the things great and small that silly people brand as imperfections and failures in His work.

Besides the considerations set forth above, we have to remember that the curse of Original Sin extends to the earth itself and to poor, dumb creatures. Had man not fallen, he could have gathered the fruits of the soil without painful exertion, and he would have been spared the sight of all the cruelty and suffering he now witnesses, with such repugnance, in the animal-world. The easy response of the earth to his efforts, and the absence of all disturbing or distressing features in his surroundings, would have enforced the single lesson of God's kindness to him. But, by his sin, he provoked God's anger. God, in His justice, condemned man to earn his bread by exhausting labour. God, in His wisdom and omnipotence, so changed the world that man, while still beholding therein the marvels of his Creator's goodness and bounty, should also be confronted with the evidence of his sin and be reminded of the need of repentance. It is not God, therefore, but man himself who is answerable for the sufferings of brute creation.

---

[11] Many men can tell how the whole course of their lives was determined by apparent trifles. Cf. the old verse: "For the want of a nail the shoe was lost / for the want of a shoe the horse was lost / for the want of a horse the rider was lost / for the want of a rider the battle was lost / for the want of the battle the kingdom was lost / and all for want of a horse-shoe nail." (G. Herbert: *Jacula Prudentum*)

OBJECTIONS FROM SCIENCE.

Palaeontology. "From palaeontology, which studies fossils, we learn that earliest man was of low brain capacity, and therefore of low intelligence, and could not have possessed those wonderful gifts which Catholics claim for him."

REPLY: Let us set up the fantastic hypothesis that some day palaeontologists may be able to identify an ancient skull of low brain-capacity as the skull of the first man. What would follow from that identification? Merely this: that Adam, when stripped down to his natural powers, as he was after the Fall, was of low intelligence, of "dark understanding" and weak memory. Before the Fall, his small brain—as, for the moment, we suppose it to have been—would not have prevented an Omnipotent God from bestowing on him all the gifts we ascribe to him. The only obstacle to God's action would have been irrationality, and that is excluded.

Ethnology. 1. "Ethnologists can point to the tools used by a race of men as an index to their culture. Earliest man possessed only the simplest tools. Therefore we may infer that Adam must have been like the lowest kind of savage."

REPLY: (a) Since Scripture scholars are uncertain as to the precise location of Eden, we may dismiss the idea that any vestiges of Adam's life before or after the Fall will ever be discovered. (b) Suppose Adam to have fashioned the first rude implements. As their inventor, he could not be compared to the later savage who inherited them from his ancestors. The first steps in the mechanical arts were the most difficult. Probably as much intelligence was required for the making of the first implement of wood or bone or stone as for the invention of the steam-engine or radio. (c) Rude implements of themselves are never a proof of feebleness of mind. If one of our learned ethnologists who has had no training in camp-life, but who knows well enough what good tools ought to be, were cast ashore on a desert island with nothing to help him but his bare hands, his efforts at tool making would be very crude, but would not entitle us to question his intellectual ability. But Adam would have had to set to work without knowing anything of the qualities of a good tool. Hence, if we were shown a set of clumsy implements as the alleged specimens of his handicraft, we should be still less justified in denying his high spiritual and mental endowments.

2. "Do not ethnologists tell us that religion began as some kind of gross superstition, a vague belief in good and bad influences, developing later into the worship of several independent spirits, and much later into the worship of a supreme divinity? If this view is correct, Adam must have known nothing of the one Supreme God."

REPLY: (a) The notion that belief in the one Supreme God is a late development belongs to out-of-date ethnology. It may be sufficiently demonstrated, employing all the modern tools of research, (1) that in the earliest form of religion known to us by ordinary human means, the one true God was worshipped by prayer and sacrifice; that the law of unbreakable monogamy[12] was acknowledged together with the great natural laws that govern the relations of parents and children and of all

---

[12] The natural law prescribing that a man should have only one wife, and a woman only one husband, and that their marriage should last until the death of either partner.

men to one another; (2) that corruptions, such as belief in magic, ancestor-worship and polytheism, are all of later date. (b) Even if these conclusions are not accepted by our opponents, it is inconceivable that the spade will ever upturn anything to prove that Adam was not a worshipper of the true God: see Reply (a) to preceding objection. We have already acknowledged the Fall of Man, which explains the degraded form of religion that took hold of man after he lost friendship with God.

GOD THE REDEEMER

CHAPTER 8

JESUS CHRIST OUR SAVIOUR

A

THE INCARNATION

Summary

I.   The solemn teaching of the Church.
II.   Jesus Christ, true God, true Man. The Hypostatic, or Personal, Union. The Holy Name. Rules of language. The human knowledge and will of Christ; His virtues and graces. The worship due to Christ as Man. Difficulties and errors.
III. The Three Offices of Christ: Priest, Prophet, King.
IV.   The miracles of Christ. Their meaning and purpose.
V.   The veneration due to the B.V. Mary and to St Joseph. Mary the Mother of God.

I

The solemn teaching of the Church. The Church teaches solemnly:

(1) that God the Son, the Second Person of the Most Holy Trinity, became Man;[1]
(2) that He was born of the Blessed Virgin Mary;
(3) that He is true God and true Man;
(4) that He is High Priest;[2]
(5) that He is Judge and Lawgiver;[3]
(6) that His Mother Mary conceived Him while still a Virgin;
(7) that as His Mother she is truly and rightly called the Mother of God;[4]
(8) that she was conceived without Original Sin;[5]
(9) that at the end of her earthly life she was assumed body and soul into Heaven.[6]

---

[1] Nos. 1, 2, 3, 6: in the Creeds.
[2] DS 261
[3] Creeds; T 1571
[4] DS 251
[5] DS 2803
[6] DS 3903

In the Council of Chalcedon (now Kadiköy, Turkey), in the year 451, the Church defined as follows:

Following the holy Fathers, therefore,
we all with one accord teach the profession of faith
in one and the same Son, Jesus Christ our Lord,
perfect both in His divinity and in His humanity,
truly God and truly man composed of body and rational soul;
consubstantial with the Father in His divinity,
consubstantial with us in His humanity,
like us in every respect except for sin (Heb 4:15);
in His divinity begotten of the Father before all ages,
in His humanity begotten of the Virgin Mary, the Mother of God,
in the last days for us and for our salvation.
We declare that the one selfsame Christ, only-begotten Son and Lord,
must be acknowledged in two natures
without commingling or change or division or separation;
that the distinction between the natures
is in no way removed by their union
but rather that the specific character of each nature is preserved
and they are united in one person and one hypostasis.
We declare that He is not split or divided into two persons,
but that there is one selfsame only begotten Son, God the Word, the Lord Jesus Christ.
This the prophets have taught about Him from the beginning;
this Jesus Christ Himself taught us;
this the creed of the Fathers has handed down to us.
As these truths, therefore, have been formulated with all possible accuracy and care,
the holy, ecumenical council has ordained that no one may bring forward or put into writing or devise or entertain or teach others any other faith.[7]

II

Jesus Christ, true God. The Church teaches solemnly that Jesus Christ is true God, the Second Person of the Most Holy Trinity, equal in all things to the Father. In the Nicene Creed she emphatically proclaims the divinity and co-eternity of the Son of God by saying that He is "born of the Father before all ages ... begotten, not made". When she says, "God from God, light from light, true God from true God", she means that He is "GOD the Son, born FROM GOD the Father, just as LIGHT comes FROM LIGHT; He is

---

[7] DS 301-3

TRUE GOD the Son, born FROM TRUE GOD the Father. In Part I, Ch. 5 & 6, we have already set forth the apologetic arguments from reason by which we can defend this great truth against the unbeliever.

Jesus Christ, true Man. The Church teaches solemnly that Jesus Christ is true Man with a body and a soul like ours. We have shown in Part I that, as Man, He belongs to authentic history. The Gospel record tells us that, like all men, He was born of a woman; that for the greater part of His life, He lived at Nazareth as the reputed son of Joseph the carpenter; that, in the three years of His ministry, He laboured and taught, journeying hither and thither, suffering fatigue, hunger and thirst, and showing the feelings and emotions of ordinary men—love, compassion, sorrow, anger, and fear; that, at length, He was seized by His enemies, tortured by them, and nailed to a Cross; that after His death He was taken down and laid in a tomb. While on this earth, He was subject, like us, to the infirmities of our nature, but, unlike us, He was subject to them not of necessity but of choice; and, unlike us, He was free from ignorance and all tendency to sin. Thus, e.g., when He was afraid in the Garden of Gethsemane (Mk 14:33) it was because He freely chose to afflict His soul with fear. As indications of these human emotions and reactions, note, e.g., the following texts: "Jesus wept (for Lazarus). So the Jews said, See how He loved him!" "When Jesus heard him, He marvelled". "He began to be sorrowful and troubled." "He looked around at them with anger, grieved at their hardness of heart". "He began to be greatly distressed and troubled."[8]

His mode of entry into this world manifests His two natures: born of no human father, the eternal Father alone being His Father, He is divine; born of the Virgin Mary, His true Mother, He is human. "Jesus was God on His Eternal Father's side, and Man on His Mother's side."[9]

The Hypostatic, or Personal, Union. (1) The Hypostatic, or Personal, Union means the union of the two natures, the divine and the human, in one Divine Person. In short, "person" answers the question, *who?*, "nature" answers the question, *what?*[10] As in us, soul and body are united in one man, so in Christ, but by a different kind of union, the two natures are united in one Person: the Person is the link by which the two natures are joined together. The two natures, the Council of Chalcedon solemnly teaches, while remaining perfectly distinct, are joined together in an unchangeable and inseparable union. The Hypostatic union began at the Annunciation when Christ was conceived in the womb of the Virgin, and

[8] Jn 11:35-6; Matt 8:10; 26:37; Mk 3:5; 14:33
[9] Rev. Arthur Klyber CSsR, *Queen of the Jews*, Remnant of Israel, 3050 Gap Knob Rd, New Hope, Kentucky 1998, p.36
[10] For the fuller meaning of *nature* and *person*, see pp.311-2.

will continue forever. It was not broken in the period between His death and Resurrection, for His Person remained united to His body in the sepulchre, and to His soul in limbo. (2) Christ acted sometimes by His human nature, sometimes by His divine nature, and sometimes by both together. He acted by His human nature, when, e.g., He walked or slept; by His divine nature, when, e.g., He cured the centurion's servant at a distance; by both natures together, when He consecrated the Blessed Eucharist: as Man, He took bread, blessed, broke, and gave to the Apostles, saying, "This is My Body"; as God, He changed the bread into His own sacred Flesh. Since Christ is one Person—and that one is a Divine Person—we can never call Him a human person.

The Holy Name. Since the Incarnation the Second Divine Person has a human as well as a divine nature, and, thus, incarnate, He is known as Jesus Christ. Jesus means, literally, "God saves" or "God is salvation." Used as a name, it may be interpreted "Saviour". The title, "Christ", is the Greek form[11] of the Hebrew, "Messiah." It means "the anointed one". In the Old Testament, men were anointed kings, priests, and sometimes prophets, as a sign of the sanctity of their office and their special consecration to God. Jesus is *par excellence* "the anointed"—"anointed", as St Peter says (Acts 10:38) "with the Holy Spirit and with power"—because He alone is the true king, priest, and prophet. He is called "Lord", in Greek "Kyrios" (Κυριος), used for the divine name "Yahweh" when the Hebrew Scriptures were translated into Greek three centuries before Christ. On the basis of this, we can say that "Jesus" is His personal name, "Christ" is His title of office, and "Lord" is His divine title.[12] It is customary for Catholics to bow their head slightly at the Holy Name of JESUS.

Rules of language flowing from the Incarnation. Because of the union of the two natures in Christ, it is true to say, e.g., that "God died on the Cross", or that "the Man Christ was omnipotent", the subject of each sentence being equivalent to "the Second Divine Person". Hence the rule that whenever, as in these sentences, either nature is so spoken of as to denote *simply* the Second Divine Person, the attributes of the other nature may be ascribed to it. This is what is technically known as "the interchange of predicates" (*communicatio idiomatum*). The rule shows us that the following statements are *wrong*: "God, as God, was crucified" ("God, as God" does not denote the Second Divine Person *simply*. It speaks of Him as He was in His divine nature, but it was not in that nature that He was crucified); "Christ as Man was omnipotent" ("Christ as Man" does not denote the Divine Person simply, but as He was in His human nature, and in that nature He was not omnipotent); "Man became God" (wrong because "man" denotes, not a Divine Person, but a human person: it says that someone who was at first a man

---

[11] Χριστος (Christos)
[12] Cf. C 209, 430, 436, 446.

Person, but a human person: it says that someone who was at first a man afterwards became God); "the humanity of Christ was divine", "the divinity was crucified" ("humanity" and "divinity" do not denote the Person of Christ but His natures). "Omnipotence itself died on the Cross": correct because "Omnipotence itself" would be understood to mean, "God Himself, God the Son".

The human knowledge, will, grace, and virtues of Christ. Difficulties answered.

THE HUMAN KNOWLEDGE OF CHRIST. The knowledge which Christ had through His *divine* nature was infinitely perfect. The knowledge which He had through His *human* nature was not infinite. It was of three kinds, viz., *experimental, infused,* and *beatific.*[13]

Christ's experimental (acquired) knowledge. His soul had the ordinary knowledge which men obtain in everyday life from the use of their senses and reason, by observing, listening, analysing, meeting people, reading, and so on.[14]

Christ's infused knowledge. "The Son in His human knowledge also showed the divine penetration He had into the secret thoughts of men's hearts. The human knowledge of Christ, on account of His union with divine Wisdom in the Person of the Word incarnate, enjoyed the fulness of knowledge of the eternal plans He had come to reveal."[15] Christ's soul was endowed with supernatural, prophetic and intuitive enlightenment enabling Him to know men's hearts, their dispositions and intentions, the past and the future. Thus He knew, for example: the unspoken objections of the Pharisees to His deeds; what the disciples were arguing about in His absence; the history of the Samaritan woman He met for the first time at Jacob's well; the death of Lazarus; the fact that the widow at the Temple was putting in her last coins; Simon Peter's future denials, repentance and martyrdom; His own death and Resurrection; the destruction of Jerusalem and the Temple within a generation; and the signs accompanying the end of the world.

Christ's heavenly knowledge (knowledge of vision). From the first moment of its existence, His soul enjoyed, like the angels and the blessed, the immediate vision of God, and in that vision beheld all things past, present, and to come. This knowledge was not infinite, but was as great as His created human intellect could receive. The Catechism teaches that the Son of God knew all things in His human mind, "*not by itself but by its union with the Word.*"[16] "Such is first of all the case with the intimate and immediate knowledge that the Son of God made man has of His Father."[17] That Christ on earth possessed this direct vision is taught also in various

---

[13] St Thomas, S.T., iii, q. 9
[14] Cf. C 472.
[15] C 473-4. Cf. Mk 2:8; Jn 2:25; 4:17-19, 29; 6:61.
[16] C473, quoting St Maximus the Confessor, *Quest. et dub.* 66
[17] C 473. Cf. Matt 11:27; Jn 1:18; 8:55.

encyclicals.[18] Our Redeemer never uttered His religious doctrine out of the conviction of *faith*, but from clear *knowledge*: "I speak of what I have seen with my Father".[19]

That Christ had heavenly and infused knowledge follows from His supreme dignity as the Word Incarnate. That He possessed experimental knowledge follows from the doctrine that He was true Man. Being true Man, He, like other men, made use of His faculties of sense and understanding. He used His eyes and ears; He observed facts, and drew conclusions from them. His experimental knowledge grew from day to day, like that of any ordinary man. However, all the knowledge so acquired was already in His possession through other channels. To adapt Himself to human conditions, He acted, as circumstances required, like common men. Thus, we may safely assume that, when a child, He allowed Himself to be taught by His Mother and St Joseph, as though He did not already know all things. Aquinas teaches that Christ did nothing but what befitted His years.[20] As we read in the Gospels, He asked questions as though seeking information, and sometimes expressed surprise at the answers He received. His experimental knowledge may be compared to His physical strength as Man. As His physical strength increased with years, so too did His experimental knowledge. As His physical strength was limited, so also was His experimental knowledge. Yet, as God, He was all-powerful and all-knowing.

CHRIST'S KNOWLEDGE OF US. "Jesus knew and loved us each and all during His life, His agony and His Passion, and gave Himself up for each one of us: the Son of God 'loved me and gave Himself for me.' He has loved us all with a human heart."[21] "He knew and loved us all when He offered His life."[22] "But the most loving knowledge with which the divine Redeemer has pursued us from the first moment of His Incarnation completely exceeds all the searchings of the human mind; for by means of that blessed vision, which He enjoyed as soon as He was received into the womb of the Mother of God, He has forever and continuously had present to Him all the members of the mystical Body, and embraced them with His saving love. ... In the manger, on the Cross, in the eternal glory of the Father, Christ sees and embraces all the members of His Church, and He sees them far more clearly, embraces them far more lovingly, than does a mother the child at her breast, and far better than a man knows and loves himself."[23]

CHRIST'S KNOWLEDGE OF HIMSELF. From the sources of Christ's knowledge given above, it is obvious that Christ knew who He was, and knew that He was true God and true Man. It is impossible that He who came to save us should Himself not

---

[18] Pius XI, *Miserentissimus Redemptor* 1928; Pius XII, *Mystici Corporis* 1943; Pius XII, *Haurietis Aquas* 1956: DS 3812, 3924

[19] Jn 8:38. Cf. Jn 1:18; 3:11; 3:31-5; 6:46; 7:29; 8:55; 10:15; Matt 11:27.

[20] S.T., iii, q. 12, a. 3, ad 3

[21] C 478. Cf. Gal 2:20.

[22] C 616

[23] Pope Pius XII in *Mystici Corporis*, 1943, Part II: DS 3812. Cf. St Thomas, S.T., iii, q. 34, a. 4.

know His own identity. The Gospels show Our Lord's perfect knowledge of Himself and His Mission: "Truly, truly, I say to you, before Abraham was, I AM.";[24] "The Son of man came … to give His life as a ransom for many."[25]

THE HUMAN WILL OF CHRIST. Being true Man, Christ had a human will like ours. He had the power of loving what His human mind represented to Him as good. Being true God, He also had a divine will. He had the power of loving what His divine mind represented to Him as good. His human mind was limited; so too His human will. His divine mind was unlimited; so too His divine will. With His divine will, He loved the Godhead with an infinite love; with His human will, He loved the Godhead, not with an infinite love, but with the highest love of which His sanctified human nature was capable. His human will was ever and in all things subject to His divine will: "I have come," He said, "not to do My own will",—i.e., His human will—"but the will of Him who sent Me."[26] His human will of its nature shrank from suffering: in the garden He cried out against the bitter chalice of pain and degradation, but He said, "Not My will, but Thine, be done."[27]

Although in Christ there were two distinct wills, each acting in its own proper way, there was but one Worker; there was but One, the Son of God—to whom the acts of both wills belonged. Hence, His least human act while He was on earth was the act of a Divine Person, and therefore of infinite value.

THE SINLESSNESS OF CHRIST. Our Blessed Lord was conceived without sin and remained free from sin all through His life. This follows necessarily from His being a divine Person. He who came to conquer Satan could not Himself be under his empire of sin in any way. In His Humanity, He was "tempted as we are, yet without sinning."[28] He claimed this sinlessness publicly: "Which of you convicts me of sin?"[29] Scripture attests to it several times, and the Church teaches the same.[30]

THE IMPECCABILITY (INABILITY TO SIN) OF CHRIST. Our Saviour was not only sinless but incapable of sin. Since sin always involves something against God, it is obvious that Christ, being God, did not, and could not, will or do something against Himself.[31]

---

[24] Jn 8:58; cf. Jn 10:30. "I AM" was the divine name revealed to Moses, "I AM WHO I AM" in Ex 3:14. Cf. C 205-6, 590.

[25] Matt 20:28

[26] Jn 6:38. The will here ascribed or appropriated to God the Father is of the Divine Nature and belongs equally to all Three Persons of the Blessed Trinity. It is the same as the divine will of Christ.

[27] Lk 22:42

[28] Heb 4:15

[29] Jn 8:46

[30] Jn 8:29; 14:30; 1 Jn 3:5; 1 Pet 2:22; 2 Cor 5:21; Heb 7:26. Cf. DS 261, 293, 301.

[31] Cf. DS 291, 434, 556.

THE CONSTITUTION OF CHRIST

One Divine Person		
The Son of God possessing:		-WHO
Two Natures joined in the Person		
DIVINE NATURE	HUMAN NATURE	
- GOD -	**- MAN -**	
Divine attributes: divine power, holiness, majesty etc.	Not Fused Not Changed Union but not Confusion	Complete, i.e., Body and Soul	-WHAT
Divine Intellect	Each Distinct & Perfect	*Human Intellect*
Divine Will	Not Divided	*Human Will*

CHRIST'S GRACE AND VIRTUES. As to the grace and virtues of our Divine Master, we must distinguish between habits and supernatural acts, between principles and effects. The works done by Him under grace, or His virtuous acts, were constantly growing into a larger total; but the source from which these acts flowed, the sanctifying grace indwelling in His soul, the grace that beseemed His dignity as the Man-God, did not, and could not, increase. "In Him dwells the Holy Ghost with such a fulness of grace that no greater can be conceived."[32]

Since Our Lord had direct knowledge and vision of the Godhead, it follows that He did not have the theological virtue of Faith, which is the blessing of "those who have not seen and yet believe".[33] Did Our Lord possess the virtue of Hope? If hope is the expectation of good, then in *some* things Our Lord did hope on earth: the establishment of the Kingdom of God, His achievement of the Redemption, His glorification and blessedness in His Resurrection, etc.[34] The virtue of Charity, of course, love of God and neighbour, He possessed supereminently.

The worship due to Christ as Man. Since Jesus Christ is a Divine Person, we owe Him not only as God but as Man, the supreme worship of adoration. Everything in His human nature is divine and adorable, because

---

[32] Pius XII, *Mystici Corporis*, Part I
[33] Jn 20:29
[34] Cf. S.T., iii, q. 7, a. 4.

it belongs to Him, the Second Person of the Blessed Trinity. But, to better excite our devotion, we may, in our act of adoration, fix our mind on Him, e.g., in relation to His Precious Blood, His Five Wounds, or His Sacred Heart. In thus adoring Him, we adore Him under so many different aspects, as it were: when we adore His Precious Blood, we adore it, not as distinct from Him, but as His own Blood which He shed for us; when we adore His Sacred Heart, we adore it, not as something apart from Him, but as the Heart symbolising the love He bears us as God and as Man. The Church invokes Christ Jesus under His various aspects in her approved Litanies: of the Holy Name, of the Sacred Heart, of the Precious Blood.

The devotion to the Sacred Heart has Biblical roots, grew greatly in the Middle Ages and later received a great impetus through a private revelation vouchsafed by Our Saviour to St Margaret Mary Alacoque (d. 1690), a nun of Paray-le-Monial, in Burgundy, France. It has been recommended by many Popes.[35]

DIFFICULTIES ANSWERED.
(1) "If Jesus was perfect from the beginning, what is meant by the words in the Gospel: 'And Jesus increased in wisdom and in stature and in favour with God and man' (Luke 2:52)?" REPLY: From the explanations given above, the answer may be easily deduced. Christ *as God* did not and could not make any advance; for, as God, He was and is infinitely perfect. But Christ *as Man* advanced in wisdom and favour, i.e., His experimental knowledge and the sum of His virtuous acts increased from day to day.

(2) "Christ as Man enjoyed the beatific vision. His happiness was greater than that of the angels. How then could He have suffered pain?" REPLY: Christ did not allow the happiness He enjoyed either as God or as Man to save Him from truly suffering. As a mountain-summit may be bathed in peaceful sunshine, while below the rocks are riven with the lightning, so Christ confined the enjoyment of the Beatific Vision within the higher part of His soul, while at the same time exposing all the rest of His human nature to the tempest of grief and affliction. This co-existence of joy with pain may be illustrated from the martyrs whose souls were filled with gladness in the midst of all their agony.

(3) "If He was not ignorant, then what did the Son of God mean when He said of the day of judgement, 'of that day or that hour no one knows, not even the angels in heaven, *nor the Son*, but only the Father.' (Mark 13:32)?" REPLY: There are two explanations, the second of which is preferable: (i) Christ knew the day and the hour in His human mind, but He did not have this knowledge *from His human nature*, His experimental knowledge.[36] (ii) Christ was using a mode of speaking— understood by His disciples, and therefore not deceptive—to express that He had not come to reveal the day and the hour of judgement. As He would tell them at

---

[35] Cf. *Haurietis Aquas*, Pius XII, 1956. See C 478.
[36] *Inter alia*, St Athanasius, *Contr. Arianos* III, 28

another time: "It is not for you to know times or seasons which the Father has fixed by His own authority."[37]

(4) "If Our Saviour was sinless, why was He baptised by John the Baptist?" REPLY: First, we must be clear that the baptism given by John prefigured Christian Baptism, but was *not* the Sacrament of Baptism. The Sacrament of Baptism removes sin and makes one a child of God. He who was the sinless and natural Son of God had no need of it, therefore. The baptism of John was a ritual cleansing to express repentance and the desire to be purified from sins in expectation of the Messiah. Jesus allowed Himself to be numbered among sinners and submitted to John's baptism to show that He had come to take our sins upon Himself and was prepared to undergo the later "baptism" of His death. St Maximus of Turin, in symphony with other Fathers, says, "Hence Christ was baptised, not so that He might be sanctified by the waters, but so that He Himself might sanctify the waters".[38] Christ's baptism illustrates what happens to us at our Baptism.

(5) "If Christ our Lord was incapable of sin, then what meaning have His temptations in the desert by the devil?" REPLY: A temptation is a test. Our Lord was tested by the devil, who pressured Him to desist from His mission. Just as a student who knows his subject perfectly cannot fail an examination but submits to a genuine test nevertheless, or just as a weightlifter will lift a heavy weight with effort and strength, so Jesus passed His tests and proved His love for God and His unfailing determination to fulfil the will of God, at whatever personal sacrifice. The difference between us and Him is that He did not have an orientation to evil. In these temptations, Christ conquered the devil on our behalf and gave us an example.

(6) "If Christ was truly God, what did He mean by saying, 'the Father is greater than I' (Jn 14:28)?" REPLY: St John, who records these words, also says that "the Word was God" (1:1), and records the confession of St Thomas, "My Lord and my God!" (20:28), and Our Lord's declaration, "Before Abraham was, I AM." (8:58). Clearly, then, these words cannot be a denial of divinity. There are two interpretations: (i) Christ was speaking *as man*, for in His Humanity and veiled glory, He was not equal to the Father. (ii) St Basil and others say the words mean that "the Son has His origin in the Father."[39] The Greek words for "greater than I"[40] mean here, "my origin, my principle". The words come from the Last Supper, when, as St John says (13:1,3), "Jesus knew that His hour had come to depart out of this world to the Father ... knowing that He had come from God and was going to God". The full sentence is, "If you loved me, you would have rejoiced, because I go to the Father; for the Father is greater than I"; that is to say: 'Although I am leaving you, if you loved me, you would be happy for me, because I am going home, to my Father, to

---

[37] Acts 1:7. Cf. C 474. Cf. St Thomas, S.T., iii, q. 10, a. 2, ad 1.

[38] *Sermo* 100 de sancta Epiphania. Cf. C 535-7.

[39] *Contra Eunom.* 1,25; St Gregory of Nazianzus, *Orat.* 30,7; St Cyril of Alexandria, *Thes. de. s. et con. Trin.*, assert. 11

[40] μειζων μου

my Origin, to the One from whom I came.' In the context, this is the preferable interpretation.

Errors.

1. Docetism (from Gk δοκεω, to seem) in the 1st and 2nd century said that Christ's human nature and sufferings were not real but only *seemed* to be so. It was condemned by several early Fathers. (C 465)

2. Arius, a priest of Alexandria in Egypt, denied the divinity of Christ. His teaching was condemned by the 1st General Council, the Council of Nicea (now Iznik, N.W. Turkey) in Bithynia, Asia Minor, in 325. (C 465)

3. Apollinaris, bishop of Laodicea in Syria, held that Christ had no rational soul, and that its place was supplied by His divinity. This teaching was condemned at the Synod of Alexandria in 362, by Pope Damasus in 375 and at the 2nd General Council, the first Council of Constantinople (now Istanbul, Turkey) in 381. (C 471)

4. Nestorius, Patriarch of Constantinople, refused to use the term *Theotokos* ("Mother of God") and was accused of teaching that there are not only two distinct natures in Christ, but two distinct persons; that Mary is the mother of Christ, the human person, but not the mother of God the Son, the Divine Person. The doctrine attributed to him was refuted by St Cyril, Bishop of Alexandria, Egypt, and condemned in 431 at the 3rd General Council, the Council of Ephesus (near modern Selçuk, Turkey), which defined that Mary is the Mother of God. (C 466)

5. Eutyches, a monk in Constantinople, erred in the opposite extreme by teaching that Christ was true God, but not true man; that He had but one nature, viz., His divine nature, and that His humanity was absorbed in His divinity like a drop of oil in the ocean. His teaching, commonly called the Monophysite heresy ("belief in one nature"), was condemned at the 4th General Council, the Council of Chalcedon (now Kadiköy, Turkey) in 451. (C 467)

6. The Monothelites (literally, "believers in one will") taught that Christ had but one will, the divine will. The 6th General Council, the third Council of Constantinople, in 681, condemned this error and defined that there are two distinct wills in Christ, the divine and the human. (C 475)

7. Some Protestants have proposed what is called the *Kenotic* theory (derived from the word *Kenosis*, from the text, "He emptied Himself"[41]), according to which God the Son is supposed to have "emptied Himself", so as to lay aside His omnipotence and omniscience when He became Man. Against this it is sufficient to say that, since Christ was God, and since God is unchangeable, Christ could never have parted with any of His divine attributes. The scriptural text simply means, as the words following it indicate, that God the Son humbled Himself by "taking the form of a servant". Pius XII condemned the error in *Sempiternus Rex* in 1951.

---

[41] Philipp 2:7, ἐκενωσεν

III

The three offices of Christ: Priest, Prophet, King.

CHRIST THE ONE MEDIATOR. By His Incarnation, God the Son is constituted the one Mediator between God and man.[42] As Mediator, He holds a threefold office: that of High Priest, Prophet, and King. Our Divine Redeemer Himself declared His threefold mission: "I am the Way (*King*), and the Truth (*Prophet*), and the Life (*Priest*)".[43]

SUPREME PROPHET. Unlike the Prophets, who announced the word of God, Christ Himself *is* the Word of God in Person. Endowed with fulness of knowledge, powers of miracle and prophecy, and impeccable holiness, He stands unique among teachers of the human race. He taught by discourses, parables, precept, miracles and example. The Apostles called Him "Master" and "Teacher", and He declared Himself to be "the light of the world."[44] He completed the Revelation made by God to the Jews and ordered it to be propagated to all mankind. He announced that certain practices given to the Jews were now over. He abolished abuses that had been tolerated, and taught a New Law that perfected the Old. He revealed the inner life of God the Holy Trinity and the means to become sharers in it. He gave a definitive Revelation that can never be superseded.

HIGH PRIEST. As High Priest *and Victim*, the Lord Jesus offers prayer and sacrifice, atones for sin, reconciles God and man, institutes sacraments, and communicates the divine life of grace. The exercise of Christ's priesthood is seen chiefly in the Redemption, covered in section B of this chapter; also in chapter 14B. In the New Testament, the Epistle to the Hebrews expounds the excellence of His priesthood.

UNIVERSAL KING. As King or Shepherd, He rules and guides His people by laws and example. His Kingship is prophesied in the Old Testament,[45] and proclaimed in the New: the angel Gabriel says, "He will reign over the house of Jacob for ever; and of His kingdom there will be no end." Jesus tells Pilate, "My kingship is not of this world. ... You say [*sc.*, rightly] that I am a King."[46] As Creator, and eternal Son of God, He is King by *natural* right. As our Redeemer, He is King by *acquired* right, for "you were bought with a price", "ransomed ... with the precious blood of Christ."[47] He holds

---

[42] Cf. 1 Tim 2:5.

[43] Jn 14:6

[44] Jn 8:12; cf. 12:46.

[45] e.g., 2 Sam 7:12-3; Ps 45 (44):6; Is 9:6-7; Dan 7:13-4

[46] Lk 1:33; Jn 18:36-7

[47] 1 Cor 6:20; 1 Pet 1:18-9

the threefold power: legislative, executive and judicial. He promulgates laws and demands obedience; He executes His decrees, imposes sanctions, and judges all men. His sovereignty is unlimited: "All authority in heaven and on earth has been given to me."[48] But His Kingdom is spiritual, "not of this world".[49] One enters it by faith and Baptism, lives in it by charity and penance, spreads it by word and example. His Kingdom is a "Kingdom of truth and of life; a Kingdom of holiness and of grace; a Kingdom of justice, love and peace."[50] He is King over our *minds*, for He is Truth itself and we must subject our thoughts to His doctrine and supreme knowledge. He is King over our *wills*, for by grace and inspiration, He subjects our free wills to the will of God. He is King in our *hearts* by reason of His love, kindness and mercy, which surpass all that we can ever imagine.[51]

The Kingship of Christ is celebrated each year on the Feast of Christ the King, on the last Sunday of Ordinary Time, the conclusion of the Church's year.[52]

In His Public Ministry, as He taught the disciples and the crowds, Our Lord mainly showed Himself as the supreme Prophet and Teacher. In Holy Week, He mainly exercised His High Priestly office, instituting the Holy Eucharist and the New Covenant, and undergoing the Passion to save mankind. In His Resurrection and Ascension, He especially manifests His glorious Kingship. Although we may separate them for the purposes of analysis, the three offices are closely connected. All three were, and are, exercised by Our Lord both on earth and in Heaven.

IV

The miracles of Christ. Their purpose and meaning.

THE MIRACLES OF CHRIST. The miracles of Christ[53] are integral to Christ's mission to reveal the Godhead, to announce the plan of salvation and to inaugurate the Kingdom of God. The purposes of the miracles are: to dispose witnesses and hearers to faith, to confirm the truth of the message and Messenger, and to illustrate Christ's teaching.[54]

Miracles are integral to Revelation. "This economy (plan) of Revelation is realised by deeds and words which are intrinsically connected

---

[48] Matt 28:18
[49] Jn 18:36
[50] *Roman Missal*, Preface of Christ the King
[51] *Quas Primas*, Pius XI, 1925, Encyclical on the Kingship of Christ: DS 3675-9
[52] In the *Missale Romanum* 1962, the Feast is on the last Sunday in October.
[53] listed on p.103.
[54] Cf. Vatican Council II: *Dei Verbum*, art. 4, Dogmatic Constitution on Divine Revelation, 1965; *Lumen Gentium*, art. 5, Dogmatic Constitution on the Church, 1964; *Dignitatis Humanae*, art. 11, Decree on Religious Liberty, 1965.

to each other, such that the deeds performed by God in the history of salvation manifest and confirm the doctrine and realities signified by the words, while the words proclaim the deeds and bring to light the mystery contained therein."[55] Christ's miracles are signs manifold in their meaning, which we may set out under the six headings below.

THE MEANING AND SIGNIFICANCE OF THE MIRACLES.[56] The miracles are divinely wrought signs indicative of many aspects of Christ and His mission: (1) *Signs of God's love.* At the most basic level, the miracles proceed from Christ's love and compassion towards human suffering and afflictions. They are a concrete revelation of God's love. Thus, for instance, Our Lord cured the man blind from birth and raised the widow's only son from death.[57]

(2) *Signs of the coming of the Kingdom.* The miracles announce that the Kingdom of God has come in the person of the Messiah, thus fulfilling the prophecy of Isaiah that the eyes of the blind will be opened, the deaf will hear, the lame and crippled will walk, the dead will be raised to life.[58] The miracles and exorcisms overcome Satan's reign and inaugurate the Kingdom of the all-powerful Messiah.

(3) *Guarantees of a divine mission and message.* A miracle or a prophecy distinguishes a true from a false prophet. "Rabbi, we know that you are a teacher come from God," said Nicodemus, "for no one can do these signs that you do, unless God is with him."[59] This is the *apologetic* value and purpose of the miracles.

(4) *Revelation of the divinity of Christ.* The miracles not only reveal that Jesus is sent by God, but that He is the eternal Son of the Father who can do the same works as the Father, such as forgive sins, and so make divine claims in all truth.[60]

(5) *Symbols of the sacramental economy.* "The miracle is the *carnal* dimension of the *spiritual* message."[61] It puts flesh on spiritual changes and claims: the forgiveness of sin—a change we cannot see—is symbolised by a visible change: the healing of a paralytic, the removal of leprosy. What paralysis or leprosy is to the body, sin is to the soul; and as it is to be delivered from such bodily afflictions, so it is to be forgiven one's sins. In overcoming the effects of sin, Christ confirms vividly that He is overcoming sin itself.[62] The

---

[55] *Dei Verbum*, art. 2
[56] Based on R. Latourelle S.J., *Theology of Revelation*, Alba House, N.Y. 1966, pp.390-403
[57] Lk 7:13; Jn 9
[58] Is 35:5-6; 29:18; 26:19. Cf. Lk 7:22.
[59] Jn 3:2. Cf. Jn 5:36-7.
[60] Jn 3:31-5; Lk 8:24-5; Mk 2:6-12
[61] R. Latourelle, *op. cit.*, p.403
[62] Mk 2:9-11

raisings from the dead symbolise spiritual resurrection. The sacraments are prefigured by the miracles. The miracle of healing the blind man, at the water of the pool of Siloam, prefigures the sacrament of Baptism which washes away sin and enables us to see Jesus with the eyes of faith.[63] The miracles of multiplying the loaves of bread prefigure the Eucharist, the Bread of Life which will be given to the believers by the Apostles. The cure of lepers prefigures the sacrament of Penance. The Apostles' anointing of the sick to heal them prefigures the sacrament of holy Anointing.[64] The outward sign signifies the inner cure, as in a Sacrament. The miraculous catch of fish is a sign of the future expansion of the Church.[65]

(6) *Signs of the transformation of the end-time.* The miracles are anticipations of the transformations to be effected in the human body and the universe at the end of time. The raisings from the dead announce and prefigure both Christ's own Resurrection and the general resurrection at the end of the world. In curing men of sicknesses, ills and afflictions, raising them from death itself, and pardoning sins, Christ is presaging the new heavens and the new earth where the just will have life and have it abundantly, and where men will live in perfect freedom as children of God, liberated from all evil and suffering, redeemed in body and soul.

These six aspects are not separate and independent; each of the miracles shows forth several or all aspects at the same time. The miracle of miracles, to which all the Gospel miracles point, is Jesus' own Resurrection. All the miracles are anticipations of the power of the Resurrection.

V

The veneration due to the B.V. Mary, to St Joseph and to the Saints. To God, and only to Him, we pay the worship of adoration, because His excellence is infinite and is all His own. We do not adore the saints, because they are mere creatures possessing nothing, not even their own existence, except as God's gift to them. Still we give them simple reverence, because they are His friends, and, in honouring them, we honour Him who is the source of all their blessedness. To Mary, as the highest and most glorious of all His creatures, we pay a special homage. She is the Mother of God; hence, all her dignity; hence, her other privileges, which we set out below. Next after her, we revere her spouse, St Joseph, the head of the household at Nazareth, to whom God Himself was obedient in the person of Jesus. Pope Leo XIII said that it is beyond doubt that St Joseph approached

---

[63] Jn 9
[64] Mk 6:13
[65] Lk 5:4-10; Jn 21:6-11

nearer than anyone else to the eminent dignity of the Mother of God.[66] Pope Pius IX in 1870 declared St Joseph 'Patron of the Universal Church'. His feast day is March 19.

The worship we pay to God is technically known as *latria*, the veneration given to the saints and angels is called *dulia*; the special veneration given to our Blessed Lady is called *hyperdulia*.

The Blessed Virgin Mary. HER IMMACULATE CONCEPTION means that her soul, from the very first instant of its existence, was free from the stain of Original Sin. This singular[67] privilege of hers was defined as a dogma[68] by Pius IX in 1854 and is celebrated on December 8 each year, nine months before the feast of her Nativity, September 8. Mary, the child of Joachim and Anna, was begotten in the ordinary human way, and, therefore, would have been stained with the sin of Adam, had not God given her soul sanctifying grace at her conception. This gift of grace was never diminished or lost by Our Blessed Lady. Throughout her life she remained free from the stain of even venial sin.[69]

By that sanctifying grace she was redeemed at the first moment of her being. It was a redemptive grace for which her Son was to pay by His death on the Cross. *We* were redeemed at out Baptism. Our redemption was a *healing* redemption, because it healed the sickness of Original Sin which had been present in our souls since our conception. Mary's redemption, on the other hand, was a *preventive* redemption, because it prevented that sickness from occurring. From this it is clear that to be conceived without sin did not mean that Mary had no need of a saviour. Rather, she was saved in the fullest possible way, *in anticipation*. Christ was her Saviour: "my spirit rejoices in God my *Saviour*."[70]

The fittingness of the Immaculate Conception: (a) As the new Eve, Mary, like Eve, was created in grace. (b) God had announced enmity between Satan and "the woman".[71] For this enmity to be complete, the new woman had to be completely free from Satan's dominion. (c) The Blessed Virgin Mary was made a fitting dwelling-place of the Most High by her Immaculate Conception; and it was fitting that from her humanity Christ drew His own human nature, which was "full of

---

[66] Encyclical *Quamquam Pluries*, 1889: DS 3260
[67] i.e., unique among *mere* human creatures after the Fall. Of course, Our Lord's conception was also immaculate, but this goes without saying.
[68] DS 2803. C 491
[69] T 1573. C 493
[70] Lk 1:47
[71] Gen 3:15

grace and truth".[72]   (d) Mary is the living image ("type") of the Church which is Christ's Bride, "without spot or wrinkle ... holy and without blemish".[73]

MARY, THE MOTHER OF GOD. Mary is the Mother of Christ. She is His Mother for the same reason that any other woman is the mother of her child. She is His Mother because He was conceived and nourished in her womb and was born of her. But her Son, Christ, is God; therefore Mary is the Mother of God,[74] as the Church solemnly defined in 431 at the Council of Ephesus (near modern Selçuk, Turkey).[75]   The Divine Maternity is celebrated in the liturgy on January 1.

There is no force in the objection that, since she did not give her Son His Divine Nature, she cannot be called the Mother of God. No woman gives her child all he has; no woman gives her child his spiritual soul—his soul is a direct gift from God. She is, nonetheless, her child's mother on that account. In ordinary conception, the first living cell, which subsequently is multiplied many times, contains elements from both parents. Therefore the body of a child comes from both parents, not the mother alone.   But since Christ had no human father but was conceived miraculously through the power of the Holy Ghost, His body came from but one source, the pure flesh of His Virgin Mother. Mary is no less her Child's Mother though His soul and Divinity did not come from her. Other women are justly called mothers of their sons, and Mary is justly called the Mother of God. Mary is the Mother of God, and God Himself made her worthy to be His Mother. Not only did He preserve her from the smallest taint of sin, but He poured out on her an abundance, beyond human comprehension, of grace and heavenly favours. He made her the second Eve, the Mother of the Living, the Mother of all those who were to be restored by her Son to the life of divine friendship. He has raised her to be the Queen of Heaven. He has given her a dignity incomparably higher than that of the highest of His Angels.

To remove any gross misconceptions: "Mother of God" does not mean eternal, or greater than God. "Mother of God" means "Mother of God the Son made man". It does not mean Mother of God the Father, nor Mother of God the Holy Ghost. The rejection by Protestants of the term "Mother of God" can only mean that they believe that (1) Jesus is not God, or (2) Mary is not His Mother, or (3) that Nestorianism was right to split Christ into two persons, and that Mary is the Mother of the human one. - Orthodox Protestants would reject all three errors, and yet illogically resist the Catholic term. If Jesus is God, and Mary is His Mother, then she is the Mother of God. For this reason St Elizabeth hailed her as, "the mother of my Lord".[76]

---

[72] Jn 1:14

[73] Eph 5:27

[74] In Greek, θεοτοκος (Theotokos: "God-bearer"); in Latin, *Dei Genetrix* or *Deiparens* or *Mater Dei*.

[75] Ephesus was the site of Our Lady's home with St John, rediscovered by archaeologists in 1891.

[76] Lk 1:43

The intellect of the Virgin Mary was not excluded from the influence of her sublime gifts. God owed it to His honour that, in all that knowledge by which the human mind is ennobled, Mary should surpass the rest of mankind. Though seemingly but a poor peasant woman, busy about the daily tasks of her humble household, she was full of divine wisdom, because she was full of divine grace. She saw more clearly than any saint or sage or scientist the manifestation of the Creator's glory in the realm of nature, and she had a vision of the beauty of His world to which no poet can ever attain.[77]

BLESSED MARY EVER-VIRGIN. The Church professes the perpetual virginity of Our Lady.[78] Jesus Christ is her first-born and only child, just as He is the first-born of all creation (Col. 1:15) and the Only Begotten of the Father (Jn 1:18). At the time of her espousal to St Joseph, Mary intended to remain a virgin. This is clear from her question at the angel's announcement that she, who was shortly to marry, was to conceive a child. "How can this be?" she asked—a meaningless question unless she had intended life-long virginity.[79]

THE ASSUMPTION. At the end of her earthly life, Our Blessed Lady was assumed body and soul into the glory of Heaven. The Assumption is celebrated each year on August 15. It was celebrated in Eastern and Western liturgies for many centuries before being defined a dogma by Pius XII in 1950.[80] The Pope deliberately left open the question of whether or not Our Lady died before her Assumption. The more common teaching of the Fathers is that she did.

The prophet Elijah was taken to heaven in a fiery chariot, in the sight of Elisha.[81] Did anyone witness the Assumption of the Virgin Mary? Possibly Saint John, but we do not know for certain. In any case, he witnesses to it in symbolic language in the Apocalypse: "Then God's temple in heaven was opened, and the *ark of His covenant* was seen within His temple ... And a great portent appeared in heaven, *a woman* clothed with the sun..." (11:19-12:1). The first Ark of the Covenant,[82] in which God dwelt in a special way, mysteriously disappeared. Mary is the new Ark of the Covenant,[83] who has also mysteriously disappeared from this earth. St John testifies that she is to be found in heaven.

While the early Church jealously guarded and venerated the relics of the martyrs and other saints, there is no tradition of relics of the Mother of God.

---

[77] Cf. St Albertus Magnus, *Mariale*, qq. 96-111, ed. Borgnet, vol. 37.

[78] C 499

[79] Giuseppe Ricciotti, *The Life of Christ*, Bruce, Milwaukee 1947, p.227

[80] DS 3903. C 966

[81] 2 Kgs 1:11-12

[82] Ex 25-27

[83] St Luke 1:43,56 parallels 2 Sam 6:9-11. "Ark of the Covenant" is one of the invocations in the Litany of Loreto.

MARY, MOTHER OF THE CHURCH AND OF ALL CHRISTIANS. *Mary our Mother.* "Mary became the Mother of Christ and our Mother when to the Angel's salutation she pronounced her meek assent, 'Behold the handmaid of the Lord: be it done to me according to thy word.' That motherhood of hers was proclaimed at the moment when it reached its complete expansion, that is, when Redemption was consummated. In the midst of the sorrows of Calvary Jesus said to her from the cross: 'Woman, behold thy son', and to St John: 'Behold thy Mother.' Through St John, these words were addressed to all the elect. Fully co-operating by her consent and sorrows in this spiritual birth of mankind, Mary became in the fullest and most perfect sense our Mother."[84]

"The Redeemer entrusts His mother to the disciple, and at the same time He gives her to him as his mother. Mary's motherhood, which becomes man's inheritance, is a gift: *a gift which Christ Himself* makes personally to every individual."[85]

"Suffering with her Son as He died on the cross, she co-operated in a wholly singular way by her obedience, faith, hope and burning charity, in the work of the Saviour to restore supernatural life to souls. For this reason she became a Mother to us in the order of grace. This motherhood of Mary in the order of grace continues uninterruptedly, from the consent which she gave in faith at the Annunciation and which she sustained without wavering beneath the cross, until the eternal fulfilment of all the elect. For, assumed into Heaven, she did not lay aside this saving office but by her manifold intercession continues to procure for us the gifts of eternal salvation."[86]

Mary Mother of the Church. In 1964, Pope Paul VI said, "We declare Mary Most Holy *Mother of the Church*, that is, of the entire Christian people, both faithful and Pastors".[87] The Blessed Virgin Mary "now continues to fulfil from Heaven her maternal function by which she co-operates in the birth and development of divine life in the individual souls of redeemed men. This truth both furnishes matter for the greatest consolation, and by the free will of God most wise, is an integral part of the mystery of human salvation; for which reason it must be held as faith by all Christians."[88]

MARY, MEDIATRIX OF GRACES. (a) Mary is called the Mediatrix of all Graces, because she is the Mother of the Redeemer who, by His Blood, has purchased all the graces that have been given, or shall be given, to man since the Fall. (b) Mary is the Mediatrix of Grace in another sense also. She became the spiritual Mother of

---

[84] *The Official Handbook of the Legion of Mary*, Ch. 5, sect. 4, Concilium Legionis Mariae, Dublin
[85] *Redemptoris Mater*, Pope John Paul II, 1987, no. 45
[86] *Lumen Gentium*, Dogmatic Constitution on the Church, Vatican Council II, 1964, art. 61-2
[87] Discourse, 21 Nov. 1964
[88] *Signum Magnum*, Pope Paul VI, 13 May 1967, Part I

men at the instant of the Incarnation, and received that title from her Son while He was dying on the Cross. Hence the belief that it is "through her hands" we receive all the graces that we seek in prayer, all the graces that lead us to the Sacraments and prepare us for their worthy reception. (c) God, in giving us Mary as our Mother—Mother of Bethlehem, Mary of Cana, Mary who stood beside the Cross—appeals to the human nature He has given us, which is so responsive to the name of "mother". It is His will that through Mary we should learn a little of the infinitely greater tenderness of His own love for us. (d) Mary never asks God for anything except what has been gained for us by her Divine Son; nor does she ask God for anything except what He Himself has inspired her to ask.

Classic Protestant objections to Catholic teaching on the Blessed Mother.

(1) "St Paul says, 'all have sinned' (Rom 3:23). Therefore, Mary too was subject to sin." REPLY: If he is speaking of *personal sin*, St Paul need not be referring to absolutely everyone; certainly he meant to exclude Christ, as well as innocent children. The Blessed Mother is simply another exception. However, his meaning is, as the full sentence shows, that all the members of the fallen human race are in need of the Redemption achieved by Christ. This, we agree, applies to Mary also.

(2) "Mary cannot be ever-virgin, since the New Testament speaks of the 'brothers of Jesus' (e.g. Matt 12:46) and 'His sisters' (e.g. Mk 6:3)." REPLY: Among the Jews, "brother" could mean blood-brother, brother-in-law, cousin, second cousin, relative, or even close friend. In some countries of Africa and Asia today, the word "brother" is used in the same broad sense. Hebrew and Aramaic, the Jewish languages used by Christ, had no particular word for "cousin". In St Matthew's Gospel, James and Joseph are called "brothers" of Jesus (13:55), but are the sons of a follower of Christ (27:56) whom St Matthew calls "the other Mary" (28:1), the wife of Clopas (Jn 19:25). If Christ had blood brothers, other sons of Mary, there would have been no need to entrust His mother to St John.[89] In the early Church barely anyone questioned the Catholic teaching on this point until a man called Helvidius about the year 380. He was solidly refuted by St Jerome.

---

[89] Cf. C 500.

B

THE REDEMPTION

Summary

I.   The solemn teaching of the Church.
II. Atonement and Redemption defined. God chose to save us by a copious Redemption; why God chose to redeem us in this way.
III. Christ proclaimed Himself our Redeemer; Christ, a willing Victim, suffered and died for us. The Redemption a mystery. Christ's work for our salvation, considered under four aspects: as a work of *satisfaction, redemption, merit,* and *sacrifice.* The prayers and supplications of Christ. His descent to the dead.
IV. The Resurrection and Ascension: completion of the Redemption. Christ's Risen Body. The significance of the Resurrection, the third day and Sunday; the Sunday precept; the Church's celebration of the Resurrection; the Resurrection wrought by the Holy Trinity. The Ascension. Pentecost.
V.   The application of the Redemption. The Cross in our life. The victory of Christ a cause for rejoicing. Personal devotion to Christ.

I

The solemn teaching of the Church. The Church teaches solemnly:

(1) that our Lord Jesus Christ, by His life and by His sufferings which ended in His death on the Cross, made satisfaction for our sins and merited for us grace and eternal life;[1]
(2) that Christ offered Himself on the Cross as a true and proper sacrifice;[2]
(3) that Christ died for all without exception, not only for the elect;[3]
(4) that in His soul, He descended to the dead;[4]
(5) that, in His body, He rose again on the third day, ascended into Heaven into divine glory, and thence sent the Holy Spirit upon the Church.[5]

II

Atonement and Redemption defined. Literally, atonement is reparation for an offence. It consists in undoing an insult or injury, or in causing offender and offended to be again *at one*, i.e., to be reunited in affection (at-one-ment). Redemption is deliverance from captivity effected by purchase. As applied to the work of Christ, the *Atonement* means: (a) the satisfaction

---

[1] The Creeds; T 1528-9, 1560-1
[2] DS 261; T 1739, 1743, 1754
[3] DS 2005. Cf. T 1522; 2 Cor 5:15; 1 Tim 2:6.
[4] Creeds. L 801
[5] Creeds

which Christ made to God for the insults offered to Him by the sin of Adam and the sins of all mankind, and (b) the reconciliation between God and man which He thereby effected. The *Redemption* means (a) the deliverance of man from slavery to Satan and from the debt of eternal punishment incurred by sin, and (b) his restoration to the dignity of the divine sonship. Either term, therefore, may be used to denote the entire saving work of Christ. As we shall see further on, we can also describe Christ's work for us on the Cross as a work of merit and as a work of sacrifice. "The Redemption has as many angles to it as liberation from sin has: if sin is a fall, redemption is raising up the fallen person; if sin is illness, redemption is a cure; if sin is a debt, redemption is payment, purchase, ransom; if sin is a fault, redemption is atonement; if sin is slavery, redemption is liberation; if sin is an offence against God, redemption is satisfaction, propitiation, reconciliation with God."[6]

The mystery of Christ's Death and Resurrection is also known as the "Paschal Mystery", because the Blood of Christ, the new Lamb of God, delivers us from sin, in fulfilment of the Paschal (= Passover) Lamb which was sacrificed and eaten by the Jews at the annual commemoration of that first Passover in Egypt, when God "passed over" and thus spared the houses marked with the blood of the lamb.[7] As Moses led the Hebrews from slavery in Egypt under the Pharaoh, to the Promised Land, so Christ the King of Israel leads His People from the slavery of sin under the devil to the Kingdom of Heaven in eternity.

We call Christ our "Saviour" for He has saved us, in essence, from four things: (1) sin (2) death (3) hell, and (4) the devil. We are saved from *sin* because, by His death, Christ expiated all sin and won forgiveness for us. We are thereby saved from *death*, the consequence of sin, for Christ has won eternal life for us and a future resurrection. In being saved from sin, we are thereby saved from *hell*, separation from God, where original and mortal sin would have left us. Christ has transferred us to the Kingdom of light and thus delivered us from sin's instigator, the *devil*, whom He conquered upon the cross, despoiling him of any lasting power over us.

God chose to save us by a copious Redemption. God, at the prompting of the divine mercy, and under no compulsion of justice, resolved to restore mankind to His favour. He might have effected His purpose in many ways. He might, for instance, without exacting anything from us, have freely admitted us once more to His friendship; or He might have been pleased to accept as sufficient atonement the acts of penance which we ourselves could

---

[6] F. Ocáriz, et al., *The Mystery of Jesus Christ*, Four Courts, Dublin 1994, p.271
[7] Cf. Ex 12; Jn 1:29; 1 Cor 5:7.

perform. But He chose none of these ways. He chose the way of superabundant redemption, so that we might do more than discharge the debt we owed Him because of our sins, and should fully earn the recovery of His friendship. For such a redemption, the following conditions were required:

(1) that the atonement should be made by a representative of the human race;

(2) that the atonement should be freely made;

(3) that the atonement should be made by one pleasing to God, and not himself bound to any reparation; and, above all,

(4) the atonement should be more pleasing to God than sin had been displeasing to Him.

Now, in our Redeemer Christ, the Son of God made Man, all these conditions were fulfilled:

(1) As Man, He represented the human race, and made Himself answerable for our sins: "The Lord has laid on Him the iniquity of us all";[8]

(2) He made the atonement freely: "No one takes (my life) from me, but I lay it down of my own accord."[9]

(3) He was pleasing to God because He was God's beloved Son; He was without sin, and was, therefore, not bound Himself to any form of reparation; and

(4) the atonement was more than equal to the offence, since every act offered by Christ on our behalf, as being the act of a Divine Person, the Son beloved of the Father, was infinitely precious in the sight of God, and availed to blot out all the sins that man had ever committed or could ever commit.

St Thomas and many theologians hold that, if we suppose God to have required of man full satisfaction for sin, the incarnation of one of the Divine Persons was necessary. They argue as follows: "Man had committed grave sin. Grave sin is infinite in malice, and could be repaired only by an act of infinite worth. An act of infinite worth is beyond the power of mere man. Hence, it was necessary that there should be a God-Man who, as Man, could truly represent, and act for, the human race, and who, as God, could perform an act of atonement infinite in value." This reasoning is based on the following principles: (1) An insult is measured by the dignity of him who is insulted; therefore, the insult of mortal sin is infinite, since the dignity of God is infinite. (2) An honour is measured by the dignity of him who confers it. Therefore, any good deed that mere man, even though aided by grace, could perform as an agreeable offering to God would be finite, and, hence, insufficient to atone for a grave sin.

---

[8] Is 53:6
[9] Jn 10:18

Why God chose to redeem us in this way. God exacted this form of Redemption to show His boundless love for us, to make us understand the hatefulness of sin, and to move our hard hearts: "God is love"; i.e., God is love itself—"In this the love of God was made manifest among us, that God sent His only Son into the world, so that we might live through Him";[10] "God, who is rich in mercy, out of the great love with which He loved us, even when we were dead through our trespasses, made us alive together with Christ"[11]—i.e., God, out of His great love for us, has, through Christ, raised us from the grave of sin to the life of grace, so that, united as brothers to His own Divine Son, we may return His fatherly love for us.

III

Christ proclaimed Himself our Redeemer. Christ Himself tells us that He came into the world to obtain pardon for our sins, and to give us a new spiritual life. "The Son of Man came", He said, "to save the lost"[12] and "to give His life as a ransom for many."[13] And again our Saviour declared: "I came that they may have life, and have it abundantly."[14] To Nicodemus, He said: "As Moses lifted up the serpent in the wilderness, so must the Son of Man be lifted up, that whoever believes in Him may have eternal life",[15] i.e., as the brazen serpent had to be set up to heal the wounds of the Israelites, so Christ had to be lifted up on the Cross to cure mankind of sin, and to give them the new life of sanctifying grace. "You were ransomed", says St Peter, "not with perishable things such as silver or gold ... but with the precious blood of Christ ... Christ also suffered for you ... He Himself bore our sins ... that we might die to sin and live to righteousness",[16] i.e., should live to be just men, the friends and sons of God. So, too, St Paul's epistles are filled with the doctrine of the Redemption as an atonement for sin and as the means of restoring us to friendship with God: "while we were enemies we were reconciled to God by the death of His Son";[17] "Blessed be the God and Father of our Lord Jesus Christ ... He destined us

---

[10] 1 Jn 4:8-9

[11] Eph 2:4-5

[12] Matt 18:11

[13] Matt 20:28

[14] Jn 10:10

[15] Jn 3:14-15. When the Israelites in the wilderness murmured against God, He "sent fiery serpents among the people, and they bit the people, so that many people of Israel died. And the people came to Moses, and said: 'We have sinned, for we have spoken against the Lord and against you; pray to the Lord, that He take away the serpents from us.' So Moses prayed for the people." God told Moses to make a brazen serpent, and set it up. God said: "every one who is bitten, when he sees it shall live". Num 21:5-8.

[16] 1 Pet 1:18-19; 2:24

[17] Rom 5:10

in love to be His sons through Jesus Christ ... In Him we have redemption through His blood."[18]

Christ, a willing Victim, suffered and died for us. CHRIST WAS A WILLING VICTIM. Christ was eager to shed His Blood for us. When He told His Apostles that "He must go to Jerusalem and suffer many things from the elders and chief priests and scribes, and be killed", St Peter, with warm-hearted solicitude for His Master, "began to rebuke Him, saying: 'God forbid, Lord! This shall never happen to you.'" But Jesus turned on him sharply and said: "Get behind Me, Satan. You are a hindrance to Me; because you are not on the side of God, but of men."[19] Peter was a scandal or obstacle, because with thoughtless compassion he sought to dissuade Him from entering on the way of the Cross. Again, He said: "I have a baptism to be baptized with; and how I am constrained until it is accomplished!"[20] "Constrained", because distressed with eagerness. The baptism of which He spoke was the baptism, or bathing, of His limbs in His precious Blood.

CHRIST SUFFERED AND DIED FOR US. While He prayed at night in the Garden of Gethsemane, He said: "My soul is very sorrowful, even to death."[21] He did not allow His Divinity to spare His human Heart a single pang. He suffered as though He were not God. Nay, He suffered all the more because He was God, because His human mind was divinely enlightened, and His human will divinely inspired. His human mind had before it a vision of all the torments in store for Him, and of the sins for which His Blood was to atone. His human will, freely but with intense agony, consented that He should bear all that was to befall Him, and that He should feel all the shame and filth and horror of our sins. How cruel the affliction of a good father or mother, when word comes of a son's or daughter's disgrace! And as the shame of a child's sin stabs his poor parents to the heart, so, but infinitely more because of His greater love and His greater sensitivity to everything evil, did our sins afflict the Heart of our brother Jesus. That Heart, the throne of innocence, the well-spring of love, was now forced to feel all the foulness of the wicked world, and began to throb with a vehemence beyond its nature, sending forth the Blood with such violence that it burst through the pores, streaming in great drops to the ground. He grieved for our sins and did penance for them, as though

---

[18] Eph 1:3-7
[19] Matt 16:21-23
[20] Lk 12:50
[21] Mk 14:34

He Himself—if we dare say it—were the sinner.[22] For our sake, as the Apostle Paul conveys, He became a thing accursed.[23] And on the morrow He was led from court to court, buffeted, spat upon, scourged at a pillar, crowned with thorns, stripped of His clothes in the sight of His Mother and all the people and nailed to a cross. There He hung, the gentlest, the kindest, the noblest of men, as though He were a criminal whose infamous deeds had justified the utmost savagery, "despised and rejected by men; a man of sorrows", as though He were "stricken, smitten by God, and afflicted. He poured out His soul to death, and was numbered with the transgressors; yet He bore the sin of many, and made intercession for the transgressors."[24] - "It is finished",[25] He said, and, bowing His head, He died. The work for which He had come was done. He had paid the penalty for our sins, and purchased for us the privilege of becoming the children of God.

The Redemption a mystery. It involves the mysteries of the Trinity and the Incarnation. It is in itself a mystery of love. We cannot understand how God loved the world so much that He suffered His Divine Son to become man and die for us. Sin is also a mystery. We speak of sin as an "offence against God", as "an insult to God", as "exciting the wrath of God", but God is unchangeably happy, and no creature can touch Him, disturb Him, or assail Him in any way; and yet the effects produced in us by sin are as though we had done all this. The creature who strikes at his Creator does not strike the Creator but himself. Sin therefore of its nature is a suicidal act. The dreadful harm it does can be known only through what faith teaches of the sufferings of Christ to repair it.

Christ's work for our salvation, considered under four aspects. The entire work accomplished for us by Christ on the cross may be considered under four aspects: (1) as a work of satisfaction or atonement, (2) as a work of redemption or ransom, (3) as a work of merit, and (4) as a work of sacrifice.[26]

(1) CHRIST'S WORK OF SATISFACTION OR ATONEMENT. Satisfaction is a reparation, equal to the offence, made to the person offended. Its value depends on the dignity of the one who makes it. Adam, by his sin, had offered a grievous insult to God. Christ, as the new Adam, the spiritual head of the human race, made satisfaction for that sin and for all the sins that had been, or would be, committed by men till the end of the world. His

---

[22] See Cardinal Newman, *Discourses to Mixed Congregations*, pp.324-342, Mental Sufferings of our Lord.

[23] Gal 3:13

[24] Is 53

[25] Jn 19:30

[26] St Thomas, S.T., iii, q. 48, aa. 1-4

satisfaction more than sufficed for its purpose, because it was of infinite value, because He, as a Divine Person, the infinitely beloved of His Father, was of infinite dignity.

(2) CHRIST'S WORK OF REDEMPTION OR RANSOM. Both "ransom" and "redemption" come from the Latin, *redemptio*, a buying back, release by purchase. A ransom is a price paid for the deliverance of a captive. Because of grievous sin, man lay under the sentence of eternal punishment, and had become a slave of the devil, exposed to all his assaults, and powerless to obtain that divine grace by which alone he can be vanquished. Christ delivered us from this cruel bondage: He paid the full price of our liberation. God's justice had demanded that the wrongful pleasure which men get from sin should be balanced or blotted out by its equivalent in voluntary suffering. That equivalent was paid to Him by His own Son in the supreme agony of the Cross. It was a payment which sufficed, in strict justice, to extinguish, for Adam and all his posterity, the debt of eternal punishment and of servitude to Satan.

St Thomas says Christ resolved to deliver us from sin, not merely by His power, but by a process of justice. Hence, though He knew that, from the fact that He was God, His smallest suffering would have more than sufficed to save us, He willed, in conformity with the will of His Father, that His human nature should exhaust itself in the agony of a just reparation.[27]

(3) CHRIST'S WORK OF MERIT. A work of merit is a work that gives a just claim to a supernatural reward. A supernatural reward is a blessing, happiness, or honour to which no creature, man or angel, could ever attain by his natural powers. For a work of merit, it is required: (1) that it be the act of a living man, (2) that it be freely done, (3) that it be in itself virtuous, (4) that the one who performs it should be a friend of God, and (5) that God should have promised the reward. Adam by his sin had become an enemy of God, incapable of a work of merit, and, therefore, unable ever to recover of his own power the gift of divine sonship which he had lost for himself and his descendants. But Christ, the new Adam, the Father of spiritual life, as the first Adam had been the father of spiritual death, came into the world to rescue the human race from its unhappy condition. His work of Redemption was a work of merit: (1) it was the work of a living Man subject to mortality; (2) it was freely done: "I lay (my life) down of my own accord. I have power to lay it down, and I have power to take it again";[28] (3) it was a work of supreme charity: "Greater love has no man

---

[27] S.T., iii, q. 46, a. 6, ad 6
[28] Jn 10:18

than this, that a man lay down his life for his friends.";[29] it was commanded by the Father: Christ said in the Garden: "not My will, but *Thine*, be done";[30] (4) Christ was the beloved Son of God; (5) the reward, viz., the recovery of divine sonship, was promised, for He had been sent to us "that they may have life, and have it abundantly,"[31] that we might be made one with Him as He is one with the Father.[32]

But Christ merited not only for us but for Himself. By humbling Himself even unto the death of the Cross, He acquired a just claim to His glorious Resurrection: "He humbled Himself and became obedient unto death, even death on a cross. Therefore God has highly exalted Him and bestowed on Him the name which is above every name".[33]

(4) CHRIST'S WORK OF SACRIFICE. In every sacrifice a suitable victim is offered to God by a priest, specially appointed by Him, to express the homage which the creature owes to his Creator.[34] The priest speaks to God in the name of the people; and the victim or gift which he places in God's hands represents the desire of the people to give themselves to God—i.e., to surrender themselves, in loving adoration and submission, to their Lord and Creator. Fallen man was unfit for the office of priest. Fallen man could find no suitable victim, no victim acceptable to God. Adam had made it impossible for himself and his sin-stained descendants to offer to God the supreme worship due to Him. (The priests of the Old Law were mere types or figures of Christ, and their sacrifices only shadows of the Sacrifice of the Cross). But Christ intervened on our behalf. He became our Priest and our Victim. As both Priest and Victim, infinitely pleasing to God, He discharged fully and perfectly the debt of worship that we owed. But, since man had sinned, it was necessary that the sacrifice should be one, not of simple adoration, but of adoration expressing itself in the form of propitiation or appeasement. Christ, both as Priest and as Victim, represented the whole human race: with Adam and all his posterity before His mind, He adored and appeased His Father, as though each one of us were speaking through His lips. In the name of each one of us, He offered to His Father, as an atoning gift, His bitter sufferings together with all the love and the grief of His human heart. Christ offered His sacrifice for the remission of sin. He could not have offered it for Himself: this is the teaching of the Council of Ephesus.[35] Nevertheless, by the human

---

[29] Jn 15:13
[30] Lk 22:42
[31] Jn 10:10
[32] Jn 17:22
[33] Philipp 2:8-9
[34] Sacrifice is dealt with more fully in Chapter 14B.
[35] DS 261

obedience which led Him to the Cross, He merited glory for Himself as man.[36]

Note. The outstanding feature in the works of atonement and ransom is our deliverance from evil; in the work of merit, it is our restoration to God's grace and friendship; in the work of sacrifice, it is Christ's substitution of Himself for each one of us in His acts of adoration and in His propitiatory sufferings. Yet, as already intimated, in each of the four works, if we look closely, we can see the entire work of Christ.

THE PRAYERS AND SUPPLICATIONS OF CHRIST. Nothing that has been said in this section should obscure the truth that the Man, Christ, was God Himself. His prayers and supplications were utterly unlike ours. Since He was God omnipotent, He need not have prayed for anything. Why then did He pray? Because He, in union with the Father and the Holy Spirit, decreed that, as Man, not only should He drink the chalice of suffering to the dregs, but that He should also cry out as a poor supplicant from the abyss of degradation and anguish, and should urge His human soul to the very limit of its power in the vehemence and ardour of His appeal for each one of us. Thus, His appeal was as real as His sufferings. It was a true human cry for mercy, though He, as God, had willed beforehand that it should be heard. Thus, we can understand why Christ prayed for Himself, why, e.g., He prayed that He might be glorified. He prayed, because He with the Father and the Holy Spirit had decreed that He should do so, and that He, as Man, should receive the glory of the Resurrection in answer to His prayer.

When He cried out, "My God, my God, why hast Thou forsaken me?", did Christ despair?[37] Since despair is a sin, this is an impossibility on the part of Christ. It was also impossible that the Eternal Father should truly forsake His Son. Why, then, did He utter that heart-rending cry? First, to indicate the depths of His anguish and desolation. Secondly, He uttered it on our behalf, in solidarity with us sinners who are far from God and the consolation of union with God. More significantly, it was the opening line of Psalm 22 (21), well known to the Jews, a prophetic psalm speaking of the sufferings of a just man who will be delivered by God.[38]

Christ addressed His prayers to God the Father, but, while doing so, He was also addressing them to Himself, the Son, and to the Holy Spirit. So, too, with His Sacrifice: He did not offer it to the Father alone, but to the Father as united to the other two Divine Persons. The Church too in some of her prayers offers the Holy Sacrifice to God the Father; in others she offers it to the Blessed Trinity. Compare the old prayers at Mass, 'Suscipe sancte Pater' and 'Suscipe sancta Trinitas'. Cf. also

---

[36] Cf. St Thomas, S.T., iii, q. 22, a. 4, ad 2.
[37] Mk 15:34
[38] Cf. C 603. The reader ought to read the Psalm in full. It is no. 22 or 21, depending on one's version of the Bible. It was written about one thousand years before Christ.

the Byzantine Liturgy, "For it is You, O Christ our God, Who offer and are offered, *Who receive* and are given".[39]

Jesus descended to the dead. Death is the separation of soul from body. Upon His death, the soul of Jesus descended to the realm of the dead, the "Limbo of the Fathers", also called "the bosom of Abraham",[40] where those like Abraham who had died in faith and grace awaited the Redemption so that they could enter Heaven. The Apostles' Creed mentions this event when it says, "He descended into hell"[41]—which means not the hell of the damned, but 'hell' as the abode of the dead deprived of the vision of God and awaiting entry into Heaven. This abode is called *Sheol* in Hebrew or *Hades* in Greek.[42] St Peter says, "the Gospel was preached even to the dead".[43] Christ the "Lord both of the dead and of the living"[44] descended to the dead to announce the accomplishment of the Redemption and to shed His glorious light upon the just who had preceded Him.

IV

The Resurrection and Ascension: completion of the Redemption. Christ's risen Body and the import of the Resurrection. Sunday, the new Sabbath. Pentecost.

Jesus did not come simply to die, but to die *and rise again*. The *fact* of His Resurrection is treated in *Apologetics* (Ch. 7, II). Here we deal with the condition of His Risen Body and the saving significance of the Resurrection. The essence of the Resurrection is the *reunion* of Christ's soul with His body, which were separated at death.

CHRIST'S RISEN BODY. Risen from the dead, Christ the Lord was immune from all suffering and enjoyed the other perfections of the glorified body: the body being totally at the command of the soul, He could penetrate the sealed tomb and closed doors;[45] He was no longer tightly bound by space and time, but free to come and go at will, to appear or vanish in a split second.[46] He could change His voice and features as He chose.[47] His body

---

[39] *Divine Liturgy of St John Chrysostom*: priest's silent prayer after the Second Prayer of the Faithful

[40] Lk 16:22-3

[41] Some translate, "He descended *to the dead*".

[42] Ps 16 (15):10; 89 (88):48; Ezek 32:21,27

[43] 1 Pet 4:6

[44] Rom 14:9

[45] Matt 27:66; Jn 20:19

[46] Lk 24:31

[47] Lk 24:15-32

was in a state of transfigured glory,[48] which the Transfiguration had prefigured,[49] but which He kept veiled from His disciples in the forty days from the Resurrection to the Ascension.[50] Our Divine Lord kept, however, the marks of His five wounds in hands, feet and side: (a) as a proof to the Apostles that it was truly He,[51] (b) as a perpetual witness to His triumphant love and sacrifice, and (c) because, bearing these glorious wounds, He intercedes with the Father in Heaven for our salvation.[52]

Our Risen Lord had no need to eat, but partook of the broiled fish to prove the reality of His body.[53] It was not in order to strengthen and nourish His flesh, since the risen body enjoys immortality and effortless agility.

THE SAVING SIGNIFICANCE OF THE RESURRECTION. The Resurrection is the greatest of all of Our Lord's miracles. "The Resurrection constitutes above all the confirmation of all that Christ Himself did and taught. All truths, even the most inaccessible to human reason, find their justification if Christ by rising again has given the definitive proof which He had promised, of His divine authority. ... Christ's Resurrection is the fulfilment of the promises both of the Old Testament and of Jesus Himself during His earthly life. ... The truth of Jesus' divinity is confirmed by His Resurrection. ...The Resurrection of the Crucified one shows that He was truly 'I AM', the Son of God and God Himself."[54] It is the sure sign that His sacrifice was accepted by God the Father, and "proves the Father's own fidelity, fulfilling the prayer which Jesus offered before entering into His Passion: 'Father, glorify Thy Son that the Son may glorify Thee' (Jn 17:1)".[55] It is also the model of our justification, our spiritual resurrection from sin.[56] "Finally, Christ's Resurrection—and the risen Christ Himself—is the principle and source of our future resurrection."[57] As Christ rose from the dead, so all the just will rise with glorified bodies at the end of time.

THE THIRD DAY. Since Christ died on Friday and rose on Sunday, our way of counting should lead us to say that He rose "on the second day" after His death. But the Creeds declare that He rose "on the third day" because the Jewish method was to include the first day when counting the number of days between two events.

---

[48] Cf. Acts 9:3.
[49] Matt 17:2
[50] St Thomas, S.T., iii, q. 54, a. 2 (or 3), ad 1
[51] Lk 24:39
[52] Heb 7:25; 9:24
[53] Lk 24:42-43
[54] C 651-653
[55] Pope Paul VI, *Gaudete in Domino*, 1975, Part III
[56] Rom 6:4; Cf. C 654.
[57] C 655

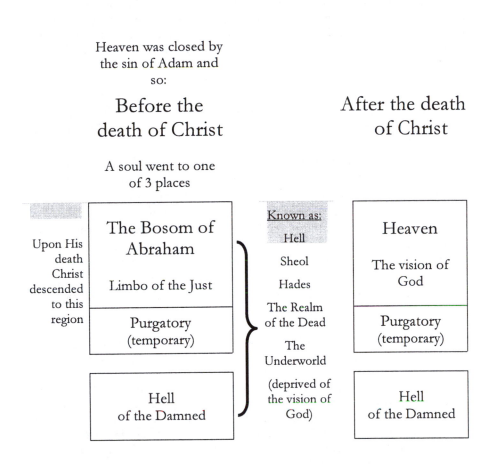

Heaven was closed by the sin of Adam and
so:

	Before the death of Christ	**After the death of Christ**
	A soul went to one of 3 places	

Upon His death Christ descended to this region

The Bosom of Abraham	Known as: Hell	Heaven
Limbo of the Just	Sheol	The vision of God
Purgatory (temporary)	Hades	Purgatory (temporary)
	The Realm of the Dead	
Hell of the Damned	The Underworld (deprived of the vision of God)	Hell of the Damned

The Apostles' Creed: "*He descended into hell*" does not include the hell of the damned.

Catechism nos. 633, 1022

THE SIGNIFICANCE OF SUNDAY. Christ observed the Sabbath rest in the tomb. He rose on Sunday because it was the first day of the Jewish week, the day that God began the work of Creation by saying, "Let there be light."[58] Christ is the true "light of the world";[59] His Resurrection is the beginning of the new creation.[60] From early times, Christians called Sunday "The Lord's Day", and set it apart for Mass, which they called "the Breaking of the Bread".[61] At the same time, Sunday became a new Sabbath announcing man's eternal rest in God.[62]

THE SUNDAY PRECEPT. With the authority given her by Christ, the Church transferred the Sabbath rest and worship to Sunday. Already by the year 107, St Ignatius of Antioch says that converts are "no longer observing the Sabbath, but living by the Lord's Day, on which also Our Life rose by His power".[63] After the conversion of Constantine in 312 A.D., what was apostolic custom became law in the universal Church, and was given civil recognition. Whereas at one time, the Church's legislation used to prohibit, on Sunday, work designated 'servile', the Church now says, "On Sundays and other Holydays of Obligation, the faithful are obliged to participate at Mass. They are also to abstain from such work or business as would impede the worship which must be given to God, the joy proper to the Lord's Day, or the due relaxation of mind or body."[64] The obligation to attend Mass is a fundamental and serious one: "Those who deliberately transgress this obligation commit a grave sin."[65]

THE CHURCH'S CELEBRATION OF THE RESURRECTION. The Church commemorates the Resurrection every Sunday, but especially on Easter Sunday, which is the first Sunday after the first full moon after March 21 (the vernal equinox, when the sun is directly above the equator), as decreed by the Council of Nicea in 325. Easter Sunday, then, occurs between March 22 and April 25 inclusively. On account of differing methods of calculating the calendar, Easter Sunday does not always occur on the same day in East and West.[66] The Resurrection (and not Christmas, as many seem to think) is the greatest and oldest Feast of the Christian Church. Its importance is emphasised in the sacred liturgy by the long preparation of Lent and Passiontide, the solemn ceremonies of Holy Week, and the following Paschaltide (Easter-time).

---

[58] Gen 1:3
[59] Jn 8:12
[60] Cf. 2 Cor 5:17.
[61] Cf. Acts 2:42,46; 20:7, 11; 1 Cor 16:2; Rev 1:10.
[62] Cf. C 2174-5.
[63] *Ep. ad Magnes.*, 9
[64] Can. 1247
[65] C 2181
[66] Cf. C 1170.

THE RESURRECTION—A WORK OF THE HOLY TRINITY. Sacred Scripture at different times appropriates the Resurrection to each of the three Divine Persons.[67] "In it the three Divine Persons at once act together and manifest their own proper characteristics."[68] We read that, "*God the Father...raised Him from the dead*". The *Son of God* says, "I have power to lay [my life] down, and I have power to take it again". St Paul says, "*the Spirit...raised Jesus from the dead*".[69]

The difference between Christ's rising and others'. Various people were raised from the dead before Christ, including at least three raised by Our Saviour Himself.[70] The differences are: He rose by His own power, they were raised by another; He rose glorious and immortal, they returned to this life, to die again. Further, He pre-announced His resurrection. His was also salvific and revelatory, and the great object of faith.[71]

THE ASCENSION. On the fortieth day after His Resurrection, our Divine Saviour ascended into Heaven in the sight of His Apostles.[72] The Nicene Creed proclaims, "He ascended into Heaven and is seated at the right hand of the Father". "This expression 'at the right hand of God'[73] is only figurative and must not be taken literally; God, being spirit, has in Him nothing that is corporal, but Holy Scriptures and the Church employ this expression to demonstrate the sublimity of the triumph granted to Christ in the sanctuary of the divinity."[74] 'At the right hand' is a Hebrew expression to signify perfect equality. "In the same way, when we say that Jesus is 'seated,' we mean to signify that He has entered for ever into possession of that eternal repose merited for Him by His glorious combats. This repose, however, does not exclude the continual exercise of the omnipotence communicated to Him by the Father in order that He may rule, sanctify and judge all mankind."[75]

The Ascension terminates Our Lord's visible sojourn on this earth. We shall not see Him with our earthly eyes until He comes again in glory, just as the Apostles saw Him go.[76] We are sad at His departure, but it was expedient for us that He go,[77] so that we might receive the Holy Spirit, cling to Jesus with deeper faith and grow in our longing to join Him. Our

---

[67] On appropriation, see p.315.

[68] C 648

[69] Gal 1:1; Jn 10:18; Rom 8:11

[70] In the O.T., 1 Kgs 17:22; 2 Kgs 4:34; 13:21; in the N.T., Lk 7:15; 9:55; Jn 11:44

[71] Cf. C 646.

[72] Acts 1:1-11

[73] Mk 16:19; Col 3:1; Heb 1:3

[74] Dom Columba Marmion OSB, *Christ in His Mysteries*, Sands & Co., London 1939, p.304

[75] Idem, *ibid.* p.304

[76] Acts 1:11

[77] Jn 16:7

Redeemer ascended into Heaven to prepare a place for us,[78] and to lead the way to Heaven above, on which we must set our hearts.[79] He ascended "to appear in the presence of God on our behalf"[80] and to occupy the royal throne of His Kingdom. The Ascension is the glorious completion of the Redemption and signifies Christ's final and irreversible entry into divine glory.

PENTECOST: THE COMING OF THE HOLY SPIRIT. On the ninth day after His Ascension, and the fiftieth after His Resurrection, Jesus Christ sent the Holy Spirit upon the Apostles, as He had promised, and filled them with truth, love and fortitude. With the coming of the Holy Spirit, the Paschal Mystery was brought to its completion. The Holy Spirit came on the day known to the Jews as the 'Feast of Weeks', also called *Pentecost*, a Greek word meaning 'the fiftieth day', for it was that many days after the Sabbath after Passover. On this day, the Jews celebrated the completion of the grain harvest, and the giving of the Covenant of Sinai.[81] Thus, on this new Pentecost, the Apostles went out to gather the harvest of souls and announce the New Covenant. After Peter preached, "those who received his word were baptised, and there were added that day about three thousand souls."[82]

The Holy Spirit, sent by the Father through the Son, is the enduring fruit of the Redemption. The Holy Spirit is the life and soul of the Body of the Church, and came to be with the Church forever. Pentecost celebrates the Gift of the Holy Spirit and His abiding presence in the Church. Pentecost is, as it were, the birthday of the Church, when she came forth publicly into the world. What Christ did once, before a few, in one small country—the Holy Spirit enables the Church to bring to all people of all places and all times. The Holy Spirit brings us to Christ and imparts to us the life won by Christ's Paschal Mystery. Christ takes us to the Father. Through Christ, in the Spirit, we have access to the Father.[83]

V

The application of the Redemption.

THE REDEMPTION IS COMPLETE ONCE AND FOR ALL. Our Divine Redeemer completed the work of our salvation at the instant of His death. From that moment onwards His work for us has been a work of

---

[78] Jn 14:2
[79] Col 3:2
[80] Heb 9:24
[81] Ex 23:16; 34:22; Lev 23:15-21; Deut 16:9
[82] Acts 2:41
[83] Cf. Eph 2:18.

application, the work of applying or giving to our souls the fruits of the Redemption. Christ our Lord does not now gain any new graces for us: while on the Cross, He gained for us every grace we need. Nor does He now make any fresh appeal for us distinct from that which He made on Calvary. "He always lives to make intercession for them",[84] but that intercession is identical with the intercession which He made for us on the Cross, and which is ever continuing to produce its effects in us.

CHRIST REQUIRES OUR CO-OPERATION. St Augustine says, "God made thee without thy aid; but, without thy aid, He does not make thee holy: He made thee, unknown to thee; but, without thy consent, He does not make thee righteous."[85] Christ redeemed us, but not in such a way that we can be saved without our co-operation. He placed the fruits of the Redemption within our reach, but we must stretch forth our hand and take them, or else they will be of no profit to us.

THE REDEMPTION ENTRUSTED TO THE CHURCH. Where shall we find the fruits of the Redemption? Who can give them to us? The Church which Christ has established. The Church herself may be called the first fruit of the Redemption. St Paul says: "Christ loved the Church and gave Himself up for her, that He might ... present the Church to Himself in splendour" - "gave Himself up for her", i.e., He delivered Himself unto death for her, to found her and to endow her with all the gifts she possesses.[86] The Church is the dispenser of the treasures of the Redemption, and Christ in a mysterious and awesome fashion has made Himself dependent on us, so to speak: "This is truly a tremendous mystery and one which can never be sufficiently meditated: namely, that the salvation of many souls depends upon the prayers and voluntary mortifications offered for that intention by the members of the mystical Body of Jesus Christ".[87]

CHRIST OPERATES VIA HIS CHURCH. Christ at His Ascension passed from the sight of men, but He is still with us invisibly in His Church. He lives in her, and through her He exercises the threefold office of Priest, Teacher, and King. As Priest, He is the principal Minister of the Sacraments, and is represented by the earthly ministers who act on behalf of the Church. As Teacher, He publishes through the voice of His infallible Church the truths which He has revealed, and which we must believe in order to be saved. As King, He conveys His commands to us in the laws which the Church tells

---

[84] Heb 7:25
[85] *Sermo* 169,11,13
[86] Eph 5: 25, 27. Cf. p.138.
[87] Pius XII, *Mystici Corporis*, 1943, Part I

us we must observe on pain of forfeiting His grace. We shall consider this in greater detail in the next chapter, on the Church.

The Cross in our life. Evil and suffering are lightened and enlightened by the suffering, death and resurrection of our Redeemer. It is His will that suffering and death, which entered the world as the penalty for sin, should be made instruments of sanctification. There is no Christianity without the Cross: "If any man would come after me, let him deny himself and take up his cross and follow me."[88]

Suffering brings self-knowledge, teaches us our misery and our absolute dependence upon God. Suffering humbles.

Suffering enables us to know and appreciate how much God loves us. The more we suffer, the more deeply we know how much Jesus Christ loved us, to suffer freely for love of us.

Suffering delivers us from superficiality, matures the heart, refines and elevates the spirit.

Suffering enables us to understand others and offer sincere consolation.

Suffering detaches us from earth, saves us from loving this passing life too much, and teaches us to seek happiness in God and in Heaven.

Suffering offered to God in, with and through Jesus Christ, purifies our souls, expiates our sins, and sanctifies us.

Suffering offered to God is a powerful prayer and means of obtaining graces for ourselves and others—above all the grace of conversion and salvation.

Suffering makes us like Jesus Christ, and wins for us a greater share of His Risen Glory.

"In the Cross is salvation, in the Cross is life, in the Cross is protection from enemies. In the Cross is infusion of heavenly sweetness, in the Cross is strength of mind, in the Cross is joy of spirit. In the Cross is height of virtue, in the Cross is perfection of sanctity. There is no health of soul, nor hope of eternal life, but in the Cross. Take up, therefore, the Cross, and follow Jesus, and thou shalt go into life everlasting. ... Because if thou die with Him on the Cross, thou shalt also live with Him, and if thou art His companion in suffering, thou shalt be His companion also in glory. ... If thou fling away one Cross, without doubt thou wilt find another, and perhaps a heavier. ... The whole life of Christ was a Cross and a martyrdom, and dost thou seek for thyself rest and joy?"[89]

The redemption and victory of Christ a cause for confidence and rejoicing. The *Exultet* of the Easter Vigil exults in the awesome mystery of the Resurrection: "Let the angelic choirs of Heaven now rejoice ... let the trumpet of salvation resound for the victory of so great a King. Let the earth also rejoice, illumined with such splendour; and enlightened by the brightness of the eternal King, let it feel that the darkness of the whole world is dispersed."

---

[88] Mk 8:34

[89] *The Imitation of Christ*, Book II, Ch. 12: a 15th century spiritual classic attributed to the monk Thomas à Kempis.

Anscar Vonier writes, "Just as there is no limit to Christ's sovereignty, so there is no limit to the possibilities of Christian sanctification, of the Christian's power to rise superior to all darkness and the captivity of sin; we not only worship the victory of Christ, but we are partakers of its virtue in our own mind, in our own members. This superiority of the Christian to all evils is, of course, a commonplace in New Testament thought; but though it be such a universal idea it is none the less marvellous. The victory of Christ operates in us; His Resurrection and His Ascension are not only future hopes, but actual spiritual phenomena of our individual Christian life. …Christ has won our battles for us long before we were born."[90]

Personal devotion to Jesus Christ. "Let it be then our chief study to meditate on the life of Jesus. … But he that would fully and with relish understand the words of Christ, must study to conform his whole life to Him."[91] To know Jesus—to know that He is the Son of God—brings eternal life to the soul. But to know Him is not merely to know Him with the cold assent of the intellect. To know Him in truth is to love Him with all the strength of our being, to make His every interest our own, to give Him without reserve our deepest affection, and to enthrone Him in our heart. It is an excellent thing to acquire a detailed knowledge of Christ and of His life on earth; excellent also to form beautiful thoughts about Him. But it is not enough. We may do all this, and yet possess no more than a mere sentimental love for Him; we may do all this, and yet be entirely displeasing to Him. We must stand the test He Himself has set us: "If you love Me, keep my commandments" (Jn 14:15). We have no love for Him, if we do not obey Him. We make no progress in our love for Him, unless we obey Him ever more willingly, ever more perfectly. We should ask Him with great humility to give us a deeper knowledge of His Sacred Heart, so that we may love all that He loves and be solicitous for His honour. An excellent means for growing in the love of Our Lord is to make the Stations of the Cross—with meditations or by speaking to Jesus in our own words at each one—a devotion which takes its origin from the Holy City of Jerusalem itself, where Christians used to retrace the steps of Our Lord during His Passion.

In true devotion to Jesus, it is not the compromisers and those who do the bare minimum who are our models, but the Martyrs. Their memory will be an inspiration to us in that hour, which is sure to come sooner or later, when, like every faithful follower of the Crucified, we shall be invited by Him to take on our shoulders, for His sake, the cross of humiliation, of

---

[90] Abbot Anscar Vonier OSB, *The Victory of Christ* (1934), Collected Works, Vol. I, pp.324-5
[91] *The Imitation of Christ*, Book I, Ch. 1

sorrow, of pain, of poverty, of rejection or unpopularity, perhaps of death itself.

Christianity is not an ideology or a programme. It is not merely a system of doctrine; it is devotion to a Person—the Sacred Person of Jesus Christ. "Grow in the grace and knowledge of Our Lord and Saviour Jesus Christ. To Him be the glory both now and to the day of eternity."[92]

---

[92] 2 Pet 3:18

CHAPTER 9

THE CHURCH

Chapters 8-10 in *Apologetics* deal with the Church as a united, holy, catholic and apostolic society set up by Christ. Ch. 11 in *Apologetics* deals with Papal primacy and the Church's teaching and governing authority. To complete our treatment of the Church, we present here her constitution and nature as the Body of Christ and People of God.

Summary

I.   The teaching of the Church.
II. The origin of the Church. The nature of the Church: the Mystical Body of Christ. The Church is a body. One Body. The Body of Christ. Christ, Founder of the Body. Christ, Head of the Body. The Church, His Mystical Body. The Church, Christ on earth. The Church, Christ's Bride. The Holy Spirit, the soul of the Church. Mary the Mother of the Church. One, holy, catholic, apostolic. The Church reflects the mysteries of the Trinity and the Incarnation. The Church in the Old and New Testament.
III. The constitution and members of the Church. The People of God. The Hierarchy: the Pope and Bishops. The Laity. Clerics. Consecrated Life - its various forms.
IV. Indefectibility of the Church. Love for the Church. The Church, a Communion of Saints. The identity of the Church. The structure of the Catholic religion

I

The teaching of the Church. The Church teaches as of Faith:
(1) that the Church was founded by Jesus Christ;[1]
(2) that Christ is the Head of the Church;[2]
(3) that the Church is the Body of Jesus Christ;[3]
(4) that the Church is visible;[4]
(5) that she is one;
(6) that she is holy;
(7) that she is catholic;
(8) that she is apostolic;[5]

---

[1] Matt 16:18; 1 Cor 3:11; Eph 2:20; V 3050; DS 3302
[2] Eph 5:23; Col 1:18
[3] 1 Cor 12:27
[4] DS 3300, T 1764, V 3013-4, 3051
[5] (5) - (8): Nicene Creed

(9) that, through the Church, Christ continues His mission as Priest, Teacher and King of His people;[6]

(10) that Christ set up in the Church a hierarchy consisting of the college of Bishops united under Peter and his successors;[7]

(11) that the Church is infallible in both her solemn and her universal teaching;[8]

(12) that it is impossible for anyone culpably outside the Church to be saved;[9]

(13) that the Blessed Virgin Mary is spiritual mother to all Christ's faithful;[10]

(14) that the Church on earth shall last until the end of time;[11]

(15) that the Church is a Communion of Saints comprising the faithful on earth, the souls in Purgatory and the blessed in Heaven.[12]

II

The origin of the Church.[13] The word *Church* means convocation or assembly. In the Old Testament, the Chosen People was known, among other names, as 'the Church of God'. The first community of Christians called itself 'the Church', thus showing that it recognised itself as heir to that original assembly. The Church's origin is in the plan of the Most Holy Trinity to reunite all things in Christ. It is a plan realised in stages in history, beginning with Adam and continuing up to Jesus Christ, the new Adam, who gathers His people into a body joined to Himself.

The nature of the Church: the Mystical Body of Christ.
THE CHURCH IS A BODY. *One, undivided, visible body.* The Sacred Scriptures assert several times that the Church is a body. Christ "is the Head of the body, the Church", says St Paul.[14] Being a body, the Church must be something one and undivided, for as St Paul says, "we, though many, are one body in Christ". As a body, the Church is something concrete and visible, not merely a spiritual and invisible union of souls. As a body, the

---

[6] Matt 28:18-20; Jn 20:21; V 3050
[7] T 1776, V 3055, 3058, 3064
[8] V 3011
[9] L 802
[10] Jn 19:26-7; DS 3262, 3275
[11] Matt 16:18; V 3050, 3056
[12] Apostles' Creed; T 1821, DS 3363
[13] The doctrine in Section II is drawn principally from *Mystici Corporis*, Pope Pius XII, 1943, Encyclical Letter "On the Mystical Body of Jesus Christ and our Union with Christ therein". That of Section III is taken mainly from *Lumen Gentium*, Vatican Council II, 1964, "Dogmatic Constitution on the Church", and the *Catechism*, 748-975. Repeated references to these three documents will not be given.
[14] Col 1:18

members of the Church live not only for themselves, but also help fellow-members for the mutual support and for the constant growth of the whole body. As, in any body, the organs have different functions to perform, so in the Church the members are different from one another but are co-ordinated within the common mission: "For as in one body we have many members, and all the members do not have the same function, so we, though many, are one body in Christ, and individually members one of another."[15]

The Sacraments of the Body. Christ has provided for the life, health and growth of the Church and each of her members by means of the Sacraments. By Baptism, new members are reborn in Christ and enter her. By Confirmation, believers are strengthened to guard the faith and defend Holy Mother Church. In the Sacred Eucharist, the faithful are nourished and fortified at a common banquet, and united by heavenly bonds to one another and to the Head of the whole Body. By Penance, sinful members are delivered from their sins and their fellow-members are saved from the danger of contagion. When they are mortally ill, the Church anoints them to heal the body, if God so wills, and strengthen the wounded soul, so that Heaven may receive new citizens and the Church receive the benefit of new intercessors. Christ has provided for the social needs of the Church by two other Sacraments. The Sacrament of Matrimony, in which husband and wife become the ministers of grace to each other, ensures the regular numerical increase of the Christian community, and the religious education of the younger members. Holy Orders consecrates to the perpetual service of God those destined to offer the Eucharistic Victim, to nourish the flock of the faithful with the Bread of Life and the food of doctrine, to guide them by the divine commandments and counsels, and to sanctify them by other holy ministrations.

Membership of the Body. One becomes a member of the Church by Baptism, and after the age of reason demonstrates this membership by three things: (1) profession of the Catholic faith; (2) acceptance of all the means of salvation, chiefly the Sacraments, and (3) union with the Pastors of the Church, and in particular, the Chief Pastor, the Pope.

Union with the Church is lost by sinning against the faith or against communion. One sins against faith by *heresy*, i.e., the obstinate denial or doubt of a revealed Catholic truth, or by *apostasy*, which is the total repudiation of the Christian faith. One sins against union or communion by *schism*, i.e., by withdrawal of submission to the Pope or from communion

---

[15] Rom 12:4-5

with the members of the Church subject to him.[16] By the penalty of excommunication, a member of the Church is cut off from communion with the Church and suffers the effects of the law for his offence. Sinners, however, are not excluded from membership of the Church. They are her members and are bound to her, even if by their own freely chosen sins they do not enjoy the graces which membership of the Church is meant to bring them.

The Church is the Body of Christ.

CHRIST THE FOUNDER OF THE BODY. The divine Redeemer founded this Body in various stages: He began to build the mystical temple of His Church when He was conducting His Public Ministry; He completed it during Holy Week and when He was crucified; it was born from His wounded Heart as He slept in death upon the Cross; He manifested and promulgated it by the visible mission of the Holy Spirit upon His disciples.

He laid its foundations during His Public Life. While preaching, Our Divine Lord chose and formed His Apostles, sending them as He had been sent by the Father, that is to say, as teachers, rulers and sanctifiers in the community of believers. He designated their chief and His vicar. He made known to them all the things which He had heard from the Father. He prescribed Baptism as the means of incorporation into the Body of the Church; and finally, at the close of His life, He instituted at the Last Supper the wonderful sacrifice and sacrament of the Eucharist.

He completed it on the Cross. As Eve was born from the side of Adam, so on the Cross, the Church, Christ's Bride, was born from the Saviour's side. The Blood and water that came forth from His side announced the sacraments of Baptism and the Eucharist, merited and given virtue by His Passion. With the death of the Redeemer, the Old Law was abolished and the New Testament took its place.[17] It was then that the Law of Christ, with its mysteries, its laws, institutions, and sacred rites, was ratified for the whole world by the Blood of Jesus Christ. So long as Our Saviour preached in a restricted territory (for He had been sent only to the lost sheep of the House of Israel),[18] both the Old Law and the Gospel (the New Law) were in force together. At the death of Christ, there occurred the transition from the Law to the Gospel, from the Synagogue to the Church, from the multitude of sacrifices to the one Victim. Although already Head of the human race from the Incarnation, it is by virtue of the Cross that the Lord Jesus exercises in all its fulness His function of headship in the Church. By

---

[16] Cf. Can. 751.
[17] Cf. Eph 2:15; Col 2:14; 1 Cor 11:25.
[18] Matt 15:24

the victory of the Cross, He purchased the Church for Himself, that is, all the members of His Body, and won for them all the divine graces, favours and spiritual blessings of the New Testament that He bestows upon them. Through the shedding of His Blood, the Redeemer merited the outpouring of the Holy Spirit upon His Church. Vivified by the Lord and Life-Giver, the Church now could not fail to be an effective instrument of the Incarnate Word and to distribute to all nations the fruits of the Redemption.

He promulgated it on the day of Pentecost. Having established the Church in His Blood, Jesus fortified it on the day of Pentecost with special power from on high. He made known and promulgated His Church by means of the visible descent of the Holy Spirit, coming with the sound of a mighty wind and with tongues of fire, just as He Himself entered upon His Public Ministry, announced by the voice of the Eternal Father and the descent upon Himself of the Holy Spirit in the form of a dove.

CHRIST THE HEAD OF THE BODY. "Christ is the Head of the Church, His Body",[19] says St Paul, and this for a number of reasons, apart from His being its Founder.

His pre-eminence. The head holds highest place. It is clear, then, that the Son of God, the Eternal Word of the Father, the first born of all creation, the first born of the dead by His Resurrection, the one mediator between God and man, is Head of the Church, since none can hold a higher place than He.[20]

He rules the Church. The head stands over the other members of the body to have them under its care. Our Redeemer wields supreme power and government over the entire Church. He guides His people providently with suitable means and right principles. During His sojourn on earth, by His laws, counsels and admonitions, He taught us that doctrine which will never pass away and which will always be spirit and life for souls. Further, He imparted to the Apostles and their successors His threefold power of teaching, governing and sanctifying men, and promised to be with them to the end of time. Thus through the Pope, the vicar of Christ, and through the other Bishops, the successors of the Apostles, Christ governs His Church in a visible and ordinary fashion. At the same time, He watches over the whole commonwealth of the Church, enlightening and fortifying her rulers, and, especially in circumstances of greater difficulty, raising up men and women of outstanding sanctity. From Heaven, He watches His

---

[19] Eph 5:23; cf. Col 1:18.
[20] Cf. Col 1:15,18; 1 Tim 2:5.

Bride struggling in this vale of tears and delivers her from the tempests and waves that would overwhelm her. Moreover, He governs the Church directly by reigning in the minds and hearts of men, and caring for each individual, providing for each one all the graces necessary for sanctification and salvation.

Christ and His Body need each other. What St Paul says of the human organism is true also of the mystical Body: the head cannot say to the feet, "I have no need of you."[21] It is clear enough that Christians stand in absolute need of their Saviour's help: apart from Him we can do nothing, and all growth is from Him.[22] Yet in His capacity as direct and invisible ruler of the Church, Our Lord wants to be helped by the members of His Body in carrying out the work of Redemption. This is not due to any need or insufficiency in Him, but rather because He has so ordained it for the greater honour of His immaculate Bride. Unaided by the Church He merited the treasure of the Redemption, but in the distribution of that treasure He not only shares this work of sanctification with His spotless Bride, but wills it to arise in a certain manner out of her labour.

The likeness between Christ and His members. The Son of God became man, that men might become sons of God. Christ and the Church form head and body for they are of the one nature. By grace, we have been made "partakers of the divine nature"[23] on earth, and in Heaven we shall be so by glory. We no longer live of ourselves, but Christ lives in us. We not only *imitate* His virtues and *follow* His teaching, but we *live* by the very same grace that sanctified His humanity, and so reproduce the power of His Passion and Death and Resurrection.

The whole Body of the Church shows forth her likeness to Her divine Founder when she teaches, governs, sanctifies and offers sacrifice, as He did. In her consecrated religious members who practise the evangelical counsels, the Church portrays in herself the poverty, chastity and obedience of her Redeemer. The manifold orders and institutions in the Church show forth Christ in various aspects of His life: contemplating on the mountain, preaching to the people, healing the sick, bringing sinners to repentance, showing compassion, feeding the hungry, and doing good to all. During her earthly pilgrimage, she resembles Christ too in His rejection, persecution, insults and tribulations.

His fulness. The head of our mortal body is endowed with the brain and all the senses, while the remainder has only the sense of touch. So too is

---

[21] 1 Cor 12:21
[22] Cf. Jn 15:5; Eph 4:16; Col 2:19; 1 Cor 3:6-7.
[23] 2 Pet 1:4

420

Christ called Head by the surpassing plenitude and perfection of His supernatural gifts, virtues and powers, whose fulness the Body draws upon. "For in Him all the fulness of God was pleased to dwell" and "from His fulness have we all received, grace upon grace."[24]

His dynamic influence. As the nerves are diffused from the head to all the members of our body, giving them the power to feel and move, so Our Saviour pours forth into the Church His power and virtue, giving to the faithful a clearer understanding and a more ardent desire of the things of God. From Him flows into the Body of the Church all the light which divinely illumines those who believe, and all the grace which makes them holy as He Himself is holy. It is His light which enlightens and guides the Pastors of the Church, that they may proclaim the deposit of faith; it is He who presides unseen at the Councils of the Church and protects them from defining error. Indeed, every salutary act proceeds from Him, the author and perfecter of our faith.[25]

THE CHURCH HIS 'MYSTICAL' BODY. We distinguish (1) the *physical* Body of Christ, which He had on earth and is now glorious in Heaven; (2) the *Eucharistic* Body of Christ, which is the same Body but in sacramental form; and (3) the *Mystical* Body of Christ, the Church.

The Mystical Body compared to physical and moral bodies. In a human body, there is but one person, and the parts cannot subsist by themselves; in the Mystical Body, there are many persons, but each member retains his own personality. In a physical body, the parts are ordered only to the good of the whole, but in the Church, as in any social body, the society exists for the good of each and every member. As in moral bodies, the members of the Church share a common purpose, means and authority, but in addition, the Church is a body by virtue of a supernatural internal principle—the Holy Spirit—really existing and operative in the whole structure and in each one of its parts, the source of her unity, filling and unifying the whole Church.

THE CHURCH IS CHRIST ON EARTH. The Apostle to the Gentiles, St Paul, calls the Church simply by the name of "Christ",[26] following herein the example of His Master who, when Saul was persecuting the Church, cried out to him from Heaven, "Saul, Saul, why do you persecute Me?"[27] It is indeed Christ who acts through the Church. It is He who baptises, teaches,

---

[24] Col 1:19; Jn 1:16
[25] Cf. Heb 12:2.
[26] 1 Cor 12:12
[27] Acts 9:4; 22:7; 26:14

decrees, governs, and appoints. It is He who sanctifies, saves, absolves, binds, and offers sacrifice.

THE CHURCH, CHRIST'S BRIDE. The Lord Jesus referred to Himself as 'the Bridegroom'.[28] Each soul personally, and the Church collectively, is espoused to Jesus Christ. So St Paul could say, "I betrothed you to Christ to present you as a pure bride to her one Husband."[29] The Church is Christ's bride, a virgin bride made fruitful, a mother of many children. He loves her as His own Body.[30]

THE HOLY SPIRIT, THE SOUL OF THE CHURCH. The Paraclete promised by Jesus and sent by the Father is the invisible principle of the union of all the parts of the Body with one another and with their exalted Head. He dwells in the Head, the Body and in all the members. Pope Leo XIII says, "since Christ is Head of the Church, the Holy Spirit is her soul."[31] St Augustine, the Doctor of Grace, says, "What the soul is in our body, so is the Holy Spirit in the Body of Christ which is the Church."[32]

MARY THE MOTHER OF THE CHURCH. The Blessed Virgin Mary is the Mother of God and the mother of the members of Christ. By her charity, she has joined in bringing about the birth of believers in Christ. Our Blessed Lady was made fruitful by the Word implanted within her, and she likewise continues to prepare the way for Christ into souls that they may be reborn as members of the Church and children of God. As a mother protects and nourishes the new life entrusted to her, introduces her babe to its family, and teaches an infant to speak, so our Mother Mary protects and nourishes our spiritual life, leads us to our elder Brother and our Father, and educates us in the school of Christ. Mary's motherhood in the order of grace began at her consent to God's plan at the Annunciation, was publicly declared by Christ upon the Cross, continued through her life as she prayed for the infant Church awaiting the Holy Spirit at Pentecost, and was carried on until her Assumption into Heaven. Her maternal intercession will continue until the last soul is gathered into its heavenly home.

THE CHURCH IS ONE, HOLY, CATHOLIC AND APOSTOLIC. The Church is *One* in government, faith and worship. She is *Holy* in her Founder, Jesus Christ, the God-Man; in her doctrine, and in the holy lives of her members. The Church is *Catholic* because her mission is universal, and she possesses

---

[28] Mk 2:19-20
[29] 2 Cor 11:2
[30] Cf. Eph 5:28-9; Rev 21:2,9; 22:17.
[31] Encyclical on the Holy Spirit, *Divinum Illud Munus*, 1897: DS 3328
[32] *Sermo* 267, c. 4, 4: DS 3328

the fulness of teaching and means of salvation. The Church is *Apostolic* in her foundation upon the Apostles;[33] in her teaching, received from the Apostles; in her Holy Orders and pastoral office handed on by the Apostles to the Bishops.[34]

THE CHURCH A REFLECTION OF THE MYSTERIES OF THE TRINITY AND THE INCARNATION. Just as the Most Holy Trinity is One in nature and Three in Persons, so the Church is One and yet composed of many members. Just as her Divine Founder has two natures, divine and human, so the Church, His Body, has both a human aspect and a divine one: but the two coalesce so as to form the one Mystery of the Church.

THE CHURCH AT CREATION, THE CHURCH OF THE OLD COVENANT, THE CHURCH OF THE NEW COVENANT.[35] The Church, the ark of salvation, embraces all the just from the dawn of history to the end of time. Thus none of the just is saved outside the Church. So St Thomas says that the just of the Old Testament, "belonged to the same body of the Church to which we belong."[36] "Already prefigured from the beginning of the world, this Church was wondrously prepared in the history of the people of Israel and in the Old Covenant, established in the last days, and manifested in the outpouring of the Spirit, and it will be gloriously consummated at the end of time."[37] "It may be said that the Church was the ... purpose and the foundation of creation; in this sense it was created before all things, and for it the world was made. ... Thus it is difficult to point to a time when the Church did not exist in humanity, at least in the state of previous design. According to the doctrine of the Fathers, a primordial Church already existed in Paradise before the fall, when the Lord went to speak with man and put Himself into relation with him. After the fall, in the first words about the 'seed of the woman' the Lord laid the foundation of what may be termed the Church of the old covenant, the Church wherein man learned to commune with God. ... Certainly the Church attained the fullness of its existence only with the Incarnation, and in this sense the Church was founded by Our Lord Jesus Christ and realized at Pentecost. On this event, the foundation of the Church was laid, but its fullness is not yet attained. It is still the Church militant, and it must become the Church triumphant, where 'God shall be all in all'."[38]

---

[33] Cf. Eph 2:20.
[34] C 811-870. See Part I, Ch. 9 for more detail.
[35] Cf. C 759-769.
[36] S.T., iii, q. 8, a. 3, ad 3
[37] *Lumen Gentium*, art. 2
[38] Sergius Bulgakov (1871-1944), *The Orthodox Church*, St Vladimir's Seminary Press, N.Y. 1988, pp.6-7

III

The constitution and members of the People of God.

THE PEOPLE OF GOD. The People of God is marked by characteristics that distinguish it from every other religious, ethnic, political or cultural group in history:

- It is the People *of God*. God has acquired this people for Himself through the Precious Blood of His Son. They are "a chosen race, a royal priesthood, a holy nation, God's own people".[39]
- *Membership* is acquired not by birth or by natural inheritance, but by faith and Baptism.
- The *Head* of this People is Jesus Christ, the King of Kings and Lord of Lords.
- The *status* of this People is that of the dignity of sons of God and citizens of His Kingdom.
- Its *law* is the new law of the Holy Spirit, with the new commandment to love one another as Christ has loved us.
- Its *constitution* is divinely ordained, that of a hierarchical body led by the Pope and bishops succeeding Peter and the Apostles.
- Its *culture* is an extension of the Incarnation, is the true worship of God in spirit and in truth, and the sanctification of all realities under the Lordship of Christ.
- It is a *priestly* People, sharers in Christ's priesthood by Baptism, and offering spiritual sacrifices to God.
- It is a *prophetic* People, adhering to the teaching of Christ and bearing witness to Him by word and deed.
- It is a *kingly* People, enjoying a royal freedom from sin, and serving its King as intimates and members of His household, entitled to all the privileges He has bequeathed to them.
- Its *mission* is to be the salt of the earth and light of the world; to gather the scattered children of God into one,[40] to call all people into itself and to spread the graces of salvation.
- Its *destiny* is the Kingdom of God in all its perfection when Christ returns in glory and hands this people, risen from the dead, over to His Father.

THE HIERARCHICAL CONSTITUTION OF THE CHURCH. In the Church, there is diversity of ministry but unity of mission. All members follow Christ and advance His Kingdom, but not all are called to be His ordained ministers. Christ Himself is the source of all ministry in the Church. When He chose the Twelve, He set them up in the form of a college or permanent

---

[39] 1 Pet 2:9
[40] Jn 11:52

assembly, with Simon Peter as head under Him. The Roman Pontiff is Peter's successor, and the Bishops of the Church are the successors of the Apostles. Together, they form one college with power of governance and teaching over the whole Church.

Papal jurisdiction. By divine institution, the Pope enjoys supreme, full, immediate and universal power over the whole Church.[41] His authority is *supreme,* for it is the highest in the Church. It is *full,* for it can be exercised in all aspects of ecclesial life. It is *immediate,* for the Pope is not bound to act through any other authority or intermediary. It is *universal,* for it extends to all members of the Church everywhere. At the same time, his authority is not absolute or unlimited, for it is received in delegation from Christ. The Pope is not Christ, but the Vicar of Christ.[42]

Episcopal jurisdiction. Each Bishop has jurisdiction over the territory or people assigned to his pastoral care. But the college of Bishops has no authority unless united with the chief Bishop, Peter's successor, the Roman Pontiff.

The threefold office of the Bishops. The individual bishops are the visible source and foundation of unity in their own particular churches. First, they have the task to *preach* the Gospel, for they are heralds of Christ, endowed with His authority to teach the true faith. In ecumenical councils, they possess the charism of infallibility when they corporately teach the faith in a solemn and definitive fashion. Likewise they infallibly proclaim the doctrine of Christ when, though dispersed throughout the world, but in unison, and in unity with the Pope, they definitively teach a doctrine as revealed or as inseparably connected with the body of revealed truth.[43] Secondly, they are the stewards of grace to *sanctify* the faithful by Baptism, by forgiving sins and offering the Holy Eucharist, and by the other sacraments. This they do personally or by assuring it through their priests. Thirdly, they *govern* their subjects by counsels and directives.

Bishops and dioceses. The Bishops succeed the Apostles in their government and teaching office. Most of the Catholic Church is divided into territories known as "dioceses", or major dioceses known as "archdioceses", each one headed by a bishop or archbishop, respectively. There are about 2,700 dioceses and archdioceses in the universal Church. The number grows year by year, as the Church grows and dioceses are sub-divided. Every five years, each bishop goes to

---

[41] Cf. *Lumen Gentium*, 22; *Christus Dominus*, 2; Can. 331; C 882, 937.
[42] See p.205 "Limits to Papal Authority".
[43] Cf. *Lumen Gentium*, 25; *Commentary* on *Ad Tuendam Fidem*, S. Congregation for the Doctrine of the Faith, 1998.

Rome to give to the Holy See a complete report on the state of his diocese. This is called the *ad limina* visit, since he goes *ad limina*, i.e., *to the thresholds* of the tombs of the Apostles Peter and Paul in Rome.

Auxiliary bishops. An auxiliary bishop is not in charge of the diocese but helps the reigning bishop in administration, government, conferring of the sacraments, and any other matter where he is needed. A *co-adjutor bishop* does the same, and generally will take over the diocese upon the retirement or death of the reigning bishop.

Cardinals. A cardinal is a cleric appointed as a voter in the election of a Pope, by special enrolment as a member of the clergy of the diocese of Rome. As in ancient times, when the Bishop of Rome died, the senior clergy of Rome would meet to elect a new Bishop of their diocese, so the cardinals gather in Rome in a private meeting, known as a "conclave", to elect a new Bishop of Rome, who by his election is Pope of the universal Church. The cardinalate is not part of Holy Orders, but is open to any cleric selected by the Pope. Generally, a cardinal is already an archbishop of a major see, but occasionally a priest is chosen to be a cardinal, and might choose to remain a priest and not be made a bishop.

THE LAY FAITHFUL. The lay faithful comprise the greater proportion of the Church on earth. The laity are those who by Baptism have been incorporated into Christ and made sharers in their own manner in the priestly, kingly and prophetic office of Christ. The laity includes all the faithful, except those in Holy Orders or in a religious state approved by the Church.

The vocation of the laity. It belongs to the laity to seek the Kingdom of God by engaging in temporal affairs and directing them according to God's will. It is their task to permeate political, social and economic life with the spirit of Christ.

Participation in Christ's priestly office. All the laity's prayers, daily work, apostolic undertakings, family and married life, relaxation and sufferings— in short, every aspect of their lives—can be offered to God by virtue of their Baptism to be spiritual sacrifices through Jesus Christ. All these can be offered to God the Father in union with the sacrifice of the Altar.

Participation in Christ's prophetic office. Lay people receive the Word of God that Christ our teacher revealed to mankind. By the grace of God they adhere unfailingly to the deposit of faith and teach it to their children and those entrusted to their care. In their lives of work, social relations and apostolate, they are witnesses to Christ by word and example.

Participation in Christ's kingly office. By self denial and obedience to God, the lay faithful become conquerors of sin, and enjoy royal freedom, being no longer slaves to sin, but sons with the Son.[44] They strive to free all temporal realities from the marks of sin and to direct them to the glory of God.

CLERICS. A cleric is a deacon, priest, or bishop, i.e., one who has received the sacrament of Holy Orders in any of its three grades. If a priest is not in a religious institute, he is called a 'diocesan' priest, because he is attached to that territory governed by a bishop. He may also be called a 'secular' priest, because he is not a religious, but is in daily contact with the world and has the worldly responsibilities of managing his own financial affairs and goods. A diocesan priest promises celibacy and obedience to his bishop.

CONSECRATED LIFE. Consecrated life is a deepening of the consecration begun at Baptism, by profession of the three evangelical counsels of *poverty*, *chastity*, and *obedience*. By poverty, one gives up personal possessions and enrichment, and shares one's goods with the community where all things are held in common. The vow of poverty fulfils the invitation of Christ, "If you would be perfect, go, sell what you possess and give to the poor, and you will have treasure in heaven; and come follow Me."[45] Chastity fulfils the invitation of Christ, made to "those to whom it is given",[46] to be celibate "for the sake of the Kingdom of Heaven".[47] Obedience to one's superior is an imitation of Christ who came to do not His own will but the will of the One who sent Him, and who prayed, "not My will, but Thine, be done."[48]

In the Church, consecrated life takes many forms, among which are the following.
Religious life. A religious order or institute is a community of men or women living by the evangelical counsels within a particular rule of life and Constitutions. Religious usually live a communal life with a specific apostolate and a particular spirituality. They may be *active* or *contemplative*. An active order or institute conducts an external work such as a school, parish, hospital, educational or charitable institution. A contemplative order or institute lives an enclosed life and focuses on prayer. Or an institute may lead a mixed life, i.e., semi-contemplative.

A female religious is a Nun or Sister. (The difference between the terms is technical only, as is the difference between an Order, Congregation or Institute). Corresponding to a Sister, on the male side, is a Brother. A

---

[44] Cf. Jn 8:34-6.
[45] Matt 19:21
[46] Matt 19:11
[47] Matt 19:12
[48] Lk 22:42; Jn 5:30

Brother is a male religious who is not ordained, but has taken the same three religious vows.

Some male religious are also priests, which means they are religious and clerical together.

Secular institutes. Members of secular institutes do not assume the religious state or habit, but, professing the evangelical counsels, remain within the world to sanctify it from within.

The eremitic life. "Without always professing the three evangelical counsels publicly, hermits devote their life to the praise of God and salvation of the world by a stricter separation from the world, the silence of solitude and assiduous prayer and penance."[49]

Consecrated virgins and widows. Christian virgins and widows, called by the Lord to cling to Him with undivided heart, may, with the blessing of the Church, live in the respective states of virginity and chastity. A consecrated virgin is betrothed mystically to Christ and is dedicated to the service of the Church.

IV

Indefectibility of the Church. Love for the Church. The Church, a Communion of Saints. The identity of the Church. The structure of the Catholic religion.

INDEFECTIBILITY OF THE CHURCH. The Church cannot fail to be the Church. When we assert her indefectibility, we mean that the Church on earth is imperishable and so shall last until the end of time.[50] We mean, further, that the essentials of her constitution, teaching and sacraments will never change.[51] This does not exclude the total demise of the Church in particular regions.

LOVE FOR THE CHURCH. We must love the Church as designed by Christ. The defects which we may perceive in the Church are not truly hers, but belong to her sinful members, and owe nothing to her constitution as willed by Christ. Her divine Founder even permits tendency towards evil to afflict the higher members of His mystical Body, for the testing of the virtue of both flock and Pastors, and for the greater merit of Christian faith in all. No one aware of his own frailty and the blight of Original Sin should be so scandalised by the sins of others as to weaken in faith or lessen in his

---

[49] C 920; cf. Can. 603 §1.
[50] cf. Matt 16:18; 28:20.
[51] L. Ott, *Fundamentals of Catholic Dogma*, Mercier Press, Cork 1957, p.296

attachment to Christ and the Church, but ought prove his love ever more by praying for those who have fallen and making loving reparation to the Heart of Jesus wounded by sin. The Church ever remains the Immaculate Bride of Christ, perfectly pure in her teaching, and unfailingly fruitful in her sacraments and spiritual doctrine. In the Church we must see Christ himself, and love her members, especially the more ailing, as Christ loves them. The charity of Christ knows no boundary of race or custom; it regards no one as a mere stranger but sees all souls as actual or potential family members in Christ. We must love the Church as our mother, and show our love by participation in her apostolic works and by fervent prayers for her chief Pastor, and for all the pastors and faithful. In addition to this, practices of mortification and the generous acceptance of suffering offered to God avail much for Holy Mother Church, for in this way, as the Apostle tells us, "in my flesh I complete what is lacking in Christ's afflictions for the sake of His Body, that is, the Church".[52] In times of crisis and need, God raises up saints and holy reformers to renew the face of the Church. Never in opposition to the Church, and never outside the Church, "the great reformers always burned with the Church's own flame when attempting to renew it."[53] They "found a remedy for the Church's evil in the Church itself, for it is only in the holiness which it possesses that there can be found a remedy for the sin which afflicts it."[54]

THE CHURCH, A COMMUNION OF SAINTS. The Apostles' Creed says, "I believe ... in the holy catholic Church, the Communion of Saints". The Communion of Saints *is* the Church. "The Saints" means "the Holy Ones", i.e., God's holy people and the holy things in the Church. St Thomas says, "Since all the faithful are one body, the good of each is communicated to the others."[55] Christ communicates His riches to the faithful. The faithful possess all their spiritual riches in common: the faith, the sacraments, charisms, charity, union with their Saviour, and even worldly goods when necessary. St Paul says, "If one member suffers, all suffer together; if one member is honoured, all rejoice together. Now you are the body of Christ and individually members of it."[56] By petitionary prayer, the faithful can procure gifts from God for one another.

This communion takes place also between the living and the dead in the Church. The Church comprises not only the faithful on earth, but also the souls in Purgatory and the blessed in Heaven. These three states are

---

[52] Col 1:24
[53] Bishop L.Z. Legaspi, O.P., *The Church We Love*, University of Santo Tomas, Manila 1982, p.174; 1997 ed., p.191
[54] Ibid.
[55] *In Symb. Apost.*, 13
[56] 1 Cor 12:26-7

often called the Church Militant, the Church Suffering, and the Church Triumphant. The Saints and Angels in Heaven inspire, befriend and succour the pilgrim faithful on earth. The faithful on earth come to the aid of souls in Purgatory, and the Saints similarly can intercede for the Poor Souls there.

The identity of the Church. Is the Church of Christ to be identified totally with the Catholic Church, or does it exist outside the Catholic Church as well? The second Vatican Council's decree *Lumen Gentium* teaches that, "This is the one and only[57] Church of Christ which we confess in the Creed to be one, holy, catholic and apostolic. ... This Church, constituted and organised as a society in this world, *subsists* in the Catholic Church, governed by the Successor of Peter and by the Bishops in communion with him, although several *elements* of truth and sanctification are found outside its structure, which as gifts proper to the Church of Christ, impel towards Catholic unity."[58] Can the Body of Christ subsist outside the Catholic Church? No, since a being can have only one subsistence. If it subsists elsewhere it is plural, divided and distinct—whereas the Catholic Church is *one*, as we profess in the Creed. The Congregation for the Doctrine of the Faith explains it thus: "When [one] asserts, 'In fact, she (the one Church of Christ) can also subsist in other Christian churches', he draws a conclusion exactly contrary to the true meaning of the text of Vatican II. The Council had instead chosen the word *subsists* precisely to clarify that there exists only one 'subsistence' of the true Church, while outside of her visible structure there exist only 'elements of the Church' which—being elements of the Church herself—tend and lead towards the Catholic Church."[59] The second Vatican Council's decree on Eastern Churches speaks of, "The holy Catholic Church, which *is* the Mystical Body of Christ"[60]—thus confirming the complete identity. Protestant 'churches' are not strictly churches, but societies of people who have taken *elements* from the Catholic Church and put them together in their own way. Documents of the Catholic Magisterium for this reason do not even call Anglican or Protestant bodies 'Churches', but only 'communions' or 'communities'.

But are not children who receive Protestant Baptism made members of their Protestant church? In reply, we must first understand that there is no such thing as Protestant Baptism: Baptism is a sacrament instituted by Jesus Christ and entrusted to His Church—the Catholic Church. Most Protestant communities have valid Baptism, because they have retained the true way of conferring it, but it remains a Sacrament of the Catholic Church nevertheless. To put this in practical terms: a baptism of an *infant* by a Protestant minister makes that child a member of the Catholic Church (the one and only Church of Christ). It is not a Protestant Baptism, but a Catholic Baptism *performed by* a Protestant.[61] *Children* of Protestants who validly receive the Sacrament of Baptism are actually made members of the

---

[57] "one and only" or "sole": Latin, *unica*
[58] *Lumen Gentium*, art. 8 (italics added)
[59] *Notificatio*, 11 Mar. 1985, approved by Pope John Paul II.
[60] *Orientalium Ecclesiarum*, 1964, art. 2 (italics added)
[61] See p.484.

Catholic Church; however, if reared in a non-Catholic denomination, they will lose some of their baptismal heritage and then only be in "partial communion" with the Church.

Lex orandi, lex credendi: the law of worship establishes the law of belief. What ceremony, then, is needed for validly baptised *infants* of parents who become Catholics? None at all. They have no need of any ceremony to signify their entrance into the Church. They are *already* her members and, thanks to their parents' becoming Catholic, will be reared in full accordance with their Baptism. As for Protestant (or Orthodox) *adults*, they are incorporated into Christ by Baptism, at whatever age they receive it, but are only in *partial* or *imperfect* communion with the Church.[62] (By Protestant or Orthodox, we mean those who are so in good faith. Catholics who have defected from the Church are not in partial communion with the Church; they are outside the Church and in mortal sin until they repent and return).[63]

We may consider the question about the one true Church, with another scenario: suppose all non-Catholic Christian denominations were to go out of existence, and the Catholic Church survive, then the Church of Christ would survive intact. But suppose the Catholic Church were to become extinct (which will never happen, of course), and all others survive, then the Church of Christ would no longer exist, but only elements of it.

THE STRUCTURE OF THE CATHOLIC RELIGION:

> We go to the Father,
> through Jesus Christ His Son,
> in His Body the Church,
> in the Holy Spirit,
> through Mary,
> with Peter.

(a) the Father is the Origin without origin, the beginning and the goal of all.

(b) Jesus Christ is the one Mediator, the Way to the Father.

(c) to be in union with the Head, we must be joined to His Body which is the Church.

(d) the Holy Spirit is the Lord and Life-Giver, the Soul of the Mystical Body, the principle of our divine life of Grace.

(e) Jesus came to us through Mary, and through Mary we go to Him. She is our Mother, to protect, sustain and nourish our Christian life.

(f) as Catholics we do all this in union with the Pope, the successor of Peter, and never apart from him, since the Lord Jesus made Peter and his successors the visible centre of unity, and shepherds of the whole flock.

---

[62] *Unitatis Redintegratio*, Decree on Ecumenism, Second Vatican Council 1964, art. 3
[63] Cf. Can. 751, 1364.

GOD THE SANCTIFIER

Under this heading we treat of Grace and the Sacraments. Christ by His sufferings and death won for us the right to be made sons of God. We are made sons of God by Sanctifying Grace, which we obtain chiefly through the Sacraments.

CHAPTER 10

GRACE

Summary

I.   The solemn teaching of the Church.
II. Sanctifying Grace: its nature; a pearl of great price; a higher life, a participation in the Divinity. It makes us children of God, brethren of Christ, and enthrones the Holy Spirit in our soul. Its beauty hidden in this life; its efficacy will be known after death. It is caused in us by God through the Humanity of Christ. With it we receive the divine virtues, the moral virtues, and the gifts of the Holy Spirit. In adults, it is preserved and increased by good works. Good works cannot be performed without Actual Grace.
III. Actual Grace: its nature; it enlightens the understanding and strengthens the will; it helps the sinner and the unbeliever to Sanctifying Grace.
IV. External Graces.
V.   Merit: true and imperfect. The just can truly merit eternal life, and an increase of Sanctifying Grace and of glory hereafter; the sinner and the unbeliever can merit, not truly, but imperfectly, the actual graces (all except the first actual grace) that lead to Sanctifying Grace.
VI. Errors: Pelagianism, Semi-Pelagianism; Lutheranism, Calvinism, Jansenism.

I

The solemn teaching of the Church. The Church teaches solemnly:
(1)   that by Sanctifying Grace, dwelling within the soul, we are made just, holy, or pleasing to God;[1]
(2)   that Sanctifying Grace is lost by mortal sin;[2]
(3)   that it is not possessed by all just persons in equal measure;[3]
(4)   that it is increased in whoever fulfils the commandments of God and the Church;[4]

---

[1] T 1528-9, 1561
[2] T 1544, 1577
[3] T 1529 (end)
[4] T 1535, 1574

(5) that the just man by good works truly merits eternal life, an increase of Sanctifying Grace and of glory hereafter;[5]

(6) that it gives whoever possesses it at death the right to a degree of eternal happiness proportionate to his good works;[6]

(7) that Grace is necessary for good works;[7]

(8) that Actual Grace prepares the sinner or the unbeliever for the reception of Sanctifying Grace;[8]

(9) that the first Actual Grace which God gives the sinner or the unbeliever is altogether gratuitous and cannot in any sense be merited.[9]

II

SANCTIFYING GRACE

Sanctifying Grace: its nature. A pearl of great price. A higher life, a participation in the Divinity.

SANCTIFYING GRACE: ITS NATURE. Sanctifying Grace, or Habitual Grace, is a supernatural[10] gift of God by which the soul is made pleasing to Him. It removes all stain of grievous sin; it gives the soul a new and higher life, and fills it with splendour. It prepares the soul for that most intimate union with God which He has destined for it in the blessedness of Heaven. It is called *Sanctifying* Grace, because it sanctifies, makes holy, with the Holiness of God Himself. It is called a *supernatural* gift, because it is something to which no creature as such can ever have any natural right or claim. It is called *Habitual* Grace, because it dwells and endures in the soul as a habitual, i.e., permanent and constant, quality (unless, of course, destroyed by sin). It is also called *Justifying* Grace because by it the sinner is "justified", i.e., made just or righteous.

Sanctifying Grace is an inward or internal gift, so described because it dwells within the soul. It is not a substance, because it cannot exist by itself. It is, therefore, what is technically called an accident (see p.298). But it is not a mere passing accident like the red colour of a cloud at sunset; it is a permanent quality like the fixed colour of a flower.

SANCTIFYING GRACE, A PEARL OF GREAT PRICE. The value of Sanctifying Grace may be estimated from the price that was paid for it: the price was the Life-Blood of the Son of God. According to St Thomas, the whole

---

[5] T 1545-6, 1576, 1582

[6] T 1582

[7] T 1551-3, 1545-6

[8] T 1526-7, 1542

[9] T 1525

[10] For the meaning of Supernatural, see p.362.

world and all it contains is of less value in the eyes of God than the grace in a single human soul.[11] Of Sanctifying Grace, the soul may speak in the words of the Book of Wisdom: "I preferred her to sceptres and thrones, and I accounted wealth as nothing in comparison with her. Neither did I liken to her any priceless gem, because all gold is but a little sand in her sight, and silver will be accounted as clay before her. I loved her more than health and beauty, and I chose to have her rather than light, because her radiance never ceases. All good things came to me along with her, and in her hands uncounted wealth."[12]

SANCTIFYING GRACE, A HIGHER LIFE, A PARTICIPATION IN THE DIVINITY. The soul of man gives him a threefold life. It enables him to grow, mature and reproduce, like a plant (*vegetative life*); to feel and move, like the lower animals (*sensitive life*); and to think, reason, contemplate, and choose freely (*intellectual life*). But there is still a higher life which he may receive, a *divine life*, a supernatural life, a life which, by a true and real change, raises him above the natural excellence of the most exalted creatures, and sets him, so to speak, on a level with God Himself; a life which places him inside the veil that God has hung between Himself and His creation; *a life which gives him a share in what is special to God Himself, a share in the knowledge God has of His own perfections and in the happiness He derives therefrom.* This life is given to him by Sanctifying Grace. The state of grace is not merely the absence of mortal sin; it is a positive acquisition and elevation. "Therefore, if any one is in Christ", says St Paul, "he is a new creation".[13] God became man, so that man might, in a sense, become God. Thus, St Peter says that, through Christ, the Father "has granted to us His precious and very great promises, that through these you may ... become *partakers of the divine nature.*"[14] St John says, "we shall be like Him, for we shall see Him as He is",[15] and the Church prays at the Offertory of the Mass that "we may be made sharers in the Divinity of Him who deigned to participate in our humanity."

Sanctifying Grace makes us children of God, brethren of Christ, and enthrones the Holy Spirit in our soul.

SANCTIFYING GRACE MAKES US CHILDREN OF GOD. A rational creature as such is not a child but merely a servant of God. Through Sanctifying Grace, God adopts him as His son: "See what love the Father has given us", says St John, "that we should be called children of God; and so we

---

[11] S.T., i-ii, q. 113, a. 9, ad 2
[12] Wis 7:8-11
[13] 2 Cor 5:17
[14] 2 Pet 1:4
[15] 1 Jn 3:2

are";[16] "God sent forth His Son", says St Paul, "that we might receive adoption as sons";[17] "we are children of God, and if children, then heirs, heirs of God and fellow heirs with Christ."[18] Christ is the Son of the Father alone; the just man is the adopted child of the whole Trinity. We speak of the Father as the author of that adoption, of the Son as its pattern, of the Holy Ghost as its conveyor. When St Paul the Apostle speaks of "adoption", he has before his mind the Roman practice by which a child was transferred by solemn process of the law from the family of his birth to the family of his adoption. He was admitted to all the dignity and intimacy of a son born of the blood; he acquired a strict right to inherit; and thereafter, he identified himself with the traditions, the honour, and the interests of his new family. Now, it is somewhat in this way that we are transferred by Sanctifying Grace from the family of mankind to the family of God: we acquire the claim of children to His affection and intimacy. We are raised, as far as possible for creatures, to His dignity. His honour becomes ours; His friends become ours; and we receive from His hands the right to enter like heirs into the possession of such a share of His Kingdom as He appoints for us.

SANCTIFYING GRACE MAKES US BRETHREN OF CHRIST. Sanctifying Grace makes us other Christs. It makes us brethren to Him and to one another. Sharing in His life, we are joined to Him as the living branches are joined to the vine-stock, or as the members of the living body are joined to its head. "Brethren of Christ" is thus no empty name. Who would forfeit that loving intimacy with Him which it denotes and with which no human friendship can be compared? "Love Him and keep Him for thy friend who, when all go away, will not leave thee, nor suffer thee to perish in the end ... Thou must at last be separated from all things else, whether thou wilt or not. Keep thyself with Jesus both in life and death and commit thyself to His care who alone can help thee, when all others fail."[19]

SANCTIFYING GRACE ENTHRONES THE HOLY SPIRIT IN OUR SOUL. The change in the soul caused by Sanctifying Grace is wrought by all Three Divine Persons of the Blessed Trinity, but, being a work of Divine Love, it is properly ascribed to the Holy Spirit.[20] His divine presence is incompatible with serious sin, "for", as the Church prays, "He is Himself

---

[16] 1 Jn 3:1
[17] Gal 4:4-5
[18] Rom 8:16-17
[19] *Imitation of Christ*, Book II, Ch. 7
[20] See note on appropriation, p.315.

the remission of all sins."[21] The Holy Spirit is the Divine Artist who makes our soul like the soul of Jesus. It is He who joins us to Jesus in the mystic[22] brotherhood. And as it is the Holy Spirit who unites Father and Son in eternal love, so it is He who unites us as other sons to the Father. It is He who draws us into membership in the Blessed Trinity. Having made us other Christs, the Holy Spirit takes up His dwelling in our soul. He makes it His temple, and sets up His throne there: "Do you not know that your body is a temple of the Holy Spirit within you, which you have from God?"[23] The Father and the Son are with the Holy Spirit in this indwelling: "If a man loves me", says Christ, "he will keep My word, and My Father will love him, and We will come to him and make our home with him."[24] The "love" of which He speaks here as uniting the soul to Father and Son is the Personal Divine Love, the Holy Spirit. St Augustine says: "Love, therefore, which is of God, is properly the Holy Spirit, by whom the Love of God is shed abroad in our hearts, that Love by which the whole Trinity dwells in us".[25]

Sanctifying Grace: its beauty hidden from us in this life; its efficacy will be known after death.

ITS BEAUTY HIDDEN IN THIS LIFE. The soul of the just man reflects the very light of the Godhead; it shines with a radiance like that of Christ Himself in His Transfiguration on the mountain. If we could behold the beauty of this precious gift of Sanctifying Grace, it would be impossible for us ever to lose it by mortal sin, for all things else—wealth, rank, power, or anything we may name—would seem to us by contrast to be as valueless as a speck of dust. But God grants us no such vision in this life. It is His holy will to try us. He wants us to believe for a little while without seeing, until at death faith is changed into sight.

A real acorn and an artificial one may seem to be exactly alike in shape, colour and weight. The real acorn can develop into a superb oak, and be the originating cause of an immense forest, whereas the other acorn, the one carved and coloured by the hand of man, can never develop into anything. Whence this immeasurable difference between them? "The acorn produced by the oak contains a principle of life; that which man's cunning hath devised, in rude imitation, is dead and destined

---

[21] "quia ipse est remissio omnium peccatorum": *Missale Romanum*, 1975, p.338: 7th week of Easter, Saturday, Prayer over the Gifts. *Missale Romanum*, 1962, *Postcommunio*, Tuesday after Pentecost
[22] "Mystic", i.e., formed by grace.
[23] 1 Cor 6:19
[24] Jn 14:23
[25] *De Trinitate* 15:18, 32.

436

only to corruption. *This may serve as an illustration of the essential, though invisible, difference between a man in grace and a man devoid of grace.*[26]

ITS EFFICACY WILL BE KNOWN AFTER DEATH. After death we shall know the true meaning of being the friend and son of God. Sanctifying Grace, when perfected by the Light of Glory,[27] will effect a change immeasurably great in our understanding and will. It will give us a direct knowledge of the infinite Beauty of God. It will teach us more than if all the wonders and mysteries of the great world of men and angels were at once unveiled to our eyes, and it will add to that divine illumination of the mind an equal ardour of the will, so that we shall ever desire, while ever finding, the perfection of happiness.

Sanctifying Grace is caused in us by God through the Humanity of Christ. Since Sanctifying Grace places us at the height inaccessible to the natural power of even the greatest of Archangels, it is clear that it can come to us from none other than God Himself. God alone—i.e., the Blessed Trinity—is the source of all Grace; but He imparts it to us through the Human Nature of Christ. Christ as Man is the living instrument of God; He is the arm of God. Or, taking another comparison, we may represent Sanctifying Grace as the light of God's omnipotent Love passing through the wounds of Christ and flashing on the human soul where it produces the image of Him through whom it comes to us. St Teresa declares, "It is clear to me that if we wish to please God and to receive graces in abundance from Him, it is God's will that these graces come to us through the hands of Christ in His most sacred Humanity, that Humanity in which His Majesty has proclaimed that He is well pleased."[28]

To put this teaching in technical language: (a) God is the *principal* cause of Grace; Christ as Man is the *instrumental* cause. This does not mean that God produces, as it were, the larger part of Grace, and that Christ produces the smaller part. "Principal Cause" means "Source-cause", the source from which all Grace comes. Christ as Man, the *instrumental* cause, adds nothing of His own to it; He is its transmitter. (b) According to St Thomas,[29] the entire humanity of Christ—His Soul and Body and Blood—co-operates in the production of Grace, and his teaching is reflected in the prayer *Anima Christi* indulgenced by the Church, "Soul of Christ, sanctify me. Body of Christ, save me. Blood of Christ, inebriate me."[30] (c) When Grace is produced by a Sacrament, two instrumental causes are at work, viz., Christ as Man and the

---

[26] Bishop Vaughan, *Thoughts for all Times*, Washbourne 1911, Vol. I, p.155
[27] Cf. p.621.
[28] St Teresa of Jesus (of Avila) *Life*, Ch. 22.6
[29] S.T., iii, q. 8, a. 2, c.
[30] *Enchiridion Indulgentiarum*, 1968, n.10

Sacrament itself. To make this clear, let us adopt the illustration of St Thomas,[31] who speaks of the human nature of Christ as "the arm of God" because it is inseparably united to Him, while he compares the Sacrament to an implement—let us say, a sculptor's chisel—held in the fingers of Christ. God, Christ as Man, the Sacrament—all three are true causes of Grace, but not in the same way: God is the principal cause, while the other two are instrumental. St Thomas in this comparison brings out the idea that the humanity of Christ is joined to God in inseparable union, and is always used by Him in the production of Sanctifying Grace. On the other hand, he wishes to convey that a Sacrament is a means which God may or may not employ. God, as we know, often gives Sanctifying Grace outside the Sacraments: "God has bound salvation to the sacrament of Baptism, but He Himself is not bound by His own sacraments."[32]

With Sanctifying Grace we receive the Divine Virtues, the Moral Virtues, and the Gifts of the Holy Spirit.

THE DIVINE VIRTUES. With Sanctifying Grace we receive the three Divine Virtues of Faith, Hope and Charity. They are called Divine or Theological, because the acts that belong to them are directly prompted by God Himself under some aspect: we believe in God because of His truthfulness; we hope in God because of His willingness to help us; we love God because of His own goodness and loveliness. Faith opens our eyes to all that we must believe and do in order to be saved; Hope buoys us up and encourages us to struggle and persevere; Charity makes us the friends of God. In heaven, Faith will be changed to sight; and, with the attainment of all we desired, the need for Hope will disappear; but Charity will remain: it draws us near to God in this life, and it will unite us ever so much more closely to Him in the embrace of love throughout the life to come.

A virtue such as spoken of here is not a *facility*, but a *capacity*, for performing good works. We may illustrate by comparing the virtues to the limbs of the body: our feet enable us to walk, our hands to grasp, but it is only by frequent exercise that we acquire a facility in performing these actions.

THE MORAL VIRTUES. The Moral Virtues are all those other virtues which are necessary for a good Christian life. They may be grouped under the four main headings: Prudence, Temperance, Justice, and Fortitude.[33]

THE GIFTS OF THE HOLY SPIRIT. The nature of the Gifts of the Holy Spirit is explained in the chapter on the Sacrament of Confirmation. These virtues and gifts enable us to act like Jesus, just as sanctifying grace, which they accompany, makes our souls to be like that of Jesus. A Christian virtue

---

[31] S.T., iii, q. 62, a. 5, c.
[32] C 1257. Cf. St Thomas, S.T., iii, q. 64, a. 7.
[33] Wis 8:7

is, in fact, a power of acting in a Christ-like way. A virtuous action is not simply a good action: it is an action such as Jesus would have performed were He in our place. Since Jesus had the beatific vision during His human life, He did not have the virtues of faith and hope: they were replaced by the light of glory and the face-to-face possession of the Godhead. Our faith enables us to share imperfectly in His knowledge, and our hope enables us to trust one day to possess the Father in vision as He always did.

Can we know if we are in Grace? No one can know with absolute certainty that he is in the state of grace: "man knoweth not whether he be worthy of love or hatred."[34] "Since it is supernatural, grace escapes our experience and cannot be known except by faith. We cannot therefore rely on our feelings or our works to conclude thereby that we are justified or saved."[35] The Psalmist prays to God, "But who can discern his errors? Cleanse me from hidden faults."[36] St Paul declares, "I do not even judge myself. I am not aware of anything against myself, but I am not thereby acquitted."[37] It may happen that by dreadful pride or spiritual blindness, a person is guilty of mortal sins, especially of omission, but is unaware of it. St Thomas says that we may conjecture from the following three signs that we are in God's favour: (a) if we find contentment and delight in the thought of God, i.e., in reflecting on His goodness and loving care of us, in uplifting our mind and heart in prayer, and in frequenting the Sacraments; (b) if we despise earthly things, i.e., if we are detached from pleasures and riches, not desiring them for their own sakes but for use in the service of God; (c) if we are not conscious of any unforgiven mortal sin.[38]

In adults, Sanctifying Grace is preserved and increased by good works.

SANCTIFYING GRACE IS PRESERVED BY GOOD WORKS. We who have come to the use of reason cannot retain Sanctifying Grace, unless we prove by our actions that we are friends of God. Christ said to His Apostles: "He who has My commandments and keeps them, he it is who loves Me ... He who does not love Me, does not keep My words."[39] We must, therefore, live as true friends of Christ. We must be obedient to His words as conveyed to us by His holy Church. We must bring forth the fruit of good works, by which are understood all the acts of virtue we perform with a supernatural motive, i.e., a motive known to us by faith.

---

34 Ecclesiastes (Qoheleth) 9:1 (Douay)
35 C 2005. Cf. T 1533-4.
36 Ps 19:12; Vulgate, Ps 18:13: "Ab occultis [erroribus] munda me".
37 1 Cor 4:4
38 S.T., i-ii, q. 112, a. 5
39 Jn 14:21,24

SANCTIFYING GRACE IS INCREASED BY GOOD WORKS.[40]   Through Sanctifying Grace we are made living branches of the vine of Christ: "I am the vine", He says, "you are the branches ... Every branch of mine that bears no fruit, He"—i.e., God the Father—"takes away, and every branch that does bear fruit He prunes that it may bear more fruit."[41]   Thus, the branch that bears fruit will be given greater strength; its divine life, which is Sanctifying Grace, will continue to increase in proportion to the good works it produces. Hence, St Peter bids us "grow in grace."[42] And, in the Book of Proverbs,[43] we read: "the path of the righteous is like the light of dawn, which shines brighter and brighter until full day", i.e., his soul becomes more and more resplendent as he grows in Sanctifying Grace. "He that is just", St John is told, "let him be justified still; and he that is holy, let him be sanctified still",[44] i.e., let him enlarge his store of Sanctifying Grace.

Good works cannot be performed without Actual Grace. Every good work we perform is an act of one or more of the virtues. The virtues are, as it were, blossoms that appear on the branch the instant it is united to the mystic vine; and as the blossoms of an orchard tree will never yield fruit without sunshine and gentle rain, so without a help from God, known as Actual Grace, the virtues given with Sanctifying Grace will never produce the fruit of good works. Deprived of this help, we should be unable to keep God's Commandments, and so should lose Sanctifying Grace, which would thus prove a useless gift. Hence we say that Actual Grace is the due accompaniment of Sanctifying Grace—that is, God is urged by His own Wisdom and Justice to give it to us. We will now consider its nature.

III

ACTUAL GRACE

Actual Grace: its nature. It enlightens the understanding. It strengthens the will.

THE NATURE OF ACTUAL GRACE. Actual Grace is a supernatural gift of God, enabling us to do something towards eternal life. It is supernatural, because it is a help towards happiness to which we, as creatures, can have no claim. It is a transient, or passing, aid, and is present in the soul only while the soul is acting. It is like the electric current which, passing for an instant through the wire wound round an iron bar, gives the bar a

---

40 And by the Sacraments, as we shall see in the next chapter.

41 Jn 15:5,2

42 2 Pet 3:18

43 4:18

44 Apoc 22:11 (Douay)

momentary magnetic power. Sanctifying Grace, on the other hand, is something permanent, and is like the electric power in a storage battery. Sanctifying Grace makes us friends of God, while Actual Grace enables us to act the part of friends.

Actual Grace makes our acts pleasing to God because it makes them like the acts of Christ as Man. Thus, for instance, when by Actual Grace a sinner is made aware of his wickedness and begins to shrink from it as something detestable, his mind and his will are freely repeating the acts of the human mind and will of Jesus. He is beginning to see and feel, though ever so obscurely, some of that dread vision of sin which filled the mind and oppressed the Heart of Jesus at Gethsemane. And when a just man is moved by Actual Grace to advance higher and higher in holiness, he is but reproducing or copying, in his imperfect way, the human acts of divine love that are constantly welling up in the Mind and the Heart of the Saviour. Hence we say that Actual Grace makes our acts pleasing to God by adding to them a divine or Christ-like quality or flavour which we could not give them from our own natural powers. Actual Grace works on our souls in a twofold manner: (1) it enlightens the understanding, and (2) it strengthens the will and reduces the attractiveness of evil. According to St Augustine, it effects "not only that we discover what ought to be done, but also that we do what we have discovered; not only that we believe what ought to be loved, but also that we love what we have believed."[45]

From the intimate union of soul and body in the living man, it follows that every act of the intellect or the will is accompanied by some vibration or movement in the nervous system. Hence, it may, perhaps, be argued that the grace, e.g., which reforms a drunkard, effects some transformation in the sensuous appetite.

ACTUAL GRACE ENLIGHTENS THE UNDERSTANDING. It helps us to perceive the truths of Faith; to keep them in mind; to reason correctly about them; to know what we should believe and do. When, for instance, we say to ourselves, "God has revealed this: I must believe it", or, "This act is sinful: God forbids it: I must not do it", or, "God will be pleased with me, and make me love Him better, if I receive Holy Communion worthily", or, "What doth it profit me, if I gain the whole world and suffer the loss of my soul?"—in all this, we are thinking the thoughts that God's grace has awoken in us. St Paul says that we are not "sufficient", i.e., able "of ourselves to claim anything as coming from us; our sufficiency is from God."[46] "God calls us", says St Augustine, "by our innermost thoughts."[47]

ACTUAL GRACE STRENGTHENS THE WILL AND LESSENS THE ATTRACTIVENESS OF EVIL. Actual Grace inspires the will with fear of God's anger, with zeal for His service, and with desire for the happiness of

---

45 *De Gratia Christi*, Ch. 12
46 2 Cor 3:5
47 *In Ps.* 102, 16

His love. It helps us to fight down our passions, and to resist the call of the world that would make us forget God in the cares of business, the amassing of wealth, or the pursuit of secular knowledge. While leaving us free to accept it or reject it, it has the power, if we obey its impulse, to bind our hearts so firmly to God that nothing outside ourselves—no suffering, no blandishment—can ever relax its hold. It gave the mother of the Maccabees the strength to witness unmoved the torture of her seven sons, and to exhort her youngest to have pity on her and to die for the faith as bravely as his brothers.[48] (God gave grace under the Old Testament in consideration of the merits of the Redeemer who was to come). It made the Apostles and the Martyrs rejoice that they were found worthy to tread the blood-stained footprints of their Master. Its power was before the inspired mind of St Paul when he said: "I am sure that neither death, nor life, nor angels, nor principalities, nor things present, nor things to come, nor powers, nor height, nor depth, nor anything else in all creation, will be able to separate us from the love of God in Christ Jesus our Lord."[49]

Actual Grace helps the sinner and the unbeliever to acquire Sanctifying Grace. The state of Sanctifying Grace is opposed to the state of sin. Both cannot exist in the soul at the same time. One excludes the other, as light excludes darkness. But there is no such opposition between Actual Grace and sinfulness, because Actual Grace does not make the *soul* holy—only Sanctifying Grace can do that—but it makes our *acts* holy. Hence it is given to the sinner and the unbeliever as well as to the just. It is in fact the very means God uses to draw all erring souls to Him. To the unbeliever, He gives sufficient light to know the truth, and sufficient strength to embrace it; to the sinner, He gives the grace of repentance. He leads both to the Sacraments, the unbeliever to Baptism, the sinner to Penance.[50]

According to the Council of Trent, we may trace, as a rule, four stages in the progress of the new convert and baptised sinner towards Sanctifying Grace: (1) from faith to fear of God's judgements; (2) from fear to trust in the divine mercy and hope of forgiveness; (3) from hope to initial love (i.e., they begin to turn to God and to desire Him as the source of every good, and to turn away from sin as the cause of ruin and misery); (4) from initial love to contrition and a firm purpose to begin a new life. If the contrition is perfect, Sanctifying Grace is at once received. Perfect Contrition contains the implicit desire of Baptism, in the case of the unbeliever, and of the Sacrament of Penance, in the case of the sinner. If the sinner's contrition is imperfect, the actual reception of the Sacrament of Penance will be necessary for the reception of grace.

---

[48] 2 Macc 7
[49] Rom 8:38-39
[50] As to how the unbeliever is led on to make his first Act of Faith, see p.283.

Complete definition of Actual Grace. We are now able to give a complete definition of Actual Grace. It is a supernatural help from God, which, working within us, enlightens our mind and moves our will to do good and avoid evil for the sake of eternal life. Another definition may also be given, viz., Actual Grace is a supernatural help from God which, working within us, enables us to perform acts that lead to the acquisition, or effect the preservation and increase, of Sanctifying Grace.

IV

External graces. The grace of which we have been speaking so far is *internal* grace, so called because it dwells or acts *within* the soul. All the other helps which God gives us towards heaven are included under the term *external* grace. Thus, the Incarnation, the Scripture, and the Church are external graces, because they are not actually present within our souls. However, in ordinary speech, we are inclined to restrict the term "external grace" to circumstances or incidents, apparently casual, which God makes use of to prepare us for the reception of His internal grace. Our birth and upbringing in a Christian household, our education at a Christian school, our easy access to a church and the ministrations of a priest, all these are great external graces, for which we should express our gratitude to Divine Providence every day we live. Any seeming accident that leads us to God is an accident only in name; it is in truth an external grace. What could appear more fortuitous than a man's entering a church to escape a shower of rain, or his purposeless glance at a religious book? Yet we know that God uses such incidents to effect the conversion of sinners. The wound which the soldier Ignatius received at the siege of Pamplona seemed to be a mere accident, but it was the natural means God employed to make him a great saint. We should not forget, however, that external grace is grace only in a loose sense. The true grace is internal and works within us. Hence, for instance, our birth in a Christian home would have been of no profit to us, had not God given us the light to see the truth of all we were taught there, and the will to love Him. St Ignatius' reading of the *Lives of the Saints* during his hours of convalescence would have been nothing more than the pastime he intended it to be, had not God's grace been at work on him. God sometimes chooses to dispense altogether with external grace and to work a miracle in the supernatural order, an instance of which is the conversion of St Paul, whose frenzy as a persecutor of the Church, "breathing threats and murder against the disciples of the Lord",[51] was suddenly changed into an equal or greater zeal for the advancement of the Kingdom of Christ.

---

[51] Acts 9:1

V

Merit, true and imperfect. To merit a supernatural reward is to have a claim to it by reason of some service or good work done. The claim may be just, or it may be merely reasonable. In the former case, one merits truly or perfectly; in the latter, imperfectly.

To merit *truly* a reward from God, we require the following conditions: (1) On our part, good works, i.e., virtuous acts done freely in the state of grace from a supernatural motive. Such acts have a special dignity or worth in the sight of God: they are the acts of His friends, performed with the aid of His Actual Grace. (2) On the part of God, the promise to reward us.

The sinner cannot merit any reward truly, because he is not in the state of grace; but, by co-operating with Actual Grace, he establishes a claim on God's mercy, and is said to merit *imperfectly* the further graces he needs for his conversion.[52]

It is only adults who can merit: "good works" cannot be performed by those who have not come to the use of reason. At death, all opportunity of merit ceases: "it is appointed for men to die once, and after that comes judgement" (Heb 9:27); "each one may receive good or evil, according to what he has done *in the body*." (2 Cor 5:10)

The good works by which we merit are not of any advantage to God: "when you have done all that is commanded you, say, 'We are unworthy servants; we have only done what was our duty'."[53] But, though God is not benefited by our works, He has promised to reward us. It is precisely because of His promise that we can truly merit.

The just man by good works truly merits eternal life, an increase of Sanctifying Grace and of glory hereafter.[54] God not only enables the just man by actual grace to perform good works, but promises him a reward for so doing. "Rejoice and be glad", says our Divine Saviour to all whom He had mentioned in the Beatitudes, "for your reward is great in heaven."[55] "Be faithful unto death", He says to us in the Apocalypse, "and I will give you the crown of life."[56] And St Paul says that God "will render to every man according to his works: to those who ... seek for glory and honour and immortality, He will give eternal life."[57] The just man, therefore, in virtue of God's promise, truly merits a reward in heaven proportioned to

---

[52] Compare what is said above with the section on the merit of Christ, pp.402-3.
[53] Lk 17:10
[54] Cf. St Thomas, S.T., i-ii, q. 114, a. 8; and T 1545-6.
[55] Matt 5:12
[56] Apoc 2:10
[57] Rom 2:6-7; cf. 2 Tim 4:8; 1 Cor 3:8; Col 3:25.

his good works.[58]   The more precious, in the sight of God, are the good works that stand to a man's credit at death, the greater will be his eternal happiness.   Since capacity for eternal happiness is given by Sanctifying Grace, it follows that the just man truly merits an increase of this grace by his good works.[59]

Note. While it is true that neither man nor angel can ever attain to the sublime elevation of holiness enjoyed by the human soul of Christ the Redeemer or by His Blessed Mother, it is still an inspiring thought that, on a lower plane of sanctity, we can, by our acts day to day, constantly increase and intensify indefinitely our measure of Sanctifying Grace. One grain of wheat may in time fill all the granaries of the world. It is so with Sanctifying Grace—yet there is a difference: the multiplication of the grain of wheat depends, not on the good-will of the sower, but on the soil and weather, and may be frustrated by unfavourable conditions, while Sanctifying Grace cannot be denied its increase, except through our own fault.

VI

The doctrines of Original Sin, the Redemption, and Grace, are so intimately related, that the denial of any one of them leads to a denial of the other two.

PELAGIANISM. Pelagius (c. 400 A.D.) held: (a) That the sin of our first parents was not transmitted to their posterity; (b) that Christ came into the world, not to restore anything we had lost, but to set up an ideal of virtue, and so counteract the evil example of Adam; (c) that we can, of our own natural powers, and without any internal assistance from God, merit the happiness of the Beatific Vision.
Observations: (1) The doctrines of Pelagius were condemned as heretical by several Popes and Councils. (2) They are refuted by the arguments given in this and the preceding chapters.   (3) His followers, overwhelmed by the reasoning of St Augustine, almost completely abandoned their master's position, and contented themselves with holding that man can truly merit the first grace. This error, called *Semi-pelagianism*, was also condemned.

LUTHERANISM, CALVINISM, JANSENISM. According to these systems, Original Sin has annihilated free will. Man is the plaything of God or Satan, of grace or of sinful desire, and is incapable of freely choosing right or wrong. Luther held that every act of man is sinful, but that he can be saved by "faith", which he understood to mean a trust that God, for the sake of Christ, will not charge us with our sins. Calvin adopted this teaching, but his more logical mind led him on to the crowning absurdity that the very saving act of faith is itself a sin.

---

[58] But remember that the reception of the Sacraments, though not technically classified among "good works", can also give him a claim to eternal life, an increase of Sanctifying Grace and of glory.
[59] Merit, though lost by mortal sin, is restored on the recovery of Sanctifying Grace: this has long been the teaching of theologians, including St Thomas. It is taught by Pope Pius XI in his document for the Proclamation of the Holy Year of 1925: DS 3670.

Observations: (1) We may regard as self-condemned any system that rests on a denial of human liberty.

(2) If every act of man were sinful, then every commandment of God, e.g., to honour and love Him, to be just, truthful, etc., would be a commandment to commit sin. The Council of Trent upheld human dignity by defining that man's will is free; that he has not been utterly corrupted by Original Sin; and that even without Grace or Baptism he is capable of morally good acts, i.e., acts of obedience to the natural law.[60]

(3) The doctrine that faith alone saves us, purports to be based on the words of St Paul: "For we hold that a man is justified by faith apart from works of law."[61] Apart from ignoring the fact that St Paul was speaking of the *Mosaic* Law, Luther falsified the text by deliberately inserting the word "alone" after "faith." By the same process, he might have proved that *grace* and not faith, is the one and only essential for salvation—for the Apostle twice says elsewhere that grace saves us: "by grace you have been saved" and "all ... are justified by His grace".[62] Or Luther might equally have picked *Baptism*, for St Peter says, "Baptism ... now saves you."[63] Or he could have picked *hope*, for St Paul says, "in this hope we were saved."[64] Or he could have selected the *name of Jesus*, for, "there is no other name ... by which we must be saved."[65] Furthermore, he completely ignored or misinterpreted St Paul's teaching on charity: "if I have all faith, so as to remove mountains, but have not love, I am nothing."[66] St Paul upheld the indispensable role of good works: "to those who by patience *in well-doing* seek for glory and honour and immortality, He will give eternal life".[67] St Paul insisted that the Mosaic Law was over, but he equally insisted on the New Law of Christ: "Bear one another's burdens, and so *fulfil the law of Christ.*"[68] He never speaks of faith *alone*, but of "faith working through love."[69] Luther called the Epistle of James, "an epistle of straw" because it so clearly opposes his teaching: St James says, "faith by itself, if it has no works, is dead" and, "a man is justified by works and not by faith alone".[70]

The heresy known as Jansenism is found in the work, *Augustinus*, written by Cornelius Jansen, Bishop of Ypres (d. 1638), but not published until two years after his death. He died in communion with the Church, professing full submission to her decrees. Man, he held, is the helpless victim of rival forces: grace urging him to what is good, concupiscence to what is evil. He acts virtuously or sinfully according to the relative strength of these forces. His followers were remarkable for the rigorous conditions they exacted of penitents and communicants.

---

[60] DS 1555
[61] Rom 3:28
[62] Eph 2:5; 2:8
[63] 1 Pet 3:21; cf. Tit 3:5.
[64] Rom 8:24
[65] Acts 4:12
[66] 1 Cor 8:2
[67] Rom 2:7
[68] Gal 6:2
[69] Gal 5:6
[70] James 2:17, 24

CHAPTER 11

DIVINE WORSHIP AND THE SACRAMENTS
IN GENERAL

Summary

I.   The solemn teaching of the Church.
II.   Definition of Sacrament.
III. The Minister and the Subject of a Sacrament.
IV.   The Sacraments are true causes of grace.
V.   The number of the Sacraments; the Blessed Eucharist, how related to the other Sacraments. The relation of prayer to Sacramental Grace.
VI.   The Sacred Liturgy. The Holy Oils. The liturgical year. The cult of the saints. Answers to objections. Christian funerals.
VII. The sacramentals.

I

The solemn teaching of the Church. The Church teaches solemnly that:
(1)   there are seven Sacraments of the New Law, neither more nor less, viz., Baptism, Confirmation, Blessed Eucharist, Penance, Anointing of the Sick, Holy Orders, and Matrimony;[1]
(2)   that all the Sacraments were instituted by Christ Himself;[2]
(3)   that they truly cause grace in whoever is fit to receive them;[3]
(4)   that the Sacraments of the New Law confer grace *ex opere operato*, i.e., by virtue of performance of the rite itself;[4]
(5)   that the Sacraments of Baptism, Confirmation, and Holy Orders imprint a *character*, or indelible mark, on the soul, and that therefore, they cannot be received more than once;[5]
(6)   that, to confer a Sacrament validly, the minister must intend to do what the Church does, but need not be in a state of grace;[6]
(7)   that it is legitimate and profitable to honour the Blessed Virgin, the Angels and Saints, and to seek their intercession before God;[7]
(8)   that it is legitimate and profitable similarly to make and venerate— without the adoration of *latria*[8]—holy images representing Our

[1] F 1310, T 1601
[2] T 1601
[3] T 1606-7
[4] T 1608
[5] T 1609
[6] T 1617
[7] T 1821, 1823
[8] latria = divine worship. See p.391.

Saviour, the Blessed Virgin, the Angels and Saints, as well as to venerate relics of Saints.[9]

II

Definition of Sacrament. A Sacrament is an outward rite instituted by Christ, the Son of God, to signify grace, and to give the grace it signifies.

"An outward rite" i.e., an outward act or action, appointed by God as a means of sanctification or worship. The word "instituted" means that the Sacraments were set up by Christ as permanent things, i.e., for frequent and public use.

A SACRAMENT IS AN OUTWARD RITE. A Sacrament is an outward rite, because it can be perceived by the senses. Christ founded a visible Church; He, therefore, gave it visible, or outward rites. Hence we find that people enter its membership by the public rite of Baptism; that its pastors are solemnly and publicly ordained; that marriages between its members take place in its presence; and, in general, that all openly profess their faith, and manifest their unity, by availing themselves of the same public rites, and by seeking spiritual life and strength at the same fountains of grace. Christ also gave us these outward rites because: (1) He wished us to know with certainty and through the evidence of our senses the exact moment His grace is given to us; "if you were without a body", says St John Chrysostom, "He would have given you simple and incorporeal gifts, but since your soul is united to a body, He gives you spiritual things in visible things."[10] (2) He wished to humble the ever insurgent pride of men by compelling them to use for their sanctification the simplest material things. He wished that we who, from the days of Adam, have been misusing His inanimate creatures for our spiritual ruin, should turn back humbly to things of the same order, and use them as instruments of holiness.[11]

THE SACRAMENTS WERE INSTITUTED BY CHRIST. Christ Himself is the institutor of all the Sacraments, (a) because He earned by His Passion, and marked off, the grace which each should confer, and (b) because He personally appointed the several sacramental rites—in detail for Baptism and the Blessed Eucharist, and in general outline for the rest.

THE SACRAMENTS CONFER GRACE. The Sacraments confer Sanctifying Grace, or an increase thereof. They also confer Sacramental Grace, by

---

[9] DS 600-3; T 1822-4
[10] *Hom. in Matt.* 82, 4
[11] St Thomas, S.T., iii, q. 61, a. 1

which is meant the "gifts proper to the different Sacraments."[12] Sacramental Grace is a new orientation of the whole supernatural organism toward the purpose intended by the individual Sacrament.[13] Sacramental Grace includes also the claim to the special actual graces that help us to attain the object of each Sacrament.

THE SACRAMENTS SIGNIFY THE GRACE THEY CONFER. The Sacraments signify, or indicate, the grace they confer, (1) because, in each, words are used which clearly point to the spiritual effect produced, e.g., "I baptise you ...", "I absolve you from your sins ..."; and (2) because, in each, the meaning of the words is enforced or illustrated by the ceremony itself. In Baptism, Confirmation, Anointing of the Sick, and Holy Orders, the words are accompanied by an appropriate action or gesture: thus, in Baptism, the washing with water signifies the spiritual cleansing; in Confirmation, the anointing signifies strengthening, and Anointing of the Sick, healing. In Holy Orders, the imposition of hands signifies the giving of the Holy Spirit. In the Blessed Eucharist, the bread and wine, over which the priest utters the words of consecration, suggest spiritual food into which they are changed. In Penance, the whole ceremony has the appearance of an act of reconciliation; the sorrowful confession of guilt at the tribunal of mercy presaging and pointing to the absolution that is to follow. Matrimony signifies grace, not exactly from the words used or any action accompanying them, but because, as we are taught by the Holy Spirit, speaking to us through the lips of St Paul,[14] Christian marriage is a figure of the union, so fruitful in spiritual gifts, of Christ with His Church.

Matter and Form. In explaining how the Sacraments signify grace, the distinction between matter and form has been deliberately omitted. The matter is that part of the Sacrament which vaguely signifies the effect produced; the form is that part which definitely signifies the effect: thus, in Baptism, the washing with water, by which some kind of cleansing is denoted, is the matter, while the form consists in the words, "I baptise you", etc. In the case of Penance and Matrimony, these terms raise special difficulties.

---

[12] C 2003. Cf. St Thomas, S.T., iii, q. 62, a. 2.
[13] Mons. A. Piolanti, *De Sacramentis*, Marietti 1960, p.71
[14] Eph 5:22-33

III

The Minister and the Subject of a Sacrament.

THE MINISTER OF A SACRAMENT. The Minister is the one who performs the sacramental rite.

Qualifications of the Minister. The Minister must be qualified for his office. Thus, for all the Sacraments except Baptism and Matrimony, he must be in Holy Orders. Baptism may be administered by a layman; Matrimony is conferred by the parties to the marriage covenant. Fuller particulars are given below in the separate treatment of each Sacrament.

Conditions required of the Minister in the act of conferring a Sacrament. (a) The Minister must employ the proper form of words, or words of the same meaning; he must perform the prescribed action; he must use the prescribed thing (e.g., water in the case of Baptism; oil in the case of Anointing of the Sick). (b) He must intend to do what the Church does, or to do as Catholics or Christians do.

If the Minister is duly qualified, and if the conditions required of him are present, the Sacrament is validly, or truly, conferred. It is not essential that the Minister be in the state of grace or even believe in the efficacy of the rite: the Church teaches that Baptism given by a heretic, Jew or pagan, is valid.[15] The condition of his soul does not affect the validity of his act. The reason is that the virtue of what he does comes, not from him, but from Christ. Christ is the Principal Minister of all the Sacraments—i.e., He works through the voice and hands of the earthly Minister.[16] As early as the third century, Pope St Stephen (253-7) declared, against the learned St Cyprian, that the Church had always held that a Sacrament can be validly conferred by a heretic. St Augustine says that whether it be Peter or Paul or Judas who administers Baptism, it is equally Christ who baptises.[17] Such a doctrine is a consolation to the laity who can, therefore, have perfect confidence in the rites of the Church without the need to know the personal state of the minister.

THE SUBJECT OF A SACRAMENT. The subject of a Sacrament is the one who receives it. All the Sacraments, with the exception of the Blessed Eucharist, exist only at the moment when they are being conferred on the subject. The Blessed Eucharist, from its very nature, does not merely consist, like the other Sacraments, in a passing action, but in the continued presence of Christ under the appearances of bread and wine; and as corporal food is

---

[15] DS 646; T 1617; F 1315; DS 2536
[16] See below, pp.452-3.
[17] *In Ioannis Evang,* tract 5, sect. 18

450

food independently of its consumption, so the Blessed Eucharist exists as spiritual food independently of its reception by the faithful in Holy Communion.

The valid reception of the Sacraments. To receive a Sacrament validly is to receive it really or truly. To receive a Sacrament invalidly is to receive it merely in appearance but not in reality. (a) To receive a Sacrament validly, the Subject *must be capable of receiving it:* thus, an infant is incapable of receiving the Sacrament of Matrimony or Penance; a woman is incapable of receiving Holy Orders. Those who have not received Baptism are incapable of receiving the other Sacraments. Even the Blessed Eucharist produces no effect whatever on the souls of the unbaptised. (b) Adults cannot receive any Sacrament validly without *the intention or will to receive it.* For infants and those who have never had the use of reason, no intention is required for the valid reception of Baptism, Confirmation, and the Blessed Eucharist.

The worthy or fruitful reception of the Sacraments. To receive a Sacrament worthily is to receive it with the due dispositions. To receive it fruitfully is to receive the graces it gives. Worthy reception is, therefore, practically the same as fruitful reception, the former expression looking chiefly to the recipient's fitness, the latter to the good effects produced.

Division of the Sacraments. The Sacraments can be divided into *Sacraments of Initiation* (Baptism, Confirmation and Blessed Eucharist), *Sacraments of Healing* (Penance, Anointing of the Sick), and *Sacraments at the Service of Communion* (Holy Orders, Marriage).[18] These last two may also be called Sacraments of Public Service.

The Sacraments can also be divided into *Sacraments of the Dead* (Baptism and Penance) and *Sacraments of the Living* (the other five). The *Sacraments of the Dead* are so called, because they raise the soul from spiritual death (absence of Sanctifying Grace) to spiritual life (presence of Sanctifying Grace). The *Sacraments of the Living* get their name from their presupposing the presence of Sanctifying Grace in the soul, which they augment or intensify.

For the *worthy* reception of the *Sacraments of the Dead,* adults require faith, hope, and at least attrition for grave sin committed.[19] For the *worthy* reception of the *Sacraments of the Living,* they must be in the state of grace. Two points may, however, be noted: (1) A Sacrament of the Dead, if received in the state of grace, gives an increase of grace like a Sacrament of

---

[18] Cf. C 1211.
[19] Since attrition is founded on faith, and must always be accompanied by the hope of salvation, it would have been sufficient to mention attrition as the only essential for the worthy reception of Baptism, or Penance by one who has committed grave sin.

the Living; (2) it is generally held that a Sacrament of the Living will give Sanctifying Grace to one in mortal sin, provided he has imperfect contrition and is unaware at the moment of his sinful state. (This doctrine has an important bearing on the Sacrament of the Blessed Eucharist, supplying us with the practical direction: "Do not abstain from Holy Communion because of a doubt." Even if he who doubts is actually burdened with grievous sin, it is none the less true that he is "unaware of his sinful state." Holy Communion together with the act of attrition will restore his soul to Sanctifying Grace. He may, therefore, approach the altar with the confidence of an invited guest).

We may also speak of the Sacraments for *individuals* and the *social* Sacraments (see below, pp.454-5).

Sacrilegious reception of the Sacraments. A person who knowingly and wilfully approaches a Sacrament of the Living in mortal sin, or a Sacrament of the Dead without proper dispositions, profanes what is most holy, and commits a grave sin of sacrilege. The holiness of a Sacrament is beyond our full comprehension; it is a source of grace, and grace is the fruit of the Precious Blood of Christ. St Paul warns the Corinthians that unworthy Communions among them were the cause of the sickness of some and the death of others: "Whoever, therefore, eats the bread or drinks the cup of the Lord in an unworthy manner will be guilty of profaning the body and blood of the Lord. ... For any one who eats and drinks without discerning the body eats and drinks judgment upon himself. That is why many of you are weak and ill, and some have died."[20]

IV

The Sacraments are true causes of grace. Christ the Son of God is the invisible Head of the Church: He teaches us through her lips; He sanctifies us through the Sacraments He has committed to her; He has made them true causes of grace. As the water of the distant reservoir gushes forth at fountains and hydrants all over a city, so the great reservoir of grace, filled for us by the Passion and Death of Christ, sends forth its living water at its appointed outlets, the Sacraments. As surely as our Saviour cleansed the leper by touching him and saying, "be clean";[21] as surely as He raised Lazarus to life with the words, "Lazarus, come out";[22] so surely does He work grace in our souls through the Sacraments. Christ as Man uttered the command of God—the command of the Three Divine Persons—when

---

[20] 1 Cor 11:27,29-30
[21] Matt 8:3
[22] Jn 11:43

raising Lazarus to life, but the power which those words called into action was the infinite power of God. Just as on earth, virtue came forth from His Divine Person through His Sacred Humanity, so now Grace comes from that same Divine Person through the medium of the Sacraments. In the Sacraments, we touch, as it were, His very hands, and hear His voice. It is He who, through them, produces the effect of grace. Neither the Minister nor the Subject is the contributory cause. This last point may be better understood from the following illustration: A king's treasure-house is filled with heavy bars of gold. A warden is in charge of the door, and opens to all who have the right of entry. Each one who comes takes away with him as much gold as he can carry. Some take several bars, others few, and others again, because of their weakness, none at all. The treasure-house is the Sacrament; the gold is the grace it gives; the warden is the Minister; those who come for the gold are the Subjects of the Sacrament, and their strength represents their good dispositions. To apply the figure in detail: as the warden turns the key effectively whether he be a loyal servant or not, so the Minister confers the Sacrament validly, whatever be the condition of his soul in the eyes of God. Again, as he who visits the treasure-house bears away as much gold as his strength allows, so the Subject of a Sacrament receives grace according to his good dispositions: the better the dispositions, the more grace is received; and, if there be no good dispositions, then no grace is obtained. Lastly, as the strength of the visitor to the treasure-house does not, as a cause, contribute one ounce or one grain to his share of gold, so the good dispositions do not contribute as causes to one's share of grace, but merely enable one to receive it in greater or less abundance; as all the gold is the gift of the king, so all the grace is the gift of God. Hence, we say, technically, that good dispositions are not a *cause* of grace but a *condition*, i.e., they do not themselves contribute anything to the grace received through the Sacrament, but merely regulate or determine the amount we are fit to receive.

THEIR FRUITFULNESS. (1) It follows from the preceding that the Sacraments may be validly and lawfully received, but with little fruit because of imperfect dispositions. A series of careless Confessions and Communions may easily end in sinful indifference to these most precious gifts of Christ, and in the shipwreck of faith. (2) Since the Sacraments are the instruments by which Christ conveys His grace to us, it follows that they are not mere signs of grace. It follows also that their holiness is the holiness of Christ Himself, and that no one, no matter how perfect his dispositions may be, can exhaust the stream of Sanctifying Grace that flows through them.

V

The number of the Sacraments. Had the Church never expressly defined that the Sacraments instituted by Christ are seven in number, the doctrine could still have been inferred with certainty from the facts of history. The Assyrian Church, whose separation dates from the fifth century, has the same seven Sacraments that we do. The oriental orthodox Churches (Armenian, Coptic, Ethiopian, Syrian, Malankara), whose separation dates later in the fifth century, have the same seven Sacraments.[23] Today the Greek and Russian (and other Byzantine) Orthodox Churches, whose separation dates from the eleventh century on, are in perfect accord with us on the divine institution, the number, the grace-giving power, and the use and identity of the Sacraments.[24] The tension between these Churches and the See of Rome over the centuries excludes the possibility of their having borrowed anything from Rome since their separation. Nor did Rome borrow anything from them. In East and West, therefore, in the first millennium, the doctrine with its practical application in the everyday life of the Christian, was recognised as an essential part of the true religion. Such agreement in belief and practice, in many and diverse countries, over an entire millennium, puts its divine origin beyond question. The Protestant Reformers of the sixteenth century presumed to remodel the Church of Christ and its institutions. By denying that the Sacraments give grace, by reducing their number from seven to three or two, and, in particular, by their rejection of the Sacrament of Holy Orders with its power to consecrate the Blessed Eucharist and to forgive sin, they left themselves but a poor remnant of Christianity. They broke the cisterns of grace given them by Christ.

Christ gave us seven Sacraments, because such is the number of our spiritual needs. The first five in the list concern Christians as individuals; the last two concern Christians as members of society.

The Sacraments for individuals. The Church on earth is the Church Militant, an army engaged in spiritual warfare. The comparison helps us to grasp the significance of the Sacraments appointed for the welfare of the individual. Through Baptism, he is born, as it were, into a race of warriors. In Confirmation, he comes of age, he takes arms, and goes forth a fully-equipped soldier to battle with the evil one. He is fed and nourished with the spiritual food of the Blessed Eucharist. If he be wounded by sin, Penance is at hand to restore him to health. In this last contest, Extreme Unction completes the healing process of Penance, removes any vestiges of weakness, and gives him strength and courage to win the soldier's reward, which, for him, is death in the state of grace and Heaven for eternity.

---

[23] The terminology and practice of the Assyrians and the other five Churches differ from Catholic usage, however, and this has misled some writers (e.g., D. Attwater) into saying they have fewer than seven. For a full explanation, see M. Jugie, *Theologia Dogmatica Christianorum Orientalium ab Ecclesia Catholica Dissidentium*, Paris 1935, Tom. V, pp.279-334. Anointing of the Sick has fallen into disuse in two of the Churches: the Armenian and Ethiopian: cf. M. Jugie, *ibid.*, p.637.

[24] Cf. S. Bulgakov, *The Orthodox Church*, St Vladimir's Seminary Press, N.Y. 1988, pp.112-5; M. Jugie, *op. cit.*, Paris 1930, Tom. III, pp.15-25; B. Leeming S.J., *Principles of Sacramental Theology*, Longmans, London 1956, pp.578-81.

The social Sacraments. Since the Sacraments are rites of a visible Church, and are designed for the welfare of its members, they may all be described as "social", but the term can be applied with particular justice to Holy Orders and Matrimony as promoting in a very special way the general well-being of the whole Christian society. The former provides the Church with a succession of bishops and priests to teach, govern and sanctify the faithful, while the latter consecrates family life, and gives parents the grace, by their instruction and good example, to give the Church a new generation of worthy members. Thus, Holy Orders perpetuates the government of the Church; Matrimony, its membership.

THE BLESSED EUCHARIST IN ITS RELATION TO THE OTHER SACRAMENTS. In the mind of St Thomas, not only the Sacrament of Holy Orders, but also the Sacraments of Baptism, Confirmation, Penance, Extreme Unction and Matrimony are, as it were, the servants of the Blessed Eucharist.[25]

Baptism is administered by the Church with the intention that its recipient should obey the command of Christ to nourish his soul on the Divine Food of the Blessed Eucharist.[26] It is conceived as preparing the soul for the Blessed Eucharist.

Confirmation completes the preparation begun in Baptism. It encourages us to come more frequently to the Lord's Table, and enables us, by its Gifts and Graces, to derive more profit from the Sacred Banquet.

Penance removes the obstacles to the worthy reception of the Blessed Eucharist.

Anointing of the Sick (or *Extreme Unction*), which the dying receive before Viaticum, helps them to a more perfect union with Christ in Holy Communion.

Holy Orders was instituted for the service of the Altar, for the Sacrifice of the Mass, for the distribution of Holy Communion and for the preparation of souls for its reception.

Matrimony, by its graces, enables couples to nurture and increase their love of Him by means of the Blessed Eucharist, and enables parents to train their children by word and example to love God above all things and to lead their children also to the Sacred Banquet.

THE RELATION OF PRAYER TO SACRAMENTAL GRACE. The question may be asked: "If the Sacrament of Baptism, e.g., gives us the right to all the actual graces essential for a good Christian life, how, then, can it be held that prayer too is necessary?" We may reply: (1) The actual graces to which Baptism gives us a claim enable us to perform all the duties of a Christian life. One of these duties is the duty of prayer, the prayer of petition as well as the prayer of praise. Thus, the actual grace which moves us to pray,—the grace of prayer, in other words—comes to us from the Sacrament of Baptism. God does, indeed, give this grace of prayer to the unbaptised and the sinner, but He gives it in special fullness to the living members of His Church, and in such a form that they are urged to ask His help to live up to the Christian ideal.

---

[25] S.T., iii, q. 65, a. 3
[26] Cf. S.T., iii, q. 73, a. 2.

Fittingness of the seven Sacraments		
Needs of the person	**Body**	**Soul**
As an individual	Birth	Baptism
	Growth	Confirmation
	Nourishment	Holy Eucharist
	Healing from sickness	Penance
	Restoration to full strength	Anointing of the Sick
As a member of a community	Leadership	Holy Orders
	Growth and continuity	Marriage

from St Thomas Aquinas (1224-1274)
Summa Theologica, III, q. 65, a. 1

(2) The claim which the Sacraments give us to obtain from God a whole series of actual graces is indeed a true claim to which God plays a special heed; but He requires us to present the claim to Him as humble servants in the form of prayer.

(3) God does not deal with us as though we were mere machines. He deals with us as living persons with understanding and will. Hence, e.g., when He gives those who have been confirmed the grace to overcome temptations against faith, He enlightens their mind to see the danger and moves their will to ask Him for further help to turn away from it. The very act of turning away from sin is in the nature of prayer, for it is a turning to God, a profession that we wish to belong to Him and not to Satan. It is so with every actual grace we receive through the other Sacraments: our conscious correspondence with it is always a form of prayer.

VI

The Sacred Liturgy. Its origin. Definition. Exterior and interior worship.

THE SACRED LITURGY. The Greek word "liturgy" originally meant a "public work or function". In the context of the Christian religion it means the participation of God's People in "the work of God", and in particular, the official, public, divine worship performed by the People of God. The celebration of the seven Sacraments forms the major part of the liturgy of the Church.

ORIGIN OF THE LITURGY. When God instituted the Old Law and Covenant, He Himself laid down provisions for sacred rites by which the Chosen People were to worship Him, the one true God. He established various kinds of sacrifice and designated the ceremonies with which they were to be offered to Him. He gave exact directions regarding the Ark of the Covenant, Feast Days and Years of Jubilee. He established a High Priest—Aaron, and his descendants—and chose the tribe of Levi to supply priests. He ordained the vestments they were to wear and decreed the sacred functions they were to perform: all this is recorded in the Books of Exodus and Leviticus. In His earthly life, Jesus Himself participated in the Temple worship and observed other Jewish rites.

Yet all this, says the Epistle to the Hebrews, was "but a shadow of the good things to come instead of the true form of those realities". Jesus Christ, the High Priest—not from the tribe of Levi, but the tribe of Judah—offered a perfect sacrifice with "His own blood, thus securing an eternal redemption." "Therefore He is the mediator of a new covenant", and "when there is a change in the priesthood, there is necessarily a change in the law as well."[27] Christ brings a new and superior priesthood and sacrifice, and a new law of worship.

CHRISTIAN LITURGY: DEFINITION. The "liturgy is ... an exercise of the priestly office of Jesus Christ, in which man's sanctification is symbolised by means of sensible signs, and effected in ways appropriate to each sign, and full public worship is executed by the Mystical Body of Jesus Christ, that is, by the Head and His members."[28] This definition includes the liturgy's essential elements: (1) it is priestly; (2) it takes place by means of external signs; (3) it includes worship of God and sanctification of man; (4) it is public; (5) it is performed by Christ and the Church.

EXTERIOR AND INTERIOR WORSHIP. The divine worship rendered by the Church must necessarily be exterior, since the nature of man as a composite of body and soul requires it to be so. Divine Providence has disposed that by things seen we may be drawn to the love of things unseen. The Church as a social body necessarily requires a public form of common worship. This common outward worship reveals and strengthens the unity of the Mystical Body. However, ritual is not an end in itself; it must both foster and be the outward expression of inward sentiments of adoration of God, submission to His divine majesty and will, and the desire to serve Him and to hand over to Him all that we have and all that we are.[29] The liturgy is both active and contemplative. Its contemplative dimension includes the

---

[27] Heb 10:1; 9:12; 9:15; 7:12

[28] *Sacrosanctum Concilium*, Constitution on the Sacred Liturgy, Second Vatican Council, 1963, art. 7. Cf. C 1070; Can. 834 §1; DS 3841. Here, "sensible" means "perceptible to the senses".

[29] Cf. Pius XII, *Mediator Dei*, 1947, Encyclical on the Sacred Liturgy, Part I: DS 3842.

sense of awe, reverence and adoration, which are fundamental attitudes in our relationship with God.

Participation in the liturgy. Excellence of the liturgy. Christ's presence in it. The Holy Trinity in the liturgy.

PARTICIPATION BY THE LAITY. The Sacred Liturgy, however impressive, is not a theatrical spectacle attended by onlookers, but an act of divine worship by ministers and faithful alike. "Mother Church earnestly desires that all the faithful be led to that full, conscious, and actual participation[30] in liturgical celebrations which is demanded by the very nature of the liturgy, and to which the Christian people, 'a chosen race, a royal priesthood, a holy nation, a redeemed people' have a right and duty by virtue of their Baptism."[31] The laity participate by performing their particular actions, by saying or singing the hymns, psalms and parts of the liturgy proper to them, by following the other texts, listening to the readings and sermon, and by offering themselves to God in union with the sacred action. Active participation does not preclude, but necessarily demands, the inner participation in silence, stillness, listening and contemplation. In the Mass, for example, the laity join with the priest in offering the saving Victim to God, and themselves along with Him. Their highest form of participation is to receive the Lamb of God in the Sacred Banquet.

EXCELLENCE OF THE SACRED LITURGY. "Inasmuch as it is a work of Christ the Priest and of His Body which is the Church, every liturgical celebration is a sacred action *par excellence*, whose efficacy no other action of the Church can equal by the same title and to the same degree." The "liturgy is the summit toward which the activity of the Church is directed, and, at the same time, the fount from which all her power flows."[32] Hence, the Church prays, "Grant us, we beseech Thee, O Lord, to frequent these mysteries worthily, for, as often as the commemoration of this sacrifice is celebrated, the work of our redemption is accomplished."[33]

THE PRESENCE OF CHRIST IN THE SACRED LITURGY. Christ is always present in *His Church*, especially in her liturgical celebrations. He is present in the person of His *minister*, who stands in His place. He is present in the *congregation*, for He has promised, "where two or three are gathered in my

---

[30] *actuosa participatio*

[31] *Sacrosanctum Concilium*, art. 14. Cf. 1 Pet 2:9; 2:4-5; C 1141.

[32] *Sacrosanctum Concilium*, art. 7, 10.

[33] *Missale Romanum*, 1975, p.341, 2nd Sunday of the year, Prayer over the Gifts. *Missale Romanum*, 1962, Secret of 9th Sun. after Pentecost. Cf. *Sacrosanctum Concilium*, art. 2; *Lumen Gentium*, art. 3. Cited in St Thomas, S.T., iii, q. 83, a. 1, and *Mediator Dei*, Part II.

name, there am I in the midst of them".[34] He is present in His *sacred Word*, since it is He Himself who speaks when the Sacred Scriptures are read in the Church. He is present in the *Sacraments*, for when anyone baptises, it is really Christ Himself who baptises. He is present in the *Sacrifice* of the Mass, for He who once offered Himself on the Cross, now offers Himself through His priests; and He is above all present in the *Eucharistic Species of His Body and Blood*.[35] The liturgy celebrates and draws upon the power of Christ's Paschal Mystery, for as St Leo the Great says, "what was visible in our Redeemer has passed over into His Sacraments".[36]

THE HOLY TRINITY IN THE LITURGY. God the Father sent His Son into the world to save it; and God the Son sent the Holy Spirit to complete His work on earth. Within the Church's worship, as in the Redemption, each of the three Divine Persons has a particular role. The Holy Spirit draws us to Christ, joins us to Him, and enables the Church to celebrate Christ's Paschal Mystery. Through Christ, in the Spirit, we have access to the Father,[37] and through Christ, we worship the Father "in spirit and truth."[38] God the Father is both the source and goal of the sacred liturgy.

Elements of the liturgy. The Holy Oils. The liturgical year. Christ's mysteries live on His Church. Feasts.

THE LITURGY IS COMPOSED OF SYMBOLS, SIGNS AND ACTIONS. As an extension of the Incarnation, the Sacred Liturgy uses the matter created by God, and involves persons, places, things and times.

In the following paragraphs, we restrict ourselves to the Roman rite, except where otherwise specified.

Persons and actions. The bishop, priest, deacon, acolytes, lectors, readers, cantor, choir (schola) and members of the congregation all have their distinctive role in the sacred action. Man's soul is active in prayer and adoration, his five senses are employed, and also his whole body in gestures and sacred movements, such as joining or extending hands in prayer, making the sign of the cross, processing, standing, bowing, genuflecting, and kneeling. The bishop, priests and ministers also perform the actions particular to their office: e.g., pouring the waters of Baptism; prostrating themselves before the altar; kissing the altar and Gospel; incensing the altar, Gospel, crucifix, relics, gifts, ministers and people; anointing with holy oil at Baptism, Confirmation, Anointing of the Sick, dedications of altars and churches; elevating the Blessed Eucharist; raising their hands in blessing, or imposing them upon the sick or ordinands.

---

[34] Matt 18:20

[35] Cf. *Mediator Dei*, Part I: DS 3840, and *Sacrosanctum Concilium*, art. 7

[36] *Sermo* 74, 2, quoted in C 1115.

[37] Cf. Eph 2:18.

[38] Jn 4:23-24

Music and language. When truly worthy of the sacred liturgy, sacred music and singing make the celebration of the Sacred Mysteries more dignified and solemn, help lift up the hearts of the faithful to God, and are conducive to rendering God glory. Through sacred music, "prayer is expressed more pleasantly, the mystery of the liturgy, with its hierarchical and community nature, is more openly manifested, the unity of hearts is more profoundly achieved by the union of voices, minds are more easily raised to heavenly things by the beauty of the sacred rites, and the whole celebration more clearly prefigures that heavenly liturgy which is enacted in the holy city of Jerusalem."[39] "The musical tradition of the universal Church constitutes a treasure of immeasurable value, exceeding that of the other arts, principally because, as sacred music joined to words, it forms a necessary or integral part of solemn liturgy."[40] In the Roman Rite, Gregorian chant is the perfect and proper expression of sacred music, and should be given pride of place.[41] As well, there is place for other kinds of sacred music, especially polyphony.[42] The traditional language of the Latin Rite is Latin, with sprinklings of Greek (e.g., "Kyrie eleison") and Hebrew (e.g., "Amen", "Alleluia", "Hosanna"). The Byzantine Greek liturgy is conducted in Byzantine Greek (c. 6th cent. A.D.), the Byzantine Russian liturgy is conducted in Old (Church) Slavonic. The Mass is not a sermon but a sacrifice, and so the use of such languages is no impediment to participation and worship. Indeed, if this were so, there would be no obligation to attend Mass either at home or abroad unless one knew the local language or the language of the liturgy. The use in Catholic rites of ancient tongues no longer in use springs from a desire to preserve ancient prayers in their original form and so maintain a universal, timeless and transcendent ritual that joins people to their ancestors in the faith, and is beyond cultural tampering, manipulation and deviations. An ancient tongue expresses the inherently 'traditional' (i.e., handed-on) nature of the sacred liturgy, it commands the respect and adherence of the faithful (unlike the vernacular translations, which have become an incessant source of division). It is beyond partiality, trivialisation and vulgarity; it rises above the ceaseless changes in living languages, thus rendering it apt to express the eternal verities upon which the liturgy depends. Its mysterious and venerable character helps transport men's minds beyond the limits of the present moment to the contemplation of the divine and the invisible.[43]

Pope Pius XII wrote in 1947: "The use of the Latin language, prevailing in a great portion of the Church, is a manifest and beautiful sign of unity, and an effective safeguard against any corruptions of true doctrine. However, the use of the mother tongue in several rites can frequently prove very profitable to the people. But the Apostolic See alone can grant permission for this."[44] In 1963, the Fathers of the second Vatican Council decreed, "The use of the Latin language, particular law remaining in force, is to be preserved in the Latin rites. But since the

---

[39] *Musicam Sacram*, Instruction on Music in the Liturgy, Sacred Congregation of Rites, 1967, art. 5

[40] *Sacrosanctum Concilium*, art. 112; C 1156

[41] Cf. *Sacrosanctum Concilium*, art. 116.

[42] Ibid.

[43] *Institutions Liturgiques*, Dom Prosper Guéranger OSB, Vol. III, ch. iii. On the qualities of the Latin language, see *Veterum Sapientia*, Pope John XXIII, 1962.

[44] *Mediator Dei*, Part I

use of the vernacular language, whether in the Mass, the administration of the Sacraments, or in other parts of the liturgy, can frequently prove very profitable to the people, a wider place may be given to it, especially in readings, directives and in some prayers and chants."[45] "Nevertheless care must be taken to ensure that Christ's faithful may also be able to say or sing together in Latin those parts of the Ordinary of the Mass which pertain to them."[46]

Sacred places. A *church* is dedicated or at least blessed before use. It symbolises that spiritual building which Christ is building up from the living souls of the faithful. The chief church of a diocese (a territory assigned to a Bishop) is called the *Cathedral*, because in it is the *cathedra* or chair of the Bishop, from which he instructs and feeds his people with saving doctrine. The *baptistery* contains the baptismal font of water blessed during the Easter vigil on Holy Saturday night. The *holy-water font* at the entrance to the church is there for us to bless ourselves upon entering the church in remembrance of our Baptism. At the front of the church is the *sanctuary*, which is the centre of liturgical action. The Lectionary (book of readings from the Word of God) is placed at the *lectern* or *ambo*. From there or from the chair or the *pulpit*, the priest delivers the homily. The *altar* is the site of the offering of the Holy Sacrifice, and is a symbol of Christ. It often contains relics of a martyr. (Since the 1960's, Mass facing the people has become commonplace, but traditionally in the liturgies of East and West, the altar faces east, whence the rising sun comes, as a symbol of our waiting for the glorious appearing of Our Saviour, the Sun of Justice.[47] By ancient tradition, the priest faces the people to greet them or address them, but then turns round to the altar, to face the same way as the people, to be their leader and mediator, as both priest and people are oriented to the Lord. The east, or the direction where priest and people face, becomes symbolically the transcendent reference point). There may be a *communion rail*, where the faithful kneel to receive Communion, separating the sanctuary from the nave or body of the church. The *tabernacle* ('tabernaculum' means tent in Latin) is the residence of Christ in the Blessed Sacrament, indicated by a sanctuary lamp (a light near the tabernacle, to signify that the Captain is in His Tent of Meeting). The *confessional* is the place for the Sacrament of Penance. Sacred places are ennobled by sacred art: sculpture, images, statues, paintings, icons, furnishings, adornments and architecture. A church may also have a *cemetery* attached where the bodies of the faithful departed await the General Resurrection.

Things. The liturgy also contains sacred signs and symbols such as bread and wine (which become the Body and Blood of Christ), water, oil, the Cross, Crucifix, palms, ashes, candles and lights. The sacred utensils and instruments include: the paten (a small plate to hold the Host), chalice (a cup to hold wine which becomes the Precious Blood of Christ), purificator (a cloth used to wipe the chalice), lavabo (or hand-towel, to wipe the priest's hands), corporal (a linen cloth on which are placed the paten and chalice at Mass), burse (a pocket-case to hold the corporal), pall (a

---

[45] *Sacrosanctum Concilium*, art. 36
[46] Ibid., art. 54
[47] cf. Mal 4:2.

square of linen placed on top of the chalice), veil (to cover the chalice), credence table (on this are placed the sacred vessels and books when not in use at Mass), cruets (to hold the water and wine), thurible (a kind of brazier suspended on chains, and swung; in it is placed the lighted charcoal), incense (a mixture of aromatic gums, held in a 'boat' and sprinkled on the charcoal to give off a sweet smoke as a symbol of the prayers going up to God, sweet-smelling before Him, like the sacrifices of old, while enveloping the people and things which belong to God; cf. Psalm 141:2), bells (rung to highlight the consecration of bread and wine, and other key points), holy water stoup (to carry holy water for sprinkling), aspergillum (with which holy water is sprinkled), Paschal candle (Risen Christ/Easter symbol, in a prominent place during Eastertide, and at baptisms, funerals), ciborium (holds the consecrated hosts for Holy Communion), pyx (a small case for the Host to be used at Benediction, or for Hosts to be taken to the sick), lunette (a little instrument, shaped like a new moon, holding the same Host), monstrance (vessel for exposing the Blessed Sacrament), reliquary (a case holding a relic of a saint), sacristy (store-room for sacred objects).

Vestments. The vestments worn by the priest are a development of the ordinary civilian clothes of the educated classes in the Roman Empire in the centuries after Christ. For Mass: over the cassock or religious habit goes first the *amice*, a rectangular cloth around the priest's neck; the *alb* is next, a long white gown going down to his feet; a *cincture* or girdle is tied round his waist; the *stole*, a long band or sash, goes round the neck and in front on both sides; the *chasuble* is the outer garment covering all the others. (If necessary, a *maniple*, a small band, is hung on the left arm). A deacon vests in the same way, but he wears the stole over his left shoulder and fastened at the right side, and his outer garment is a *dalmatic*. A priest on the sanctuary, not celebrating a particular rite, wears choir dress: a cassock (soutane), with a white linen *surplice*, or his religious habit. A server may be dressed similarly. At processions, Benediction and other rites, the celebrant may wear a *cope*, a large semi-circular garment reaching to the feet behind, and joined at the front of his neck. When processing with a ciborium or monstrance, or giving the blessing at Benediction, he wears a *humeral veil*, a shawl worn over the shoulders which also covers the hands when he is carrying something. A bishop wears a *skull cap*, and on occasions may carry a *crozier* (a staff, since he is Shepherd of his people), wear a *mitre* (a tall pointed hat, reminding us of his headship—shaped like the tongues of fire that descended upon the Apostles at Pentecost), an episcopal *ring* (symbolising his union with his church, his diocese), and a *pectoral cross* (suspended from his neck).

Liturgical colours. *White* for Holy Thursday, the Easter and Christmas seasons, Trinity Sunday, certain feasts of Our Lord, His Mother, Virgins, the Angels, and Saints who are not martyrs; also funerals. *Red* for Palm Sunday, Good Friday, Pentecost, feasts of the Cross, Apostles, Evangelists and martyrs. *Violet* for Lent and Advent, All Souls' Day, funeral of an adult, requiem Masses, and other penitential occasions. *Green* for Ordinary Time and days of no assigned feast or season. *Black* may be worn on All Souls' Day, at Masses for the Dead and at the funeral of an adult. *Gold* may stand for white, red or green.

THE HOLY OILS. In four of the Sacraments, Holy Oils are used. There are three kinds: the Bishop consecrates one and blesses two, on Holy Thursday or earlier, at the "Chrism Mass" or "Mass of the Oils". The three oils are:
(1) *Oil of Catechumens*, used at the ceremony of Baptism before the Sacrament itself is conferred upon infants. It may be used to anoint adult catechumens some time before their Baptism;[48]
(2) *Oil of the Sick*, used in Anointing of the Sick;
(3) *Chrism*, a mixture of oil and balsam (or other aromatic substances), consecrated by the Bishop, and used in the three Sacraments that confer a character, viz., Baptism, Confirmation, and Holy Orders (at ordination to Priesthood and the Consecration of a Bishop); also used at dedications of churches and altars. At Baptism, the top of the head of the newly baptised is anointed with Chrism (as an anticipation of the Confirmation to follow in later years: hence omitted if Confirmation is to follow immediately).[49] At Confirmation the forehead is anointed.

The oil referred to in all these cases is olive oil, or if unavailable, any other vegetable oil.[50] The spiritual significance of the various anointings can be understood from the various uses of oil: oil *penetrates* things, even stone (as in the rites of dedication of a church and altar). Thus it symbolises the Holy Spirit which penetrates Christ the Messiah (the "Anointed One"), or a share in the Divinity and holiness which penetrates us in the form of Grace; also the sacredness which penetrates the object. Oil *strengthens* and *heals*, as in oil used by athletes and by the wounded and sick. It *illuminates*, as when used in lamps; it *nourishes* when used with food, and gives a *pleasing fragrance* in perfumes.[51]
    The Oils of Catechumens and the Sick may be blessed by a priest in a case of necessity. Only a bishop may consecrate Chrism. The Holy Oils must be renewed yearly after the Mass of the Oils and placed in metal cases, usually marked by the letters: B, C, I. "B" means the oil used at the start of the ceremony of Baptism; it may also be marked "Cat." for Catechumens, or "O.C." for Oleum Catechumenorum (Oil of Catechumens), or "O.S." for Oleum Sanctorum (Oil of the Saints). "C" or "Ch." means the oil of Chrism; or "S.C." for Sacrum Chrisma (Sacred Chrism). "I" or "O.I." means "(Oleum) Infirmorum", the Oil of the Sick. The holy oils are kept in a receptacle known as the ambry (or aumbry).

SACRED TIMES AND SEASONS: THE LITURGICAL YEAR. In the course of the year, the Church celebrates the Incarnation, Birth, Passion, Death and Resurrection of Jesus Christ, and related mysteries. She also commemorates the life and privileges of the Blessed Virgin Mary, and the Saints and Angels. The Liturgical Year begins with the First Sunday of

---

[48] R.C.I.A., *Ordo Initiationis Christianae Adultorum*, 1972, nn. 206-7, 255-6, 340
[49] Cf. C 1242.
[50] Can. 847
[51] See also C 1293-4.

Advent and concludes on the Saturday after the Feast of Christ the King. The basic liturgical year grew up in the first centuries of Christianity, centred around the Paschal mystery, and, later, the Birth of Christ. Thus our Church year has the two poles of Easter and Christmas, each one preceded by a period of preparation (Lent, Advent), and succeeded by an extended celebration of the mystery (Paschaltide, Christmastide).

The chief points of the year take place in this order:
1. Advent: four weeks preparing for the Feast of Christmas (the Birth of Our Lord), after which come Epiphany, and the Baptism of the Lord.
2. Ordinary Time begins.
3. Lent, the season of preparation for Easter, begins (in February or March) with Ash Wednesday, and lasts 40 days. Palm Sunday.
4. Holy Week, including the Easter Triduum: Holy Thursday, Good Friday, Holy Saturday. EASTER SUNDAY.
5. Eastertide of 50 days, including the Ascension of the Lord (40th day), and going up to Pentecost.
6. Ordinary Time resumes. Feasts following Pentecost: Trinity Sunday, Corpus Christi, Sacred Heart of Jesus.
7. Last Sunday of Ordinary Time: Feast of Christ the King. Advent follows and thus the new Church year begins.

In the Roman Missal of 1962, the liturgical year was divided thus:
A. Christmas section
1. Advent: 1st Sunday of Advent to Dec. 24.
2. Christmastide: Dec. 25 to Jan. 13.
Sundays after Epiphany: Jan. 14 to Saturday before Septuagesima[52](9th Sunday before Easter).
B. Easter section
1. Septuagesima to Shrove Tuesday.[53]
2. Lent: Ash Wednesday to Saturday before the First Passion Sunday (the Sunday before Palm Sunday).
3. Passiontide: First Passion Sunday to Easter Night.
4. Paschaltide: Easter Night to Saturday after Pentecost.
Sundays after Pentecost: Trinity Sunday to Saturday before Advent.

CHRIST LIVES AGAIN IN THE CHURCH DURING THE LITURGICAL YEAR. "In the sacred Liturgy, the whole Christ is proposed to us in all the conditions of His life, namely, as the Word of the Eternal Father, as born of the Virgin Mother of God, as He who teaches us truth, heals the sick, consoles the

---

[52] A Latin word meaning '70th', since that Sunday is close to the 70th day before Easter.
[53] So named, since that was a day for 'shriving', i.e., confessing one's sins.

afflicted, who endures suffering and who dies; as He who rose triumphantly from the dead and who, reigning in the glory of Heaven, sends us the Spirit as Paraclete and, finally, who lives in His Church forever: 'Jesus Christ is the same yesterday and today and forever'."[54] The mysteries of Christ are ever present and active as shining examples of Christian perfection, as well as sources of divine grace, due to the merit and prayers of Christ. Each mystery brings its own special grace for our salvation. We are in communion with the mysteries of Jesus: for He lived His life not for Himself but for us; because in them He presents Himself as our model; and He enables us to live in Him all that He lived, and He lives it in us.[55]

Interspersed throughout the year are the feast days of the Angels and Saints, chief among whom is Our Lady. These feasts can be seen in the calendar at the front of any Missal. Sunday remains the pre-eminent feast day of the Resurrection of Our Lord.

Grades of feasts. The highest celebration is a *Solemnity*, generally for major celebrations of Our Lord or Our Lady. Then comes a *Feast* for lesser celebrations and feast days of Apostles other than Peter and Paul. A Saint may be celebrated with a *Memoria*, some of which are obligatory, others optional. If a saint's day arises during a major season, there will simply be a *Commemoration*, involving just one mention during the Mass. The 1st, 2nd, and 3rd class Feasts of the 1962 calendar correspond to the Solemnity, Feast, and obligatory Memoria of the new calendar.

Liturgical books. Regulation of the liturgy.

THE LITURGICAL BOOKS. The liturgical books of the Roman Rite:

1. The *Missal* (sometimes called the *Sacramentary*) contains the texts of the Mass. The *Lectionary* contains the readings for Mass, and is, strictly, a part of the Missal. The *Gradual* contains the parts of the Missal needed by the choir, with the music.

2. The *Pontifical* contains rites celebrated by a bishop (pontifex, in Latin): Confirmation, ordinations, consecration and blessing of holy oils, consecration of virgins, blessing of abbots and abbesses, dedication of churches and altars, and other episcopal ceremonies.

3. The *Ritual* contains the rites for the Sacraments of Baptism, Penance, Anointing of the Sick, Matrimony; also funerals, processions, exposition and Benediction; blessings of persons, places and things; and exorcism.

4. The *Ceremonial of Bishops* provides the normative rules of ceremonial applying to all involved in the liturgy, and describes ceremonies at which the Bishop officiates: Mass, Liturgy of the Hours, the other Sacraments, sacramentals such as blessing of abbots and abbesses, dedication and blessing of churches, other episcopal ceremonies, as well as the ceremonial at councils and synods. It is not a book used at ceremonies, but describes them.

---

[54] (Heb. 13:8) Pius XII, *Mediator Dei*, Part III. Cf. also DS 3855.
[55] Cf. DS 3855; C 519-521. The doctrine is found in Dom Columba Marmion OSB, *Christ in His Mysteries*, Sands & Co., London, 1939, pp.11-14.

5. The *Breviary*, or *Divine Office*, or *Liturgy of the Hours*, contains the Psalms and prayers recited by clerics and certain religious. Since it is the official Prayer of the Church, the Church encourages the faithful to pray at least a portion of it privately or in common. The Psalms form the major part of the Liturgy of the Hours. Those who pray the Breviary prolong the worship Christ gave to His Father on earth, as they use the very prayers that Christ Himself said, and pray to God in the words that He Himself inspired.

6. The *Martyrology* is a calendar listing the martyrs and saints for each day of the year, with information about some of them.

REGULATION OF THE LITURGY. "Regulation of the sacred liturgy depends solely on the authority of the Church, which resides in the Apostolic See, and, as laws may determine, on the bishop … and Conferences of Bishops. Therefore, no other person at all, not even a priest, may add, remove, or change anything in the liturgy on his own authority."[56] "The liturgy is a constitutive element of the holy and life-giving Tradition. For this reason, no sacramental rite can be modified at the will of the minister or community, or changed at their convenience. The Church's supreme authority itself cannot change the liturgy at will, but only in the obedience of faith and in religious respect for the mystery of the liturgy."[57]

The cult of the Saints. Replies to objections. Christian funerals. The earthly and heavenly liturgy.

THE CULT OF THE SAINTS. God commands us to honour our father and mother. The Holy Spirit praises the saints of the Old Testament,[58] and also bids us, "Let us now praise famous men … Their bodies were buried in peace, and their name lives to all generations. Peoples will declare their wisdom and the congregation proclaims their praise."[59] The Church honours the martyrs and saints who are our heroes in the faith, friends of Christ and intercessors in Heaven. We praise and honour them because God Himself has honoured them. We seek their intercession, because in Heaven they have not ceased to care for their struggling brethren here below, who are hoping to join them. We venerate their images and shrines because they remind us of their holiness and virtues. The angels, too, are our protectors and intercessors before God, and we honour them for their supernatural dignity and closeness to God. Countless are the miracles, favours and graces that God has granted to those who ask the angels and saints to pray for them. The Church's faith finds practical expression in the celebration of the feasts of the angels and saints. We offer Masses *to* God *in honour of* the saints to thank Him for the graces He gave them, and to

---

[56] *Sacrosanctum Concilium*, art. 22. Cf. Can. 838.
[57] C 1124-5
[58] Hebrews 11
[59] Ecclesiasticus (Sirach) 44:1,14-15

beseech their intercession. We never offer the Mass *to* a saint. We offer it to God alone.[60] There are thousands upon thousands of saints. Each one has a feast day, but clearly not all of them can be celebrated in the liturgical calendars. The Church, therefore, chooses some for universal commemoration, and leaves others to be venerated publicly or privately in particular regions, religious societies or groups.

The saints are given to us for inspiration, imitation, instruction and intercession. Apart from commemoration by ceremonies and prayers, it is important also to read lives of the saints in order to be inspired by their example, to seek to imitate their virtues, to see how the Gospel can be applied to all states and situations of life, and to be moved to seek the benefit of their patronage and intercession.

Relics. The Church has solemnly defined that it is legitimate to honour the bodies and relics of the saints. This practice goes back to Old Testament times: the Jews respected the bodies of the dead, and Moses took the bones of Joseph with him from Egypt for burial in the Promised Land.[61] God showed His favour with the holy men of old by working miracles through them, even after their death. The mantle of Elijah was used to work miracles after his departure from this life.[62] A dead man whose body was cast into the grave of the prophet Elisha, upon touching the prophet's bones, came back to life at once.[63] The New Testament records that the very shadow of St Peter was enough to cure the sick.[64] Even during St Paul's lifetime, God worked miracles through objects used by him: his handkerchiefs and aprons were taken to the sick, who were thereupon cured and delivered.[65]

The relics of the saints' bodies are venerated because "they have been living members of Christ and temples of the Holy Ghost"[66] and will be raised up again in glory on the Last Day. Veneration is naturally extended to objects closely connected to them. A first class relic is something from the body of a saint; a second class relic is from some clothing or article used by the saint; a third class relic is something touched to a first or second class relic. "It is forbidden to sell sacred relics."[67]

Of course, the greatest 'relic', or object of worship in the Catholic Church, is the Blessed Sacrament. Christ left not just a memento, not just a

---

[60] T 1744. Cf. St Augustine, *The City of God*, Bk XXII, ch. 10.
[61] Ex 13:19
[62] 2 Kgs 2:13-14
[63] 2 Kgs 13:21
[64] Acts 5:15
[65] Acts 19:11-12
[66] T 1822; cf. 1 Cor 3:16; 6:19; 2 Cor 6:16.
[67] Can. 1190 §1

piece of His corpse, or a piece of something He used, but His very Self, true God and true Man, in the Blessed Eucharist.

True and false devotions. "Chain letters" containing prayers, demanding copies and distribution, and promising favours, are superstitious nonsense and should be thrown away; likewise for any leaflet claiming that temporal favours are *absolutely* guaranteed by a formula of prayers or days. God answers our prayers when and how He wills. We cannot constrain Him with some formula of prayers or days. The Lord Jesus told parables about people who kept on badgering their neighbour or their judge until they got what they wanted. These parables teach us that answers to prayer do not come as fast as we would like. Commendable, however, is a *Novena*, a prayer offered over nine days to obtain a particular favour. This is in imitation of the original novena, the nine days from the Ascension to Pentecost, spent in prayer by the Apostles and the Virgin Mary, in expectation of the Holy Spirit. If a day is missed during a novena, it can be made up by adding a day at the end. The important thing is not the number of days but persistence in asking. In such prayers, while we should pray with trust and confidence, we must always remember that our Heavenly Father knows already what we need[68] and does not require detailed explanations, that His thoughts are not our thoughts,[69] that even if Divine Providence does not grant us exactly what we want, we will certainly receive something even better.[70] Jesus taught us persistence in prayer, but also to pray, "Thy will be done".

Classic Protestant objections to veneration of the Saints.

(1) "It is wrong to venerate Mary and the Saints and seek their intercession, since the 1st Commandment says, 'You shall have no other gods before me' (Ex 20:3) and St Paul says, 'there is one mediator between God and men, the man Christ Jesus' (1 Tim 2:5)." REPLY: Already in the Old Testament, Moses appealed to God in the name of his ancestors: "Turn from Thy fierce wrath ... Remember Abraham, Isaac and Israel, thy servants".[71] In the Second Book of Maccabees 15:14, a former high priest, Onias, has a vision of the deceased prophet Jeremiah, and says of him: "This is a man who loves the brethren and prays much for the people and the holy city". This book is not in the Protestant Bible, but is nevertheless a witness to Jewish belief. Christ confirmed this Jewish belief when He insisted that the dead of this world are not dead before God: "He is not God of the dead, but of the living."[72] In the Old Testament, the prophet Zechariah heard an angel intercede for Israel.[73] Christ accordingly taught of the angels' interest in our salvation: "there is joy before the angels of God over one sinner who repents."[74] St John depicts the angels presenting the prayers of the Christian faithful to God.[75] Thus it is clear we may

[68] Matt 6:8
[69] Isaiah 55:8-9
[70] Lk 11:13
[71] Ex 32:12-3
[72] Matt 22:32
[73] Zech 1:12
[74] Lk 15:10
[75] Rev 5:8; 8:3-4

seek the intercession of the angels. The early Christians sought the intercession of their brethren in Heaven, as testified by the ancient inscriptions on the tombs in the Catacombs, e.g., "Januaria, enjoy your happiness and pray for us."[76] As explained above,[77] we do not adore or worship Mary and the Saints; we honour and venerate them, for God Himself has honoured them with sanctity on earth and glory in Heaven. (Some older books may use the word 'worship', which at one time was broader in its meaning, as seen in the old marriage rite: "with my body I thee worship…". "Your Worship" has been a title of honour for judges and mayors. To 'worship' is to ascribe 'worth'). Honouring the Blessed Virgin Mary is simply the fulfilment of what she prophesied: "henceforth all generations will call me blessed."[78] Jesus Himself said, "if anyone serves Me, the Father will honour him."[79] As many of the Psalms do, we praise the Creator for His work in His creatures. As for mediation, or intercession, St Paul tells the Colossians, "we have not ceased to pray for you".[80] Now, if a Christian on earth can pray for others, why can he not pray for them once in Heaven? St Jerome, in the year 406, said the same: "If the Apostles and martyrs while still in the body can pray for others, when they should still be concerned for themselves, how much more will they do so after their crowns, victories and triumphs?"[81] The unique mediation of Christ is not undermined by any such doctrine: Christ shares His intercessory power with us, just as He shares His priesthood, His glory, and His goodness with us.

(2) "It is forbidden to make statues and icons of the Saints, for God forbade the making of images in the book of Exodus (20:4-5)." REPLY: By the same argument, we ought destroy all pictures, photos and images of persons living and dead. God forbade the fashioning of idols *for false worship*, but not images as such. Indeed, God Himself commanded Moses to make two statues of Cherubim (angels), with wings and faces, for the Ark of the Covenant.[82] God also commanded Moses to make a bronze serpent, which the Israelites had only to look at, to be healed of snake-bite.[83] With God's approval, King Solomon built his house with images of cherubim, lions and oxen.[84] The presence of statues in churches is no more idolatrous than Nelson's Column at Trafalgar Square. The heresy which condemns the use of statues and icons is called "iconoclasm" (literally, "image-breaking"). It was condemned at the 7th General Council, the Second Council of Nicea in 787, which solemnly decreed it is legitimate to use and reverence, without adoration in the strict sense, holy images of Our Saviour, the Mother of God, the Angels and Saints,

---

[76] L. Hertling S.J. & E. Kirschbaum S.J., *The Roman Catacombs and their Martyrs*, DLT, London 1960, p.194
[77] pp.390-1, 466
[78] Lk 1:48
[79] Jn 12:26
[80] Col 1:9
[81] *Contra Vigilantium*, 6
[82] Ex 25:18-20
[83] Num 21:8-9
[84] 1 Kgs 6:11-3,23-35; 7:25,29,36

"since the veneration of the image refers to the original, and the one who honours the image honours the person of the one depicted in it."[85]

CHRISTIAN FUNERALS. The purpose of a funeral is (1) to pray for the soul of the deceased; (2) to bring God's consolation to those who mourn; and (3) to dispose of the body ritually and reverently in expectation of the resurrection.[86] - For a deceased Catholic, a Requiem Mass is most suitable, for in the Eucharist, "the Church expresses her efficacious communion with the departed: offering to the Father in the Holy Spirit the sacrifice of the death and resurrection of Christ, she beseeches that His child be purified of his sins and their consequences, and be admitted to the Paschal fulness of the table of the Kingdom."[87]

Eulogies and attempted 'canonisation' (declaration that the deceased "is in heaven") are out of place at a Catholic funeral, and offer false consolation to family and mourners. What the dead need are prayers, not praise. It is no consolation to a soul in Purgatory to be lauded on earth when a congregation should be praying for its eternal repose. Violet or black vestments are appropriate at the funeral of an adult, since they express the penitential character of the liturgy: the deceased has undergone the separation of soul and body, and after any necessary purgation, is awaiting the fulness of the Redemption in the general resurrection. Black is also the traditional colour of mourning. On the other hand, white vestments emphasise the hope of the resurrection.

"The Church earnestly recommends that the pious custom of burying the bodies of the deceased be retained; she does not, however, forbid cremation, unless this is chosen for reasons contrary to Christian doctrine."[88] The practice of cremation re-entered the Western world at the time of the so-called Enlightenment, originally as an act of defiance against the doctrine of the resurrection of the body. If cremation is chosen for this or any other anti-Christian reason, the Church will not grant ecclesiastical burial.[89]

THE EARTHLY AND THE HEAVENLY LITURGY. "In the earthly liturgy, we take part in a foretaste of that heavenly liturgy which is celebrated in the Holy City of Jerusalem, toward which we journey as pilgrims, where Christ is sitting at the right hand of God, Minister of the holies and of the true tabernacle. With all the warriors of the heavenly army, we sing a hymn of glory to the Lord; venerating the memory of the saints, we hope for some part and fellowship with them; we eagerly await the Saviour, Our Lord

---

[85] DS 600-1
[86] Cf. Can. 1176 §2.
[87] C 1689
[88] Can. 1176 §3
[89] Can. 1184 §1

Jesus Christ, until He, our life, shall appear and we too will appear with Him in glory."[90]

VII

The Sacramentals.[91]

DEFINITION AND TYPES. "Sacramentals are sacred signs by which—after a certain likeness to the Sacraments—certain effects, especially spiritual ones, are symbolised and obtained by the intercession of the Church."[92] Sacramentals have been appointed by the Church to give spiritual and temporal blessings. They are of two kinds, *permanent* and *transient*.

Permanent sacramentals are *things* that have been blessed, such as holy water, medals, and rosary beads.

Transient sacramentals are sacred *actions* performed by the ministers of the Church with her authority. These are of four kinds: *consecrations, dedications, blessings* and *exorcisms.*

By *consecration*, Christians enter upon a sacred state of life (not a Holy Order), as, e.g., consecration to a life of virginity.

By *dedication*, things are withdrawn from profane use and dedicated to the service of God, e.g., churches, cemeteries, altars, and chalices. A dedication renders an object sacred, and to violate it is a sin of sacrilege.

By *blessing*, the grace or protection of God is invoked on persons, as at Benediction with the Blessed Sacrament, at the blessing given by a priest or bishop, or on things, as at the blessing of crops. (The action of the priest in blessing rosary-beads is a *transient sacramental* and belongs to this class. The set of beads when blessed is a *permanent sacramental*). Certain blessings are called 'constitutive' blessings because, by them, objects are *constituted* as sacred, as with dedications. To violate them is sacrilege. The same cannot be said for other ordinary blessings, such as of a house, car, field, etc.

An *exorcism* is an order of banishment addressed to an evil spirit in the name of Christ and the Church.

HOW THEY DIFFER FROM THE SACRAMENTS. The sacramentals differ in many ways from the Sacraments: (a) The Sacraments were instituted by Christ; the sacramentals have been instituted by the Church. (b) The Sacraments give Sanctifying Grace. The sacramentals, though incapable of conferring that precious gift, are still an important means of access to the divine mercy and favour: they give Actual Grace; they enable us to obtain pardon for venial sin; they procure for us temporal blessings; and, as appears from the words of the Roman Ritual, they afford us a special

---

[90] *Sacrosanctum Concilium*, art. 8
[91] Can. 1166-1172
[92] Can. 1166

protection against the power and influence of evil spirits. (c) The sacramentals are not causes of grace. Their efficacy depends partly on the dispositions of whoever uses them, and partly on the good pleasure of God, who is moved by them, because they bear with them the petition of His Spouse, the Church. Her prayer is more powerful than that of any individual, however holy. (d) God has commanded us to receive the Sacraments at due time. We are under no such command to receive or use the sacramentals, but they are recommended to us by the Church as profitable for our spiritual and temporal welfare.

Some of the more popular sacramentals are: the Miraculous Medal, the Brown Scapular, blessing before and after childbirth; the blessing of throats on the feast of St Blaise (Feb. 3); Enthronement of the Sacred Heart; crossing oneself with holy water or sprinkling it in church and at home; blessing of a home, of children and of the sick; blessed statues and images. Every home ought to have a Crucifix and other inspiring images of Jesus and Mary.

Their origin in Christ. Christ, as we read in the Sacred Scriptures, blessed little children; He blessed the loaves and fishes; and He expelled evil spirits. The Church in her sacramentals continues to exercise His power: Christ lives in her and, through her, He acts as He acted while on earth.

Their antiquity. Many of the sacramentals are as old as the Church herself. Holy water—a reminder of our Baptism—is of great antiquity, for we find that, even in the fourth century, the faithful were wont to take it with them from the churches for use in their homes.

Reverence for them. No good Catholic will refuse to avail himself of the sacramentals or will treat them with disrespect: St Paul says that "nothing is to be rejected if it is … consecrated by the word of God and prayer."[93] A sacramental no longer desired should be discarded respectfully, by burial or burning.

---

[93] 1 Tim 4:4

CHAPTER 12

BAPTISM

Summary

I.   The solemn teaching of the Church.
II.   Baptism defined. How it is conferred. Its Minister and its Subject. Its Ceremonies. The office of sponsor. Christian name.
III. Its effects: grace and the Sacramental Character. The "revival" of Baptism. Invalid baptism.
IV.   It is absolutely necessary for salvation either in fact or in desire. The Baptism of the Holy Ghost, or Baptism of Desire. The Baptism of Blood.
V.   Baptism directly instituted by Christ.
VI.   Solution of difficulties.

I

The solemn teaching of the Church. The Church teaches solemnly:

(1) that Baptism is a Sacrament;[1]
(2) that it imprints a Character, or indelible mark, on the soul and cannot be repeated;[2]
(3) that water is necessary for its administration;[3]
(4) that it removes all stain of Original Sin and all stain of Actual Sin, together with the punishment due to it;[4]
(5) that concupiscence or an inclination to sin, however, remains after Baptism;[5]
(6) that Baptism is necessary for salvation;[6]
(7) that it can be validly received by infants;[7]
(8) that children when they grow up are not free to reject the Baptismal promises made for them by their sponsors.[8]

---

[1] T 1601
[2] T 1609
[3] T 1615
[4] T 1513, 1515
[5] T 1515
[6] T 1618
[7] T 1514, 1626
[8] T 1627

II

Baptism defined, how it is conferred; its ceremonies. The minister of Baptism and its subject. Sponsors. Christian name.

DEFINITION. Baptism (sometimes called "christening") is the Sacrament which makes us Christians and children of God.

HOW IT IS CONFERRED. Baptism is given by pouring water on the head of the person to be baptised while reciting the words: "I baptise you in the name of the Father, and of the Son, and of the Holy Spirit." The words used in the Eastern Catholic liturgies are: "The servant of God is baptised in the name of the Father and of the Son and of the Holy Spirit."[9] The Sacrament may also be conferred by a threefold immersion of the body, or at least of the head, as was the common practice in the Church down to the twelfth century, or by sprinkling with water (aspersion). The last method, however, was very rarely used, and is not recommended.

SOLEMN AND PRIVATE BAPTISM. Solemn Baptism is Baptism accompanied by all the ceremonies prescribed by the Church. Private Baptism consists of the bare essentials, viz., the pouring of water and the recital of the proper words. Solemn Baptism is given in a church. Private Baptism, which is given in an emergency or in the absence of a Catholic minister, may be given anywhere. (After a Private Baptism, if the opportunity arises, the other ceremonies are "supplied" by a Catholic minister in a church. The Baptism itself, of course, is not repeated).

THE CEREMONIES. At an infant Baptism in the Latin Rite, after the preliminary rites, the prayer of exorcism is said over the infant, who is then anointed on the breast with the Oil of Catechumens.[10] The baptismal water is blessed, if not already. The parents and godparents renounce Satan and sin, and profess the faith, on behalf of the child. After the Baptism itself, the child is anointed on the crown of the head with sacred Chrism,[11] clothed with a white garment as a sign of having "put on Christ",[12] and its parents and sponsors are presented with a candle lit from the Easter candle. The 'ephphetha' prayer is said over the baby's ears and mouth, and the mother and father are blessed by the ordained minister.

THE MINISTER OF BAPTISM. The ordinary minister of Baptism is a priest or deacon.

Private Baptism may be lawfully conferred in case of necessity by any person—man, woman, or child. Since whoever baptises must have the

---

[9] C 1240
[10] For "Oil of Catechumens", see p.463.
[11] For "Chrism", see p.463.
[12] Gal 3:27

intention of doing what the Church does, it follows that he or she must possess the use of reason. It is preferable to have a Catholic perform the baptism, but anyone of any or no religion can do so validly.[13] The case of necessity arises: (a) when there is immediate danger of death; or (b) when, in the absence of a minister, Solemn Baptism cannot be given without difficulty or long delay.

The minister of Baptism has the duty of ensuring that the details of the Baptism are recorded in the parish register. When a layman gives Baptism, he should endeavour to secure, if possible, the presence of two witnesses and should draw up a baptismal certificate to which he and they should affix their signatures, and should send it without delay to the priest in charge of the district or to the Bishop. The certificate could be worded: "On ... (*give full date*), at ... (*name the place*), I baptised ... (*full name of child*), the son/daughter of (*give parents' names; if unknown, say so*) by pouring water on its head, saying at the same time: 'I baptise you in the name of the Father and of the Son and of the Holy Spirit.' Signed: (*name and address of baptizer*). Witnesses: (*their signatures and addresses*)".

THE SUBJECT OF BAPTISM. The subject of Baptism is anyone who has not yet received it.

BAPTISM IN THE NEW TESTAMENT. Jesus instructs His Apostles, "baptise ... in the name of the Father and of the Son and of the Holy Spirit".[14] We read in Acts 2:38, 10:48, of Baptism "in the name of Jesus Christ". This does not mean that the Apostles said: "I baptise you in the name of Jesus Christ." The phrase, "in the name of Christ", was a *term* for Baptism, distinguishing the Baptism instituted by Christ from that of John the Baptist.

THE OFFICE OF SPONSOR. The Church requires that, if possible, at least one sponsor or godparent be present at Solemn Baptism; also, at Private Baptism, if a suitable person can be easily found. The Church permits the presence of two godparents, one male and one female, but no more than two. It is part of the sponsors' office to make a profession of faith in the recipient's name during the ceremony. Their obligations do not end at the baptismal font; they are strictly bound to watch over the subsequent career of their spiritual child, to see that he is instructed in all the duties of the Christian life and fulfil the promises which were made of him at Baptism. This duty, however, binds only when the parents or guardians neglect to discharge it. To undertake the office of sponsor, one must be: (1) appointed by the parents or guardians, or, if necessary, by the parish priest or minister of Baptism, and intending to assume the obligations in question; (2) at least sixteen, unless the priest or minister admits an exception; (3) a Catholic who has received Confirmation and Communion and lives a suitable life of faith; (4) not

---

[13] DS 1315
[14] Matt 28:19

labouring under an ecclesiastical penalty; (5) not a parent of the child.[15] - A non-Catholic cannot be a godparent, but may act as co-witness.

CHRISTIAN NAME. At least one of the names given should be that of a Saint. A patron Saint provides a model of charity for the Christian and assures the benefits of that Saint's prayer from Heaven.[16] Names taken from the entertainment world are totally unsuitable for a child who is to be taken from the world to become one of the "sons of light".

III

The effects of Baptism: Sanctifying Grace, the virtues and gifts, remission of all sin & punishment, Sacramental Grace, the Sacramental Character. The "revival" of Baptism. Invalid baptisms.

The effects of Baptism may be summarised under the following headings:
SANCTIFYING GRACE. Through Baptism we are given a new birth: by our natural birth, we are children of our parents, by our spiritual or supernatural birth in Baptism, we become children of God and heirs to His Kingdom. This is effected by *Sanctifying Grace*.

THE VIRTUES AND GIFTS. Accompanying Sanctifying Grace are the *theological virtues* of Faith, Hope and Charity,[17] by which we believe in God, hope in Him and love Him. The *moral virtues*, also given, enable us to grow in goodness, especially by the cardinal virtues of prudence, justice, fortitude and temperance. At the same time we are given the power to live and act under the divine prompting through the *gifts of the Holy Spirit*.[18]

REMISSION OF ALL SIN AND PUNISHMENT. Sanctifying Grace, infused into our soul at Baptism, removes every trace of sin, *original and actual*, and extinguishes any debt of *temporal punishment* which we may have incurred through actual sin committed before Baptism.

SACRAMENTAL GRACE. Along with Sanctifying Grace we receive *Sacramental Grace*, the orientation to live as an adopted child of God. This Grace gives also the right to a series of actual graces which, if properly used, will enable us to live the new life of Brotherhood with Christ, of membership in His Mystical Body, by faithfully following in His footsteps and obeying all His commands.

---

[15] Can. 872-4
[16] Cf. C 2156, 2165.
[17] Cf. 1 Cor 13:13.
[18] C 1266. See p.488.

THE SACRAMENTAL CHARACTER AND INCORPORATION INTO THE CHURCH. A Sacramental Character is some permanent change made in the soul, specially fitting it for spiritual work. Since Baptism imprints a Character, it cannot be repeated: as we can be born but once of our natural parents, so we can be born but once into the Church of God. By the Baptismal Character: (1) we are made members of the body whose head is Christ, i.e., we become citizens and subjects of the Church, and sharers in the priestly, prophetic and royal mission of Jesus Christ;[19] (2) we become capable of receiving the other Sacraments; we become capable of joining with the priest in the Church's great act of public worship, viz., the Sacrifice of Mass; and we become capable of participating in all the special blessings bestowed by Christ on the Church on our behalf. Baptism is, as it were, a compact between God and man: God gives spiritual life and promises all the means necessary to preserve and increase it; man, on his side, renounces sin, and undertakes to lead a good Christian life as a faithful member of the Church. It is the solemn teaching of the Church that the Character is indelible, which means that it is permanent at least for this life; the teaching that it is permanent also for the life to come, though not defined, is regarded as certain.

Note. *Unbaptised* would-be converts, though they may possess faith, hope, and charity, cannot *co-offer*, in the strict sense, the sacrifice of the Mass.[20] Their acts of adoration, however pleasing they may be to God, are not accepted, as ours are, by the Divine Victim on the altar, who gives them a higher value, and so presents them to the Eternal Father.

"REVIVAL" OF BAPTISM. Baptism validly, but unfruitfully, received, can "revive", i.e., can produce the grace proper to it, as soon as the recipient has the required dispositions. This "revival" or recovery is made possible by reason of the Baptismal Character which remains in the soul. It is effected sometimes with the aid of the Sacrament of Penance, sometimes without it, as will be understood from the following cases: (1) A man about to be baptised forgets that he has committed a grave sin of which he has never repented, and fails to make an act of attrition; it is only after Baptism that he perceives the omission. Such a person, by an act of attrition, can remove the obstacle to the operation of the Sacrament, and so receive all its graces. (2) If a man knowingly and wilfully receives the Sacrament of Baptism without attrition for grave sin, he commits the heinous crime of sacrilege. His assent to that crime must necessarily continue for some moments after the reception of the Sacrament: the Baptism is valid and cannot be repeated, but he must go to Confession and be absolved of this sin of sacrilege. The Sacrament of Penance forgives the sin committed after Baptism but not before it. Simultaneously with that forgiveness, his Baptism produces its full effect, viz., the remission of all

---

[19] Can. 204
[20] See p.522.

sins committed before Baptism. The principle underlying this reasoning is that the Divine Mercy could not permanently exclude the repentant sinner from the graces of the Sacrament. Note that the word "revival" is given inverted commas to indicate a certain want of aptness. Strictly taken, it implies that the Sacrament is restored to life, as though at some time previously it had been "alive", when it was not. A better term would be "vitalisation" or "vivification."

INVALID BAPTISM. An invalid baptism is a ceremony devoid of the effects listed above. Some fringe Protestant groups and modern sects have invalid baptism, either because they do not baptise at all, or because they have changed the Trinitarian formula. Among them are Quakers, Unitarians, Jehovah's Witnesses, the Salvation Army, Christian Scientists, Christadelphians, Pentecostals, and the New Church (of Emmanuel Swedenborg).[21]

CONDITIONAL BAPTISM. If a person has a reasonable doubt about the validity of his baptism, he may be baptised by a priest conditionally, thus: "If you have not been baptised, I baptise you in the name of... etc."[22] Similarly, if there is a doubt whether death has taken place, a person who had been willing to be baptised may be baptised with water thus: "If you are alive, I baptise you... etc." When death is certain, no sacrament may be administered; sacraments are for the living.

IV

The necessity of Baptism for salvation. The Baptism of infants. Timing. The substitutes for Baptism.

THE NECESSITY OF BAPTISM FOR SALVATION. By "salvation" we mean, as has already been explained, the enjoyment of the Beatific Vision. The Church teaches that Baptism is necessary for the salvation of both adults and infants. Its necessity for adults is defined by the Council of Trent, which says, "If any one says that Baptism is optional, that is, not necessary for salvation, let him be anathema."[23] (The word "optional", *liberum*, indicates that the Council speaks here only of an adult, of one who is capable of making a free choice).

The necessity of Baptism for infants follows: (1) from the condemnation of the Pelagians[24] who held that infants were saved without Baptism; (2) from the ancient rule of the Church that all, infants as well as adults, should be immediately baptised when there was danger of death; and (3) from the comprehensive words of Christ, "unless one is born of water and the Spirit, he cannot enter the kingdom of God." (Jn 3:5).

---

[21] Cf. J.M. Huels OSM, *The Pastoral Companion*, Franciscan Press, Illinois, 1995, p.342.
[22] Can. 869
[23] DS 1618
[24] See p.445.

Baptism makes us members of Christ, members of His Mystical Body. It is only those thus united to Him who can be saved.[25]

THE BAPTISM OF INFANTS. "The practice of infant Baptism is an immemorial tradition of the Church."[26] Some Protestant groups have abandoned the practice and even condemned it as un-Biblical. However, three passages of the Acts of the Apostles speak of the Baptism of a whole household or family,[27] and there is explicit testimony to the practice from the second century on.[28] As circumcision of the infant Jews signified entry into the Old Covenant, so its fulfilment, Baptism, introduces infants into the New Covenant.[29]

TIMING. Because of the absolute necessity of Baptism, the Church has made a law requiring that all infants should be baptised "within the first weeks".[30] Her command imposes a grave obligation on parents and guardians. To delay Baptism beyond the first few weeks is sinful. Absence of relatives or the desire for a particular priest is *no excuse* for delay. If there is danger of death, the child should be baptised immediately; this is a case of necessity in which anyone may lawfully administer the Sacrament.

THE SUBSTITUTES FOR BAPTISM. The words of Christ Himself show us that He accepts the Baptism of Desire and the Baptism of Blood as substitutes for the Sacramental Baptism of water.

The Baptism of the Holy Ghost (Baptism of Desire). By Baptism of the Holy Ghost we mean an act of perfect contrition or perfect charity made by an adult who has not received Sacramental Baptism. It is termed Baptism by analogy, or comparison, because it resembles the Sacrament in producing Sanctifying Grace in the soul and in blotting out Original Sin and grave actual sin. It is called Baptism of the Holy Ghost, because the Holy Ghost causes grace in the soul directly and not through the medium of any sacramental rite. It is also spoken of as Baptism of Desire, i.e., desire of the Sacrament of Baptism.

It is Catholic doctrine that it has this power, as is proved from the words of Christ: "he who loves Me will be loved by my Father, and I will love him";[31] of Mary Magdalen He said, "her sins, which are many, are forgiven, for she loved much", and turning to her He added, "Your sins are forgiven you";[32] to the penitent thief who had expressed sorrow for his crimes, resignation in his sufferings,

---

[25] See p.169.
[26] C 1252
[27] Acts 16:15; 16:33; 18:8. Cf. 1 Cor 1:16.
[28] Cf. C 1252.
[29] Cf. Col 2:11-12.
[30] Can. 867
[31] Jn 14:21
[32] Lk 7:47,48

and belief that Christ after death would reign as a King, He addressed the words, "Truly, I say to you, today you will be with Me in Paradise."[33] Baptism of Desire does not imprint the Sacramental Character; therefore, it does not make one a member of the visible Church (nor does it necessarily remit all the temporal punishment due to sin). Hence, the obligation remains of receiving the Sacrament at the earliest opportunity.

The Baptism of Blood. Baptism of Blood is martyrdom suffered by one who has not been baptised. (1) Martyrdom, whether of baptised or unbaptised persons, is the endurance of death or deadly suffering for the sake of Jesus Christ. There are, therefore, two requisites: (a) the martyr must be put to death or endure sufferings that lead to death; (b) the persecutor must inflict death or deadly violence through opposition to the Church, the Catholic Faith, or a Christian Virtue. (A Christian killed for refusing to commit a sin against the virtue of chastity is a martyr; so, too, a Christian who suffers death rather than commit the sin of perjury or apostasy). In the case of adults, it is furthermore required: (c) that they endure death or deadly violence from a supernatural motive and do not try to save their lives by resistance; (d) that they have made acts of Faith and Hope, and that they have at least attrition for grave sin committed. Hence a person with these dispositions, if, while unconscious, he is slain from hatred of Catholicism, is a martyr: his attrition, by which he detests sin "above every other evil", carries with it the implicit intention to suffer death rather than offend God by denying the faith.

Note. Christ was slain by the enemies of truth, the enemies of God, and offered no resistance. The martyr's death is like the death of Christ; hence its great fruitfulness for the soul. Resistance, so far as it spoils the likeness to our Saviour's Passion, is inconsistent with martyrdom; that likeness is not, of course, spoiled in the case of one who resists an unchaste assailant solely for the purpose of escaping sin and defilement. Soldiers who fall on the battle-field, fighting for God or virtue, may be martyrs, but since, in their case, it would be difficult to establish that there is no admixture of any merely human motive, such as self-protection or the desire of distinction, the Church follows the rule that those who die as combatants must not be honoured as martyrs.

It is Catholic doctrine that the Baptism of Blood blots out Original Sin, and all actual sin together with the punishment due to it. This is evident: (a) *from the words of Christ*: He has absolutely promised salvation to those who give their lives for the Gospel: "he who loses his life for My sake will find it";[34] and again He says, "So everyone who acknowledges me before men, I also will acknowledge before my Father who is in heaven";[35] (b) *from the Tradition of the Church*: the Church honours as martyrs in heaven several who were never baptised: the Holy Innocents massacred by Herod; St Emerentiana (c. 304); one of the Forty Martyrs of

---

[33] Lk 23:39-43
[34] Matt 10:39
[35] Matt 10:32

Sebastea (A.D. 320); and some others. St Augustine says, "it would be an affront to pray for a martyr: we should rather commend ourselves to his prayers."[36]

Martyrdom does not imprint the Sacramental Character. Hence, an unbaptised martyr could not receive Holy Communion or any other sacrament in his last moments without first receiving Sacramental Baptism.

Notes. The title "Baptism of Blood" reminds us of the words of Christ when He spoke of the outpouring of His Blood as a "baptism" (Lk 12:50); but though He was condemned to death by Caiaphas on a charge of blasphemy, His death should not be described as a "martyrdom", but rather as a "sacrifice" (See p.403).

Since the substitutes for Baptism are rightly held to imply a desire of its reception, the doctrine of the Church on the necessity of the Sacrament can be expressed in a form that excludes all exceptions, viz., *the Sacrament of Baptism received in fact or in desire is absolutely necessary for salvation.*

THE FATE OF INFANTS WHO DIE WITHOUT BAPTISM. It has been the common teaching of theologians that infants who die without Baptism cannot be admitted to the beatific vision of Heaven, since they have not been cleansed of Original Sin; nor suffer the pains of Hell, since they are free of personal sin. After death they must, therefore, enter a state of natural, but not supernatural happiness, known as Limbo. This doctrine is taught by St Augustine and St Thomas Aquinas. ("Limbo" in common parlance means, "no man's land; a state of uncertainty". That is not the meaning here). Aquinas explains that exclusion from Heaven does not necessarily mean a state of suffering, but in this case includes the enjoyment of natural goods.[37] Nor is there any injustice, since man does not have a *right* to the beatific vision; it is not *due* to his nature as such. The Council of Carthage in 418 condemned the Pelagians for denying the need for infants to be baptised for the remission of sin.[38] The Council of Trent repeated this condemnation.[39] The Second Council of Lyons and the Council of Florence (both General Councils) presumed this teaching on Limbo to be true when they defined that the penalty of those who die "in Original Sin only" is different from those who die in personal mortal sin.[40] If no-one dies in Original Sin only, then these dogmatic definitions are worthless. The Council of Florence declared against the postponement of the Baptism of infants, "since it is not possible for them to be saved by any other remedy than the sacrament of Baptism".[41] The *Roman Catechism* teaches that it is sinful to delay Baptism unnecessarily, "since infant children have no other means of salvation except Baptism".[42] Pope Pius VI adopted this common teaching on Limbo against the Jansenist synod of Pistoia.[43] Pope Pius XII insisted that the gratuity of the

---

[36] *Serm.* 159, c. 1

[37] *De malo*, q. 5, a. 3; *Comm. in Sent.* II, d. 33, q. 2, aa. 1, 2

[38] DS 223, 224. Cf. 903-4, 1349.

[39] DS 1514. Cf. 1524.

[40] DS 858, 1306. The same doctrine is upheld in DS 184, 219, 780, 926.

[41] DS 1349

[42] *Roman Catechism*, Part II, "Baptism". On the *Roman Catechism*, see p.643, n.133.

[43] DS 2626

supernatural order means that God can have created rational beings without necessarily ordaining them to the beatific vision.[44] The same Pope said, "Under the present economy there is no other way of giving this [supernatural] life to the child who is still without the use of reason. ...In the case of a grown-up person, an act of love may suffice for obtaining sanctifying grace and making up for the lack of Baptism. To the child still unborn or the child just born this path is not open."[45] The *Instruction on Infant Baptism* says, "The Church has thus shown by her teaching and practice that she knows no other way apart from Baptism for ensuring children's entry into eternal happiness."[46] Various theories about how infants may receive grace without Baptism have been put forward. There is no need to list them here. (One theory is that they receive an enlightenment before or upon death, enabling them to make a choice. This theory is totally inadmissible, since it means they could be saved *or damned*). *However, none of these theories may be taught as a certainty, and no-one may refuse or delay Baptism on the grounds of any such theory.*

The *Roman Missal* cautions the celebrant at the funeral of an unbaptised baby: "In catechesis, care must be taken that the doctrine about the necessity of Baptism not be obscured in the minds of the faithful."[47] The *Catechism of the Catholic Church* says only that we are permitted to *hope* that there be a way of salvation for such infants; it gives no assurances.[48] The *Code of Canon Law* presumes the necessity of Baptism for a dying infant, when it lays down, "In danger of death, an infant of Catholic or even non-Catholic parents is lawfully baptised, even against the parents' will."[49]

The happiness of Limbo. In that state, they are as fully happy on the natural level as human nature can be, a state akin to the happiness of Adam and Eve in Paradise. The souls in Limbo are not in an infantile state; they are fully mature, and immortal, as their bodies will be at the General Resurrection.[50]

V

The Sacrament of Baptism was instituted by Christ. PROOF FROM THE SOLEMN TEACHING OF THE CHURCH. The Church in the exercise of her infallible authority declares the institution of the Sacrament of Baptism by Christ to be a doctrine given to her by God Himself. This proof alone suffices for Catholics; the proof from Sacred Scripture is added to give fuller instruction.

PROOF FROM SACRED SCRIPTURE. The Scriptures show that Christ himself personally instituted the Sacrament of Baptism. He said to Nicodemus, "unless one

---

[44] *Humani Generis*, 1950: DS 3891

[45] Discourse of 29 Oct. 1951

[46] *Pastoralis Actio*, art. 13, Sacred Congregation for the Doctrine of the Faith, 1980

[47] *Missale Romanum*, 1975, p.913

[48] C 1261

[49] Can. 868 §2; Cf. Eastern canons (CCEO) 681 §4.

[50] Cf. St Augustine, *Enchiridion*, Ch. 85.

is born of water and the Spirit, he cannot enter the kingdom of God.";[51] and to the Apostles, "Go therefore and make disciples of all nations, baptising them in the name of the Father and of the Son and of the Holy Spirit" (Matt 28:19). These texts show that Christ definitely proclaimed the necessity of Baptism, and showed precisely how the rite was to be administered: Christ, therefore, is the institutor of this Sacrament in all its essential details. That the Apostles understood their Master to speak, not of a figurative baptism, but of a true washing with water, is clearly conveyed in Sacred Scripture: we read in Acts how Philip, having converted the treasurer of queen Candace of Ethiopia, went down with him into some water by the wayside and baptised him;[52] and how Peter, seeing the wonders wrought on Cornelius and his household, the first Gentile (= non-Jewish) converts, exclaimed, "Can any one forbid water for baptising these people?"[53]

VI

Solution of objections and difficulties. (1) "The Catholic method of Baptism by pouring water is un-Biblical, since in the New Testament and in the early Church, Baptism was performed by total immersion in water." (A common objection by Fundamentalists and Evangelicals). REPLY: (a) For Catholics, the power of the Catholic Church to determine what does and does not constitute Baptism, removes the force of this objection entirely. The Catholic Church teaches that Baptism by infusion (pouring) fulfils the command of Christ as fully as any other recognised method. (b) It is not true that Baptism by full immersion into the water was the only method originally used. St Paul baptised at very short notice a jailer and his family after midnight (Acts 16:33); it is not reasonable to suppose that there was always a man-size tub and loads of water, or a deep river nearby, in which to be baptised. The *Didache* of the 2nd century mentions use of running water, but if not, "then pour water on the head thrice in the name of the Father and of the Son, etc." (Ch. 7). St Cyprian (d. 258) recognises Baptism by infusion for the sick.[54] It is not true that full immersion remained common even in the early Church: of the dozen or more 3rd and 4th century baptisteries excavated in Greece, only two have fonts a metre or so deep, and most are under 50cm, i.e., knee-deep *if full*. The same pattern is true of baptisteries found in Syria, Palestine, Egypt and N. Africa.[55] A fresco from the first half of the 3rd century in the Catacombs of St Callistus, Rome, shows a baptism being performed in water a few inches deep. From all these it is clear that an adult candidate stood in a shallow pool, and some water was gathered from it and poured over his head.

---

[51] Jn 3:5

[52] Acts 8:26-39

[53] Acts 10:47

[54] *Ep.* 69, 12

[55] Cf. J.G. Davies, *The Architectural Setting of Baptism*, Barrie and Rockliff, London 1962; S.A. Stauffer, *On Baptismal Fonts: Ancient and Modern*, Grove Books, Nottingham 1994; Bellarmino Bagatti OFM, *The Church from the Circumcision: History and Archaeology of the Judaeo-Christians*, Franciscan Printing Press, Jerusalem 1984, p.245; Id., *The Church from the Gentiles in Palestine: History and Archaeology*, Francisc. P. Press, Jerusalem 1984, pp.301-8.

(2) "At our Baptism, our sponsors promised that we would lead Christian lives. How can we be bound by a promise given without our knowledge and consent?" REPLY: The obligation to lead a Christian life is not imposed on us by our sponsors' promises, but by the Sacrament itself: as we, by our physical birth and without our consent, are made members of a family and a nation, so, by our spiritual birth and without our consent, we are made members of the household of God. As we are bound to love and obey our parents and are entitled to receive from them corporal nurture, so we are bound to obey the Church, and are entitled to our share of the blessings Christ has given her for us; and as a man by ingratitude or disobedience can never cease to be the child of his parents, even if they bar him from their house, so he can never cease to be a child of the Church, no matter how disloyal or disobedient to her he may be. She may, by excommunication, sentence him to exclusion from her sacred rites, but she cannot cancel his baptism. She cannot deny that he is still her child. She cannot and will not refuse to restore him, on due repentance and submission, to all that he has lost.

(3) "It is an injustice and a violation of personal freedom to be baptised unawares. Baptism should be proposed when a child is old enough to choose for himself." REPLY: By the same argument, no child should be made to rise, eat, or sleep, take medicine, bathe, learn how to speak, or go to school—until he freely desires to do any of these things. Parents must necessarily make choices for their children. Good parents want to pass on to their children the best that they can offer. One could only object to infant Baptism on these grounds if Baptism and the Faith were a curse and not a blessing. Moreover, every individual, whether baptised or not, is, as a creature, already bound by indefeasible duties to God and His representatives.

(4) "Does it not seem that children who receive Protestant Baptism are bound to practise the Protestant religion?" REPLY: (a) There is no such thing as Protestant Baptism. Baptism is a sacrament instituted by Christ and entrusted to His Church, the Catholic Church. Some Protestant communities have valid Baptism (because they have retained the true way of conferring it) and their children who validly receive the Sacrament are made members of the Catholic Church.[56] The Church, however, from motives of prudence and charity, does not exercise jurisdiction over them, i.e., she does not use her right to command their obedience. (b) A Protestant child is bound to obey his parents and superiors, until he discovers that they are in error. If he lives according to his conscience, God in His own time will give him all the light and grace he needs for salvation.

(5) "If Baptism can never be administered without faith, what is the advantage of baptising children when they cannot possess or profess faith?" REPLY: The advantages are set out above: the remission of Original Sin, the bestowal of sanctifying grace, the pledge of salvation, etc. Baptism is no less the sacrament of faith with infants, since they are baptised in the faith of the Church, and the sacrament also confers upon them the virtue of faith, which will grow and mature as they are reared in it. In His Public Ministry, Our Lord conferred benefits upon

---

[56] See pp.430-1.

children for the sake of their parents' faith, e.g., He raised Jairus' daughter from the dead, He delivered a desperate man's son from a demon.[57]

(6) "The Gospels do not record when the Apostles received Baptism. Were they baptised and by whom?" REPLY: At some time in His Public Ministry, Christ must have baptised His Apostles, but He did not require any ceremony to do so. He, the God-Man and author of Grace, needed no ritual to confer all that the rite of Baptism gives. He simply had to will it, for it to happen. The Council of Trent teaches solemnly that Christ made the Apostles priests (with the fulness of the priesthood as bishops) at the Last Supper,[58] but that does not mean that He necessarily imposed hands upon them one by one. The same applies for His baptism of them some time earlier. He may or may not have employed water and a formula of words. It had certainly taken place earlier, for Baptism is a requisite for ordination. "God has bound salvation to the sacrament of Baptism, but He Himself is not bound by His own sacraments."[59]

---

[57] Lk 8:41-2, 49-56; Mk 9:14-29. Cf. Lk 7:11-5.
[58] DS 1752
[59] C 1257; cf. St Thomas, S.T., iii, q. 64, a. 7.

CHAPTER 13

CONFIRMATION

Summary

I.   The solemn teaching of the Church.
II. Confirmation defined. Its Minister and its Subject. How it is conferred.
III. Its effects: grace; the Gifts of the Holy Spirit; the Sacramental Character. The "revival" of Confirmation.
IV. Confirmation was instituted by Christ. Proof (1) from the solemn teaching of the Church; (2) from S. Scripture; (3) from Tradition.

I

The solemn teaching of the Church. The Church teaches solemnly:

(1) that Confirmation is a Sacrament;[1]
(2) that its ordinary minister is a Bishop;[2]
(3) that it imprints a Character, or indelible mark, on the soul and cannot be received more than once;[3]
(4) that it gives us an increase of grace and strengthens us in the faith.[4]

II

Confirmation defined. Its minister and its subject. How and when it is conferred.

DEFINITION. Confirmation is the Sacrament that completes Baptism and gives the grace to live as strong and perfect Christians. Baptism is the Sacrament of spiritual birth; Confirmation, as its name suggests (con-*firm*), is the Sacrament of spiritual strength. In the Eastern Churches it is called "Chrismation" (anointing with chrism) or "Myron", which means chrism.

ITS MINISTER. In the Latin Church, the ordinary minister of Confirmation is a Bishop. It can also be conferred by a priest upon a Catholic in danger of death, or, if he has the faculty, upon an adult whom he is receiving into the Catholic Church.[5] A priest may also be given the faculty for other occasions. In the Eastern Churches, any priest can confirm at the appointed time.

---

[1] T 1601
[2] T 1630
[3] T 1609
[4] F 1319
[5] Can. 883

ITS SUBJECT. Its subject is anyone who has been baptised but not yet confirmed.

HOW IT IS CONFERRED. The Bishop imposes his hand on the recipient and anoints his forehead with chrism in the form of a cross, while reciting the words: "Receive the seal of the Gift of the Holy Spirit."[6] The blow on the cheek which the Bishop then gives became customary about the 12th century. It may be interpreted both as a substitute for the ancient "kiss of peace" and as a reminder that, "as a valiant combatant, he should be prepared to endure with unconquered spirit all adversities for the name of Christ."[7]

A candidate for Confirmation, where possible, has a sponsor to help him to live as a true witness of Christ and be faithful to the duties inherent in this sacrament.[8] The requirements in a sponsor are the same as for Baptism, and it is desirable that it be one of the godparents again.[9] It is also customary at Confirmation to take the name of a Saint whom one would like to adopt as a patron.

WHEN IT IS CONFERRED. In the early Church, it was customary to give Confirmation and the Blessed Eucharist to children immediately or soon after Baptism—as is still the practice of the Eastern Churches. Eastern priests, therefore, always have the faculty to confirm. In the Latin Church, the administration of these Sacraments is usually postponed until the child has reached the age of reason and is sufficiently instructed. Confirmation is postponed so that the Bishop can confer it personally.

III

The effects of Confirmation: Grace. Closer union with the Church. The gifts of the Holy Spirit. The Sacramental Character. The "revival" of the Sacrament.

INCREASE OF SANCTIFYING GRACE. The primary effect of Confirmation, as of all Sacraments of the living, is a great increase of the Divine Life of Sanctifying Grace, and, consequently, a closer and more intimate union with God who dwells in our soul. This indwelling is appropriated to the Holy Spirit.[10]

---

[6] "Accipe signaculum doni Spiritus Sancti." For "chrism" see p.463.
[7] *Roman Catechism*, Part II, "Confirmation". On the *Roman Catechism*, see p.643, n.133.
[8] Can. 892
[9] Can. 892-3
[10] On "appropriation", see p.315.

SACRAMENTAL GRACE. The Sacramental Grace of Confirmation disposes the recipient energetically to profess, defend and propagate the Faith received in Baptism. It includes also the right or claim which the Sacrament gives us to the special spiritual helps or Actual Graces which, if we avail ourselves of them, enable us to lead a more saintly life undeterred by human respect or other worldly obstacles.

CLOSER UNION WITH THE CHURCH AND HER MISSION. Confirmation binds the baptised more perfectly to Christ and the Church. The special strength of the Holy Spirit given in it assists them and obliges them more strictly to spread and defend the faith publicly by word and deed.[11] To clear up a common misunderstanding: it is not we who 'confirm' our Baptism by choosing Confirmation; rather, it is the Holy Spirit who confirms us.

THE GIFTS OF THE HOLY SPIRIT. In Confirmation, as the Council of Florence teaches, the Holy Spirit is given to us for our spiritual strengthening,[12] a strengthening which is effected in a most particular way through the Gifts of the Holy Spirit.

The Gifts of the Holy Spirit always accompany Sanctifying Grace: they were, therefore, given to us at our Baptism; but in Confirmation they are given to us in a fuller or more perfect form. To understand their purpose, we may compare the soul to a sailing ship, the gifts to the sails, and the impulses of the Holy Spirit to the favourable winds of heaven. At Baptism the ship of the soul was given its suit of sails, but the sails were small. At Confirmation they are enlarged so that they may more perfectly respond to the impulse of God's grace. At Baptism we were given a certain disposition to be moved by divine light and inspiration; at Confirmation that disposition is perfected, so that we are enabled to respond easily to the fuller and more precise Actual Graces we need for final perseverance, for the heroic deeds of a martyr or the heroic life of a saint. Because of venial sin, the Gifts of the Holy Spirit may be impeded or contracted, like sails that are furled or reefed. Hence, the great importance of not offending God even in the slightest way.

The Gifts of the Holy Spirit, as the Prophet Isaiah foretold (11:2-3), were bestowed on our Saviour; they are bestowed on us also. They shine in our soul, because it reflects His image. They are all conferred on us in the same instant. They are seven in number, viz: the Gifts of *Wisdom, Understanding, Counsel, Fortitude, Knowledge, Piety* (or *Godliness*), and *Fear of the Lord.* They endow us with good dispositions and greater docility, opening

---

[11] C 1285
[12] DS 1319

wide our intellect and will to the inflow of Actual Grace. In other words, they enlarge our power to receive Actual Grace.

Through these Gifts, as through so many broad inlets, the Holy Spirit, unless resisted, will pour generously into our soul all these Actual Graces which shall enable us: to dwell with pleasure on the Beauty and Majesty and Infinity of God (*Wisdom*); to grasp and hold in our mind all the great truths presented to us by God's Holy Church (*Understanding*); to show good sense in the custody of our soul by shunning bad company, dangerous occasions and everything that might imperil our spiritual life (*Counsel*); to be true to our Faith, to profess it boldly, and, with the superb courage of a martyr, to welcome death in testifying to its truth (*Fortitude*); to see the hand of God in the happenings of the world, to see His likeness in all created things, but at the same time, to realise that no creature deserves to be loved for its own sake, or can be of any profit to us, unless it lead us to our Creator (*Knowledge*); to serve God with joy, to say our prayers in spite of hurry or weariness, to receive the Sacraments, to join with devotion in the Holy Sacrifice of the Mass, to look on God as our Father and on all men as our brothers (*Piety* - Godliness); to entertain a profound though filial fear of God, to meditate on the great disaster of losing His love, and of being separated from Him for all eternity (*Fear of the Lord*).

Through the Gifts of Wisdom, Understanding, Counsel, and Knowledge, Actual Grace is given to the *intellect*; through the Gifts of Fortitude, Piety, and the Fear of the Lord, it is given to the *will*.

Carefully distinguish between (the natural virtue of) *Wisdom* and the *Gift of Wisdom*, (natural) *Understanding* and the *Gift of Understanding*, etc. The Gift of Wisdom enables us to respond easily to all the Actual Graces we need for the acquisition of divine Wisdom. Wisdom may be termed the fruit of the Gift of Wisdom; the Gift is bestowed on us in full measure at Confirmation, but the fruit might not appear until many years later. So with the other Gifts.

THE SACRAMENTAL CHARACTER. Like Baptism, Confirmation imprints an indelible mark on the soul, and, therefore, cannot be repeated. Confirmation is, as it were, a spiritual coming of age, and as we can come of age physically but once, so we can come of age only once in the spiritual sense. The Baptismal Character marks us as a *Disciple* (follower) of Christ, while the Character given in Confirmation enrols us as an *Apostle* (missionary) of Christ, fully equipped for the apostolate. By appropriation,[13] we may say that Baptism gives the seal of Christ, and Confirmation gives the seal of the Spirit.

THE "REVIVAL" OF CONFIRMATION. It is commonly held that those who are so unfortunate as to receive the great Sacrament of Confirmation in the state of mortal sin may, by due repentance and Confession, obtain the

---

[13] see p.315.

precious gifts of grace it conveys. The sacramental character is already present, and will operate upon repentance.

THE NECESSITY OF CONFIRMATION. The Church teaches that although Confirmation is not a necessary means for salvation, still "the faithful are bound by obligation to receive this sacrament at the proper time."[14] Hence, no one should refuse Confirmation or unduly postpone it. So much depends on our receiving it worthily that we should exercise the greatest care in our preparation for it, using our best endeavour to acquire an accurate knowledge of doctrine and to put ourselves in the proper disposition by Confession and Holy Communion. When the Apostles were awaiting the descent of the Holy Spirit at Pentecost, for many days they "with one accord devoted themselves to prayer".[15] For each of us our Confirmation is our Pentecost, and it comes but once. Confirmation is obligatory for anyone being advanced to Holy Orders, and highly desirable for a man and woman going to be married.

IV

The Sacrament of Confirmation was instituted by Christ. PROOF FROM THE SOLEMN TEACHING OF THE CHURCH. The Church in the exercise of her infallible authority declares the institution of the Sacrament of Confirmation by Christ to be a doctrine given to her by God Himself. This proof alone suffices for Catholics. The following proofs are added for fuller instruction.

PROOF FROM SACRED SCRIPTURE. (1) Christ's promise to send the Holy Spirit on His Apostles (Acts 1:8) was fulfilled at the first Pentecost.
(2) This ineffable gift was intended for all the faithful as well: St Peter addressing the multitude said: "Repent, and be baptised every one of you in the name of Jesus Christ for the forgiveness of your sins; and you shall receive the gift of the Holy Spirit. For the promise is to you and to your children and to all that are far off, every one whom the Lord our God calls to Him."[16]
(3) The Apostles communicated this gift to them by a rite distinct from Baptism: "Now when the Apostles at Jerusalem heard that Samaria had received the word of God, they sent to them Peter and John, who came down and prayed for them that they might receive the Holy Spirit; for it had not yet fallen on any of them, but they had only been baptised in the name of the Lord Jesus. Then they laid their hands on them and they received the Holy Spirit."[17] This passage shows: (a) that the Apostles conferred the gift of the Holy Spirit by laying on of hands and by prayer, i.e., by a visible rite; (b) that the rite was distinct from Baptism, the people of Samaria having already been baptised by the deacon Philip; (c) that its administration was reserved to the Apostles, probably in their capacity as bishops, otherwise Peter and John would not have gone to Samaria in a time of persecution

---

[14] Can. 890
[15] Acts 1:14
[16] Acts 2:38-39
[17] Acts 8:14-17

at the peril of their lives; (d) that the rite must have been instituted by Christ Himself, for it is only He who could have endowed it with its grace-giving power.

(4) The rite consisted in prayer and the laying on of hands. Very early on, anointing also was made part of the rite.

(5) The only rite in present use which can claim identity with the rite administered by the Apostles is our rite of Confirmation. If the identity of the two rites is denied, the absurd conclusion follows that a rite regarded as of such great importance by the Apostles was afterwards abandoned as useless by the Church. The same arguments may be adduced from Acts 19:5-6: "they were baptised in the name of the Lord Jesus. And when Paul had laid his hands upon them, the Holy Spirit came on them".

PROOF FROM TRADITION. No one doubts that in the time of St Augustine (d. 430), Confirmation was exactly as it is today: "The Sacrament of Chrism", he says, "is one of the visible signs and, like Baptism itself, is most holy."[18] As to the earlier ages, the testimony of only a few witnesses, out of a very large number, need be quoted:

(a) St Cyril of Jerusalem (d. 386), devoting a special *Catechesis* to the praise of Confirmation, says, "As the bread of the Eucharist ... is no longer mere bread but the Body of Christ, so this holy ointment, after the invocation of the Holy Spirit, is no longer plain ointment ... but the chrism of Christ, which, by the presence of the Godhead, causes in us the Holy Spirit. This symbolically anoints your forehead, ... but the soul is sanctified by the holy and life-giving Spirit."[19]

(b) St Cyprian (d. 258), commenting on the passage from Acts quoted in (3) above, says: "The Samaritans who had already obtained legitimate ecclesiastical Baptism did not require any further Baptism. Peter and John merely supplied what was wanting, namely that by prayer and the imposition of hands the Holy Spirit should be poured forth on them. This is also the practice with us: those who are baptised in the Church are presented to the Bishops, and, through our prayer and the laying on of hands, they receive the Holy Spirit and are made perfect by the seal of the Lord."[20]

(c) Tertullian, writing c. 210, says: "The body is anointed, that the soul may be made holy; the body is marked with a sign, that the soul may be protected; the body is over-shadowed by the laying on of hands, that the soul may be enlightened by the Holy Spirit."[21]

---

[18] *Contra litt. Petiliani*, ii. 239
[19] *Catech.* 348, *myst.* 3: PG 33,1089
[20] *Ep.* 73, 9
[21] *De resur. carnis*, 8

Non-Catholic witnesses. The ancient oriental Churches and the Byzantine Orthodox Churches all have the Sacrament of Confirmation.[22] The Gnostic heretics as far back as the first half of the second century practised the rite of anointing and laying on of hands.[23] These alone would suffice to establish decisively the tradition of the Church.

---

[22] See p.454.

[23] F. Dölger, *Das Sakrament der Firmung,* Theol. Stud. der Leo-Gesellschaft, 1906, p.4 f.

CHAPTER 14

THE BLESSED EUCHARIST

A

THE REAL PRESENCE OF CHRIST
IN THE BLESSED EUCHARIST

Summary

I.   The solemn teaching of the Church.
II. Proof of the Real Presence:
     (1) from the words of Christ;
     (2) from the faith of the Apostolic and early Church, evidenced by the
          words of St Paul and the Fathers, by *the discipline of the secret*, by the
          symbols and illustrations found in the catacombs, and by the belief of
          non-Catholic Easterners;
     (3) from the lateness and insignificance of the errors opposed to it.
III. The Real Presence, produced by Transubstantiation. Its completeness. Its
     duration. Its adorableness. Reverence for It.
IV. Difficulties answered.

I

The solemn teaching of the Church. The Church teaches solemnly:
(1) that the Holy Eucharist is a Sacrament instituted by Christ;[1]
(2) that in the Blessed Eucharist, Christ Himself—His Body and Blood,
     His Soul and Divinity—is really, truly, and substantially, present under
     the species (accidents, appearances) of bread and wine;[2]
(3) that His presence is effected by transubstantiation, i.e., by a change in
     the substance of bread and wine into the Body and Blood of Christ;[3]
(4) that He is wholly present both under the species of bread and under
     the species of wine; that, when the sacred species of the bread or wine
     are divided, He is wholly present in each part or division;[4]
(5) that the Real Presence begins the instant the consecration is
     completed; that it is not restricted to the moment in which the Blessed
     Eucharist is being received; that it continues in the hosts that may be
     reserved after Holy Communion has been given;[5]

---

[1] T 1601
[2] T 1651
[3] T 1652
[4] T 1653
[5] T 1654

(6)   that Christ in the Blessed Eucharist is to be worshipped with the supreme worship due to God Himself.[6]

For a Catholic, it is sufficient to know that the Church teaches the above doctrine infallibly. The following proofs, therefore, are not necessary, but they are useful as giving a knowledge of Sacred Scripture and Ecclesiastical Tradition.

II

Proof of the Real Presence from the words of Christ. The words used by Christ when He promised the Blessed Eucharist, and when He actually instituted it, prove that He is really present therein.

CHRIST'S WORDS OF PROMISE. We read in the sixth chapter of St John's Gospel how Jesus fed a multitude of five thousand men with five loaves and two fishes; and how, on the following night, He walked upon the waters, and rejoined His disciples as they were crossing the lake to Capernaum. The next day, we are told, He again addressed the multitude, who had followed Him in ships to that city. By the multiplication of the loaves and fishes, He had proved to them His love and consideration for them, and His dominion over the laws of nature: He had thus prepared their minds and hearts for His doctrine of the heavenly food of the Blessed Eucharist. "Do not labour", He said to them, "for the food which perishes, but for the food which endures to eternal life, which the Son of Man will give to you".[7] And, when they said, "Lord, give us this bread always",[8] He continued: "I am the Bread of Life; he who comes to Me shall not hunger, and he who believes in Me shall never thirst."[9] He then tells them clearly that the Bread is His Flesh: "the Bread which I shall give for the life of the world is My Flesh."[10] And when they objected saying, "How can this man give us His Flesh to eat?",[11] He insists on the literal truth of His words, telling them with still greater emphasis that they must not only eat His Flesh but drink His Blood: "Truly, truly, I say to you, unless you eat the Flesh of the Son of Man and drink His Blood, you have no life in you; he who eats My Flesh and drinks My Blood has eternal life, and I will raise him up at the last day. For *My Flesh is food indeed, and My Blood is drink indeed*. He who eats My Flesh and drinks My Blood abides in Me, and I in him."[12] Many of His disciples thought this "a hard saying",[13] and would not accept it. Jesus said to them, "Do you take offence at this?"[14] i.e., "Are you shocked at what I have said?" If (in line with modern heresies) they had thought that by "eating His Flesh and drinking His

---

[6] T 1656
[7] Jn 6:27
[8] Jn 6:34
[9] Jn 6:35
[10] Jn 6:52
[11] Ibid., v. 53
[12] vv. 54-57
[13] v. 61
[14] v. 62

Blood", He merely meant that they were to take His doctrine and commands into their mind and heart, they would not have been shocked. They were shocked, precisely because they understood Him to speak of the true eating of His Body and drinking of His Blood. If they had mistaken His meaning, He would have shown them their error. He would have disowned the doctrine they ascribed to Him. But He did not disown it. Instead, He insists again on the divine character and value of the Food to which they object. But they are not satisfied, because He has not withdrawn or mitigated the command to eat His Flesh and drink His Blood. The stumbling-block still stands in their path; and so they leave Him and walk with Him no more.[15] Then turning to the Apostles He said, "'Will you also go away?' Simon Peter answered Him, 'Lord, to whom shall we go? You have the words of eternal life; and we have believed, and have come to know that You are the Holy One of God.'"[16] Those noble words, so full of loyalty and love, we adopt as our own, promising to be faithful to Jesus no matter who may be unfaithful to Him.

The exact words which He addressed to them were as follows:
A. "Do you take offence at this? Then what if you were to see the Son of Man ascending where He was before?"
B. "It is the spirit that gives life, the flesh is of no avail".
C. "the words that I have spoken to you are spirit and life."
D. "But there are some of you that do not believe." (6:61-64).
That is to say:
(a) "Are you shocked at what I have said? Will you still be shocked even when you see that My Flesh is the Flesh of One who shall ascend into Heaven?"
(b) "It is the spirit of My Divinity that gives life, or makes My Flesh a life-giving Food. Mere human flesh such as you are thinking of profits nothing."
(c) "The words I have spoken to you promise you a Food which will make you one with Me in spirit and life."
(d) "But I know that some of you do not believe that I am the Son of God and can do what I have promised."

CHRIST'S WORDS OF INSTITUTION. Jesus fulfilled His promise at the Last Supper. He had been longing for that hour to come: "I have earnestly desired to eat this passover with you before I suffer".[17] Taking bread He "blessed, and broke it, and gave it to the disciples and said, 'Take, eat; this My body.' And He took a cup, and when He had given thanks He gave it to them, saying, 'Drink of it, all of you; for this is My blood of the covenant, which is poured out for many for the forgiveness of sins.'"[18] Jesus uttered those words at a most solemn moment: He was delivering His last address, His last wishes and commands, to the Apostles, for on the morrow He was to be put to death. He spoke in the very plainest speech to the simple and childlike men who sat at the table with Him. The words were in themselves unmistakable, but they were doubly so in the light of the promise already made that

---

[15] v. 67
[16] vv. 68-70
[17] Lk 22:15
[18] Lk 26:26-28

He would given them His Flesh to eat and His Blood to drink. The Apostles believed, as we believe, that when He said, "This is My Body, ... This is My Blood", the bread and the wine were changed into His Body and Blood.

Proof of the Real Presence from the faith of the Apostolic and early Church. The faith of the Apostolic and early Church in the Real Presence of Christ in the Blessed Eucharist is attested by the words of St Paul and the Fathers; by "the discipline of the secret"; the symbols and illustrations found in the catacombs; and the belief of non-Catholic Eastern Christians. The fact that the Church from the very beginning believed in the Real Presence proves that her doctrine must have been delivered to her by her Founder.

THE WORDS OF ST PAUL AND THE FATHERS.
(a) St Paul says: "The cup of blessing which we bless, is it not a participation in the Blood of Christ? The bread which we break, is it not a participation in the Body of Christ?" "Whoever, therefore, eats the bread or drinks the cup of the Lord in an unworthy manner will be guilty of profaning the Body and Blood of the Lord."[19]
(b) St Ignatius of Antioch (once in Syria; now Antakya, Turkey: d. 107) says: "The Eucharist is the Flesh of our Saviour Jesus Christ, Flesh which suffered for our sins and which the Father, in His goodness, raised up again."[20]
(c) St Justin Martyr (d. 167): "We take this not as ordinary bread nor as ordinary drink. But just as Jesus Christ our Saviour ... had Flesh and Blood for our salvation, so have we been taught that the food consecrated by the word of prayer coming from Him ... is the Flesh and Blood of that Jesus who was made Flesh."[21]
(d) St Irenaeus (d. c. 202): "Wine and bread are by the word of God changed into the Eucharist, which is the Body and Blood of Christ."[22]
(e) St Hippolytus of Rome (d. 235): "He has given us His own divine Flesh and His own precious Blood to eat and to drink."[23] Later evidence of this kind is abundant.

THE DISCIPLINE OF THE SECRET. Except when the needs of controversy demanded plain speaking, it was the custom among Christians during the first centuries, and particularly from the end of the second to the beginning of the sixth, to conceal from the heathen the more sacred and mysterious rites of religion and especially the real nature of the Blessed Eucharist. This practice has been termed, "the discipline of the secret" (*disciplina arcani*). Such secrecy in regard to the Blessed Eucharist would have been unnecessary if it were merely a sacred meal to commemorate the Last Supper—for sacred meals were common among pagans, and were not believed to be the banquet of the Body and Blood of the Saviour. As an instance of the veiled language used, we may quote the following from a 4th century inscription: "Take the food sweet as honey of the Saviour of the saints, eat and drink holding

---

[19] 1 Cor 10:16; 11:27
[20] *Ep. ad Smyrn.* c. 7
[21] *Apol.* I, 66
[22] *Adv. Haer.* 5:2,3
[23] *In Proverb.* 9:2

the fish in thy hands."[24] The true meaning of this was plain to a Christian, but not to an unbeliever. The "fish" was the secret name of the Saviour, because the Greek word for fish gives the initial letters of "Jesus Christ, Son of God, Saviour".[25] The "fish" is said to be held in the hands, because the Sacred Host was received in the right hand supported by the left, and then conveyed to the mouth.

SYMBOLS AND ILLUSTRATIONS FOUND IN THE CATACOMBS. In the crypts of Lucina, in the Catacombs of St Callistus, Rome, a fish symbolising Christ is represented as bearing on its back a basket of bread and a cup of red wine. As one commentator explains: what appears on the surface is bread and wine; what sustains this appearance beneath the surface is the living Christ. This beautiful illustration of the Real Presence is dated late in the 2nd century. Another in the same Catacombs, towards the end of the 2nd century, shows us a table on which are laid a fish and a piece of bread: on the left, a figure representing Christ or a priest is consecrating the bread, and on the right a woman with outstretched arms is adoring or returning thanks.[26] A very similar fresco is found in the Catacombs of Priscilla, also in Rome.

THE BELIEF OF EASTERN NON-CATHOLICS. The Eastern non-Catholic Christians have always most emphatically professed their faith in the Real Presence. On the significance of their testimony, see p.454.

Proof of the Real Presence from the lateness and insignificance of the errors opposed to it. THE LATENESS OF THE ERRORS. For fully a thousand years, the doctrine of the Real Presence was virtually unopposed: Christ, who promised to be with His Church all days even unto the end of time, would not have allowed His children to live in the grossest of error and idolatry during all those centuries.

THE INSIGNIFICANCE OF THE ERRORS. When the doctrine was at length assailed, all the skill and determination of its opponents, who left no stone unturned to destroy it, produced no argument worthy of consideration.

(1) Berengarius (d. 1088) held that the words, "This is My Body", meant "This is not My Body but a figure of it": that is to say, Christ never gave men His Flesh to eat, and therefore violated the promise He had most distinctly made. This interpretation at once aroused the indignation of Christendom. It was branded as directly contradictory to the ancient faith of the Church and the teaching of Christ himself. It was withdrawn by its author, who died repentant.
(2) Some five centuries later the doctrine was attacked by the Protestants. Martin Luther (1483-1546) seems at first to have held the traditional teaching of the Church, but later maintained that Christ is present in the Blessed Eucharist only at the moment of its reception in Holy Communion. He forgot that Christ simply

---

[24] Epitaph of Pectorius, in J. Quasten, *Monumenta eucharistica, etc.* pars I, Bonn 1935, pp.24-6
[25] Fish: ἰχθυς, acronym of Ἰησους χριστος θεου υἱος σωτηρ
[26] L. Hertling S.J. & E. Kirschbaum S.J., *The Roman Catacombs and their Martyrs*, DLT, London 1960, p.239

said, "This is My Body", and not, "This will be My Body when you receive it." Ulrich Zwingli (1484-1531) revived the doctrine of Berengarius. John Calvin (1509-1564) proposed the far-fetched theory that the words, "This is My Body" mean, "This is not really My Body, but when you receive it, you receive into your souls a spiritual influence from the Body of Christ which is in Heaven." Andreas Osiander (1498-1552) thought that, as God became Man, so He became bread. Hence, "This is My Body", would mean, "This is not My Body, but bread to which My Divinity is united." This teaching is called *impanation* ("becoming bread", *panis*) a term modelled on *incarnation* ("becoming flesh", *caro*). *Companation*, or *consubstantiaion*, held by many Lutherans, means that the substance of bread and the Body of Christ exist together in the Eucharist.

These are but a few of a great number of conflicting interpretations invented by the Reformers to place as wide a gulf as possible between themselves and the Church they had abandoned. In more recent times, people have refused to give the words of Christ their true meaning, chiefly because they measure God's power by their own. What seems impossible to them must, they think in their folly, be impossible to God.

III

The Real Presence, produced by Transubstantiation.
Its completeness. Its duration. Its adorableness. Reverence for It.

THE REAL PRESENCE, PRODUCED BY TRANSUBSTANTIATION. When Christ said "This is My Body ... This is My Blood", the substance of the bread and the wine was changed into His Body and Blood. Of the bread and the wine, nothing remained but the accidents, that is, the size, shape, weight, colour, taste, and all else that could be perceived by the senses.[27] This mysterious change is called Transubstantiation.

The term "Transubstantiation" appears to have been first used by Hildebert of Tours (c. 1097), and was adopted by the Fourth Council of Lateran and by the Council of Trent. Its equivalent Greek form[28] was admitted into the official terminology of the Greek Orthodox Church in 1643, which proves that "Transubstantiation", though a new word, represented an idea as old as Christianity itself. Had the idea been as new as the word, and therefore a mere Roman invention, the Greeks would have been the very last to give it countenance.

We may illustrate the difference between substance and accidents as follows: I hold a bar of iron in my hands. It has a certain size, shape, weight, colour, and hardness. None of these things makes it iron. Not its size or shape, for, clearly, it may change in either respect and still be iron. Not its weight, for its weight depends on gravity, and varies according to the distance from the centre of the earth. In fact, at a certain point outside the earth, it loses

---

[27] On *substance* and *accident*, see p.298.
[28] μετουσιωσις

the centre of the earth. In fact, at a certain point outside the earth, it loses all weight. Not its colour, for that changes with the temperature; under moderate heat it will become red, and under intense heat, a glowing white. Not its hardness, for when it is cast into a furnace, it becomes a liquid. If then it is not iron because of size, or shape, or hardness etc., what is it that makes it iron? It is its substance. The substance remains fixed amid many changes; it is an unchanging thing, whereas the changeable dress it wears constitutes its *accidents*. With every change in the iron bar, there is a corresponding change in the molecules of which it consists. Yet each molecule, throughout all the changes it suffers, continues to be iron. As in the entire bar, so in each molecule, there is that unchanging thing which we call substance. *Substance* is not a hard or heavy thing; it is something invisible, a power that supports the accidents. It is something like a soul, which cannot be grasped by the senses, but by the mind alone; and, like the soul, it is present in its entirety in every part, however small, of the body to which it belongs.

THE COMPLETENESS OF THE REAL PRESENCE. By the completeness of the Real Presence we mean that the entire Christ is present both under the species of bread and under the species of wine, and also under each part of either species. It is Christ gloriously risen from the dead Who is present.

The entire Christ is present under each species. At the words, "This is My Body ... This is My Blood", the bread Christ held in His hands became His Body, and the wine in the chalice, His Blood. But, as Body and Blood were united at that time in the living Christ, under the species of the bread was the entire living Christ, true God and true man, and so too with the wine. At that Last Supper, as at Mass, the *bread* became the *Body* of Christ, and co-present were His Blood, soul and Divinity. The *wine* became the *Blood* of Christ, and co-present were His Body, soul and Divinity.

The entire Christ is present under each part of either species. When bread or wine is divided, each division is true bread or true wine. Each division therefore, contains the true substance of bread and wine. But in the Blessed Eucharist, Christ is present instead of the material substances. Therefore, when the Blessed Eucharist is divided, Christ is present in His entirety in each part or division. This doctrine is clearly taught in the Sacred Scripture where we read that Christ gave the consecrated chalice to His apostles, saying, "This is the cup of My Blood", and that all drank of it.[29] Each one, therefore, received, in the portion which he drank, the Blood of the Saviour, and (as follows from the preceding paragraph) in receiving the Precious

---

[29] See Mk 14:23.

Blood, he received the entire living Christ, true God, true Man.

THE DURATION OF THE REAL PRESENCE. From the defined doctrine that Christ gave His Apostles His sacred Body and Blood under the species or accidents of bread and wine, and under no other species, we draw the conclusion, universally held, that as long as the species remain unchanged after the Consecration, the Real Presence continues; and that when, by corruption or fermentation, they become altered into species of a different kind, the Real Presence terminates, and the substances proper to the new species enter in. The species follow the laws they would follow if the substances of bread and wine were behind them. Exposure to the air will change wine to vinegar. Thus, if the consecrated chalice were kept uncovered for a considerable time, the accidents of wine would disappear, and with their disappearance the Real Presence would cease. Bread when eaten is gradually changed in the process of digestion, and a moment comes when it is no longer bread. Hence, it is only for some minutes after Holy Communion that the Real Presence stays with us.

THE ADORABLENESS OF THE REAL PRESENCE. We can and ought to adore our Divine Lord in the Blessed Eucharist: "No one", says St Augustine, "eats this flesh without having first adored it."[30] The practice of this great devotion received its first decided impetus in the 12th century, after the condemnation of Berengarius, when the custom was introduced of reserving the Sacred Host in the Tabernacle with the express purpose of enabling the faithful to adore it outside the Mass. A still further advance was made by Pope Urban IV in 1264. At the request of Bl. Juliana of Liège, he instituted the Feast of Corpus Christi, for the office and Mass of which St Thomas Aquinas (d. 1274) composed the well-known hymns, *Verbum Supernum*,[31] *Pange Lingua*, and the sequence, *Lauda Sion*. Within a century of that date, the custom was established of exposing the Blessed Sacrament in the monstrance and of bearing it in solemn processions through the streets and public places. This custom gave rise to the rite of Exposition and Benediction now so familiar in the Church. During the last few hundred years, numerous orders and societies have devoted themselves to the perpetual adoration of Jesus hidden in the Tabernacle.[32]

---

[30] *In Ps.* 98, 9

[31] To be distinguished from the Advent Hymn of the fifth or sixth century which begins with the same words. The two concluding stanzas of St Thomas' hymn are sung at Benediction (*O Salutaris Hostia,* etc.).

[32] Observe how God uses the assaults of heretics for the development of His holy doctrine and the stimulation of piety.

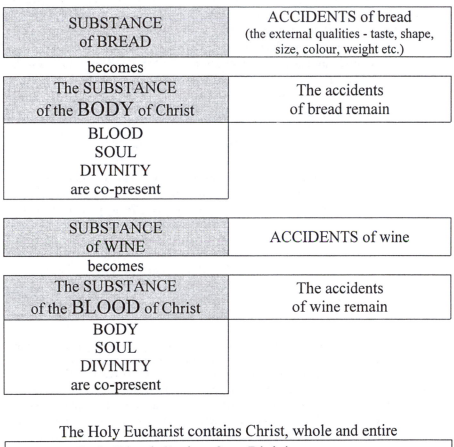

SUBSTANCE of BREAD	ACCIDENTS of bread (the external qualities - taste, shape, size, colour, weight etc.)

becomes

The SUBSTANCE of the **BODY** of Christ	The accidents of bread remain
BLOOD SOUL DIVINITY are co-present	

SUBSTANCE of WINE	ACCIDENTS of wine

becomes

The SUBSTANCE of the **BLOOD** of Christ	The accidents of wine remain
BODY SOUL DIVINITY are co-present	

The Holy Eucharist contains Christ, whole and entire

Body Blood, Soul	&	Divinity
True Man	&	True God

Jesus Christ

This change of substance is called by the Church:
TRANSUBSTANTIATION

Catechism: 1374, 1376, 1377.

REVERENCE FOR THE REAL PRESENCE. The Blessed Sacrament is, as Pope Paul VI said, "the living heart of our churches."[33] It is His presence which makes our churches unique, and set apart from every other building. Reverence for His presence is an inviolable duty of every Catholic. Talking in church should be restricted to the brief and the necessary. Prolonged conversation in church is out of place, just as to spend one's time talking to friends during a visit to an important person would be discourteous and offensive. A reverent genuflection towards the tabernacle upon entering and leaving church indicates our adoration of Our Lord and Our God. Visits to Our Lord in the Blessed Sacrament are a most efficacious means of growing in intimate friendship with Him and of drawing greater fruit from Mass and Holy Communion.

IV

Answers to difficulties against the Real Presence. (1) "It seems impossible that the same body could be present at the same time in Heaven and in all the consecrated Hosts throughout the world." REPLY: (a) We may admit that the ordinary human body, subject to the laws of nature, cannot be present simultaneously in different places. But here, there is question of no ordinary body but of one united mysteriously to God, the Master of nature and its laws. The physicist knows nothing whatever of such a Body. No one knows what such a Body may be capable of; no one can disprove its exemption from the laws of nature; no one can show that it is restricted like natural bodies to a single position in space. Other bodies are subject to the laws of space, but to this Body the laws of space are obedient.
(b) There is only one soul in man, wholly and entirely present at once in many places, in the eyes, in the ears, and in every organ and member of the body, and yet the soul has no dimensions and occupies no space. We make no difficulty in accepting such a truth, because we can give sound arguments from reason in support of it.[34] Admitting it, we can understand the opinion of those philosophers who hold that God could, if He chose, create several distinct human bodies, all vivified by the same identical soul, so that what might seem to be the acts of many different individuals would all belong to a single consciousness and proceed from a single will. Now, the glorified Body of Christ in many distinct Hosts may be compared to such a soul: while remaining one and the same, it is present at the same time in different places.
(c) Take the following illustration: "A man writes a book on foreign travel; he gets fifty thousand copies printed; he gives a copy to fifty thousand different people. Now, in a book we have two totally distinct things—in the first place, we have the story, the narrative, the facts recounted, which I call the truth of the book; and, in the second place, we have the paper, the leaves, the type, the letterpress, the punctuation, which do not indeed constitute the truth, but which are merely the

---

[33] *Credo of the People of God*, 1968, art. 26
[34] See p.68.

channel by which the truth is conveyed to us. The first I call the *substance* of the book; the latter I call the *accidents*. Put these fifty thousand copies of the book into the hands of fifty thousand different men. What is the result? Well, the result is, that each man possesses (1) the *entire* truth, and (2) the *exact* truth, and (3) the *same* truth. The accidents may be different in each, but the substance is the same; and, not only similar, but identical. Each book may vary in size, weight, type, paper, material, binding, and so forth. It makes no difference. There is not one truth in one volume, and another in another, but the same truth is present wherever there is a copy of the book; and if there be fifty thousand copies, then the same truth, whole and entire and identical, is equally present in fifty thousand different places. And further, whether a man receive but one copy, or whether he receive fifty copies, or even the whole edition of fifty thousand volumes, he will have the same truth, neither more nor less than if he had received but one. So in the Blessed Sacrament, if one hundred particles are consecrated, the incarnate Wisdom of God is present under each, just as the wisdom of any author is present in each of a hundred volumes ... This is of course a mere illustration and not to be pressed too far; for whereas in a book the truth is merely expressed by signs, in the Blessed Sacrament, the Eternal Truth, i.e., the infinite God is substantially present in His Human and Divine nature."[35]

(d) Cardinal Newman says, "Catholics do not see that it is impossible at all, that our Lord should be in Heaven and yet on the Altar; they do not indeed see *how* it can be, but they do not see *why* it should not be; there are many things that exist, though we do not know *how*,—do we know *how* anything exists?—there are many truths which are not less truths because we cannot picture them to ourselves or conceive them; but at any rate, the Catholic doctrine concerning the Real Presence is not more mysterious than how Almighty God can exist, yet never have come into existence."[36]

(2) "It seems absurd that the Body of our Saviour could be so reduced in size as to dwell within the small dimensions of a Host." REPLY: (a) The difficulty is solved by removing the misunderstanding that underlies it. The dimensions of the Host are accidents; they are not part of the substance of bread. Accidents (size, colour, weight, etc.) can be perceived both by the mind and by the senses; substance can be perceived by the mind alone. Substance has no size, no dimensions, and, to that extent, may be regarded as like a soul. Christ's Body, therefore, since it replaces the substance of bread, cannot be said to be affected by the size of the Host. How this can be, we do not know, but, as Cardinal Newman says, "Why should it not be? What's to hinder it? What do I know of substance or matter? Just as much as the greatest philosophers, and that is nothing at all."[37]   (b) An analogy: an encyclopaedia of ten large printed volumes may be committed to a single CD-Rom. The compact disk can contain the entire text, the diagrams, illustrations and photographs—all that is in the "hard copy"—and, as a result, we have the *exact same*

35 Bishop Vaughan, *Thoughts for all Times*, Washbourne 1911, Vol. I, p.123
36 *Discourses to Mixed Congregations*, XIII, p.266
37 *Apologia*, p.239 (Ch. V, Position since 1845)

encyclopaedia, the only difference being that it exists *in a different form*. Similarly, we have Christ's body in the Holy Eucharist, *in sacramental form*, but no less real for that.

(3) "Since the Blessed Eucharist produces the effects of ordinary food and drink, does it not seem that the substance of bread and wine must be present?" REPLY: The appeasing of hunger, the allaying of thirst, and any such immediate effects, must be ascribed to the species alone. God, who miraculously sustains the species of bread and wine, gives them all that their own proper substance could give them. He provides them with whatever support they need for their existence and activity. It may be added, however, that, before actual nutrition is effected, the sacred species will disappear and, with them, the Real Presence. They are supplanted by a new species, and the Real Presence by some natural substance.

The difficulty is sometimes given a very gross form by adversaries who deny that Christ could be present in a liquid which may actually cause intoxication. (a) They fail to observe that precisely the same objection could be urged against the presence of God in poisons, in the microbes of disease, and in the bullets of assassins; yet every true believer in God knows that not one of these things could exist without His sustaining presence. (b) Those Protestants who reject the Real Presence admit at the same time that what they call "the Sacrament of the Lord's Supper" is something holy, something blessed by God. Obviously, therefore, their objection can be turned against themselves. They can be asked to explain how what is holy can produce the effect they mention.

(4) "Does not Christ in the Blessed Eucharist expose Himself to the insults of blasphemers?" REPLY: He does, but, if we may say so, no insult ever deterred Christ Jesus from showing His love for man: He did not refuse to come on earth, though He knew that some of His people would nail Him to a cross; so, He did not withhold from us this most precious gift of the Blessed Eucharist, though He knew that wicked men would reject it or use it for His dishonour. The very fact that our kind and patient Saviour exposes Himself to insult and ingratitude in this adorable Sacrament should urge us to increase our love for Him a thousandfold.

(5) "Since God is everywhere, what is the need of the Blessed Eucharist? Would not God be present in the Host even though unconsecrated?" REPLY: (a) God is present in the unconsecrated Host as He is present in all His creatures. But this presence does not endow them with any powers over and above their natural ones, since its immediate effect is merely to sustain them in their ordinary existence and action. The Lord Jesus' presence in the Blessed Sacrament is, however, ordained to an effect entirely different from that of God's sustaining presence in bread— namely, the spiritual nourishment of our souls. God is present in all His creatures, but no mere creature can be adored, because its activity is its own, not God's. The only creature that is adorable is the Human Nature which is united to the Second Divine Person. It is adorable, because the acts done by means of it are the acts of God Himself. (b) God became Man. He did so, because He knew that by living, labouring, suffering, and dying, as a mortal, He could best win our love. Likewise, He gave us the Blessed Eucharist to touch our hearts with the knowledge that He, the Man of Sorrows, who was born, who was crucified for our sakes, and who rose

from the dead, is still with us. God is indeed everywhere, but the Sacred Humanity of Christ in the Blessed Eucharist is not everywhere.

B

THE SACRIFICE OF THE MASS

Summary

I.   The solemn teaching of the Church.
II. Sacrifice among the Jews: God, the institutor of the Jewish sacrifices. The place of offering. The Jewish Priesthood. The different kinds of sacrifice. The meaning and value of the sacrifices of the Old Law. The Sacrifice of the Covenant, the Pasch, and the Day of Atonement. The privileges of the Jews extended to Christians, but in fuller measure. Christ the fulfilment of the Old Testament sacrifices.
III. Definition of sacrifice.
IV. The Sacrifice of the Cross: Christ proclaimed at the Last Supper His intention to offer His life for us. He offered Sacrifice on the Cross. It was a true and perfect Sacrifice. Christ, the High Priest of the human race. Christ our Paschal Lamb. The Resurrection and the Ascension in relation to the Sacrifice of the Cross.
V.   Christ at the Last Supper instituted a sacrificial rite as a memorial and representation of His Death on the Cross. The sacrificial rite is the Mass. The two-fold consecration. The Mass is a true Sacrifice, the same Sacrifice as that of the Cross, but without bloodshed. The Priest, the People, the Victim, and the Altar of the Mass. The Mass prefigured in the sacrifice of Melchizedek, and foretold by Malachi.
VI. The blessings of the Mass. The excellence of the Mass.
VII. The teaching of the Fathers. Replies to objections against the Mass.
VIII. Additional remarks on the Mass.

I

The solemn teaching of the Church. The Church teaches solemnly:

(1) that Christ at the Last Supper instituted the Mass, a true, visible sacrifice, such as the nature of man requires;[1]

(2) that Christ bequeathed the Mass to His Church to represent and commemorate for all time the Sacrifice of the Cross, not only as a sacrifice of praise and thanksgiving, but also to be of avail for the remission of sins and of the punishment due to them, and for the benefit of the living and the dead;[2]

(3) that Christ established a special priesthood for its celebration;[3]

(4) that Christ, through the ministry of His priests, offers Himself in the Mass as He offered Himself on the Cross; but that, whereas He

---

[1] T 1740
[2] T 1740, 1743, 1753
[3] T 1739-40, 1752

506

offered Himself with bloodshed on the Cross, He offers Himself, without bloodshed on our altars;[4]

(5)   that, this difference apart, the Sacrifice of the Mass is the same sacrifice as that of the Cross, for there is the same Priest, the same Victim, the same offering;[5]

(6)   that it is legitimate to offer Mass to God in honour of the Saints and in order to obtain their intercession with Him;[6]

(7)   that it is not necessary for Mass to be said in the local language;[7]

(8)   that the traditional ceremonies, vestments and external signs which the Church uses in the celebration of Mass are conducive to true piety.[8]

II

It is important to treat of the Jewish sacrifices before the beginning of the study of the Sacrifice of the Mass. Like them, the Mass is a true sacrifice under the form of a sacred rite: it is an outward means of worship appointed by God for frequent and public use.[9]

The Sacrifice of Calvary, as offered by Christ in Person, with the shedding of His precious Blood, was not a sacred rite: it was offered but once, and was not to be repeated. In its essentials as a sacrifice, however, it is continued in the Mass, and was prefigured in the sacred rites of the Jews.

Since Judaism foreshadowed Christianity, familiarity with the ancient sacrifices prepared the Apostles and the first Christians for the doctrine of the sacrifice of Calvary and the Sacrifice of the Mass.

Sacrifice among the Jews.

GOD, THE INSTITUTOR OF THE JEWISH SACRIFICES. God commanded the Jews to worship Him with sacrifices. He set forth all the details of these sacred rites. He ordered that they should be offered in one place alone and through the hands of a specially appointed priesthood.

THE PLACE OF OFFERING. All sacrifices were offered within the precincts of the Tabernacle, a tent-like structure, brilliant with curtains of fine linen and many colours and decorated with cherubim.[10] It was erected on an oblong plot of ground within an enclosure or court of the same shape. It was divided into two parts by a veil. The outer chamber was called Holy; the inner, the Holy of Holies. On entering the Holy, one saw to the right the table on which was laid the weekly offering of bread, the twelve Loaves of Proposition—one for each of the twelve

---

[4] T 1743
[5] Ibid.
[6] T 1744, 1755
[7] T 1749, 1759
[8] T 1746, 1757
[9] See p.448.
[10] Ex 26:1. Description in Ex 25-27

tribes. On the left, was the seven-branched candlestick, and, in front, the altar of incense built of setim wood and overlaid with gold. In the Holy of Holies stood the Ark of the Covenant, on which was laid a cover of the purest gold. This cover, overshadowed by the outstretched wings of two figures representing Cherubim, was called the Mercy-seat or Propitiatory. Above it, God hung a bright cloud. This was His throne, the visible sign of His merciful presence among His people. The Tabernacle with its apartments was reproduced in the Temple.

The great Temple, which thenceforward took the place of the Tabernacle, was completed by Solomon c. 970 B.C. About five years after his death it was plundered of its treasures by Shishak, King of Egypt.[11] It was destroyed by the Chaldeans under Nebuchadnezzar in 586 B.C., and rebuilt on a smaller scale by Zerubbabel in 515 B.C.[12] Herod the Great set about repairing and beautifying it 20 B.C., a work which was finished only within a few years of the final destruction of the building by Titus in 70 A.D.

THE JEWISH PRIESTHOOD. All who ministered in the temple were of the tribe of Levi. Of these, only the descendants of Aaron could offer sacrifice. One was chosen as the High Priest. Arrayed in splendid vestments, he presided at the more solemn feasts. He alone was permitted to enter the Holy of Holies. This he did on the Day of Atonement (Expiation), which occurred once a year.

THE DIFFERENT KINDS OF SACRIFICE. From the nature of the offerings, sacrifices were termed bloody or unbloody (i.e., with or without bloodshed).

The bloody sacrifices. In the bloody sacrifice, an animal was slain by whoever wished to have it offered, or by the temple attendants. The slaying of the victim preceded the Sacrifice proper and did not form part of it. The blood was received by the priest, who disposed of it as the rite prescribed. Of the bloody sacrifices, the chief was the Holocaust, offered on the Altar of Holocausts which stood outside the Tabernacle but within the enclosure. (Between the Altar of Holocausts and the Tabernacle was the Brazen Laver, the vessel in which the priests washed before ministering). It was the great public act of divine worship, and was offered up for the whole people every day, morning and evening. After the blood had been poured out beside the altar the entire victim was burnt, to signify the supreme dominion of God over creatures. Bloody sacrifices were also offered to obtain forgiveness of sin (*sacrifices for sin or trespass*), or to praise and thank God and beg His blessings (*sacrifices of peace*). The former were offered on behalf of private individuals, and so too, as a rule, were the latter. The distinguishing feature of sin-offering was that the blood was sprinkled on the Altar of Holocausts, the altar of incense, or the Ark, according to whether it was offered, respectively, for the people, priests or the High priest. Certain parts of the victim were burnt on the altar while the rest, if offered for the people, could be eaten by the priests. If offered for the priests, it had to be burned outside the camp. The distinguishing feature of the Peace Offering was the sacred banquet. After certain parts had been burnt on the altar and the blood poured out,

---

[11] 1 Kgs 14:25-6
[12] Ezra 3:8ff.

the rest was eaten by the offerer and his friends and others, especially the Levites and the poor.

The unbloody sacrifices. In these sacrifices, the following things were offered: (1) cereal foods, such as roasted ears of corn, flour and cakes of unleavened bread, all of them sprinkled with salt and tempered with olive oil; (2) wine; (3) frankincense. Generally speaking, these offerings were a subordinate accompaniment to the sacrifices with bloodshed. The wine was poured out beside the altar. Usually, but not always, a portion of the food, with a little incense added, was burnt on it. The incense, when offered alone, was entirely consumed on the special altar reserved for it. The unbloody sacrifices are also known as *clean oblations.*

THE MEANING AND VALUE OF THE SACRIFICES OF THE OLD LAW. *Their meaning.* The Jews, by obeying the Commandment of God to offer Him sacrifice, thereby professed in act their subjection to Him the one true God, the God of Love, the Creator of all things. The very rites themselves were the outward sign of this acknowledgement. First, as to the bloody sacrifices: blood was thought to be the seat of life. In offering the blood, therefore, the priest offered the life of the animal, and the life of the animal was a symbol of the soul of man: the Lord said, "the life of the flesh is in the blood ... I have given it to you, that you may make atonement with it on the altar for your souls".[13] In the bloody sacrifice for sin, there was the further notion that the sinner who caused it to be offered held himself guilty of death: he identified himself with the victim, and transferred his sins to it by confessing them while he held his hand on its head. As to the unbloody sacrifices: food and drink are necessary for the support of life; hence, such offerings indicated the dependence of human life on God. In both kinds of sacrifice, the rite showed that man surrendered himself to God or desired union with Him as his Master and Owner, his loving Lord, the Perfecter of his happiness: by the sprinkling or effusion of its blood, the life of the animal was regarded as passing from the hand of man to the hand of God (symbolised by the altar). The wine was given to God by being poured out, and the bread or other such food by being blessed and by being withdrawn from its ordinary use.

Their value. Sin was remitted and grace obtained through the sacrifices of the Old Law, not, however, of their own intrinsic efficacy, but in virtue of the Sacrifice of the Cross of which they were figures. They were not causes of grace like our Sacraments: they produced their effect by operating on the understanding and will of the sinner, by appealing to him like some inspired preacher. They brought him into God's presence, as it were. They served to remind him of all that God had done for his people, of the great destiny He had marked out for them, and of the hatefulness and ingratitude of sin; and so they helped to touch his heart. God then gave him the grace to make an Act of Perfect Love, or Perfect Contrition, by which alone in those days sin could be forgiven.

---

[13] Lev 17:11

THE SACRIFICE OF THE COVENANT, THE PASCH, AND THE DAY OF ATONEMENT. These three festivals or solemnities require special mention, because they are referred to in important texts from the New Testament quoted further on.

The Sacrifice of the Covenant. In Exodus 24, Moses wrote the Lord's words to him in the book of the covenant. He sent young Israelites to offer sacrifices, took half of the blood of the sacrifices and poured it upon the altar. After he read the book of the covenant to the people, they promised their obedience to it, and Moses then sprinkled the rest of the blood upon the people, saying, "Behold the blood of the covenant which the Lord has made with you". Then Moses and Aaron and two others, with seventy elders of Israel, went up the mountain and "they beheld God, and ate and drank."

The Pasch or Passover. The Pasch (literally, "a passing by") was the most solemn of the Jewish festivals, and is set out in Exodus 12. It commemorated Israel's deliverance from the bondage of Egypt and the preservation of the first-born of the Hebrews whom the angel of God spared ("passed by") while he slew the first-born of the Egyptians. The festival, which could be celebrated only at Jerusalem, was of seven days duration and occurred at the time corresponding to our Holy Week. Strictly speaking, the name Pasch applies only to this preliminary rite; the seven days which followed were called the Feast of Unleavened Bread. The opening ceremony was the most important: on the eve of the first day (our Holy Thursday), at sunset, a year old male lamb without blemish, chosen four days previously (on our Palm Sunday), was slain, and its blood was poured out at the foot of the altar by the priest. With a wooden cross set within the ribs, it was roasted at a fire. Care was taken that no bone should be broken. A lamb was thus prepared as a sacred banquet for each family or, as convenience might direct, for groups of ten or twenty persons. Cups of red wine, mingled with a little water, together with cakes of unleavened bread and bitter herbs, were set on the festive board, and all were regarded as sanctified by their association with the lamb. Psalms and prayers were recited. Unlike the celebration in Egypt, the meal was not consumed in haste, but at ease and in a spirit of religious joy. It was a meal of thanksgiving, a "eucharist." It resembled a banquet after a *sacrifice of peace*, the guests at which believed themselves to be guests of God.

The Day of Atonement. This day of solemn atonement or propitiation (in Hebrew, *Yom Kippur*) was instituted for the expiation of all the sins and irreverences committed by the people during the course of the preceding year. It was observed as a most rigorous fast, all food being prohibited from the previous evening to the evening of the festival. The High Priest, clothed in linen vestments and wearing a linen mitre, offered a calf for the sins of his own household, and two goats, only one of which was slain, for the sins of the people. He twice entered the Holy of Holies, taking with him on the first occasion the blood of the calf, and on the second the blood of the goat, to be sprinkled upon the Mercy-seat (Propitiatory), or poured out as the rite prescribed. Then laying his hands on the head of the live goat, he confessed the sins of the people over it, and had the animal driven into the wilderness, as a sign that the people had renounced evil and had obtained forgiveness. (Only the chief points in the elaborate ceremony are mentioned here.

For the full account, telling of preliminary ablution, the incense, and the manner of applying the blood, see Leviticus 16).

THE PRIVILEGES OF THE JEWS EXTENDED IN FULLER MEASURE TO US. So far, enough has been said to indicate the nature of the great privileges enjoyed by the Jews. They had, in the cloud over the Mercy-seat, the sign of the presence of God in their temple. They had sacrifices by which they could adore Him, beseech His help, and plead for forgiveness of sin. And yet the grace they received was but a trickle compared with that great flood of blessings which has come to us through Christ, the Son of God, who dwells invisibly amongst us as our Priest and Victim, our Teacher and our King.

CHRIST THE FULFILMENT OF THE OLD TESTAMENT SACRIFICES. In the New Testament, Christ's death is closely connected to the three central Jewish sacrifices mentioned above: (1) the Sacrifice of the Covenant; (2) the Passover; and (3) the Day of Atonement. In turn, we see: (1) Christ says at the Last Supper, "this cup ... is the new covenant in My Blood."[14] The Letter to the Hebrews brings out the importance of the new covenant, and Our Lord's superiority to Moses. (2) Jesus is the "Lamb of God, who takes away the sin of the world."[15] The Last Supper takes place at the time of the festival of the Jewish Passover. (3) The Letter to the Hebrews in particular compares the ritual of the Day of Atonement with the death of Christ whose precious blood and sacrifice are efficacious once and for all. St Paul speaks of Christ Jesus as being made a sacrifice of propitiation.[16] The goat upon whom the High Priest imposed all the sins of the people was sent into the wilderness to die. This 'scapegoat' was a 'type' (symbolic preview) of the promised Redeemer who took upon Himself all the sins of mankind and took them away in His death outside the Holy City of Jerusalem.

III

Definition of sacrifice. The Jewish sacrifices helped the Apostles to understand the Sacrifice of Christ. Judaism was the preparatory school of Christianity. The elementary lessons which the Apostles had learned from the Temple ritual were not to be set aside, but preserved and enlarged. No doubt the enlargement brought the flash of divine enlightenment and the glow of divine love into a dull and cold picture, transforming gross material things into things spiritual, but it left the outlines unchanged. Though it spoke of God's new and greater mercy to fallen man, it did not alter the general conceptions of man's duty to God; least of all did it change the essential features of sacrifice.

The essential features in the Jewish sacrifices were the following:

---

[14] Lk 22:20; 1 Cor 11:25
[15] Jn 1:29
[16] Rom 3:25. Cf. 1 Jn 2:2; 1 Jn 4:10.

(1) Some material thing, representing man or human life, was offered as a gift to God. The gift was called "the victim", "the host", "the oblation", and sometimes even "the sacrifice", the word "sacrifice" being used in that case to denote what was only a part of the sacrifice.

(2) A priest offered, or handed over, the victim to God by bringing it into contact with the altar in one of the ways already described.

(3) The offering of the victim was designed to express: man's complete surrender of himself and his will to God; man's acknowledgement of God's supreme and fatherly dominion over him; and man's desire to be united to God in love. The effect or fruit of the sacrifice was to secure a renewal or increase of God's friendship. The outward rite was not a mere sign: it increased the value of the worshipper's acts.

From all this we may deduce our definition of sacrifice: "A sacrifice is a public action in which a priest offers or transfers to God a visible gift or victim, in order to signify God's supreme and fatherly dominion over us, our total dependence on Him, and our childlike submission to His will." We shall find that this definition is verified in the Sacrifice of the Cross and the Sacrifice of the Mass.

By "total dependence on God" we mean that to Him we owe all that we are and have and hope for—that is, that He is the Creator and Sustainer of our whole being and of all powers of acting, thinking and willing; the Giver of every good thing we possess, whether spiritual, intellectual, or physical; the Giver of the eternal happiness for which we hope.

Our Adoration of God in sacrifice naturally carries with it acts of Thanksgiving, Petition, and Atonement or Expiation. How can we, His creatures, adore Him without thanking Him? How can we who are utterly dependent on His goodness adore Him without beseeching the continuance of His mercy towards us? How can we adore Him without desiring to make satisfaction to Him for our sins? Any one of these acts may be the dominant note in a particular sacrifice and give it a special designation. Thus, e.g., the perfect Sacrifice of Christ is called a Redemptive Sacrifice, because primarily it is a Sacrifice of Expiation. Similarly, the Mass is called a Eucharistic Sacrifice, because, before all else, it is a Sacrifice of Thanksgiving for the Redemption.

IV

In Chapter 8, we gave our attention chiefly to the sufferings that Christ bore for our sake. In the paragraphs below we explain more fully the nature of the great Sacrifice which He offered to God for us.

The Sacrifice of the Cross. CHRIST PROCLAIMED AT THE LAST SUPPER HIS INTENTION TO OFFER HIS LIFE FOR US. Christ said to His Apostles at the Last Supper that His Body would be delivered for them—that is, delivered up to death for them—and that His Blood, the Blood of the New Testament, would be shed for them and for many unto the remission of sins.[17] ("For *many*", as opposed to a *few*. St Paul says Christ "died for all"[18]). As the Old Testament, the ancient pact of God with the Israelites, was sealed with the blood of animals offered in sacrifice, so too the New Testament, a new pact between God and all mankind, was to be sealed with the Precious Blood shed in the Sacrifice of the Cross.[19]   The Apostles whom Christ addressed were to be His messengers to all the nations of the earth. They and their successors were to carry His words to the men of all ages unto the end of time. Thus, through them, Christ at the Last Supper made known to the whole world His intention to suffer death in sacrifice for us. St Gregory of Nyssa says that Christ offered Himself at the Last Supper to make it clear that He freely accepted the work of the Redemption, and that it was not imposed on Him by the treachery of Judas, the hostility of the Jews, or the sentence of Pilate.[20]

CHRIST OFFERED SACRIFICE ON THE CROSS. Christ fulfilled on the Cross the promise He had made at the Last Supper. He "gave Himself up for us", says St Paul, "a fragrant offering and sacrifice to God";[21] "in Him we have redemption through His Blood, the forgiveness of our trespasses";[22] He "gave Himself as a ransom for all".[23] "Christ also died for sins once for all", says St Peter, "that He might bring us to God".[24] In the Epistle to the Hebrews, we find it set forth as a fundamental truth and insistently repeated that the many sacrifices of the Old Law were only figures of the one, all-sufficing Sacrifice of the Cross. To quote just a single passage: "if ... the blood of goats and bulls ... sanctifies for the purification of the flesh, how

---

[17] 1 Cor 11:24; Lk 22:20; Matt 26:28
[18] 2 Cor 5:15; 1 Tim 2:6
[19] Heb 9:19-20
[20] *Or. Ia in resurrectionem*, PG 46, 612.   Cited in Fr Maurice de la Taille S.J., *Mysterium Fidei*, 1921, p.43; Eng. ed. *The Mystery of Faith*, Sheed and Ward, Book I, 1940, p.62; Book II, 1950.
[21] Eph 5:2
[22] Eph 1:7. Cf. Col 1:14.
[23] 1 Tim 2:6
[24] 1 Pet 3:18,22

much more shall the Blood of Christ, who through the eternal Spirit offered Himself without blemish to God, purify your conscience?"[25]

THE SACRIFICE OF THE CROSS, A TRUE AND PERFECT SACRIFICE. In the Sacrifice of the Cross, Christ was at once the Priest and the Victim, divinely chosen and appointed for each of these offices. It was a Redemptive Sacrifice; therefore, He did not offer it for Himself but for us sinners. As our representative, and with a heart full of love for us and of grief for our sins, He outwardly offered and surrendered His life to God:[26] (1) to show that God was the Master and Owner of the life of each one of us, our Creator and Lord; (2) to praise, thank, and glorify God on our behalf; (3) to plead with God that we might be restored to divine friendship through the gift of Sanctifying Grace; and (4) by His sufferings, to make reparation to God for all our sins.

As a *Priest*, He offered His life to God; as a *Victim*, He gave it. He was perfect as a Priest, because with His human and His Divine nature He was perfectly fitted to act as a Mediator between God and man: from the perfection of His understanding and His Will, and from the infinite value of His acts, He, as Man, was able to offer to God on our behalf an adoration and an atonement so perfect that God laid aside His anger, so to speak,[27] and placed the privilege of divine sonship once more within our reach.

He was perfect as a Victim, not only because of His dignity as God and Man, but because He was a living, conscious Victim, submitting to His executioners, accepting to His last breath freely, fully, and with infinite love, every suffering inflicted on Him: "He makes himself an offering for sin";[28] "I lay down My life ... I lay it down of My own accord. I have power to lay it down".[29] The slaying of the Divine Victim of the Cross was not the Sacrifice proper; the Sacrifice proper consisted in Christ's offering of Himself to God as Victim. Christ did not slay Himself; He was slain by the Jews. Even in the Jewish Sacrifices the victims were not slain by the priests but by the Temple attendants.

In the Jewish sacrifices, it was the altar, a structure of wood, or of wood and metal, that sanctified the gift laid on it;[30] but Christ the Victim, who was Holiness itself, had no need of any such extrinsic sanctification. His own sacred Body was the *Altar*, and the Blood that streamed out on it was the sign that He had offered His life for us. Thus, Christ was not only the Priest and Victim, but also the Altar of His Sacrifice.

---

[25] Heb 9:13,14
[26] That is, to the Blessed Trinity: see pp.404-5.
[27] On all such expressions, see "Immutability", pp.302-3.
[28] Isaiah 53:10
[29] Jn 10:17-18
[30] Cf. Matt 23:19.

The Church sometimes speaks of the Cross of Calvary as the Altar of Christ's Sacrifice,[31] and sometimes of Christ Himself as the Altar, e.g., the 5th Preface of Easter which says, "Christ showed himself to be the Priest, Altar and Lamb".[32] The Cross was a secondary altar. It did not sanctify the Victim but derived its sanctification from Him.

CHRIST, THE HIGH PRIEST OF THE HUMAN RACE. Among the Hebrews, the High Priest offered sacrifice for them alone: Christ, the High Priest of the human race, offered sacrifice for all mankind. The Jewish High Priest offered the sacrifice of Atonement year by year; he died, and was replaced by another. Christ offered but the one Sacrifice, which He still continues to offer; He died, but He is not replaced. He died; but yet He still lives, and is represented by others, His earthly priests. Thus in the Epistle to the Hebrews we are told that of Him the Lord said "'Thou art a priest for ever'. ... The former priests [i.e., the Jewish High Priests] were many in number, because they were prevented by death from continuing in office; but He [Christ the High Priest] *holds His priesthood permanently, because He continues for ever ... since He always lives to make intercession for them.* For it was fitting that we should have such a High Priest, holy, blameless, unstained, separated from sinners, exalted above the heavens. He has no need, like those high priests, to offer sacrifices daily, first for his own sins, and then for those of the people".[33] The Jewish High Priest entered the Holy of Holies, a tabernacle made by men, taking with him the blood of calf or goat. Christ, our High Priest, went up to the true Holy of Holies, not made by human hands, and there offered at the throne of the Divine Majesty His own most precious Blood. The offering made by the Jewish High Priest was but a passing thing: the offering made by Christ will continue for ever.

CHRIST, OUR PASCHAL LAMB. St John the Baptist, pointing to our Saviour, said: "Behold the Lamb of God, who takes away the sin of the world!"[34] Those prophetic words, uttered at the beginning of Christ's public life, were verified at its close: at the Last Supper He revealed Himself as the Lamb who was to give His life for our redemption, the Lamb whose Sacrifice was to be commemorated and renewed in the new Pasch of the Blessed Eucharist. The first Paschal Lamb was slain to deliver Israel from the slavery of Egypt, and its blood, spread on the door-posts, saved the first-born of every Hebrew family from death: Christ, our Paschal Lamb, was slain to save mankind from the bondage of Satan. His Blood was cast upon the earth so that the destroying vengeance of God[35] might pass by all the dwellers thereon to the end of time. "You were ransomed", says St Peter, "not with perishable things such as silver or gold, but with the precious Blood of Christ, like that of a Lamb without blemish or spot."[36] Of the blessed in Heaven, the Holy

---

[31] e.g., Council of Trent: DS 1743; Cf. also C 1182.

[32] *Missale Romanum*, 1975, p.409; *Pontificale Romanum* 1962, Ordination of subdeacon, exhort., *Adepturi*; *Breviarium Romanum*, Nov. 9, end of Off. Dedic. Basilic., Lesson IV. Cf. Fr. de la Taille, *Mysterium Fidei, Elucid.* XIII, *The Mystery of Faith*, Sheed and Ward, Book I, pp.215 ff.

[33] Heb 7:21-7; cf. 8:1; 10:21.

[34] Jn 1:29

[35] On such expressions, see "Immutability", pp.302-3.

[36] 1 Pet 1:18-19; cf. 1 Cor 5:7.

Spirit says: "These are they who have come out of the great tribulation; they have washed their robes and made them white in the Blood of the Lamb."[37]

THE RESURRECTION AND THE ASCENSION IN RELATION TO THE SACRIFICE OF THE CROSS. The Sacrifice of Christ ended at the moment of His death on the Cross. It was crowned and glorified by His Resurrection and Ascension. The Resurrection showed that Christ was what He had claimed to be, the Son of God. It was the divine approval of His life and work. It was the evidence that God had accepted His Sacrifice. By the Ascension, Christ passed from the eyes of men to the Kingdom of Heaven. He entered the true Holy of Holies where He exercises, and ever will exercise, His office of High Priest, making intercession by showing His wounds to the Father. He is there, a perpetual Victim, no longer suffering but glorified; and it is as a glorified Divine Victim that He descends on our altars at Mass.

St Thomas, on Heb 7:25, says that Christ intercedes for us "by presenting to His Father the Humanity to which He (the Son) is united and which He immolated on the Cross, and by manifesting His desire for our salvation." Christ's intercession for us in Heaven is not distinct from the intercession He made for us on the Cross. While on the Cross, He gained for us every help we need for our salvation.[38]

V

Christ at the Last Supper instituted a sacrificial rite as a memorial and representation of His death on the Cross. "For I received from the Lord", says St Paul, "what I also delivered to you, that the Lord Jesus on the night when He was betrayed took bread, and when He had given thanks, He broke it, and said, 'This is My Body which is for you. Do this in remembrance of Me.' In the same way also the cup, after supper, saying, 'This cup is the new covenant in My Blood.[39] Do this, as often as you drink it, in remembrance of Me.' For as often as you eat this Bread and drink the Cup, you proclaim the Lord's death until He comes."[40] Therefore, by the words spoken by Christ at the Last Supper, and by the consecration of the bread and the wine which those words effected, He signified that, on the Cross, His Blood would be completely separated from His Body. Thus, He placed before His Apostles a representation of His death, and when He said to "do this for a commemoration" of Him, He instituted a sacrificial rite, a memorial of His Sacrifice, which was to be repeated by them and their successors to the end of time.

---

[37] Apoc 7:14
[38] See pp.410-1.
[39] St Luke adds, "which shall be shed for you", 22:20. St Matthew has, "This is my Blood which shall be shed for many unto the remission of sins", 26:28.
[40] 1 Cor 11:23-26. "Until He comes", i.e., "Until He comes again in glory."

It can be shown that Christ offered a true, bloodless sacrifice at the Last Supper. We can regard it as, in itself, a distinct sacrifice or as but the beginning and formal offering of the Sacrifice of the Cross. In either case, the Last Supper and the Cross are bound together in close union. As the bishops at the Council of Trent agreed, what Christ began at the Supper, He completed on the Cross. It is indeed obvious that it was at the Supper that Christ made clear His intention to offer His life in sacrifice for us on the Cross.[41]

The new rite was well named the Eucharist (literally, "the thanksgiving") because of the thanks offered by Christ before consecrating the bread and the wine: raising His eyes to Heaven,[42] He thanked His Father for man's Creation, for man's Redemption, and for all the blessings that were to flow from it through the Church and the Sacraments.

The bread was unleavened. It was the bread hallowed by the figurative Paschal Lamb. The Pasch was celebrated in the first month of the Jewish year, the month later called Nisan, but first designated by the Scripture as the month of Abib, which means the month of "the new corn" (Deut 16:1), a title of deep significance, since it was to be the month of the Passion and the Eucharist, when Christ was to be crushed and ground and given as Divine Food to men. Bethlehem, where He was born, means "the house of bread." Thus, His place of birth and the time of His death are closely linked with the Blessed Eucharist. The Wine of the Last Supper was spoke of by the ancient patriarch Jacob on his death-bed. To each of his sons, the heads of twelve tribes, he addressed words of prophecy; but to Judah he delivered the sublimest message, foretelling that he would be praised by his brethren, that they would bow down before him, and that from him would be descended the Messiah who would "wash his garments in wine and his vesture in the blood of grapes" (Gen 49:8-11). The words in their surface-meaning seemed to say nothing more than that, in the days of the Messiah, there would be a great abundance of good things, and that wine would be as plentiful as water. But, with the eye of faith, we can see that "the Blood of the Grape", the red wine of Judah, is "the Blood of Christ the Vine", the Blood that was given at the Last Supper, the Blood that drenched the garments of the Son of God in the Garden of Gethsemane, the Blood of the Paschal Lamb "who takes away the sin of the world."

The Mass is the sacrificial rite instituted by Christ at the Last Supper. At the Mass, bread and wine are on the altar, and the priest repeats the words and actions of Christ at the Last Supper: he takes the bread in his hands and says: "(Jesus Christ our Lord), the day before He suffered, took bread in His holy and venerable hands, and raising His eyes to Heaven, to Thee, God, His Almighty Father, He gave thanks to Thee. He blessed it, broke it, and gave it to His Disciples, saying, 'Take and eat of this, all of

---

[41] Cf. Fr. de la Taille, *The Mystery of Faith*, op. cit., Book I, pp.136-61.

[42] This detail has been preserved in the Latin Church: see the rubric (direction) in the Missal at the Roman Canon.

you: for this is My Body, which will be given up for you.' In like manner, ... taking in His holy and venerable hands this precious chalice, He again gave thanks to Thee; He blessed it, and gave it to His disciples, saying, 'Take and drink, all of you: for this is the chalice of My Blood of the New and everlasting Covenant, which shall be shed for you and for many unto the remission of sins. Do this for My commemoration.' The mystery of faith."

"The mystery of faith." The Blessed Eucharist involves the mysteries of the Trinity and the Incarnation, and the mystery of Transubstantiation. It is fittingly called "the mystery of faith", because it is faith's severest test and faith's greatest triumph, as well as the embodiment of the Faith. The Mass is often spoken of as "the celebration of the Divine Mysteries"; the plural is used because of the double consecration.

THE TWO-FOLD CONSECRATION. The words of the priest, and the appearances of bread and wine, represent Christ as in the state of death. The separate consecration of the bread and wine symbolises the violent separation of Jesus' Body and Blood on the Cross. Pope Pius XII explains, "the Sacrifice of our Redeemer is shown forth in an admirable manner by external signs which are symbols of His death. For by transubstantiation ... His Body and Blood are both really present: now the Eucharistic species, under which He is present, symbolise the violent separation of His Body and Blood. Thus the commemorative representation of His death, which actually took place on Calvary, is repeated in every Sacrifice of the altar, seeing that by separate symbols Christ Jesus is symbolically shown in a state of victimhood."[43] St Thomas teaches the same: "Since the achievement of our salvation took place through Christ's passion and death, by which His blood was separated from His flesh, we are given the sacrament of His body separately under the appearance of bread, and the sacrament of His blood under the appearance of wine; so that in this sacrament we have the memory and the representation of the Lord's passion."[44] The Fathers of the Church compare the double consecration to a two-edged mystic sword. Thus St Gregory Nazianzen says to a fellow bishop: "Cease not to pray and plead for me when you draw down the Word by your word, when using your voice as a sword, you divide by a bloodless cutting the Body and Blood of the Lord."[45] That the entire Christ with His Body and Blood, Soul and Divinity, is present under the appearances of bread and the appearances of wine is due to the fact that, in the living, glorified Christ, His human nature and His divine nature are indissolubly united: wherever His Body is, or

---

[43] *Mediator Dei*, 1947, Part II: DS 3848
[44] *Summa Contra Gentiles*, Book IV, ch. 61
[45] *Ep. clxxi ad Amphil.*, PG 37, 282

wherever His Blood is, He is present in the completeness of His Humanity and in the fullness of His Divinity.

The Mass is a true sacrifice, the same sacrifice as that of Christ on the Cross, but without bloodshed. At the Supper, when the Lord Jesus had consecrated the bread and the wine, He said to His Apostles, "Do this for a commemoration of Me." Thus He made them priests with the power to do as He had done, and they transmitted that power to others down to our day, together with the command of Christ to exercise it.

THE MASS IS A TRUE SACRIFICE. Looking at the Mass with the light of faith, we see that it possesses all the requisites for a sacrifice:
(1) Christ, the Victim, is present—the Victim, offered by Himself at the Supper and on the Cross—the Victim who, by His very command to the Apostles, declared Himself to be a perpetual Victim, a Victim, therefore, capable of being offered to the end of time. "The virtue of that Victim continues for ever", says St Thomas.[46]
(2) The offering is made in an outward and public manner at an altar by a priest commissioned for the purpose by Christ.
(3) The priest, in the name of the Church, offers the Victim to the Eternal Father: "We offer to Thy glorious Majesty", he says, "a pure Victim, a holy Victim, an unspotted Victim, the Holy Bread of eternal life, and the Chalice of perpetual salvation".[47] He offers for the same sacrificial ends for which the Victim was offered at the Supper and on the Cross, for the salvation of the whole world and "for the remission of sins".[48] He offers the Victim for the purpose of adoring, praising, and glorifying the Father Almighty (*adoration*), of thanking Him for His past mercies and favours (*thanksgiving*), of beseeching His help and blessings (*petition*), of appeasing His anger and gaining His friendship (*propitiation*), and of obtaining release from the punishment due to sin (*satisfaction*). These purposes are expressed in the *Gloria*, the *Pater Noster (Our Father)*, the Eucharistic Prayer and other parts of the Mass.

THE MASS IS THE SAME SACRIFICE AS THAT OF THE CROSS, BUT WITHOUT BLOODSHED. It is obvious that, at Mass, Our Lord does not come on earth to renew over and over again, in every detail, what took place on Calvary: "Christ being raised from the dead will never die again; death no longer has dominion over Him."[49] Thus we may speak of Mass as a "renewal" or "re-presentation" of Calvary, but we avoid the words "repetition" or "re-

[46] S.T., iii, q. 22, a. 5, ad 2: based on Heb 10:14.
[47] Roman Canon (1st Eucharistic Prayer): first prayer after the Consecration.
[48] Words spoken at the consecration of the Chalice.
[49] Rom 6:9

enactment". How then is the Mass the *same* sacrifice as that of the Cross, and yet not identical in every respect with it? It is the same sacrifice, because in both there is the same *Victim*, the same *Priest*, the same *Offering*.

The *differences* are that in the Mass, however, Christ as Priest offers through the ministry or agency of the priest of the Church, and His offering is not accompanied by the shedding of His Blood. Moreover, the Cross is the source of all the grace that has been given to man since the Fall, and of all the grace that shall be given to him till the end of the world; the source, too, of the Church herself and her Sacraments, including the very Sacrifice-Sacrament of the Mass.

The Sacrifice of the Cross is renewed in Holy Mass, but without bloodshed, giving us a daily opportunity of uniting ourselves with the Lord Jesus, Offerer and Victim.

The priest, the people, the Victim and the altar of the Mass.

THE PRIEST OF THE MASS. (a) The Mass, as the Church defines, is offered by Christ through the ministry of the priest. Thus Christ is the Principal Priest of the Mass, and the earthly priest is His agent. But he is a true agent; he truly consecrates or offers, just as he truly absolves. He is the agent or minister of Christ, since it is from Christ he has received the "character" of the priesthood. He is the minister of the Church, since he is her deputy, acting in her name and for the benefit of all her children. Hence, he never acts as a private individual when celebrating: his Mass may be offered under a forest-tree or in some poor shack in the desert, with no one at hand to answer it or assist at it; even so, it is still a public action, the action of an official commissioned by the public or visible society of the Church, and the blessings gained at the lonely altar are borne by God's angels to all her faithful members throughout the world.

(b) To offer the Victim is to hand over the Victim to God, to present Him as our gift to God. This is done by the priest at the Consecration. And since it is the priest alone who has the power of consecrating, it is the priest alone who has the power of direct offering.

(c) The priest's power to offer the sacrifice of the Mass comes from the "character" which was impressed on his soul at his ordination, whereby he was given a likeness to Christ, the great High Priest, the Offerer of the Sacrifice of the Cross. Even if he be unworthy of his exalted office, his unworthiness will not deface the image of Christ within him, nor will it impede his power of offering, nor make the Victim less acceptable to God. The Mass, as the Council of Trent solemnly teaches, "is not defiled by the unworthiness or wickedness of those who offer it."[50] The power of the

---

[50] DS 1742

THE ELEMENTS OF A SACRIFICE	CALVARY	MASS
Priest	Jesus Christ	Jesus Christ (via the priest)
Community	The nascent Church	The Church
Gift (Victim) pure and consecrated	Jesus Christ Himself	Bread & Wine: - Body & Blood of Christ Unleavened plain bread; pure wine, not distilled
Holocaust of Victim	Bloodshed until death	Bloodless - death signified by separate consecrations
Altar	The Cross	Altar
Recipient	God the Father	God the Father
Partaking	Anticipated at the Last Supper	Holy Communion
Reasons (Motives)	Adoration Thanksgiving Atonement Petition	Adoration Thanksgiving Atonement Petition

The Holy Eucharist is the Sacrament of Christ's Body and Blood
OFFERED, CONTAINED, RECEIVED

Offered	it is called	the Mass
Contained	it is called	the Blessed Sacrament
Received	it is called	Holy Communion

laity to act as co-offerers via the priest comes from the "character" impressed on their souls in Baptism.

THE CHRISTIAN PEOPLE CO-OFFER THE MASS. The priest offers, but the laity have the power of co-offering, i.e., the power of attaching their offering to that of the priest. "Taking part in the Eucharistic Sacrifice, the source and summit of the whole Christian life, the faithful offer the divine Victim to God and themselves along with Him."[51] It can be inferred from the teaching of the Council of Trent, and is expressly stated by later Popes, that the Universal Church (excluding only those members who are sinners and do not desire the grace of repentance) offers, and is offered in, the Mass.[52] The Catechism says, "The Church, which is the Body of Christ, participates in the offering of her Head. With Him, she herself is offered whole and entire."[53] In short, every Mass is offered by Christ as the Principal Priest, and by the Universal Church. It is visibly offered by: the officiating priest, who acts as minister of Christ and the Church; by those who assist at the altar; by the congregation present; and by those who cause the Mass to be celebrated.

The words of the Mass themselves tell you that at Mass you are not present only as one praying to God, but that you are actually joining with the priest and with Christ in offering the Sacrifice. In the prayer, *Orate fratres*, the priest says, "Pray, brethren, that my sacrifice *and yours* may be acceptable before God the Father Almighty." In the Roman Canon (1st Eucharistic Prayer), he says, "Be mindful, O Lord, of Thy servants and all here present for whom we offer to Thee or *who offer to Thee* this Sacrifice of praise". He commends to God, "This oblation, then, of our [priestly] service, and *of all Thy household*". He says, "We Thy servants, *and all Thy holy people*, *offer* the pure Host".

The ministerial priesthood and the priesthood of the laity. In the sense explained, all the laity are priests, and St Peter (I, 2:9) speaks of the Christian people as "a royal priesthood". God spoke in a similar manner of the Jewish nation as "a kingdom of priests" (Ex 19:6), yet no one can deny that to the Levites alone was reserved the charge of the religious ceremonies in the Temple, and that it was only a descendant of Aaron who could perform the sacrificial rite. Neither the words of St Peter nor those of Exodus refer to laymen, as distinct from priests, but to an entire people spiritually united by sacrifice in the worship of their God and King. The Christian laity, though co-offerers of the Mass, have no power to perform the sacrificial rite of the Consecration. They share in the priesthood of Christ by baptism, but they are not ministerial priests as those in Holy Orders. In necessity, a layman can baptise, but under no circumstances at all could a layman or deacon say Mass.

---

[51] *Lumen Gentium*, Dogmatic Constitution on the Church, Vatican Council II, 1964, art. 11
[52] T 1743, 1744, 1747, 1748; Pius XI, *Miserentissimus Redemptor*, 1928; Pius XII, *Mediator Dei*, 1947, Part II.
[53] C 1368; cf. 1372

THE VICTIM OF THE MASS. Christ is the Victim of the Mass; but He does not die nor suffer again at Mass. He is presented to God as the Lamb, once slain, who lives forever, as the Crucified, Risen and living Victim, perfectly pleasing to our Heavenly Father, as the great Mediator between God and man. We, by the "character" stamped on our souls in baptism, are joined to Him as secondary victims. As bread is made from many grains of wheat, and wine from the juice of many grapes, so we—the members of the Church, forming one body with Christ as our Head, associating our wills with His—present ourselves as co-victims with Him to the Eternal Father. From the very nature of sacrifice, this must necessarily be so: in every sacrifice the victim represents the offerers. They hand it over as a gift to God, accompanied by the gift of their self-surrender, i.e., of their complete subjection to Him, their acceptance of His law, and their desire of union with Him.

THE ALTAR OF THE MASS. The altar at which the priest celebrates has been consecrated or dedicated with great solemnity by the bishop, so that, like the Cross of Calvary, it may be a secondary altar of Christ's sacrifice. But Christ Himself is the true or chief Altar, and it is in that capacity that He receives and attaches to Himself our offering of ourselves as sharers in His Victimhood.

The Mass, prefigured in the sacrifice of Melchizedek, and foretold by Malachi.

THE SACRIFICE OF MELCHIZEDEK. Melchizedek, whom the Scriptures call a "priest of God Most High",[54] blessed Abraham after his victory over the four Kings, and offered a sacrifice of bread and wine, the first great figure of the unbloody sacrifice of the New Law. "Who", says St Cyprian, "is more a priest of the Most High God than our Lord Jesus Christ who offered a sacrifice to God the Father, and offered the same that Melchizedek offered, namely, bread and wine, that is, His Body and Blood."[55] Since Christ offered this unbloody sacrifice at the Last Supper, and will continue to offer it to the end of time, He is called "a priest for ever according to the order of Melchizedek",[56] i.e., "like Melchizedek".

THE PROPHECY OF MALACHI. Through the mouth of the Prophet Malachi, God condemns the Jewish priests, because they had offered Him unworthy victims, "polluted food", animals "lame", "blind" or "sick". He angrily rejects the levitical sacrifices, and foretells that their place will be taken by a clean oblation which shall be offered up all over the world: "I have no pleasure in you, says the Lord of hosts, and I will not accept an offering from your hand. For from the rising of the sun to its setting My name is great among the nations, and in every place incense is offered

---

[54] Gen 14:18
[55] Ep. 63, *ad Caec.* n. 4
[56] Heb 7:17; cf. Ps 110:4 (109:4).

to My name, and a pure offering; for My name is great among the nations, says the Lord of hosts."[57]   God spoke in these words of a new sacrifice, an unbloody sacrifice, one that should be pleasing to Him, and, therefore, one of His own institution.   It was to be offered at every hour and in every place.   Observe how wonderfully His prophecy has been fulfilled: at every hour of our day, dawn is breaking in some part of the world, and with it comes the daily Mass, the clean oblation, the great sacrifice founded by His Divine Son.

VI

The blessings of the Mass.

OUR GIFT TO GOD IN THE MASS.   Since, through the promise of Christ, the Church can never lose her holiness, she infallibly gives God in every Mass the supreme worship of adoration.   But she is never holy in all her members;   and even if she were, her holiness would be a finite holiness;   it would not be as the infinite holiness of the Divine Victim she offers. Hence, our gift of worship to God in the Mass is never infinite in value.

GOD'S GIFTS TO US IN THE MASS.   The gifts or benefits we receive from God through the Mass are commonly called its *fruits.*   They consist in the appeasement of God's anger (*propitiation*), the extinction of the debt of temporal punishment (*satisfaction*), and the reception of blessings, which include an increase of Sanctifying Grace and other favours (*impetration*).

The *fruits* of the Mass, in regard to their recipients, can be divided into *general, special, ministerial* and *personal.*   The first go to the entire Church;   the second to those present;   the third, to those for whom in particular the priest offers the Mass;   the fourth, to the priest himself.   As to the *general fruit*: the Church on earth benefits according to the measure of her sanctity, which may vary considerably from age to age.   The greater her sanctity, the greater the benefit received by each one of the faithful from every Mass that is celebrated, and the greater the relief granted to the souls in Purgatory.   As to the other *fruits*, they are limited only by the dispositions of those who receive them.   But note that the *fruits* of the Mass, though proportioned to the dispositions, are of far greater value than any that could be derived from private prayer with the same dispositions, because in the Mass Christ Jesus *works with us* in a very special way.

One who is a friend of God and has no affection for venial sin can undoubtedly obtain through the Mass, not only a great increase of Sanctifying Grace, but also a full discharge of his debt of temporal punishment.   But in regard to this latter point, what is true of the living may not be true of the dead: a Mass offered for a soul in Purgatory will certainly

---

[57] Mal 1:10-11, cited by Trent: DS 1742

524

benefit that soul,[58] but to what extent we cannot say. Through the Mass, also, a friend of God can obtain from Him any temporal favour which would not be an obstacle to holiness or spiritual advancement.

The Mass does not remit sin directly, but indirectly. To those in the state of grace, it can give that greater glow of charity which takes away venial sin. To those in the state of mortal sin, it can give the grace of contrition. Even the greatest criminal on earth can obtain that grace, if he sincerely asks God for it through the Mass. The only sinner who can gather no fruit from the Mass is one who seeks no friendship with God. Yet the Church obliges such a one to Sunday Mass, not in the desire to add to his load of guilt, but in the hope that, even by physical presence, he may catch some gleam of God's love and be touched to penance.

The more your will corresponds to the will of Christ in the Garden when He said: "Not My will but Thine be done", the greater will be the fruit which you will derive from the Mass. All good Christians take up the Cross of Christ and follow Him. In other words, all accept and practise that form of self-denial which consists in the substantial observance of God's law, i.e., in refraining from grievous sin. But we should try to push out the frontier of that self-renunciation by avoiding all deliberate venial sins. In that struggle towards the higher sanctity, the Mass will be your chief aid; you will draw from it the great and strong graces given to those who as victims seek a closer resemblance to the Victim of the Cross.

The excellence of the Mass. The Mass is superior even to the abiding presence of our Blessed Lord in the Most Holy Sacrament. We may kneel before Him as He is in the Tabernacle, like the shepherds kneeling at the crib of Bethlehem long ago. We may draw close to Him, and plead with Him, like the sufferers who thronged round Him while He was on earth, begging for the touch of His great holy hand. We may join in the hosannas of a great multitude at the high festival, when He, our Lord and King, is being borne through the city streets. But through Mass, though celebrated in the humblest circumstances, we can do much more than all this, because *in the Mass He gives us a greater help to adore God than He gives us at any other time.* The Mass is superior to all other religious exercises, to all private prayers and penances: "no work", says the Council of Trent, "can be performed by the faithful, so holy, so divine, as this tremendous mystery."[59]

In the life of Our Blessed Lord, there was one moment beyond all others. He called it His "hour". It was the hour in which He gave His life for us on the Cross. In the Mass, we are with Him at that supreme moment. We

---

[58] D. Prümmer O.P., *Manuale Theologiae Moralis*, vol. III, n. 242
[59] *Decretum de observandis et vitandis in celebratione Missarum*, 17 Sept. 1562

stand with His Mother at the foot of the Cross, and we ask God through Him to apply to our souls all the blessings of the Redemption. Fix your thoughts on the Mass at which you will be present next Sunday. Your Saviour had that Mass and you before His mind on the Cross. He saw your utter dependence on the Divine Omnipotence for your being and life, for your every act and thought,—and He adored God for you. He saw your indebtedness to the Divine Mercy for all the graces bestowed on you, including the very privilege of your being present at that renewal of His Redemptive Sacrifice,—and He thanked God for you. He saw your weakness and your needs—and He besought God's help and blessings for you—the precise help and blessings you ought to desire in the hour of that Sunday's Mass. He saw the marks of imperfections, or perhaps, the stain of guilt, on your soul, together with your unpaid debt of temporal punishment—and He made full atonement and expiation for you, so that you might be cleansed and relieved by His sufferings. At next Sunday's Mass, all the help He gained for you through His own sublime acts will be available for you. *Your* acts will be pitifully feeble—weakened by distractions, perhaps, and wanting in fervour—but He, the Divine Victim, will take them in His own holy hands. He will winnow them of their deficiencies; and to their little worth, He will add all the glowing love of His Sacred Heart, all that perfect submissiveness to the Divine Will that was His on the Cross, and thus drawing them up to a resemblance to the acts He made in your name, He will present them to the eternal Father. Thus, through the Mass, our acts of adoration, praise, thanksgiving, atonement, satisfaction, and petition, receive a new and special efficacy. Thus, through the Mass, we can obtain far more surely than through any other means the grace of contrition in the hour of need, the grace of more perfect sanctity, and all temporal blessings not in conflict with our spiritual well-being.

The Mass, according to St Francis de Sales, is "the centre of the Christian religion, the mainspring of devotion, the soul of piety, an ineffable mystery which embraces the untold depths of divine charity".[60] It is the very life of the Church, the secret of her holiness and her vitality. No wonder that the spirits of darkness should have inspired the heretic with hatred for the Mass, for they know that when they strike at the Mass, they strike at the heart of the Church. No wonder that Pope Urban VIII should say that, if the angels could envy man anything, it would be his power to offer the Holy Sacrifice. No wonder that the faithful in all the ages of persecution, from the days of the Catacombs to recent times, were willing to pay with their lives for the privilege of assisting at Mass. Go back in thought to the penal era in Ireland: at daybreak in some mountain fastness you see a little group

---

[60] *Introduction to the Devout Life*, Part II, Ch. 14

of men, women, and children, clustered round a rude altar at which a hunted priest is celebrating the Sacred Mysteries. They take no heed of the cruel blasts of winter. So intent are they on the progress of the great Sacrifice that their persecutors come upon them unawares: the ravening wolf descends on the flock of Christ, and their blood commingled with the very Blood of the Lamb is borne by Him to the high throne of God. Think of the martyrs of England and Wales: how they risked everything, including their very lives, if only they could have a priest, if only they could assist at Mass. No need to say that we, their descendants in the faith, should never fail in loyalty to the Mass; that we should never tarnish their proud name by indifference to the most precious gift of Christ.

VII

The teaching of the Fathers. The early Fathers are at one with Catholic teaching on the Sacrifice of the Mass. To cite but a few:

(a) St Clement c. 96 A.D. speaks of "those of the episcopate who have blamelessly and holily offered its Sacrifices."[61]

(b) St Justin Martyr c. 155 quotes God's prophecy to Malachi (1:10-12) and says, "He is speaking at that time of the sacrifices offered to Him in every place by us, the Gentiles, that is, of the Bread of the Eucharist and likewise of the Cup of the Eucharist".[62]

(c) St Irenaeus, writing 180-199, says Christ "took from among creation what is bread, and gave thanks, saying, 'This is My Body'. So too the cup, which is from the creation to which we belong, He confessed to be His Blood. He taught the new Sacrifice of the new Covenant, which Malachi, one of the twelve prophets, had indicated beforehand."[63]

(d) St Cyprian of Carthage (d. 258) says, "the Blood of Christ is not offered if there is no wine in the cup; nor is the Sacrifice of the Lord celebrated with a legitimate consecration unless our offering and sacrifice corresponds to the Passion".[64]

(e) St John Chrysostom c. 387 says, "When you see the Lord immolated and lying upon the altar, and the priest bent over that Sacrifice praying, and all the people reddened by that Precious Blood, can you think that you are still among men and on earth? Or are you not lifted up to Heaven?" "Thus there is one Sacrifice. By this reasoning, since the Sacrifice is offered everywhere, are there, then, a multiplicity of Christs? Not at all! Christ is one everywhere. He is complete here, complete there, one Body. And just as He is one Body, and not many, though offered everywhere, so too there is one Sacrifice."[65]

---

[61] *Ep. ad Cor.* 44
[62] *Dial. cum Tryph.* 41
[63] *Adv. Haer.* IV, 17, 5
[64] *Ep.* 63, 9
[65] *De Sacerd.* III, 4; *Hom. in Heb.* 17, 3 (6)

(f) St Augustine in 408: "Was not Christ immolated only once in His very Person? In the Sacrament, nevertheless, He is immolated for the people not only every Easter Solemnity, but every day".[66]

Replies to objections against the Mass. Various objections against the Mass have been brought forward by Protestants. We deal with them, chiefly because they afford an opportunity of repeating and summarising our doctrine.

A. "In the Epistle to the Hebrews, we are taught that under the Old Law there were many sacrifices, offered by a succession of High Priests, whereas under the New there is only one sacrifice and one High Priest, Christ, who has no successors. This doctrine cannot be reconciled with the Catholic system of many priests offering many sacrifices."
REPLY: (1) We have but one High Priest, Christ. He has no successor, but He has representatives who act with His power and authority. Though unseen, He is still with us. He still acts as our High Priest. His earthly priests are only His ministers, His visible agents. As the judges and officials of a Kingdom are not the successors of their King, but his representatives, so our priests are not the successors, but the representatives, of Christ. "And therefore Christ alone is the true Priest, the others but His ministers."[67] (2) Further, they do not offer many sacrifices, but one and the same sacrifice. Under the Old Law, one High Priest succeeded another, and at each sacrifice a new victim was offered. Under the New, in the Sacrifice of the Mass, Christ Himself, the same for ever, fills the office of High Priest and Victim.

B. "The Epistle to the Hebrews, again, teaches that Christ by His one Sacrifice atoned for all the sins of men. Hence, there is no room for the sacrifice of the Mass."
REPLY: "Christ by His one Sacrifice atoned for all the sins of men." Yes, but each individual did not thereby receive remission of sin. Christ, by His death on the Cross, filled, as it were, a great cistern with His merits. He connected us with that cistern by means of the Mass and the Sacraments. It was His plan that we Christians should obtain forgiveness of sin by making use of the Mass and the Sacrament of Penance. Through the Sacrifice of the Mass, we get the benefit of Christ's intercession for us here and now. Through the Sacrament of Penance, we get the benefit of the atonement He made for our sins.

C. "You say that man is bound to offer frequent sacrifice to God to adore, praise, thank Him, and beg His blessings, and that the Mass is the sacrifice by which all this is done. But Christ's death on the Cross discharged all these duties for us, and so no subsequent sacrifice is required."
REPLY: (1) One might just as well argue that, since Christ prayed for us, *we* need never say a prayer. Christ's *internal* act of adoration on the Cross has not exempted us from the obligation of personally adoring God in our hearts. Neither has Christ's *external* act of adoration, His Sacrifice, dispensed us from the duty of offering

---

[66] *Ep.* 98, 9
[67] St Thomas, *Comm. in Heb.*, 7, 4; cf. C 1545.

sacrifice to God. We must be imitators of Christ in regard to the outward as well as the inward act. We imitate Him in respect of both by means of the Sacrifice of the Mass. (2) Our opponents admit that the Jewish sacrifices were instituted by God, yet, if their objection were sound, this could not have been so; for Christ's one sacrifice, it could be contended, satisfied the obligations of all men, before and after His time, from the beginning of the world to the end. (3) Sacrifice has been so common at all times and in all parts of the world as to give rise to the saying, "No sacrifice, no religion." The impulse to adore God in this precise way belongs to our very nature, and must have been implanted there by God Himself. He gave us a body as well as a soul, and He wishes us to worship Him with both. He wishes us to express outwardly, by gesture, as well as by word, our internal acts of worship. This we do in the Sacrifice of the Mass.

D. "According to Catholics, the Sacrifice of the Cross does not benefit us directly, but indirectly through the Mass. That is to say, the Sacrifice of the Cross is not all-sufficient, but requires some instrument to produce its effect on us. The Mass, therefore, is derogatory to the Sacrifice of the Cross" (i.e., the Mass depreciates, or lessens the value of, the Sacrifice of the Cross).

REPLY: (1) Protestants teach that we receive the benefit of the Sacrifice of the Cross by an act of faith. But, according to their argument above, even this act of faith is disrespectful to the Sacrifice of the Cross; for it is the instrument that conveys its blessings to us. (2) The Mass is in no sense derogatory to the Sacrifice of the Cross, because it is a representation and continuation of it, and derives all its efficacy from it. It is not an instrument separated from Calvary; on the contrary, it is Calvary brought to us.

VIII

A FEW ADDITIONAL REMARKS ON THE MASS. (1) The Mass, as given to us by Christ, consists of the Consecration and the Communion. The essence of the Sacrifice, according to the common teaching, is found in the Consecration: the priest's communion may be compared to the eating of the Paschal Lamb, which ceremony was not the sacrifice proper, but the sacred banquet that followed it. The priest, however, unlike the laity, must always receive Communion at the Mass he offers, and must receive under both kinds.

(2) At the very moment when the twofold Consecration has been completed, the Sacrifice is offered; the Divine Victim is handed over to God by the priest in the name of the Church. St Thomas uses the word *consecrare* as equivalent to *offerre*. He says, "this Sacrament comes into being at the consecration of the Eucharist, in which (consecration) the Sacrifice is offered to God".[68] Since it would be impossible for us, with our human limitations, to make all our acts of adoration, etc., in that fleeting instant of time, we may make them at our leisure before and after the Consecration. We make them in a most solemn way at the Offertory, and continue doing so until just before the *Agnus Dei* ("Lamb of God"), when the

---

[68] S.T., iii, q. 82, a. 10, ad 1

prayers for Communion begin. The Church herself does the same; she makes her various acts of praise, petition, and thanksgiving, all through the Mass.

(3) You will notice that, before the Consecration, the priest may pray that by the power of the Holy Spirit the bread and the wine be changed into the Body and the Blood of Christ. This prayer is an expression of desire for the presence of the Victim. The Consecration is effected by the words, "This is My Body", "This is the Chalice of My Blood". In the Byzantine rite, this prayer invoking the Holy Spirit (the *epiclesis*) to change the elements is made *after* the Consecration. This is because the Eucharistic Prayer forms a unity, and not everything can be expressed at once. Hence, some things must precede, and others must follow, the Consecration. It would be a mistake to analyse the sequence of the prayers too literally. Thus, "the words of the Epiclesis are to be taken as referring, not to the time at which they are spoken, but to the time to which they are related. That which happens in one single moment in the consecration, is liturgically developed and explained in the subsequent words of the Epiclesis."[69]

(4) As has been so often said, all grace comes to us through Christ our Lord. It is His grace, therefore, that gives us the good dispositions which we require for the fruitful reception of the Sacraments. But, as noted on p.453, when we actually receive a Sacrament, Christ gives us a further grace which is not caused by our dispositions, though its amount is determined by them. The same is true of the Mass: the good dispositions we bring with us are His gift to us, yet they are not the cause, but the measure, of the greater gift we get from Him through actual assistance at the Holy Sacrifice.

---

[69] L. Ott, *Fundamentals of Catholic Dogma*, Mercier Press, Cork 1957, p.393

C

THE BLESSED EUCHARIST AS A SACRAMENT

Summary

I. The teaching and legislation of the Church.

II. The Sacrament of the Blessed Eucharist defined. Its Minister and Subject.

III. Holy Communion: how far necessary for salvation. Frequent Communion. Communion under one kind. The significance of Communion. Intercommunion. 'Communicatio in sacris'.

IV. The effects of Holy Communion: it gives an increase of Sanctifying Grace; it produces a union of love between Christ and the soul; it reinforces the unity of the mystical body; it is the food and medicine of the soul; it produces spiritual gladness; it is a pledge of our glorious resurrection.

V. Preparation and thanksgiving.

I

The solemn teaching and the legislation of the Church.

The solemn teaching of the Church. The Church teaches solemnly:

(1) that the Blessed Eucharist is a Sacrament;[1]

(2) that it gives an increase of grace to those who receive it worthily; that its effect on the soul resembles that of food on the body, supporting, strengthening, refreshing, and delighting it; that it helps us to avoid mortal sin, and to overcome all imperfections;[2]

(3) that it is a pledge, or token, of the everlasting happiness that shall be ours;[3]

(4) that no one except the priest celebrating Mass is bound to communicate under both species.[4]

The legislation of the Church. The Church has decreed:

(1) that the subject, a Catholic, must not only be in the state of grace to receive worthily, but must have abstained from all food and flavoured drink for one hour before Communion, excepting only water and medicine;[5]

---

[1] T 1601
[2] T 1607, 1638; F 1322
[3] T 1638
[4] T 1726-29, 1731-33
[5] Can. 919 §1

(2)   that all the faithful who have come to the use of reason are bound to receive Holy Communion at least once a year in Paschal tide,[6] and, if possible, at the hour of death;[7]

(3)   that no one should approach the Altar until he has obtained remission of all mortal sins in the Sacrament of Penance; if then he be conscious of having committed some mortal sin since his last Confession, he must abstain from Holy Communion;[8]

(4)   that one may receive Holy Communion a second time in the same day, provided that one is assisting at the second Mass;[9] a third time *only* if danger of death arises later that day.[10]

Exceptions to the Eucharistic fast.   No fast at all is required of the elderly, the sick and those who are charged with their care.[11] (From 1973 until the promulgation of the 1983 Code, the rule was a quarter-hour fast). Piety and reverence require that alcohol be avoided beforehand. The law of fasting does not bind those who receive in order to prevent irreverence, e.g., if a church were attacked, and there was a probability that the ciborium might fall into sacrilegious hands.

Paschal tide: the period from Palm Sunday to the Second Sunday of Easter (Low Sunday). Those who have failed to fulfil the Paschal precept to receive Communion are bound to receive as soon as possible. For a just cause, it may be deferred.[12]

Note on freedom from mortal sin.   A person conscious of mortal sin may go to Communion, says canon 916, "if there is a grave reason, and no opportunity to confess; in which case he must remember the obligation to make an act of perfect contrition,[13] which includes the resolve to go to Confession as soon as possible." This could arise if, e.g., a person in a *concealed* mortal sin is expected to accompany others to the Altar. Note, however, that he should not abstain from Holy Communion because of a grievous sin which he forgot to tell in his last Confession, provided he was sorry for all his sins and can answer yes to these two questions: "Would I have told that sin if I had remembered it?"   "Am I now resolved to tell it in my next

---

[6] Can. 920
[7] Can. 921
[8] T 1647; Can. 916
[9] i.e., taking part as one praying or following the Mass, at least from the Offertory. Can. 917.
[10] Can. 921. See C 1388 and its footnote in the 1997 edition.
[11] Can. 919 §3
[12] Can. 920 §2. Cf. *Rituale Romanum* V, iii, De Communione Paschali, 2. In certain places, the Paschal precept may be fulfilled from the 4th Sunday of Lent to Trinity Sunday.
[13] See p.547.

Confession?" Such a sin has been forgiven. There remains only the grave obligation to confess it next time.

II

The Sacrament of the Blessed Eucharist defined. Its minister and subject.
The Sacrament of the Blessed Eucharist is the Body and the Blood of Christ under the appearance of bread and wine. The other Sacraments exist only in the instant of their conferring. They are actions, and therefore transient, whereas the Blessed Eucharist consists in the continued presence of Christ. It not only gives grace like the other Sacraments, but contains the very Author of grace.

THE MINISTER OF THE SACRAMENT. We distinguish between the Minister of Consecration and the Minister of Distribution. The former is the priest who confects or consecrates the Blessed Eucharist at Mass; the latter is the priest or deacon who distributes it to the faithful.

In cases of grave necessity the laity may be allowed to give themselves Holy Communion (as, e.g., during the early persecutions the people were permitted to take the Blessed Eucharist to their homes, and communicate themselves privately), but the Church has always held it as an Apostolic rule that the Bread of Life should be dispensed only by the consecrated hand of the priest.[14] A lay person may assist in the distribution of Holy Communion only where there is such a large number of communicants that Mass would be prolonged excessively, or where the sick are too numerous or too distant for the ordained ministers to go themselves.[15]

THE SUBJECT OF THE SACRAMENT. The subject in the Latin Rite is any baptised Catholic who has reached the age of reason and can distinguish the Body of Christ from ordinary food.[16] In the Eastern Churches, Holy Communion is given to infants after Baptism.

---

[14] T 1648
[15] *Immensae Caritatis*, S.C.D.S., 1973; *Ecclesiae de mysterio*, Instruction on collaboration of the non-ordained, Vatican City 1997, art. 8. Can. 230 §3; 910 §2
[16] Can. 913. See "The Subject of a Sacrament", pp.450-1.

III

Holy Communion: how far necessary for salvation. Frequent Communion. Communion under one kind. The significance of Communion. Intercommunion. 'Communicatio in sacris'.

NECESSITY FOR SALVATION. Christ Himself has said, "unless you eat the Flesh of the Son of Man and drink His Blood, you have no life in you".[17] The Church interpreting this command and putting it into a more definite shape, requires all adults to receive Holy Communion at least once a year in Paschal time. Those who wilfully disobey her, disobey Christ, and "shall not have life in them", but those who disobey her through ignorance or no grave fault will not be punished.

FREQUENT COMMUNION. Daily Communion was an ordinary practice of the Church in early centuries. Later, it was recommended by the Council of Trent[18] and, still more earnestly, by the decree of Pope St Pius X: "It is the desire of Jesus Christ and the Church", he says, "that all Christ's faithful should approach the sacred banquet daily ... No one can be excluded from the Table of the Lord who is in the state of grace, and approaches with a right and devout intention."[19] A "right intention", he explains, consists in the sincere purpose of pleasing God, of being more closely united to Him in charity, and of seeking in this heavenly Food a remedy against all spiritual weakness and defects.[20] In short, the *only* conditions are that a Catholic observe the fast, be in a state of grace, and have a right intention.

Older books requiring marital abstinence beforehand, and any other practices, are superseded by this definitive decree, which concludes by saying that all controversy is henceforth forbidden as to what dispositions are required.

COMMUNION UNDER ONE KIND. The priest celebrating Mass must communicate under both species. This is necessary in order to carry out fully the rite established by Christ. But, though necessary for the Sacrifice, it is not necessary for the Sacrament; we can obtain all the graces of Holy Communion by receiving under either species, since Christ is wholly present under each. He Himself has said, "He who eats this bread will live for ever."[21] In the early ages of the Church, it was customary to administer the Blessed Eucharist under the species of bread alone to the sick and to confessors imprisoned for the faith. During the fifth century, Communion under both species was actually prescribed by Pope St Leo. The Manichaeans in those days asserted that wine was the creation of the spirit of evil.

---

[17] Jn 6:53
[18] DS 1638, 1649
[19] Decree of 1905 on daily Communion: DS 3375, 3379
[20] DS 3380
[21] Jn 6:58

The decree was issued to condemn their teaching, and to secure a public profession of faith in the Real Presence of Christ under this species. In the Latin Rite, Communion under one kind did not become the prescribed form for the faithful generally until about the twelfth century, when its practical convenience began to be clearly recognised. It is difficult to procure wine in sufficient quantities for use all over the world, and difficult also to preserve the sacred species for any length of time; add to this the danger of spilling, the repugnance many feel to communicating from the same chalice, and the danger of spreading disease.

THE SIGNIFICANCE OF COMMUNION. Communion is the highest expression of unity *with* the Church, as well as being a sign of the unity *of* the Church. "Now the other sacraments, as indeed all ecclesiastical ministries and works of the apostolate, are bound up with the Holy Eucharist and are directed towards it. For in the Blessed Eucharist is contained the entire spiritual good of the Church".[22] St Thomas says, "The Eucharist is, as it were, the completion of the spiritual life and the end of all the sacraments."[23] Following St Paul's phrase, *anathema sit*,[24] the doctrinal declarations of the Church have traditionally ended with an *anathema*, meaning in practical terms an excommunication from the Holy Eucharist for whoever does not believe the dogma. The ultimate aim of doctrine is not doctrine itself, but Eucharistic Communion and Its fruits.[25]

Since Holy Communion is the greatest sign and efficacious symbol of the unity of the Mystical Body, the Church, only someone in communion with the Catholic Church can rightly participate in it; otherwise the sign is falsified. Sharing of Holy Communion between different churches rightly takes place *after* unity has been reached. To practise it before such unity is achieved is a dishonest denial of the separation between churches. It is a pretence that unity exists where it does not, and is thus an obstacle to a search for genuine unity.

INTERCOMMUNION. *Reception of Communion at Protestant services.* "Eucharistic intercommunion with these communities is not possible."[26] For a Catholic to receive an Anglican or Protestant Communion is gravely sinful and absolutely forbidden, for a number of reasons. First, such a Communion is not a real Communion in the Catholic sense, since it does not contain the true Body of Jesus Christ; and generally these communities themselves make no such claim. Those communities "have not preserved the genuine and integral substance of the Eucharistic mystery, principally because of the

---

[22] *Presbyterorum Ordinis*, Decree on the Ministry and Life of Priests, Second Vatican Council, 1965, art. 5

[23] S.T., iii, q. 73, a. 3

[24] Gal 1:8,9, "let him be anathema": ἀνάθεμα ἔστω

[25] Cf. J.D. Zizioulas, *Being as Communion*, St Vladimir's Press, N.Y., 1985, p.117.

[26] C 1400

absence of the sacrament of Orders".[27] Secondly, such a Communion is a sin of indifferentism and scandal. Thirdly, it may imply defection insofar as it gives formal, public witness that one now adheres to a non-Catholic body. Fourthly, it is a serious sin against the virtue of religion, because it is an unauthorised participation in a communion service not authorised by the Church of Christ, and as such is subject to a penalty.[28] The simple fact is that Catholics and Protestants have a totally different faith regarding the Eucharist.

"COMMUNICATIO IN SACRIS": *Communion in separated Eastern Churches.* Since these have the true priesthood and the Blessed Eucharist, a certain sharing in the sacraments (*communicatio in sacris*) is possible.[29]
The Church has given the following directives to cover various situations:
A. What is permitted to Catholics:
1. *Catholics may receive Communion, penance and anointing of the sick from an Eastern non-Catholic priest when the following conditions are all fulfilled:* (a) it is physically or morally impossible to approach a Catholic minister; (b) necessity requires or a genuine spiritual advantage suggests it; (c) the danger of error or indifferentism is avoided; (d) there is no objection from the eastern Church itself; and, further, (e) for Communion, one must be free from mortal sin, and observe the Eastern discipline concerning prior Confession, the frequency of Communion, and the Eucharistic fast.[30]

2. *Catholics may receive Communion, penance and anointing of the sick from a minister of a separated Church or ecclesial community in the West[31] when the following conditions are all fulfilled:* (a) it is physically or morally impossible to approach a Catholic minister; (b) the minister has been validly ordained according to Catholic teaching on ordination; (c) they are properly disposed, i.e., observing the customary Eucharistic fast and any need for prior Confession; (d) there is danger of death or some other grave necessity, e.g., imprisonment or persecution.[32]

B. What is permitted to non-Catholics:
1. *Eastern non-Catholic Christians may receive Communion, penance and anointing of the sick from a Catholic minister when:* (a) they spontaneously ask for them; (b) they are

---

[27] *Unitatis Redintegratio*, Decree on Ecumenism, Second Vatican Council, 1964, art. 22. Cf. C 1400.
[28] Cf. Can. 1365.
[29] C 1399
[30] Cf. Can. 844 §2; *Directory for Ecumenism*, Pont. Council for Promoting Christian Unity, 1993, art. 123-4.
[31] E.g., the Polish National Church (in the USA); Society of St Pius X (of Archbishop Lefebvre)
[32] Cf. Can. 844 §2; *Directory, etc.*, art. 132.

properly disposed; and (c) due consideration is given to the discipline of the eastern Churches for their own faithful in such cases.[33] - "Properly disposed" for Communion means that one holds Catholic faith in the Eucharist, observes the Eucharistic fast, is free from mortal sin, and is not in an objectively invalid marriage, i.e., contrary to divine law (as might be the case with someone 'remarried' in an Orthodox church).

2. *Non-Catholics of a separated Church or ecclesial community in the West may receive Communion, penance and anointing of the sick from a Catholic minister when the following conditions are all fulfilled:* (a) they cannot approach their own minister; (b) they spontaneously ask for them; (c) they manifest Catholic faith in the sacrament; (d) they are properly disposed; (e) there is danger of death or some other grave necessity, e.g., imprisonment or persecution.[34] - Again, "properly disposed" for Communion means that one observes the Eucharistic fast, is free from mortal sin, and is not in an objectively invalid marriage. The local ordinary (bishop) or the episcopal conference can establish norms to judge other situations of grave and pressing need.[35]

In all of the above, "non-Catholic" means someone who is so in good faith. It never means someone who has defected from the Catholic Church. A Catholic turned heretic, schismatic or apostate is automatically excommunicated, i.e., may not go to Holy Communion.[36]

IV

The effects of Holy Communion.

HOLY COMMUNION INCREASES SANCTIFYING GRACE AND GIVES SACRAMENTAL GRACE. Every time we communicate worthily, we receive an increase of Sanctifying Grace, that "eternal life" given here below, which not even death itself can interrupt, but which death will make bloom into eternal glory. The better our dispositions, the greater the increase. If we approach the Altar resolved to conquer our self-love, resolved to take the Cross of Christ on our shoulders, and, for His sake, to keep His law and to belong to Him entirely, then our dispositions are perfect, and we lay our souls wide open to a vast increase of God's radiant Grace. With the increase of Sanctifying Grace there is given also a more intimate and active presence of the Three Divine Persons in our souls. The presence of the Sacred Humanity of Jesus ceases as the process of digestion takes its ordinary course, but this presence of the Blessed Trinity continues, and is only removed by grave sin. Holy Communion is, therefore, the sacrament of our growth in supernatural life and in our union with the Father, Son and Holy Spirit. Every time we communicate worthily we also receive

---

[33] Can. 844 §3; *Directory*, art. 125
[34] C 1401; cf. Can. 844 §4; *Directory*, art. 131.
[35] Cf. Can. 844 §§4, 5; *Directory*, art. 130.
[36] Cf. Can. 751, 1364.

Sacramental Grace, perfecting and disposing the soul by charity for union with God in Christ. By this Grace also we are given a claim to all those generous Actual Graces which will help to keep us safe in God's love, and to live our lives in childlike docility to Him.

HOLY COMMUNION PRODUCES A UNION OF LOVE BETWEEN CHRIST AND THE SOUL. After receiving the Blessed Eucharist, as long as the species of bread remain, Christ dwells within us. Not only do we obtain a great increase of Sanctifying Grace, but His soul is united to ours in some mysterious way. His Soul breathes into ours its own spirit of Divine Love, so that we may say with St Paul: "It is no longer I who live, but Christ who lives in me."[37] This is what we desire when we say the words, "Soul of Christ, sanctify me". St Cyril of Alexandria says, "Just as if someone were to entwine two pieces of wax together and melt them with a fire, so that both are made one, so too through participation in the Body of Christ and in His Precious Blood, He is united in us and we too in Him."[38]

HOLY COMMUNION REINFORCES THE UNITY OF THE MYSTICAL BODY. By uniting us with Christ, it unites us thereby *with all the faithful*: "Because there is one Bread", says St Paul, "we who are many are one body, for we all partake of the one Bread."[39] As bread is made of many grains of wheat, and wine from the juice of many grapes, so, through this mystic food and drink, all who partake of it are made one in Christ: the same spirit of Christ dwells in all, and draws all together into a perfect union. Speaking of this Sacrament as that which forms the faithful into the Church, the body of Christ, St Augustine exclaims, "O Sacrament of piety! O sign of unity! O bond of charity!"[40] St Thomas says, "Now the sacrament of the Eucharist belongs chiefly to charity, since it is the sacrament of ecclesial unity, containing Him in Whom the whole Church is united and consolidated, namely Christ. Therefore the Eucharist is, as it were, the origin and bond of charity."[41]

HOLY COMMUNION IS THE FOOD AND MEDICINE OF THE SOUL: IT HELPS TO BLOT OUT VENIAL SINS AND PRESERVES US FROM MORTAL SIN. *It is the food of the soul.* As a lamp needs oil to keep it burning, so does the body need food to keep it alive. Every part of it is being constantly worn away, and must be constantly renewed. The process of waste must be balanced by the process of reparation. The soul, too, in regard to its spiritual life, is subject

---

[37] Gal 2:20
[38] *In Ioann.*, 10, 2
[39] 1 Cor 10:17
[40] *In Ioann. Tract.*, 26, 13
[41] *Comm. in Sent.* iv, d. 45, q. 2, a. 3 (= S.T. Suppl. q. 71, a. 9)

to an incessant decline in fervour caused by the venial offences which we daily commit; and what food does for the body, the Blessed Eucharist does for the soul by giving it new energy, fervour, and life. So the Council of Trent says, "It is like an antidote whereby we are delivered from daily faults, and preserved from mortal sins."[42] But in this comparison, St Augustine notes a point of difference: material food is absorbed into the body, and is converted into living tissue, whereas what may be termed the opposite process is effected by the Blessed Eucharist; for it is not Christ who is made like unto us, but we who are made like unto Christ.[43]

It is the medicine of the soul. As medicine can render the body proof against the microbes of disease, so the Blessed Eucharist can preserve the soul from mortal sin. It closes our ears to temptations from without, and stifles the flame of carnal desire that burns within. It is in this latter effect that we chiefly feel its wholesome power. Impurity is the principal disease of the human soul, the disease that sets us against God, gives us a distaste for His service, blinds us, pins us to the earth, and degrades us. Frequent Communion is the best medicine for that dread disease which turns the steps of so many towards Hell.

HOLY COMMUNION PRODUCES SPIRITUAL GLADNESS. By spiritual gladness we do not mean a feeling of joy or sweetness, although this is often the effect of Holy Communion, but rather a greater alacrity, a keener willingness, to do all that Christ and His Church command us. Those who have made a careful preparation and receive the Sacrament worthily may not perceive this effect, for God often denies His consolation to those He loves, so that by their patience they may merit greater grace. Still, though no such increase be observed, it is none the less really given. Every good Communion brings us a great step nearer God: the virtues of Faith, Hope, and Charity are strengthened, so that the soul sees divine truth better, trusts more firmly in the goodness of God, and is warmed by a closer approach to the sunshine of His Love.

HOLY COMMUNION IS A PLEDGE OF OUR GLORIOUS RESURRECTION. In Holy Communion the body becomes ennobled, because it is brought into contact with the Sacred Species, and, therefore, indirectly with the living Flesh of Christ. Being the abode and tabernacle of Christ in this life, it is fitting that it should not see final corruption, but should share with Him in the privilege of a glorious resurrection. He Himself has said: "He who eats My Flesh and drinks My Blood has eternal life, and I will raise him up at the

---

[42] DS 1638
[43] *Confess.*, VII, 10, 16

last day."[44] The Body of Jesus in Holy Communion is His Crucified *and Risen* Body—as glorious, fresh and immortal as on the first Easter Sunday when He arose triumphant from the tomb, overcoming the shackles of death.

V

Preparation and thanksgiving. PREPARATION FOR COMMUNION. Need we speak a word on the necessity of being free from mortal sin when we approach the Altar? St Paul says, "Whoever, therefore, eats the Bread or drinks the Cup of the Lord in an unworthy manner, will be guilty of profaning the Body and Blood of the Lord. … For any one who eats and drinks without discerning the Body eats and drinks judgement upon himself",[45] i.e., acting as though he did not recognise that the Body of Christ is here. An unworthy Communion is a dreadful act of sacrilege and ingratitude: it is the traitor's stab, the kiss of Judas. But we should not rest satisfied with refraining from such an insult. The more we empty our soul of all affection even for venial sin, the greater will be the inflow of grace. Before receiving we should ask ourselves: Who is it that comes to me? (The Son of God Who was born at Bethlehem and died on Calvary and rose again. I believe He is here in the Blessed Sacrament. I adore Him). Why does He come to me? (Because He loves me, and wants to make me like Himself). To whom does He come? (To a poor sinner. I am sorry from my heart for having offended Him. I love Him all the more for coming to one so imperfect.)

THANKSGIVING AFTER COMMUNION. After receiving we should spend some time in prayer. During the first few minutes we should try to pray without a book, making acts of faith, adoration and thanksgiving, offering ourselves to God and begging His grace. We should then take up our prayer book and read the prayers after Holy Communion with deep attention. Those moments during which Christ is really present within us are amongst the most precious of our lives. Our private prayers have then a virtue which they have at no other time: as Jacob held the fleet angel fast and would not let him go, saying, "I will not let you go, unless you bless me",[46] so we should cling to our Saviour, and not let Him leave us, until He gives us all He so much desires to give, if we but ask Him. We should ask for ourselves and for others, for the welfare of the entire Church, for the living and for the dead.

---

[44] Jn 6:54
[45] 1 Cor 11:27-29
[46] Gen 32:26

CHAPTER 15

PENANCE

Summary

I.   The solemn teaching and legislation of the Church.
II.   The Sacrament defined. Its Minister and its Subject. Effects. Conditions for its valid reception.
III. Mortal and Venial sin. Contrition. Its qualities. Two kinds of Contrition: Perfect Contrition and Attrition. Examination of Conscience. Honesty in Confession.
IV.   Charity: how to arrive at Perfect Contrition.
V.   Institution of the Sacrament of Christ: Proof: (1) from the solemn teaching of the Church; (2) from Sacred Scripture; (3) from the tradition of the Church; (4) from reason (negative argument from history).
VI.   Changes in the Church's method of administering the Sacrament. Devotional Confession. First and Second Rites of Reconciliation. General absolution. The sin against the Holy Spirit.
VII. Indulgences.

I

The solemn teaching and the legislation of the Church.

THE SOLEMN TEACHING OF THE CHURCH. The Church teaches solemnly:

(1) that Penance is a Sacrament instituted by Christ for the remission of sin committed after Baptism;[1]

(2) that the words of Christ, "Receive the Holy Spirit. Whose sins you shall forgive, they are forgiven them; and whose sins you shall retain, they are retained", refer to the power of forgiving and retaining sin in the Sacrament of Penance;[2]

(3) that it is only a priest or bishop who possesses this power; that he exercises it as a judge, with true authority to hear the self-accusation of the sinner, to give or withhold absolution, and to impose such penances as he thinks fitting;[3]

(4) that three acts are required of the penitent for the complete and perfect remission of sins, viz., Contrition, Confession, and Satisfaction;[4]

(5) that contrition conceived from such motives as the fear of hell, the loss of heaven, the filth of sin, and accompanied by a purpose of

---

[1] T 1701
[2] T 1703. Jn 20:22-23
[3] T 1684-85, 1709-10, 1700, 1715
[4] T 1704

amendment, provided it excludes the affection for sin, is true sorrow, and prepares one to receive the grace of the Sacrament;[5]

(6) that by divine law the penitent must make a definite and specific confession of all grave sins, even those of thought, which he can call to mind; that private, or auricular confession, as practised in the Church from the beginning, is not a human invention or opposed to the ordinance of Christ;[6]

(7) that a debt of temporal punishment often remains after sin has been forgiven, but that it may be cancelled by temporal afflictions willingly borne, by penitential works, and by the penance given by the priest, for by such sufferings we are made like unto the suffering Christ, who alone can give our actions the power to satisfy Divine Justice;[7] that the debt of temporal punishment may also be remitted by the indulgences granted by the Church;[8]

(8) that, for those who have fallen into grave sin after Baptism, the Sacrament of Penance is the only gate of salvation; that though "it sometimes happen that contrition is perfect through charity and reconciles man with God before the Sacrament of Penance is actually received, nevertheless the reconciliation itself is not to be ascribed to contrition alone but to contrition together with the desire it includes of receiving the Sacrament";[9]

(9) that it is correct and profitable to confess venial sins;[10]

(10) that the Church has the power from Christ to grant indulgences;

(11) that indulgences are profitable to Christians.[11]

THE LEGISLATION OF THE CHURCH. (1) The Church has made a law requiring all the faithful who have come to the use of reason, to receive the Sacrament of Penance at least once a year.[12] This law only binds those who are guilty of mortal sin. The sacramental confession of venial sin is never obligatory. This law was first made by the Fourth Council of Lateran, 1215. It is not satisfied by a bad confession. (2) The priest who hears confessions is absolutely bound to observe complete secrecy, and never to betray a penitent in any way by word or deed, or to use confessional knowledge to the detriment of the penitent. This is the "seal of confession", the inviolable seal, which enables penitents to come forward

---

[5] T 1705
[6] T 1706-7
[7] T 1712, 1691, 1693, 1715
[8] T 1835
[9] T 1677
[10] T 1680
[11] (10) & (11) T 1835
[12] Can. 989

for Confession without fear of exposure or reprisal. Also bound to silence is an interpreter for Confession, or anyone who learns of confessional sins in any way.[13]

II

The Sacrament defined. Its minister and its subject. Its effects. Conditions for its valid reception. Examination of conscience.

THE SACRAMENT DEFINED. Penance is the Sacrament by which the priest remits sins committed after Baptism to those who confess them with sorrow, and are willing to perform the works of satisfaction he imposes. In the Latin rite, the priest gives absolution, or remission of sin, by pronouncing the words, "I absolve you from your sins".

ITS MINISTER. (1) The minister of the Sacrament of Penance is a duly authorised priest or bishop. By "duly authorised", we mean that he must have jurisdiction or faculties, i.e., he must have received the right to exercise the power of forgiving sin. Jurisdiction is the right to act as judge or to exercise authority over subjects. A priest in the confessional is like a judge, and as a judge cannot condemn or acquit except in the court to which he has been appointed, so a priest who is not provided with proper authority cannot validly absolve.[14]
(2) The Pope has jurisdiction from Christ over the entire Church; a bishop in communion with him has jurisdiction over his own subjects and diocese, and the bishop communicates it to his pastors and other priests. In her solicitude for the eternal welfare of souls, the Church grants faculties to all validly ordained priests, even if deposed from office or outside her communion, to absolve anyone who is in immediate danger of death.[15] Generally, a priest who has faculties for confessions in one region, can exercise them everywhere.[16]

ITS SUBJECT. Its subject is any Catholic who has committed sin after Baptism. This presupposes the age of discretion, i.e., about seven years.[17] "Children must go to the Sacrament of Penance before receiving first Holy Communion."[18]

---

[13] Can. 983-4. St John Nepomucene (c. 1340-93) is one of the priest martyrs to the confessional seal. After death, his tongue was miraculously preserved incorrupt.
[14] Can. 966
[15] Can. 976
[16] Can. 967 §2
[17] Can. 989
[18] C 1457. Cf. Can. 914.

ITS EFFECTS. For those guilty of *mortal* sin, the effects are:[19] (1) forgiveness of sin, and reconciliation with God, by which the penitent recovers grace; (2) reconciliation with the Church, wounded by the sinner's evil deeds; (3) remission of the eternal punishment incurred by mortal sin, viz., everlasting loss of God and exclusion from the Kingdom of Heaven.

They also receive the benefits received by those guilty of *venial* sin only: (4) forgiveness of venial sin; (5) remission, at least in part, of temporal punishments resulting from sin, viz., the expiation required in this life or the next; (6) "peace and serenity of conscience with strong spiritual consolation";[20] (7) Sacramental Grace to help one expiate sin and to struggle with fortitude in the Christian battle.

CONDITIONS FOR ITS VALID RECEPTION. To receive the Sacrament validly, three acts are required of the penitent, viz., Contrition, Confession, and Satisfaction.

Contrition is the true sorrow which we conceive for having offended God by sin. (Fuller treatment in the next section of this Chapter.)

Confession is the declaration of our sins to the priest, in order to obtain forgiveness. When we have *mortal* sins to confess, our confession must, *as far as memory serves*, be complete, specific, and numerical. (1) *Complete*, i.e., all grave post-baptismal sins, not already mentioned in a good confession, must be told. (2) *Specific*, i.e., the precise nature of the sin must be stated: it would not suffice, e.g., to confess, "I have sinned against my neighbour", without explaining how exactly he had been injured, whether in person, property, or good name. (3) *Numerical*, i.e., the number of times each grave sin has been committed must be given.

Satisfaction is the voluntary acceptance of the penance imposed by the priest. The object of this penance is to discharge (in part at least) the debt of temporal punishment that often remains after sin has been remitted. A severe penance, e.g., five decades of the Rosary, if imposed for mortal sin, is of grave obligation.

Further points on confession. (a) In the case of necessity, e.g., weakness at death, a complete confession is not required: a sign suffices. (b) A priest gives conditional absolution to a Catholic who is on the point of death and is incapable of making any confession by word or sign. It is assumed that in such a case, the past life of the dying person, or the faith which he has professed, indicates sufficiently his desire of confessing his sins in his last moments. But since there is no actual confession, the

---

[19] Cf. C 1468-70, 1496.
[20] T 1674

absolution is of doubtful validity and the help of the Sacrament of Extreme Unction is required: see next Chapter. (c) A doubtful sin is one as to which there is uncertainty in regard to its commission or its gravity or whether it was previously confessed. If the doubt is supported by a good reason, confession is not obligatory, though for the penitent's peace of conscience it is usually advisable. (d) Sins which we have forgotten to confess are forgiven. They are included in our contrition— and *their guilt never returns*. The obligation of confessing them, when remembered, alone remains and must be fulfilled, unless our confessor decides otherwise. If he decides that it would not be to our spiritual advantage to review the past, we must submit to his judgement, and keep our soul in peace.

EXAMINATION OF CONSCIENCE. A good catechism or prayer-book will set forth how in particular the Commandments of God and the Precepts of the Church may be violated. A good Examination of Conscience enables us to identify how we have offended God, and to recall sins deserving of mention. One method is to run through the Ten Commandments, keeping in mind what each one enjoins and prohibits, so as to identify sins of commission and omission. Or one may consider one's life and actions in the light of the seven deadly (capital) sins, of which the first three are of the spirit, and the next four of the flesh: pride, envy, anger, lust, covetousness (=avarice, greed), gluttony, sloth (=laziness). Again, we may see how we have offended against the seven contrary virtues, which in corresponding order are: humility, brotherly love, meekness, chastity, liberality (=generosity), temperance, diligence.

HONESTY IN CONFESSION AND SPIRITUAL DIRECTION. A good confession requires humility and courage. There is nothing to be gained by confessing with euphemisms or roundabout expressions. A telling of sins in direct and plain language is pleasing to God and profitable to the soul. There is nothing a priest has not heard before. In confession and spiritual direction, honesty is a key virtue, and dissimulation is a trap. "Whoever conceals a temptation from his spiritual director shares his secret with the devil."[21] St Alphonsus often used to say, "A temptation disclosed is half overcome."[22] St Ignatius of Loyola says the devil is like a secret lover who is afraid of being made known. As soon as one reveals his suggestions and intentions to the confessor, he is unmasked and undone.[23]

III

Sin: mortal and venial. Contrition. The qualities of contrition.

SIN. A sin is any wilful thought, word, deed or omission against the law of God.

Mortal Sin. Mortal or grave sin is any serious violation of the Law of God. It is the choice of an inferior good in place of God and His friendship, and

---

[21] Bl. Josemaría Escrivá, *Furrow*, no. 323
[22] *Practice of Love of Jesus Christ*, cap. 17.1 *& al. loc.*
[23] *The Spiritual Exercises*, Discernment of spirits, Week I, Rule 13

thus destroys grace and charity in the soul. It is called "serious" or "grave" because of its gravity; it is called "mortal" because it is deadly, and kills the divine life within the soul. Three conditions must be met for a sin to be mortal: grave matter, full knowledge, deliberate consent.[24]

Venial Sin. A venial sin is a minor violation of the Commandments, or a failure to meet the requirements of God's law in a less serious matter, or a major transgression but without full knowledge or consent. "Venial" means "pardonable". It does not deprive of grace, but does weaken charity. Scripture distinguishes between mortal and venial sin: "All wrongdoing is sin, but there is sin which is not mortal."[25]

CONTRITION. *Definition.* Contrition is the true sorrow which we conceive for having offended God by sin. We can have contrition only for our own sins; we cannot have contrition for another's sins, though we may be sorry about them. Contrition, of its very nature, implies detestation of sin and a firm purpose of amendment. We must share in God's hatred of sin, and we must be resolved not to offend Him again. Contrition is the first and most necessary condition for the forgiveness of sin. God will not pardon us any sin, great or small, unless we are sorry for it.

In the rest of this Section III, whenever we speak of "sin" without qualification, we mean "grave sin" or "mortal sin".

THE QUALITIES OF CONTRITION FOR GRAVE SIN. Contrition must possess four qualities:

(1) it must be *internal,* i.e., it must be genuine sorrow and not mere outward show;

(2) it must be *universal,* i.e., it must cover all mortal sins of which the penitent is guilty; it must be a sincere turning to God and away from such sins, and must, therefore, be accompanied by a firm purpose to avoid them and to avoid dangerous occasions of sin—for "he that loveth danger shall perish in it."[26]

(3) it must be *supernatural,* i.e., (a) it must be inspired by grace, for without grace we can do nothing towards eternal life; and (b) it must spring from some motive revealed to us by faith, as e.g., the fear of hell or the goodness of God as made known to us in the life and sufferings of Christ. If this latter condition is fulfilled, we need have no misgiving to the former: if our motive is correct, God will most certainly give us the grace necessary to make our act of sorrow pleasing to Him;

---

[24] C 1857

[25] 1 Jn 5:17

[26] Ecclesiasticus 3:27 (Douay) = Sirach 3:26

(4) it must be *supreme*, i.e., the penitent must adjudge sin to be a greater evil than any evil of this life, i.e., greater than any evil he may have to encounter in avoiding sin, and he must detest it accordingly. Contrition, therefore, comes from a judgement of the intellect, followed by the approval of the will. It need not necessarily excite anything in the nature of physical pain or passionate grief, such as one suffers from a wound or the death of a relative: any good Christian mother, though *feeling* less love for God than her son, would yet prefer to see him die rather than save his life by committing a mortal sin. She cannot help being drawn to him by a strong emotional love. Still, her reason, enlightened by grace, tells her that an insult to God is an infinitely greater evil than the death of her child.

The two kinds of contrition for grave sin. There are two kinds of Contrition, viz., Perfect and Imperfect (or Attrition). Contrition is derived from *conterere*, to grind thoroughly, and is often used to denote Perfect Contrition. Attrition is from *atterere*, to grind against, and does not convey the meaning of grinding completely.

PERFECT CONTRITION. *Definition*. Perfect Contrition is contrition founded on Charity or the perfect love of God. In Perfect Contrition, we grieve for our sins because they are hateful to One who is Himself infinitely lovable and whom we love above all things *for His own sake*. But, though this love is unselfish, we need not exclude the thought of the great blessings His friendship will give us. The Church has condemned the opinion that perfect Charity must be *absolutely* disinterested.[27]

Perfect Contrition immediately reconciles the sinner to God, because it contains the desire of the Sacrament. Christ Himself said: "He who loves Me will be loved by My Father, and I will love him".[28] Of the penitent woman at His feet, He said: "Her sins, which are many, are forgiven, for she loved much".[29] Love of God, therefore, restores us to His friendship. The love of God necessarily carries with it the desire to keep all His commandments, one of which is, according to the solemn teaching of the Church, that all grievous sins committed after Baptism be confessed in the Sacrament of Penance. Hence, the desire of receiving the Sacrament is contained, at least implicitly, in the act of Perfect Contrition.

ATTRITION. *Definition*. Attrition or Imperfect Contrition is contrition that springs from any supernatural motive lower than that of perfect Charity, e.g., the filth and horror of sin, the loss of eternal happiness, or the pains of

---

[27] DS 2351 ff.
[28] Jn 14:21
[29] Lk 7:47

hell. The filth of sin does not mean its sordid details, physical or natural; it means the defilement which, in God's sight, is caused in the soul by sin— not physical, but moral defilement. The motives of Attrition do not call us to unselfish friendship with God. They appeal to our self-interest by showing us the evil consequences of sin to ourselves, e.g., when we are shocked by the filth of sin, we are thinking chiefly of the wretched plight in which we find ourselves as outcasts from God, no longer His children, and with no claim on His loving care. When we dread the loss of eternal happiness, we do not have distinctly before our minds the nature of that happiness arising from a loving union with God, but we conceive it in a vague way as something very precious to us. When we tremble at the thought of eternal torments, our minds are more fixed on God's terrible chastisement, than on the love to which He would draw us by cutting us away from sin. Attrition may be justly described as selfish sorrow for sin. Yet it is true sorrow. It is grounded on Faith and Hope, and God is pleased with it. Every true motive of Attrition brings *God* clearly before our mind and urges us to sorrow for having offended *Him*.

The qualities of Attrition. Attrition must have all the qualities we have ascribed to Contrition. It must be *internal, universal, supernatural, supreme.* It is a sincere and thorough change of heart, a turning to God, and away from sin. The motives we have set forth (the fear of hell, the loss of heaven, etc.) lead the sinner (1) to see the error of his ways: to regard sin as the one and only true defilement of the soul or as the bar to his eternal happiness, or as the cause of eternal damnation; (2) to detest sin as the greatest of all evils; and (3) most important of all, to desire reconciliation with God. We mark the third effect as the most important, because the Sacrament of Penance, being the Sacrament of reconciliation, cannot be received validly unless reconciliation is truly desired.

Attrition disposes one for forgiveness of sin. When the sinner has made such an act of Attrition as we have described, he is fit to receive the Sacrament of Penance. Without the Sacrament, he could not obtain pardon for sin, because his sorrow is not inspired by the perfect love of God. Still, his Attrition would seem necessarily to involve some love of God, however imperfect: he cannot completely turn away from sin as his enemy without perceiving, at least obscurely, that he is turning to God as his friend; he cannot desire reconciliation without seeking, or beginning to seek, friendship with God. (Contrition necessarily implies the hope of pardon. Hence the sorrow of Judas, because it was devoid of hope, was not true Contrition.)

Pardon, through Attrition, does not remove the obligation of making Acts of Charity. We know from our basic catechism that we are bound to make frequent Acts of Charity, as well as of Faith and Hope. The chief commandment of the Jewish Law was: "Thou shalt love the Lord thy God with thy whole heart and with thy whole soul and with thy whole mind." That, too, is our chief commandment, reaffirmed by Christ Himself.[30] It would, therefore, be a grievous mistake to suppose that, because the sinner can obtain pardon in the Sacrament of Penance without that perfect contrition which we have described, he is freed in any way from the obligation of making acts of divine Charity. He is as much bound as one under the Old Law, and has less excuse for failing in his duty: the Sanctifying Grace he receives at absolution gives him the *virtue* of Charity, and is followed by many actual graces that enable him to make *acts* of that virtue. Furthermore, he has, in the Passion of our Saviour, a greater incentive to divine love than any that can be found in God's dealings with His chosen people. In the Christian life which he is now beginning anew, he will make his acts of Charity as easily and as frequently as his acts of faith: God has so constituted us that, with His grace, our mind readily accepts His revealed truth, and our heart as readily gives Him the supreme love we owe Him as our Creator, our Father, and our Friend.

IV

Charity: how to arrive at Perfect Contrition.
CHARITY. The love we should have for God is twofold: (a) we should love Him because of all the blessings He has given us and because of the happiness He desires to bestow on us in Heaven. This is the imperfect love of gratitude and hope. (b) We should also love Him above all things and for His own sake because there is no limit to His goodness and lovableness. This is the perfect love of Charity.

Since our love of God is exercised through our will—the higher part of our will—it is not necessary that we should feel a glow of affection for Him, though we should pray that this great favour may be granted to us. It suffices that, along with the firm purpose of never offending Him by mortal sin, we truly desire to see Him loved and honoured by all men, for, in so desiring, we show that we have made His interests our own, that we are looking beyond our personal advantage—in brief, that we love Him for His own sake. Every time we say the first part of the "Our Father" with full sincerity, we make this generous act of Perfect Love. We pray that we and all men may bless the name of Him who is our Father and our God, and that the Kingdom of His Church may spread throughout the world, so that

---

[30] See Matt 22:37; Mk 12:30.

He may be enthroned in every heart, and may behold in the daily lives of us all the perfect fulfilment of His holy will.

In loving God perfectly, we love all men as sincerely as we love ourselves; obviously so, since we desire for ourselves and for them the greatest happiness conceivable. But we desire it for the sake of God. We desire it because we want Him to have friends worthy of His love. Hence, Charity is defined as "the love of God above all things for His own sake, and the love of ourself and our neighbour for the sake of God."

HOW TO ARRIVE AT PERFECT CONTRITION. Under the Old Law, Perfect Contrition was the only means of recovering Sanctifying Grace. Under the New Law, those who are unable to receive the Sacrament of Penance must apply the same remedy: hence, for one dying in the state of mortal sin without the ministrations of a priest, there is no other means of salvation. Under the Old Law it was easy to make an act of Perfect Contrition; under the New Law it is still easier, because we know so much better how great is God's love for us, and how worthy He is to be loved for His own sake. The following gives in outline one of the many methods of making an act of Perfect Contrition: (1) Humbly ask God to help you by His grace to love Him as He should be loved. (2) Try to understand how hateful mortal sin must be to Him, since He has to punish it, with eternal torments. (3) Reflect that it was to save you from Hell and to give you a happiness greater than the mind of man can conceive, that He sent His own beloved Son into the world. (4) Think of Jesus and what He did for you: He died on the Cross to make up for your sins and to gain your love. (5) Remember that Jesus who lived and died for you is God Himself, and ask yourself, Is He not worthy to be loved for His own sake? (6) Conclude by making an act of Perfect Contrition in some simple form, e.g., "Jesus, true God, You died on the Cross for me. Jesus, true God, Your Heart is full of love for me. I love You for Your own sake and above all things. I am bitterly sorry I ever offended You, and I will never offend You again."

V

The Sacrament of Penance was instituted by Christ.
PROOF FROM SOLEMN TEACHING OF THE CHURCH. The Church, in the exercise of her infallible authority, declares the institution of the Sacrament of Penance by Christ to be a doctrine given to her by God Himself. This proof suffices for Catholics. The following proofs are inserted for fuller instruction.

PROOF FROM SACRED SCRIPTURE. Christ appeared to the Apostles after His resurrection, and said to them, "'Peace be with you. As the Father has sent Me, even so I send you.' And when He had said this, He breathed on them, and said to

550

them, 'Receive the Holy Spirit. If you forgive the sins of any, they are forgiven; if you retain the sins of any, they are retained.'"[31]

(1) Christ thus made the Apostles judges of sinners, with power to grant or withhold absolution; and in giving them this power, He gave them the authority to prescribe all that its exercise demanded,—authority, therefore, to require men to confess their sins, and to submit themselves to examination as to their dispositions, their sorrow, their purpose of amendment, and their willingness to "bear fruits that befit repentance."[32] For how, in most cases, can a sin be known except through the self-accusation of the penitent? And how can it be decided whether absolution is to be given or refused except after personal interview and inquiry? Strictly speaking, in no case can we know for certain that sin has been committed except through the sinner's own avowal. No matter how criminal his outward act may have been, it does not follow that the full consent of his will went with it. His guilt is a secret of his conscience, and can be revealed by him alone. Therefore the Apostles had to know, judge and absolve.

(2) The power of forgiving sin in the Sacrament of Penance was not given to the Apostles alone, but to their lawful successors as well. Observe the solemn words of Christ, "As the Father has sent Me, even so I send you." He sent them, therefore, clothed with His own power. And to whom did He send them? To all nations, even to the consummation of the world. As long, therefore, as the world shall last, the Apostles shall be with us, exercising the power of forgiving sin through their living representatives, the bishops and priests.

(3) The same Lord also told Peter that he must forgive, "seventy times seven."[33] Would the Church, His Body, not forgive sinners as her Lord told its leader to forgive others?

(4) St Paul tells the Corinthians who are already believers, "We beseech you on behalf of Christ, be reconciled to God."[34] There must be some means, therefore, for reconciliation with God even for sins committed after Baptism. St John presumes the same, for he too addresses Christians: "I am writing this to you so that you may not sin; but if any one does sin, we have an advocate with the Father, Jesus Christ the righteous".[35]

(5) St Paul denounces a public sinner in the Church at Corinth and says he is to be excommunicated: "you are to deliver this man to Satan for the destruction of the flesh, that his spirit may be saved in the day of the Lord Jesus."[36] Note that the baptised man is guilty of a heinous sin after Baptism, but may still be saved via this medicinal punishment and an ultimate reconciliation with the Church. In other

---

[31] Jn 20:21-23
[32] Lk 3:8
[33] Matt 18:21
[34] 2 Cor 5:20
[35] 1 Jn 2:1
[36] 1 Cor 5:5

words, St Paul was well aware of forgiveness of mortal sin committed after Baptism via his ministry in the Church. The Protestant idea that a simple invocation of the Lord Jesus will put things in order, makes nonsense of this Church practice, more fully evidenced in the centuries immediately thereafter (see below).

(6) The evidence from the New Testament texts[37] may be summarised thus: "Every sin calls for penance; but no sin, not even the gravest, is excluded from forgiveness, provided that sincere penance is performed. Prayer and works of mercy are means for obtaining the remission of sins. Personal prayer receives efficacious support from the intercession of the faithful as its counterpart. Joined to prayer is confession of sins. Where the sins are grave, the rulers of the Church are obliged to admonish the guilty, and, if this proves fruitless, to exclude them from the community. If the excommunicated person is converted the Church grants him her forgiveness, and this is a guarantee of 'forgiveness in heaven' also, in accordance with the promise of the Lord."[38]

(7) Proof from typology: to the early Jewish converts to Christianity, the Sacrament of Penance did not appear as a startling innovation. A rite accompanied by the confession of sin was one of the many Jewish practices which by divine ordinance passed quite naturally into the religious life of the New Israel, the Church. Under the Old Law, a sinner offered sacrifice for sin,[39] the priest decided according to the gravity of the sin—therefore after an avowal on the part of the repentant sinner— whether the victim presented was of sufficient value or not.[40] When Jews confessed their sins before John the Baptist and were symbolically washed clean by him, there was no shock at the ritual; something like it was already a part of Jewish life, and was carried over into the new dispensation. A Jewish convert could see at once how the New Law fulfilled the Old: he still had to go to the priest and admit his guilt, and still had to hope for pardon in the blood of a Victim—no longer a beast of the herd, but the Lamb of God, offered once for all, possessing a power of propitiation available at every moment.

Similarly, the Old Testament practice for dealing with lepers was a divinely ordained prefiguring of this Sacrament. The leper had to present himself to the priest, was judged to be unclean, was separated from the Jewish community, but, if purified again, could present himself to the priests who would judge if this were so, and if so, could rejoin the community. After this, the priest made a guilt offering on his behalf.[41] This clearly is an image of the contraction of sin, confession of guilt to the priest, removal from Communion with the Church, forgiveness, return to Communion, and atonement before God.

---

[37] Matt 18:15-18; Jn 20:21-23; 1 Cor 11:31f.; 5:5; 2 Cor 2:5-11; 7:10f.; Gal 6:1f.; 1 Tim 1:20; 2 Tim 4:2; 2:25; 2 Thess 3:6,14-16; Tit 3:10; James 1:21; 2:13; 5:19f.; 3:2; 1 Jn 1:8; 2:1f.; 5:16; 2 Pet 3:9; Rev 2:2,5,14-16,20; 3:1-5,15-19

[38] Mons. B. Poschmann, *Penance and the Anointing of the Sick*, Herder, Freiburg 1964, pp.18-19

[39] Num 5:6-8

[40] Lev 5:10-11,18; 6:2-7

[41] Lev 13-14; cf. Lk 5:12-4; 17:11-5.

PROOF FROM THE TRADITION OF THE CHURCH. The Church has always believed that the Sacrament of Penance was instituted by Christ. This may be briefly proved as follows:

From the belief of non-Catholic Eastern churches. All the Eastern churches not in communion with Rome have the Sacrament of Penance, which shows that at the time of their separation, no-one questioned its institution by Christ.

From the condemnation of heresies. In the second century, the Montanists were expelled from the Church because they contested her right to forgive the sins of idolatry, adultery, and murder. So too were the Novationists, in the third century, who taught that there was no pardon for a denial of the faith.

From the Fathers and early writers. (a) St Ignatius of Antioch (d. 107): "Now God forgives all who repent, so long as their repentance turns to union with God and to communion with the bishop."[42]
(b) Tertullian wrote a work *On Penance* c. 200-6 in which, in a long passage, he describes the Christian process of repentance, confession, and satisfaction for sin by public acts of penance.[43]
(c) Origen (d. 254): "The layman who falls into sin cannot by himself wash away his fault. He must have recourse to the levite; he needs the priest. At times, he applies to one even greater: he needs the pontiff's help, that he may obtain the remission of sins."[44] Note that even in those days there appears to have been a practice of reserving certain sins to a higher authority, just as at present a few heinous crimes are reserved to the Bishop or Pope.
(d) St Cyprian (d. 258): "I entreat you, brethren, that each one should confess his own sin while he who has sinned is still in this world, while his confession may be received, while his satisfaction and the absolution given by the priest are still pleasing to the Lord."[45]
(e) Lactantius (c. 240-c. 320): "it must be known that the true Catholic Church is that in which there is confession and repentance, which treats in a wholesome manner the sins and wounds to which the weakness of the flesh is liable."[46]
(f) St Pacian, Bishop of Barcelona (d. 390), admonishes sinners "to cease to hide their wounded conscience", and to follow the example of "the sick who do not fear the physician, though he cut and burn the secret parts of the body". He also says: "'God alone', you say, 'can remit sin.' Quite correct. But what He does through His priest, is done by His power."[47]
(g) St Ambrose (d. 397): "Sins are forgiven through the Holy Ghost. Certainly, but men lend Him their ministry ... they forgive sins, not in their own name, but in the name of the Father, the Son, and the Holy Ghost."[48]

---

[42] *Ad Philad.* 8
[43] *De Paenitentia,* 9
[44] *Hom. in Numeros,* 10, 1; cf. *Hom. in Lev.* 2, 4.
[45] *De lapsis,* 28, 29
[46] *Div. Institut.* lib. IV, c. 30
[47] *Libellus exhort. ad poen.* 6-8; *Epist. ad Sympr.* i, 6; iii, 7
[48] *De Spiritu Sancto,* iii, 137

(h) St Leo the Great (d. 461) sharply condemns insistence on public confession as "opposed to Apostolic rule ... since it suffices that guilt of conscience be revealed to priests alone in secret confession."[49] And in a passage too long for quotation, he fully describes all the essentials of the Sacrament as we know it.[50] In the later centuries, the evidence becomes more and more abundant.

PROOF FROM REASON. An obligation so distasteful to human nature as confession could never have been imposed on the Church by a Pope or Council without creating a vast upheaval. There would have been schisms and revolts everywhere, and the date of the innovation would be as well known as that of the French Revolution or of any other great events of secular history. But there is not a trace of anything of the kind. The absence of all protest during the centuries that elapsed from the founding of the Church to the Reformation fifteen centuries later, is a conclusive proof that the practice of Confession was always regarded as a sacred duty imposed by none other than Christ Himself.

VI

CHANGES IN THE CHURCH'S METHOD OF ADMINISTERING THE SACRAMENT OF PENANCE. The Church has always claimed the right to determine, according to the needs of the age, the just conditions under which she will administer her Sacraments, a power given to her by Christ when He said, "Whatever you bind on earth", etc.[51] Hence we are prepared to find that, in the case of the Sacrament of Penance, she has not adhered to a uniform practice.

Difference in order. In the early Church, the sacrament took place with its parts in the following order: (1) contrition (2) confession (3) penance (4) absolution. Today, the sacrament takes place in this order: (1) contrition (2) confession (3) absolution (4) penance. All four parts are essential to the sacrament, but their order can be adapted as the Church determines.

Public Confession. Until about the year 500, a *public* sinner had first of all to make a private avowal of guilt to the bishop or priest. He then made a public avowal, and received a penance to be performed in public, after the fulfilment of which he was absolved. For *private* sin, private confession sufficed, as may be inferred from the strong statement of Pope St Leo quoted above. Occasionally, public avowal of a private sin was recommended by the confessor as an act of humiliation. From the year 500 onward, the practice of public confession became more and more restricted.

Canonical Penances. For the first four centuries severe penances, lasting for years or even a lifetime, were imposed for very grave sins. They are called Canonical Penances, because they were prescribed by the canons or laws of the Church. The

---

[49] *Ep.* clxviii; cf. DS 323.
[50] *Ep.* clxviii; *Ep.* cviii
[51] Matt 18:18

penitent was excluded from Holy Communion, and, perhaps also, from the Mass of the Faithful (the part of the Mass that begins at the Offertory). He was bound to rigorous fasts. He was not allowed to marry, and, if already married, he had to live apart from his wife until death. He had to beseech the prayers of the poor and the afflicted, to lie in sackcloth and ashes, and, in the Western Church, to wear distinctive dress. In effect, he was withdrawn from the ordinary pursuits of life, and became like one who had entered a religious order. In the later centuries, until about 1200, penances of a milder type were inflicted, but never of such a kind that the nature of the sin committed could be inferred from them, e.g., the penitent was required to go on a pilgrimage, or to make a retreat in a monastery. After the twelfth century, all traces of public Canonical Penances disappear. It was a rule of the Church, observed for many centuries, that, except in cases of urgency, absolution should be deferred until the penance had been performed.

Many questions connected with the history of the Sacrament of Penance still remain obscure, for lack of clear evidence. There is still some uncertainty as to the frequency of Confession in the early Church, but authorities are agreed that it was common in the ancient Celtic Church of Great Britain and Ireland, and that its use on the Continent received a great impetus from the fiery zeal of Columbanus and his Irish monks at the end of the sixth century. [52]

DEVOTIONAL CONFESSION. "Devotional Confession" or "Optional Confession" is the name we give to the Sacrament of Penance as received by those who have nothing to tell but venial sins, or sins forgiven in a previous confession. In the early ages, Christians had recourse to the Sacrament of Penance only when weighed down with the guilt of grievous sin, and devotional Confession did not exist. This latter practice, which had its origin in a keener realisation of the graces given by the Sacrament, began in the monasteries at some period later than the fourth century, and gradually spread to the laity.

We can free ourselves from venial sin at any time by acts of charity or sorrow, or by acts of the particular virtue in which we have failed, but we can do so with greater profit in the Sacrament of Penance, because it gives us an immediate increase of Sanctifying Grace. (Good acts, outside the Sacrament, may be more than sufficiently fervent to blot out venial sin. If so, they will increase our store of Sanctifying Grace, but the increase will not be so great, and may not be immediate).[53] The Sacrament also gives us Sacramental Grace, which impresses in the soul a penitential attitude, helping us to expiate sin and to struggle with fortitude and resolution to sin no more. This Grace includes a claim to those actual graces which help us to avoid deliberate venial sin, and a total or partial release from the debt of temporal punishment.

Those who have only venial sins to confess should note most carefully that their sorrow must be a *true* sorrow: it must contain the purpose of amendment; it must be internal, supernatural, and supreme. It need not be universal, i.e., it need not extend to all the venial sins the penitent may have committed. To ensure this

---

[52] On the history of Penance, see the article, "Penitence" by C. Vogel in *Encyclopedia of the Early Church*, James Clarke & Co., Cambridge, 1992. See also C 1447-8.
[53] Cf. St Thomas, S.T., i-ii, q. 114, a. 8, ad 3.

true sorrow, they should fasten their mind on some fault which they really desire to correct. Otherwise they may come to regard Confession as a matter of routine, and be exposed to the grave danger of committing sacrilege. A sorrowless confession is invalid, and, if intentional, is sacrilegious. To guard against such a profanation of God's Holy Sacrament, they should mention in every Confession some sin of their past life for which they are truly sorry: re-confessed sins of our past life are always a valid matter for absolution, since, though God has pardoned them already, He is willing to pardon them over and over again as often as they are avowed with fresh sorrow. If, however, a repeated mention causes torment or scruple, it should be omitted.

In devotional Confession, our sorrow may be perfect or imperfect. If it is imperfect, its chief motives would be: (a) the fear of God's chastisements, i.e., the fear of having to suffer at His hand either in this world or in Purgatory; (b) the fear of spiritual decay, i.e., the fear that God will not be as generous to us in the bestowal of actual graces, that the love of God in our heart will lessen, that we will weaken in our power to resist the temptation to sin, and thus find ourselves drifting towards the dread verge of mortal sin.

The Church recommends frequent Confession. "For a constant and faster advancement along the necessary path of virtue, we highly recommend the pious practice of frequent confession, introduced by the Church under the guidance of the Holy Spirit; for by it true self-knowledge is increased, Christian humility grows, bad habits are uprooted, spiritual negligence and apathy are prevented, the conscience is purified, the will strengthened, salutary spiritual direction is obtained, and grace is increased by the efficacy of the sacrament itself."[54]

THE FIRST AND SECOND RITES OF RECONCILIATION. The First Rite of reconciliation is confession in its most common form: private confession to a priest followed by one's penance in private. The Second Rite is a communal ceremony with common prayers, and readings, followed by private confession to one of the priests present, and then final prayers in common. In this Rite, the Church emphasises the communal nature of sin's effects, the duty of the Church as a whole to labour for the conversion of sinners, and this aspect of the sacrament, viz., that absolution from grave sin reconciles us with God *and with the Church* wounded by our sins.[55]

GENERAL ABSOLUTION ('THIRD RITE').[56] General absolution means absolution of a number of people together, without prior individual confession. It is only permitted where (1) danger of death threatens, and there is no time for the priests present to hear individual confessions, or (2) given the number of penitents and the paucity of priests, confessions cannot be heard within an appropriate time, and penitents will be deprived of the sacraments for a long time. Hence, a large gathering for some

---

[54] Pope Pius XII, *Mystici Corporis*, 1943, Part II: DS 3818
[55] Cf. *Lumen Gentium*, art. 11, Vatican Council II, 1964.
[56] Cf. C 1483; S. Reid, *General Sacramental Absolution*, St Austin Press, London 1998.

occasion is not sufficient reason.[57] Examples of situations where a priest could give a general absolution are: a priest on an aircraft that is headed for a crash; a priest visiting a territory only briefly whose inhabitants cannot have access to a priest *for a long time* and are too numerous to hear one by one; a chaplain with armed forces about to go into battle. Note, however, that the Church does not dispense Catholics *able to confess* from the God-given obligation to confess mortal sins. A Catholic absolved at a general absolution is still bound *by divine law* to confess any mortal sins at the next opportunity if and when it arises. Absolution is given him by the Church *on this condition*. If he has no intention to confess mortal sin when able, he does not truly receive absolution[58]—just as in a normal Confession, he does not truly receive absolution if he has no intention to perform the penance. The freely chosen rejection of one of the four parts during the sacrament vitiates the sacrament. In cases of general absolution, the Sacrament of Penance is taking place with its parts in this order: (1) contrition (2) absolution (3) confession—when possible (4) penance—when possible.

THE SIN AGAINST THE HOLY SPIRIT. *Objection.* "Not all sins can be forgiven in the sacrament of Confession, for Christ said, 'whoever speaks against the Holy Spirit *will not be forgiven*, either in this age or in the age to come.' (Matt 12:32)."[59] *Reply.* In the context, Christ was referring to the obstinacy of the Pharisees who, against the dictates of their own conscience, ascribed His miracles to Satan, and closed their hearts against the grace of faith and repentance. The Angelic Doctor, St Thomas Aquinas,[60] amongst others, enumerates six sins against the Holy Spirit: (1) *Presumption*—presuming upon God's mercy that one will be saved while refusing to do what God commands for salvation, or presuming to save oneself without divine aid. (2) *Despair*—despairing of the mercy of God, and thus not asking for it; this was the sin of Judas. (3) *Obstinacy in sin*, i.e., mortal sin—hardening one's purpose in sinning, which, if not repented of, leads to damnation. (4) *Final Impenitence*—a shamelessness leading to a refusal to be penitent even at the moment of death. (5) *Resisting the known truth*—this was the sin of the Pharisees referred to above. They had seen Christ's claims verified by plain miracles, and still refused to believe or follow Him. If we refuse to acknowledge in practice the truth of a doctrine or a commandment necessary for salvation, if we dishonestly affect not to know it or to be unconvinced of it, even after hearing it plainly, we cannot be saved. (6) *Envy of another's spiritual good*—a malicious desire for the spiritual downfall of another, which means that one has set oneself up in opposition to God's grace in the world and the growth of grace in others.

To express it simply: the sin against the Holy Spirit is a sin against the grace of faith and repentance offered by the Holy Spirit. It is unforgivable, not because of any defect in the infinite mercy of God, but because the sinner in some way does not want to be forgiven, and closes his heart against the mercy of God.[61] Bishop

---

[57] Can. 961
[58] Can. 962 §1
[59] Cf. Mk 3:29; Lk 12:10.
[60] S.T., ii-ii, q. 14, a. 2
[61] Cf. C 1864, 2091-2.

Fulton Sheen expressed the unforgivable sin as the sin of rationalising or justifying one's sins.

VII

Indulgences. INDULGENCE DEFINED. "An indulgence is a remission before God of the temporal punishment due to sins whose guilt has already been forgiven".[62] Though sanctifying grace is restored to the soul by absolution, the penitent, unless his sorrow is so intense as to be in itself a most severe affliction, still remains answerable for a debt of temporal punishment. This debt is sometimes fully discharged by the penance imposed in Confession, but there is, as a rule, a residue which must be removed either in this life or the next: in this life, by well-borne suffering or by gaining indulgences; in the next, by the pains of Purgatory. An indulgence is not a pardon of sin; still less is it a permission to commit sin.[63]

THE CHURCH HAS POWER TO GRANT INDULGENCES. The Church teaches solemnly that she has received from Christ Himself the power to grant indulgences.[64] While this statement is sufficient proof for Catholics, the doctrine may be briefly proved as follows:

(1) Christ said to the Apostles, "Whose sins you shall forgive, they are forgiven", and "Whatever you bind on earth, shall be bound in heaven, and whatever you loose on earth shall be loosed in heaven."[65] This general spiritual power of forgiving sin and granting indulgences is called "the power of the Keys", because of the expression used by our Lord in His promise to St Peter: "I will give you *the Keys of the Kingdom of Heaven*, and whatever you bind on earth... etc."[66] He therefore gave His Apostles and their successors the power to loose all spiritual bonds, to relieve the faithful of all spiritual debts—the debt of temporal as well as of eternal punishment. This power resembles that possessed by the State which can remit the death penalty, substitute a lighter for a heavier punishment, or grant complete amnesty.

(2) The Church's manner of acting, even in the early ages, shows that she was authorised by God to remit the temporal punishment due to sin. During the times when Canonical Penances were inflicted, she frequently lightened, abbreviated, or entirely remitted them. She would not have done so, had she not believed that her act was valid in the eyes of God, and that, at her ruling, He accepted the lighter for

---

[62] Pope Paul VI, *Indulgentiarum Doctrina*, Apostolic Constitution on the Revision of Indulgences, 1967, Norm 1. Cf. C 1471.

[63] These gross absurdities, one would fancy, are quite unworthy of mention, but they have not yet disappeared from the writings of some controversialists.

[64] Council of Trent, *Decree on Indulgences*: DS 1835

[65] Matt 18:18

[66] Matt 16:19

the graver penalty. This will be all the better understood if it be borne in mind that, at that period, it was her practice not to admit the sinner to final reconciliation, until he had fully performed the work of satisfaction imposed on him.

(3) The proof of the Church's power to grant indulgences is confirmed by the doctrine of the Communion of Saints. In a living body, a limb enfeebled by illness falls into debt, as it were, and receives help from its healthier neighbours; thus, the weaker members are benefited by the stronger. Now, according to the doctrine of the Communion of Saints, we are knit together into the great spiritual union of the Church; we share membership with the saints and the blessed in Heaven; we have Christ as the Head of our organism and the source of its life. It would, therefore, seem reasonable that the process observable in the physical body should have its counterpart in the spiritual; that the weak should be aided by the strong; that the wealth of the rich should be available to discharge the debts of the poor. But where is this spiritual wealth found, and by whom has it been accumulated? In the Treasury of the Church, where it has been deposited by Christ and the saints. Christ, by the Sacrifice of the Cross, has enabled us to pay all our debts of temporal as well as eternal punishment. He has filled, with inexhaustible merits, what the Church aptly calls her Treasury. There, too, are stored merits arising from the sufferings of our Blessed Lady, the Mother of Sorrows, and from the sufferings and penances of the saints and the pious faithful of every age who have made more than the necessary satisfaction for themselves.

INDULGENCES: HOW DIVIDED, BY WHOM GRANTED, HOW GAINED.
(1) Historically we may roughly divide indulgences into ancient and modern: the ancient, extending over the first twelve centuries; the modern, from about the end of the thirteenth century to the present day. The ancient indulgences were commutations (reductions) of the Canonical Penances, and were, therefore, granted only to penitents who had been guilty of grievous sin, and who were thus enabled to satisfy the Justice of God by prayers, alms-deeds, or pious pilgrimages. The modern are of wider application, being offered to all who are liable for any debt of temporal punishment.

Modern indulgences are variously divided:
(a) *Plenary* and *Partial*. *Plenary* remits the whole temporal debt, *partial* only a part. For many centuries, the latter were described as indulgences of a certain number of days or years. An *indulgence of 100 days*, for example, denoted a remission of as much of the temporal debt as would have been discharged in ancient times by a *Canonical Penance lasting 100 days*. An *indulgence of 7 years and 7 quarantines* denoted the remission that an ancient *Canonical Penance of 7 years and 7 quarantines* would have gained (a quarantine is 40 days). In 1967, Pope Paul VI abolished the measurement of days and

years, and decreed that henceforth all indulgences be simply either plenary or partial.[67]

(b) *Real, Local,* and *Personal:* These are now very rare. *Real,* when they are attached to things as, e.g., rosary beads or crosses; *Local,* when attached to places as, e.g., a church or a shrine; *Personal,* when specially granted, e.g., to the members of a religious community or confraternity.

(c) Indulgences *for the living* and *for the dead:* the former benefit the living who gain them, the latter may benefit the dead for whom they are offered. We say *may* benefit, because the Church has no authority to remit the punishment of the souls in Purgatory. An indulgence for the dead, therefore, produces its effect only by way of intercession. God may or may not ratify such an indulgence or apply it to those prayed for. An indulgence cannot be applied to another person still living.

(2) All indulgences can be granted by the Pope; a Bishop also, if he expressly has this power in law or has the faculty from the Pope.[68]

(3) CONDITIONS FOR GAINING INDULGENCES. "To be capable of gaining indulgences, a person must be baptised, not excommunicated, and in the state of grace at least upon completion of the prescribed work. To gain them, however, a capable subject must have at least the general intention of gaining them, and must fulfil the prescribed works at the time and in the manner determined by the terms of the grant."[69]

Enchiridion of Indulgences: Norms and Grants. This manual, issued by the Sacred Apostolic Penitentiary, Rome,[70] lists all the universally indulgenced works and prayers, and conditions for the same. Any previous ones not included in its norms are abolished. This official manual of indulgences lists three General Grants of Indulgences related to prayer, almsgiving and fasting:
"I. A partial indulgence is granted to the faithful who, in the performance of their duties and in bearing the trials of life, raise their mind with humble confidence to God, adding—even if only mentally—some pious invocation.
II. A partial indulgence is granted to the faithful who, in a spirit of faith and mercy, give of themselves or of their goods to serve their brethren in need.
III. A partial indulgence is granted to the faithful who, in a spirit of penance, voluntarily deprive themselves of what is licit and pleasing to them."

---

[67] *Indulgentiarum Doctrina,* Apostolic Constitution on the Revision of Indulgences
[68] Can. 995
[69] Can. 996
[70] 1st & 2nd ed. 1968; 3rd ed. 1986; 4th ed. 1999

Every sin has consequences:

Eternal punishment for mortal sins	&	Temporal punishment for all sins, mortal or venial
Being deprived of communion with God and so incapable of eternal life		To purify the unhealthy attachment to creatures, and to make amends for the harm done, penance is done either on earth or in Purgatory
Forgiveness takes away the guilt of sin…		
and takes away the eternal punishment. The person is restored to friendship with God and again made an heir to the kingdom of Heaven.		but does not take away all the temporal punishment. This purification takes place by prayer, suffering, charity. **An indulgence** takes away some or all of this temporal punishment by drawing on the treasury of the Church

An Analogy

The son's theft from his father's business had two consequences

Permanent penalty for the son's serious theft	&	Short term penalty for the effects of the theft
He was sacked from the business, and so lost his chance to inherit it		He put money before his loyalty to his father and the business and he needs to make amends for the harm done to the business
The Father's forgiveness took away the guilt of the son's theft…		
and cancelled the penalty of dismissal. He was restored to friendship with his father, and was again made an heir to the business.		Being forgiven did not automatically undo all the harm. So he has to work extra hours to repay the money. The son's indulgent father has reduced the penalty. He said: "Just do one week's extra work and I will make up the rest of the money from the family's investments."

Partial Indulgences. "The faithful who, at least with contrite heart, perform an action to which a partial indulgence is attached, obtain, in addition to the remission of temporal punishment merited by the action itself, an equal remission of punishment through the intervention of the Church."[71] Many of the Church's best known prayers have a partial indulgence attached, e.g., the Angelus, Memorare, Grace at Meals, the Litanies, Eternal rest, Hail Holy Queen, Come Holy Spirit, etc. Indeed, *all* prayers are covered under the first of the General Grants listed above. A partial indulgence can normally be gained any number of times in a day.

Plenary Indulgences. To gain a plenary Indulgence, apart from performing the specific work required, three conditions must be fulfilled, within eight days before or after the specific work:[72] (a) sacramental Confession; (b) reception of Holy Communion; (c) prayers for the intentions of the Supreme Pontiff. One Our Father and one Hail Mary for the Pope's intentions suffice, but the faithful are free to recite any other prayer for this purpose. In addition, all attachment to sin, even venial sin, must be absent.

If not all the conditions are met, the indulgence will be partial. A plenary indulgence can be gained only once in the course of a day, but a second time if danger of death arises.[73] Deserving of special mention are the following works to which a plenary indulgence is attached by the Church: adoration of the Blessed Sacrament for at least half an hour; devout reading of the Sacred Scriptures for at least half an hour; making the Way of the Cross; recitation of the Rosary in a church or public oratory, or the same in a family group, a religious Community or pious Association. To the dying, any priest has the faculty to impart the Apostolic Blessing with its plenary indulgence.[74]

(4) THEY ARE SPIRITUALLY HELPFUL. The Church teaches solemnly that indulgences are "salutary to the Christian people",[75] i.e., spiritually helpful. They are helpful not only because of the remission of temporal punishment which they effect, but also because of the intrinsic excellence of the conditions which must be fulfilled in order to gain them—since one must be in the state of grace, at least when the last of the prescribed exercises is being performed. The good works enjoined (e.g., prayer, fasting, alms-deeds) must be conscientiously performed, and sacraments (if included in the terms of the indulgence) must be worthily received. There must also be an intention of gaining the indulgence: supernatural favours are never

---

[71] *Indulgentiarum Doctrina*, Ch. V, art. 5
[72] *Enchiridion of Indulgences*, Norms, nos. 26-7, 29
[73] *Enchiridion, etc.*, Norms, no. 24
[74] Cf. Can. 530 3⁰; *Enchiridion, etc.*, Norms, no. 28
[75] T 1835

forced on any adult, but must be voluntarily accepted. For such acceptance, however, it suffices that one had at some time in the past the general intention of gaining all the indulgences one could. Experience has taught that indulgences are a great stimulus to piety and the penitential spirit: they turn Christians' thoughts to the gravity of sin, the obligation of atonement, the need of fervent prayer and good works, and the necessity of preparing to receive in the spirit of Christ the Sacraments of Penance and the Blessed Eucharist. Besides, the desire to gain indulgences is an implicit act of faith in the Church's divine authority to bind and loose.

CHAPTER 16

ANOINTING OF THE SICK

Summary

I. The solemn teaching of the Church
II. The Sacrament defined. How conferred. Its minister and its subject. Its names.
III. The effects of the Sacrament
IV. The Sacrament of Anointing of the Sick was instituted by Christ: proof (1) from the solemn teaching of the Church; (2) from Sacred Scripture; (3) from Tradition.

I

The solemn teaching of the Church. The Church teaches solemnly:
(1) that Anointing of the Sick (or Extreme Unction) is a Sacrament instituted by Christ;[1]
(2) that it confers grace, remits sin, and comforts the sick;[2]
(3) that its minister is a priest;[3]
(4) that St James speaks of this Sacrament in his epistle.[4]

II

The Sacrament defined. How it is conferred. Its minister and its subject. Its names.

THE SACRAMENT DEFINED. Anointing of the Sick, also called Extreme Unction, is the Sacrament through which those in danger of death from bodily illness or infirmity receive, by the anointing with holy oil and by the prayer of the priest, the grace of God for their spiritual strength and consolation, and often also a divine assistance by which they are restored to health.

HOW IT IS CONFERRED. In the Latin Rite, the priest confers the Sacrament by anointing the forehead and palms while saying: "Through this holy anointing and His most tender mercy, may the Lord help you by the grace of the Holy Spirit, that, freed from sin, He may save you and graciously

---

[1] T 1716
[2] T 1717
[3] T 1719
[4] T 1716, 1718. James, Chapter 5.

raise you up."[5]   In the Byzantine rite, the priest says during the several anointings, "Heal your servant from the ills of body and soul by means of this anointing".   Since the forms have differed over times and places, it may be inferred that Our Lord did not determine the precise prayer which should be recited.

A single unction suffices for the validity of the Sacrament.   Any suitable part of the body may be anointed if the forehead and hands are bandaged or out of reach.[6] "The minister is to perform the anointings with his own hand, unless a grave reason urges the use of an instrument."[7]   By instrument is meant the use of cotton, a cloth or glove, etc.[8]

ITS MINISTER.   The minister of Anointing of the Sick is any priest and only a priest.[9]

The anointing of sick people by the laity, once a practice in earlier centuries, was not the Sacrament, but a sacramental—just as sprinkling with holy water is a sacramental, an extension of Baptism, but is not the Sacrament of Baptism itself.

ITS SUBJECT.   The subject of Anointing of the Sick is "any one of the faithful who, having attained the use of reason, begins to be in danger of death through illness or old age."[10]   In the case of a child, unless it is certain that he has not yet attained the use of reason, Extreme Unction should be given.   As the primary purpose of the Sacrament is to strengthen the soul weakened by sin and temptation, it cannot be administered to those who have never been capable of committing sin.

The danger of death must arise from bodily infirmity.   Hence, soldiers going to battle or prisoners about to suffer the death penalty, cannot be anointed;   but a soldier dying of wounds can, of course, be anointed;   so, too, a prisoner who has passed from the executioner's hands, provided a hope remains that death has not yet actually taken place.

Since Anointing of the Sick supposes the presence of spiritual life which is to be strengthened, the subject must be in the state of grace in order to receive it fruitfully.   But should it happen that he has only attrition for grave sin committed and becomes unconscious before the arrival of the priest, or is unable to make his confession even by a sign, Anointing of the

---

[5] "Per istam sanctam Unctionem et suam piissimam misericordiam adiuvet te Dominus gratia Spiritus Sancti, ut a peccatis liberatum te salvet atque propitius allevet."
[6] Cf. Can. 1000 §1.
[7] Can. 1000 §2
[8] A. Cuschieri, *Anointing of the Sick: A Theological and Canonical Study*, Uni. Press of America, 1993, p.106
[9] Can. 1003 §1
[10] Can. 1004 §1

Sick will restore him to Sanctifying Grace. Without at least attrition for grave sin, the Sacrament produces no effect. Hence, it "is not to be conferred upon those who obstinately persist in a manifestly grave sin."[11]

For a dying person who is conscious and capable, the Last Sacraments are administered in this order, if possible: Penance, Anointing of the Sick, and, last of all, Viaticum (Holy Communion). The Commendation of the Dying (special prayers) may be said at any time before or after these sacraments, until death occurs.

ITS NAMES. In the first millennium, this Sacrament had no specific name, but there are references to its sacred oil as "Blessed Oil", "Oil of Faith"[12] and "Oil of the Sick". Peter Lombard (c. 1100-1160) was the first to call it "Extreme Unction". The word *extreme* applied to unction meant either the *last* (*extrema*, in Latin) unction or anointing, after those given at Baptism and Confirmation; or that the sacrament was often given to those *in extremis* (in their last moments). The Greek Church calls this Sacrament *Euchelaion*,[13] which means "Oil of Prayer". The second Vatican Council said it "may also be better called Anointing of the Sick".[14] This name was adopted in the Roman ritual for the Sacrament issued in 1972.

III

The effects of Anointing of the Sick.

SPIRITUAL EFFECTS. (1) It gives an increase of Sanctifying Grace; (2) by means of actual grace, it excites such confidence in the divine mercy that the recipient is enabled to bear more easily the inconveniences and pains of sickness; (3) it unites the gravely sick person to the Passion of Christ, for his own good and that of the whole Church; (4) it assists him to resist more easily the assaults of the Evil One; (5) it remits venial sin and removes what is termed "the remains of sin",[15] by which is meant the weakness of will and the depression caused by sinful habits in the past; (6) it cancels the debt of temporal punishment wholly or in part according to the recipient's dispositions; (7) it also remits mortal sin in the case already explained (under "Its subject").[16]

PHYSICAL EFFECT. It may restore the recipient to health, when, as the Council of Trent says, "it is expedient for the soul's salvation."[17] This effect, by no means rare, as medical experience attests, cannot be

---

[11] Can. 1007

[12] A. Cuschieri, *op. cit.*, intro., p.36

[13] εὐχελαιον

[14] *Sacrosanctum Concilium*, Constitution on the Sacred Liturgy, 1963, art. 73

[15] T 1696

[16] T 1696, 1717; C 1520-3, 1532

[17] DS 1696

satisfactorily explained as solely the result of the great peace of mind given by the Sacrament; the improvement often begins while the sick person is still unconscious. On the other hand, it need not be ascribed to any direct miraculous intervention on the part of God, but rather to a special activity of His ordinary Providence by which He aids and stimulates in a natural, though quite exceptional way, the recuperative powers of the patient. The prayers which the priest recites after the anointing may ask God to heal the sick man. These prayers have a special sacramental efficacy, but they do not appeal for the performance of a miracle. It will, therefore, be understood that, even for the patient's physical welfare, it is most important to summon the priest before his system is so enfeebled that recovery without a manifest miracle would be impossible.

The responsibility of those in charge of the sick. If the patient is conscious when the priest arrives, he can be properly prepared for Anointing of the Sick, and will derive all the more benefit from its reception. If he is aware of his serious condition, he should ask himself for the priest; but if he fails to do so, the responsibility devolves on his friends or attendants. They should send word to the priest at once; to delay would be both foolish and unkind. The priest is helped by God's grace to deal with sick people, to remove their apprehensions, and to prepare them to receive the consoling Sacrament of Christ with joy and gratitude.

IV

The Sacrament of Anointing of the Sick was instituted by Christ.
PROOF FROM THE SOLEMN TEACHING OF THE CHURCH. The Church, in the exercise of her infallible authority, declares the institution by Christ of the Sacrament of Anointing of the Sick to be a doctrine given to her by God Himself. This proof suffices for Catholics. The following proofs are added for fuller instruction.

PROOF FROM SACRED SCRIPTURE. St James says: "Is any among you sick? Let him call for the elders [presbyters, priests] of the Church, and let them pray over him, anointing him with oil in the name of the Lord; and the prayer of faith will save the sick man, and the Lord will raise him up; and if he has committed sins, he will be forgiven."[18] The rite of which St James speaks is manifestly our Sacrament of Anointing of the Sick: (a) The rite is performed by the priests of the Church and consists of prayer and anointing; (b) it relieves the sick man and causes forgiveness of sin; (c) it is administered in the name of the Lord, i.e., by the command or through the power of Christ; (d) the inspired instruction here given by St James clearly indicates the divine institution ("in the name of the Lord"), for Christ alone has the power to make an external sign be a cause of grace. We may take it that St

---

[18] James 5:14-15

James, in speaking of "presbyters" instead of "a presbyter", did not absolutely require the presence of several priests for the valid administration of the Sacrament. If he did, very many Christians would die without its consolations.

During our Blessed Lord's Public Ministry, He sent the Twelve out on mission, and they "anointed with oil many that were sick and healed them."[19] This was not the sacrament itself, but prefigured it. Anointing of the Sick is the Church's continuation of the healing ministry of Our Saviour. It may confer renewed strength or even recovery from illness. And it always confers, upon the well-disposed, that more important healing of which the Lord's miracles were a sign: deliverance from sin and its effects upon the soul.

PROOF FROM TRADITION. Early testimony is scanty for several reasons: Anointing of the Sick was generally regarded as the complement of Penance, which is how Origen (d. 254) depicted it; it was not preceded by the lengthy instruction and preparation that occurred before Baptism, Confirmation and Communion—hence we have no lengthy discourses on it as for the first three Sacraments; it was not considered a part of the basic instruction of a Christian; it was not administered in church; it was not the object of controversy, requiring defence and exposition; and the earliest commentary on the Epistle of James that has come down to us is that of the Venerable Bede (d. 735).[20] Still, we may cite the following early witnesses:

(1) The *Apostolic Tradition* of Hippolytus c. 215, has a blessing by the bishop said over oil which will be used for the sick.[21]

(2) Origen refers to this Sacrament, saying it fulfils what St James describes.[22]

(3) Aphraates the Persian Sage (c. 280- c. 345) says that olive oil is used by Christians to "anoint the sick".[23]

(4) The Sacramentary of Serapion (c. 350) contains a prayer said over oil, asking God to bestow the power of His Son upon it, that it may "be effective for the casting out of every disease and every bodily infirmity, … for good grace and remission of sins, … for health and integrity of soul, body and spirit".[24] The prayer illustrates that its use was frequent and that the doctrine held was as ours today.

(5) St John Chrysostom (d. 407), quoting the words of St James, says the dignity of the priesthood springs from the power of forgiving sin, which, in one of its forms, is exercised in the Anointing of the Sick.[25]

(6) A letter of Pope Innocent I to Decentius, Bishop of Gubbio, Italy, 19 March 416, answers his query about the text of James 5, and assures him that a bishop, as much as the priests, may administer this anointing: "if the bishop is able to do so, or thinks it suitable, he should personally visit the sick person and bless him and anoint him with the chrism without delay".[26]

---

[19] Mk 6:13
[20] Mons. B. Poschmann, *Penance and the Anointing of the Sick*, Herder, Freiburg 1964, p.236
[21] G. Dix (ed.) *The Apostolic Tradition*, SPCK, London 1968, V, p.10
[22] *Hom. in Lev.* 2, 4
[23] *Treatises*, 23, 3
[24] F.X. Funk, *Didasc. et Const. Apost.*, Vol. II, p.191
[25] *De Sacerd.* III, 6
[26] DS 216

(7) The non-Catholic Eastern Churches: Anointing of the Sick is administered at the present day by all of them, with the exception of the Ethiopian and Armenian churches, who, however, as their ancient books testify, recognised the Sacrament at the time of their separation.[27]

---

[27] M. Jugie, *Theologia Dogmatica Christianorum Orientalium ab Ecclesia Catholica Dissidentium*, Paris, 1935, Tom. V, p.637

CHAPTER 17

HOLY ORDERS

Summary

I.   The solemn teaching of the Church.
II. The Sacrament defined. Its minister and its subject. How the Sacrament is conferred.
III. The effects of the Sacrament, general and particular. The powers and graces received by the Deacon, the Priest, and the Bishop.
IV. The different kinds of Orders: Sacramental and non-Sacramental; Major (Holy) and Minor. The Ministries. Male ordination. Deaconesses. The celibacy of the clergy.
V.   The Hierarchy of Orders. The Hierarchy of Jurisdiction.
VI. The Sacrament of Holy Orders was instituted by Christ: Proof: (1) from the authority of the Church; (2) from Sacred Scripture; (3) from Tradition; (4) from reason. - Replies to objections.

I

The solemn teaching of the Church. The Church teaches solemnly:
(1) that Holy Orders is a sacrament instituted by Christ;[1]
(2) that it imparts the Holy Spirit and imprints an indelible mark or character on the soul;[2]
(3) that in the New Testament there is a visible and external priesthood;[3]
(4) that Christ conferred the priesthood upon the Apostles at the last Supper;[4]
(5) that through this sacrament, there is set up in the Church, by divine ordinance, a hierarchy consisting of Bishops, Priests, and Ministers;[5]
(6) that the Episcopate is superior to the Priesthood; that the Bishop has power to confirm and ordain;[6]
(7) that the Priest has power to consecrate and offer the Body and Blood of the Lord, and to forgive sin.[7]

---

[1] T 1601, 1773
[2] T 1774
[3] T 1771
[4] T 1752
[5] T 1776
[6] T 1777
[7] T 1771

II

The Sacrament defined.   Its minister and its subject.   How the Sacrament is conferred.

THE SACRAMENT DEFINED.   Holy Orders is the Sacrament which imparts to a man the gift of the Holy Spirit, so as to enable him to perform validly and worthily the sacred functions of deacon, priest, or bishop.   The sacrament, therefore, can be conferred in three degrees: diaconate, priesthood, or episcopate.

ITS MINISTER.   The minister of this Sacrament is a Bishop.

ITS SUBJECT.   The subject is any baptised person of the male sex.
For *valid* ordination to the diaconate, the man must be baptised.   For *lawful* ordination to the priesthood, the candidate must be a deacon.   For *valid* ordination to the priesthood he need not be a deacon, because the power given with priesthood includes that of diaconate.   For ordination to the episcopate (office of bishop), a man must first be a priest.

HOW IT IS CONFERRED.   The Sacrament is conferred by the imposition of hands and prayer.   Thus, like all the other Sacraments, it is constituted by two factors.[8]   The imposition of hands, or laying on of hands, shows that some kind of power is being given.   The words of the prayer show that it is a sacred ministerial power, and express what kind of power.

"The imposition of *hands*" denotes the use of the right hand alone or both hands together.   Besides "the imposition of hands", there is also, as will be noted below, "the extension of hands", which describes the action of the Bishop in stretching out his right hand or both hands towards the candidate or the newly ordained.   It is regarded as introducing or continuing the imposition of hands, and has the same meaning.   When Christ prescribed the imposition of hands for the giving of Holy Orders, He prescribed nothing unfamiliar to the Apostles: they knew that Moses, at the command of the Lord, laid his hand on the head of Joshua to appoint him as his successor;   and they had seen Christ Himself impart a blessing or restore health in the same way.[9]

The ceremonies and prayers that follow are those of the Roman Rite.
The rite of conferring Diaconate.[10]   During the preliminary ceremonies, the candidate promises to observe celibacy, to pray the Liturgy of the Hours daily, and to respect and obey his Bishop.   The Bishop alone lays hands upon the man's head in silence, then with hands extended over him, says the prayer of ordination, including the

---

[8] Pius XII, Apostolic Constitution, *Sacramentum Ordinis*, 1947: DS 3859
[9] Num 27:18,23; Mk 10:16; Lk 13:13
[10] = deaconship, deaconate

essential prayer: "Send forth the Holy Spirit upon him, Lord, we beseech, that he be strengthened by the gift of Thy sevenfold grace to carry out faithfully the work of Thy ministry."[11]

Other prayers and ceremonies follow as appointed by the Church: the new deacon is vested in stole and dalmatic, and is presented with the Book of the Gospels.

The rite of conferring Priesthood. After preliminary ceremonies, during which the deacon to be ordained priest renews his promise of respect and obedience to his Bishop, the Bishop lays both hands on the candidate's head in silence. The priests then do the same, one by one. Then the Bishop alone, with hands extended over the ordinand, says the prayer of ordination, the essential part of which is: "Grant, we beseech, Almighty Father, to this Thy servant, the dignity of the Priesthood; renew the Spirit of holiness deep within him; may he hold, O God, the office of second rank received from Thee and by the example of his behaviour afford a pattern of conduct".[12]

The other ceremonies, though obligatory, are not of its essence: the newly ordained priest is vested in stole and chasuble, the Bishop anoints the palms of his hands with Chrism,[13] and presents him with the paten holding the host, and the chalice containing wine and water. The priest then, conjointly with the ordaining prelate, celebrates Mass, and, for the first time, consecrates the Body and Blood of Christ.

Conferring the Episcopate. No one may consecrate a bishop without a mandate from the chief Bishop, the Pope.[14] The principal consecrating bishop must have at least two other consecrating bishops with him: a rule made by the Council of Nicea in 325. These other two bishops also impose hands and recite the essential prayer.[15] In the absence of others, one bishop alone suffices to confer the episcopate.

The rite of conferring it. After preliminary ceremonies, during which the priest chosen to be Bishop promises to discharge the episcopal office faithfully, and promises obedience to the Successor of Peter, the consecrating Bishops in turn lay both hands on the head of the priest in silence. The principal consecrator places the open Book of the Gospels upon the head of the Bishop-elect; two deacons hold the Book above his head while the principal consecrator, with hands extended over the Bishop-elect, recites the prayer of consecration. All the consecrating Bishops recite the essential prayer: "And pour out upon this chosen one that power which is from Thee, the governing Spirit whom Thou didst give to Thy beloved Son Jesus Christ, whom He gave to the holy Apostles, who established the Church in every place to be Thy temple for the unceasing glory and praise of Thy name."[16] This is the Sacrament of Holy Orders in its plenitude.

---

[11] Pius XII, *Sacramentum Ordinis*, 1947: DS 3860; Paul VI, Apost. Const., *Pontificalis Romani*, 1968

[12] Idem

[13] For "Chrism" see p.463.

[14] Can. 1013

[15] Pius XII, *Episcopalis consecrationis*, 1944

[16] Paul VI, *Pontificalis Romani*, 1968. Cf. C 1586.

Outside the essential rite, and yet of great moment, other rites follow: the new Bishop's head is anointed with Chrism, he is presented with the Book of Gospels, and is invested with his episcopal ring, mitre and pastoral staff (crosier).

III

The effects of the Sacrament of Holy Orders. IN GENERAL: the effects of the Sacraments of Holy Orders are: (1) the Sacramental Character; (2) Sanctifying Grace, and (3) Sacramental Grace.

The Character. "This sacrament configures the ordinand to Christ by a special grace of the Holy Spirit, so that he may be Christ's instrument for His Church. By ordination is received the capacity to act as a representative of Christ, Head of the Church, in His triple office of priest, prophet and king."[17] The sacramental character not only marks the soul indelibly, but also gives the power required for the exercise of the Order conferred. Because of this indelible mark, a second reception of the same ordination or a return to a truly lay state is impossible.

Sacramental Grace perfects the souls of God's ministers by directing and strengthening them to perform their different duties of instructing, ruling and sanctifying the faithful. This Grace orients the soul of the priest to the sentiments and works of spiritual fatherhood. Sacramental Grace consists also in the claim to special actual graces, or series of actual graces, which the Bishop, Priest, or Deacon needs for the worthy discharge of his sacred functions.

IN PARTICULAR: (a) The Deacon receives the power of preaching the Gospel effectively, of worthily and reverently assisting the Priest and the Bishop at Mass, of exercising the ministry of charity and of faithfully fulfilling his other duties.

It is the office of a deacon to: administer solemn Baptism; be custodian and distributor of the Blessed Eucharist; bring Viaticum to the dying; officiate at marriages and bless them in the name of the Church; officiate at funerals and burials; administer sacramentals and certain blessings; preside over the worship and prayer of the faithful, e.g., Benediction and Vespers; preach to the people and instruct them; and assist in works of charity and functions of administration.[18] A deacon may give those blessings explicitly allowed him by the liturgical books, but none outside the liturgy.[19]

---

[17] C 1581
[18] Cf. *Lumen Gentium*, Dogmatic Constitution on the Church, Vatican Council II, 1964, art. 29.
[19] Pont. Com. Decr. Conc. Vat. II Interp., 3 Dec. 1974, A.A.S., LXVI (1974) p.667. Cf. Can. 1169 §3.

(b) The Priest receives the power of forgiving sin in the Sacrament of Penance, and of offering the great Sacrifice of the Mass. He is made another Christ, a living representative of the Redeemer whose work he continues. A priest is essentially a mediator, a sharer in Christ's mediation. To God, he offers Christ's sacrifice and man's prayers, petitions, repentance and needs. From God, he brings Christ Himself and His truth, love, grace and mercy.

His office includes all that assigned to a Deacon; as well, to administer Anointing of the Sick, and, when necessary, Confirmation. As a co-operator with the Bishop, a Priest has the pastoral charge to teach, sanctify and govern the portion of the Lord's flock assigned to him.[20]

It is the sacred character received through the sacrament of Holy Orders which distinguishes the Catholic priest from a Protestant minister. A minister holds an office deputed to him by his community, does not receive Holy Orders, and does not have—nor claim to have—the power to consecrate the Body and Blood of Christ or to forgive sins. The distinctive character in the soul is the basis for the distinctive clerical dress required of the priest.[21] His wearing of priestly dress is a proclamation of Christ, an outward sign of his consecration by and to Christ, and makes him recognisable and available to God's people.

(c) The Bishop receives the power of confirming and ordaining. He is given the plenitude of the Priesthood and is made a Successor of the Apostles.

The office of a Bishop includes all that belongs to a Deacon and Priest. Moreover, he regulates the celebration of the Sacraments, especially the Eucharist, and the discipline regarding Penance. He governs and legislates for the particular church (diocese) assigned to him, gives judgement for his subjects, regulates the good order of the apostolate, and teaches his people in the name of Christ.[22]

THE BISHOP'S POWER OF ORDERS. It is through our Bishops, therefore, that the sacred power bestowed by Christ on His Apostles to consecrate the Blessed Eucharist, to absolve from sin, to confirm, and to give the Holy Unction to the dying, is always kept alive in the Church. Through his power of ordaining, the Bishop is enabled to provide his diocese with priests. Through his priests, in turn, he causes people to be born into the Church. He feeds them with the Bread of Life, and tends them in spiritual illness.

UNION WITH THE CHURCH AND CO-OPERATION WITH GRACE. The Deacon or Priest's power to teach effectively the truths of faith remains inactive until his Bishop has appointed him to preach. Only then does he become associated with

---

[20] Cf. *Lumen Gentium*, art. 28.
[21] Can. 284
[22] Cf. *Lumen Gentium*, 25-27.

the successors of the Apostles, whom alone Christ commissioned to teach all nations. Only then are men bound to listen to him. But even then, his power of preaching will not fully assert itself without that zeal which is the fruit of Sacramental Grace. Something similar may be said of his power to assist worthily in the Sanctuary. Lawful appointment joins him to those whom Christ ordered to sanctify men by sacred rites, but it is only by co-operating with Sacramental Grace that he can acquire for himself, and communicate to the congregation, the true spirit of reverence for the ceremonies of the Church and the Mysteries which they illustrate.

IV

Major and Minor Orders. The ministries. Male ordination. Deaconesses. The celibacy of the clergy.
There have been eight Orders in the Roman Church, viz., the Order of Bishop, Priest, Deacon, Subdeacon, Acolyte, Exorcist, Lector (Reader), and Porter (Door-keeper).
MAJOR ORDERS. The Episcopate, the Priesthood, and the Diaconate are conferred through the Sacrament of Holy Orders. They are sometimes known as Major Orders, to distinguish them from Minor Orders. These latter were not instituted by Christ, but by the Church, and are therefore not part of the Sacrament.

THE MINOR ORDERS. By the middle of the 3rd century in Rome, there were subdeacons, acolytes, exorcists, lectors and porters[23]—offices which became known collectively as the minor orders. Their names suggest the duties originally attached to them. The *Subdeacon* was one step lower than a Deacon, assisted at the altar, and by later legislation was bound to celibacy and the recitation of the Divine Office (the Breviary, the Liturgy of the Hours). In the West, from the 13th century, the Subdiaconate was regarded as a Major Order, even if not instituted by Christ. The *Acolyte* ministered to the Subdeacon. He had charge of lighting the candles for Mass, helped at the serving of the wine and water, and was the bearer of letters from one Christian community to another. It was the *Exorcist's* duty to exorcise evil spirits. The *Lector* read portions of the Sacred Scripture for the people, and instructed children in the rudiments of doctrine. The *Porter* had the custody of the sacred edifice. He called the faithful to service by ringing the bell, and helped to preserve order among the congregation.

For many centuries, before minor orders were conferred, the candidate for priesthood received the first *Tonsure*, a ceremony by which he was set apart and became a cleric. Over time the minor orders became only steps by which a candidate approached Major or Holy Orders. The office of Exorcist was discharged by a priest specially authorised by his bishop, and the duties connected with the other minor orders were fulfilled chiefly by the laity.

---

[23] Eusebius, *Eccl. Hist.* VI, 43, 11

HOLY ORDERS	
and the administration of the Sacraments	
Sacrament	**Administered by**
Baptism	Bishop, Priest, Deacon *or anyone in an emergency*
Confirmation	Bishop Priest *with permission or in an emergency*
Holy Eucharist	Bishop or Priest *celebrate Mass*
Penance	Bishop Priest *provided he has faculties from the Bishop*
Anointing of the Sick	Bishop or Priest
Holy Orders	Bishop
Matrimony	Bride & Groom *confer the Sacrament upon each other. The Bishop, Priest or Deacon only officiate.*

THE MINISTRIES. In 1972, in the document *Ministeria Quaedam*, Pope Paul VI abolished the subdiaconate and minor orders in the Western Church, and replaced them with *lector* and *acolyte*, henceforth to be known as "ministries", open to laymen. At the same time, the ceremony of Tonsure was abolished, and replaced by a rite of "candidacy". Entrance into the clerical state now takes place at diaconate. Before diaconate, a candidate will have first received the two ministries.

Laymen[24] may receive the stable ministry of *acolyte* in a liturgical rite, appointing them to serve at the altar and to assist, where needed, in the distribution of Holy Communion, and, in the absence of a deacon or priest, in presiding at liturgical prayers, conferring Baptism and exposing the Blessed Sacrament. Laymen may similarly receive the stable ministry of *lector*, principally to exercise the ministry of the word of God.

The Eastern Churches retain the minor orders. Each of them has some of the following: subdeacon, acolyte, exorcist, lector, porter, cantor. The Roman Church retains them in the Traditionalist clerical communities operating under the provisions of *Ecclesia Dei*.[25]

MALE ORDINATION. *The Church's constant tradition.* "Only a baptised *man* receives sacred ordination *validly*."[26] A woman cannot be ordained validly. In continuity with the Jewish Synagogue, the Church has always excluded women from the service of the altar. This is not her own regulation; it was established so by her Divine Founder. A few heretical sects in the first centuries entrusted priestly functions to women, or had priestesses, and were condemned by the Fathers for

---

[24] 'viri laici', Can. 230 §1. For their functions, see Can. 230, 910 §2, 943.
[25] Apostolic Letter of John Paul II, 1988
[26] Can. 1024: 'solus vir'

this innovation.[27] Regarding herself as bound by her Founder's will for the ministry as He established it, the early Church's witness is unanimous on this subject. Early canonical documents also evidence the mind of the Church.[28] St Chrysostom, in his classic work on the priesthood c. 387 A.D., says simply, "Divine law has excluded women from the ministry".[29] Until very recent times, male priesthood enjoyed peaceful and universal acceptance in the Church both of the East and West, and did not require extended defence or explanation. All non-Catholic Eastern churches are at one with the Catholic Church on this doctrine. Over the centuries, some writers have proffered weak arguments to explain the Church's position, but the Church has not depended upon them. In any case, a truth is not disproved by an invalid argument in its defence. The points that follow are taken mainly from a document of the Magisterium issued to offer considerations in explanation of the Church's position.[30]

The attitude of Christ. Christ's attitude to women differed markedly from that of other Jews. He let the legally impure woman touch His cloak to be cured, He let the woman who was a public sinner wash and dry His feet in the house of the Pharisee, He pardoned the adulteress, He forbade men to divorce their wives and upheld the marriage bond as applying equally to men and women, He was accompanied by women followers, He appeared first to women when risen from the dead and commissioned them to inform the Apostles.[31] Being the divine Son of God, Christ was not bound by His culture and times in His decision to choose only men for the Apostolic college. In fact, this was a counter-cultural decision, since the ancient pagan religions regularly had their priestesses. Even the great Mother of God, the perfect embodiment of the Church, was not invested with the powers and dignity of the priesthood. Below we shall see why.

The practice of the Apostles. The Apostles and their successors continued in this tradition, while always availing themselves of the services of women in evangelisation, instruction and works of charity. Several of them are mentioned in the New Testament, such as Phoebe, Priscilla, and Lydia. There was never any question, however, of making them presbyters or official preachers of the Word. The Holy Spirit, speaking through St Paul, says: "the women should keep silence in the churches ... For it is shameful for a woman to speak in church ... what I am writing to you is a command of the Lord." "I permit no woman to teach or to have authority over men":[32] women are excluded from the *teaching* and *governing* mandate of Holy Orders by reason of "a command of the Lord". St Paul writes not out of

---

[27] Tertullian, *De Praesc. Haer.* 41, 5; *De Virg. Veland.* 9, 1; *De Baptismo* 17,5; Firmilian Caes. in Cyprian, *Ep.* 75; Origen, *Fragm. in 1 Cor.* 74; St Epiphanius, *Panar.* 49, 2, 1;

[28] *Didasc. Apost.* 3, 6, 133; *Const. Apost.* III, 6 & 9; Hippolytus, *Trad. Apost.* 11; Laodicea, can. 11

[29] *De Sacerd.* III, 9

[30] Cf. *Inter Insigniores*, S. Congregation for the Doctrine of the Faith, 1976.

[31] Matt 9:20-2; Lk 7:37ff.; Jn 8:11; Mk 10:2-12; Lk 8:1-3

[32] 1 Cor 14:34-7; 1 Tim 2:12

mere prejudice; it is he who authors one of the most vigorous texts in the New Testament on the equality of men and women as children of God.[33]

The role of women. The Church has always profited from the valuable services of women in the instruction of the faithful, service of the sick and needy, and the works of the apostolate. As the work of spreading the Gospel in Apostolic times was facilitated by the exertions of devout women, so it is continued today by the nuns and sisters of the numerous orders and congregations. There are women, such as Sts Clare, Gertrude the Great, Birgitta of Sweden, Catherine of Siena, Angela Merici, Teresa of Jesus (of Avila), Margaret Mary Alacoque, Therese of Lisieux, and Mother Teresa of Calcutta, who have bequeathed an outstanding heritage to the Church. Lay women also direct home and family life. They are the bearers of culture and form the souls of their children for life. Many of the saints were indebted under God for their sanctity to the influence of pious mothers, and much of the good that there is in the world can be traced to the same source. It is noteworthy, too, how many of the great mystics and recipients of divine messages for the renewal of Christian and priestly life have been women.

The teaching of the Church. In 1994, Pope John Paul II promulgated an Apostolic Epistle, saying that in this matter, "which pertains to the Church's divine constitution itself ... we declare that the Church has no faculty whatsoever to confer priestly ordination on women, and that this judgement is to be held definitively by all the faithful."[34]

The basis for male priests only. The priest must be a man because he represents a man, Jesus Christ, and by his ordination acts *in persona Christi Capitis*, in the very person of Christ the Head, who is the *Bridegroom* of His Bride, the Church.[35] Here we see why the ordination of the Blessed Virgin would not make sense: she represents the Church *as Bride*, not the Church's Head and Groom. The ultimate reason for ordination of men only to represent Christ as Head, lies, therefore, in the fact that God the Son became a man and not a woman. He became a man in order to be the *Husband* of the Church and at the same time the perfect image of the *Fatherhood* of God.[36] A woman cannot be a Christian priest, because she cannot be a husband and father. This leads us to the question of why God is called *Father*.

First, let us keep in mind how children stand in relation to their father and mother. The child is conceived and grows *outside* the father and is clearly distinct from him. The child is conceived and grows *within* the mother. God has revealed that He is to be called *Father*, for a father more than a mother is an image of the transcendence and might of God. A woman, on the other hand, more than a man, is an image of those other immanent and tender qualities of God in His relations with the human race. These various divine qualities have been demonstrated in the Incarnation and the sending of the Holy Spirit.

---

[33] Gal 3:26-8
[34] Epistola Apostolica *Ordinatio Sacerdotalis*. Cf. C 1577, 1598.
[35] Cf. 2 Cor 11:2; Eph 5:23-32; Jn 3:29; Rev 19:7, 9.
[36] Cf. Jn 1:18; 14:8-10; Col 1:15; 2 Cor 4:4; Heb 1:1-3.

In human generation, the man is the (1) initiating, (2) self-giving and (3) fecundating partner; the woman, correspondingly, is receptive, co-creative and fruitful. In the relationship between God and man, God is the (1) Initiator (2) who gives Himself and (3) is the Lord and Life-Giver. Thus, God the Father is properly called *Father*, is represented by Christ, and described in male terms. The responsive, co-operating fruitful Church is most appropriately called *Mother*, is represented by the Virgin Mary, and described in female terms. A woman cannot become fruitful of herself, without man; the human race cannot by itself become spiritually fruitful or holy without the grace of God. Nature is an image of grace, and grace does not destroy but perfects and elevates nature.

But if the First Person of the Trinity is given a female title, then God will be reduced in men's minds to an immanent world-spirit that is barely distinguishable from the world itself. Thus it is that those who call God "Mother" very soon degenerate into Earth-worship. The God-Man, Adam-Eve, Jesus-Mary, Christ-Church couplets are primordial in the Christian religion. It is impossible to reconstitute them without denying Revelation and changing the religion itself.

DEACONESSES. St Paul says to the Romans, "I commend to you our sister Phoebe, a deaconess of the church at Cenchreae ... for she has been a helper of many and of myself as well."[37] While this is the first use of the word *deaconess*, the ecclesiastical institution of deaconess as a state of life did not arise until much later, i.e., after 200 A.D. The word *deaconess* until then could mean a servant or helper in a broad sense. There were deaconesses in several of the churches of the East from the third century on. They were officially instituted or commissioned to assist in the instruction and baptism of women, and visiting of sick women who needed bathing and desired Holy Communion. In other regions, some religious, especially abbesses, were made deaconesses. The *Apostolic Tradition* of Hippolytus c. 215 A.D. says, "A deaconess does not bless, nor perform anything belonging to the office of presbyters or deacons, but is only to keep the doors, and to minister to the presbyters in the baptising of women, for the sake of decency".[38] The priest anointed the head or forehead of a woman after Baptism, but for decency's sake, the deaconess used to perform the additional anointings that followed.

The office and meaning of deaconess varied greatly from one church to another and one region to another. Some regions never had them at all: deaconesses were unknown to the church in Egypt, to the Maronites and the Slavs, and they appeared only belatedly among the Armenians. The Latin Church had no deaconesses in the first four centuries. Deaconesses in the east and west gradually declined in numbers until they disappeared some time probably in the 11th century.[39]

The rank of deaconess was an ecclesiastical institution not part of the Sacrament of Holy Orders. This is seen by the essential diversity of ways of instituting deaconesses, by the wide variation in their functions, and by the differing explanations regarding them—for whatever pertains to the essence of a Sacrament

---

[37] Rom 16:1-2
[38] *Trad. Apost.* VIII, 28
[39] Cf. A.G. Martimort, *Deaconesses: An Historical Study*, Ignatius Press, San Francisco 1986.

is essentially the same in matter, form and doctrine throughout the Church. What was uniform was that deaconesses never taught or preached in public, and administered no sacraments, except that they sometimes gave Holy Communion to the sick or in convents. We have seen above that a woman cannot receive sacramental ordination.[40] That a woman cannot be a deacon follows from the fact that the diaconate is a part of Holy Orders.[41] A deaconess was not a female deacon, therefore.

THE CELIBACY OF THE CLERGY.[42] The celibacy of the clergy takes its origin from the example and teaching of Christ. His Church, which is His Virgin Bride and His pure Body, is fittingly served by a virginal priesthood. Among Jews, the priesthood was hereditary, yet even in the Jewish Dispensation where the priest fathered children to whom his functions descended, continence was prescribed during his time of service in the Temple.

In the early Church, many, if not all clerics—whether celibate, married or widowed—observed perfect continence after ordination. Naturally, therefore, the consent of a married man's wife was required before he entered upon Holy Orders. It is an undisputed fact that *after* ordination there could be no marriage for widowed or celibate clerics—a regulation which seems only to make sense if conjugal abstinence was demanded even of married clerics. St Paul declares that a deacon, presbyter or bishop must be a "husband of one wife",[43] the reason being that a second marriage after widowhood was a sign that a man could not live in the dedication demanded of a cleric. The Synod of Elvira, Spain (c. 300), was the first to legislate in written form this ancient norm of continence for single and married clerics. Thereafter in the West, other local councils enacted similar legislation. In the East, the contrary practice spread of allowing clerics to remain with their wives. From the 7th century on, in both West and East, generally only monks or single clerics were elevated to the episcopate. By the 13th century, the Western Church had generally ceased ordaining married men. The Eastern Churches, however, continued to do so, as they do today, but generally selected unmarried priests to be bishops, or else required that bishops live apart from their wives. In the West, since the Second Vatican Council, married men are able to become permanent deacons.

The Latin Church in requiring celibacy of her candidates for the priesthood is influenced chiefly by considerations such as the following: (1) The state of virginity is holier than that of marriage, as the Church has defined,[44] and is, therefore, more desirable in those who minister at the altar. This is testified by the lives of Our Lord and the Blessed Virgin, and by the words of St Paul.[45] (2) Celibate clergy have

---

[40] C 1577, 1598

[41] C 1536, 1538, 1554, 1570, 1572-4, 1576, 1600

[42] The historical evidence can be found in: C. Cochini, S.J., *The Apostolic Origins of Priestly Celibacy*, Ignatius Press, San Francisco 1990; R. Cholij, *Clerical Celibacy in East and West*, Gracewing, U.K. 1989; Cardinal A. Stickler, *The Case for Clerical Celibacy*, Ignatius, San Francisco 1995; S. Heid, *Zölibat in der frühen Kirche*, Schöningh, Paderborn 1997.

[43] 1 Tim 3:2,12; Tit 1:6

[44] T 1810

[45] 1 Cor 7:32-34; cf. Matt 19:12; Apoc 14:4.

renounced marriage for the sake of the Kingdom of Heaven and so can serve God with an undivided heart. They are not distracted from their work by family affections and cares, and are free to work wherever they are needed. (3) Celibacy in the priest is a sign and stimulus of charity, and a singular source of spiritual fruitfulness in the world. The celibate priest is a sign of the mystical marriage of the Church to Christ and is better fitted for a broader acceptance of fatherhood in Christ.[46] Celibacy is most fitting in him who, by ordination, is configured to Christ the Head and Spouse of the Church. (4) The priest's vow of chastity wins for him the respect of his people. It disposes them to listen to his instructions, and to approach him with confidence in the confessional.

But does not the Church deprive herself of potential priests by not choosing married men who have a priestly vocation from God? In answering this, we ought first be clear that a vocation to the priesthood from God is confirmed *via the Church* and never outside the Church or contrary to her. The Church is free to choose whom she will for the priesthood, and commits no injustice in not choosing married men. To consider things in their proper light, we should say rather that all men *first* have a vocation either to the celibate or the married state; and it is from those who have a celibate vocation that the Roman Church chooses *some* to be priests, if they are willing. No injustice is committed, since no one, married or celibate, has a right to the priesthood. It is an Order conferred upon some, but not upon all.

The Latin Church's law of celibacy may be stated as follows: (a) No one in Holy Orders can contract valid marriage. (b) No married man in the Latin Church can receive the Priesthood licitly without permission of the Holy See, which is rarely granted and only for specified cases. From the time of Pius XII on, exception has been made when a married Anglican or Protestant minister becomes a Catholic and offers himself for the priesthood.[47]

The Eastern Churches in communion with Rome nearly all permit married men to receive Diaconate and subsequently Priesthood, but not the Episcopate. They do not allow those already in Holy Orders to marry. Their preference for unmarried men for the Episcopate is a proof that they regard virginity as the higher state. *Common to both East and West, both Orthodox and Catholic, is the tradition that once a man is ordained, he cannot then marry. This applies also after the death of a cleric's wife.* Eastern Church candidates for priesthood are normally bound to celibacy when they are training in Latin Rite territories.

V

The hierarchy of Orders. The hierarchy of jurisdiction. In general, we mean by hierarchy (literally, "sacred government") the ministers or officials of the Church, arranged in ranks according to the degree (1) of spiritual

---

[46] *Lumen Gentium*, 42; *Presbyterorum Ordinis*, Decree on the Ministry and Life of Priests, 1965, art. 16

[47] Can. 277, 1042 n.1, 1047 §2 n.3

power (Orders), or (2) of sacred authority (jurisdiction) which they possess.[48]

Christ charged His Church with the duty of teaching and governing men, and of sanctifying them by the administration of the Sacraments. The Church teaches and governs through the hierarchy of jurisdiction. She sanctifies through the hierarchy of Orders.

THE HIERARCHY OF ORDERS (*Spiritual power*). The hierarchy of Orders consists of Bishops, Priests, and Ministers[49] of the Church. The Deacon is inferior to the Priest, the Priest to the Bishop. Every Priest is also a Deacon. Every Bishop is at once Bishop, Priest, and Deacon. The Papacy is not a holy Order. The Pope, therefore, so far as the power of Orders is concerned, ranks no higher than a Bishop.

The Council of Trent, in defining that the hierarchy of Orders is of divine institution, did not mean that Christ gave the Church three distinct classes of ministers, but three distinct degrees of spiritual power. All these three degrees were possessed by each of the Apostles, the first Bishops of the Church, on the very day of her foundation, and later, according to the ordinance of Christ, were given by them, in whole or part, to others as need arose. In the Church there must always be Bishops, but there need not be Priests or Deacons as such.

THE HIERARCHY OF JURISDICTION (*Sacred authority*). Jurisdiction is authority to *teach* and *govern*. In every well-ordered society, the degree of authority to be exercised by each official must be clearly marked out. Otherwise, nothing but confusion would arise. In the Church, all good order and efficiency would vanish if every Bishop were to teach, make laws, and administer the Sacraments in any part of the world he pleased. Hence the necessity of a hierarchy of jurisdiction. Jurisdiction goes with the office held. As instituted by Christ Himself, it consists of the Bishops of the Church with the Pope at their head. The Pope is the successor of St Peter. The Bishops, not taken singly, but collectively and in union with the Pope, are the successors of the Apostles. The jurisdiction of a Bishop is confined to his own subjects and diocese. That of the Pope extends to the universal Church. The Pope receives his jurisdiction directly from Christ. The Bishop receives jurisdiction from the same divine source, upon his consecration as a Bishop.

---

[48] Power of Order: cf. Can 274 §1; power of governance: cf. Can. 135.
[49] "Ministers", i.e., Deacons and members of the Orders below Diaconate.

The Bishop retains his jurisdiction as long as he remains loyal to the Holy See and to its teaching. If he becomes schismatic or heretical, and is cut off from the Church by solemn condemnation, he loses all authority. Although forbidden to minister, he may validly, though sacrilegiously, consecrate and ordain, but he cannot even validly administer the Sacrament of Penance—he has no jurisdiction.[50] The Bishop is the father of his subjects. And as a father is head of his household, so is the Bishop head of his diocese, its ruler and its authentic teacher on faith and morals. As an individual, he does not possess the gift of infallibility, yet this will cause no anxiety to his subjects, who know that, in any case of error, the supreme head of the Church can intervene to protect them. But, pending an appeal to the Pope, the clergy and the laity are bound to obey the Bishop, because he has authority (1) to teach Catholic Doctrine, and (2) to decide whether any particular question belongs to the sphere of faith or morals. To deny him this latter power would be tantamount to asserting the Protestant claim to the right of private judgement.[51]

The Bishops of the Church taken collectively constitute what we have already called, "The Church Teaching",[52] and are infallible (1) when they are assembled under Papal authority in General Council; and (2) when, though dispersed throughout the world, they are at one with the Pope in teaching that a doctrine forms part of the Deposit of Faith or is to be held definitively.[53] In either case, they teach as a united body, as the successors to the College of the Apostles, and must, therefore, be infallible.

The jurisdiction of the Apostles. The word "Apostle" (literally, "one who is sent"), like the word "Pope", denotes jurisdiction, or sacred authority—not sacred power (Orders). Each Apostle had universal jurisdiction: Christ said to them, "Go and teach *all* nations", Matt 28:19. Except in the case of St Peter, this was a personal and intransmissible privilege. It was required by the needs of the infant Church, and was exercised under St Peter's direction. St Peter possessed the privilege in virtue of his office as head of the Church. Hence, he alone was able to transmit it to his successors.

Bishops as successors of the Apostles. The Apostles were unique, in that they were appointed directly and personally by Christ our Lord, were the original eyewitnesses of His life, works and Resurrection, and were each filled with the Holy Spirit at Pentecost. They possessed exceptional prophetic knowledge of revelation and by divine assistance announced the Christian message infallibly. Certain of them were chosen by God to write or dictate inspired books of the New Testament. The

---

[50] See p.543.
[51] pp.199-200
[52] p.183
[53] pp.185-6

Apostles alone were able to set up as foundation builders what Christ the architect had appointed for His Church. They alone could promulgate certain sacraments at the due time, i.e., authoritatively announce the sacraments that Christ instituted and when they were to be received.[54] These particular apostolic powers ceased at the death of the last Apostle, traditionally said to be St John. The Church is built on the Apostles, her foundation stones; it is not said to be built on the Bishops. The Bishops have received none of this uniqueness. They also differ from the Apostles in that, as individuals, they have restricted jurisdiction and limited teaching power. Nevertheless, we call them, collectively, the "successors of the Apostles", for their power comes in a line of succession from the Apostles.

VI

The Sacrament of Holy Orders was instituted by Christ.

PROOF FROM THE SOLEMN TEACHING OF THE CHURCH. The Church, in the exercise of her infallible authority, declares the institution of the Sacrament of Holy Orders by Christ to be a doctrine given to her by God Himself. This proof suffices for Catholics. The following proofs are added for fuller instruction.

PROOF FROM THE SACRED SCRIPTURE. *By a visible rite consisting of prayer and the imposition of hands, the Apostles ordained helpers and successors.* (a) We read of the first deacons that "seven men of good repute, full of the Spirit and of wisdom", were chosen, and were "set before the Apostles" who "prayed and laid their hands upon them."[55] One of the seven was St Stephen, the first Martyr. Another was St Philip, who preached and baptised in Samaria. (b) When St Paul and St Barnabas were about to set forth on their first mission, the heads of the Church at Antioch "after fasting and praying ... laid their hands on them and sent them off."[56]

This rite conveyed divine grace. (a) The text just quoted about Sts Paul and Barnabas is, in full: "the Holy Spirit said, 'Set apart for me Barnabas and Saul for the work to which I have called them.' Then after fasting and praying they laid their hands on them and sent them off. So, being sent out by the Holy Spirit, they went down to Seleucia".[57] Therefore, through this rite of prayer and the imposition of hands, Sts Paul and Barnabas were made the envoys of the Holy Spirit, i.e, they were empowered by Him to preach and sanctify. (b) St Paul says to St Timothy: "I remind you to rekindle the gift of God that is within you through the laying on of my hands".[58] As the context shows, St Paul is speaking of the grace to discharge the

---

[54] Charles Journet, *The Church of the Word Incarnate*, Sheed and Ward, London 1954, pp.130-48; Id., *Petit Catéchisme sur l'Église*, Ch. III, qq. 9-11, Fribourg 1968.
[55] Acts 6:3-6
[56] Acts 13:3
[57] Acts 13:2-4
[58] 2 Tim 1:6

duties of a bishop. St John Chrysostom paraphrases the words thus: "Excite anew the grace you received for the purpose of ruling the Church."[59]

Those who received this rite had authority to teach, sanctify and rule. They had to teach and preach (1 Tim 5:17), administer sacraments (Acts 19:4-6; Jam 5:14-5; 1 Cor 1:16), care for the flock of Christ (Acts 15:22; 20:28), give directives (Acts 15:6ff.; 1 Cor 5:3-4; 11:17,33-34), receive obedience from the faithful, watch over their souls, and render an account for them (Heb 13:17; 1 Tim 3:1-6). The deacons instructed and gave baptism (Acts 8:26-38).

This rite is the Sacrament of Holy Orders. From the above we infer: (1) that the Apostles marked out helpers and successors by the imposition of hands, a gesture signifying the transmission of power or authority; and (2) that this visible rite communicated the grace to fulfil the offices of the ministry. But, the capacity to confer divine grace must have been given to the rite by Christ Himself; hence, this rite is a Sacrament. It is a visible sign instituted by Christ to give grace. Our proof is confirmed by the statement in the Acts of the Apostles,[60] that Sts Paul and Barnabas "appointed presbyters [πρεσβυτεροι = priests] for them in every church". Sts Paul and Barnabas were, therefore, bishops in our sense of the word, i.e., they had received at their ordination the power to ordain others.

Objection. "The words 'priest' and 'bishop' are not used of Christian ministers in the New Testament." *Reply:* That depends on which translation you use. In any case, our argument does not stand or fall upon the occurrence of any particular word or translation, but on the meaning or content of those words. In the New Testament, as shown above, certain men were ceremoniously empowered to teach the believers, administer sacraments and lead the Church. Such men would be called priests in our use of the word. The two words used for those men in Greek were 'presbyteros' and 'episcopos'.[61] Presbyteros can be translated as priest, elder or presbyter. Episcopos can be translated as bishop, overseer, supervisor, or guardian. The two words were used interchangeably, but by the time of St Ignatius of Antioch, in 107 A.D. (see below), they were already being distinguished: episcopos regularly represented a higher rank than presbyteros. Presbyteros became 'presbyter' and 'priest' in English. Episcopos became 'bishop': likewise in other languages.[62] In Latin, the word, 'sacerdos' was also used for priest, from the words meaning, 'to give the sacred'.[63] St Paul speaks of himself as "a *minister* of Christ Jesus ... in the *priestly* service of the Gospel".[64]

PROOF FROM TRADITION. The proof from tradition that the Sacrament of Holy Orders, as we have it today, was instituted by Christ, is clear and decisive, and need

---

[59] *Hom. in 2 Tim.*, 1
[60] 14:23 (RSV, adapted)
[61] See, e.g., Acts 14:23; 20:28. In Greek: πρεσβυτερος, ἐπισκοπος
[62] French: prêtre, évêque; Italian: prete, vescovo; German: Priester, Bischof.
[63] 'Sacer' (sacred) + 'dare' (give). Priest and bishop in Spanish: sacerdote, obispo.
[64] Rom 15:16: minister: λειτουργος (leitourgos); serve as a priest: ἱερουργεω (hierourgeo)

not be fully drawn out. East and West, the Sacrament was regarded from the earliest centuries, not as a mere ceremony, like that observed at the appointment of magistrates and civil officers, but as the means whereby the spiritual power of the Apostles was conveyed to each generation of the Church's ministers.

Testimony of the Fathers and early writers: (a) About the year 96, St Clement, Bishop of Rome, draws a parallel between the Old Testament's triad of High Priest, priests and levites—and the New Testament's triad of Bishop, priests and deacons.[65]

(b) St Ignatius of Antioch (d. 107) speaks of the bishop as one who has "acquired his ministry, not from himself, nor through men", and that he is to be regarded "as the Lord himself"[66] i.e., (i) one cannot be made a bishop merely by human appointment; and (ii) a bishop is like our Divine Lord in possessing a spiritual power not given to other men. - In six of his seven letters written while conducted by soldiers to Rome for martyrdom, St Ignatius mentions the triad of, "the *bishop* and his assistants, the *presbyters* and *deacons*",[67] regularly speaking of "bishop" in the singular, and the others in the plural.

(c) St Cyprian (d. 258) declares that bishops are the successors of the Apostles by ordination.[68] He says also: "Since by the imposition of hand (sic) we receive the Episcopate, that is, the Holy Ghost as the guest of our heart, let us offer no cause of grief to Him who shares a dwelling with us",[69] i.e., we Bishops have received a special gift of the Holy Ghost consisting of an indwelling presence or power not given to others. He quotes the judgement of Clarus, Bishop and Confessor: "The meaning of our Lord Jesus Christ is plain when He sent His Apostles and entrusted to them alone *the power given to Himself by His Father*, whose successors we (Bishops) are, governing the Church of God with the same power."[70]

(d) Firmilian (d. 269), Bishop of Caesarea, says, in a letter to St Cyprian, that the power of forgiving sin was bestowed on the Apostles, then on the churches and the bishops who have succeeded the Apostles by successive ordination.[71]

(e) A contemporary of St Ambrose (d. 397), probably Pope Sylvester I (d. 335), writes: "Who gives the episcopal grace, brother? You answer without hesitation, God. But still God gives it through man. Man imposes hands; God bestows the grace."[72]

---

[65] *Ep. ad Cor.*, 40
[66] *Ep. ad Philad.*, 1; *Ephes.* 6
[67] *Ep. ad Philad.*, salut; cf. *Ep. ad Trall.* 3, 1; et al.
[68] *Opera Cypriani* (ed. Hartel), *Ep.* 66, p.729
[69] Ibid. *App.* 94, 3
[70] Ibid. *Sent. Episc.* n. 79
[71] Ibid. *Ep.* 75, p.821
[72] *De dignitate Sacerd.* 100:5

(f) St Gregory of Nyssa (d. 395) says of a newly ordained priest, that "he who was but yesterday one of the people suddenly becomes ... the dispenser of hidden mysteries ... Though in outward appearance he is the same as before, by a certain unseen power and grace, he is transformed into a higher being."[73]

(g) St John Chrysostom (d. 407), in his great work on the Priesthood, says, "Priests have received a power which God has given neither to angels nor archangels."[74]

Testimony of the Councils of the Church. The General Council of Chalcedon in 451, at which a great concourse of prelates from all over the Church was assembled, forbade the ordination of unworthy candidates to the Episcopate, the Priesthood, or the Diaconate, and condemned certain impious bishops who had conferred Orders for a gift of money, because "they had exposed for sale *an unpurchasable grace.*" Many similar decrees and prohibitions were issued by subsequent Councils.

Testimony of the separated Eastern Christians. The Eastern non-Catholic Churches, as already stated, have the Sacrament of Holy Orders. They are as zealous and emphatic in maintaining its divine institution as Catholics themselves.

ARGUMENT FROM REASON. We have already seen that Christ appointed the Apostles and their successors to the end of time to be His representatives on earth, to teach and govern all mankind, and to make them holy by means of sacred rites.[75] It is plain that those who are raised to such a sublime office need a very special grace to discharge their duties worthily; and it would seem to be entirely in conformity with the plan of Christ that they should receive that grace, not in some utterly hidden way, but through an outward rite signifying the spiritual effect produced. Christ commanded that by the Sacrament of Baptism people should be made members of His Church, that by the Sacrament of Penance their sins should be forgiven, and that by the Sacrament of the Blessed Eucharist they should be fed with His precious Body and Blood. Hence, we can infer that He also instituted a Sacrament of Holy Orders, a public rite which would signify the bestowal of grace and power on those chosen to be the rulers of His Church, teachers of His message, dispensers of His mysteries, and the ministers or guardians of His Sacraments.

Objection against the transmission of the power of Orders. The following objection is drawn out at length and with much ingenuity by Macaulay in his review of Gladstone's work, *The State and its Relations with the Church.* We may put it as follows: "A bishop, to prove that he has valid Orders, must be able to trace his spiritual ancestry back to the Apostles. In most instances, this would indeed be a difficult feat. Even though accomplished, it would not suffice: for it would still be necessary to establish that every bishop in that long line of descent from the Apostles was validly baptised and ordained."

---

[73] *Orat. in Bap. Christi,* PG 46, 582
[74] *De Sacerd.* III, 5
[75] See pp.132-6.

REPLY: (1) For a Catholic, the objection has no force whatsoever: at the words of Christ, "behold, I am with you all days, even to the consummation of the world" (Matt 28:20, Douay), all its specious fabric turns to dust. Christ will be always with the Church, so that she can never fail in her work of making men holy. The great instrument which He gave to her to discharge that office is the spiritual power of the Episcopate, which He decreed should be transmitted from the Apostles to their successors to the end of time. He who issued the decree will see to its fulfilment. He will guard the transmission of His Holy Orders, either by securing that there be no invalid rites, or if He permits such to occur, by directly supplying the power Himself which they fail to give.[76] A Catholic, therefore, believes in the ordination of his priests and bishops, not because of any historical argument, or because he knows that the Church takes extreme care to preserve her rites from invalidity and to repair defects, but because she who speaks with the voice of Christ offers him her priests and bishops as truly ordained.[77] Certain Anglicans argue in the following way: (a) "We can prove historically that we have valid Orders; (b) having valid Orders, we have the same spiritual power as the Apostles, and are, therefore, members of the true Church." That is, they say: "We are members of the true Church, because our Orders are valid." Our argument is the exact reverse: "Our Orders are valid, because we are members of the true Church." That is to say, because Christ is always with us, He will provide for the validity of our Orders. The perpetual support of Christ shields the Church's faith from all possibility of error and guarantees the validity of her Orders.

(2) Even if Anglicans succeeded in the difficult and, it would seem, utterly impossible, task of tracing their Orders step by step back to the Apostles and of showing that there had not been one single instance of failure in rite or intention, their conclusion would not follow. Valid Orders without the divine authority to exercise them would not make their church a branch of the Church of Christ. Rome gave the English Church the divine authority to exercise Orders, and Rome withdrew it.[78] Moreover, Rome has declared that the Orders conferred by England's apostate bishops at the time of the Reformation were invalid.[79] Hence, however much it may use the words, the Anglican communion today has neither priests nor bishops.

Objection to the title 'Father'. "Priests ought not be called 'Father', since Jesus said, 'call no man your father on earth, for you have one Father, who is in heaven' (Matt 23:9)." REPLY: By the same slavishly literal interpretation, no-one should refer to his male parent as his father, even though Our Lord Himself elsewhere spoke about people's fathers.[80] Similarly, we should prohibit the title, "Mister" (= old English for "Master"), or "Teacher", since the verse following says, "Neither be called masters" [or, "teachers", in some translations]. For the same reason, most

---

[76] St Thomas, *Comm. in Sent.* iv, d. 24, q. 1, a. 2, qcla 3, ad 2 (= S.T. Suppl. q. 35, a. 3, ad 2)
[77] Cf. T 1778.
[78] See Newman's *Essays Critical and Historical*, vol. II, pp.86 ff.
[79] DS 3319
[80] e.g., Matt 10:21; 19:5; 19:19; 19:29; 23:32; Jn 6:49; 8:56

Christians by now ought to be one-handed, for Scripture says, "if your hand causes you to sin, cut it off".[81] To answer the objection directly: priests are rightly called "Father" since they possess spiritual fatherhood, because of which St Paul could say, "I became your father in Christ Jesus".[82] The meaning of Christ's saying above is that human fatherhood is as nothing before the Fatherhood of God.

The deeper question is: which sayings of Christ are to be interpreted literally and which ones figuratively? Fundamentalists claim to take everything literally, and yet refuse to do so when they read, "this is my Body", and "What therefore God has joined together, let not man put asunder."[83] Only the Church, to whom the Bible belongs, can guide us as to what is literal and what is not. Those who have forsaken the guidance and wisdom of the Catholic Church finish up in the most bizarre and illogical interpretations.

---

[81] Mk 9:43

[82] 1 Cor 4:15. Cf. 2 Cor 6:13; 1 Thess 2:11; 1 Tim 1:2; 1:18; 2 Tim 1:2; Acts 7:1; 1 Jn 2:13-14.

[83] Mk 14:22; 10:9

CHAPTER 18

MARRIAGE

Summary

I.   The solemn teaching of the Church.
II.   The Sacrament defined. Its Ministers and its Subjects.
III.   Differences between marriage and other contracts. The nature of the bond: marriage a Covenant in Christ and the Church. The effects of the Sacrament. The obligations it imposes. Marriage, the family, the Church and society.
IV.   Marriage is a Sacrament instituted by Christ: Proof: (1) from the solemn teaching of the Church; (2) from Sacred Scripture; (3) from Tradition; (4) from Reason.
V.   The unity and indissolubility of Marriage. The Fathers on indissolubility.
VI.   The qualities of married love. The purposes and goods of marriage. Sins against marriage.
VII.   Dissolution. Separation. Divorce. Annulment. The Pauline privilege. The privilege of the faith.
VIII. The Church's exclusive control over Christian Marriage. The rights of the State: so-called civil marriage and divorce.
IX.   The impediments of Matrimony.
X.   Matrimonial consent.
XI.   The form of the celebration of Marriage.
XII.   Mixed marriages. Summary.
XIII. Marriage and religion. The dignity of Christian Marriage. Obedience to the Church's teaching. Preparation for marriage.

I

The solemn teaching of the Church. The Church teaches solemnly:
(1)   that Matrimony is a Sacrament instituted by Christ;
(2)   that it confers grace;[1]
(3)   that a Christian is forbidden by divine law to have several wives at the same time;[2]
(4)   that the Church has power to create impediments making it unlawful or impossible for people to contract marriage in certain circumstances;[3]
(5)   that the marriage bond cannot be broken by adultery;[4]
(6)   that the marriage bond cannot be broken by heresy, difficult cohabitation, or desertion;[5]

---

[1] (1) and (2): T 1801
[2] T 1802
[3] T 1804
[4] T 1807

(7) that the Church has power to grant a separation of husband and wife, i.e., permission to live apart, but not to contract a new marriage while both parties are still living;[6]

(8) that clerics in Holy Orders, and religious who have taken a solemn vow of chastity, cannot contract a valid marriage;[7]

(9) that marriage not yet consummated is dissolved by the solemn religious profession of either party.[8]

II

The Sacrament defined. Its ministers and its subjects.

THE SACRAMENT DEFINED. Matrimony is the Sacrament which unites a Christian man and a Christian woman as husband and wife, and gives them grace to fulfil the duties of the married state. It is a sacred covenant, i.e., a binding agreement, by which two baptised persons, a man and a woman, undertake to live faithfully and affectionately together as husband and wife from that moment forward until parted by death, and to rear their children in the love and service of God.

Sacramental Marriage and Natural Marriage. Between a couple both baptised, a valid marriage is always a Sacrament, whether they know it or not.[9] When one or both are unbaptised, marriage is not a Sacrament, but a natural contract, also recognised by God and the Church. A natural marriage is transformed into a sacramental one upon the baptism of both partners, or—if one is already baptised—the other partner.

ITS MINISTERS AND ITS SUBJECTS. The contracting parties themselves are, at the same time, the Ministers and the Subjects of the Sacrament. At the marriage there is a mutual giving and a mutual acceptance:[10] under the former aspect, the contracting parties are the Subjects of the Sacrament; under the latter they are its Ministers. Therefore, the priest or deacon who assists at the marriage is not its Minister, but is present as the Church's official representative.

---

[5] T 1805

[6] T 1808

[7] T 1809

[8] T 1806. A marriage is consummated after the man and the woman have actually lived together as husband and wife.

[9] Leo XIII, *Arcanum divinae sapientiae*, Encyclical on Christian Marriage, 1880: DS 3145-6

[10] In technical terms, the mutual giving is the "matter", the mutual acceptance the "form".

III

Differences between Marriage and other contracts. The nature of the bond. The effects of the Sacrament. The obligations it imposes. Marriage and society.

DIFFERENCES BETWEEN MARRIAGE AND OTHER CONTRACTS. At the most basic level, marriage is a type of contract, since it is an agreement entered into by two people. However, whereas a contract is an exchange of *things*, a covenant, in a certain sense, is an exchange of *persons*. What a man and woman promise to each other in marriage is not just an agreed amount of time, services or goods; rather, they give *themselves* to each other. There are other differences also: (1) Marriage is a sacred and religious contract, not merely a legal convention. (2) Marriage is also a natural contract—not established by man, but by God. (3) At times, contracts can be sealed by legal guardians or representatives, but marital consent must be given by the parties themselves. (4) Some contracts can be changed by law or by agreement, but neither Church, nor State, nor the parties themselves, are free to change the essential properties of marriage. (5) Unlike other contracts, marriage cannot be terminated by mutual agreement.

THE NATURE OF THE BOND: MARRIAGE A COVENANT IN CHRIST AND THE CHURCH. In the Old Testament, marriage was established by God as a sacred, exclusive and permanent partnership between a man and woman—ordained to procreation, mutual help and right ordering of carnal instincts. However, both Jews and pagans fell into divorce and polygamy, which God tolerated until the coming of the Redeemer, who restored marriage and elevated the covenant of marriage to the dignity of a Sacrament. Revelation teaches that between two baptised people, such a covenant is now a living image of the everlasting covenant between Our Lord Jesus Christ, the Divine Bridegroom, and His Immaculate Bride, Holy Church—a marriage He began at the Incarnation and consummated upon the Cross. It is St Paul who develops this significance of marriage as a union of love which mirrors the Christ-Church relationship.[11] Just as the nuptial union of Christ with His Bride the Church (a) is born of that generous *self-giving*, (b) through which Jesus of His purest and overflowing love gives Himself *forever* (c) to *one* Spouse alone, (d) to make her *fruitful*, till the entire Body of the faithful is built up:—so Christian Marriage (a) is born of that mutual *self-giving* expressed externally in the marriage vows and in the marital union of flesh thereafter, (b) through which an *indissoluble* bond is set up, lasting until death, (c) shared exclusively by this *one* man and this *one* woman, (d)

---

[11] See Eph 5:21-33.

who, as servants of God, will *bring forth children* for the formation and increase of God's family in the Kingdom of Heaven.

THE EFFECTS OF THE SACRAMENT. Matrimony, being a symbol of Christ's union with His Church, manifestly presupposes the state of grace in its recipients. Those who receive it worthily obtain (1) an increase of Sanctifying Grace, and (2) the Sacramental Grace of the sacrament: a grace of conjugal union, elevating their natural mutual inclination, and orienting them to the supernatural virtues and operations that will perfect their union and life together. The Sacrament "adds special gifts, good impulses, and seeds of grace, amplifying and perfecting the powers of nature".[12] The Sacramental Grace gives an increase in the virtues of charity and justice, and is a remedy for concupiscence (disordered desire). It also gives a right to all the actual graces necessary for faithfully performing the duties of the married state.

It would be a very grave misfortune if one were to receive the Sacrament of Matrimony while stained with mortal sin. The marriage bond would indeed be valid, but devoid of grace. It is commonly held, but it is not absolutely certain, that, on a subsequent recovery of Sanctifying Grace, the sacrament "revives", and gives one a title to the actual graces referred to—though, perhaps, not as full a title as worthy reception would have given. But who would face such a risk, and think of offering a gross insult to God at the very outset of one's career? Who would think of entering sacrilegiously a state of life on which the salvation of many souls may depend?

THE OBLIGATIONS IT IMPOSES. *The duties of the husband and wife to one another.* The primary duties of husband and wife to one another bind under pain of mortal sin. They must help one another to lead good Christian lives, and support one another in the necessities and duties of life. They should share any riches with each other, and, if necessary, be willing to share any poverty. The marriage vows express this mutual support, sharing and fidelity: "I take you … to have and to hold, from this day forward, for better, for worse, for richer, for poorer, in sickness and in health, till death do us part."

Men and women are equal in personal dignity, but as husbands and wives, and fathers and mothers, are different and complementary in their roles or function within the family. To the husband, God has entrusted the headship in marriage. A wife should submit to her husband as the head of the household, and the husband should love his wife as much as himself: the Holy Spirit says, "Wives, be subject to your husbands, as to the Lord. For the husband is the head of the wife, as Christ is the Head of the

---

12 Pope Pius XI, *Casti Connubii*, 1930, Encyclical on Christian Marriage, Part I: DS 3714

Church, His Body, and is Himself its Saviour. As the Church is subject to Christ, so let wives also be subject in everything to their husbands. ... Even so husbands should love their wives as their own bodies. ... For no man ever hates his own flesh, but nourishes it and cherishes it". "Husbands, love your wives, and do not be harsh with them."[13] A misunderstanding of the nature of authority leads some to contradict or ignore these texts of Sacred Scripture relating to spouses. To appreciate the Apostolic teaching, we must realise that the headship of a husband is not that of a tyrant, but of one who devotes himself to the good of his wife and of their marriage and family, in imitation of Christ who laid down His life for His Spouse: "Husbands, love your wives, as Christ loved the Church and gave Himself up for her".[14] The husband's headship is not the privilege of getting his own way, but the responsibility of leadership for the good of the couple. In other words, his authority is ordered toward service. If, for whatever reason, he cannot fulfil his responsibility, the duty devolves on his wife. Both are equally bound to each other in the duty of dwelling together, and the duty of marital affection: again, the Holy Spirit says, "husbands, live considerately with your wives"; "Train the young women to love their husbands".[15] The marriage vows demand absolute loyalty in affection and intimacy. Spouses are seriously bound to avoid anything that can endanger their mutual fidelity.

The actual grace that flows from the Sacrament enables them to discharge these duties. It strengthens their mutual love and loyalty; it fosters in them the spirit of patience and unselfishness; it gives them constant help to lead holy lives, to give good example to one another, and thus save their souls.

Their duties to their children. As parents, husband and wife are bound to provide for the physical well-being of their children, but are far more strictly bound to provide for their spiritual needs: they should make the home a place of peace and holiness, a true nursery of the Church. They should bring up their children in the love and service of God, and give them a truly Catholic education. Within the home, they must teach the love of neighbour, as manifested by rules of politeness, by self-control, performance of duty and acts of kindness and consideration. They must furnish the home with good wholesome literature, and religious books and magazines. They must forbid any literature, television or videos stained by vanity, graphic violence or lust. They should promote family unity by regular contact with relations, they should foster friendship with other good Catholic families, and avoid bringing into the sanctuary of the home anyone

---

[13] Eph 5:22-4, 28-9; Col 3:19
[14] Eph 5:25
[15] 1 Pet 3:7; Titus 2:4

or anything that threatens Catholic family life. Daily prayer, ideally the Rosary, is a source of great blessing for the family. Parents can lead their children, too, in bed-time prayers. In short, in spiritual things, parents have the duty to teach their children, give them good example, and pray for them.

The actual grace parents receive through the Sacrament enables them to fulfil these important obligations. It encourages habits of thrift and industry so that they may better provide for the material needs of the household. It gives them divine light and guidance, a great tenderness, patience, and love, so that they may help to save the souls of their children. In a family, the spouses' first duty is to each other and to their children. Any service rendered to others should never interfere with their primary duties.

Thus, while God lays a heavy and life-long task on husband and wife, He gives them the grace to bear it. But He will increase that help and bestow it far more generously in response to fervent and constant prayer.

MARRIAGE, THE FAMILY, THE CHURCH AND SOCIETY. "Each family which gathers at the altar to share in the Sacrifice of the Mass is a strong cell in the Mystical Body, the domestic church. But such a family is also the strongest cell in society at large. The natural unit of society is the family. When families are stable and united, so the society made up of those families will enjoy stability and peace. This social sacrament of Marriage is therefore 'social' in the broadest sense, as the centre of Christian ministry to human society. ... People often remark on the witness value of the good Christian family as an example. But that witness goes beyond example to the very structure of society and the positive contribution offered to society by people who are mature and secure because they were formed in a Christian home. In such a domestic church we also find the transmission, not only of Catholic morality, but also of the rich heritage of culture and civilization which the Church has nurtured over the centuries."[16] Indeed, the Church has been described as 'the family of the families of God'.[17]

IV

Marriage is a Sacrament instituted by Christ.

PROOF FROM THE SOLEMN TEACHING OF THE CHURCH. The Church, in the solemn exercise of her infallible authority, declares the institution of the Sacrament of Matrimony by Christ to be a doctrine given to her by God Himself. This proof suffices for Catholics. The following proofs are added for fuller instruction.

---

[16] P.J. Elliott, *What God Has Joined: the Sacramentality of Marriage*, Alba House, N.Y. 1990, pp.224-5
[17] Ibid. p.225

PROOF FROM SACRED SCRIPTURE. St Paul says: "the husband is the head of the wife, as Christ is the Head of the Church ... Husbands, love your wives, as Christ loved the Church and gave Himself up for her, that He might sanctify her... This (viz., Marriage) is a great mystery, and I mean in reference to Christ and the Church".[18] According to these inspired words of the Apostle, Christian Marriage is to be regarded as an image, reflection, or sign of the union between Christ and the Church. Hence, Christian Marriage must be a holy union, pleasing to God, and, therefore, blessed with the gift of Sanctifying Grace. Christ Himself, through whom all grace comes to us, must have attached to it the power of conferring such a gift. Christian Marriage has, therefore, all the requisites of a sacrament: (1) it is an outward rite, because the marriage covenant is made outwardly in words or their equivalent; (2) it signifies Sanctifying Grace, because it signifies what is most holy, viz., the union of Christ with the Church; (3) it gives, by the appointment of Christ, the grace it signifies.

PROOF FROM TRADITION. (1) In the fifth century, the doctrine that Marriage is a sacrament was universally admitted: (a) It was taught expressly by St Augustine, who shows that Matrimony, like Baptism and Holy Orders, is a permanent source of grace.[19] (b) It is held by all the non-Catholic Eastern Churches who separated from Rome in this period.

(2) Representations found in the Catacombs, dating from the fourth century or earlier, prove that marriage between Christians was regarded as a sacred rite. In one of these ancient memorials, a sarcophagus found in the Villa Albani, Rome, Christ is seen behind the bride and groom, and the inscription says, "Almighty God bound them together in sweet Matrimony".[20]

(3) Tertullian c. 200-6 writes to his wife, "How shall we be able to describe the happiness of that marriage which the Church performs, the sacrifice ratifies, the blessing seals, the angels declare and the Heavenly Father recognises?"[21]

(4) At the end of the first century, St Ignatius of Antioch testifies to the sacred character of Matrimony thus: "It is right for men and women who marry to be united with the consent of the bishop, that the marriage may be according to the Lord and not according to lust",[22] i.e., marriage is not a mere business agreement, or a compact suggested by low desire; it is something sacred, because, according to Ignatius, it ought to receive the approval of the bishop, and thus be made pleasing to God.

---

[18] Eph 5:23-32. "This (i.e., Marriage) is a great Sacrament" (Douay). - This sentence alone in the Douay translation is not in itself a proof of our doctrine. "Sacrament", in the language of St Paul, meant "something holy and mysterious"; it had not yet arrived at its technical meaning.

[19] *De bono coniug.* 18, 21; 29, 32; *De nupt. et conc.* I, 11, 13; 21, 23; *In Io. Ev. tract.* 9, 2

[20] L. Hertling S.J. & E. Kirschbaum S.J., *The Roman Catacombs and their Martyrs*, DLT, London 1960, p.242

[21] *Ad uxorem*, (2, 8) 2, 9

[22] *Pol.* 5

ARGUMENT FROM REASON. (a) *Marriage, an unbreakable bond.* Christ, as we shall see in Section V, declared marriage to be an unbreakable bond. This doctrine being admitted, reason demands that marriage should be a sacrament. It is undeniably a solemn and exacting moment, under any circumstances, when a man and woman deliberately surrender themselves, body and soul, to the keeping of each other while life shall last; and this (reserving the supreme claim of duty to the Creator) is the matrimonial contract. But who would be encouraged to make themselves over, without condition or stipulation, to a fallible being—and not for a season, but for life? The mind shrinks from such a sacrifice, and demands that, as religion enjoins it, religion should sanction and bless it. It instinctively desires that either the bond should be dissoluble, or that the subjects should be sacramentally strengthened to maintain it.[23]

(b) *Marriage, the foundation of the Christian home.* The Church depends, for her continued existence and normal increase, on the offspring of Christian parents; they are her agents in the education of her children. The Christian home, when it is all that it should be, is truly the domestic Church. There the children get their first knowledge of God, the Creator of Heaven and earth. They are told that it is God who has given them to their parents, and made their parents love them. They learn how Christ was born at Bethlehem, and how He died on the Cross for us. They are taught how to pray. Their parents show them by the example of their lives what religion really means in practice, and give their character a bent for holiness. They lay in them the foundations of a good Catholic life. Nor does the influence of the Christian home cease with infancy: while the children are approaching manhood or womanhood, virtuous parents help to keep them from evil company and temptation. They guide them in the choice of career. They are at all times the children's sincere friends and advisers. In brief, as long as they live, they try to keep and guard their children for God. The Christian home thus forms a most important part in the plan of Christ for the salvation of souls. It is, therefore, a reasonable conclusion that He must have blessed marriage in a very special way; that He must have attached Sanctifying Grace and special gifts to the marriage pact, and a right to all the actual graces necessary for its worthy fulfilment; in other words, that He must have elevated marriage to the dignity of a sacrament.[24]

V

The unity and indissolubility of Marriage.

These are the two essential *properties* of Marriage.[25]

THE UNITY OF MARRIAGE. The unity of marriage consists in having only one man and one woman as partners to the covenant.

The unity of marriage is opposed to polygamy and polyandry. Polygamy means having two or more wives at the same time; and polyandry, two or more husbands.

---

[23] Cf. J.H. Newman, *Callista*, start of Ch. xi.

[24] Cf. Encyclical of Pius XI on the Christian Education of Youth, *Divini Illius Magistri,* 1929.

[25] Cf. above, "The solemn teaching of the Church". Cf. Can. 1056.

The latter has never been expressly condemned by the Church for the sufficient reason that even pagans regard it as an abomination. The former was tolerated or permitted during the age of the Patriarchs and under the imperfect Mosaic Law, but, under the New and perfect Law, it was abolished by Christ when He said to the Pharisees: "Whoever divorces his wife and marries another, commits adultery against her; and if she divorces her husband and marries another, she commits adultery."[26] If then it is unlawful to marry again during the lifetime of the first partner, much more unlawful is it to have two or more marriage partners simultaneously. St Paul repeats his Master's doctrine, and says of those not called to virginity: "each man should have his own wife and each woman her own husband ... To the married I give charge, not I, but the Lord, that the wife should not separate from her husband (but if she does, let her remain single or else be reconciled to her husband)—and that the husband should not divorce his wife."[27] The practice of keeping several wives in the same household leads to many evils, the chief of which are domestic unhappiness, the absence of true home life for parents and children, and the enslavement and degradation of women.

The Protestant reformers Luther and Melanchthon allowed the Landgrave Philip of Hesse in 1539 to marry another woman while his lawful wife was still alive; and some of their followers of the present day, against the clear teaching of Christ, make no difficulty in availing themselves of the same licence.

THE INDISSOLUBILITY OF MARRIAGE.   Marriage is indissoluble or unbreakable, i.e., the bond of valid marriage cannot be undone either by the contracting parties themselves or by any merely human power. This is true of all marriages, whether between Catholics, baptised non-Catholics, or pagans. "What therefore God has joined together", says Christ, "let no man put asunder."[28] It is more plainly so with Christian Marriage, which is an image of the indissoluble union between the Lord Jesus and His Church. To say that a consummated sacramental marriage could be dissolved is equivalent to saying that Jesus could sever Himself from His Church and abandon her.

The Pharisees asked our Lord: "'Is it lawful to divorce one's wife for any cause?' He answered, 'Have you not read that He who made them from the beginning made them male and female, and said, 'For this reason a man shall leave his father and mother, and be joined to his wife, and the two shall become one.'? So they are no longer two but one. *What therefore God has joined together, let no man put asunder.'* They said to Him, 'Why then did Moses command one to give a certificate of divorce, and to put her away?' He said to them, 'For your hardness of heart Moses

---

[26] Mk 10:11-12; cf. Lk 16:18.
[27] 1 Cor 7:2, 10-11
[28] Matt 19:6

598

allowed you to divorce your wives, but from the beginning it was not so."'[29] By these words Christ abolished the permission for divorce given under the Old Law.

Objection. Having expressed Himself in the words quoted above from St Matthew, Christ continued thus: "And I say to you, whoever divorces his wife, *except for unchastity,* and marries another, commits adultery."[30] The Greek Orthodox and other non-Catholic Eastern Christians, and most Protestants, argue from this that marriage may be dissolved because of adultery,—but this interpretation is impossible, since:
(1) it is condemned by the Church's solemn teaching;
(2) the very next sentence shows that the Lord does not regard the marriage as over: "he who marries a divorced woman commits adultery";[31]
(3) it is opposed to the clear statements of Our Lord made elsewhere. In Luke 16:18 and Mark 10:11-12, Jesus says plainly, "Whoever divorces his wife and marries another, commits adultery";
(4) it is opposed to the teaching of St Paul in 1 Cor 7:10-11 quoted above; also 1 Cor 7:39; Rom 7:2-3;
(5) if it were correct, it would encourage an unhappy spouse to commit adultery, since it would allow not only the innocent but the guilty party to marry again.[32]

How, then, is the text to be interpreted? What did our Lord mean by saying, "except for unchastity"? The Church has ruled out any interpretation which would allow divorce and remarriage, but has not given any definitive explanation. A number of explanations are possible, among which are the following:[33]
(a) The clause, "except for unchastity" is an aside, a mere passing comment on the words, "whoever divorces his wife",—so that the meaning is: "whoever puts away his wife—a proceeding justified by her unchastity—and marries another, commits adultery." In other words, a separation from bed and board may be permitted, but not another marriage. This is the interpretation of St Jerome, St Augustine and St John Chrysostom, among others.
(b) Our Lord was referring to the "unchastity" of concubinage, which means a marriage that is not genuine and does not bind its partners in a definitive fashion.
(c) The Greek word for "unchastity" used here—πορνεια (porneia)—refers to the unchastity of an incestuous marriage, a marriage contracted within the degrees of kinship forbidden by Leviticus 18. Anyone involved in such a marriage would be entitled to put away his putative "wife", and remarry according to the law of Christ.[34] (This is probably the meaning also of the word "unchastity" [porneia] in Acts 15:29 where the Apostles instruct the Gentile converts about what part of the Mosaic Law still binds).

---

[29] Matt 19:3-8
[30] Matt 19:9. Almost the same sentence occurs in Matt 5:32.
[31] Matt 19:9; 5:32
[32] Cf. St Jerome, *In Matt. comm.* III, c. 16, v. 19.
[33] At least twelve have been proposed, not all of them acceptable to the Catholic Church. Cf. R.F. Collins, *Divorce in the New Testament,* Minnesota 1992, pp.199-205.
[34] The interpretation proposed by J. Bonsirven S.J. in his French work, *Mariage,* 1948. It has been followed in several translations of the Bible into various languages.

THE FATHERS ON INDISSOLUBILITY. The early Fathers are unanimous on the permanence of marriage. The only discordant texts are in an anonymous writer known as Ambrosiaster, and one ambiguous and perhaps spurious passage in St Epiphanius.[35] By taking certain other quotes of the Fathers out of context, it is easy to present a good-looking argument that the Fathers did not hold the teaching of the Catholic Church. We cannot answer all such arguments here, but suffice to say that learned books such as those given in the footnote have taken all relevant texts into account.

VI

The qualities of married love. The purposes and goods of marriage. Sins against marriage.

QUALITIES OF MARRIED LOVE. "Truly, conjugal love most clearly manifests to us its true nature and nobility when we recognise that it has its origin in the highest source, as it were, in God, Who 'is Love' and Who is the Father, 'from Whom all Fatherhood in heaven and on earth receives its name'."[36] Pope Paul VI spells out the qualities of married love: (1) Married love is *human*, and therefore both of the senses and the spirit. Hence, it is a product not only of natural instinct and inclinations; it also and primarily involves an act of free will. Through this act of free will, the spouses resolve that their love will not only persevere through daily joys and sorrows, but also increase. (2) Conjugal love is *total*; it is a very special form of personal friendship whereby the spouses generously share everything with each other without undue reservations and without concern for their selfish convenience. The spouses love each other, not just for what each receives from the other, but for the other's sake. (3) Conjugal love is *faithful* and *exclusive* to the end of life. Such indeed is how the bride and groom conceive marriage when they take their vows. (4) Married love is *fruitful*, since the whole of the love is not contained in the communion of the spouses, but looks beyond itself and seeks to raise up new lives.[37] "The institution itself of marriage and married love are ordained by their very nature to the procreation and education of children and in them it reaches its crowning glory."[38] "Offspring are indeed the supreme gift of marriage and contribute immensely to the good of the parents themselves."[39]

THE PURPOSES OF MARRIAGE. God has implanted a natural instinct in both sexes for close companionship and intimacy, which leads naturally to

---

[35] Cf. G.H. Joyce S.J., *Christian Marriage*, Sheed and Ward, London 1948, pp.304-31; H. Crouzel S.J., *L'Église primitive face au divorce*, Beauchesne, Paris 1971.
[36] *Humanae Vitae*, Pope Paul VI, 1968, art. 8. Cf. 1 Jn 4:8; Eph 3:15.
[37] Cf. *Humanae Vitae*, art. 9.
[38] *Gaudium et Spes*, Vatican Council II, 1965, art. 48
[39] *Gaudium et Spes*, art. 50

marriage. In marriage, man and woman give and receive mutual help in sharing and bearing the duties and difficulties of life. In this union, they satisfy the natural desire to found a family and to bestow their love and the best of what they have upon their children, born as the fruit of their love. Further, within marriage, human passions are well-directed and elevated to a noble purpose.

THE GOODS OF MARRIAGE. St Augustine writes, "These are all the blessings of marriage, on account of which marriage itself is a blessing: offspring, conjugal faith and the sacrament."[40]

Children. God's original command, "Be fruitful and multiply" (Gen 1:28), makes of man and woman in wedlock His co-operators in the creation by His omnipotence of new human beings. As Christian parents, they are called not merely to preserve and propagate citizens of earth, but children of God and citizens of Heaven—man's true destiny. The Church commends and encourages the generosity of those couples who have a large family.[41]

Faith. Faith here means conjugal fidelity, the faithful pledging of conjugal union in one flesh by husband and wife to each other, and to no other. The blessing of fidelity is guaranteed by unity, chastity, charity and honourable submission.

Sacrament. The blessing of the sacrament includes both *indissolubility* and *grace.* The ultimate foundation for this unbreakable perpetuity of consummated Christian Marriage is its mystical signification of the union between Christ and the Church. The grace of this sacrament "perfects natural love, confirms an indissoluble union, and sanctifies the married couple."[42] The indissolubility of the marriage is the guarantee of the permanent availability of the grace. Marriage "is a sacrament like to that of the Eucharist, which is a sacrament not only when it is being conferred, but also whilst it endures; for as long as the married parties are alive, so long is their union a sacrament of Christ and the Church."[43]

SINS AGAINST MARRIAGE. It is only in the light of the permanent, faithful and fruitful union between Christ and His Spouse the Church, of which Christian marriage is the image, that one can properly evaluate sins against Marriage.

Adultery and Infidelity; Desertion of a faithful spouse. To say that infidelity or adultery, or desertion of a faithful spouse, is admissible in marriage is to say that Christ could withdraw His love, betray or abandon His Church, violate

---

[40] *De bono coniug.*, cap. 24, n. 32. Cf. Encyclical of Pius XI, *Casti Connubii*, 1930.
[41] Cf. *Gaudium et Spes*, art. 50; C 2373.
[42] T 1799
[43] St Robert Bellarmine, *De controversiis*, tom. III, *De Matrim.*, controv. II, cap. 6

the covenant He made with her, and renege on His promise to be with her all days.

Contraception. To say that a husband and wife could licitly render their conjugal acts sterile is to say that Christ could render the Sacraments unfruitful and sterile by depriving them of the power to confer the divine life of grace.

Sterilisation. To say that a husband or wife could licitly be sterilised is to say that Christ could sterilise the Church or destroy a healthy member of His Body, the Church.

VII

Dissolution. Separation. Divorce. Annulment. The Pauline privilege. The privilege of the faith.

DISSOLUTION. The Church never dissolves, and has never claimed power to dissolve, a marriage entered into by two Christians, if the parties have actually lived together as man and wife.

SEPARATION. The Church sometimes permits a *separation* of husband and wife because of cruelty or adultery, but cannot permit either to marry again during the lifetime of the other. "Though it be allowed, because of adultery", says Pope Eugene IV (1431-47), "to obtain a separation, it is not permissible to contract a new marriage, since the bond of lawful wedlock is perpetual."[44] Permission to separate is obtained from the local Bishop, but one may leave upon one's own authority if there is danger in delay.[45] Other causes also justify a separation of husband and wife: leaving the Catholic Church to join a non-Catholic denomination; denying the children a Catholic upbringing; living a criminal and ignominious life; causing grave danger to soul or body of the partner. In all these cases, however, if the evil ceases, conjugal life must be resumed. To separate from one's lawful spouse for good reason is no sin; sometimes it is a moral necessity. Even so, one must separate with a view to a future reconciliation if and when possible.[46] It is best to consult with the Bishop or one's pastor before taking any steps to leave one's spouse, in order to attempt a reconciliation and to avoid rash decisions that have more harmful results in the long term.

DIVORCE. The State, needless to say, has no power to dissolve the marriage bond *even between non-Catholics, whether baptised or unbaptised.* After a separation of husband and wife, the parties may apply to a civil court, and go through a form of so-called divorce, but merely to secure the protection or aid of the

---

[44] *Decretum pro Armenis*: F 1327
[45] Can. 1153 §1
[46] Can. 1151-1155

civil law in regard to property, maintenance, and the custody of the children.[47] To seek a civil "divorce" for good reason is no sin. Again, it is wise to consult the Bishop or pastor before making such a serious move. A separated or divorced person is morally bound to avoid company-keeping that would be a temptation to seek entrance into a new and invalid union. Such conduct is a source both of temptation and of scandal. A separated or deserted spouse who remains faithful is also a very important witness to Christ and Christian Marriage.

"ANNULMENT" OR DECREE OF INVALIDITY. An ecclesiastical marriage tribunal may decide, after detailed examination, that a marriage apparently valid is not really so.[48] This decision cannot be spoken of as a dissolution of the marriage. It is a *declaration of invalidity*, i.e., a declaration that in fact, from the very start, there was *no* marriage tie in the particular case, because of the absence of some condition necessary for validity. This is what is commonly called an "annulment"—but more correctly, a declaration of nullity. No marriage is being *made* null; rather, it is being declared never to have existed, to have been null and void from the beginning. To be declared null, it must be ascertained that some essential element was missing *on the wedding day itself*. Whatever happens afterwards is irrelevant, except insofar as it manifests what was missing on that day. This book cannot present the complex process of ascertaining nullity. When the need arises, recourse must be had to those people appointed to handle cases. A person whose marriage has been declared null is free to marry again, *provided there is no continuation or repetition of the very defect (or some other defect) which would make a new marriage also null*. Moreover, he or she must discharge the natural obligations of the previous union, i.e., look after one's children and ensure that the former partner is not reduced to poverty. A decree of nullity will also note if one of the parties is forbidden to marry until certain conditions are met.

THE PAULINE PRIVILEGE. A marriage between two unbaptised persons is sacred, but is not one of the seven Sacraments. In such a marriage, if one party becomes a Catholic, and the other refuses to live in peace with the convert, the Catholic may seek permission from the local Bishop to make use of the Pauline privilege.[49] By this privilege, the Catholic party may seek freedom to enter into a new marriage with another person, by which the first non-sacramental marriage is at once dissolved. This is called the Pauline privilege, because it is fully set forth by St Paul in 1 Cor 7:12ff. He introduces it with the words, "I say, not the Lord", i.e., "I do not quote the words of Christ, but I speak as an Apostle with His authority." Under the Pauline privilege, therefore, it is not man that "puts asunder", but God. Before it can be invoked, the converted party must inquire of the other (1) whether he or

---

[47] Can. 1154
[48] Can. 1671-1691
[49] Can. 1143-1147

she is willing to become a Catholic, and, if not, (2) whether he or she promises to live in peaceful wedlock without insulting or attacking the Catholic religion of the partner. It is only when a negative answer is returned to both questions that the Catholic partner can be granted the privilege.

THE PRIVILEGE OF THE FAITH. In certain cases, by the "privilege of the faith", sometimes called the Petrine privilege, a marriage in which one of the parties is unbaptised "can be dissolved by the Roman Pontiff in virtue of his ministerial power"[50] (i.e., his power as vicar of Christ), thus freeing the parties to marry again.[51] This privilege is not available to those who have received a dispensation to enter a natural bond of marriage in the Catholic Church.

Non-consummation. If a couple enter marriage but do not live together as husband and wife, the marriage may be submitted to the Pope for dissolution, should there be a just cause.[52]

VIII

The Church's exclusive control over Christian Marriage. The rights of the State. Civil marriage and divorce.

THE CHURCH'S EXCLUSIVE CONTROL OVER CHRISTIAN MARRIAGE. Matrimony is a Sacrament; the Church is, therefore, its sole custodian. She has always claimed the right to determine the conditions under which a marriage may be contracted lawfully or validly.[53] (Without entering into the historical question, we find her asserting her claim as far back as c. 300 A.D. at the Council of Elvira, a local council, in Spain. A claim made at such an early date, and frequently repeated in subsequent years, must have been based on the authority of the Apostles). Reason itself approves this doctrine: in secular matters, in order to safeguard the temporal welfare of its citizens, the State frequently requires certain conditions as necessary for a lawful or valid contract, and no one questions its right to do so. Thus, e.g., we find that, in many countries, with a view to protecting minors from unscrupulous money-lenders, the State enacts that debts incurred by them have no force in law; or the State may declare a contract null under the law of equity, or null for lack of witnesses or lack of clarity. So, too, as regards the matrimonial contract, the Church, in defence of higher interests, must possess a similar power to require conditions for validity or liceity.

---

[50] Pope Pius XII, Allocution to the Holy Roman Rota, 3 Oct. 1941
[51] Cf. Can. 1148-1150. J. Abbo & J. Hannan, *The Sacred Canons*, Herder 1960, vol. II, p.391; L. Chiappetta, *Il Codice di Diritto Canonico*, Dehoniane, Roma 1996, vol. II, pp.412-5
[52] Can. 1142
[53] See opening section above, "The solemn teaching of the Church" (4).

THE RIGHTS OF THE STATE. The State has no rights except in regard to what is extrinsic to the Sacrament: e.g., it can require that it be notified when a marriage takes place; it can give a wife exclusive ownership of her dowry, where applicable; and, on the death of one partner, it can apportion the property among the surviving spouse and children.

CIVIL MARRIAGE. Between Christians, whether Catholic or non-Catholic, marriage is always a religious act and always a Sacrament. For them there is no such thing as a non-sacramental marriage.[54] The practice of wedding in the presence of a secular magistrate was introduced into France by Napoleon I, and thereafter spread widely through Europe and beyond. It was repeatedly condemned by the Supreme Pontiffs.

(a) As regards *Catholics*, Civil Marriage or marriage in a registry office or town hall, etc., is no marriage at all. The civil law may compel them to go through a rite of marriage in the presence of a civil functionary (some time either before or after the church wedding)[55] to secure the legitimacy of their marriage in the eyes of the State, but they must regard the ceremony as only a civil formality which in no way makes them husband and wife. The civil ceremony may be necessary to ensure the protection of the civil law for spouses and children in matters of property, money and inheritance.

(b) Between two baptised non-Catholics (*Protestants*) free to marry, the marriage vows may be taken by them anywhere (church, park, registry office, etc.) and without any witnesses. The ceremony constitutes them man and wife and confers on them the Sacrament of Matrimony.[56]

(c) As regards the *unbaptised*, in whose case there is question merely of a natural or non-sacramental marriage, it is generally held that the State may be entitled to lay down conditions even for validity, and so require, e.g., that such marriages should be contracted in the presence of its officials.

CIVIL DIVORCE. As stated above, the State has no power to dissolve any genuine marriage bond. Decrees of so-called divorce are an affront to God and an attack upon the institution of marriage. Through the Prophet Malachi, God says, "the Lord was witness to the covenant between you and the wife of your youth, to whom you have been faithless, though she is your companion and your wife by covenant. ... And what does He desire? Godly offspring. So take heed to yourselves, and let none be faithless to the wife of his youth. For I hate divorce, says the Lord the God of Israel."[57] The State may make laws to regulate property, maintenance, and custody of the children, for the benefit of those who have chosen to separate. It

---

[54] Leo XIII, *Arcanum Divinae Sapientiae*, 1880: DS 3145-6
[55] as in Belgium, e.g.
[56] See p.591.
[57] Mal 2:14-16

cannot, however, dissolve the marriage itself. Still more odious are laws whereby one spouse may unilaterally 'divorce' the other, even against the will of the other party. In many modern civil enactments, marriage is the only contract which may be reneged at will and routinely 'dissolved', regardless of the harm to men, women and children.

IX

To enter into marriage, the two partners must: (a) be legally capable (b) manifest their consent, and (c) do so in a valid ceremony. We will now consider these three requirements in turn. This section will consider the impediments to legal capability. Section X will explain the requisites of matrimonial consent. Section XI will examine the form of the celebration of marriage.

The impediments of Matrimony. Impediments, or obstacles to marriage, make a person incapable of validly entering marriage. For a marriage to be valid, *both* parties must be free of impediments. We mention the impediments below, but do not state in all cases how far the Church dispenses, or who has the authority to give a dispensation from them (e.g., one's Bishop, or the Pope). The Church does not dispense without a reasonable cause. This outline cannot answer all questions concerning marriage laws. When the question of marriage becomes practical, timely application should be made to one's parish priest, from whom the necessary information may be obtained. If there is any practical question or doubt, a prospective couple should see a priest or canon lawyer at the earliest opportunity, and avoid making premature plans.

The following impediments are listed in the *Code of Canon Law*.[58]

Age. A man must have turned sixteen; a woman, fourteen. (In many countries this minimum age has been raised). This is meant to ensure sufficient maturity and freedom. Marriages arranged between children are valid as long as the parties themselves consent at the time of marriage itself. *Existing marriage.* A person already bound by an existing marriage tie cannot marry again. From what has been said above, it is plain that this impediment is not removed by civil divorce. Entrance into a second unauthorised 'marriage' is mortally sinful, and bars Catholics from Holy Communion, until repentance.[59] (If the previous marriage was invalid or dissolved, this must be established in law before a new marriage can take

---

[58] Can. 1083-1095, 1103. Throughout this Chapter, unless otherwise stated, we refer only to Latin (Roman) Catholics, not Eastern Church Catholics, whose marriage laws differ slightly. For any practical marriage questions, Eastern Catholics should consult their own priests.
[59] C 1650

place. It is not enough to be personally convinced that one's previous marriage was invalid. The so-called 'internal forum solution', by-passing the process of ascertaining nullity, is not accepted by the Church).

Consanguinity (relationship by blood). Close blood relations cannot marry validly. Divine law prohibits marriage between a parent and child. The Church has specified also that no marriage can take place between any two direct descendants (grandparent-parent-child, etc.). Nor is marriage possible between: a brother and sister; half-brother and sister; uncle and niece; aunt and nephew; first cousins.[60] A dispensation from the Church is never granted for marriage between direct descendants, or brother (or half-brother) and sister.[61] Marriage between first cousins requires a dispensation from the local bishop.[62]

These impediments arising from kinship are established partly by God and partly by the Church in order to safeguard family life. Thus the natural intimacy which develops between family members and the larger circle of relations will not go beyond its proper boundaries, and the healthy affection proper to a family will remain unaffected by the desire to find a conjugal partner within it. Further, inbreeding can result in serious genetic defects or deformities. Marriage between close relations was necessary and unavoidable at the beginning of the human race, but was closed off once the necessity had passed.

Disparity of cult. This means that one party is not a Christian. A Catholic cannot validly marry an unbaptised person unless the Bishop grants a dispensation. Conditions apply for Mixed Marriages (see below). The conditions aim at protecting the faith of the Catholic, the faith of the future children, and the harmony of the spouses.

Abduction. A woman abducted or held in order to be married cannot marry validly unless she freely chooses marriage after being separated from her abductor and established in a safe and free place.

Crime. One who kills one's own or another's spouse, with a view to marrying a particular person, cannot validly enter that marriage. Similarly, accomplices in such a crime cannot marry later on. The Church has no desire to help murderers enjoy the purpose or effects of their crime.

Impotence. If, before marriage, there is a permanent incapacity for the conjugal act, on the part of the man or the woman, the marriage is invalid. If there is a doubt about the matter, the marriage may take place.

Affinity. This refers to the relationships arising from marriage: 'in-laws', 'step-child', etc. A widow cannot marry her deceased husband's father, or her step-son. A widower cannot marry his deceased wife's mother, or his step-daughter. (In the Eastern Churches, a widow/er cannot marry a brother/sister-in-law. Further, in the

---

[60] Can. 1091
[61] Can. 1078 § 3
[62] Can. 1078 § 1

Eastern Churches, *spiritual relationship* is an impediment, as it once was in the Latin Church: a sponsor or god-parent cannot marry a god-child or a parent of the god-child[63]).

Adoption. The legal relationship arising from adoption rules out marriage between an adopted person and a direct ascendant (legal parent or grandparent), or a legal brother or sister. As with consanguinity and affinity, the Church here desires to preserve the purity of family relations.

Public propriety. When a couple live together after an invalid marriage or in a notorious or public concubinage, neither party is free later on to marry a child or parent of the former partner. This would offend against public propriety.

Holy Orders and Vows of Chastity. A deacon, priest, or bishop, or a religious man or woman who has taken a public vow of perpetual chastity, cannot validly marry while bound by that vow.

X

Matrimonial consent. Defects in consent. Public expression of consent.[64]

MATRIMONIAL CONSENT. The mutual giving and receiving of consent makes the marriage. "Matrimonial consent is an act of the will by which a man and woman by an irrevocable covenant mutually give and receive one another in order to establish a marriage."[65] For consent to be valid, the couple must at the least be aware that marriage is a permanent partnership between a man and a woman, ordered to the procreation of children through their intimate co-operation.[66]

DEFECTS IN CONSENT. Consent to marriage is vitiated (rendered null) by incapacity or a serious defect in knowledge or the will:

Incapacity. Incapable of marriage are they who lack sufficient use of reason, or labour under a grave lack of due discretion, or suffer from a severe psychological illness that makes them incapable of taking on the essential duties of the married state.

Defects in knowledge. (1) Ignorance of what marriage is, as set out a few lines above, under "Matrimonial consent". (2) Error concerning the identity of the person, or a quality of the person directly and principally intended. E.g., Marcus wanted to marry Marcia, not her identical sister, Martha! Or, Scholastica married Polycarp, only because she thought he was a soldier, when in fact he was not. Again, a marriage would be invalid if a woman is proceeding to marry her fiancé only because she falsely thinks he has

---

[63] Code of Canons of the Eastern Churches, can. 809 §1, 811 §1
[64] Can. 1095-1107
[65] Can. 1057 §2
[66] Can. 1096

finished his studies and has a job. (3) Deceit or fraud perpetrated in order to secure consent, concerning a quality of the other party which of its very nature can seriously disrupt the marriage. E.g., Lydia dishonestly said she was a practising Catholic, when Boniface said he would only ever marry such.

Defects of will. (1) Force or fear: the consent to marriage cannot be valid or genuine if extracted by force or grave fear. (2) Conditional consent: marriage is invalid if contracted subject to a condition regarding a future event. E.g., a marriage is invalid if one says, "I mean to marry you today, as long as you inherit that money some day." If the condition regards the past or present, a marriage will be invalid if that condition in fact does not exist. (3) Simulation, total or partial: pretended consent is no consent at all. If one or both parties by a positive act of the will excludes marriage, or an essential element or property of marriage, then the marriage is invalid. Partial simulation means taking marriage vows with an intention to exclude fidelity, or permanence, or openness to having children. Total simulation exists when marriage itself is not desired, e.g., marrying purely to gain citizenship of a particular country and nothing else. Until proven otherwise, the presumption is that the parties mean what the vows say.[67]

Dangers to consent also arise from pre-matrimonial contracts (fixing arrangements before the marriage in case of divorce). They spring from mistrust between couples, undermine their determination to maintain fidelity "in good times and in bad", and weaken, if not vitiate, a genuine consent to the permanent bond of marriage. Any couple who feels the need for a pre-matrimonial contract should discuss this openly with the minister of marriage.

THE PUBLIC EXPRESSION OF CONSENT. In the marriage ceremony of the Latin Rite, the three questions put to the couple enable them to express their free consent to the essential elements, properties and duties of marriage: 1. Unity: "Have you come here freely and without reservation to give yourselves to each other in marriage?" 2. Indissolubility: "Will you honour each other as man and wife for the rest of your lives?" 3. Openness to Fertility: "Will you accept children lovingly from God, and bring them up according to the law of Christ and His Church?"

---

[67] Can. 1101 §1

XI

The Catholic form of the celebration of Marriage. Whom it obliges. Exceptions.

NORMAL FORM OF CELEBRATING A MARRIAGE.[68] The normal form, known as the "canonical form", is the exchange of vows in a Catholic ceremony before a Bishop or any delegated Priest or Deacon, in the presence of two other witnesses.

WHO IS BOUND BY IT. All Catholics, i.e., those baptised or received into the Catholic Church are bound to this form of marriage.

EXCEPTIONS. (1) With a dispensation given by the Bishop in special cases, a Catholic may marry a non-Catholic in a non-Catholic ceremony that is civilly recognised. This is called dispensation from canonical form. (2) Those who have formally defected from the Catholic faith are not bound by the canonical form. (3) "Extraordinary form": when observance of the form is impossible, a Catholic may marry in the presence of two witnesses, without a delegated priest or deacon. This is permitted when there is a danger of death, or when it is judged that no delegated Catholic minister can come within one month. Such cases may arise in remote districts, or in times of persecution or warfare. In such a case, if an undelegated priest or deacon can be found, he should be asked to officiate, and should send a record of the marriage to the parish priest or bishop. His presence, however, is not required for validity but for lawfulness. If no Catholic minister is available, the married couple and the two witnesses are bound to see that a record of the marriage is sent to the proper quarter.

XII

Mixed marriages.[69] A marriage between a Catholic and a baptised non-Catholic Christian is called a mixed marriage. There is "disparity of cult (worship)" where one partner is not baptised. The Church prefers that Catholics marry Catholics: to share the same religion is one less factor for division and one more factor for unity. In a mixed marriage, the division which sadly afflicts Christians can display itself in the heart of the home. Division in religion can manifest itself on Sundays and at times of family prayer: grace before meals, rosary, etc. Differences of belief can plague decisions about married behaviour, the rearing and education of children, and family priorities.[70] It is important to be realistic about such differences before entering upon a mixed marriage.

---

[68] Can. 1108-1123
[69] Can. 1124-1129
[70] Cf. C 1633.

To summarise:

1. *Catholic* + *Catholic*, in a Catholic ceremony—valid, sacramental marriage.

2. *Catholic* + *Catholic*, in a non-Catholic ceremony—invalid.

3. *Catholic* + non-Catholic Christian, in a Catholic ceremony—valid, sacramental marriage, but permission is required from the Bishop or his delegate.

4. *Catholic* + unbaptised, in a Catholic ceremony—valid, natural marriage, provided a dispensation is obtained from the Bishop or his delegate.

5. *Catholic* + non-Catholic Christian, in a non-Catholic ceremony—valid, sacramental marriage, provided a dispensation from canonical form is obtained from the Bishop or one who has a mandate from him.

6. *Catholic* + Orthodox Christian, in an Orthodox ceremony—valid, sacramental marriage; licit if approved by the Catholic authority; otherwise illicit but still valid.[71]

7. *Catholic* + unbaptised, in a non-Catholic ceremony—valid, natural marriage, provided the dispensations are obtained from the Bishop or one who has a mandate from him.

8. Non-Catholic Christian + non-Catholic Christian, in any ceremony—valid, sacramental marriage, provided divine law is observed.

9. Non-Catholic Christian + unbaptised, in any ceremony recognised by the State—valid, natural marriage, provided divine law is observed.[72]

10. Unbaptised + unbaptised, in any ceremony recognised by the State—valid, natural marriage, provided divine law is observed.

*   *   *

Divine law binds all people. *Church law* binds only Catholics. The essential divine law here, i.e., God's law, is that both the man and woman must not be already validly married to someone else.

In marriage law, "Catholic" means someone who was baptised a Catholic or received into the Church, and has not defected from it by a formal act (Can. 1086 §1).

By "Christian" is meant someone validly *baptised*, not simply one who professes Christian faith.

---

[71] Code of Canons of the Eastern Churches, can. 834 §2

[72] Nos. 8 & 9 apply to Protestants but not to non-Catholic *Eastern* Christians, who may be bound by their own Church's legislation for their marriage to be valid: Code of Canons of the Eastern Churches, can. 780, 781.

CONDITIONS FOR A MIXED MARRIAGE.   Before a mixed marriage, the Catholic partner is to declare that he or she is prepared to remove dangers of defecting from the faith, and is to make a sincere promise to do all in his or her power to ensure that all the children be baptised and reared in the Catholic Church.   The other party is to be informed in good time of the promises and obligations of the Catholic party.[73]

The Church rejoices when, in a mixed marriage, the day comes when husband and wife are one also in membership of the Catholic Church and can receive Holy Communion together at the same altar.   Even should that day never come, the Church greatly appreciates the help that non-Catholic spouses give in the religious education of the children, and is very grateful when the non-Catholic partner joins the other family members at Sunday Mass, prayer, and Church activities.

XIII

Marriage and religion.   The dignity of Christian Marriage. Obedience to the Church's teaching.   Preparation for marriage.

MARRIAGE BREAKDOWN AND RELIGION.   In many Western countries, 1 in 3, or even 1 in 2 marriages ends in divorce.   Only in God can the help and strength be found to resist the force of this plague and bad example. Among couples who go to church every Sunday, divorce occurs at the rate of about 1 in 25;   and among couples who go to church every Sunday and have some time of prayer together at home during the week,—about 1 in 50.   Father Patrick Peyton, the great crusader for the daily family Rosary, popularised the slogan, "The family that prays together, stays together." God who is love, and the source of all love, teaches married couples how to love, and love faithfully.   When married couples are closest to God, they are closest to each other.   Their love then is built on the rock which weathers all storms.   A practical fidelity to Christ and His Church is the surest guarantee for a happy and lasting marriage.

THE DIGNITY OF CHRISTIAN MARRIAGE.   God consecrates the priest to be His helper on earth.   He invests the priest with a share in His own divine power of mercy and forgiveness.   He gives him the keys to open the Kingdom of Heaven to souls.   Likewise, God blesses husband and wife to be His helpers in preparing those who are one day to stand around His throne.   He lets the shadow of His creative power come down upon them. He calls them to be the living image of His own Fatherhood and Providence, and to be the instruments whereby the Kingdom of Heaven shall be peopled.   Christian marriage is the foundation of the Christian

---

[73] Can. 1125

home and the nursery of the Church. Marriage is a vocation to holiness. "Christian spouses, therefore, are fortified and, as it were, *consecrated* for the duties and dignity of their state by a special sacrament; fulfilling their conjugal and family mission by virtue of this sacrament, and imbued with the spirit of Christ, by which their whole lives are suffused with faith, hope and charity, they thus advance more and more upon their own mutual perfection and sanctification, and so together render glory to God."[74]

OBEDIENCE TO THE CHURCH'S TEACHING. On the subject of marriage and the preparation for it, the Church sets forth the grave obligations of husband and wife to one another and to their children. She condemns the false and shameful views that teem in the books and magazines of the modern world, and she warns us against the dangers arising from uncontrolled intimacy outside of marriage. She conveys her teaching to us through the Pope and Bishops, through the united voice of faithful theologians, and sometimes to the individual through a confessor or spiritual director. She speaks to us in the name and with the authority of her Divine Founder, our Lord Jesus Christ, who is always with her. Her teaching, therefore, is His teaching. Hence, when the Church explains the divine law in regard to marriage and the preparation for it, and declares this or that to be sinful, *all Catholics are bound to accept her ruling: to resist it is to resist God Himself.* Young people in particular should ponder this truth: at a time of crisis in their future lives, it will nerve them against the attractions of the world and the call of passion, and will save them from a shameful betrayal of their Redeemer.

PREPARATION FOR MARRIAGE. The best preparation for marriage, apart from the fulfilment of one's particular religious duties, is a life of chastity and the faithful fulfilment of one's daily duties. A lazy and selfish life is no preparation for the generosity and sacrifices demanded of spouses. Unchastity before marriage can weaken one's ability to promise chastity within marriage. A Catholic who has not been confirmed should endeavour to receive this sacrament before marriage, if possible. To receive the sacrament of marriage itself fruitfully, spouses are earnestly recommended to go to Confession beforehand.[75]

The choice of marriage partner should be based on the *virtues* of the other person. Merely external and worldly qualities and talents must never be the chief factor. Affection and passions come and go; the attachment must be founded upon virtue and love, which is the desire for the true good of another. Married love, as St Thomas says, is the highest form of

---

[74] *Gaudium et Spes*, art. 48
[75] Can. 1065

friendship.[76] The love between husband and wife leads them to desire the happiness of each other, even more than their own. Of a potential partner, one must ask oneself: will this person be a good father or mother to my children?

The most serious step in life is Ordination or Marriage. In each case a grave obligation is assumed which, if not fulfilled, will bring down a terrible judgement, because the souls of others are involved. Neither should be approached without prudent advice, calm reasoning, and fervent prayer. Marriage is the making or marring of life: a wise marriage may bring earthly happiness and will set one on the road that leads to heaven; a foolish marriage will certainly bring suffering and sorrow, and may lead to hell. No one should speak flippantly of marriage, or treat it as a subject of levity. Such idle talk produces false and harmful notions. It distorts the judgement and may issue in the gravest unhappiness. It is encouraged by the dread enemy of the human soul, working through suggestive films, novels, and magazines, and is a gross irreverence to the great Sacrament which Christ has founded. One of the consequences of Original Sin is the escape of the passions from the natural control of reason. Many people are inclined to look at marriage from a merely natural standpoint, and are attached to it by worldly pleasure, which they find in the experience to be an empty illusion. The true happiness of husband and wife rests on divine grace. It consists in mutual sympathy and help in the practice of religion and in the ordinary affairs and troubles of life. It is at its highest when they see themselves surrounded by innocent children dependent on them for every care, and when they realise that they are the invisible agents of God in a great spiritual work; that He is revealing through them His love and tenderness for the little ones He has given them.

Hence, with what jealous, reverent care young people should guard their affections; in what a Catholic spirit they should spend the serious time of engagement; how well they should prepare themselves for this revered Sacrament, the symbol of the unique and fruitful love of Christ for His Spouse, the Holy Church!

---

[76] *Summa Contra Gentiles*, Book III, ch. 123

GOD THE AWARDER

CHAPTER 19

THE LAST THINGS

Summary

I.   The solemn teaching of the Church.
II. The purpose of man's creation. Death. The Particular Judgement. Eternity.
III. Heaven: an abode of perfect and everlasting happiness. Its happiness comes from the direct Vision of God. Its happiness cannot be adequately described. The Light of Glory.
IV. Hell: an abode of eternal suffering. The fire of Hell. The torments of Hell cannot be adequately described. Objections against the doctrine of Eternal Punishment, based on apparent inconsistency with Divine Justice and Goodness, and the happiness of the Blessed. Replies. The moral value of the doctrine of Eternal Punishment.
V.   Purgatory: an abode of purification. Proof of the doctrine from the definition of the Church, from Sacred Scripture, from Tradition, from reason. Succouring the dead.
VI. The end of the world. The resurrection of the body. All men will rise from the dead: proved from Sacred Scripture and Tradition, shown to be not in opposition to reason. The nature and properties of the risen body.
VII. The General Judgement. On the Last Day Christ will judge and sentence all mankind. The purpose of the General Judgement. A new heaven and a new earth.

I

The solemn teaching of the Church. The Church teaches solemnly:

(1) that death is a punishment for sin;[1]
(2) that the just who depart this life free from all debt of temporal punishment are at once admitted, but not all in the same degree, to the Blessed Vision of God in Heaven;[2] that they have a clear and direct knowledge of the Divine Essence and attributes and of the Three Divine Persons;[3] that their happiness will last for all eternity;[4]
(3) that demons, and men who die in the state of mortal sin, suffer eternal punishment in Hell;[5]

---

[1] T 1512
[2] Pope Benedict XII in the year 1336: DS 1000
[3] F 1304-5
[4] DS 1001
[5] Athanasian Creed; DS 858, 1002, F 1306

(4) that the souls of the just who have not fully discharged their debt to God's justice are cleansed in Purgatory after death before their admission to Heaven;[6]

(5) that the souls in Purgatory can be relieved by the suffrages of the living[7] (i.e., by Masses, prayers, alms-deeds and other good works);

(6) that on the Last Day all men will rise from the dead in the bodies which they had in this life;[8]

(7) that Jesus Christ will return to earth gloriously on the Last Day;[9]

(8) that everyone will be arraigned before the judgement seat of Christ, and sentenced by Him according to their deserts.[10]

II

The purpose of man's creation. Death. The Particular Judgement. Eternity.

THE PURPOSE OF MAN'S CREATION. God has placed us in this world to know, love, and serve Him, and thus to merit Heaven. He has taught us that from Him we have come, that to Him we go, and that in Him alone we can find the happiness for which we long. We are here in a state of trial, doing battle. God, by His Sacraments and His graces, has given us the weapons we need, the strength to use them, and the desire of victory. He has created us and destined us for Paradise,[11] not to enrich Himself but to manifest His goodness.

DEATH. Through sin, death has come into the world.[12] All men must die, since all have sinned in Adam: "you are dust, and to dust you shall return."[13] But though death is certain for all, no one knows *when, where,* or *how* he will die. We must, therefore, be prepared at all times: "You also must be ready; for the Son of man is coming at an hour you do not expect."[14] You can live and die but once: "it is appointed for men to die once".[15] With death, the time for merit is at an end: "night comes when no one can work."[16] *You will die either as the friend or foe of God, and will continue to*

---

[6] T 1580

[7] F 1304; T 1820

[8] L 801

[9] The Creeds

[10] The Creeds

[11] "Paradise" sometimes refers to the Garden of Eden, but here means Heaven: cf. Lk 23:43; 2 Cor 12:3; Rev 2:7.

[12] Rom 5:12

[13] Gen 3:19

[14] Lk 12:40

[15] Heb 9:27

[16] Jn 9:4

be His friend or foe for all eternity: "if a tree falls to the south or to the north, in the place where the tree falls, there it will lie."[17] But Christ, by taking away the sins of the world, has robbed death of its terror. There is nothing in Christian death to make us tremble: "by dying He has destroyed our death; by rising again He has restored our life."[18] He has made it the gate through which we must pass to Him. Death is only fearful for those who bear the thought of having to face God in a state of mortal sin—for "the sting of death is sin".[19]

THE PARTICULAR JUDGEMENT. Immediately after death, the Particular Judgement takes place at which each one's eternal destiny is decided: "it is appointed for men to die once, and after that comes judgement".[20] When your soul has left the body, it will be brought before the throne of God, who will pass sentence on you. If you died in a state of grace, you will be saved; otherwise, condemned. The good and evil you have done during your life will be examined in the light of His justice. He will give you reward or punishment, according to your deserts; He will cast you into the Hell of the damned or summon you to share with Him in the happiness of Heaven, either at once or after you have been cleansed in the fire of Purgatory.

ETERNITY. After death the soul enters eternity, a form of duration that never comes to an end. It is not a multiple of time: we may set down a million years for every grain of sand on the shore, for every leaf of the forest, for every drop of water in the ocean; we may multiply these millions together as often as we please, but at the end of our calculation we are no nearer to understanding eternity than we were when we began. No number of squares superimposed will give a cube: no number of centuries added together will give eternity. A square is no part, no measure of a cube: a century of years is no part, no measure of eternity.

III

Heaven, an abode of perfect and everlasting happiness. The souls of those who die in the grace of God are admitted into Heaven either immediately or after their release from Purgatory. There in that abode of His blessedness they shall enjoy in company with the angels and saints a perfect and everlasting happiness: "they shall see His face, and His name shall be on their foreheads. And night shall be no more; they need no light

---

17 Ecclesiastes (Qoheleth) 11:3
18 Easter Preface
19 1 Cor 15:56
20 Heb 9:27; see also F 1304-6, T 1545-6.

of lamp or sun, for the Lord God will be their light, and they shall reign for ever and ever."[21] Their happiness shall never be clouded by grief: "God shall wipe away every tear from their eyes, and death shall be no more, neither shall there be mourning nor crying nor pain any more, for the former things have passed away."[22] Their happiness shall never end: "the righteous will go into eternal life";[23] they shall receive from the "Prince of Pastors" "an imperishable wreath",[24] "the unfading crown of glory."[25] They cannot themselves destroy their happiness by sin: in this world men crave for happiness but never find it; they commit sin because to their dark understanding it seems to promise the fulfilment of their desire; but, in Paradise, the blessed do not seek for happiness, because they have found it in its perfection. Their longings and desires are at rest in God, so that even the thought of turning away from Him by sin can never approach them. The Church celebrates the glory of all the saved on November 1, All Saints' Day.

The happiness of Heaven comes from the immediate vision of God. "For now we see in a mirror dimly, but then face to face. Now I know in part; then I shall understand fully, even as I have been fully understood."[26] Now we know in part; for through our natural faculties we see God as in a weak and blurred reflection: all the power and majesty and beauty we behold in the wide world about us, from the stars in heaven to the flowers of the field; all the high and noble achievements of men in science, literature, and art; all the love and devotion that have ever burned in the human heart, and all the joy that has ever shone there—all drawn together and intensified indefinitely—is so far below the inexhaustible Source and Author of all as hardly to deserve the name of image or shadow. Now we know in part; for in all that God has told us of Himself in the many precious revelations He has vouchsafed to man, we see Him but obscurely. Even the great unfolding of His love manifested to us in the life and death of His own Divine Son gives us only an imperfect vision: faith sets us within a narrow circle of light, while above and all around, the impenetrable darkness of mystery baffles our reason. "But then I shall know even as I am known."[27] We shall pass into a state utterly unlike the present. We shall see God as even as He sees us—immediately, clearly, with nothing to intercept or obscure the vision: "Beloved, we are God's children now; it does not yet appear what we shall be, but we know that when He appears we shall be like Him, for we shall see Him as He is."[28] In the Beatific Vision, the

---

[21] Apoc 22:4-5

[22] Apoc 21:4

[23] Matt 25:46

[24] 1 Cor 9:25

[25] 1 Pet 5:4

[26] 1 Cor 13:12

[27] 1 Cor 13:12 (Douay)

[28] 1 Jn 3:2

veil shall be withdrawn from the truths of faith.[29] We shall know the mystery of the Creation, why God made the world, how He sustained it in being, how He guided its every movement, linking it all together in perfect unity, triumphing and manifesting His glory even in His rebellious creatures. We shall know the true nature of Grace and its wondrous workings in the mind and heart of every man. We shall know the mysteries of the Trinity,[30] the Incarnation, and the Redemption. We shall see down into the depth of God's wisdom, justice, power, beauty, and love. (To know God and His Mysteries is not the same as to comprehend them fully. Because He is infinite, God can be fully known only to Himself). Thus clasped to Him for all eternity, each soul will find a complete happiness, living in Him as it were, living a life of ceaseless and varied activity, passing from knowledge to knowledge, and from joy to joy, and united in loving association with Mary ever Blessed, with the Angels and Saints.

The happiness of Heaven cannot be adequately described. It is difficult to describe to another a pleasure which he has not actually experienced, to convey to him, for instance, in words alone the sensation produced in us by the fragrance of a flower or the taste of a fruit. Still, we may succeed to some extent by telling him it is like such and such a perfume or flavour with which he is already familiar. The task is vastly more difficult when we deal with one who does not possess the use of that sense through which the pleasure has come to us. Such is the case when we try to tell a blind man of our delight in looking at a great stretch of landscape in the hour after sunset. He hears us speak of the objects within sight, of mountains, woods, and water, of the play of light and shade, of the richness of colour, the verdure of the rolling plain, and of the peace that seems to breathe at that hour from earth and sky. But all our rapture tells him no more than this: that, if he had his sight, he would enjoy a new and great pleasure which may be compared in some vague way to that which he feels when he listens to a beautiful harmony. We, however, when we try to understand the happiness of heaven, are in a worse case even than the blind man trying to understand colours. He knows at least that though the pleasure of seeing is quite dissimilar from that of hearing, yet in intensity both pleasures are much the same. We, on the other hand, are endeavouring to conceive a happiness which is not only altogether unlike, but infinitely beyond anything we have ever felt, for the Holy Spirit tells us that "what no eye has seen, nor ear heard, *nor the heart of man conceived*, what God has prepared for those who love Him."[31] Still, though it is plain that

---

[29] Solemnly taught by Pope Benedict XII, who says that "the vision and the enjoyment of the Divine Essence put an end to acts of faith and hope": DS 1001

[30] The Trinity is expressly mentioned in the solemn teaching of the Council of Florence: the just in Heaven "clearly behold the One and Triune God Himself, as He is": DS 1305.

[31] 1 Cor 2:9

anything like an adequate idea of Heaven is impossible, we may form some conception of it from considerations such as the following:

(1) *The sufferings of this life are but a poor price to pay for the happiness of Heaven.* Once we begin to know the greatness of God, we can appreciate the saying of St Alphonsus Liguori: "God is cheap at any price."[32] Christ told His followers that they would be like lambs among wolves, calumniated, reviled, persecuted, imprisoned and scourged. Yet He said to them, "Blessed are you when men revile you and persecute you and utter all kinds of evil against you falsely on My account. Rejoice and be glad, for your reward is great in Heaven."[33] All that is hard to flesh and blood was to be their portion—yet they were to make light of it. They were to rejoice at it, because it was but a little price to pay for the reward of Heaven. St Paul tells us what he endured for the Gospel of Christ:[34] five times he received the scourging of thirty-nine lashes; thrice he was set upon and beaten with rods; stoned once; three times he was shipwrecked; "a night and a day adrift at sea"; his life was at the mercy of the robber, the Jew, the Gentile, and, cruel thought, the traitor within the fold; cold and ill-clad, he was worn with pain, labour, scant sleep, hunger, and thirst; and besides all this, his mind and heart were ever on the rack, fearing, praying, and planning for the welfare of so many widely dispersed Christian communities. *He* knew what suffering was; yet, what does he say? "The sufferings of this present time are not worth comparing with the glory that is to be revealed to us"[35]—not even worthy of mention when set beside the reward promised by God to His faithful servants.

(2) *The blessed in Heaven have outgrown the pleasures of this world.* Toys and childish games were a source of pleasure to us in our early years. When we grew up, we turned to other amusements, and perhaps wondered how we could have taken our early pastimes so seriously: "When I was a child", says St Paul, "I spoke like a child, I thought like a child, I reasoned like a child; when I became a man, I gave up childish ways."[36] So will it be with those who enter God's Kingdom. They will realise that at last they have arrived at true adulthood, that they have outgrown all the pleasures that fastened them so passionately to earth and made the leaving of it so bitter to them. They will cast from themselves all the trivial things of their past. They will have gone out of the land of shadow and darkness. Within their minds there will be a great out-flashing of light. They will have found Him who alone is

---

[32] *Practice of Love of Jesus Christ* (maxims at end) & *al. loc.*
[33] Matt 5:11-12; Lk 10:3
[34] 2 Cor 11:24 ff.
[35] Rom 8:18
[36] 1 Cor 13:11

Truth and Beauty and Omnipotence, and who will use His very Omnipotence to fill them with every joy.

The Light of Glory. Sanctifying Grace alone does not enable the soul to see God. If it did, the just in this life would behold Him. Something further is therefore required, which is called the Light of Glory. It is a force or power imparted to the intellect of the blessed in Heaven, like a new eye, enabling them to see God as He is. Its intensity will depend on the degree of Sanctifying Grace which each one possesses at death. Each soul will therefore receive all the happiness it is capable of receiving; and no soul can envy another that receives more: Illustrations: (1) The small cup and the large cup are both filled to the brim by the torrent. One contains more than the other, yet both are equally full. (2) Suppose several people look at a beautiful picture or listen to a great musical work; all go away thoroughly delighted, yet owing to differences in capacity and training, some will see or hear more in the work than others, and derive a greater pleasure from it.[37]

Degrees of glory in Heaven. Our Lord Jesus Christ is King of Saints; second to Him in glory is the Blessed Virgin, the Queen of Saints; after them comes Saint Joseph, the Head of the Holy Family. Each saint is ranked according to the degree of charity and merits that he possessed at the end of his life. The Council of Florence declares that the souls of the just, "clearly behold the One and Triune God Himself, as He is, but in accordance with the difference of their merits, one more perfectly than the other."[38] Our Lord told parables in which servants of the same Master received differing rewards for different responsibilities.[39] He spoke of those who are greater and lesser in the Kingdom of Heaven.[40] He declared He would reward each one according to his works,[41] and told the Apostles, "In my Father's house there are many mansions."[42]

Note. *Borrowed or transferred expressions*. Of all the senses, sight is the noblest, because it seems to give us the clearest and most definite knowledge of material things. Hence, we are prone to use the terms proper to it of the higher faculty, the intellect, and to speak as though the intellect had "eyes" and could get from God "light to see" the truth. All such expressions are borrowed or transferred: they have been borrowed from the sense of sight, and given to the intellect to which they do not strictly belong. They represent our weak efforts to convey a meaning too deep for human language.

---

[37] The analogy of two different vessels being both full to capacity is at least four centuries old: cf. James Boswell, *Life of Samuel Johnson*, Everyman ed. 1946, Vol. I, footnote at pp.315-6 (A.D. 1766 Aetat. 57).

[38] DS 1305

[39] Matt 25:14-30; Lk 19:11-27

[40] Matt 5:19; 18:4; Lk 7:28; Mk 10:31

[41] Matt 16:27

[42] Jn 14:2 (Douay)

The 'lights' given by God; the 'vision' of God. 'The light of Reason' is the natural power given us by God the Creator to distinguish between right and wrong. 'The light of Faith' is the power given to the soul by God the Sanctifier to know and embrace the truths of faith. 'The light of Glory' is the power given to the intellect by God to know Him with an intimacy of which no creature, without His special aid, would be capable. But 'light' strictly understood is something material, and can only vaguely describe a movement or power of the understanding. So, too, when we speak of the 'vision of God', of 'seeing Him face to face', our words are not strictly exact; still, they are the least imperfect we can find. Using his natural reason, even at its highest level, man knows God only through His works, knows Him only 'at a distance', or 'as hidden under an impenetrable veil'. But the souls of the blessed enjoy a direct knowledge of Him. They share in some way in the knowledge which He has of Himself. So we say that they 'stand in His presence', that they 'gaze upon Him in His unveiled Majesty', that they 'behold Him face to face'.

IV

Hell, an abode of eternal suffering. Salvation is not automatic upon the death of Christ. The Council of Trent declares, "Although it is true that 'He died for all' (2 Cor 5:15), not all, however, receive the benefit of His death, but only those to whom the merit of His Passion is communicated."[43] The souls of those who die in mortal sin are cast at once into Hell. Each will suffer according to its deserts—some more than others, therefore.

(1) *In Hell, the wicked will suffer the pain of loss.* St Alphonsus says, "If God is lost, all is lost."[44] In this life, sinners rejected God for sin; in Hell, they will know what they rejected. They will see that they have missed the one thing that can make them happy, the one thing which they need and can never obtain. That the living man needs food, air and water, is a truth only too distressingly illustrated in authentic narrative: we have read many a time, how a group of castaways after days in an open boat under a blazing sun, driven mad with hunger and thirst, have thrown lots to see which of them should be put to death, so that the others might eat his flesh. We have heard of how desperate passengers on sinking ships have fought and scrambled and trampled one another to death in the race for the passages to the surface. These incidents, which one shudders to record, are our comment on the simple statement that man needs food and air; but how shall we illustrate the truth that man needs God? Man's desire to eat and breathe is a desire of his animal nature, while his desire for God is a desire of his whole being. In the living man, the desire for air and sustenance is always present, always more or less awake, and, if frustrated, leads to

---

[43] DS 1523
[44] *Practice of Love of Jesus Christ* (maxims at end) & *al. loc.*

dreadful suffering. In man after death, the desire for God which he now can hardly feel, will suddenly spring into full activity. His whole being will flame up with an intense craving, with a hunger and a thirst for God, of a force and vehemence infinitely beyond anything within mortal experience. After judgement, the sinner will feel himself fiercely, madly, borne and swept onwards by every faculty within him towards his Creator; but, held down pitilessly with his guilt, he will struggle in an agony of suffocation. He will rage with the frenzy of a parched and famished beast in sight of the food and drink that cannot be reached. St John Chrysostom says: "Unbearable is the fire of Hell—who does not know it?—and dreadful are its torments; but, if one were to heap a thousand hell-fires one on the other, it would be as nothing compared with the punishment of being excluded from the blessed glory of Heaven … and of being compelled to hear Christ say, 'I know you not'."[45]

(2) *They will suffer the pain of sense.* In this life they rejected God for a created thing; in Hell, God will employ a created thing to punish them. They will be tortured by a physical agency which the Sacred Scriptures call fire. Our Lord says that at the end of the world, "the Angels will come out and separate the evil from the righteous, and throw them *into the furnace of fire*; there men will weep and gnash their teeth."[46] "If your hand causes you to sin", He says, "cut it off; it is better for you to enter life maimed than with two hands to go to Hell, *to the unquenchable fire*."[47] He tells us too of the rich man and of the beggar Lazarus who lay at his gate: "The poor man died and was carried by the Angels to Abraham's bosom. The rich man also died and was buried; and *in Hades*, being *in torment*, he lifted up his eyes, and saw Abraham far off and Lazarus in his bosom. And he called out, 'Father Abraham, have mercy upon me, and *send Lazarus to dip the end of his finger in water and cool my tongue; for I am in anguish in this flame.*' But Abraham said, 'Son, remember that you in your lifetime received your good things, and Lazarus in like manner evil things, but now he is comforted here, and you are in anguish. And besides all this, between us and you a great chasm has been fixed, in order that those who would pass from here to you may not be able, and none may cross from there to us.'"[48] St John writes in the Apocalypse that the wicked "shall drink the wine of God's wrath", that they "shall be tormented with fire and brimstone in the presence of the holy

---

[45] *Hom. in Matt.* 23, 9
[46] Matt 13:49-50
[47] Mk 9:43
[48] Lk 16:19-26

Angels, and in the presence of the Lamb. And the smoke of their torment goes up for ever and ever; and they have no rest, day or night".[49]

The pain of sense includes not only the pain of fire but every pain distinct from that of loss. It includes, therefore, all that the damned soul will suffer from remorse of conscience, from the memory of lost opportunities, from the thought of the wretched pleasures of this life purchased at the price of eternal happiness. It includes all that it will endure from association with demons, hateful to the soul as the soul is hateful to them. There is no sufferer on earth we pity more than one who is unloved and never hears a kind word. Yet, unknown to us, God may give such a person many consolations. But what of the soul in Hell? It will never again hear the voice of pity. It is left to brood on its misery, alone and for ever.[50]

(3) *They will suffer for all eternity.* Christ speaks of Hell as the place "where their worm does not die, and the fire is not quenched."[51] He calls it "Gehenna",[52] Greek for "Valley of Hinnom", a deep ravine on the south-west side of Jerusalem, long a dumping ground for corpses, human waste, and rotting matter—hence a place synonymous with incessant fire and every revulsion. He tells us that God will pass sentence on the wicked, saying to them: "Depart from Me you cursed into the eternal fire prepared for the devil and his angels".[53] He contrasts the fate of the bad and the good in the words: "And they will go away into eternal punishment, but the righteous into eternal life."[54] "Eternal" or "everlasting" is sometimes used loosely in Sacred Scripture to denote a long, but not endless, period. This, however, as St Augustine points out, is not its meaning here. It must, he says, mean "eternal" in the strict sense, and for the following reason: the two expressions "everlasting punishment" and "everlasting life" occur in the same sentence; "everlasting" must, therefore, bear the same meaning in both. All admit that "everlasting life" means "never-ending life." All must therefore admit that "everlasting punishment" means "never-ending punishment."[55]

Note on the Parable of Lazarus. The parable of the rich man and the beggar is Our Lord's impressive illustration of the truth that He punishes the grave abuse of worldly wealth with unending torments. But He does not intend us to accept all the

---

[49] Apoc 14:10-11

[50] Dante depicts on the entrance into Hell an inscription, "Abandon all hope, ye who enter here": *The Divine Comedy*, Inferno III, 9.

[51] Mk 9:48

[52] e.g., Mk 9:43; Matt 23:33; cf. 2 Chron 33:6.

[53] Matt 25:41

[54] Ibid., v. 46

[55] *The City of God*, Bk XXI, Ch. 23

dramatic details as literally true. He does not require us to believe that there could have been a respectful interchange of words between Abraham and a soul in Hell, nor that a disembodied spirit could have cried out for "a drop of water" to cool its "tongue", nor that a damned soul is solicitous for the salvation of its surviving relatives. What He *does* require us to believe is that, even if, *on an impossible supposition*, a lost soul could make a piteous appeal for the very slightest relief, its request would be denied. (The contention by some that the rich man is in Purgatory is untenable. His sin of hard-heartedness was mortal, not venial. In the parable, Abraham says there is a great chasm between them that "none may cross from there to us". If the rich man is saved and awaiting Heaven, then the whole point of the parable is lost).

Attempts to circumvent the doctrine of Hell. Origen in the 3rd century, and some others who followed him, held that at the end of time there would be a universal restoration, in which all the devils and the damned would also be saved. This error was condemned at the Synod of Constantinople in 543, and on other occasions.[56] A different form of the error has been proposed by some, who say that Christ's descent to the dead included the damned, to offer them salvation. This error is contrary to the Church teaching already given. It makes nonsense of Hell, and it is specifically ruled out in the Catechism: "Jesus did not descend into hell to deliver the damned, nor to destroy the hell of damnation, but to free the just who had gone before Him." [57]

The same, and others, have proposed that while Hell exists for demons, possibly no human being has gone or ever will go there, for, as St Paul says, God "desires all men to be saved".[58] But the same Apostle tells us that the condemned "shall suffer the punishment of eternal destruction and exclusion from the presence of the Lord".[59] Numerous other texts could be cited. It will suffice to quote Our Lord: "all who are in the tombs will hear His voice and come forth, those who have done good, to the resurrection of life, and *those who have done evil, to the resurrection of judgement.*"[60] "Enter by the narrow gate; for the gate is wide and the way is easy, that leads to destruction, and *those who enter by it are many.*"[61] The fate of one man, Judas, was specifically declared by Our Lord, on two occasions: "I have guarded them [the apostles], and none of them is lost but the son of perdition";[62] "woe to that man by whom the Son of Man is betrayed! It would have been better for that man if he had not been born."[63] These dreadful words of Our Lord cannot refer to the sin of betrayal, which His infinite mercy would have been willing to forgive, but to the eternal damnation of Judas who despaired instead of seeking forgiveness. Look

---

[56] DS 409, 411, 485, 587, 1011, 1077. The heresy is known as ἀποκατάστασις (apocatastasis - universal restoration).
[57] C 633
[58] 1 Tim 2:4
[59] 2 Thess 1:9
[60] Jn 5:29 Here "judgement" means "condemnation".
[61] Matt 7:13
[62] Jn 17:12
[63] Matt 26:24. Cf. Acts 1:25.

closely at the words of Jesus: these words could never have been uttered about a man who reached eternal salvation.

Some in their naiveté and false compassion assure us that God will give the damned a second chance. Will He? No, He will not; He has told us so Himself. They have had their chances in this life. God gives every person sufficient grace for salvation. It is a revealed fact that upon death the human will is fixed. It is sheer delusion to hope for a repentance in the next life: "there is no repentance for men after death", says the Catechism.[64] "*Immediately* after death the souls of those who die in actual mortal sin descend into Hell".[65] The only way open to salvation for the damned is by the path of humility and contrition—but this they will not and can not take. Our Lord's numerous parables warning us to be ready for a judgement by the Master—a judgement which comes suddenly and admits of no appeal—have been given to us so that we may be ready, because after judgement *it is too late*. To cling to the wishful thinking that God in His mercy must offer us a second chance is to destroy the meaning and purpose of all these parables spoken by Divine Truth Himself.

The fire of Hell. The fire of Hell is something real. Yet, as the Fathers tell us, it is not identical with the fire of this world. Lactantius says: "The nature of that everlasting fire is different from this fire of ours which we use for the necessary purposes of life, and which ceases to burn, unless it be sustained by the fuel of some material. But that divine fire always lives by itself, and burns without nourishment."[66] St Ephraem[67] and St Basil[68] declare that the fire of Hell causes darkness, and incessantly torments its victims without destroying them. St Augustine says that, while not corporeal, it resembles a corporeal thing.[69] Whatever its nature, God has given it the power of acting on pure spirits and disembodied souls. Though we know it only from its effects, and though we know these effects themselves very imperfectly, we may be assured that "fire", the name given to it by Christ, conveys to us the best idea of its nature that we are capable of conceiving.

The torments of Hell cannot be adequately described. No tongue can describe the happiness of Heaven: no tongue can describe the horrors of Hell. It is a grievous mistake to suppose that the dreadful pictures of Hell drawn by preachers, writers and artists are mere fabrics of the imagination, mere senseless exaggerations with no relation to the truth. The details presented may not indeed correspond with the facts, but they help us to stretch our mind towards the awful reality. They put before us sufferings we know of, so that we may get some idea of sufferings similar in their nature, but far more intense (*the pain of sense*), and of other and inconceivably greater sufferings of a different and higher order (*the pain of loss*). Ponder over the words of our Saviour Himself: they are the most appalling ever uttered by human

---

[64] C 393, quoting St John Damascene.
[65] DS 1002. Cf. C 1035.
[66] *De Div. Inst.* 7, 21
[67] *Serm. Exeg., Opera*, Vol. II, p.354
[68] *In Psal.* 28, 7 n. 6
[69] *De Genesi ad Litteram*, 12: 32,61

lips, and He that spoke them did not exaggerate. His description of the damned as separated from happiness by an impassable chasm, as gnawed by the undying worm, as afflicted with burning thirst, as tortured in flames, as flung into unquenchable fire, as sent away to unending Hell, gives us, when fully understood and expanded, more than all we find in sermons and religious epics.

Saint Faustina Kowalska (1905-1938) describes Hell thus: "the first torture that constitutes Hell is the loss of God; the second is perpetual remorse of conscience; the third is that one's condition will never change; the fourth is the fire that will penetrate the soul without destroying it—a terrible suffering, since it is a purely spiritual fire, lit by God's anger; the fifth torture is continual darkness and a terrible suffocating smell, and, despite the darkness, the devils and the souls of the damned see each other and all the evil, both of others and their own; the sixth torture is the constant company of Satan; the seventh torture is horrible despair, hatred of God, vile words, curses and blasphemies. These are the tortures suffered by all the damned together, but that is not the end of the sufferings. There are special tortures destined for particular souls. These are the torments of the senses. Each soul undergoes terrible and indescribable sufferings, related to the manner in which it has sinned. There are caverns and pits of torture where one form of agony differs from another…".[70]

Replies to difficulties against the doctrine of eternal punishment.

A GENERAL REPLY TO ALL DIFFICULTIES. Many who deny the existence of Hell have no difficulty in believing in Heaven; but on what basis do they believe in Heaven? "Why", they would say, "it is in the Bible, it is taught by Christ and the Church". So, too, is Hell taught by the Bible, by Christ and the Church. Heaven *and* Hell: it is both or neither. We cannot believe Christ when He speaks of things we are glad to hear, but disbelieve Him when He tells us things we would rather not know. God commands us to believe in the eternity of Hell. We admit the doctrine raises many difficulties; so does the doctrine of the Most Holy Trinity; so does the doctrine of the Blessed Eucharist. Yet it is precisely because the doctrine is difficult to our feeble understanding, our faltering reason, that we glorify Him in accepting it. - Any denial of Hell entails a denial of free will: it means that souls are saved even against their will. It means that God coerces them into the Kingdom of Heaven. Salvation is a gift—and like all gifts, it can be refused.

A. *"Eternal punishment seems opposed to Divine Justice."*
1. "How can a sin committed in a moment of time deserve an eternity of punishment?"
REPLY: (a) It is not reasonable to hold that the duration of the punishment should be determined by the length of time it took to commit the offence: theft, forgery, or manslaughter may be committed in an instant, and yet such crimes are justly punished by imprisonment for many years. (b) The suggestion that a good man may at the end of a long life be surprised into a single mortal sin and be cast into Hell,

---

[70] *Diary of Bl. Sr. M. Faustina Kowalska*, Marian Press, Massachusetts 1996, par. 741. Cf. St Teresa of Jesus (of Avila) *Life*, Ch. 32.

need cause no apprehension. Mortal sin is a violation of the law of God committed (1) in a serious matter; (2) with clear knowledge, and (3) in full freedom and with full consent. Sometimes we see a man who has long been honoured for his virtue, die apparently the death of the unjust; but what to us seems a grave sin may be due to some merely physical weakness, break-down, or aberration. God reads the heart; He will send no man to Hell who does not fully deserve it. But if he who has all his life enjoyed the blessings of God's friendship turns against Him in the end knowingly, freely, and deliberately, he is guilty of the blackest ingratitude and can expect no forgiveness after death.[71] The supposition is indeed improbable, and might never be realised in fact. (c) God does not suffer from ignorance like a human judge; He knows us through and through. He will make full allowance for the obstacles in our path, for human frailty and ignorance, for evil surroundings, and for inherited tendencies to sin. He will judge us with perfect but humane or kindly justice. - St Thomas says, "God judges men through the Man Christ, so that judgement may be milder for men".[72] God judges men in His human nature, not because He as Man has more pity for them than He has as God, but because He desires to remind them that, in Him, they have a Judge who has felt all their weaknesses—who has felt the stress of temptation and the edge of suffering.

2. "Is not all punishment designed for the correction of the wrongdoer? If so, is not eternal punishment unjust?"
REPLY: (a) There are four purposes of punishment, not simply one: expiation, protection of society, rehabilitation, and deterrence. Not all punishment is designed for the correction of the offender. The State will sentence a man to life imprisonment or even execution. In such a sentence, the primary object is obviously not that of reforming the criminal. Nor can it be said that the sole object is to offer his example as a warning to the evil-minded. The State has something further in view: it intends to make him expiate his crime, to do to him somewhat of what he has done to another; and citizens approve, saying, "That is right. Justice has been done." Even in the lesser punishments inflicted by the civil arm, this element of expiation enters in: for instance, when a thief is sent to prison for ten years, the object is not merely to deter others from crime or to hold the malefactor in detention for a period nicely calculated as sufficient for his reform, but to make him pay for his guilt. Crime disturbs the balance of justice: punishment restores it. The criminal owes a debt to justice: he must pay it to the last penny. Apply this to the doctrine of eternal punishment. A man dies in rebellion against God: he must suffer a penalty equal to his crime. But how are we to estimate the penalty? Only by humbly taking the words of God Himself: He has issued a most solemn and emphatic warning that the impenitent sinner deserves eternal punishment, and we must believe it. In this life, we walk by faith, and believe God is just. In the next, we shall *know* He is just, and perhaps there may be many who, to their cost, will know it too late. (b) The objection assumes that lost souls are capable of reform. This is false. As we say below in our reply to the next objection, the will of the sinner, for reasons which we cannot fathom, is, as a consequence of its very nature,

---

[71] Cf. Ezek 18:23-26.
[72] "ut sit suavius iudicium hominibus" S.T., iii, q. 59, a. 2; see Heb 4:15-16.

fixed after death in perpetual hatred of God; and this perpetual hatred demands in justice a perpetual punishment. To ask God to refrain from punishing the wicked in Hell would be like asking Him to deny the truth that they died in rebellion against Him.

B. *"Eternal punishment seems opposed to Divine Goodness and Mercy."*

1. "How can we reconcile Divine Goodness and Mercy with the doctrine of eternal punishment?"

REPLY: (a) If God were to release the damned, His Mercy would be stultified. The wicked could defy Him, saying, "We trampled on Your Law. We had our own way in spite of You. We knew that Your Mercy would not allow You to punish our defiance of You with the eternal torments of Hell. We have triumphed over You." (b) By dying in mortal sin, the damned have eternally disqualified themselves for deliverance. When a man commits a mortal sin, he deliberately thrusts God and His commandments aside. He is no longer God's servant. He has chosen himself as his own lord and master. And if he dies without reversing his choice, that choice becomes final for all eternity. He will never cease to be a rebel against God; he will never cease to be unfit for the Kingdom of Heaven. The Divine Mercy, therefore, cannot release him. (c) The lost soul is no object of pity. It is fixed in eternal selfishness. It regrets its sins, merely because they have made it suffer, but not because they were offensive to God. It will never bow its will to say: "Father, forgive me". It will never appeal to the divine mercy for relief. It would gladly be rid of its suffering, but only on condition of retaining its attitude of independence of God. (d) The doctrine of Hell does not misplace the doctrine of the infinite Mercy of God. God in His Mercy offers souls the chance of salvation, without coercing them against their will. Those who resist His Mercy will receive His Justice.

2. "Why cannot God break the rebellion of the lost soul by giving it an overwhelming grace of repentance? Or why does He not of His pity annihilate it and end its misery?"

REPLY: God can do neither of these things because they are absurd. When all that is now hidden is revealed, we shall see that to convert or annihilate a lost soul would involve an absurdity comparable to that of constructing a square circle. In this present life, we can see clearly that a figure ceases to be a circle it if is transformed into a square. After death, we shall see that God's release or annihilation of a lost soul would demand such a change in Him that He would cease to be God. For God has pledged Himself not to deprive man of his liberty and existence, even if he misuses these gifts. God in His justice will not destroy the integrity of human choice. After death we shall see also, as St Thomas says, that the divine mercy extends even to the wicked in Hell by making their punishment less than their deserts.[73] People often presume that the damned will do anything to be delivered;

---

[73] *Comm. in Sent.* iv, d. 46, q. 2, a. 3, ad 1: etiam in eis [sc. damnatis] misericordiae locum habet, inquantum citra condignum puniuntur. - "even in them [the damned], He shows mercy, insofar as they are punished less than they deserve." = S.T. Suppl. q. 99, a. 2, ad 1. Cf. ibid., a. 3, ad 4; a. 5, ad 1.

yet the only way open to salvation is by the path of humility and contrition—but this they will not and can not take.

C. *"It would seem that the contemplation of eternal suffering must destroy the happiness of the Blessed."*

"How can the Blessed be happy if they see those whom they loved on earth suffering eternal punishment?"

REPLY: The happiness of the Blessed in Heaven cannot be marred by the sufferings of those who were their friends on earth. The friendships of this life are not proof against grievous wrong: if, for instance, a man learns that his parents have been robbed and murdered by one whom he thought his dearest friend, is not the bond of friendship broken? Such a crime we recognise as destructive of affection, but the crime of one who dies as God's enemy will appear far more heinous to the Blessed in Heaven. For them, it will bear the character of a most grievous personal wrong utterly extinguishing every claim to their regard. They will perceive the obstinacy and black ingratitude of the sinner. They will see how he spurned God's graces, and how he hardened his heart against the sufferings of Christ. They will behold him after death with his will set in eternal hostility to his Creator. So the very thought of retaining any vestige of friendship for such a one will seem to them to be an insult to the God they love. They will feel as little pity for a lost soul in Hell, as men on earth feel for the sufferings of Satan. They will be united to God more closely, more lovingly, than a child is united to its parents; His honour will be their honour; His friends, their friends; His enemies, their enemies; His affections will be their affections, and they will see all things with His eyes. For the saints in Paradise, earthly ties have been transformed, and are as nothing compared to heavenly ties. They are just as happy to see in Heaven people from different nations and epochs, as their own family members. They look upon the other saints as their true brothers and sisters, united by supernatural bonds in consummate happiness. The absence of a onetime family member who is not saved can only appear to them as the absence of an uninvited and unwelcome guest, the absence of an alien who has no place there, of one with whom there is no real basis for contact or unity. Even if—on an impossible supposition—one of the damned could join the Blessed in Paradise, the saints could only say with Our Lord, "I do not know you."[74]

Boswell: "One of the most pleasing thoughts is, that we shall see our friends again." Johnson: "Yes, Sir; but you must consider, that when we are become purely rational, many of our friendships will be cut off. Many friendships are formed by a community of sensual pleasures: all these will be cut off. We form many friendships with bad men, because they have agreeable qualities, and they can be useful to us; but, after death, they can no longer be of use to us. We form many friendships by mistake, imagining people to be different from what they really are. After death, we shall see every one in a true light. Then, Sir, they talk of our meeting our relations: but then all relationship is dissolved: and we shall have no regard for one person more than another, but for their real value. However, we

---

[74] Matt 25:12; cf. 7:23; Lk 13:27.

shall either have the satisfaction of meeting our friends, or be satisfied without meeting them."[75]

The moral value of the doctrine of eternal punishment. God has created no one for Hell. Thus, we may put the Catholic doctrine of Eternal Punishment in a homely way by saying that He did not make Hell to put us into it, but to keep us out of it. He has created every one of us for Heaven, and He has given us every help to get there. Among these helps, one of the greatest is His revelation of the eternal torments of Hell. He has shown us that sin leads to Hell, so that knowing this we may, by our own free-will, and aided by His grace, learn to shun and hate what would bring us there. If someone of agreeable manners sought our society with no other object than to rob us and ruin us, we would avoid him and come to hate the attractions with which he sought to ensnare us. In like manner, we come to detest sinful pleasure, knowing that it is but the bait that tempts us into the dread trap from which there is no escape. The more we meditate on Hell, the nearer we shall be drawn to God. We should pray for a salutary fear of the divine judgements: "The fear of the Lord is the beginning of wisdom"; "by the fear of the Lord a man avoids evil."[76]

After meditation on the Passion, there can be no more profitable meditation than that on the four Last Things: Death, Judgement, Heaven, Hell.[77]

> Death: than which nothing is more certain;
> Judgement: than which nothing is more strict;
> Hell: than which nothing is more terrible;
> Heaven: than which nothing is more delightful.[78]

V

Purgatory, an abode of purification. Purgatory is a place or state of punishment where the souls of those who have died in the state of grace, but who still owe something to divine justice, suffer for a time before they are admitted into Heaven. The debt to God's justice may arise from venial sin unrepented of, or from satisfaction still due after the guilt of mortal sin has been remitted. Its duration and intensity differ for each soul. St Thomas says that the length of time is according to the degree of attachment to sin, and the intensity of pain according to the degree of guilt.[79] (By analogy: in this life, deeply rooted vices take *longer* to eradicate,

---

[75] J. Boswell, *The Life of Samuel Johnson*, Everyman 1946, Vol. I, p.419, A.D. 1772, Aetat. 63
[76] Prov 9:10; 16:6
[77] Study of the Last Things is called "Eschatology", from the Greek word ἐσχατα (eschata): last things.
[78] Cf. Pope John XXIII, *Journal of a Soul*, p.448.
[79] *Comm. in Sent.* iv, d. 21, q. 1, a. 3, qcla. 3, ad 1: "acerbitas poenae proprie respondet quantitae culpae; sed diuturnitas respondet culpae radicationi in subjecto." = S.T. Suppl. appendix, q. 2, a. 8 [or 6], ad 1

guilt.[79] (By analogy: in this life, deeply rooted vices take *longer* to eradicate, and major transgressions are punished with *harsher* penalties). The souls in Purgatory are called "Poor Souls" because they do not have the resources to help themselves. They are called the "Holy Souls" for they are the souls of those who died in a state of grace or holiness. At every Mass, during the Eucharistic Prayer, the Church prays for the dead. On All Souls' Day, November 2, she has the Commemoration of All the Faithful Departed. On that day the Church concedes her priests the privilege of saying three Masses for the dead.[80]

The pains of Purgatory. The poor souls in Purgatory suffer the pain of loss, because, while detained there, they are deprived of the Beatific Vision of God. This temporary deprivation is a most severe punishment. The consciousness of being so close to God, now loved with an intense ardour, and of being unable to go to Him, causes dreadful suffering, which is enhanced by the sense of unworthiness and by regret that the opportunities of purging the soul before death were not availed of. Nevertheless, the suffering of souls are cheered by the light of hope, by the certainty of release. Their agony is not the agony of the damned, not an agony of rage and despair, but an agony accepted with perfect resignation, borne with unyielding patience, an agony of love.

It is commonly taught, but it is not of faith, that the poor souls suffer also a pain of sense, caused by some agency similar to the fire of Hell. How their sufferings compare with the sufferings of this world, we cannot tell: St Bonaventure says that "the severest pain of Purgatory exceeds the most violent known on earth".[81] St Augustine says, "though we be saved by fire, that fire will be more severe than anything a man can suffer in this life."[82] St Thomas, following him, asserts that "even the slightest suffering of Purgatory exceeds the worst suffering of this life."[83] - From all that is written above, one can see how absurd and mistaken is the view of some that Purgatory simply means the final agony before death.

Proof of the doctrine of Purgatory. PROOF FROM THE SOLEMN TEACHING OF THE CHURCH. The Church teaches as a revealed truth that the souls of the just who have failed in this life to pay in full their debt to God's justice are cleansed in Purgatory, to fit them for admission to Heaven. The Church says this infallibly in the name of God. Hence, God Himself testifies, through the Church, to the

---

[79] *Comm. in Sent.* iv, d. 21, q. 1, a. 3, qcla. 3, ad 1: "acerbitas poenae proprie respondet quantitae culpae; sed diuturnitas respondet culpae radicationi in subjecto." = S.T. Suppl. appendix, q. 2, a. 8 [or 6], ad 1

[80] *Incruentum Altaris*, Apostolic Constitution of Pope Benedict XV, 1915. Cf. *Ordo pro anno liturgico*, Vatican City 1998-99, at 2 Nov.

[81] *In IV Sent.*, d. 20, a. i, q. 2

[82] *Enarrat. in Ps.*, 37, 3

[83] *Comm. in Sent.* iv, d. 21, q. 1, a. 1, qcla. 3 (= S.T. Suppl. appendix, q. 2, a. 3 [or 1])

existence of Purgatory. This proof suffices for Catholics. The following proofs are added for fuller instruction.

PROOF FROM S. SCRIPTURE. *Preliminary note.* The word *Purgatory* is not found in the Bible; nor are the words *Incarnation, Trinity, consubstantial, omniscient, miracle,* or *Bible* itself. What matters is not the word itself, but the content and meaning of the word. The Bible is replete with evidence for Purgatory:

(1) When Judas Maccabeus, after his victory over Gorgias, went to bury the few Jews who had fallen, he found under their coats tokens of the idols of Jamnia. In seizing this booty, they had probably been actuated by mere greed, never thinking of the contamination they suffered by appropriating objects connected with idolatrous worship. Still, such objects "the law forbids the Jews to wear. And it became clear to all that this was why these men had fallen. ...[Judas Maccabeus] took up a collection ... to the amount of two thousand drachmas of silver, and sent it to Jerusalem to provide for a sin offering." Obviously, he believed that these men were not lost eternally, but that they were in some state or abode of temporary detainment, and could be relieved by the prayers of the living. The Holy Spirit through the inspired writer approves of his action and the belief that prompted it, saying: "it was a holy and pious thought. Therefore he made atonement for the dead, that they might be delivered from their sin."[84]

(2) Matt 12:32: Our Blessed Lord said: "whoever speaks against the Holy Spirit will not be forgiven, either in this age or in the age to come." "The age, or world, to come" means life after death. Hence, according to our Saviour Himself, there are other sins that can be pardoned after death. This is the interpretation of St Gregory the Great.[85] Note, too, that the Lord presumed that His Jewish listeners already knew what He meant by forgiveness in the next life.

(3) Matt 12:36: "on the day of judgement, men will render account for every careless word they utter". This follows the passage just cited about words that will not be forgiven at all. Manifestly, "careless words" do not merit Hell, but there will be a penalty for them, the Saviour warns. Hence, after judgement, and in the next life therefore, there must be a place of temporal punishment for minor faults.

(4) Matt 5:21-6: Christ warns about the coming judgement and its severity. He warns, in the language of a parable, that it is like a court case, and so we are advised to be reconciled and repentant here on earth, lest we be forced to undergo the full rigour of the law, for, "put in prison ... you will never get out till you have paid the last penny".[86] This is a clear reference to the payment which must be made here or hereafter. Note that the detention is temporary, for at the end there is a release. It can, then, be neither heaven nor hell.

---

[84] 2 Macc 12:40-43,45
[85] *Dialog.* 4, 41; cf. C 1031, Mk 3:28-30; Lk 12:10.
[86] Cf. Lk 12:57-9.

(5) Matt 18:23-35 is a parable about an unforgiving debtor whom the King "handed over to the torturers till he should pay all his debt." The King, as in so many parables, is an image of God, who expects us sinners, like the man in the parable, to forgive others as we have been forgiven, but who will make us pay our debts in full here or hereafter, if we demand full justice from others. The analogies of torture, prison, and debts—however unpleasant—fit Purgatory perfectly!

(6) Lk 12:42-8 is a parable about judgement and differing rewards and punishments. The servant found faithful at his Master's return, "his Master will set over his household" (= reigning with Christ in *Heaven*); the servant who beat the others and is drunk, the Master "will punish him and put him with the unfaithful" (= dismissal, permanent exclusion from the household, i.e., *Hell*). "And that servant who knew his Master's will, but did not make ready or act according to his will, shall receive a severe beating" (= the severe temporal punishment of *Purgatory* for the repentant but guilty, after which one is restored to the Kingdom again). "But he who did not know, and did what deserved a beating, shall receive a light beating." (= a less severe purgation because of ignorance, followed by reconciliation with Christ the Good Master: a hint of how God may deal with those in invincible ignorance).

(7) 1 Cor 3:14-5: St Paul says, "If the work which any man has built on the foundation [i.e., on Christ, v.11] survives, he will receive a reward. If any man's work is burned up, he will suffer loss, though he himself will be saved, but only as through fire." St Paul is speaking of the judgement of believers. (Unbelievers do not build on the foundation, viz., Christ, so he does not mention them here). Faithful Christians who have built on the foundation "will receive a reward", since their work "survives" the test. Faulty Christians, whose inferior work cannot withstand searching scrutiny, "will suffer loss"—not eternal, but only temporary, for they too "will be saved, but only as through fire." Again, a clear reference to the temporary punishment of Purgatory.

(8) 2 Tim 1:16-8: St Paul prays for the household of his onetime helper Onesiphorus, who has obviously died. Then he offers a prayer for Onesiphorus himself: "may the Lord grant him to find mercy from the Lord on that Day". Here we have an example of prayer for the dead.

(9) Behind the Protestant rejection of Purgatory are two notions: (a) since *Christ's* sacrifice has made expiation for sin, then *we* need not suffer or expiate anything ourselves; (b) forgiveness by God means no reparation is required. - We will answer these two notions in turn. As to (a): Christ told His Apostles that as He was persecuted, they too must face persecution.[87] He said that anyone who wants to follow Him must take up his cross.[88] The Apostles said that "through many tribulations we must enter the Kingdom of God."[89] St Paul said, "in my flesh I complete what is lacking in Christ's afflictions for the sake of His body, that is, the

---

[87] Jn 15:20
[88] Mk 8:34
[89] Acts 14:22

Church."[90] Hence, the baptised, precisely because they are baptised into Christ's *death* and resurrection, must participate in His Passion in various ways according to their age and vocation. Sins committed before Baptism are completely remitted as to guilt *and* penalty, but for sins committed after Baptism, there is not the same indulgence. Pardon will come, but atonement must still be made. It is not that our prayers and sufferings have any intrinsic value, but that they have a value before God insofar as they are joined to the one Mediator's intercession and atonement.

As to (b): this is contrary to reason and Revelation. Forgiveness does not necessarily mean cancelling the penalty to be suffered or compensation to be made. On the *human* level: a man may forgive, and restore to friendship, his neighbour who maliciously broke his window, but can still demand payment to repair it. In *S. Scripture*, there are numerous examples where, even after repentance, the sinner must pay the price and suffer a penalty for his actions. In 2 Sam 12:13-4, Nathan informs King David that God forgives his sin, but because of his sin, the child born to him must die. Later, David takes a census of the people against the will of God, repents of it and begs God's pardon, but the next day God tells the prophet Gad to tell David that he must choose one of three punishments for his sin.[91] Other examples could be recounted.[92]

PROOF FROM TRADITION. (1) *Jewish belief.* Though Protestants deny the inspiration of the Books of Maccabees, the quotation given above, regarded merely as a statement of secular history, proves that the Jews believed in Purgatory. Moreover, in another book, recognised by Protestants, we read of King David and his men fasting for the dead: "they mourned and wept and fasted until evening for Saul and for Jonathan his son and for the people of the Lord and for the house of Israel, because they had fallen by the sword."[93] Prayer for the dead has been practised by Jews uninterruptedly to the present day. When Jews from around the world gathered at the Auschwitz-Birkenau death camp on 25th January 1995, fifty years after its closure, they offered prayers for the victims who had died there.

(2) *The Early Church's prayer for the dead.* The belief of the early Church is evident from the immemorial custom of praying for the dead: e.g., (a) Tertullian (c. 215) bids a widow "pray for [her husband's] soul and ask that he may, while waiting, find rest ... and have sacrifice offered for him every year on the anniversary of his death."[94] In another work, dated the year 211, he says, "We offer sacrifices for the dead on the anniversaries of their death."[95]
(b) The Sacramentary of Serapion (c. 350), in its Anaphora (Eucharistic Prayer), prays, "We beseech Thee also on behalf of all the departed, whom we

---

[90] Col 1:24
[91] 2 Sam 24:10-16
[92] *Adam* in Gen 3:17-9; Wis 10:1; *Miriam* in Num 12:9-15; *Moses* and *Aaron* in Num 20:12; 27:12; *Ahab* in 1 Kgs 21:20-9; *Hezekiah* in 2 Kgs 20.
[93] 2 Sam 1:12 (= Vulgate 2 Kgs 1:12)
[94] *De monogamia,* 10
[95] *De corona,* 3, 3

commemorate here also … grant unto them a place and dwelling in Thy Kingdom."[96]

(3) *Belief of the Fathers.* (a) Origen (d. 254), commenting on St Paul's desire to die that he might be with Christ (Philipp 1:23), says, "For my part, I cannot speak thus, for I know that, when I go hence, my wood will have to be burned."[97]

(b) Tertullian says, "we understand that 'prison' indicated in the Gospel to be the underworld, and interpret 'the last penny' (Matt 5:26) as meaning every small sin which has to be expiated there in the interval before the resurrection". He repeats the same thought elsewhere.[98]

(c) St Cyril of Jerusalem (d. 386) explains the ceremonies of the Church to new believers, saying, "we also make mention of those who have already died … for we believe that it will greatly benefit the souls of those for whom the petition is offered up, during the presentation of this holy and solemn Sacrifice."[99]

(d) St Augustine of Hippo (354-430) wrote a special treatise, "On the Care to be Exercised for the Dead." He says that "the universal Church … observes the custom of giving a place to the commemoration of the dead in the prayers of the priest at the altar."[100] His mother, St Monica, on her death-bed said to him: "This one request I make to you, that, wherever you be, you remember me at the altar of the Lord."[101] (She was buried originally in Ostia, where she died, and later her body was taken to the Church of St Augustine, Rome). In his *Enchiridion* of 421 A.D., Augustine says, "some of the faithful may be saved through a certain purgatorial fire, some more slowly and others more quickly, according to the greater or lesser degree with which they loved corruptible goods."[102]

(e) St Caesarius of Arles (d. 452) says in a sermon, "If we neither give thanks to God in tribulations nor redeem our own sins by good works, we shall have to remain in that purgatorial fire as long as it takes the aforesaid lesser sins to be consumed".[103]

(f) St Gregory the Great (d. 604): "We are bound to believe that for certain lesser faults there is a purgative fire before the final judgement".[104]

(4) *Ancient inscriptions.* The inscriptions in the Catacombs, some dating from the second century, are exactly like those we find in any Catholic graveyard. They beseech the mercy of Christ for the dead, and appeal to the living to pray for them. The most ancient epigraphs are in the Catacombs of Priscilla, Rome. Among countless examples there: "Peace to you, Octavia, in peace"; "Peace, Celestina"; in the Catacombs of St Callistus, Rome, "Felicola, peace to you in the Lord".[105] The famous monument known as the Epitaph of Abercius, erected c. 200 A.D., in

---

[96] F.X. Funk, *Didasc. et Const. Apost.* Vol. II

[97] *Hom. in Jer.* 20, 3. Cf. H. Crouzel S.J., *Origen*, Harper & Row, San Francisco 1989, pp.242-6.

[98] *De Anima*, 58; cf. Ibid., 35; *De Res. carnis*, 42.

[99] *Catech. Mystagog.* (23) 5, 9

[100] *De cura gerenda pro mortuis*, I, 3

[101] *The Confessions of St Augustine*, Book 9, c. 2

[102] *Enchirid.* 69

[103] *Sermo.* 179, 2 (ed. Morin). (104 in PL 39)

[104] *Dialog.* 4, 41; cf. C 1031.

[105] A. Ferrua S.J., *The Unknown Catacomb*, Geddes & Grosset, Scotland 1991, pp.16-7

Phrygia, Asia Minor (now Turkey), concludes with the words: "Let every comrade who understands this pray for Abercius."[106] Other examples from the Catacombs: "May you live in peace"; "May you live in God"; "I do not deserve to be united with the Lord. By your prayers obtain for me that God pardon my sins."[107]

(5) *The non-Catholic Eastern Churches.* *All* of these Churches have prayers and suffrages for the dead. E.g., the Assyrian *Liturgy of Theodore of Mopsuestia* prays, "that by Thy grace, O Lord, Thou wouldst grant pardon to all the children of the holy catholic Church who have passed from this world in the true faith, for all the sins and offences which they committed in their mortal bodies in this world". A Syrian Jacobite liturgy prays, "Remember, O Lord, those who have died, and grant rest unto them who were clothed with Thee at Baptism and received Thee from the altar."

We may argue, as we did for the Apostolic origin of the seven sacraments, that without the definitions of the Councils of Lyons, Florence and Trent, the doctrine of Purgatory could still be inferred with certainty from the facts of history. The Assyrian Church, whose separation dates from the fifth century, the oriental orthodox Churches (Armenian, Coptic, Ethiopian, Syrian, Malankara), whose separation dates later in the fifth century, the various Byzantine Orthodox Churches, whose separation dates from the eleventh century on—all have public and official prayers for the dead,[108] asking that God in His mercy "would grant them a place of refreshment, light and peace", as the Roman Canon (4th cent.) puts it. The tension between these Churches and the See of Rome over the centuries excludes the possibility of their having borrowed any doctrine or practice from Rome since their separation. In East and West, therefore, in the first millennium, the doctrine with its practical expression in the Divine Liturgy and Christian monuments was recognised as an essential part of the true religion. Such agreement in belief and practice, in many and diverse countries, over an entire millennium, puts its Apostolic origin beyond question. - The sixteenth century Protestant Reformers, by attacking the doctrine of Purgatory and forbidding prayers for the faithful departed, denied many Christians what is one of the most natural and consoling practices for those who mourn the dead. It is no surprise that among Protestants the practice has made a steady return.

ARGUMENT FROM REASON. The Holy Scriptures tell us that "nothing unclean shall enter" into Heaven,[109] and that "on the day of judgement men will render account for every careless word they utter."[110] From what we know of human nature, is it

---

[106] The two fragments of this monument, discovered in 1883, were presented to Pope Leo XIII on the occasion of his Episcopal Jubilee by the Sultan of Turkey, Abdul Hamid. The inscription refers also to the Primacy of the Roman See and the Real Presence in the Blessed Eucharist.

[107] L. Hertling S.J. & E. Kirschbaum S.J., *The Roman Catacombs and their Martyrs*, DLT, London 1960, p.194

[108] The evidence is presented fully in M. Jugie, *Theologia Dogmatica Christianorum Orientalium ab Ecclesia Catholica Dissidentium*, Paris, Tom. IV, 1931, pp.166-70; Tom. V, 1935, pp.341-4, 774-82.

[109] Apoc 21:27

[110] Matt 12:36

not reasonable to say that, of those who die in the grace of God, very many are still bearing venial sin? Such cannot enter Heaven, for they are not undefiled; nor can they be cast into Hell, for they are not enemies of God. There must, therefore, be a middle state in which they can be purified.

Succouring the dead. (1) It is the faith of the Church that we who are on earth can relieve the souls in Purgatory by Masses, prayers, good works, and indulgences. The Mass produces its effect of its own efficacy, and does not depend for its value on the piety of the earthly priest who offers it. On the other hand, prayers and good works are of no avail for the suffering souls, unless offered by one in the state of grace. When a person who is in the state of grace says a prayer devoutly or performs some good work with a supernatural intention, his act bears a threefold fruit, *meritorious, impetratory* and *satisfactorial:* (a) *meritorious,* i.e., it merits an increase of Sanctifying Grace and eternal glory: this fruit is for himself alone; (b) *impetratory,* i.e., it works as a petition for God's graces: this he can apply for the benefit of others; (c) *satisfactorial,* i.e., it helps to blot out the temporal punishment due to sin: this, also, he may surrender in favour of another. It is the satisfactorial fruit which God accepts for the relief of the souls in Purgatory (not that we can be certain that He will apply it fully for the relief of the particular soul for whom we pray). On Indulgences, see p.558.

(2) The prayers in the Missal show that the dead are helped by the intercession of the Angels and Saints, and especially by the powerful advocacy of the Blessed Virgin Mary and St Michael the Archangel.

(3) It is certain that the poor souls cannot shorten their purgatory by their own prayers. It may be that they can pray for us. The Church in her liturgy never appeals for their intercession; but, on the other hand, she has never censured the practice of asking them for help. But whether they can help us or not while still in Purgatory, God will reward our charity in praying for them. For He has said: "Blessed are the merciful, for they shall obtain mercy".[111] "It is therefore a holy and wholesome thought to pray for the dead, that they may be loosed from sins."[112] Once in Heaven, they will, no doubt, gratefully intercede for those who prayed for them. "Our prayer for them is able not only to help them, but also to make their intercession for us efficacious."[113]

TIME IN PURGATORY. Time is the measure of change, and since souls in Purgatory are undergoing purification, we can say that there is time there—not a time of this

---

[111] Matt 5:7
[112] 2 Macc 12:46 (Douay)
[113] C 958

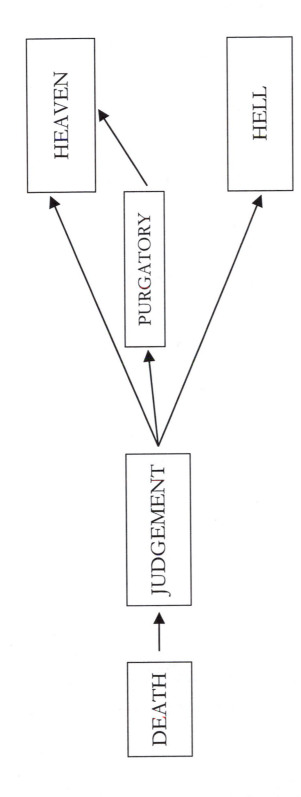

"Upon death, each man receives his eternal retribution in his immortal soul, in a particular judgement that refers his life to Christ: entrance into the blessedness of Heaven, either immediately or via a purification, – or immediately to everlasting damnation." Catechism #1022

world, however. It is purgatory-time, if you will, of a different dimension, in which each soul passes through spiritual instants, which do not correspond to earthly time.[114] An indulgence of 300 days, for example, as one sees in prayerbooks or on holy cards, does *not* mean "300 days off Purgatory". (See "Indulgences" pp.559-60 for explanation).

THE END OF PURGATORY. Purgatory will cease at the Last Judgement. How, then, shall those alive at the end of the world be purified? St Thomas answers that the final sufferings and the fire of the general conflagration at the end of the world[115] will serve as a purgation, and its intensity will compensate for its short duration.[116]

REINCARNATION. A human being lives an earthly human life only once: there is no reincarnation after death. A soul cannot return to its human body except by a miracle and divine intervention. It is impossible for a human soul to inhabit an animal body. Nor can a human person reappear later as another person; this is a contradiction in terms. Reincarnation is contrary to reason and the Bible.[117]

VI

The Last Things of the World:[118]
- The end of the world, time and history by the general conflagration;
- The general resurrection;
- The return of Christ in glory;
- The general judgement;
- The final exclusion of the damned;
- The glory of the blessed in a new heaven and a new earth.

The end of the world. St Peter says: "the day of the Lord will come like a thief, and then the heavens will pass away with a loud noise, and the elements will be dissolved with fire, and the earth and the works that are upon it will be burned up. Since all these things are thus to be dissolved, what sort of persons ought you to be in lives of holiness and godliness?"[119] Science admits the possibility of such a dread conflagration, and mentions

---

[114] Cf. St Thomas, *Comm. in Sent.* iv, d. 44, q. 2, a. 3, qcla 3, ad 5 (= S.T. Suppl. q. 84, a. 3, ad 5).
[115] "… the elements will be dissolved with fire, and the earth and the works that are upon it will be burned up." 2 Pet 3:10
[116] *Comm. in Sent.* iv, d. 47, q. 2, a. 3, qcla 2, ad 5 (= S.T. Suppl. q. 74, a. 8, ad 5)
[117] Cf. Heb 9:27; C 1013.
[118] Cf. C 668-82, 1038-44.
[119] 2 Pet 3:10-11

any causes that may bring it to pass; divine Revelation assures us of its certainty. The exact day is known to God alone.[120]

All men will rise from the dead. The Church teaches solemnly that on the last day all men will rise from the dead in the same bodies which they had in this life. The Apostles' Creed says, "I believe in ... the resurrection of the flesh and life everlasting." The Nicene Creed says, "I await the resurrection of the dead and the life of the world to come." This is one of the chief doctrines of the Christian faith. It is the plain teaching of Sacred Scripture and Tradition, and it can be shown to be not in opposition to reason.

PROOF FROM SACRED SCRIPTURE. Our Saviour said: "The hour is coming ... when the dead will hear the voice of the Son of God ... and come forth, those who have done good, to the resurrection of life, and those who have done evil, to the resurrection of judgement."[121] Christ refers particularly to the resurrection of the wicked when He warns: "fear him who can destroy both soul and *body* in hell."[122] St Paul says that as surely as Christ rose from the dead, so surely also shall we: "Now if Christ is preached as raised from the dead, how can some of you say that there is no resurrection of the dead? But if there is no resurrection of the dead, then Christ has not been raised; if Christ has not been raised, then our preaching is in vain and your faith is in vain."[123] He says moreover, "there will be a resurrection of both the just and the unjust."[124]

PROOF FROM TRADITION. Abundant evidence from the Fathers is available to prove that the early Church believed in the Resurrection of the just. As to the Resurrection of the wicked, let the testimony of Tertullian suffice, who says that Christ will come in glory to reward the good and punish the wicked, "after both have risen and resumed their bodies."[125]

THE DOCTRINE OF THE RESURRECTION IS NOT OPPOSED TO REASON. (1) *The Resurrection is not impossible to God's Omnipotence.* St Cyril of Jerusalem (d. 386) says: "God created us out of nothing; why should He not be able to re-awaken that which is destroyed?"[126] (2) *It is fitting that the good and the wicked should rise again.* Of the good, St Irenaeus (d. 202) says: "How can it

---

[120] Cf. Mk 13:32.
[121] Jn 5:25-29
[122] Matt 10:28
[123] 1 Cor 15:12 f; cf. Rom 6:3 f; 8:11; Acts 17:18; 24:15; 26:8,23
[124] Acts 24:15
[125] *De Praescript.* 13
[126] *Catech.* 18

be asserted that the flesh which is nourished with the Body and Blood of our Lord shall not partake of His life?"[127]

Of both the good and the wicked it may be argued that their bodies which in this life served as the instruments of their virtues or vices should also share in their rewards or punishments in the life to come.

THE NATURE AND PROPERTIES OF THE RISEN BODY. The Church, as already stated, solemnly teaches that all men will rise from the dead in the same bodies which they had in this life. But in what sense the same? "An objection might be made", says Newman, "that since the component particles of our body are ever changing during life, that since on death they are dissipated to the four winds, the *same* body cannot be raised; what is *meant* then by its being called the *same* body?"[128] He lets St Paul answer, who, speaking of the resurrection of the just, says: "And what you sow is not the body which is to be, but a bare kernel, perhaps of wheat".[129] The Apostle compares the earthly body to a seed, the risen body to the plant that springs from it. Look at a tree with its stem, branches, foliage, flowers, and fruit. All that you behold is contained in some way in the little seed from which it grew; yet how noble is the one, how insignificant the other! The tree is the same as the seed, yet how different! Such, according to St Paul, is the relation of the risen body to the natural body. It is the same body, yet how changed by the power and love of God! "What is sown", he says, "is perishable, what is raised is imperishable. It is sown in dishonour, it is raised in glory. It is sown in weakness, it is raised in power. It is sown a physical body, it is raised a spiritual body."[130] As in this life the soul has the power of transmuting mere senseless things, food and drink, into the substance of the living man, and of making them co-operate in noble thought and action; so, at the resurrection of the just, the soul enraptured by the vision of God will have the power of transforming and ennobling the body, so that it will become a worthy associate in an infinitely higher life. The body will shed its imperfections like a husk; it will become inaccessible to pain, disease, or death; its senses and faculties will be raised to nobler capacities. St Thomas says that the full happiness of the soul will overflow to the body, perfecting the senses in their operations.[131] While remaining a true body, it will be given powers which will make it resemble a spirit. It will shine for ever in beauty and radiance like the glorified Body of our Saviour, "who", as St Paul says, "will change our lowly body to be like His glorious body".[132] That wonderful change which the Apostle compares to the development of the plant from the seed may also be illustrated from nature's transmutation of carbon into a diamond. What once was carbon, resembling nothing better than a thimbleful of coal-dust, is now a flashing gem, fit for a royal diadem.

What is true of the resurrection of the just is true also, but in a very different sense, of the resurrection of the wicked. They too will rise with the same bodies

---

[127] *Adv. Haer.* IV, 18
[128] *Lectures on Justification* (3rd ed. 1874) IX, p.211
[129] 1 Cor 15:37
[130] Ibid., vv. 42-44
[131] S.T., i-ii, q. 3, a. 3
[132] Philipp. 3:21

they had in this life, but they will rise in dishonour. In their case, the natural body will not reveal its capacity for ennoblement, but for utter degradation. Their hatred of God will manifest itself in their appearance, making them hideous and repulsive like the demons with whom they must consort forever. The fire of Hell will burn their bodies without consuming them.

The *Roman Catechism*[133] sets forth these properties of the risen body under six headings. The first two are common to all the risen, while the next four are enjoyed only by the saints, i.e., all those in Heaven:

(a) Integrity: the bodies of all will be restored in their integrity, complete with all their members and faculties. Infants and unformed babies, as well as the aged, will all rise again in completeness, in full bodily maturity and perfection.

(b) Immortality: "before the resurrection they were subject to the law of death, but once restored to life, they shall, without distinction of good and evil, be invested with immortality."

(c) Impassibility: "shall place them beyond the reach of suffering anything disagreeable or of being affected by pain or inconvenience of any sort." St John declares, "death shall be no more, neither shall there be mourning nor crying nor pain any more".[134]

(d) Clarity (Splendour): "the bodies of the Saints shall shine like the sun.[135]... This brightness is a sort of radiance reflected on the body from the supreme happiness of the soul."

(e) Agility: "the body will be freed from the heaviness that now presses it down, and will be capable of moving with the utmost ease and swiftness, wherever the soul pleases".

(f) Subtility: "by which the body shall be completely subject to the dominion of the soul, and serve her, and be ever ready to follow her desires."

These qualities can be deduced from the writings of St Paul (1 Cor 15:37, 42-44): "what you sow is not the body which is to be, but a bare kernel" [the dead body, like a seed planted, comes up with all its hidden possibilities brought to fruition, in *integrity*]. "What is sown is perishable, what is raised is imperishable [*immortality & impassibility*]. It is sown in dishonour, it is raised in glory [*clarity*]. It is sown in weakness, it is raised in power [*agility*]. It is sown a physical body, it is raised a spiritual body [*subtility*]."

DIFFICULTY: "What of those whose bodies have been devoured by cannibals, or in some way become part of others' bodies? How can they receive their own bodies again?" REPLY: In this life, our body cells are always being renewed; we do not retain the same particles of matter all through life. The matter of our body is ours

---

[133] promulgated by Pope Pius V in 1566, three years after the closure of the Council of Trent (i.e., the Tridentine Council); hence often called the *Catechism of Pius V* or *Catechism of the Council of Trent*. The teaching and quotations following are taken from Part I, art. 11.

[134] Rev 21:4

[135] See Matt 13:43.

by virtue of its present union with the soul. Similarly, at the resurrection, the matter joined to our soul will thereby be constituted our body.

Note. We profess in the Creed, "He shall come again in glory to judge the living and the dead". By "the living and the dead" is meant all people: those who will have died already, and those alive at the end of the world. Will those then alive be exempt from the general law of death? The Roman Catechism answers that those alive shall then die, and at once rise again.[136]

VII

On the Last Day, Christ will come again to earth to judge and sentence all mankind. It is the faith of the Church, expressed in the Apostles' Creed and other early professions of belief, that after the General Resurrection, Christ will come again in glory to judge the whole human race. Few truths are more prominently set forth in Sacred Scripture than this. Time and again the New Testament speaks of the "Second Coming" of Christ as the universal Judge, in contrast with His "first coming" as the Redeemer.[137] In St Matthew's Gospel, we read His own words: "When the Son of Man comes in His glory, and all the angels with Him, then He will sit on His glorious throne. Before Him will be gathered all the nations, and He will separate them one from another as a shepherd separates the sheep from the goats, and He will place the sheep at His right hand, but the goats at the left."[138] All that is hidden will be revealed. The deeds of every man will be made known, yet the sins of the just will not be revealed in such a way as to cause them shame or unhappiness,[139] for as St Gregory says, it will be to sing of the Lord's mercies forever.[140] And Christ will pass sentence. To the just He will say: "Come, O blessed of My Father, inherit the Kingdom prepared for you from the foundation of the world", and to the wicked: "Depart from Me, you cursed, into the eternal fire prepared for the devil and his angels". Straightaway the sentence will be executed: "And they will go away into eternal punishment, but the righteous into eternal life."[141] The wicked shall be cast body and soul into hell and buried for ever there. The elect, clothed in the glory of their resurrection, shall join the company of angels, and enter with Jesus into the eternal Kingdom of the blessed. St John in the Apocalypse, relating his vision of the General Judgement, says,

---

[136] Part I, art. 11. Cf. St Thomas, *Comm. in Sent.* iv, d. 47, q. 2, a. 3, ad 3; d. 43, q. 1, a. 4 (= S.T. Suppl. q. 74, a. 7, ad 3; q. 78, a. 1).

[137] See e.g., Acts 17:31; 24:15; 1 Cor 15:23; 1 Thess 2:19; 2 Thess 1:7; 2:8; 1 Tim 6:14; 2 Tim 4:1.

[138] Matt 25:31-33

[139] St Thomas, *Comm. in Sent.* iv, d. 43, q. 1, a. 5, qcla 2, ad 3 (= S.T. Suppl. q. 87, a. 2, ad 3)

[140] *Moralium*, IV, 36

[141] Matt 25:34,41,46

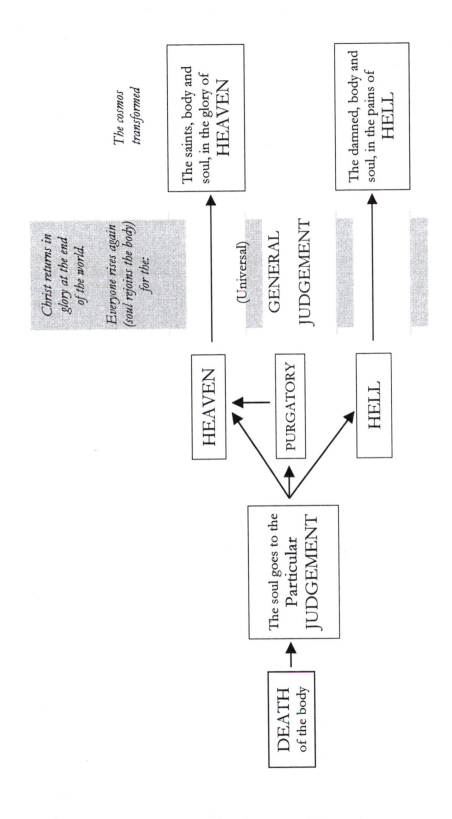

"Then I saw a great white throne and Him who sat upon it … And I saw the dead, great and small, standing before the throne, and books were opened. Also another book was opened, which is the book of life. And the dead were judged by what was written in the books, by what they had done. … And if anyone's name was not found written in the book of life, he was thrown into the lake of fire." And he was shown the home of the blessed, the City of Light: "And the city has no need of sun or moon to shine upon it, for the glory of God is its light, and its lamp is the Lamb. By its light shall the nations walk. … But nothing unclean shall enter it … but only those who are written in the Lamb's book of life."[142]

The purpose of the General Judgement. The General or Universal Judgement will not change the judgement already given to each person upon death. The Particular Judgement will reveal to each individual the wisdom and justice of God's dealings with him personally. The General Judgement will reveal to him the wisdom and justice of God's dealings with every member of the human race. Further, it will reveal to all the majesty of Christ and the glory of the elect. On the Last Day, Christ who was once spurned, spat upon, nailed to a cross, rejected by faithless children whom He had fed with His doctrine and helped with His graces, will appear before all mankind in the might of the Godhead, compelling every knee to bend in homage to Him. On that day also, the elect will shine as the stars of heaven: they who were once belittled and despised by sinners, they who were once clothed in the infamy of their Master, will now share in His triumph. The Holy Spirit declares that the wicked, seeing them, "will be shaken with dreadful fear … They will speak to one another in repentance, and in anguish of spirit they will groan, and say, 'This is the man whom we once held in derision and made a byword of reproach—we fools! We thought that his life was madness and that his end was without honour. Why has he been numbered among the sons of God? And why is his lot among the saints? So it was we who strayed from the way of truth, and the light of righteousness did not shine on us, and the sun did not rise upon us. We took our fill of the paths of lawlessness and destruction and we journeyed through trackless deserts, but the way of the Lord we have not known. What has our arrogance profited us? And what good has our boasted wealth brought us? All those things have vanished like a shadow, … like a ship that sails through the billowy water, and when it has passed no trace can be found, nor track of its keel in the waves; … So we also, as soon as we were born, ceased to be, and we had no sign of virtue to show, but were consumed in our wickedness.' Such things as these the sinners said in Hell … Because the hope of the ungodly man is like chaff carried by the wind … But the righteous live for ever, and their reward is with the Lord; the Most High takes care of them. Therefore they will receive a glorious crown and a beautiful diadem from the hand of the Lord".[143]

---

[142] Apoc 20:11-15; 21:23-27
[143] Wisdom 5:2-17 (v.14, Douay)

A New Heaven and a New Earth. After describing the General Judgement, St John says: "Then I saw a new heaven and a new earth; for the first heaven and the first earth had passed away, and the sea was no more. And I saw the holy city, new Jerusalem, coming down out of heaven from God, prepared as a bride adorned for her husband; and I heard a great voice from the throne saying, 'Behold, the dwelling of God is with men. He will dwell with them, and they shall be His people, and God Himself will be with them; He will wipe away every tear from their eyes, and death shall be no more, neither shall there be mourning nor crying nor pain any more, for the former things have passed away.' And He who sat upon the throne said, 'Behold I make all things new'."[144] Will the earth, then, be utterly destroyed? In what sense are we to interpret God's promise to "re-establish all things in Christ",[145] to make "new heavens and a new earth"?[146] Will the earth which, as St Anselm says, "once harboured in its bosom the Body of Our Lord", which was watered by His precious Blood and by the blood of the saints, be made anew so as to be a fit residence for the innocent and the blessed? Or will all the matter of the universe be at length united, every particle of it, to living spirits, and thus actively participate in manifesting the justice and wisdom of God? These are questions which no man can answer: revelation is silent, and it is idle to speculate.

> "TO THE ONLY GOD, OUR SAVIOUR
> THROUGH JESUS CHRIST OUR LORD,
> BE GLORY, MAJESTY, DOMINION, AND AUTHORITY,
> BEFORE ALL TIME AND NOW AND FOR EVER. AMEN."

Jude, v.24

---

[144] Apoc 21:1-5
[145] Eph 1:10
[146] 2 Pet 3:13

COMBINED INDEX TO BOTH PARTS

This index does not include some of the more obvious subjects
which may be found by consulting the chapter titles,
and the summaries at the start of each chapter.

I

SUBJECTS

Missale Romanum: see "Roman Missal."
"Missing link," 352
Missions, defended, 170, 171
Modalists, 316
Modernism/Modernists, 265-6, 292
Monarchians, 316
Monogenism, 358
Monophysites, 168, 177, 386
Monothelites, 208, 386
Mortal sin, 432, 532, 542, 544, 545-6, 606, 615, 622, 627-8, 629
Muratori, fragment of, 92
Murder, 350
Musicam Sacram, 460
Mycenae, 273
Mystici Corporis, 169, 380, 381, 383, 411, 416, 556

Natural Religion: see "Religion."
Natural selection, 343
Nature, notion of, 48-9, 299, 311, 378
Nestorianism, 177, 386, 392
"New Age," 60-1
Nicea, Council of/Nicene Creed, 184, 191, 316, 318, 377-8, 386, 572, 641; Second
Council of, 160, 318, 469-70
Nihilism, 60
Nostra Aetate, 108-9
Notes of the Church: one, holy, catholic, apostolic, 139ff., 149-50, 153-4, 161-2, 164-8,
174-7, 415, 422-3

Oils, Holy: three kinds, 463, 474, 564, 566, 568
Old Testament, history summarised, 252-5; compared to the New, 257-9, 418
Omnipotence, God's, 48, 304
Omnipresence, God's, 48, 302
Omniscience, God's, 48, 303
Orange, Second Council of, 184, 276, 278
Order, Sacrament of Holy, 417, 506, 541, 570ff.; rite of conferring diaconate, 571;
priesthood, 572; episcopate, 573-4; the power received by deacon, 573; priest, 574;
bishop, 574; Sacramental and non-sacramental orders, 575; exclusion of women from H.
Order, 576-80
Ordinatio Sacerdotalis, 578
Ordo Initiationis Christianae Adultorum, 463
Oriental Churches: see "Eastern Churches."
Orientalium Ecclesiarum, 178, 430
Original Sin, 360ff., 445, 476, 484
Orthodox Churches, how differ from Catholic Church, 160-2; status of, 430-1; see also
"Eastern Churches."

Pagan religion & myths, 335, 358, 367, 374-5
Pagans' contempt for early Christians, 234-5
Pain and suffering, 53-4, 367-8, 372-3, 412
Palaeontology, 374

PERSONS

Pio, Bl. Padre, 220, 224
Piolanti, A., 449
Pius IV, Profession of, 184
Pius V, Pope St, 365, 643
Pius VI, Pope, 481
Pius VII, Pope, 233
Pius IX, Pope Bl., 184, 247, 265, 275, 292, 534, 643
Pius X, Pope St, 184, 248, 265, 292, 534
Pius XI, Pope, 380, 388, 445, 522, 593, 597, 601
Pius XII, Pope, 169, 190, 197, 248, 261, 328, 335, 356, 357, 358, 380, 381, 383, 384, 386, 393, 411, 416, 457, 459, 460, 465, 481, 482, 518, 522, 556, 571, 572, 581, 604
Plato, 54, 73, 75, 91
Pliny, 234
Plutarch, 87
Polycarp, St, 86, 87, 269
Poschmann, 552, 568
Prümmer, 525

Quadratus, 104

Raphael, St, 320, 321
Reid, S., 556
Reimarus, 264
Renan, 123
Ricciotti, 93, 95, 264, 393
Richard of St Victor, 180
Riesenfeld, Harald, 94
Ritschl, A., 265
Roberson, R.G., 159, 177
Robert Bellarmine, St: see "Bellarmine."
Robinson, J.A.T., 93, 96
Rolland, Philippe, 95
Rumble, Dr Leslie, 172, 198

Sabellius, 316
Santamaria, B.A., 60
Sartre, Jean-Paul, 60
Schweitzer, 265
Ségur, 233
Seneca, 74
Shakespeare, 328, 329
Sheed, Frank, 291
Sheen, Fulton, 558
Shepherd of Hermas, 86
Sixtus IV, Pope, 214
Socrates, 75, 123, 125
Sophocles, 91
Spencer, Herbert, 59
Stauffer, S.A., 483
Stephen, Pope St, 450